Organizational behavior
THEORY and APPLICATION

THE IRWIN-DORSEY SERIES IN
BEHAVIORAL SCIENCE

EDITOR   JOHN F. MEE   *Indiana University*

ARGYRIS   *Interpersonal Competence and Organizational Effectiveness*

ARGYRIS   *Organization and Innovation*

CARZO & YANOUZAS   *Formal Organization: A Systems Approach*

CUMMINGS & SCOTT   *Readings in Organizational Behavior and Human Performance*

GUEST   *Organizational Change: The Effect of Successful Leadership*

KELLY   *Organizational Behaviour*

KUHN   *The Study of Society: A Unified Approach*

LAWRENCE & SEILER, WITH BAILEY, KATZ, ORTH, CLARK, BARNES, & TURNER   *Organizational Behavior and Administration: Cases, Concepts, and Research Findings*   rev. ed.

LYNTON & PAREEK   *Training for Development*

MASLOW   *Eupsychian Management: A Journal*

MASSARIK & RATOOSH   *Mathematical Explorations in Behavioral Science*

O'CONNELL   *Managing Organizational Innovation*

ORTH, BAILEY, & WOLEK   *Administering Research and Development: The Behavior of Scientists and Engineers in Organizations*

PORTER & LAWLER   *Managerial Attitudes and Performance*

PRICE   *Organizational Effectiveness: An Inventory of Propositions*

RUBENSTEIN & HABERSTROH (eds.)   *Some Theories of Organization*   rev. ed.

SCOTT   *The Management of Conflict*

SEILER   *Systems Analysis in Organizational Behavior*

WHYTE   *Organizational Behavior: Theory and Application*

WHYTE & HAMILTON   *Action Research for Management*

Organizational behavior
THEORY and APPLICATION

WILLIAM FOOTE WHYTE, Ph.D.
Professor of New York State School
  of Industrial and Labor Relations, and
Professor of Sociology
Cornell University

1969
RICHARD D. IRWIN, INC., and THE DORSEY PRESS
Homewood, Illinois
Irwin-Dorsey Limited, Georgetown, Ontario

This book is based in part on the author's previous text *Men at Work*

First Printing, July, 1969

Library of Congress Catalog Card No. 72–78391
Printed in the United States of America

Preface

THIS BOOK started out to be a revision of *Men at Work*. As I worked on the project over a two-year period, with the invaluable stimulation of weekly meetings with two groups of graduate students, the revisions became more and more drastic until, when the whole project was done, it seemed reasonable to call this a new book.

The book consists of 33 chapters, with not a single one appearing in the exact form of *Men at Work*. To assess the extent of changes, I sorted the chapters out in the following categories:

Completely new: 19 chapters (1–8, 14, 18, 24–28, 30–33).

New but incorporating old material: 4 chapters (9, 10, 11, and 13).

Major revisions: 3 chapters (17, 19, and 22).

Small revisions: 7 chapters (12, 15, 16, 20, 21, 23, and 29).

The title, *Organizational Behavior*, seems to me the best general term for the field in which I find myself. The subtitle, *Theory and Application*, needs a word of explanation. I feel that I have gone considerably beyond *Men at Work* in the effort to present a coherent theoretical framework. I have not done an "applied book" in the sense of a "how-to-do-it" manual. Such a manual, I feel, gives only a spurious impression of practicality. I have undertaken, in chapter after chapter, to consider the practical implications of the analysis, and I have devoted a final chapter to the problems of establishing behavioral science research in industry.

A major structural change in the book is found in the seven chapters of Part VIII, "Introducing Change." While the other chapters in this part represent reworking of old material, four out of the seven are completely new. With "The Industrial Research Laboratory" and "The Development Process" I have entered into an area of great and increasing importance which was not dealt with at all in *Men at Work*. "Managerial Succession" presents a comparative analysis of four cases, whereas the *Men at Work* chapter on this topic dealt with only one. "The Decision-Making Process" represents an attempt to use my own theoretical framework on the decision-making literature.

While *Men at Work* contained only tantalizing fragments on organizational behavior in other cultures, I have here devoted to it a long chapter which undertakes to examine, along the same dimensions of analysis, three very different cultures: the United States, Japan, and Peru.

This book also represents a new approach to methodology and theory. I am not here aiming to teach students how to do research, but, with

"Strategies of Research in Organizational Behavior," I am attempting to give students some understanding of the way the data they will be examining have been gathered. On the theoretical side, I have integrated certain ideas regarding "Transactions" with the concepts I was using in *Men at Work* and have sought to apply the resulting framework throughout the book.

The present book also goes a good deal further than *Men at Work* in examining a broad range of research projects.

Men at Work was built primarily out of research that I had either done myself or with which I had been closely associated. While a good deal of the Whyte research is to be found in the present volume, I have gone much further here in incorporating the work of other people. I have also gone somewhat further toward making this an interdisciplinary approach, although there is no concealing the fact that I am a sociologist, and naturally I am much influenced by this background and general point of view.

I have also made substantial changes in the form of presentation. Instead of having a set of questions at the end of each major section of the book, I have developed them for each chapter, which should make for a more effective teaching instrument. I do not think it very useful to ask questions that require the student simply to reproduce material he has read. But what are the alternatives? We want the student to learn to use the ideas in the book in analyzing new situations. In some textbooks, the authors attempt to lead the student in this direction by presenting cases after each chapter or section of the book and focusing the questions on the cases. I find two difficulties in this approach. In the first place, if the book is designed as a text rather than a case book, the cases must necessarily be presented in very brief form, which provides the students with a rather condensed and abstracted slice of reality. In the second place, I have found myself putting so many of what I consider my most interesting and useful cases into the chapters that I have very little ammunition left over for brief cases to offer to students.

The alternative that I have adopted points the students toward gathering their own case material. It seems to me likely that the student will learn more by trying to apply the analysis in this book to his own experience or to the experience of another individual, whom he interviews for this purpose, than is likely to be the case when he simply sits down to examine a case presented in a paragraph or two in a book. On the other hand, such an analysis of own or other experience is a more taxing assignment for the student than simply answering a question or two about a case presented in the book. Therefore, the instructor would hardly be able to give out this type of assignment for every chapter.

In this book, a number of cases from my own research or that of others appear in several chapters. So as to help student and teacher to pull the threads of a case together, I have prepared an index of cases for the end of the book.

This book depends very much upon the discussion sessions I carried on with graduate students. The 1967 group consisted of Giorgio Alberti, Richard Clarey, Richard Dunnington, Eustace Theodore, Peter Weissenberg, and Nicholas Yarmoshuk. The 1968 group consisted of William Button, Allen Hundert, Sean Kelly, John Kimberly, and George Westacott.

I am indebted to my wife, Kathleen King Whyte, for her critical comments and suggestions on many of the chapters, for participating in the discussion groups, and for providing the refreshments for the evening meetings.

I am very much indebted to my secretary, Mrs. Katherine Anderson, for her dedicated and highly efficient service at all stages of getting the book done, including the final typing under a good deal of time pressure.

Ithaca, New York   WILLIAM FOOTE WHYTE
June, 1969

Table of contents

PART I.   HISTORICAL AND THEORETICAL BACKGROUND . . .   1

1. The nature of our field of study   3

Forerunners: Taylor and Weber. U.S. social science origins.
Ushering in the modern period. Expansion and diversification.
Event-process analysts. The social structuralists. Organizational
surveyors. Group dynamicists. Decision-making theorists.
Psychiatric analysts. Technological structuralists. Where do
we stand now? Prospects for the field. Introducing the author.

2. Strategies of research   25

Broad comparative studies. Experimental studies. Interview-
observational methods. Interviewing and observation: possibilities. Interviewing and observation: limitations. The questionnaire survey: possibilities. The questionnaire survey:
limitations. Conclusion.

3. The structuring of the work environment   55

Technology and work flow. Work flow and the nature of the
job. Impact of technology on formal organization structure.
Specific determinants of structure. On formal versus informal
organization. Job placement and mobility systems. The compensation system. Describing and evaluating jobs. Rate setting
for incentive systems. Predictability and programming. On the
progress of scientific thinking. On the implications of structuring.

PART II.   FRAMEWORK FOR ANALYSIS   87

4. Interactions and activities   91

Micro-interaction and the cronograph. Personality and organization. Foremen in interaction. Vertical or horizontal interactions. Relating activities to interaction. Leaders and followers.
Leadership and status. Aspects of activities. Summary and
conclusions. Social implications.

5. Sentiments and symbols   128

The nature of sentiments. The framework of time. The investment-rewards relationship. Social relativity. Other ways of

dealing with sentiments. Relating Maslow and Herzberg to our framework. On the importance of structural effects. Symbols. Summary and conclusions.

6. Transactions   147

1. Positive exchange. 2. Trading. 3. Joint payoff. 4. Competitive. 5. Negative exchange. 6. Open conflict. 7. Bargaining. Dynamic tendencies. How are transactional values determined? What is power? On identifying transactional types and measuring values. Level of analysis. Transactions in relation to IAS. Summary and conclusions.

PART III.   GROUPS AND INTERGROUP RELATIONS   171

7. Groups: membership and structure   173

The Nortons. "Banana time." One department, many groups. Ethnicity and group pressures. Summary and conclusions.

8. Groups: offense and defense   205

1. Bulldogs versus Red Devils. 2. The Esso intergroup experiments. 3. The work group versus management. 4. The problem of the grinders. 5. The case of the steel containers. Summary and conclusions.

PART IV.   INDIVIDUAL AND GROUP IN THE ORGANIZATION
            CONTEXT   229

9. Supervisor, waitress, and the work group   231

Status and mobility opportunities. Ellen Geiger's story. Ann Lindstrom's story. Ann's initial adjustment to Chandler's. Ann and her friends under pressure. Ann prepares to quit. Aftermath of Ann's departure. Analysis of the case. Summary and conclusions.

10. Group leader, work group, and management   252

Historical perspective. Team composition and work operations. Work flow problems. Management-worker relations. Working conditions and the job itself. The card-ranking method. Jack Carter's card sort. Quantitative measures of leadership. Team leadership, Carter style. How did Jack Carter get that way? Summary and analysis.

11. Man, group, and process   277

The man who walked off the job. Technology and process. Personal and organizational history. The union drive. Sloan's last six weeks. How analyze the case? 1. Sloan's rapid rise. 2. Reactions to blocked progress. 3. Failure of group efforts. 4. The final six weeks. 5. The final day. General conclusions on Sloan. Technology, work process, and symbols.

PART V. VERTICAL RELATIONS 301

12. The first-line supervisory position 303

"The" foreman does not exist. The changing nature of foreman positions. Moving up from worker to foreman. The college-trained foreman. Status symbols in the supervisory relationship. Status and positive exchange transactions. Communication, interaction, and the initiation of activities. Summary and conclusions.

13. Supervision, morale, and productivity 318

Does virtue pay off? Differences in supervisory jobs. "General" versus "close" supervision. The programming of behavior. Participation management. Conceptual clarification. Conclusions.

14. The supervisor in the social system 331

From success to failure. Technology and work flow. Vertical and nonvertical relations. 1947–48: The pattern of success. What changed? 1949–50: The pattern of failure. Views of steward and foreman. Walker's transactional deficit. General conclusions.

PART VI. LATERAL AND DIAGONAL RELATIONS 347

15. Maintenance and operating organizations 349

The standardization program. The area coordination system. The struggle at Milo. Conclusions.

16. Cost control, production, and people 368

What do budget symbols mean to people? Problems with budgets. The impact on people. The budget-making process. Summary and conclusions.

17. The role of the personnel man 379

The evolution of the personnel department. How to organize the personnel department. The nature of personnel functions. Personnel counseling. Training. The personnel man as human relations consultant. Summary and conclusions.

18. Patterns of lateral and diagonal relations   399

1. Work flow. 2. Buy-sell relationships. 3. Service relationships.
4. Scheduling. 5. Auditing and standard setting. 6. Stabilization.
7. Advisory relationships. Combinations, natural and unnatural.
Lateral or diagonal relations? Changing work flow and status
relations. Power and performance. Summary and general conclusions.

PART VII.   UNION-MANAGEMENT RELATIONS   417

19. Enter the union   419

1. The union organization drive at Hi-Test. In the "good old
days." The company union. The Masters crack-down. The
situation at Hi-Test. New supervision at Hi-Test. The campaign. Local management's counteroffensive. The farewell
party. Negotiating for the company union. Management's
eleventh-hour effort. Analysis. Long-run changes. Changes in
interpersonal relations. 2. Symbolism for changing management
sentiments. Summary and conclusions.

20. The evolution of union-management relations   457

The rise and fall of Frank Vitucci. The decline of the steward.
The union meeting. How much centralization? The meaning
of grievances. The evolution of rules. Loyalty: dual or divided.
Conclusion.

21. Work unit cohesion and militancy   479

1. Smelting versus chemical division. The case of the caustic
plant. Post-war adjustments. The new management approach:
1953–57. Conflict cases. Analysis. 2. The rise and fall of the
grinders. The environment. The social system: 1941. The union
enters. The fruits of organization. Technological, physical, and
personnel changes. A cut in prices. Management's new offer.
State of the social system. Analysis. 3. The Benton blowing
room. Analysis. Summary and conclusions.

22. Patterns in union-management relations   514

A scheme for analysis. Union-management reciprocity. Problems at lower levels. The scheme as a guide to data. Summary
and conclusions.

23. The collective bargaining process   528

Symbolic equivalence of status. Attacking the man who isn't
there. Encouraging full expression. Building a pattern of agreement. Safety valves. Symbolism of common interests. Making
the institutional framework clear. The role of the international

representative. Getting the contract accepted. Launching the agreement. The problem of manipulation. Conclusion.

PART VIII. INTRODUCING CHANGE 559

24. On introducing change 561

1. Changing work team composition. Introducing a new product. Making the Amicon tube. Automation and the new IRR. Summary and conclusions.

25. Changing organizational size, composition, and character . . 571

1. Size and structure: a restaurant case. 2. The evolution of the Electrical Equipment Company. 3. Changing ethnic composition. 4. Changing organizational character. 5. Symbols and the introduction of change. Summary and conclusions.

26. The industrial research laboratory 595

Grafting on the research function. Scientist or administrator? Management policies. Who chooses the problem? Differences between lab and shop. The supervisor as lab group representative. A new strategy for supervisor-subordinate relations. Little man versus big company. Summary and conclusions.

27. The development process 619

The race to develop radar. Downstream and upstream relations. Coordination through liaison positions. Coordination through authority. Coordination through restructuring interactions. Coordination through negotiation. Coordination through group discussion. Role and functions of the engineer. Forms of engineering organization. Instability of work groups. Engineers as internal entrepreneurs. Summary and conclusions.

28. Managerial succession 640

Framework for analysis. 1. Chandler's Restaurant. 2. The Gypsum case. 3. The automotive assembly case. 4. The precision manufacturing case. General conclusions. On the nature of succession.

29. On the meaning of delegation 673

Measuring delegation. The picture two years later. What accounts for the changes? Conclusions.

30. The decision-making process 685

The traditional approach. The impact of information. The Bay of Pigs. On the indeterminacy of facts. Structural effects. The decision maker as hero. Choosing a dean. Feedback or justification? Implications for administrative action. Summary and conclusions.

PART IX.   PROGRESS REPORT 705

31.   What have we learned so far? 707

The process of learning what was not true. The human relations movement. Bringing in technology, work flow, and formal organization structure. The end of human relations? Standards for assessing progress. Summary and conclusions.

32.   An intercultural context for organizational research . . . 717

The selection of cases. Dimensions of comparison. 1. Peru. 2. Japan. 3. The United States. On the pitfalls of oversimplification. Conclusions and implications.

33.   On the application of behavioral science research in
organizations 764

Intervention strategies. Lessons learned. On the establishment of organizational research inside organizations. Case A: Western Electric Company. Case B: from research program to operating program. Case C: who is carrying the ball? Case D: the expendable program. Case E: basic is best. Case F: from small beginnings. Lessons from the cases. Problems of recruiting and maintaining research talent. Prospects for organizational behavior research in industry.

INDEXES 787

Index of cases 789

Index of subjects 791

Part I

HISTORICAL AND THEORETICAL BACKGROUND

In Part I the reader will encounter a three-pronged introduction to the field of organizational behavior.

The first chapter presents the field in historical terms. We review briefly some of the most important work of the past that has led to the emergence of organizational behavior as a distinctive field of study.

The second chapter examines the research methods that are commonly used to develop the data to be analyzed in this book. The aim here is *not* to make students into researchers. I simply assume that anyone who hopes to use research findings intelligently should have some understanding of the ways in which they were gathered.

The third chapter sets the stage in terms of technologies, organization structure, and management systems and procedures. Here we are concerned simply with what management is trying to accomplish in order to provide a background for the understanding of behavior as we bring our actors onto the scene in subsequent chapters.

1. The nature of our field of study

WHAT IS the nature of our field of study?

We can define the central content of the field and establish its boundaries by an arbitrary personal decision or we can go about it operationally, asking what people have done and how they have done it. I shall follow the latter approach.

In this chapter, I shall present a brief outline of history, designed to answer the question: *What* have people done as they have studied men at work? In the next chapter, I shall seek answers to the question: *How* do people go about studies in this field?

The origins of the field are diverse in time and in academic discipline. It may be useful to think of this history in two periods, with the year 1940 marking the dividing line between them. It was not until the 1940's that our field of study took on something like the shape that we know today, with courses and seminars suddenly appearing and multiplying in college and university curricula. The period before 1940 reveals to us a number of threads of development which remained intellectual fragments until later students of men at work sought to bring them together for the light they might throw on this newly evolving field of study.

Forerunners: Taylor and Weber

While almost any field of study can be traced back, with some plausibility, to Aristotle, the earliest intellectual ancestor that it seems useful to us to recognize is the engineer, Frederick Winslow Taylor (1856–1915).[1] In the early 1880's at the Midvale Steel Company, he began his studies at the humble task of observing workers with shovels. Taylor noted that, although the substances shoveled varied widely in weight, the shovels used by the workers were all of the same size and design. In a series of trials through which he worked out an optimum model shovel for each

---

[1] F. W. Taylor, *The Principles of Scientific Management* (New York: Harper & Bros., 1911). For an account of Taylor's life and work, see F. B. Copley, *Frederick W. Taylor, Father of Scientific Management* (New York: Harper & Bros., 1923).

3

weight of substance handled, Taylor was able to bring about substantial increases in productivity of the workers without increasing the physical burden on them. In fact, Taylor argued that better matching of the characteristics of tasks, tools, and men could yield increased output at a reduced cost of physical effort. This matching was to be achieved through observation and measurement; hence the title he gave to his new field: Scientific Management.

From shovels, Taylor went on to more complex problems. He examined the characteristics of metals and of tools used to cut them to determine the appropriate matching of tool and substance and the optimum machine speed for each operation. He observed that workers had different styles of performing the same task, with different levels of efficiency. He noted the nature and sequence of activities in each work cycle and timed each movement with a stop watch. Thus he sought to determine the best way to put the motions of the work cycle together and to establish a standard time for the completion of the cycle.

Taylor and his associates felt that they could increase output by paying workers by the piece produced. For this purpose, they needed to have measures that would enable them to set prices or piece rates.

Taylor did not limit his attention to the worker level. He and his associates worked out systems of work flow designed to get the materials to the right work station at the right time and with minimum cost. The control of the work flow involved the devising of paper forms to record the steps in the process.

The approach of Taylor and his associates was based upon certain assumptions regarding workers and management and their work.

1. The one best method of doing a particular job can be scientifically determined.
2. Wherever possible at the work level, complex jobs should be subdivided into their elementary components. Work should proceed most efficiently when each worker had only a simple and repetitive job to do.
3. Workers were to be trained so that they could perform each job in the standardized form established by management.
4. The discretion of workers concerning their work was to be reduced to a minimum. The planning and control of activities was to be carried on at higher organizational levels.
5. Workers were viewed as responding *as individuals* to economic incentives. Payment should therefore be based upon the number of units produced by each individual worker.

These ideas remain part of the thinking and practice of many management people even today. Not all of Taylor's notions were generally adopted. For example, he presented the idea of functional foremanship, having a number of supervisors responsible for different aspects of the worker's performance. This notion violated the concept of "unity of command," which is now often thought to be a self-evident principle of administration. (We shall question it later.)

Other theorists, while rejecting the functional foremanship idea, built upon Taylor's approach by evolving theories of administration that emphasized control of activities and precise allocations of authority and responsibility. It was assumed that authority should be commensurate with responsibility—that is, if a man had responsibility for getting a given job done, he had to be given authority so that he could require the compliance with his directives of those upon whose performance he depended to get the job done.

It was assumed that, to keep adequate control of activities, close supervision of subordinates was required. This led to theories concerning the optimum span of control: the number of subordinates who should report to a given superior. While it was recognized that a manager can adequately supervise a larger number of people when the activities of his subordinates do not depend upon each other, and thus the optimum number should vary with the presence or absence of this interdependence, it has been generally assumed that, at least at higher levels of the organization, no more than five or six individuals should report to an executive.

While Taylor and others of his school worked with a good deal of empirical data, they were primarily concerned with constructing a normative system—an outline of the way people in industry *should* behave. They fully recognized that behavior often did not turn out as planned, even when management people sought to follow their principles. These failures they tended to explain away with the assumption that the principles and procedures had not been properly applied. It remained for later investigators to study behavior at work without using the assumptions of scientific management, thus coming out with data that serve to question the validity of these assumptions.

Today behavioral scientists use Taylor more as a foil for criticisms than as a source of knowledge or inspiration. We are inclined to point out that in concentrating on the individual Taylor completely disregarded social organization, and that he had so low a regard for the worker that he advocated simplifying and programming the worker's behavior so completely as to leave no room for self-expression. While these criticisms are sound, we should not allow them to obscure the pioneering role Taylor played. When he came on the scene, management was considered simply an art, and the customs of the organization in large part dictated the actions of supervisors and executives. Taylor was the first to gain a hearing for his conviction that management could be guided by science. Faulty and incomplete as was his theoretical framework, at least he built his conclusions upon painstaking observation of behavior on the shop floor.

A contemporary of Taylor, Max Weber (1864–1920), the eminent German economist and sociologist,[2] evolved an approach to the study of organization that has a number of points in common with the scientific management school. While his major work dealing with organizations, *Wirtschaft und Gesellschaft*, was not published until 1921, after his death, Weber was developing his theories before the turn of the century.

Weber was concerned with the study of what he called bureaucracy. While in common conversation, we often hear the word used as an epithet, denoting endless procedures and "red tape," neither Weber nor sociologists following his theories have interpreted the word in that way.

Weber used the term simply to point to a phenomenon of growing importance even in his time: the large organization with fixed positions linked together in a hierarchical pyramid, with specialization and division of labor, and with established rules and regulations governing behavior. Weber cited these features as characterizing bureaucracies:

I.   There is the principle of fixed and official jurisdictional areas, which are generally ordered by rules, that is, by laws or administrative regulations. . . .

II.   The principles of office hierarchy and of levels of graded authority mean a firmly ordered system of super- and subordination in which there is a supervision of the lower offices by the higher ones. . . .

III.   The management of the modern office is based upon written documents (the files). . . .

IV.   Office management, at least all specialized office management—and such management is distinctly modern—usually presupposes thorough and expert training. . . .

V.   When the office is fully developed, official activity demands the full working capacity of the official, irrespective of the fact that his obligatory time in the bureau may be firmly delimited. . . .

VI.   The management of the office follows general rules, which are more or less stable, more or less exhaustive, and which can be learned. . . .

Weber goes on to speak of the bureaucratic career: office-holding as a "vocation." The individual does not move in and out of the organization. He is appointed by a superior authority and, in the normal course of circumstances, he moves up to higher levels, again by appointment of superiors, based upon length of service and an ability to conform to the norms of the bureaucracy.

To Weber, this was not a description of any particular organization but rather an ideal type—a theoretical model which could be useful insofar as it pointed to important and commonly present features of organizations. There seems no doubt that Weber was pointing out in a

---

[2] For an account of Weber's life and work, see H. H. Gerth and C. Wright Mills, *Max Weber* (London: Oxford University Press, 1946). The summary of Weber's view of bureaucracy is taken from this book and also presented in A. H. Rubenstein and C. J. Haberstroh (eds.), *Some Theories of Organization* (rev. ed.; Homewood, Ill.: Richard D. Irwin, Inc. and The Dorsey Press, 1966), pp. 70–81.

useful way the important differences between bureaucracies and organizations of people held together through personal relationships around a particular leader. The impersonality and rationality of modern industrial and governmental organizations are indeed important features, but even those who cite Weber in their studies in recent years have been impelled to point out certain ways in which his "ideal type" does not conform to the realities of many—if not most—modern organizations. As we shall see, they question the rigidities of organization depicted, the lack of attention to processes of change, and the exclusive concentration on hierarchy, to the consequent neglect of diagonal and horizontal relations.

U.S. social science origins

Among U.S. social scientists, the first to get into the field and maintain a continuing set of activities were the industrial psychologists. It has been their function to devise tests which will measure the aptitudes and abilities of individuals in relation to the jobs they perform. While much useful work along this line has been done, it has been increasingly recognized that the aptitudes and abilities of an individual, as measured by tests, often have a low level of predictability regarding the success of the individual on the job. Performance is so influenced by relations of the individual to the group and to management that knowledge of his aptitudes and abilities will provide little predictive power.

Labor economists began studies of industrial relations in the late 19th century. To them we owe much of our knowledge concerning union history and administration—topics which were not touched upon at all by the other investigators and groups of investigators so far mentioned. As unionization in the mass-production industries gained momentum in the 1930's, labor economists generally turned their attention to bargaining relations between unions and managements. In this period they gave little attention to relations at the plant level, which have been the major focus of attention of sociologists, psychologists, and anthropologists in recent years.

Ushering in the modern period

If these earlier activities have all left traces of influence within our field of study, the concentrated period of exploration and development may be dated from the research program of the Western Electric Company and the Harvard Business School, conducted from 1927 to 1932. These two institutions were brought together in a remarkedly ambitious program by Elton Mayo, a psychologist from Australia, who had already gained some experience in industrial studies in his own country and in the United States. Mayo provided the general plan of the research program and carried the major responsibility for developing and maintaining the relationship between the university and the company. Principle researchers were Fritz J. Roethlisberger (for Harvard) and William J. Dickson (for the company).

Management and the Worker[3] has come to be recognized as a classic in social science research and, for a number of years after its publication in 1939, most of what was known about the relations among workers and between workers and management in the work place was contained in this volume and in related studies growing out of the research program. In fact, the first textbook in our field, Burleigh B. Gardner's *Human Relations in Industry*,[4] appearing in 1945, is to a very large extent based on an interpretation of the Hawthorne works, where the Western Electric studies were done, and a discussion of the research findings of these studies, supplemented by Gardner's own experience with the counseling program of the company. Gardner placed such a heavy reliance upon the Western Electric materials for the very good reason that, at the time he wrote, the literature contained little else that would give students and professors a picture of life in the industrial plant.

At a time when it was commonly believed that experimentation on human beings was impossible, Mayo and his associates carried out a series of systematically planned experiments in the Hawthorne works. The key experiment of this series will be reviewed briefly in Chapter 2, as we consider the methods they used to gather data in our field.

At a time when systematic observation of human groups had been limited to the work of anthropologists studying primitive tribes, Mayo and his associates arranged to gather continuous observational data on several work groups over a period of many months.

The Hawthorne studies had a marked impact upon theorizing about behavior in industry. They clearly showed the limitations of the economic man concept then being applied by proponents of the scientific management school. They showed that workers did not simply respond as individuals to the money incentives offered them. They demonstrated that productivity of workers had to be explained in social as well as economic and technological terms. While they were not the first to recognize the social phenomenon of restriction of output, they presented, in their study of the bank wiring room, the most intimate picture that had so far been brought forward of the way in which output norms were evaluated and enforced by members of the work group. Such studies led the investigators and those that followed them to recognize the importance of informal groups in industry and to look beyond the formal charts of organization structure and the official statements of authority and responsibility in order to determine what was going on in the plant.

---

[3] Fritz J. Roethlisberger and W. J. Dickson, *Management and the Worker* (Cambridge, Mass.: Harvard University Press, 1939).

[4] Burleigh B. Gardner, *Human Relations in Industry* (Homewood, Ill.: Richard D. Irwin, Inc., 1945).

While this work put economic man in a broader social context, it had the same implications for psychological man. The investigators had aptitude tests on members of the work group they were observing, and they found that the productivity of individual workers bore no relationship to their aptitude scores. It was only as they examined the relations of the individual to the work group that they could make sense out of the productivity records.

The Western Electric program demonstrated the possibilities of research on human behavior at the plant level, and the major report of this program came out at a most opportune time for the future development of the field. World War II stirred widespread interest in problems of morale and motivation in our armed forces and on the home front.

Another social science classic, *The American Soldier*,[5] emerged out of the survey program carried on by sociologists and psychologists within the military. The book was significant not only for its substantive and theoretical findings but also for the methods the investigators developed for the study of large organizations. It was apparent that the field methods and techniques of analysis used in studying military organizations could, with some modifications, be applied to studies of industrial organizations. In the exceedingly tight labor market of World War II, many companies suffered from high labor turnover, and some management people even became so concerned about problems of keeping workers on the job that they invited social scientists into their plants for study and consultation.

The 1940's brought forth university centers to concentrate research on the human problems of industry. First on the scene was the Committee on Human Relations in Industry, established at the University of Chicago in 1943, with anthropologists W. Lloyd Warner and Burleigh B. Gardner as chairman and executive secretary, respectively. Other members of the Committee in 1943 were Everett C. Hughes, Allison Davis, Robert C. Havighurst, and George C. Brown. E. Wight Bakke established his Labor-Management center at Yale University in 1946. Bakke was already well known for his studies of the effect of prolonged unemployment upon English and U.S. industrial workers and their families.

While he established no center or institute in a formal sense, Douglas McGregor, at Massachusetts Institute of Technology, led some of the most able investigators into this field of study. McGregor, himself, in collaboration with anthropologist Conrad M. Arensberg, had begun a pioneering study of the human problems of communication and work satisfaction accompanying the rapid growth of an industrial organization.[6]

---

[5] Samuel A. Stouffer, *et al.*, *The American Soldier: Studies in Social Psychology in World War II* (2 vols.; Princeton, N.J.: Princeton University Press, 1949).

[6] Douglas McGregor and Conrad M. Arensberg, "Determination of Morale in an Industrial Company," *Applied Anthropology*, Vol. 1, no. 2 (1942), pp. 12–34. This case is one of the five discussed at length in George C. Homans, *The Human Group* (New York: Harcourt Brace, 1950).

In 1946 Rensis Likert established the Institute for Social Research at the University of Michigan to concentrate research effort upon studies of industrial and governmental organizations. Meanwhile, Kurt Lewin had established the Research Center for Group Dynamics at Massachusetts Institute of Technology. While his group was concerned with group processes in other settings, it also gave some attention to the study of industry and was responsible for the Harwood experiments, which have become recognized as classics in the field. Upon the death of Lewin, his associates moved in a body to the University of Michigan to establish the Research Center for Group Dynamics within Likert's Institute for Social Research, alongside the Survey Research Center, which specialized in organizational surveys. Likert himself had come into this field through opinion and attitude surveys he had developed while working within the U.S. Department of Agriculture.

The Ohio State Leadership Studies, under the direction of Caroll Shartle, also came into being at this time. This program contributed particularly to theory and methodology in the study of the man-boss relationship in industry, and out of this program also came one of the most impressive studies of the effects of human relations training that has yet been made.

Expansion and diversification

The decades of the 1940's and 1950's witnessed a broad exploration of the field. While in 1940 our knowledge of the human problems in industry was very largely limited to a giant factory manufacturing telephone equipment, the following years brought a rapid extension of research in other types of work situations. The range within manufacturing was extended into petroleum, steel fabrication, chemicals, plastics, utilities, and several other industries. In the service industries, we find studies of restaurants, department stores, a hotel, and a delivery service company, among others. Research was also carried forward in government departments, and in the decade of the fifties there was a proliferation of studies of hospitals.

We also expanded greatly the range of roles in organizations on which we have research data. At the beginning of this period, our knowledge was concentrated primarily at the worker level and upon blue-collar workers. Over the period of years, our studies have moved gradually up the hierarchy. By the mid-1940's, some of us were concentrating attention upon foremen. Studies of higher levels of management came later and are now a major focus of attention. Over the years, we have also accumulated research data upon specialists in industry: engineers, accountants, personnel men, and purchasing agents. Scientists in industry and government have been the last to be included in such studies, but we are now getting some concentrated attention focused upon these key functionaries of modern industrial organizations.

At the time of their appearance, the main publications of the Western Electric research program were vigorously attacked by some critics for not giving some attention to the important role of unions in industry. The investigators at Hawthorne neglected the union for the very good reason that they were making work-group studies in a plant that was not unionized, except (at the time) by a company union which apparently played little role in the workplace. Since that time various investigators have focused their attention particularly on union-management relations. There have been studies of official and wildcat strikes and of the conditions of cooperation or conflict between union and management in a variety of industries.

Until approximately 1960, U.S. investigators focused their attention for analysis and theorizing almost exclusively upon studies done in the United States, where indeed the bulk of research activity in this field has been concentrated. Even before this period, we began to get first-rate studies from England, and, for purposes of comparison with our own U.S. data, we can now turn not only to England but also to France, Japan, Latin America, India, Poland, Yugoslavia, and a number of other parts of the world.

Our field has been studied by investigators coming out of different disciplines and applying a number of different methodologies and schemes of theoretical analysis. While any set of categories is bound to oversimplify reality, it may help us to order our thinking if we look at the field in terms of seven schools of thought and activity; representative of these are event-process analysts, structuralists, organizational surveyors, group dynamicists, decision-making theorists, psychiatric analysts, and the technological structuralists.

Event-process analysts

I select this title because those that I see following this approach devote their main attention to the study of particular (and recurring) events and the examination of social processes. We might call this the "social-anthropological approach" because it has been shaped primarily by anthropologists such as W. Lloyd Warner, Burleigh B. Gardner, Eliot D. Chapple, Conrad M. Arensberg, and F. L. W. Richardson, Jr. On the other hand, there have been men professionally identified as sociologists, such as Everett C. Hughes, George C. Homans, Melville Dalton, Donald Roy, and Orvis Collins, who have gathered their data through interviewing and observation (generally without the use of questionnaires) and who have similarly concentrated upon events and social processes.

The Society for Applied Anthropology, founded in 1941, has provided a meeting ground for anthropologists, sociologists, social psychologists, and specialists in other disciplines who have been concerned with pursuing this approach to organizational research. The Society's journal, *Human Organization* (called *Applied Anthropology* until 1949), has been the leading publication for organizational studies stemming from this approach.

The social structuralists

While the event-process analysts sought first to build their theoretical formulations out of their own intimate and detailed examination of interpersonal relations in the workplace, what we may call the structuralist approach grew out of the revival of interest in the broad and general theories of organization propounded by the great social theorists of earlier days such as Max Weber and Robert Michels. In this tradition, the starting point is some broad theoretical formulation which the research man seeks to test in some organizational situation. In general, there has been little concern with problems of immediate, interpersonal relations at the work site. For example, Lipset, Coleman and Trow[7] set out to examine the two-party political democracy of the International Typographical Union as an apparently deviant case for Michels' "Iron Law of Oligarchy." Bendix,[8] in *Work and Authority in Industry*, presents an analysis of the relationship between managerial ideology and systems of authority on both sides of the iron curtain. In *TVA and the Grass Roots*, Selznick[9] is concerned with examining ways in which a large organization makes adjustments to its social and economic environment, and how this affects its internal functioning and the development of its policies.

While studies coming out of this tradition of general organization theory have tended to concern themselves with social units far above the level of the immediate work place, apparently this is not an inevitable consequence of this point of view. Gouldner[10] launched himself out of the Weberian theory into an intimate and detailed analysis of a gypsum plant, and Blau used the same takeoff point for his close-range study of employees in two government agencies. In fact, Blau[11] represents something of a link between the structuralists and the event-process analysts, for as his work has continued on the level of detailed examination of interpersonal events, his interest in the Weberian theory seems to have dropped by the wayside in favor of attempts to build theory out of the analysis of interpersonal events and social processes. Here he and George Homans,[12]

---

[7] S. M. Lipset, James S. Coleman, and Martin Trow, *Union Democracy* (Glencoe, Ill.: The Free Press, 1956).

[8] Reinhard Bendix, *Work and Authority in Industry* (New York: John Wiley & Sons, 1956).

[9] Philip Selznik, *TVA and the Grass Roots* (Berkeley: University of California Press, 1949).

[10] Alvin Gouldner, *Patterns of Industrial Bureaucracy* (Glencoe, Ill.: The Free Press, 1955).

[11] Peter Blau, *The Dynamics of Bureaucracy* (Chicago: The University of Chicago Press, 1955).

[12] For the theories of Homans, see *The Human Group* (New York: Harcourt Brace, 1950).

one of the leading theorists of the event-process analysis group, have come close together.

Organizational surveyors

Two more or less integrated approaches have grown out of social psychology; the organization surveyors and the group dynamicists represent these. Let us first consider the surveyors.

While other aspects of organization are now receiving increasing attention, the largest volume of such research over the years has been devoted to studies of organizational leadership, focusing especially upon the immediate man-boss relationship. The particular problem has been to explore possibilities for the development of nonauthoritarian or democratic leadership patterns in industry and to determine whether these are compatible with high levels of productivity and efficiency.

Research men have relied primarily upon the questionnaire survey method. To a much lesser extent, experimentation has been used, and even in such cases the questionnaire survey has been the primary instrument used to measure the changes brought about. There has been little concern with describing or analyzing the social process whereby the changes were brought about.

The survey researchers have been concerned with measuring attitudes and perceptions and with relating these both to the demographic characteristics of their informants and to "hard criterion variables" such as productivity, absenteeism, and turnover. They have not generally been concerned with relating attitudes and perceptions on the one hand, or hard criterion variables, on the other, to the social process in which their informants are involved.

The leading theorists of this school have been Rensis Likert and the late Douglas McGregor. Likert reported and reinterpreted many of the findings of his own Michigan research program, and those of others, in *New Patterns of Management*[13] and *The Human Organization*.[14] McGregor, in *The Human Side of Enterprise*,[15] presented his view of participative management and popularized the notion of two competing theories, theory x and theory y.

Group dynamicists

Group dynamics had its principle origin in the small group experiments of the late Kurt Lewin and his Research Center for Group Dynamics and has been carried forward particularly by Dorwin Cartwright, J. R. P.

---

[13] Rensis Likert, *New Patterns of Management* (New York: McGraw-Hill Book Co., 1961).

[14] Rensis Likert, *The Human Organization* (New York: McGraw-Hill Book Co., 1967).

[15] Douglas McGregor, *The Human Side of Enterprise* (New York: McGraw-Hill Book Co., 1960).

French, Jr., and Alvin Zander. Training and research along these lines has been immensely stimulated by the National Training Laboratories in Bethel, Maine, and other regional centers.

Some years ago, dealing entirely with cases in industrial plants, Norman Maier published a book whose title, *Principles of Human Relations*,[16] suggested that the whole of organizational behavior consisted of group discussion training methods. In recent years, the most active exponents of the group dynamics approach to industry have been Robert Tannenbaum, Chris Argyris, Warren Bennis, Robert Blake, and Herbert Shepard.

The focus of attention has been upon the group discussion process and upon the effects that certain types of group discussion have upon the attitudes and behavior of the individual participants. Like the organization surveyors, the group dynamics people think in terms of autocratic versus democratic leadership.

Recognizing that an industrial organization necessarily has a hierarchy of authority and being concerned about the apparent effects of authority upon the freedom and development of the individual, people in this field have been exploring the possibility of modifying the autocratic aspects of large organizations through group discussion and participation methods which, it is hoped, enable the participants in the discussion to gain a better understanding of themselves and the organizational world around them and to change behavior and attitudes in this world.

Followers of this approach emphasize empathy or sensitivity: the ability to understand the other fellow and to respond in terms of that understanding. There is also great concern with the content of verbal communications, with authenticity, the extent to which members of the group express what they think and feel regarding their relations with other members and regarding the social situation in which they find themselves.

By whatever names they are called, group discussion approaches to human relations training have become very popular in recent years. Of course, most such training goes on without any built-in research component. There are, nevertheless, people who are concerned with doing research on these new approaches to training.

Decision-making theorists

The most recent arrivals on the organizational behavior scene are the decision-making theorists. The field owes much of its popularity to the pioneering work of James G. March and Herbert A. Simon. Besides giving a systematic review and summary statement, in propositional form, of a wide variety of research done by others, their book, *Organizations*,[17]

---

[16] Norman Maier, *Principles of Human Relations* (New York: John Wiley & Sons, 1952).

[17] James G. March and Herbert A. Simon, *Organizations* (New York: John Wiley & Sons, 1958).

organizes the thinking of the authors around decision making. The focal point of their analysis is the *individual:* how he decides whether to remain in the organization or to leave it, to produce more or less, and so on.

Research methods in this field involve primarily the building of models to illustrate the forces coming to bear on the individual as he makes his decision. Research men have been much concerned with developing mathematical formulations to represent the impact of these forces upon the individual and thus upon his resultant decision. Simon recently has been carrying the analysis beyond the drawing of diagrams and the assigning of values to the forces so represented. He has been concerned with simulating human mental processes with the computer.

Psychiatric analysts

While this school has been small in numbers of adherents, it has produced several influential studies. The original center of activities was the Tavistock Institute of Human Relations in London. The first major study was Elliott Jaques' *The Changing Culture of a Factory.*[18] In his study of a worker-management consultation program in a large unionized metalworking plant, Jaques sought to apply some of the insights and procedures used in psychotherapy with individual patients to group and organizational situations. His data were gathered largely from the observation of innumerable committee meetings at department and plantwide levels. His consultancy role involved occasionally discussing with group participants what he saw going on and, finally, reviewing his manuscript with all the groups involved.

Some years later, Cyril Sofer, also from Tavistock, described a number of his cases of research and organizational therapy in *The Organization from Within.*[19]

Leading exponents of this approach in the United States have been Abraham Zaleznik[20] and David Moment of the Harvard Business School. In a variety of leadership and organizational studies, they have been concerned with relating intrapersonal with interpersonal processes.

Technological structuralists

Charles R. Walker got the idea that the technology of the organization must have important effects upon human relations in the workplace. Stated in this way, the idea seems simple—if not too simple—but the point

---

[18] Elliott Jaques, *The Changing Culture of a Factory* (New York: The Dryden Press, 1952).

[19] Cyril Sofer, *The Organization from Within* (Chicago: Quadrangle Books, 1962).

[20] Abraham Zaleznik, *The Dynamics of Interpersonal Behavior* (New York: John Wiley & Sons, 1964); David Moment, *Human Dilemmas of Leadership* (New York: Harper & Row, 1966).

is that not until Walker set up his Technology Center at Yale had anybody decided that technology was important enough for organizational behavior to deserve a special research emphasis.

Beginning in the late 1940's, Walker and his associates carried out a series of studies[21] that have made the automotive assembly line the best known technology, from the standpoint of social research. They then moved on to make one of the earliest (and best) studies in the now popular field of automation.[22]

In England, Joan Woodward[23] carried out a study of the relationship between technology and the formal structure of the organization. This work has had a major impact upon organization theory. In Chapter 2, we will describe the way she carried out the study, and in Chapter 3, we will consider some of her findings.

Where do we stand now?

Out of this welter of activity, growing out of a number of different approaches, have come certain main lines of theoretical development.

"Participation Management" has come to be a title for a large body of research and interpretation of research concerning the exercise of leadership in organizations. Men pursuing this line of theory have been concerned with examining different patterns for the exercise of authority in relation to the attitudes and the productivity of subordinates. This approach will be assessed in later chapters on supervisory leadership.

Out of event-process analysis has grown a body of interaction theory, which bases its interpretation of behavior and attitudes on the patterns of interpersonal relations which the organizational participants have experienced. It is this theoretical approach, combined with exchange theory, which will guide our analysis beginning in Chapter 4.

Exchange theory views behavior as being based upon an exchange of values in interpersonal relations. Theorists using this approach seeks to explain behavior and attitudes of organizational participants in terms of the exchange of values among them. The outline of this approach in modified form will be presented in Chapter 6.

Theorists have not only been concerned with explaining harmonious or conflictful relations among individuals. They have recognized that much of the conflict to be observed in industrial organizations is highly organized and must be viewed in terms of intergroup or interorganizational

---

[21] Charles R. Walker and Robert Guest, *The Man on the Assembly Line* (Cambridge, Mass.; Harvard University Press, 1952). Charles R. Walker, Robert H. Guest, and Arthur N. Turner, *The Foreman on the Assembly Line* (Cambridge, Mass.: Harvard University Press, 1956).

[22] Charles R. Walker, *Toward the Automatic Factory* (New York: Harper & Bros. 1957).

[23] Joan Woodward, *Industrial Organization: Theory and Practice* (London: Oxford University Press, 1965).

relations. Theorists in this problem area have been giving attention both to day-to-day relations between union and management and to the more dramatic confrontations between groups that take place in the process of bargaining for a new contract. We shall explore research findings and theoretical implications on both levels in Parts II and III and in later chapters on bargaining.

Recent years have brought striking changes in theories concerning the process of management. The early theory of Max Weber and also the scientific management school focused attention upon the formal structure of the organization and upon principles of authority and of control of activities. Some modern theorists are now arguing that the old theories were based upon a mechanistic conception of organization that is unrealistic, that the older theorists concentrate excessive attention upon the line of authority, and that they fail to place the formal organization structure in that broader context which must necessarily shape it and influence its effectiveness. These modern theorists look upon formal organization in relation to the mission (the tasks the organization is built to carry out), the technology through which work gets done, and the market upon which the organization depends. These theorists are giving increasing attention to lateral and diagonal relations at various levels of the organization. In the coordination of activities, they examine a process of negotiation or exchange which appears to go on quite apart from the exercise of authority.

As long as we concentrated our research on organizations in the United States, we could not determine the generalizability of our findings. Would the propositions we stated regarding the behavior of men at work prove valid in any country? Or were these propositions applicable only in our own country? Recent research has indicated that some generalizations at least need modification if they are to be applied in other cultural settings. There is now in process a reexamination of organization theory in order to place it in an intercultural context. We will consider these developments in the final part of this book.

When this book is published, it will be exactly three decades since *Management and the Worker* signalled the establishment of a new field of study. If our field is still relatively young, are there nevertheless signs that it is approaching scientific maturity?

We may take three indicators of maturation:

1. *The decline of arguments over ethics.* The emergence of the field was greeted by a barrage of arguments against the ethics of its principle investigators. Some were charged with promoting a kind of "cow sociology," showing management how to "manipulate" the workers so as to make a union unnecessary. It was said that we pursued an ideal of perfect harmony, through "good communications," under a managerial elite and disregarded the conflicting interests that necessarily arise in complex organizations.

In the first decade or so, an article along these lines would appear about once a year.[24] I cannot recall seeing a single one in the last decade.

Why did the arguments stop? Because the ethical issues were settled? Hardly, because it is the nature of ethical issues that they are never really settled. Because nothing new remained to be said? Perhaps, but a lack of new arguments rarely puts an end to argumentation.

I am inclined to attribute the decline of argumentation to three influences:

a) The literature in our field has grown to cover a broad range of problems and interest groups. It deals with conflict as well as with collaboration. If it is useful to managers, so also is it useful to union leaders and union organizers.

b) In the 1930's and 1940's many social scientists felt that the union movement was *the* major force supporting democracy and social justice in the United States. By the 1960's the battlefront for social justice had shifted to the problems of civil rights and economic and political opportunities for minority groups. Management and unions were involved in the struggle, but many union leaders had come to be regarded as defenders of the status quo (or the "white establishment") rather than standard bearers for progressive forces. The social scientist no longer had to identify with unions in order to be considered ethically sound by some of his former critics.

c) Our field is no longer the academic threat that it seemed to be in the early years. The field was opened up in the 1940's with a great burst of enthusiasm. Young professors and graduate students rushed in, and in so doing, deserted the established professors and the established fields. While money was not easy to raise in these early years, it could be secured from private industry far more readily than from government. Project organizers could therefore offer bright students more money and more attractive fieldwork opportunities than what was available with what had hitherto been the academic establishment. Getting into this field early also meant better teaching jobs and more rapid promotions. A man might make the jump from assistant professor to full professor in five years or

---

[24] See, for example, Herbert Blumer, "Sociological Theory in Industrial Relations," *American Sociological Review*, Vol. 12, (1947), pp. 271–78; Daniel Bell, "Adjusting Men to Machines," *Commentary*, Vol. 3 (1947), pp. 79–88; Wilbert Moore, "Current Issues in Industrial Sociology," *American Sociological Review*, Vol. 12 (1947), pp. 651–57, and "Industrial Sociology: Status and Prospects," *American Journal of Sociology*, Vol. 13 (1948), pp. 382–91; C. Wright Mills, "The Contributions of Sociology to Studies of Industrial Relations", *Industrial Relations Research Association Proceedings*, Vol. 1 (1948), pp. 199–222; Clark Kerr and Lloyd H. Fisher, "Plant Sociology: The Elite and the Aborigines," in Mirra Kamarovsky (ed.), *Common Frontiers of Social Sciences* (Glencoe, Ill.: The Free Press, 1957); also Reinhard Bendix and Lloyd H. Fisher, "The Perspectives of Elton Mayo," and George C. Homans, "Some Corrections to 'The Perspectives of Elton Mayo.'" Published earlier, this debate is most accessible in Amitai Etzioni (ed.), *Complex Organizations* (New York: Holt, Rinehart & Winston, 1964).

less, thus arriving at the top of that line of promotion in his early or mid-thirties rather than eight to 10 years later. Those who were either unwilling or unable to join in the new enterprise naturally felt threatened.

This "boom" condition no longer prevails. Some of those who were in our field early have moved on to other interests. New people continue to come in, but they are now entering a more or less established field that no longer offers exceptional advantages in research funds, jobs, and promotions. While social research money from private industry is still available, this source is now dwarfed by the federal government, not to mention the foundations. Financial support for good graduate students in good graduate schools is now so generally available that our field no longer offers any substantial financial advantages.

2. *The decline of competing schools of thought.* In a mature science, we do not have competing schools of thought. There is agreement on a general body of knowledge and disagreement only on the frontiers of knowledge.

We have not reached that point, but we can see movement in that direction. While I have been able to sort out some of the leaders of our field into seven groupings, the word "schools" is perhaps misleading even at this point, for I have not made the division along doctrinal lines (as is usually done in delineating schools of thought). I have simply sorted people in terms of problem interests and styles of research.

Even this preliminary sorting will not stand too close scrutiny, for we will find individuals placed in one box who might perhaps also be placed in another box. I have already noted the difficulty in placing Peter Blau. While I have put Elliott Jaques with the psychiatric analysts, his recent work on *Measurement of Responsibility*[25] has nothing to do with psychiatry. Jaques simply found a problem he considered interesting and important and developed the methods and theoretical notions to throw light on it.

It may be characteristic of a good man in this field (or others) that, once classified, he does not "stay put." As old-timers shift their interests and as newcomers make their contributions, it is becoming increasingly difficult to sort people out into "schools" or other groupings. This difficulty in itself may be a sign of increasing maturity of the field.

3. *Evolving consensus over the nature of the field.* People who approach the field from different disciplines are coming to agree that the organization has certain properties that distinguish it from informal groups, communities, or simple aggregates of individuals. Whether our current problem focus is on workers, supervisors, engineers, or executives, we increasingly see the necessity of examining each category of individuals against the context of the organization. The notion of *mutual depend-*

---

[25] Elliott Jaques, *Measurement of Responsibility* (London: Tavistock Publications, 1956); see also *Equitable Payment* (London: Heinemann, 1961).

ence is also gaining ground: The organization is seen as a social system made up of mutually dependent parts. This means that if a change is introduced into one part of the system, we should expect to observe changes in other parts also.

At this point, the consensus breaks down. There are disagreements as to how to specify the parts whose mutual dependence is to be examined and as to what observations and measurements need to be made in order to describe and analyze this state of mutual dependence.

Prospects for the field

It is customary for the social scientist to speak with humility and acknowledge that he does not really know much. Certainly, if we compare our field with the natural sciences, we have every reason to be humble. On the other hand, if we compare our field now to our state of knowledge concerning men at work approximately three decades ago when *Management and the Worker* first appeared, we can record substantial progress. It will be our task to describe this progress, as we attempt to arrange the findings of research in a meaningful pattern.

While we can take at least modest satisfaction for the amount of knowledge that has been acquired by research men in this field, we can take much less satisfaction concerning the amount of knowledge which is currently being applied in the administration of organizations. The problems of applying behavioral science knowledge to administration will be considered in our final chapter.

How fast can we expect the field to advance in the future? The answer depends in large measure upon the quality and quantity of people now being attracted into the field, and on that point we will hazard no guess. But it also depends upon the inherent characteristics offered the research man by the study of human behavior in work organizations. I shall argue that work organizations offer certain strategic advantages for the development of the behavioral sciences that are difficult if not impossible to match in other types of research sites.

A work organization provides us with a definite structure to examine. While we make no assumption regarding the relationship between the organization chart and the pattern of human relations actually to be observed, we can expect at the outset that there is a definite pattern and that we can determine what it is relatively quickly and economically. This is the case because we have before us a limited number of people interacting with each other and carrying on activities that are highly repetitive. The human events we wish to observe, inquire about, and measure occur with a high frequency. In many other research sites, these events occur with a much lower frequency and in a much less patterned form.

The organization produces its own measures of certain activities and aspects of participation: records of productivity, scrap loss, turnover, absenteeism, and the like. While these records are seldom produced by management in just the form that can be used by organizational behavior research men, the researchers can often develop quite respectable data on "hard criterion variables" from material that they do not have to gather themselves. Consider for example, the case of my colleague, Ned Rosen[26] who has written a book on his experiment with the rotation of factory foremen among eight production lines. While the experiment also involved observation, interviewing, and the application of before and after questionnaires, the production data from about 70 men, calculated on a weekly basis, are crucial to the research design. This is a large statistical job, but no time and money were spent in gathering the data. They were mailed weekly to Cornell from the factory. Imagine the problems and expense that would be involved if Rosen had to provide a staff to make and record these measures himself.

The methods for applying and analyzing questionnaire surveys or interview schedules to organizations are now highly developed. Furthermore, it is far easier and less expensive to use such instruments in an organization than it is in a community, which presents all the problems of sampling and of securing the cooperation of each individual informant.

While the presence of an observer may always have some effect upon the behavior observed, it has proven possible to observe for extended periods of time within the organization with a minimum of disturbance to that organization. Furthermore, the organization is a relatively open field site once diplomatic problems of gaining acceptance have been resolved. Much of the behavior the researcher would wish to observe is highly visible.

The personal interview has a potential in a work organization that is difficult to match in other research sites. The subjects of study are known to each other and have established interpersonal relations. Thus it is relatively easy in an interview to question informant A about his relations with B, C, D, E, and F, move on to B and ask him about his relations with A, C, D, E, and F, and so on. When we seek to study a community through interviewing a sample of its inhabitants, we find we are dealing with a large number of loosely connected or unconnected personal networks, so that we do not get the rapid buildup of complementary information that is available to us as we interview people who interact frequently with each other.

While the difficulties of conducting experiments in work organizations are well known, most other social units outside of the laboratory present even greater difficulties as experimental sites. If we do not limit our interest in change to experiments, we will find many people within the

---

[26] Ned Rosen, *Leadership Change and Work Group Dynamics: An Experiment* (Ithaca, N.Y.: Cornell University Press, 1969).

organization constantly seeking to introduce changes. We can learn what they are trying to change, observe the change process, and analyze outcomes. Furthermore, since the complex organization is made up of mutually dependent parts, we have an opportunity of examining not only the immediately observable effects but also the repercussions taking place in parts of the organization not directly acted upon. In many other field sites, it is much more difficult to follow the impact of change, beyond the immediately observable effects.

If others are not introducing the changes we would like to observe, we can approach people in key organizational positions to try to persuade them to try out the steps that our theories indicate would be productive. In most other sites for research, we do not have such opportunities to exercise control over the phenomena we wish to study.

Finally, the problems of theory and method posed by the work organization are such as to invite the cross-fertilization of a number of approaches out of which a truly integrated body of knowledge may arise. Uncoordinated and parochial as we have been in studying organizations, we have found the confrontation of different methods and theories highly stimulating. It is my hope that this sort of stimulation may eventually lead to better integrated and more productive efforts. We shall be wasting resources and holding back the development of science if we do not learn to exploit more fully the tremendous research potential the work organization offers us.

Introducing the author

While the college professor might like to assume an air of Olympian detachment and claim to be able to examine his field without prejudices, we should recognize that he, just as much as the industrial worker or executive, is influenced by the position he holds and the social experience he has acquired. To the extent that the student is to learn from me, he should begin by placing me within this general field.

Early in my graduate career at Harvard, I had a seminar with Elton Mayo, which stimulated my interest in industry as a field of study. In this period, I was strongly influenced by social anthropologists Conrad M. Arensberg and Eliot D. Chapple, which led me to an interest both in their methods of research and theories and to an interest in the study of industry.

While I received my Ph.D. in sociology at the University of Chicago (1943), social anthropology was my minor field, and as a student I worked equally closely with anthropologist W. Lloyd Warner and sociologist Everett C. Hughes.

I launched my first industrial study in the petroleum industry when I was at the University of Oklahoma in 1942, which puts me close to the top of the seniority roster among those still active in the field. When I returned to the University of Chicago in 1944, to undertake a study in the restaurant industry, I also became a member of the Committee on Human Relations in Industry. When Gardner left the University in 1946 to found his own consulting and research organization, I served from 1946 to 1948 as executive secretary of the committee. Since 1948 I have been at Cornell University's New York State School of Industrial and Labor Relations in what has become an interdisciplinary department and is now called "Organizational Behavior."

This background makes it obvious that I belong in the box with the event-process analysts, and yet I have done my best to confound my own typology. Outside of industry, I have had some involvement in small-group research, and some of my industrial studies have focused on the work group. Like other event-process analysts who have also been concerned with the study of small groups, I have never ventured to apply the experimental method, which is a distinguishing feature of the work of the group dynamicists. While my own experience and knowledge is weak on the side of organizational surveys, I did make one foray into this field in 1955, and since 1962 I have been more or less continuously involved with organizational studies that have involved survey methods.

My international experience began with a U.S. company in Venezuela on a study of supervisory development and of company-community relations in 1954–55. In 1956 I carried on a brief study of supervisory development in Quebec. Since 1961 I have been more or less continuously involved in organizational and community studies in Peru.[27]

References

For historical background, see the articles on Frederick W. Taylor, Max Weber, and Elton Mayo in the *Encyclopedia of the Social Sciences*.

For material on the Western Electric Company research program see:

Mayo, Elton. *The Social Problems of an Industrial Civilization*. Boston: Harvard Graduate School of Business Administration, 1945. This gives the background of Mayo's thinking in this and earlier industrial research and presents his interpretation of the main Western Electric findings.

Roethlisberger, Fritz J., and Dickson, William J. *Management and the Worker*. Cambridge, Mass.: Harvard University Press, 1939. Still today this book is regarded as a classic in the field.

Landsberger, Henry A. *Hawthorne Revisited: Management and the Worker, Its Critics, and Developments in Human Relations in Industry*. Ithaca: New York State School of Industrial and Labor Relations, 1958. A valuable critique of the Hawthorne study and of trends in the field.

Carey, Alex. "The Hawthorne Studies: A Radical Criticism," *American*

---

[27] This chapter is based, in part, upon my article, "A Field in Search of a Focus," *Industrial and Labor Relations Review*, Vol. 18, no. 3 (April, 1965), pp. 305–22.

Sociological Review, Vol. 32, no. 3, (June, 1967), pp. 403–16. While the critics cited in footnote 23 primarily used general ethical or philosophical arguments, Carey carried out a painstaking analysis of the Hawthorne data to challenge some of the main conclusions of that research program.

Discussion questions

1. This field has gone by various titles. Among them, for example, are: Human Relations in Industry (or just Human Relations), Industrial Sociology, Industrial Social Psychology, Managerial Sociology, Managerial Psychology, Formal Organizations, Bureaucratic Structures, and Organizational Behavior. Select one of these which seems to you most appropriate—or make up your own. Discuss the implications of your title for the content of the field.

2. Examine one of the critiques of work in this field (you may select from the items listed under footnote 23). What are the principal criticisms of the author? Suppose you wish to determine (*a*) whether the criticisms were valid at the time the article was published, and (*b*) whether they are valid at the present time. As you progress in your study of this field, what are the chief questions you should keep in mind in order to arrive at a judgment of the validity of the criticisms?

3. How does this field of study relate to other fields? Select *one* discipline for comparison: for example, anthropology, psychology, sociology, economics, political science, business administration, or public administration. To what extent do you find overlap between the two fields in the topics of interest to both? To what extent do the specialists in these two fields have similar or different scientific objectives? Practical objectives?

4. The volume of research in this field has developed far more rapidly in the United States than in any other country. What conditions in the United States have especially favored this rapid growth?

2. Strategies of research

FOR A STUDENT to understand the findings of research in organizational behavior and to evaluate the interpretations drawn from the data, he needs to have some understanding of the way the data were gathered. It is not my aim to tell the student how to do research. I shall simply seek to tell him enough about the ways in which research is done so that he will be able to examine the findings of such research with more critical appreciation. I shall point out that there is no "one best way" to do research on organizational behavior. There are a number of different methods that may be and have been applied to the field. Each method has certain strengths but also certain limitations. Since the findings of any study are dependent upon the methods used, it is impossible to make an intelligent evaluation of findings without some background of knowledge regarding the methods used in the study.

Broad comparative studies

When we think of research methods, we are inclined to think first of how the investigator gets data directly from the individuals or subjects of his study. Indeed, most research in this field has built upon such close range methods. Nevertheless, there are ways in which we can study organizations from a distance and thereby get a perspective which is impossible when we are immersed in the study of a particular work situation. Let us therefore look first at the approach that may be taken by investigators who examine numbers of organizations from a distance.

Clark Kerr and Abraham Siegel[1] asked: How do we explain the frequency of industrial conflict? They began with the impression that strikes were not evenly distributed from industry to industry. They set out to gather statistics on the frequency of strikes over a period of years in the United States and internationally, industry by industry.

---

[1] Clark Kerr and Abraham Siegel, "The Inter-Industry Propensity to Strike," in Arthur Kornhauser, Robert Dubin, and Arthur Ross (eds.), *Industrial Conflict* (New York: McGraw-Hill Book Co., 1954).

They found indeed that there was a definite pattern which persisted over the years and showed marked similarities from one country to another. For example, they found that there had been persistent conflicts internationally in the longshore industry, whereas the clothing industry had been reasonably peaceful.

How could such differences be explained? The study was probably more important for what it disproved than what it proved. Up to this time, many students of organizational behavior had been inclined to explain the level of conflict between union and management in terms of the interpersonal understandings and social skills of the union and management leaders. Could we now say that the leaders in the clothing industry were skillful in understanding people, whereas the leaders in the longshore industry were a bunch of bunglers? Such an explanation would be too farfetched to be credible. Note that Kerr and Siegel's findings do not rule out the influence of interpersonal skills and understandings, but they do definitely emphasize that other powerful factors must be involved.

For their explanation, Kerr and Siegel examine the homogeneity or heterogeneity of worker groupings on the job or in the community. Strike prone industries, they argue, are those in which most workers work in close proximity on the same or similar jobs, in which they live in close association in communities where they are cut off from intimate contact with other types of workers or with management people. At the other extreme, heterogeneity leads to more peaceful union-management relations: workers who do a wide variety of jobs and are scattered through the community among other types of people are less likely to strike.

This is an oversimplification of the Kerr-Siegel argument, but for present purposes we are primarily concerned with illustrating the value of the methods used. When we are studying a single plant, the presence or absence of strikes is such a "lumpy" variable that we are unable to treat it statistically. We may seek to explain a particular event as best we can, but as we remain within the context of the local situation, we are likely to be overly impressed by the personal interpretations of the people with whom we talk and not to give due weight to the influences that we cannot so directly perceive. It is only when we stand off to get perspective through examining a large number of situations, looking for similarities and differences, that we are likely to perceive the forces that may be obscured in individual situations.

A British sociologist, Joan Woodward,[2] directed a large-scale study designed to contribute to knowledge regarding factors influencing the structure of industrial organizations and patterns of staff-line relations. Woodward and her associates gathered data on 203 manufacturing firms in South Sussex.

---

[2] Joan Woodward *et al.*, *Industrial Organization: Theory and Practice* (London: Oxford University Press, 1965).

The first results were disappointing. She found much variability, but no clear patterns emerged. For example, she found little relationship between the size of the work force and the number of levels of authority in the firm.

Looking for some factor that might sort out the cases in more meaningful form, Woodward decided to focus on technology. This involved first setting up types of technology so as to have objective standards for the categories into which she would sort her cases. When this had been done, she looked for comparisons from type to type. She now found systematic relationships between type of technology and certain aspects of formal organization structure. In the next chapter, we will show the major influence that such findings have had upon our field.

After carrying out a number of in-plant studies, concentrating on union-management relations, Leonard Sayles[3] became interested in the problem of work group cohesion. In every plant that he had studied, he had the impression that the militancy of workers was not randomly distributed among the individuals of the plant, that some departments displayed a great deal of internal unity and exercised almost constant pressures upon management, some alternated between disorganization and apathy and sporadic outbursts of concerted activity, whereas still other departments had a long history of quiescent relations with management.

Sayles suspected that such patterns which persisted over long periods of time could not be the products of chance. He resolved to see what factors in the work situation could be associated with the patterns. For this purpose, clearly he had to go beyond the individual case and seek a large enough number of cases to give him the range of data he would need. While he suspected that technology and the nature of jobs involved had something to do with these findings regarding cohesion and militancy, he did not pick the plants to be included in terms of technological differences. Rather, he approached the problem the other way around. He selected plants of which he had some background knowledge and where he had possible access to management officials and union leaders, and then interviewed certain key people in management and in the union to gather his data regarding the behavior of work groups.

While Sayles did gather his data primarily through personal interviews, he was not concerned with getting an understanding of the individual who spoke to him. He rather used each individual as an expert witness regarding the behavior of work groups. Note that he was not asking the witness to pass judgment on this behavior; he was asking him simply to report whether he had noticed differences in the plant from department to department regarding the tendency of workers to stick together and exercise pressure on management. He reports that in most cases the witness had no trouble in answering the question, he had indeed found

[3] Leonard Sayles, *Behavior of Industrial Work Groups*, (New York: John Wiley and Sons, 1958).

persistent differences among departments in these respects. Where Sayles was able to interview union leaders as well as management officials in the same case, he found a high degree of correspondence in their reports regarding the behavior of departmental work groups.

When Sayles sorted out all these departmental groups in terms of their tendency to stick together, he set up four types of groups, within each type finding certain important characteristics of the nature of jobs and technology held in common. In a later chapter, when we get to the study of work group cohesion, we will consider Sayles' findings. Here, we are simply concerned with illustrating the value of an approach which involved getting data from a large number of units without making an intensive study of a single one of them. This broad scale study gave Sayles a perspective on factors influencing work group cohesion that could hardly have been gained through immersion in a small number of cases.

Experimental studies

The experimental method is a classic method of the natural sciences—even though there are some sciences such as astronomy which have attained a high degree of development without any use of experimentation. It is often thought that one of the handicaps we face in social research is that "you can't experiment on human beings." To say that it is impossible to experiment on human beings is simply not true. Many important experiments have been performed, and social scientists are constantly trying new ones. Nevertheless, when humans seek to experiment on other humans, they encounter certain problems that do not need to be faced when experiments are carried out on animals or on physical elements. There are ethical and legal restrictions which limit our freedom to experiment as freely on human beings as we might otherwise wish. In general, the social experimenter must assume responsibility for the well-being of his subjects and may not knowingly subject them to conditions which could result in serious physical or psychological damage. Furthermore, we are limited by the conscious awareness of the subjects that they are taking part in an experiment. We assume that the pigeon or even the ape upon which man experiments is not conscious of taking part in an experiment. With few exceptions, human beings taking part in social experiments have been aware that they were being subjected to an experiment—even though the experimenter sought to mislead them as to the purposes of the experiment. We need to consider the possibility that this "artificial" condition of the experiment may limit our ability to apply the inclusions of the experiment to "natural" conditions.

The experimenter has his greatest freedom in manipulating his experimental subjects in the conditions of the small-groups laboratory. There is now a rich literature on small-group experiments, that has been fruitful for the development of theory. On the other hand, many if not most of these experiments have been carried on under such highly artificial conditions as to pose serious questions regarding the transferability of findings to a natural situation. In many cases, not only have the subjects known that they were participating in an experiment, they have been selected so that they did not know each other in advance, and they have been allowed to communicate only by means of written messages—so that the experimenter has complete control and knowledge regarding the situation. For purposes of academic convenience, the subjects are usually college students, which leaves social class differences largely unexplored. Outside of the laboratory, the behavior that we would like to be able to explain or control is generally that which takes place among people who already know each other well and who are allowed to communicate in any fashion which suits them. We are also interested in the impact of social class differences on group behavior.

As we move from the laboratory to field conditions, we gain the advantages of a more natural setting, but we are likely to lose the tight control over the experimental situation that is possible to establish in the laboratory. Let us consider how some distinguished experimenters have coped with field problems.

In the first place, the field experimenter in organizational behavior faces the necessity of persuading the responsible administrators of the organization to cooperate in establishing the experimental conditions. It takes a combination of an ingenious, persistent and persuasive experimenter and an imaginative and cooperative executive or set of executives to get together on such a program. When cooperation from the top is secured, the experimenter still has the task of explaining to the prospective participants what is to happen and why. He must do this in such a way as to get their cooperation and yet not fully reveal to them the purpose of the experiment. He is afraid that if they really know what he is up to, what psychologists call the "demand characteristics" of the experiment will influence the results. That is, the subjects, knowing what the experimenter is after, may just possibly be so cooperative that, consciously or unconsciously, they help to give him the results he is looking for. Finally, the experimenter in the field situation faces the problem of having limited control over the variables in a complex organization. Ideally, the experimenter would like to vary the values of one variable while he holds others constant except the dependent or output variable. In a real life situation, we find that one change that we consciously introduce may be linked to a number of other influences so that the effects we seek may be due not to the experimental variable but to some other variables whose impact we did not intend to measure.

There are four characteristics of a good field experiment:

1. The experimental conditions are reasonably close to those which might otherwise prevail in the organization. In this case, we have greater

confidence in applying conclusions of our experiment to behavior in nonexperimental situations.

2. The investigator provides us with a good description of behavior taking place before, during the experimental period, and after the conclusion of the experiment.
3. The investigator specifies clearly the nature of the changes that were introduced.
4. The investigator provides good measures of behavior and/or attitudes before the experiment, during the period of the introduction of the experimental change, and after the conclusion of the experiment.

Let us look first at the Western Electric Company experiments, which can be taken for a beginning point in research in human relations in industry or organizational behavior, more than 40 years ago.

The now-famous Western Electric Company—Harvard Business School research program began in the late 1920's with a rather traditional focus of interest. The researchers were concerned with studying the effects of varying physical conditions upon worker productivity.

Let us review the experimental program as summarized recently by two of the research pioneers, F. J. Roethlisberger and W. J. Dickson:[4]

THE ILLUMINATION EXPERIMENTS—INCONCLUSIVE RESULTS

From the results of the original illumination experiments reported first by C. E. Snow[5] and then later in *Management and the Worker*,[6] it was difficult to conclude just what the effect of illumination on productivity was. Some of the results of these experiments seemed to say that it was positive, some that it was zero, and some that it was "screwy." For example, sometimes an improvement in illumination was accompanied by an improvement in output, and then again, sometimes a positive increase in one did not produce an appreciable increase in the other. And then—this is the screwy part—quite often when the illumination intensity was decreased, output did not go down but remained the same and in some cases increased. In the face of these ambiguous results, all the experimenters drew one firm conclusion and some became curious.

The firm conclusion was to the effect that in the complex industrial setting it is difficult to test for the effect of a single variable, such as, for example, the effect of illumination on productivity. To do this it is necessary to control or eliminate all the factors influencing the dependent variable other than the one being studied. In most cases outside of a laboratory—and even sometimes there—this is often very difficult to do. But of all these factors, the greatest and most difficult to eliminate is the effect of the experiments or the

---

[4] W. J. Dickson and F. J. Roethlisberger, *Counseling in an Organization* (Boston, Mass.: Harvard Graduate School of Business Administration, 1966), pp. 20–23.

[5] C. E. Snow, "Research on Industrial Illumination: A Discussion of the Relation of Illumination Intensity to Productive Efficiency," *The Tech Engineering News*, November, 1927.

[6] F. J. Roethlisberger and W. J. Dickson, *Management and the Worker* (Cambridge: Harvard University Press, 1939), pp. 14–18.

experimenters themselves on the subjects being studied—what was then referred to as the "psychology of the human individual."

After having said this, however, some experimenters became curious as to
why they should have had the effect they did upon those with whom they
experimented. What was this effect that they had wrought inadvertently such
that even when the illumination changes went in a negative direction, i.e., to
lower and lower levels of illumination intensity, productivity changes remained the same and even in some cases increased? (Two girls, it will be
remembered, continued producing at their former high level even after the
intensity of illumination had decreased to "moonlight.")[7] Being good experimenters, however, they did not feel qualified to speak outside of the framework of their experiment, so little was said; just a few eyebrows were raised.

Here then we have the early observations and statements made about the
Hawthorne effect before it was named. From them it can be seen that, on the
one hand, a factor called "the psychology of the individual" was making for
trouble—that is, ambiguity in drawing conclusive results from what at that
time was considered to be good experimental design (i.e., approved by all
accredited industrial psychologists in the twenties)—while, on the other
hand, it was making for the birth of a new curiosity about and interest in
this factor which one might have thought the industrial psychologists in the
first place would be trying to understand rather than to eliminate.

THE RELAY ASSEMBLY TEST ROOM—THE BEGINNINGS OF A SEARCH

But the Hawthorne effect might never have been born, i.e., named, had it
not been reinforced by another study called the Relay Assembly Test Room.
As this experiment has been reported by many persons in many books, we can
afford to be brief.

In this study,[8] five girls who were assembling telephone relays agreed to be
placed in a separate room and to be submitted to different conditions of
work, e.g., to the introduction of rest pauses of varying frequency and
duration and to changes in the length of the working day and week. Thirteen
experimental periods of different working conditions of the above kind were
introduced in the first two years. Output was carefully measured, the time it
took each girl to assemble a telephone relay of about 40 parts (roughly a
minute) being automatically recorded. The purpose of the experiment was to
see what effect these different working conditions had on output.

During the first 11 experimental periods, as conditions of work improved,
output rose steadily. Here was strong confirmation of the hypothesis that
fatigue was the major factor limiting output. But in Period 12 (about one and
a half years later), when the experimenters went back to the original conditions of work (a 48-hour week with *no* rest pauses), average hourly output
did not drop appreciably. And in Period 13, when the morning rest period
was reinstituted, both output and the morale of the girls reached a new high.

In short, there was no simple correlation between variation in the output
of these girls and variation in their physical circumstances. This was confirmed by many other studies made of these girls about whom a great deal of

---

[7] *Ibid.*, p. 17.

[8] *Ibid.*, pp. 19–127.

data besides their output and the different experimental working conditions had been collected.[9]

Here again we had an experiment with positive results (i.e., improved output) which could not be attributed to single changes in the physical circumstances of the subjects. This finding caused some consternation in both academic and industrial circles. It meant that all experiments in which a single change had been introduced with promising results now became suspect. It meant, for example, that all experiments in which improvements in lighting, heating, sound, noise, rest periods, methods, etc., that had been made which had been accompanied for a while by an improvement in output were now in jeopardy. Their results were inconclusive because they could have been contaminated by the Hawthorne effect. The workers might not have been responding to the better working conditions per se; they might have been responding to an *awareness of the special treatment* created by the artificial experimental condition.

Some students have explained the results in terms of the "Hawthorne effect." According to this theory, the girls felt that they got special recognition through being part of the experiment and thus were responding more to the prestige gained through participation in the experiment than to the specified experimental conditions. Others have noted the drastic differences in the social situation of the work place enjoyed by these girls in the regular department. In fact, the foreman had little contact with them at all. The observer developed an informal, friendly relationship with the girls and even consulted them at several points regarding the course of the experiment. That this consultation was more than an idle gesture is shown by the fact that on occasion the girls were allowed to veto ideas the experimenters wanted to try out.

However the explanations might differ in detail, the results of the twelfth period clearly showed the importance of social influences on productivity. Mayo and his associates, F. J. Roethlisberger and W. J. Dickson, now went on to design studies into the social differences in work groups operating under more usual factory conditions. These studies, together with the test room report, have become classics in social science research.

Now let us review the Western Electric experiments in terms of our criteria. On the second and fourth points, we are provided with a detailed and comprehensive description of the test room situation before, during, and after the introduction of the experimental changes.[10] Focusing on productivity as a dependent variable, we have extraordinarily detailed and precise measures through the whole experimental period. On the first point, we have noted that the test room constituted a highly artificial

---

[9] T. N. Whitehead, *The Industrial Worker* (2 vols.; Cambridge, Mass.: Harvard University Press, 1938).

[10] However, a recent critic argues that vital changes were overlooked. See Alex Carey, "The Hawthorne Studies: A Radical Criticism," *American Sociological Review*, Vol. 32, no. 3 (June, 1967).

situation. Therefore, while results were of great interest, it was difficult to see how they could be applied to other work situations. On point three, the experimenters provided us with a clear specification of the nature of the changes that were introduced as part of the experiment. As we have already noted, apparently it was not these changes which gave rise to the striking increases in productivity. On the other hand, the investigators provide such a full observational account of the test room situation before, during, and after the introduction of various combinations of rest pauses and refreshments that we are able to infer the nature of the other changes that seemed to be associated with the increases in productivity.

The Western Electric story illustrates some of the difficulties involved in field experiments. We see that changes in one variable may occur in response to changes in variables that were not taken into account by the experimenter. On the other hand, it is the extraordinary virtue of the Hawthorne study that the investigators provide us with such well-documented accounts of what took place that we can use their data to reach conclusions regarding organizational behavior that are not based upon the manipulation of the experimental variable. When the experimenters found themselves at a dead end in trying to determine the effect of rest pauses and refreshments, they were able to turn attention to the social changes that had taken place in the work group and thus open up a whole new field of investigation.

A few years later, stimulated by the pioneering social psychologist, Kurt Lewin, Lester Coch and John R. P. French, Jr.,[11] undertook an experiment to determine the effect of participation in decision-making on the part of workers in the introduction of technological and work methods changes in a plant in the clothing industry. Research entry into the Harwood Manufacturing Company was facilitated by the fact that its President held a Ph.D. in psychology and had become very much interested in the work of Lewin and his group.

Members of management at Harwood and social scientists had recognized that, while it was necessary to introduce changes in technology and methods of work to raise productivity in the long run, the immediate effect of the introduction of such changes seemed to be a drop in productivity that tended to be much more marked than could have been explained by an allowance for the workers to learn the new ways. The introduction of methods changes seemed to give rise to a disturbance that was quite above and beyond the technical necessities of learning the new way of working. It seemed clear that there were social and psychological problems involved in the introduction of such changes as they were customarily handled in the plant. In this period, the Harwood manage-

---

[11] Lester Coch and John R. P. French, Jr., "Overcoming Resistance to Change," *Human Relations*, Vol. 1, no. 4 (1948), pp. 512–32. Also available in a number of collections. See, for example, Dorwin Cartwright and A. Zander (eds.), *Group Dynamics: Research and Theory* (2nd ed.; (New York: Harper and Row, 1960).

ment, like other managements, had no thought of involving the workers in any way in the introduction of the changes. It had been management's practice to make the necessary engineering studies, make its own plans in full detail, and simply announce and explain the changes to workers at the time they were being put into effect.

What would happen if the changes were introduced in a different way —if the workers were invited to discuss the changes with members of management and even to participate in working out how the changes should be introduced? In order to test this new approach, the investigators decided upon two somewhat different experimental approaches. The experiment involved trying out two forms of employee participation. In one, "total participation," Alex Bavelas met with all the girls on several occasions to discuss the intended changes and to get their suggestions as to how the changes should be carried out. The other approach involved having Bavelas meet with elected representatives of the groups affected for a similar type of discussion. The representatives were then to return to the groups and discuss the changes with group members. Other groups facing similar changes were kept out of the participation process so as to serve as control groups. The results showed the control groups responding to the change in the manner in which management had become familiar, with reduced output, greater absenteeism and turnover, and increased expression of worker dissatisfaction. The experimental groups responded with a drop in output at the time of the introduction of the change, but they recovered quickly and their output soon exceeded the standards that they had met before the change. The total-participation group experienced a sharper drop but also made the more impressive recovery and stabilized at a higher level.

The Harwood experiments provide one advantage not present in the Hawthorne cases. At Harwood, the experimenters were dealing with a natural setting. The production workers involved in the experiment were those on the regular production lines. They were going through the annual process of change in styles of garments produced. Having a social scientist conduct a discussion group with workers is, to be sure, an unusual phenomenon for a factory, but we can assume that, if the investigators provided us with a good description of how Bavelas conducted these meetings, it should be possible to train company supervisors to carry on the same activity. It is at this point that we run into problems with the Harwood case, for we find no description of the discussions carried on by Bavelas. We learn only that these were "democratic groups discussions." Anyone who has observed a number of different individuals trying to lead a "democratic group discussion" will recognize that those three words do not specify behavior with any degree of precision. We find quite different styles of leadership among individuals who are attempting to behave in a democratic fashion. Until we can specify with much more precision what constitutes the "democratic group discussion" that is our experimental variable, we will not fully understand what it was that produced the changes which the experimenters have been able to measure with precision. We shall explore the implications of this criticism when we deal with supervisory leadership in later chapters.

At the same time, this unfortunate vagueness on the side of the experimental variable should not prevent us from recognizing the importance of the Harwood experiments. From the customary approach of simply announcing to workers what changes in job methods were to be introduced and then instructing them in the new methods, the worker involvement in group discussion represented a marked change in organizational behavior. Furthermore, the figures show a striking difference between experimental groups and control groups in the productivity levels achieved and in worker attitudes regarding the experiences they were going through. These results suggested that a restructuring of interpersonal relations between workers and authority figures in industry could result in productivity increases and favorable changes in worker-management attitudes. These findings led to the opening up of research and writing concerning "participation management," which has become the most popular theory of management to those American executives who take an interest in the findings of behavioral science research. Much of this book will be devoted to an assessment of the possibilities and limitations of this approach.

A major experiment carried out on a large insurance company developed this basic idea in more systematic form. With the cooperation of management, secured through a vice president of the company, Nancy Morse and Everett Reimer[12] set out to build contrasting types of managerial leadership and control in two closely matched large departments of clerical workers. The changes to be introduced were carefully laid out by the researchers, in collaboration with key management people, and the research team provided a training program for supervisors to help insure that each supervisor was able to carry out the style of leadership called for in his particular department. In one department, the research staff worked systematically with management people to have them lower the level at which decisions were made and to involve employees in the discussion of these decisions. Improvements in work efficiency were to grow out of a discussion and study process in which the workers themselves participated fully. In a matched department, the decision-making level was systematically raised, and the work methods studies associated with scientific management were brought into play. That is, efficiency experts studied the jobs as they were then being performed and worked out a new set of procedures designed to make the work more efficient. In this department, workers were not consulted about the changes introduced.

---

[12] Nancy Morse and Everett Reimer, "The Experimental Change of a Major Organizational Variable," *Journal of Abnormal and Social Psychology*, Vol. 52 (1956), pp. 120–29.

Productivity was measured in each department before the experiment and after it had been carried out for a year. Questionnaires were used to elicit employee sentiments.

The questionnaires showed workers responding much more favorably toward their supervisors and toward the job itself in the groups where decision making had been decentralized, but the productivity results were not nearly so clear-cut. Productivity went up in the groups where the level of the decision-making had been lowered, but it went up even more in those groups where the level had been raised. This suggests that, under certain circumstances, centralization of authority may elicit even more productivity than a decentralized, participative approach—but at a possibly heavy cost in negative sentiments. However, this generalization regarding productivity must be questioned in this case as we note the nature of the productivity measure. In these particular work groups, the amount of work to be done was fixed so that working harder or more efficiently would not increase productivity. Productivity could only be increased through reducing the number of employees performing this fixed volume of work. The involvement of employees in group discussions with management is likely to strengthen sentiments of employee loyalty to each other as well as to management, so it hardly was to be expected that the employees would suggest that some of their numbers be laid off or transferred to other departments. In this type of situation, the work force is only reduced as new employees are not hired to replace those who quit their jobs. On job operations where the amount of work to be done is not fixed, the participative approach might prove superior in productivity as well as in worker satisfaction.

The insurance company experiment is impressive in several respects. It was carried out in a natural setting, and its success required the cooperation of important management people in implementing the changes. While we still have rather little in the way of observational material about the nature of the discussion process in the participative approach, we do have specification of the levels at which decisions were made in the two contrasting departments, and we have good measures of the productivity and the attitudinal responses to the changes introduced. Furthermore, the experiment is interesting in showing that productivity and worker attitudes do not necessarily move together, as many students of the field would have liked to believe. It is comforting to assume that high performance goes with "democratic leadership," but unfortunately life is too complicated for such a simple conclusion.

We should not leave the insurance company case without noting certain important and unplanned changes that followed upon the conclusion of the experiment. In the months after the conclusion of the experiment, the workers in the participative department apparently found their participation so satisfying that they sought to extend it into areas of decision-making that higher management was not inclined to allow. This led to disturbances within the department and later even to the discharge of the vice president who had been the key man in working with the experimenters on the research program. The participative management approach in this department was abandoned.

We should not think that these unplanned changes discredit the results of the experiment. Those results were well described and systematically measured. The subsequent unplanned changes illustrate the validity of the general approach we plan to take to the study of organization. We assume an organization is made up of mutually dependent parts, so that the change introduced in one part will have repercussions in others. We see here that a change that was successfully carried out in the participative department was not limited in its effects to that department. As we see the new managerial approach at the departmental level coming into conflict with management sentiments, policies, and procedures at the higher levels, we can appreciate the difficulties of introducing a change in one part of the organization, without being able to change other related parts. We also face, for the first time in the literature, the problem of limitations on participation. While we shall explore the participative approach in more detail later, we may here note that it is not easy to start a new pattern of activities and interactions with employees and then expect them to stop at the limits established by management.

The final experiment to be considered here, and also the most recent one, is that carried out by Ned Rosen[13] and his associates in a furniture plant. In the course of some consulting activity with the company, Rosen became especially interested in the upholstery department which had eight production lines, each one being supervised by a foreman. While the tasks of each line were not identical, since some models of furniture were more likely to be assigned to one line than another, Rosen recognized that he had found eight production units that were as closely matched as any he was likely to find in manufacturing industry. This led him to consider the possibility of an experiment to resolve the "chicken-egg" problem of supervisory leadership and productivity: is the work group's level of productivity an outcome of the foreman's leadership style, or is the foreman's leadership style an outcome of the work group's productivity level?

If plant management could be persuaded to rotate the foreman, chang-ing each man from one to another production line, according to a pattern established by the experimenter, there would at least be an opportunity to separate the "chicken from the egg." Furthermore, if this could be done as part of a "normal" management program, there was a possibility of carrying out research in which the subjects were unaware of participating in an experiment.

---

[13] Ned Rosen *et al.*, *Leadership Change and Work Group Dynamics: An Experiment* (Ithaca, N.Y.: Cornell University Press, 1969).

When Rosen broached these ideas to the plant manager, he was delighted to find them accepted with equanimity and even with interest. The manager said that on past occasions foremen had been switched from one line to another, although he had never changed all the foremen at once. The experiment could simply be made to appear as a larger scale instance of events that had happened before. It would not be necessary to consult the foremen on these changes, for that had not been done in the past. He and his superintendent could simply meet with them on a Friday afternoon and tell them that on Monday morning each of them would be supervising a different production line.

Rosen proceeded to set in motion the research design that he already had formulated. Two graduate students spent a two-week period in the department observing foremen, workers and work activity and carrying on informal interviews with foremen, and workers regarding the nature of the work and problems of supervision. On the next to last day, all the workers filled out a questionnaire aiming at exploration of their sentiments toward the job, toward fellow workers, toward their particular work group, and toward the foremen. As part of this exercise, each worker was asked to rank the eight foremen. Thus Rosen could determine the average ranking of each foreman on the basis of the total department vote, and he could also determine how each work group ranked its own foreman in relation to the other seven.

These operations had been preceded by a meeting that Rosen held with members of management and with the union leaders regarding the research objectives of the Cornell group. At this time, Rosen phrased his interest in general terms of exploring worker problems and worker supervisory relations. Nothing was said about an experimental change to be introduced.

The closer the foreman-switching time was to the initial research operations, the more confident Rosen could be that the worker survey evaluations of the foremen were those that were in effect at the time of the switching. On the other hand, the closer the switching to the initial research period, the greater the likelihood that the workers and foremen would connect the two events. The reactions then to the foreman-switching would be contaminated by worker and foreman reactions to the intervention of the Cornell research people. To avoid this contamination, Rosen waited a period of roughly one year, hoping he could assume that the worker evaluations of the foremen remained stable during this period. This seemed a reasonable assumption for he was dealing with long-service workers and long-service foremen.

During the waiting period, Rosen and the graduate assistant looked over the productivity records to make sure that they would have adequate measures of output for periods preceding and following the experimental change. Rosen also worked out his design for foreman-switching. Ideally, Rosen would have liked to give four groups foremen that they preferred to their previous foremen and four groups foremen that they rated lower than their previous foremen. For technical reasons that need not detain us here, the final design involved giving two groups foremen that they preferred to their previous foremen and the other six groups foremen that they reported that they liked less well.

During all this period, Rosen did not appear in the plant. The plant manager sent him production records weekly through the mail. They talked several times on the phone, and they worked out the final plans for the experimental change in a meeting in a hotel room in a neighboring city.

Sixteen weeks after the foreman-switching, Rosen and his research assistants again appeared on the scene and readministered the questionnaire similar to the one they had applied a year earlier. Subsequent interviewing of the men indicated that at this point perhaps one out of three of the men jumped to the conclusion that Cornell had had something to do with the foreman-switching, but they all reported that this possibility had not occurred to them at the time.

The outcome? We shall not undertake to present here a full account of the findings. Let us simply note the productivity outcomes: following the change, productivity rose generally through the department. With a single exception, each line achieved a higher average rate of production than it had in the 16 weeks previous to the switching. There was no correlation between the productivity outcome for a given group and the ranking it gave its new foreman, compared to the one it previously had.

While a single experiment can hardly be conclusive, the results in this case suggest that in many situations the foreman is not as influential in the productivity outcome of his group as the literature of organizational behavior has led us to think. Productivity is the outcome of a complex set of variables. In some situations, the supervisory style of the foreman may be an important variable whereas in others it may be insignificant. This suggests that in future research we need to be more discriminating to discover the types of situations within which the foreman's influence is high and those types within which it is low. It will not be helpful to try to draw conclusions about *the* foreman.

If we review the Rosen experiment in terms of the criteria stated above, we find that it meets the best standards on three out of four items. Of all the field experiments in organizations, this is the one that most closely approximates "natural conditions." The subjects in the experiment did not know that an experiment was going on nor did they even know that any research was in progress at the time of the critical change. Rosen provides us with a clear specification of the changes he introduced in the foreman-switching. He also has good measures of productivity before and after the change. He has attitudinal measures for before and after—although in this case the "before" data are for a year previous to the change. He gives us a good description of the situation in the department as of some months before the introduction of change, and he provides data based on observation and interviewing regarding the post-change period—but these data were gathered four months after the change had been introduced.

How did the workers and the foremen experience the change at the time? To what extent did they behave differently following the change, compared to before it? Rosen was well aware of the desirability of gathering these data on an observational basis at the time of the change instead of trying to reconstruct the situation retrospectively. To put an observer in the situation at the time of the change would immediately have communicated to the workers and the foremen that the change was an experiment, and to this extent the natural field conditions would have been sacrificed.

Our discussion of these cases should lead us to several conclusions. In the first place, we see how extraordinarily difficult it is to carry out a good experiment in an organization. Even when the experimenter over-comes the resistances and hesitations of executives and secures permission and cooperation for his experiment, he finds the real world of the field situation much more complex than the world he can create in the labora-tory. In dealing with this complexity, he generally finds that he cannot maximize on all of the important conditions of a good experiment at the same time. Furthermore, the complexity of the field situation is such that the manipulation of a given experimental variable will only produce the predicted outcome if it is examined in the context of other variables. No simple cause-effect relations are found here.

Since experiments in the field are so difficult to carry out, it is fortunate that we do not have to rely entirely upon experimentation for our research findings. On the other hand, a review of these four cases indi-cates that even when the experiment has not produced a clear finding regarding the impact of the experimental variable it may be extraordinar-ily productive in challenging old conceptions and opening up new lines of research. In fact, it is not unrealistic to date the birth of our field from the twelfth experimental period of the Hawthorne study when the Test Room girls were deprived of their rest periods and refreshments and yet productivity remained at a high level. This made it dramatically evident that the productivity changes could not be explained in terms of rest periods and refreshments. In looking elsewhere, the experimenters took the first steps in exploring the field of organizational behavior.

While possibilities of introducing experiment into an organization are quite limited, we should not assume that we can only study change if we ourselves introduce it. In fact, change is taking place all of the time in industry. The alert investigator can keep in touch with developments in organizations around him to examine the changes that have taken place and even, when he has advance notice, to follow the course of introduc-tion of change. Furthermore, while he may not be able to establish the conditions that would permit him to call his study an experiment, if he finds that decision makers in the organization are not taking actions that he would like to observe, he can propose such steps to them and in this way increase the range of changes that are open to his study.

Even if the investigator does perform a field experiment, he finds himself using other research methods for the gathering of data in connection with the experiment. To measure the before-and-after situation, he must apply some methods of measurement. To describe the social process that takes place before, during, and after the experimental change, he must have some means of observing events and also of getting participants to tell him what they think is going on.

There are two main lines of approach to such data gathering. We shall consider first interview-observational methods and then take up the questionnaire or survey methods.

Interview-observational methods

Interview-observational methods are particularly valuable for providing depth of penetration into the life of an organization. They are useful for exploratory studies of situations that are not well known to the investigator, so that he is not yet in a position to be precise and systematic about the variables he wishes to study. They are not limited in value to the exploratory phase, as we shall see later.

The most intimate view of the organization is secured by the participant observer: the investigator who gathers his data while serving as a genuine member of the organization. While this role is not frequently practiced these days in organizations, some of the best data we have on worker response to incentive systems and on informal relations among members of management and between management and the union come from the observations of participant observers.

Over a period of years, Donald Roy served as a blue-collar worker in factories, construction gangs, and oil fields. In the maintenance department of a large steel mill, Melville Dalton served as a checker who measured the output and computed the pay of workers on incentive.

This approach has certain important advantages. In the first place, it may enable the investigator to gain access to situations which he would not have been allowed to enter if he had asked management for permission to come in and make a study. Does this mean that the intellectual interests of the participant observer are completely unknown to those he is observing? Not necessarily. The workers around Roy knew that he had a good deal more education than they, and they seemed to assume that he had fallen on hard times and needed the job and in addition had some intellectual interest in what factory life was all about. Some workers and members of management in the steel mill knew that Dalton was taking courses for an advanced degree at the University of Chicago. They cast him in the respected role of a student working his way through school—which indeed he was. While Dalton was getting his degree in sociology, he found it expedient to describe himself as an industrial psychologist, for he discovered that some of the management people could not distinguish between sociologist and socialist.

The special virtue of the participant observer approach is the depth of penetration it permits into the life of the organization. A skillful participant observer may discover significant data that the research man from outside of the organization would not know enough to look for or that would be hidden from him.

Sometimes discovery grows out of introspection. For example, on one factory job where there was a great deal of conflict between workers and management over the administration of the incentive or piece-rate system, Roy became aware one day of a satisfaction he was getting out of certain piece-work jobs that had not been noted by any students of organizational behavior. On jobs where he could "make out" (make just enough pieces to get the maximum bonus acceptable to his work group without having to hold back so as to avoid going beyond the group norm), Roy found himself playing a game against the clock. He set his goal and then, hour by hour, kept track of the number of pieces he made as time passed. He checked his watch at frequent intervals to see whether he was ahead of the clock or dropping behind. In this way, Roy reports that he got a feeling of accomplishment that was otherwise absent in a dull job. He also reports that when he had a rate on which he could just make out, the time seemed to go much faster than it did when he had jobs on which he felt he had to hold back production, or on jobs where no matter how hard he tried, he knew he could not make out. As he discovered these reactions in himself, Roy checked with fellow workers and found that they were likewise playing a game against the clock and in that way gaining certain satisfactions beyond simply the earning of money.

At the time when Roy made his discovery, I had been involved in research for several years on worker reactions to incentive systems, and it had never occurred to me to ask a worker a question to probe for this type of experience. The outside investigator does not know enough to ask about reactions to a given phenomenon unless he is aware of the existence of that phenomenon.

While we are not indebted to participant observers for discovering the existence of informal group ties in industry, we have received from them some of the most intimate accounts in the literature of the unofficial part of factory life. Roy's[14] "Banana Time—Job Satisfaction and Informal Interaction" has become a classic study of the life of a small work group. Dalton's[15] studies of unofficial and informal relations between staff and

[14] Donald Roy, in *Human Organization*, Vol. 18, no. 4 (Winter, 1959–60), reprinted in Warren Bennis *et al.* (eds.), *Interpersonal Dynamics: Essays and Readings on Human Interaction* (Homewood, Ill.: The Dorsey Press, 1964).

[15] Melville Dalton, *Men Who Manage* (New York: John Wiley and Sons, 1959).

line and between management and the union served to open up a new area of study. Since some of the "deals" between members of management or between managers and union leaders were in violation of the union contract or management official policies, a research man entering from the outside would have found it much more difficult to break through the accounts of how life was supposed to be in the plant.

The role of the participant observer is not without its problems. In the first place, it is hard work. To have research data that he can later report to his behavioral science colleagues, the participant observer must keep a work diary. Since he has neither the time nor the opportunity to write this diary while on the job, he has to write up his notes from memory after he leaves work. I can well remember a period when Roy was putting in 10 hours a day at the plant and two hours a night at the typewriter after coming home.

The participant observer also faces a possibly serious limitation in the territory he can cover with his study. Subject to the understandings he reaches with management and union leaders, the research man from outside may follow his problem interests throughout the plant and even call on members of management and workers when they are on the job. The participant observer, while at work, is limited to the territory of his particular job. The severity of the limitation depends upon the nature of the job the participant observer holds. As a turret lathe operator, Roy had to spend his time among the small group that worked in his department and could only observe other people when they came into his orbit. In his steel mill job, Dalton had much more freedom to follow his interests. As a checker on the incentive program, he had the responsibility of measuring the work output of each man in a large maintenance department. Dalton thus had freedom to move about the department and to talk with every worker as he went about doing his job. Since he had no responsibility for setting the rates, against which the men were often complaining, the workers did not hesitate to accept him and to talk freely with him. Dalton did his paper work in an industrial engineering office which brought him into contact with industrial engineers and with members of line management. From this base, Dalton was even able to fit in interviews with members of management up to five levels above the bottom. They apparently talked to him rather freely on the assumption that, through sharing their knowledge and experience with him, they were helping him work his way through school—as indeed they were.

The participant observer may have more difficulty in maintaining perspective in a study than does the research man using any other method. As a participant, he is able to penetrate through the formal and superficial aspects of life around him, but the more he participates the more he may come to think, feel, and act like the people with whom he is participating. Commenting upon his experience as participant observer in a community study, sociologist Robert Johnson has reported how he began as a "nonparticipating observer" and later found himself acting as a "nonobserving participant." While this influence would inevitably be felt, the research man need not surrender to it. The task of writing up notes after getting out of the work situation helps to bring back his perspective. It is also important for him to have a life line of communication to other research men. As he tries to explain to them what he is experiencing and observing and as they question him on his study, he again finds himself beginning to ask questions about aspects of work life that he had come to take for granted.

While investigators who have played the role of participant observer in industry to the extent of holding down a regular plant job are rather rare, much valuable work has been done by research men who have operated on a semiparticipant basis. After gaining entry to the plant or union, the investigator seeks to spend enough time with his subjects of study and to make himself agreeable enough to them so as to establish an informal relationship that encourages free expression as he interviews them. While he does not work at a management or bench job, he shares smokes, coffee, and lunch room breaks with those who are working on the job. Otherwise, he tries to arrange to "hang around" so that he will not get in the way of the work and yet will have a chance to observe what is going on and even talk to men while they work—if the noise level and the degree of concentration required on the job permit such interaction.

The interviewing approach the investigator takes has often been described as nondirective. I feel that this is a misnomer, for it suggests that the interviewer leaves the informant completely free to talk about whatever he wishes. If this approach were really followed, it would be impossible to get systematic data from a number of different informants, for each man would be talking about different topics. Furthermore, the investigator would find that he was making informants anxious by the vagueness of his interests, and they would tell him (as I have been told myself), "You tell me what you want to know, and I will do the best I can to answer your questions."

It would be more appropriate to call this approach semistructured, for the investigator has definite lines of interest to pursue, but he varies his approach according to the situation and the reactions of his informant. Furthermore, he is always alert to pick up clues for topics that the informant wants to talk about and which had not occurred to the investigator.

Interviewing and observation: possibilities

The methods of interviewing and observation are particularly suitable for studies of sequences of events and of interpersonal relations. They give us answers to the question posed by anthropologist Eliot D. Chapple: "Who did what, with whom, when and where?" From the record of particular activities and personal interactions, we can draw inferences of a general nature regarding social processes.

One of the great strengths of interviewing and observation is that they provide a detailed picture of how life is lived in the work situation and of how a given institution actually functions. It is hard to imagine how we would go about describing to students the industrial environment and the human problems we find there if we were not able to draw upon the interviewing and observational data provided us by such people as Melville Dalton, Donald Roy, Leonard Sayles, George Strauss, Chris Argyris, Charles Walker, Robert Guest, Peter Blau, and Ann Douglas. From their work we have built up our picture of worker reactions to incentive systems, informal relations and power struggles within management and between management and union, managerial leadership patterns, the human problems of the local union, human relations within a government agency, the relation of workers and supervisors to technology and technological change, and the process of mediation. If we go back to the main point of origin of our field, the Western Electric study, we must recognize that, while an experiment was meant to yield the main conclusions of that study, actually the work of Roethlisberger and Dickson[16] provided a rich body of observational data concerning the nature of work groups, the formations of norms of behavior in the workplace, and worker-management relations.

While the importance of the contributions I have mentioned will be generally accepted, some might argue that the interviewing and observational approach, although necessary to fill in descriptive data regarding the nature of industrial life, is of steadily declining value now that this background has been filled in. Therefore it should give way to more rigorous "scientific" methods.

This point of view might be defensible if we could assume an unchanging work environment, so that once we thoroughly understood the environment, we could move on to more systematic measurements of the reactions of individuals to that environment. In a rapidly changing civilization like ours, we can never assume that the environment of the workplace is sufficiently well known, nor that its problems will remain constant. We hear it constantly said that automation is changing the nature of jobs and the nature of relations among workers and between workers and management, and among various levels and specialties of management. Unless we have systematic descriptions of these new and changing work environments, we shall be in the position of measuring the reactions of individuals with only a vague idea as to what it is they are reacting to.

Interviewing and observation: limitations

One of the limitations of these methods is suggested by the question: are you a storyteller or are you a scientist? No one will deny that, with

---

[16] F. J. Roethlisberger and W. J. Dickson, *Management and the Worker* (Cambridge, Mass.: Harvard University Press, 1939).

intensive interviewing and observation, you get "rich data" which make for interesting reading and stimulate many insights. We might say that this approach provides us with the sort of understanding of a particular situation that it is not possible to duplicate with other methods.

The problems arise when we seek to move beyond understanding into systematic comparisons and toward the statement of laws or uniformities. Some of the richness of a particular case must be pushed aside if we are to reach systematic statements that will hold from case to case.

This is not to say that it is impossible to quantify data gathered by these methods. If we interview a number of informants who have been involved in the same situation under study, we can draw certain general conclusions regarding quantities of interactions and activities at several different points in time. The checking and cross-checking of the retrospective statements of various informants yields only a rough approximation of the quantities we are trying to measure. This means that, if we are concerned with small changes, we cannot rely upon interviewing for this purpose. It is only where we are concerned with establishing that major changes have taken place that we can use interviewing for the establishment of quantities.

For finer and more valid measures, we can turn to observation. The work of Charles Walker, Robert Guest, and Arthur N. Turner with *The Foreman on the Assembly Line*[17] shows us the possibilities of quantitative observational studies. If only we possessed comparable observation studies for foremen in other types of work situations, our knowledge of the supervisory process and of foremen-worker relations would be advanced far beyond its present position.

Interviewing can also give us data of a subjective nature, concerning the attitudes or sentiments and beliefs of informants. In fact, the personal interview can provide a good deal more depth in this area than it is possible to gain through the questionnaire. To counterbalance the values of the depth we must note two difficulties or limitations. In the first place, to gain the advantages of depth, we have to pursue a flexible approach as described earlier. This presents us with obvious difficulties when we try to make quantitative statements regarding the responses of a number of informants to nonidentical stimuli. We also should recognize that the personal interview method is far more consuming of the researcher's time than is the questionnaire survey. The researcher may devote a whole hour to interviewing a single informant, whereas he can sometimes arrange to apply a rather lengthy questionnaire to 30 or 50 or more informants in the same length of time. Furthermore, this is not only a matter of efficiency in utilization of time. In some situations, sentiments or attitudes may change rather rapidly. If the researcher studies a department of 30 men and seeks

---

[17] Charles Walker *et al., The Foreman on the Assembly Line* (Cambridge, Mass.: Harvard University Press, 1956).

to have an hour interview with each of them, taking into account problems of scheduling and of time for writing research notes, it may take two weeks to cover the whole department. He cannot then assume that his last informant was responding to the same situation as his first informant. Furthermore, he must recognize that past and future informants will be discussing their interviews during this period, with unknown effects upon future interviews.

Observation presents us with a still more severe time problem. While an informant in an interview may talk about events that took place days, weeks, months, or even years earlier, in an hour of observation time, the observer obviously can only observe what takes place in that hour. He must invest many hours in order to build up quantities of observational data that he can usefully analyze.

We can sum up our conclusions regarding interviewing and observation in this way. For providing us with detailed descriptions of the situations we wish to study, these methods are indispensable. In a reasonably short time with these methods, we can gain an impressionistic picture of what is going on and of the general nature of the human problems involved. In the hands of a skilled clinician, this impressionistic picture may be exceedingly valuable in providing guidance for action decisions. As we seek to go beyond impressionistic pictures towards systematic scientific statements, we have seen that there are certain possibilities but also that they are extremely demanding in time. We have also encountered certain problems in assuring comparability of data across informants.

The questionnaire survey: possibilities

The questionnaire survey is particularly suitable for studies of attitudes, values, beliefs, and perceptions of informants.

When once the diplomatic problems have been solved, the researcher can apply his questionnaire to large numbers of people in a short time. The application of the questionnaire is not, of course, all there is to the field work with this method. If anything useful is to result, a good deal of time has to be spent in constructing and pretesting the instrument. The diplomatic problems of getting it into the field may also be formidable and time-consuming. Nevertheless, we should recognize that the method offers great efficiency in the data gathering process.

The method also lends itself readily to quantification. Recent years have shown a great growth of statistical methods for the analysis of survey data. Development of data processing machines and computers has made it possible to analyze great volumes of data with enormous speed. Here again a word of caution should be inserted. A machine is still not a satisfactory substitute for the human brain. While it is now possible to correlate everything with everything else and see what comes out, this is not an efficient way of proceeding. In fact, some of my colleagues refer to this as the "gigo approach"—gigo standing for "garbage in, garbage out." Even with the computer, we have to have a good strategy of analysis or we will bury ourselves under our own figures. Nevertheless, we cannot deny the extraordinary possibilities for scientific research with a survey instrument that are provided us by modern knowledge of statistics and by modern data processing machines.

The third great strength of the questionnaire is the power it offers for comparative studies: comparisons among individuals, between groups, between organizations within our own culture, and even between organizations in different cultures. With the questionnaire, we can subject a large number of people to precisely the same set of objective stimuli, thus making possible an enormous range of comparisons. To be sure, we cannot assume, even in our own culture, that a given question means the same thing to all informants. While this is a complication, it can be considered a productive one, for as we compare responses of informants across various questions we can learn much about what the questions mean to them and thus about the differing orientations towards life that they have.

The questionnaire survey: limitations

Let us now turn to the limitations of the method. As I have been pointing out, the questionnaire is particularly useful for getting at the subjective states of informants: their sentiments, beliefs, and perceptions of the world around them. But this very strength can lead us into a dead end street. With the questionnaire, we can make elaborate analyses of the perceptions our informants have of the world around them, without having any independent data as to the nature of that world they are perceiving. In other words, we study their reactions without learning what it is they are reacting to. However much we learn about how certain beliefs, attitudes and perceptions are related to each other, these findings remain within the subjective world of informants and do not allow us to break out and connect the subjective with the objective.

There are ways to break out, but if we remain within the confines of the questionnaire, the escape may be more apparent than real.

One common strategy is to compare the subjective responses of informants to "hard criterion variables" such as figures for absenteeism, turnover, productivity, and so on. While such efforts are certainly valuable, at best they provide only a partial solution to our problem. In the industrial plant, absenteeism, turnover, and productivity (like attitudes, values, and perceptions) are themselves outcomes of the social process that is going on in the plant. We are thus comparing one outcome with another. Ordinarily, we would rather learn something about the social process that gives rise to each type of outcome.

Can we get at the social process through the questionnaire? Most organizational surveys attempt to do this. Researchers do not confine themselves to attitudinal questions to determine how the informant feels about the union or how he regards his supervisor. They ask also questions referring to behavior and interaction—for example: How often do you attend your union meeting? How closely does the supervisor supervise you? Below each question will appear a range of possibilities to check, in one case for the frequency of meeting attendance, and in the other case a specification of degrees of closeness of supervision.

The procedure then seems straightforward. You correlate reported attendance at union meetings with expressed attitudes toward the union, toward the union leaders, and toward other items that you suspect may be related to meeting attendance. Similarly, you correlate reported closeness of supervision with attitudes toward supervisor in order to determine whether the supervisor who is reported to supervise closely is highly regarded or poorly regarded by his subordinates.

So far so good, but we have skipped over a key assumption on which the procedure is based. The assumption is that in reporting how often they attend union meetings or how closely their supervisor supervises them, the informants are reasonably close to objective reality—that is, reasonably close to what a trained observer would find if he checked attendance at union meetings or if he made intensive and quantitative studies of the relationship between the supervisor and his subordinates. As far as I know, this assumption has been checked in practice in only one study, and there the results were most disturbing.

The case involved a local union of approximately 500 members which was being studied through interviewing and observation by George Strauss. Attendance averaged approximately 30 members, so Strauss had no difficulty in making his own observational record of attendance at each meeting he attended through a year of field study. Toward the end of this year, Lois Dean[18] mailed a questionnaire to all of the members and, thanks to the prodding of Strauss, received a return of over 50 percent. Exclusively for our research purposes, we placed a code on the questionnaire so that we could identify each informant. This enabled us to compare the informant's questionnaire report on his meeting attendance with what Strauss had observed during the previous year.

Some small proportion of reporting error could be disregarded, but the discrepancies discovered by Dean were not small. Of the total informants, 29 percent reported falsely on their meeting attendance: 26 percent reported some frequency of attendance yet had never been observed at the meeting, while 3 percent denied attending meetings but had actually been observed at such meetings.

---

[18] Lois Dean, "Interaction Reported and Observed: The Case of One Local Union," *Human Organization*, Vol. 17, no. 3, (Fall, 1958), pp. 36–44.

The 3 percent "negative dissemblers," as Dean called them, represented such a small number (seven cases) that the researcher could only speculate about their characteristics. (Were they perhaps company spies?) On the other hand, the "positive dissemblers" were quite a substantial group (68 cases), almost twice as large as the "positive truth tellers" (36 cases) who had actually attended meetings as they claimed.

In the ordinary questionnaire survey, it would not have been possible to separate the dissemblers from the truth-tellers. The researcher who then wanted to examine the relationship between meeting attendance and attitudes would unwittingly have put into his box for meeting attenders almost twice as many who had not attended meetings as those who had. No one would do research in this sloppy fashion—if he knew he was doing so. The point is that the researcher who uses the questionnaire survey alone cannot know what he is doing on the particular issue in question here.

We have much the same problem with questions regarding closeness of supervision and other aspects of the supervisor's behavior. Our Peruvian utility questionnaire[19] clearly shows us that the workers in the plant we studied prefer a supervisor that they see as supervising them closely. What does this finding mean? Are they reporting that they like the type of behavior that U.S. workers generally dislike? Or do they have a different conception from the U.S. as to the nature of close supervision? We can never expect to answer those questions until we get in and observe a supervisor in action with his subordinates and interview both parties regarding the supervisory relationship.

The need for checking the relationship between reported behavior and observed behavior is obvious enough in a culture different from our own, but are we on safe ground in assuming that we know what a U.S. worker means when he says that his supervisor supervises him closely? I am not claiming that if we had parallel observational data we would find the reported close supervisor no different from the one reported as exercising general supervision. This would be improbable indeed. On the other hand, observation might well lead us to discovering more than one type of close supervisor and more than one type of general supervisor. It might show us that we had been submerging significant differences through lumping together distinguishably different supervisory styles.

Observation might also tell us a good deal about the conditions in a work environment conducive to close supervision and those conducive to general supervision. In this way, we could distinguish between leadership style which may be a personal phenomenon and the environmental conditions which may promote one or another type of supervision.

There is another limitation to the questionnaire survey method which

---

[19] William F. Whyte and Lawrence K. Williams, "Supervisory Leadership: An International Comparison," International Management Congress, New York, 1963. Reprint No. 143. New York State School of Industrial and Labor Relations.

may not be inherent in the method itself but tends to be associated with the way the method is generally used. The problem is that the method tends to lead us toward an oversimplified distorted view of the nature of organizations. If we examine the literature of organizational surveys, we find that the questionnaire has been used primarily for the study of the man-boss relationship. That is, questionnaires usually have series of items regarding the nature of the job itself, the pay, the company, and so on, but the major area of interpersonal concern is that of the man and his boss. This condition probably arises in part out of the requirements of the questionnaire method itself.

To be able to make statistical analyses of our findings, we need to have a large number of informants in the same position in the organization, reporting on and reacting to individuals occupying another standardized position. There are more workers than anybody else in most organizations, and every group of workers has a supervisor, so it is convenient to ask workers about this supervisor. If the organization is large enough, the researcher can move one step up the line and ask foremen about their immediate boss.

There are three things wrong with this kind of an approach:

1. If we implicitly assume that all foremen positions in the organization are much alike, we may attribute to supervisory style differences among foremen that are more properly explained in terms of the nature of the technology, work flow and nature of work in their departments. That is, we may be comparing men whose jobs are drastically different: for example, the assembly line foremen and the machine shop foreman.
2. We may limit our comparisons to supervisory jobs that are as near to identical as possible, and this has been done in some cases. This takes care of the criticism on point one, but it leaves out of account the differences in supervisory behavior that are related to differences in the nature of the supervisory jobs, and this we are coming to think is an important area of investigation.
3. While we cannot deny that the man-boss relationship is an important one, it is not worth the preponderant attention it has been receiving. The organization is not simply a series of man-boss relationships. The supervisor has to relate himself not only to his own boss and to his subordinates but also to industrial engineers, production engineers, accountants and cost control specialists, production planners, and so on within management, not to mention union leaders at various levels. In other words, the organization is made up of an interdependent network of human relations. It is unrealistic and misleading to single out the vertical line of authority for such exclusive attention.

The questionnaire tends to be little used in these other relationships in the network because we often find that the numbers of people involved are so few that the ordinary data processing approach will not serve us. I am not saying that the questionnaire cannot be used except in studying vertical relationships. I am saying that it is not so easy to use it outside of the vertical dimension and that much more effort needs to be given to tailor making new instruments for these new areas of investigation. This means also that the development of new instruments must depend upon interviews and observations to provide a foundation of knowledge regarding the new areas to be covered.[20]

Conclusion

This exploration of research methods suggests certain conclusions for students. The student should recognize that the findings of a research project can only be as good as the methods used to get at those findings. He must always ask himself whether the particular approach used gives enough confidence in the findings of the study so that the investigator's conclusions can be accepted.

The student should realize also that each method has its own special problems or limitations as well as its strong points. In the case of an experiment, he faces the extrapolation problem: to what extent is it legitimate to generalize from the perhaps somewhat artificial situation of an experiment to what otherwise goes on in the organizational world? He must also ask whether the experimenter has given him an adequate account of the social process on which the experiment was based and has not been content with simply making before and after measures.

With the more intimate interview-observational methods, while recognizing the advantages of depth penetration, the student should note the possibilities of bias and selective observation on the part of the investigator. Recognizing that such an investigator is in a position to give an account that "feels" realistic, the student must ask for the evidence behind the feeling.

In the case of the survey or questionnaire, with all its tremendous advantages in quantification, the student should recognize that the investigator is dealing primarily with expressions of attitudes or perceptions. He should realize that the investigator who uses the questionnaire alone can tell him how workers perceive the foreman, but he has no evidence regarding the way the foreman is behaving.

For potential research men in the field of organizational behavior, the principle moral of this discussion is that there is no one best way to do such research. The investigator should select his method or methods in

---

[20] Some of the discussion of the possibilities and limitations of interview-observation and survey methods is taken from Whyte, "Toward an Integrated Approach for Research in Organizational Behavior," Proceedings of the Sixteenth Annual Meeting of the Industrial Relations Research Association, 1963. Reprint No. 155. New York State School of Industrial and Labor Relations.

terms of the nature of the problem. He also needs to ask how much is known about the problem. If the situation of interest to him is largely unexplored, he must select methods appropriate for exploratory work. If the problem area has already received a good deal of research attention, he may decide that it is time to try to do a study that is sharply focused on a very small number of variables or even to do a crucial experiment. He also needs to learn to be flexible in the methodology he uses so as to avoid the research blind alleys that trap the one-method man.

This chapter should help the student to improve his critical judgment of research reports. He should read such reports with certain questions in mind. For example:

1. What method(s) did the investigator use?
2. Were the method (or methods) most appropriate for the problem studied?
3. Were the method (or methods) appropriate for the level of knowledge existing regarding the problem at the time the study was made? That is, did the investigator seek to test specific propositions when it would have been more appropriate to conduct an exploratory study designed to discover propositions worth testing? Or did he do an exploratory study on a problem already well explored?
4. Do the method or methods used permit the investigator to draw the conclusions that he states? Here I am not thinking of tests of statistical significance which, though important, are beyond the scope of this book. I am thinking of the logical relationship between data and conclusions drawn from data. For example, does the investigator draw quantitative conclusions (at least implicitly) without having clear cut quantitative data to support them? Or does he state conclusions regarding behavior when he only has data on perceptions and attitudes?

References

On research methods, see:

Adams, Richard N. and Preiss, J. J. (eds.). *Human Organization Research*. Homewood, Ill.: The Dorsey Press, 1960. A book of readings with emphasis upon interview-observational methods.

Sellitz, Claire; Jahoda, M.; Deutsch, D.; and Cook, S. W. *Research Methods in Social Relations*. New York: Holt-Rinehart and Winston, 1961. A good general introduction with broad coverage but special emphasis on surveys.

Discussion questions

1. For research in organizational behavior, discuss the possibilities and limitations of the following methods:

   a) Broad comparative studies, data being gathered from public or company records or from interviewing of a few "key informants" in a large number of cases.

    b) Field experiments.

    c) Interviewing and observation, including participant observation.

    d) Questionnaire or survey methods.

    2. Select a research report for critical examination. Regarding this report, answer the questions posed at the end of this chapter. If you conclude that the investigator used the appropriate method or methods on all counts, nevertheless consider the possibilities and limitations he would have faced if he had sought to use different methods.

3. The structuring of the work environment

BEFORE WE BRING our actors onto the stage, we need to set that stage for them. The purpose of this chapter is to describe the environment within which the drama of organizational behavior is acted out and to make some preliminary assessment of the way some aspects of environment affect the actors.

Who are the actors of concern to us? In this and other early chapters, there are workers and supervisors. High-level management people will be considered later, since the problems facing higher management can be better understood if we begin our description and analysis at the level where the basic work of production or service gets performed.

In our terms, the setting of organizational behavior consists of the following five elements:

1. Technology and work flow.
2. Formal organization structure.
3. Job placement and progression system.
4. Compensation system.
5. Management-designed programming of desired worker and supervisor behavior.

We begin by delimiting the field in two ways. First we must distinguish between the *givens* and the *explicanda:* those aspects which are to be accepted without explanation and those that are to be explained. In scientific work, it is always necessary to determine which is which and not to try to explain everything all at once. Thus, we shall make no attempt to explain why management decides to produce one line of products rather than others, to buy or build a particular type of machine for its production, to institute a system of piece rate payments, and so on. While such matters could be made the objects of research, they are not our concern. Such decisions are assumed here, not explained. We then go on to ask what impact such decisions have on workers and supervisors.

In this chapter we further delimit our field of concern in the following ways: in describing the environment, we shall give some attention to how certain aspects of this environment affect workers and supervisors, and what certain types of managerial decisions and activities are intended to achieve. How workers and supervisors react to this environment in which management places them will be considered in subsequent chapters. We will present the environment at this point in static terms. In a sense, this is unrealistic for life is constantly changing, particularly in modern industry. Nevertheless, since it is difficult to present structure and change at the same time, we will concentrate here on the structural presentation and consider change processes later.

Finally, we will concentrate upon the environment of large and complex organizations, characterized by a number of levels of authority, division into departments or other units, and by some formalization of rules of behavior, procedure and policies. While the theoretical framework to be presented in Parts II and III should apply just as well to the small and simple organization, it is only when we reach higher levels of size and complexity that it becomes necessary to establish organizational behavior as a distinctive field of study. If we are examining an organization so small and simple that the owner is in direct and frequent contact with all of his employees, we can proceed as if we were studying a small informal group 'or an association or club in the community. It is only when we get to the level where the members of the organization are so diverse and so separated from each other in space and in differentiation of functions that the organization's problems can no longer be worked out by the informal adjustments of face-to-face interaction. It is at this point that we need to develop systematic ways of examining the relation of individual to group, group to group, individual to organization, and group to organization.

Technology and work flow

By *technology* we mean the machines, processes, equipment, and supplies that are used in the work operation. The word sounds imposing enough to make us think of large machines of enormous power, and indeed the term covers such elements, but it also refers to the most simple levels. In our terms, the spindle on which the waitress places her order in the kitchen or service pantry is part of the restaurant's technology, as also are the order blanks she uses and the pen or pencil with which she writes.

By *work flow* we mean the sequence of activities carried out in patterned form whereby the product moves from its earliest stages through to final completion or whereby a series of people perform interdependent tasks in the provision of a service to the customer.

We begin with technology and work flow because it is these elements that tend to determine, within certain limits, the jobs to be performed in the organization and the relations to be built and maintained among certain organization members. Of course, it is not enough to recognize that technology and work flow have an important impact upon people. We have to ask what types of technology and what arrangements of work flow have particular effects, and this faces us first with a problem of classification. We need to sort out the elements in the field so that under technology type A we place operations that we expect to have similar effects upon people and different effects from what we expect for type B.

It seems useful for our purposes to deal with four general types: office, service, manufacturing, and continuous process. Of course, many large organizations contain two or more types, and even some relatively small plants may contain two types, as we shall note.

Office organizations are generally subunits of manufacturing, continuous process, or service organizations, but they are sufficiently distinctive in the work performed to deserve special treatment. In many governmental agencies the primary operations are of an office nature: the preparation, circulation, and filing of papers. Unfortunately, up to this point, studies of offices have been so few that we will not be able to include them in our discussion in a meaningful way.

While all types require some link between their operation and the customer, the distinguishing feature of the service type is that the customer is physically on the premises and interacting with a relatively high frequency with personnel of the organization. A retail specialty store or a department store fall into this type.

Restaurants are generally thought of as falling in the service category, but they are more properly classified as a combination of manufacturing and service. The food the restaurant serves the customers is ordinarily manufactured on the premises. In a busy restaurant, this necessitates a minute-by-minute coordination of production with service and creates especially severe problems of coordination along the flow of work. Hotels are a still more complex combination, for the hotel usually has one or more restaurants which have to be coordinated with other hotel operations. Also, most hotels have a laundry department which is similar to a small manufacturing plant. While products are not produced here, the washing and ironing activities involve machine operation and worker tasks that are similar to what we see in manufacturing.

Manufacturing involves such a range of activities that it seems useful to specify certain subtypes. We shall follow the distinction made by Joan Woodward[1] between unit and small-batch production on the one hand and mass production on the other. In unit production, the plant is engaged in the custom manufacturing of individual items. Each item is built to the customer's specifications. While, over a period of months, the plant may manufacture a number of units quite similar to designs produced in the past, the orders for any design are not sufficiently numerous to permit the

---

[1] Joan Woodward, *Industrial Organization: Theory & Practice* (London: Oxford University, Press, 1965).

standardization of operations. In small-batch production, several identical items are manufactured at the same time, but the orders are not large enough to make it practical for the plant to build its technology and work flow around any particular order. Unit and small-batch production are considered together here, for Woodward found they exhibited important similarities in organization structure.

In mass production, as the name implies, we have plants engaged in producing a large volume of units that are either identical or so similar that it is practical for management to build the technology and work flow around these particular items of production.

Continuous process operations differ from all others in two important respects. While under special conditions we sometimes have manufacturing plants operating with three shifts per day and a restaurant that never closes, it is the very nature of the continuous process organization that the activities must be constantly manned. In petroleum and chemicals, the plants cannot be shut down without incurring heavy start-up costs. Continuous process industries are also distinctive in their separation of the worker from physical contact with the product. The flow goes through tubes and machines untouched by human hands, and it is the responsibility of the workers to monitor the operations.

Work flow and the nature of the job

The work flow has important effects upon the nature of the job. In the restaurant, the worker himself (waiter or waitress) moves about providing the work flow in his person. This provides great freedom of physical movement but places upon the worker the sometimes complex problems of coordination that, in other work systems, are handled by the technology itself or are organized by management (moving materials to the workplace, while the worker remains more or less stationary).

In the department store, the work flow is generally at a very simple level. The salesperson may be responsible for seeing that his shelves are kept supplied with the appropriate merchandise, but this can usually be handled by occasionally checking with storeroom personnel. The close timing of moment-to-moment coordination of the flow of materials necessary in the large restaurant is not required of the department store. The salesperson, while not covering the mileage of waiter or waitress, is likely to have considerable freedom of physical movement. The complexities of his job primarily involve the customer relationship. (Here we are confining our attention to the bottom level of the organization. Of course, a department store buyer has a highly complex job, involving interacting with people in a number of different organizations and planning ahead so that saleable merchandise will arrive at the store in the right quantities at the right prices and at the right times.)

In the continuous process industries, the work flow is built into the equipment itself, and the worker does not handle the material, except possibly for running an occasional test. His job is to monitor this flow, diagnosing how the process is going from automatic charts and meters and tests. Here the worker has considerable freedom of movement. He may be able to keep an eye on the charts and meters from a distance. In many such situations, he is expected to intervene only when the process goes beyond certain pre-established limits. Therefore, the better the process is going, the less he has to do. He is primarily paid to observe and to make a diagnosis on the basis of what he observes. The physical actions he takes are exceedingly simple. His skills are intellectual rather than manual.

On the assembly line, the work flow comes in terms of physical objects, on which the worker has to perform physical operations. Here we must distinguish between automatic, conveyor belt lines and worker-paced flows. The automotive assembly line is the most widely known and most studied of assembly technologies. Here the pace is controlled by management decision, establishing the speed at which the line must move. In such a situation, the worker's freedom of physical action is exceedingly limited. He can work a few seconds ahead, moving a few feet up the line, or he can drop a few seconds behind, moving a few feet down the line, but he cannot go far either way without bumping into the man before him or after him in the flow. While the line is moving, he cannot leave his workplace without calling upon the foreman to have a relief man stand in for him. Except during work breaks, he can interact only with the men before and after him on the line and the two or three men opposite, as well as the foreman.

Many assembly lines are subject to a much greater worker influence in the control of work pace. Such is the case when workers sit at long tables, with each worker performing his operation or operations and then passing the object to the next person downstream in the work flow. Here the flow does not have to be as exactly coordinated as in the conveyor belt operation, for the worker does not need to pick up the object and begin work on it immediately that the person before him in the flow has finished his operation. We may observe such tables with objects waiting for action at each point between workers on the line. Here workers tend to have far more freedom of movement than on the automatic assembly line, since the worker can be away from his job for a few minutes without shutting the whole line down. On the other hand, the efficient function-ing of the line depends upon a smooth flow of objects from point to point. If any worker goes substantially slower than the rest, unfinished parts will pile up at his workplace, and the "bottleneck" will become evident to the foreman as well as to the other workers.

The technology and work flow also have important effects upon supervisory and managerial jobs. Let us illustrate here simply with the role of the first-line supervisor.

Where the supervisor is in charge of a department made up of workers on worker-paced jobs he needs to have a good deal of contact with the worker in order to make work assignments, to check on quality, and to try to maintain an adequate level of productivity. A supervisor in a conveyor belt assembly line operation has quite a different role. The workpace is controlled by the speed of the conveyor, and that in turn is set by higher management. Beyond assigning a man a place on the line, the supervisor has no functions in the distribution of tasks. The nature of the task is determined by the position on the line and by the particular model which is being worked on. Here the supervisor has some responsibility to see that the workers are supplied with the appropriate parts and tools, but he can judge the needs to a considerable extent by observation, without initiating any contact with the workers. In fact, it has been found in several assembly line studies that interaction between workers and foremen tends to be initiated primarily by workers. The technology and work flow provide the structuring of the worker's job so there is little obvious need for the supervisor to initiate interaction with the worker. We find that the interactions initiated by the workers arise particularly out of major and minor emergencies—letting the foreman know that a given tool is not functioning properly, that certain supplies are needed, that the way the work has been done in previous stages makes the task of the individual difficult and so on.

In continuous process industry, with experienced and trained men on the job, there is little need for interaction between the supervisor and the men. Here again the technology and work flow provide the basic structuring of the job, and the meters and charts which indicate to the workers how the process is running also provide the supervisor with much of the information he needs to evaluate progress and problems. At the end of each shift, he may receive a set of charts that record the state of the process minute by minute throughout the eight-hour period. If the charts indicate routine operations, he may not need to concern himself further with what went on during this shift. If the charts show wide fluctuations, he can take this information as an indication that he should get out into the plant and talk to the men about the problems. If he wants to know how things are going before the end of a shift, he can simply step into the control room and take a quick look at the charts. Presumably on such occasions there will be at least a few moments of conversation between supervisor and workers, even when operations are routine, but in my studies of such a plant, I can recall several days when the whole shift went by without any contact between workers and a foreman who was highly popular with them. Nobody thought this absence of interaction significant enough to be worth a comment.

In the restaurant industry, supervisor-worker interaction will be channeled in part by the workflow (from customer to kitchen and back) and in part by the time of day. There is likely to be a period of interaction on a group basis between service supervisor and waiters or waitresses at the beginning of the workday to get things organized. In a busy restaurant, during the rush hour, the tasks performed by waiters and waitresses do not require any interaction with the supervisor and, in fact, a skillful supervisor will not intervene during this period to try to initiate activities for them, recognizing that they have their hands and heads full with the handling of relations with customers, checkers, bartenders and service pantry personnel. The interventions that do take place, in the case of a skillful supervisor, will be those tending to take the pressure off the waiters or waitresses, the supervisor speaking to new customers to tell them that their waitress will get to them shortly so as to relieve their impatience, the supervisor taking an order for a harrassed waitress to save her steps, and so on.

Impact of technology on formal organization structure

By *formal organization structure* we mean the lines of authority in an organization, the distribution of people among different departments, divisions, or other units, and the assignment of tasks to individuals and organizational units.

We have now arrived at what the early theorists of the scientific management movement consider the starting point of all organizational inquiry. In the early years, these theorists were trying to establish universal organization principles, that would hold regardless of differences in work flow and technology. In fact, little attention was given to the relationship between technology and work flow on the one hand and formal organization structure on the other. Thus in 1927, Mary Parker Follett wrote:[2]

. . . whatever the purpose towards which human endeavor is directed, the principles of that direction are nevertheless the same.

This point of view led to a search for those fundamental principles mentioned in Chapter 1: The span of control, the unity of command (one man-one boss), and the necessity for a sharp distinction between line and staff functions.

In the 1940's and 1950's, this view of fixed principles came under increasingly heavy attack. James C. Worthy[3] of Sears, Roebuck and Company used the Sears experience as ammunition to argue against the span-of-control principle. While he noted that this principle allowed for some variation in the ratio of supervisors to subordinates, depending upon the complexity and interdependence of the tasks of subordinates, he

---

[2] H. Metcalf and L. Urwick (eds.), *Dynamic Administration* (New York: Harper & Bros., 1942), cited in Woodward, *Industrial Organization*, p. 55.

[3] James C. Worthy, *Big Business and Free Men* (New York: Harper & Bros., 1959).

argued that the application of this principle would mean providing one supervisor for a small number of subordinates. Worthy pointed out that if this "law" were actually followed, it would lead everywhere, for large organizations, to very long organizational hierarchies, with many levels of authority. This would complicate the problems of communication up and down the line of authority.

Worthy pointed out that the span-of-control principle rested upon one crucial but unstated assumption: that people need close supervision. Examining the structure of Sears department stores, Worthy was able to show that a broad, flat structure was entirely feasible and in fact appeared to be superior to the long chain of command, both in terms of morale and of productivity.

On the other hand, we find that the Sears mail order house does not present the flat structure idealized by Worthy but rather shows many levels of authority with much narrower spans of control than found in the department stores. These differences in structure within the same large company suggest that it is unrealistic to try to devise universal principles of organization structure. We can expect our theory building to proceed more effectively if we begin with the assumption that the nature of the work carried out and the technology and workflow available to channel this work will determine, within limits, the formal structure that is appropriate for a given organization.

If we state the proposition in extreme form, it implies that, since every organization is unique in some respects, every organization needs to have a structure especially tailored to its needs, and therefore no general principles are possible. Every case would be a law unto itself and no general propositions would be possible.

If we stake out our objective somewhere between that of achieving universal propositions and that of "understanding" the unique case, we open the doors to an important line of scientific development, which has been pioneered by Joan Woodward.[4]

In Chapter 2 we describe how Woodward and her assistants arrived at their important discoveries. In summary, she found that variability in the formal organization structures among the firms examined was so large that it was clearly impossible to arrive at any universal generalizations. It was only when she sorted the firms out into different technological types that uniformities in formal organization structure appeared.

While Woodward gives no cutting point to separate small- from large-batch production, her data suggest that most batch plants she studied produce either in such small batches or in such large batches that we can expect to find few cases that fall in between where the allocation to a given type is problematical. Woodward also deals with combined systems such as the process production of crystalline substances subsequently

---

[4] Woodward, op. cit.

prepared for sale by standardized production methods. We will not enter into these complexities here, since in this chapter we are simply seeking to illustrate the connection between the nature of work and the nature of the organizational structure.

Woodward shows that the span of control varies with the type of production system:[5]

In unit production firms the number of people directly responsible to the chief executive ranges from two to nine, the median being four; in large batch and mass production firms, the range was from four to thirteen, the median being seven, and in process production firms, the range was from five to nineteen, the median being ten.

If we look at the other end of the organization, checking the ratio of first-line supervisors to workers, we also find wide differences among types. In 24 unit production or small-batch production plants, the first-line supervisor had an average of 23 people working for him.

In 31 large-batch or mass production plants, the average number of workers reporting to a single supervisor was 50. In the dimensional products or continuous process plants, the ratio is one first-line supervisor to approximately 13 workers.

These wide differences both at the top and bottom levels clearly cannot be accounted for by random variation. There seems to be something about the type of production system that favors the development of a certain pattern of span of control.

The traditionalist in organization theory might argue that the departures by type from the ratios that would be indicated by classical theory have come about not through some inherent logic of the production system itself but rather through a failure of organization planners to apply the design standards that would bring them superior results. If we accept this argument, we would have to explain why it is that organization planners in a certain type of production system consistently deviate from the supposedly correct ratios in a single direction. Furthermore, for 80 firms, Woodward has gathered figures and evaluations of outside knowledgeable persons to distribute them in three categories in terms of economic success: above average, average, and below average. In looking at the ratios between first-line supervisors and workers, she finds that in each of the three types, the firms that are rated above average have ratios extremely close to the average for their type, whereas the "below average" firms in success for each type have ratios that are markedly above or below the average for their type. Even granting the difficulties in arriving at valid and reliable comparative estimates of the success of firms, the figures presented by Woodward show such striking differences between firms she rates as above average and those she rates as below average in

[5] Woodward, *op. cit.*, pp. 52–3.

respect to their supervisor-worker ratios that it is quite implausible to assume that these differences represent random variations.

Also at the top level, Woodward found meaningful relationships between success, span-of-control ratios, and type of production system. She notes:[6]

All the successful firms in which the span of control of the chief executive was 10 or more were process production firms.

Woodward's findings also tend to undermine the accepted maxims regarding staff-line relations and regarding the need for each man to have only a single boss.[7]

Eight of the twelve firms in which the status and prestige of the specialists were so high that it was impossible, in practice, to distinguish between advice, service and control, on the one hand, and executive responsibility on the other, were process production firms.

She notes that, while the personnel manager was officially responsible to one person,[8]

. . . he regarded other senior executives as his superiors and their requests as executive instructions.

In this case, whether we regard the personnel manager as having only one boss or as having several depends upon whether we are looking at the organization chart or at day-to-day behavior. But Woodward found two cases in which even the organization chart showed department heads being directly responsible to five individuals. Significantly enough, both firms with this functional kind of organization were in process industries. At the top, we find a chief executive, and immediately below him a programming manager, chief chemist (responsible for quality control), maintenance engineer, personnel manager, and works accountant. Each of these five men has authority over the same 30 department supervisors.

The type of production system may also determine the presence or absence of certain specialized management departments. This is most clearly the case with regard to production control. In the unit product and small batch systems, we find a lack of differentiation between functions of planning, execution, and control. There is little specialization. The translation of objectives into activity sequences is relatively simple, and generally the organization of work is delegated to the shop level. Dimensional products or process systems have the control of production built into the technology itself, and the operating jobs involve primarily a monitoring of the flow of production. There is thus no need for a separate production control department. In fact, production control systems tend to be concentrated in large-batch and mass production systems.

---

[6] Woodward, *op. cit.*, p. 71.
[7] Woodward, *op. cit.*, p. 65.
[8] Woodward, *op. cit.*, p. 116.

Specific determinants of structure

As has happened before in our field, the new research in this particular program area has served to demonstrate more what is *not* true than what is true. We are now ready to dump some of the most cherished maxims of classical management theory into the trash can. Have we nothing left to take the place of these discards?

We do indeed see some new uniformities emerging. This emergence seems to be taking place in two stages. First, particularly through the work of Woodward and her associates, we are discovering that there is a pattern underlying organizational structures and that this pattern relates to the nature of the work to be done, and the technology and work flow through which this work is channeled.

At this stage, we know what structural properties to expect in a plant of a given type of production system, but we do not know why these particular structural properties (and not quite different ones) should be found in this particular production system. The next step, which now lies before us, is to discover the causative factors between the production system and the organization structure. On this point, our knowledge so far is fragmentary and our conclusions are largely speculative. Nevertheless, let us explore some of the factors that may be important in this relationship in order to get a better idea of where our field may be moving in the future.

Basing his work on the foundation established by Woodward, Edward Harvey[9] seeks to specify further the relationships between "Technology and the Structure of Organizations." His analysis of 43 industrial organizations verifies Woodward's conclusions as he shows that "relationships between an organization's technology and internal structure fall into distinct patterns."[10] To convert technology into a variable, Harvey selects the characteristics which he calls technical diffuseness-specificity. He illustrates in this way:[11]

Technical diffuseness implies a firm in which a number of technical processes yield a wide range of products. Furthermore, the actual products included in this range are more likely to vary from year to year as the result of model changes in technological processes.

As a corollary, technical specificity suggests a plant in which only one or a very small number of products is constantly produced.

Since Harvey's findings generally tend to confirm those of Woodward, why should we accept the new concepts, definitions, and variables he suggests? He agrees that generally technical diffuseness corresponds to

---

[9] Edward Harvey, *American Sociological Review*, Vol. 33, no. 2 (April, 1968), pp. 247–59.

[10] *Ibid.*, p. 247.

[11] *Ibid.*, p. 249.

"made-to-orderness" which is characteristically found in unit production, while specificity corresponds to process production such as found in a refinery. But he points out that a unit production plant might produce one or a few products on a long-run basis and thus be technically specific, in his terms. He thus feels that he has made a conceptual advance in pointing to the technical diffuseness-specificity dimension and expressing it in the form of a variable. In other words, he has taken a step to abstract out of the global mass suggested by the term, technology, a dimension that can be expressed and measured in variable form.

For the purposes of his study, Harvey uses technical diffuseness-specificity as his independent variable. He posits four dependent variables:

1. Subunit specialization in organizations (the degree to which specialized functions and responsibility are set apart and formally recognized in the organization structure).
2. The number of levels of authority.
3. The ratio of managers and supervisors to total personnel.
4. Program specification in organizations. This he defines in the following terms:[12]

Programs are defined as a mechanism or rules in terms in which an attempt is made to give directions to organizational activity. Specification refers to the variable extent to which such programs are detailed or spelled out.

He goes on to identify "three major areas of organizational programming."[13]

a) role programming, by which is meant the formalization of duties and responsibilities as a sense of job specification.
b) Output programming, by which is meant the formal delineation of steps through which raw materials pass in the course of becoming the organization's outputs.
c) Communication programming, by which is meant the formal specification of the structure, content, and timing of communication within the organization.

Harvey states the relationships he has found between the independent variable and his four dependent variables in the following words:

As technical specificity increases, (1) the number of specialized subunits in the organization increases; (2) the number of levels of authority in the organization increases; (3) the ratio of managers and supervisors to total personnel increases; and (4) the amount of program specification in the organization increases.

Going from Woodward to Harvey, we have taken further steps toward abstraction and the specification of variables to be used in the

[12] *Ibid.*, p. 250.
[13] *Ibid.*, p. 250

measurement of relationships. We have not said anything about why the particular relationships should exist or why the social processes observed should proceed in the observed form.

In an effort to bridge the gap between specification and measurement of variables and explication of process, let us look at just one element of structure: the span of control. What factors make for a large span of control? What factors make for a small one? Research and experience suggests the following five factors:

1. The complexity of the job for supervisior and for subordinate

A supervisor can more easily supervise a given number of subordinates who are all doing a simple job than he can with the same number of subordinates who are doing a complex job. Similarly, if the supervisor's job in itself is quite complex, he will have less time available to devote to his subordinates and therefore will need to limit the number working for him. If we wish to go beyond this apparent common sense statement, we need to have some way of measuring the complexity of jobs. Gerald D. Bell[14] has provided a conceptual approach to this measurement problem. According to his research, complexity is made up of four factors, as follows:

a) The degree of predictability of work demands. If the demands of the job are highly predictable, men can be trained to meet these demands in routine fashion and little checking or guidance from the supervisor will be needed. If the demands are highly unpredictable, then unanticipated problems will often arise, necessitating consultation between supervisor and subordinate.

b) Amount of discretion provided for in the position. Discretion here is measured in terms of the number of decisions the individual can make without checking with the superior. The larger the number, the more the discretion the individual.

c) The responsibility of the job holder. Here Bell measures responsibility in the method proposed by Elliott Jaques[15] which involves the measurement of the amount of time that can be expected to elapse between the decision to act by the job holder and the evaluation by superiors of the effectiveness of his actions. At low levels and with relatively unskilled work, we generally find that the time elapsed between actions and checking by a superior is very short, perhaps only a few minutes and rarely more than a few hours within the same work day. At high levels in the organization, individuals will make decisions whose effectiveness cannot be assessed for months and even years.

[14] Gerald D. Bell, "Determinants of Span Control," *American Journal of Sociology*, Vol. 73, no. 1 (July, 1967).

[15] Elliott Jaques, *Measurement of Responsibility* (London: Wm Heinemann, Inc., 1956).

d) The number of tasks performed by the job holder. Here the greater the number of tasks to be performed, the greater the complexity of the job.

Bell comes to this conclusion:[16]

The findings suggest that when subordinates' jobs are highly complex, span of control is decreased. Similarly, the more complex the supervisor's job, the lower his span of control.

Bell reached these findings on the basis of a study of a large community hospital. Would we come to the same conclusions if we applied his methods to the study of manufacturing organizations? That remains to be seen. However, it is important to note that Bell has defined his terms in a sufficiently general and abstract fashion so that they may be applied to the study of any organization. He has provided us with tools that may readily be put to scientific test in other work settings.

2.   Visibility of results

It is now fashionable to declare that the executive should manage in terms of results. That is, he should judge the results achieved by subordinates and not concern himself with the methods they utilize—unless the results are unsatisfactory. The argument is that this approach to management allows the subordinate to exercise his ingenuity and develop his own way of meeting problems, which helps to build effective performance. In terms of this logic, the superior only intervenes to check on methods used and advise upon changes if the results are not satisfactory.

This might well prove to be a universally valid proposition of management—were it not for one untenable assumption. The assumption is that results are more or less equally visible to superiors on all sorts of jobs. Of course, this assumption is contrary to fact. On some jobs, results (or what pass for results in the eyes of superiors) are highly visible, whereas on other jobs, how the jobholder is performing is not at all obvious to the superior.

This aspect of visibility of results helps to explain the flat organizational structure that has been characteristic of Sears department stores. The primary measure of effectiveness of a sales person and of a sales department is the volume of sales. Management keeps running records of performance throughout the organization. It is therefore easy for any superior to check the results of an individual or a department at frequent intervals without even making personal contact with those whose performance is being checked. The supervisor checks not only the sales volume for the period in question. He can readily check that volume against the volume achieved in other periods to determine whether the

---

[16] Bell, *op. cit.,* p. 100.

trend is up or down. In case the general trend of buying in the community is downward, the supervisor can check whether the individual or his department has held its own or fared better or worse than other individuals or departments. At higher levels, management has voluminous data for checking the performance of store against store, and these comparisons can be strengthened by inclusion of data regarding the buying power in communities in which the stores being compared are located.

In this type of situation, it is quite practical for the supervisor to leave the individual or department alone for considerable periods of time, as long as the records show good results. This means that a given supervisor can supervise more people than would be possible in situations where results are not so highly visible.

3.   Interdependence and coordination

Between two organizations of the same size and number of employees, we can expect that the organization whose activities are more highly interdependent will need a larger number of supervisory personnel and will have a longer hierarchy of authority. This variable of interdependence would also help to account for the sharp differences between the structures of Sears' department stores and mail order houses. The department store is made up of a number of selling units which share in the physical space but can function largely independently of each other. If problems arise in one department, their effects will not be observed in other departments—or at least the effects will be slow in appearing. In the mail order plant, on the contrary, there is a long and complicated flow of work to be coordinated, and a breakdown at any point can have serious repercussions throughout the entire system. It is therefore important to have supervisory personnel available for quick action.

4.   Technological versus human control of interdependent activities

An automotive assembly plant generally contains large numbers of workers and a relatively small number of management personnel. Given the fact that the operations of assembling an automobile are highly interdependent, how is it possible to operate the plant with such a small complement of management personnel? The answer is to be found in the nature of the technology itself. We might say here that the coordination is engineered into the conveyor belt assembly line. The worker does not have to ask his foreman what he is to do next. The line brings to him the object to be worked on, so identified as to make clear the operations to be performed, and the worker simply responds to the work flow. If automobiles were not produced on this assembly line basis, it would be necessary to have far more supervisory and managerial personnel in order to coordinate the activities.

5.   Personnel requirements of the technology

In continuous process industries, a few men at the operating level may be responsible for guiding the flow of thousands of gallons of the product. For example, we may have three men working in one operating unit and with a foreman supervising them. There may be no other unit in the same area suitable for the foreman's attention, and yet, in order to coordinate the activities of this unit with other units, it may be necessary to have a particular individual in charge. If a more primitive technology were employed, we might find 15 to 20 men producing the same output under a given foreman. In our hypothetical case, the foreman is responsible for only three men, but for a very elaborate technology that is producing a large volume of product.

The introduction of a case in continuous processing suggests another dimension of analysis. If an automotive assembly plant operates more than one shift, the second shift will have the same number of first-line supervisory personnel as the first shift—though the higher levels of management will not be so duplicated. In a continuous process plant, we often find one foreman responsible for all three shifts. To cover a seven-days-a-week operation, the plant will need four regular crews of three men each, with replacements being available in case of absence and vacations. Thus the three men on a shift for whom the foreman is responsible can grow to 14 or 15 when we consider continuous operations. This does not mean, of course, that the foreman works 24 hours a day. It does mean that he has what is often known as "24-hour responsibility." In such a case, his working hours will generally overlap parts of the first and second shifts, so that he can be in touch with two out of the three shifts on any given day. It is understood that he is to be called on the third shift only if some emergency arises.

On formal versus informal organization

Some years ago, we probably would have begun this chapter with a discussion of formal versus informal organization, for we might say that our field of study originated with the discovery of this assumed conflict. Scientific management theorists devoted all their attention to formal organization, as if to suggest that if the designers of organizations only knew the correct principles for setting them up, desired behavior would naturally result. After the Hawthorne studies, for several years investigators were busy demonstrating that the shape of the formal organization and the nature of formalized procedures of management did not determine worker behavior. This led to the concept of "informal organization" and to a concentration of research attention upon the informal as opposed to the formal. While no one actually wrote this, the early discussions of informal organization gave the impression that management's formal allocations of authority and establishment of rules and regulations, policies and procedures, had no effect upon behavior.

As so often happens in the social sciences, reaction against one extreme view led people to go to the opposite extreme. Now we need to come back to a more balanced view.

Does this mean that we should examine both the formal and the informal organization? I question the wisdom of this way of dichotomizing our field. It suggests that we ought to be able to observe and distinguish between formal and informal behavior. I once undertook to do this myself, and I found the effort confusing and unproductive. At the extremes, the distinctions seem clear enough: we see the foreman giving the worker an order in connection with the job (formal behavior). During a coffee break, we observe a group of workers away from their machines, talking about the next World Series game (informal behavior). As we move in from those two extremes, we quickly arrive at an area where we think we see formal and informal elements appearing together. In fact, it may be a characteristic of the most effective superior-subordinate relationships that formal and informal elements are inextricably mixed. If indeed we cannot make any firm objective discrimination at the behavioral level, then we should abandon this effort to dichotomize behavior.

I prefer to leave behavior entirely out of any definition of *formal organization structure*. By those terms, I mean only such elements as can be determined without behavioral observation. For example, we see an organization chart with vertical lines drawn from factory manager to production superintendent to general foreman to foreman to workers. We see that personnel men are not indicated on the chart to be in the same department as the production superintendent and his subordinates. We note further that the personnel men are physically housed in a different area from those concerned with production. We read the job descriptions, which tell us (in management's view) what workers are supposed to do and how they are supposed to do it. We read the rules and procedures established by management concerning the distribution of authority and responsibility. If we do not find an organization chart and written records on job description, rules, and procedures, we ask key management people to tell us what the structure of the organization is and how it is supposed to operate. In other words, in our terms the *formal organization structure* is the explicit management theory of the nature and functioning of the organization.

We make no assumption regarding the extent to which the behavior we observe in the plant will conform to this formal management theory. In this problem area we simply observe the behavior that takes place and then compare it with management theories of what should happen. The closeness of fit or the magnitude of the discrepancies are matters for empirical determination.

At the same time, we assume that the management formal theory of the organization will have important effects upon the behavior we observe, for this theory expresses itself in the decisions made by management regarding the number of levels of authority, the separation or combining of different functions and departmental units, the specification of the nature of jobs, and so on. All these matters are inevitably of great concern to members of the organization, but they may be best examined by observing behavior among workers and between workers and members of management and comparing these observations with management theories of how the organization is supposed to be structured and to operate. Any attempt to divide all of behavior into formal and informal categories is bound to lead to confusion.

Job placement and mobility systems

Any organization needs to make provision for the filling of its positions, and this means establishment of channels through which individuals move from one position to another and of standards to determine who shall move where.

Until recently it was taken for granted that the hiring of personnel was strictly a technical problem. Those responsible for recruitment and hiring had the responsibility of trying to attract the most highly qualified individual for the positions open, and they were expected to establish procedures for judging the relative qualifications of applicants. Similarly, employment agencies, both public and private, operated under the assumption that it was their responsibility to send to employers the best available candidates for the position open.

When companies and employment agencies follow this approach, the inevitable result is a skimming of the cream off the labor market, with individuals not fitting in this preferred category having to take the most undesirable jobs or being classified as "unemployable," which, in our society, is practically synonomous with "useless." Renewed federal government emphasis upon the poverty problem and the problems of urban ghetto areas, combined with the widespread disturbances in these areas, have led to efforts in companies and employment agencies to change recruitment policies. Under the directorship of Frank Cassel, the United States Employment Service began developing programs to persuade employers to hire those who did not meet their ordinary standards and to provide special assistance to such workers. Similarly, a number of companies developed programs to recruit people who in the past would not have received any employment consideration. A few firms even took steps to set up subsidiaries in slum areas to bring the jobs to the people. In effect, some managements have determined that their company should accept a social responsibility that was not even contemplated only a few years earlier.

The positional system established by the company does more than allocate individuals to the jobs that need to be done. It also indirectly allocates the relative satisfaction jobholders will get out of their jobs. While the correlation is far from perfect, various studies have shown that those holding high-level jobs (both within the work force and within management) tend to have higher levels of satisfaction with their work than those at the lower levels. Differences in financial rewards are only one factor (though an important one) in accounting for these differential satisfactions, which we shall explore more in detail in later chapters.

We can assume that nearly always there will be more individuals seeking promotion than there are promotions available. Therefore, management needs to apply some standards for the selection of candidates. Management is naturally inclined to seek to fill promotional positions in terms of ability, and that in turn requires the setting up of standards and procedures for judging ability and for defending the ability criterion against other standards.

What possibilities for upward mobility does the organization offer? It is part of our democratic ideology to assume that there should be free upward movement, and individual progress should be simply based upon a combination of effort and ability. There has indeed been a great deal of mobility in the United States, but it is important to distinguish between individual-lifetime mobility and intergenerational mobility. Can a man starting as a janitor rise up to be plant manager or company president (individual-lifetime mobility)? Or can the son of a janitor, after graduating from college, enter management and rise to the top (intergenerational mobility)? In the former case, we assume that the rise of the one-time janitor is due to ability and devotion to the job, supported only perhaps by some on-the-job training. In the latter case, the college degree serves as a passport for the individual to move into management.

While there is now a growing literature on intergenerational mobility for the United States and for some other countries,[17] our concern in the field of organizational behavior is primarily with individual-lifetime mobilty. What prospects for such mobility does the organization offer? Different types of organizations are radically different in this regard.

Some types of organizations are structured in horizontal and impermeable segments. For example, in the hospital we hardly expect that, through ability and diligence, the man who begins his career as an orderly will become a nurse and then eventually rise into the ranks of doctors. Nurses and doctors are hired directly into these positions, the primary qualification being their professional education.

Even where promotions are possible within the worker ranks, we encounter large differences among types of companies. In some plants, the worker finds that upon entering at the bottom with reasonable competence and devotion to the job, he may expect to move up three or more

---

[17] "Occupational Mobility," in S. Nosow and William H. Form (eds.), *Man, Work, and Society: A Reader in the Sociology of Occupations* (New York: Basic Books, 1962), chap. X, pp. 333–72. See also Peter Blau and Otis Dudley Duncan, *American Occupational Structure* (New York: John Wiley & Sons, 1967).

positions over the course of years. In other plants, such possibilities are not open simply because nearly all the available jobs are at the same level. For example, in automotive assembly plants it is the almost universal desire of men who have a regular position on one of the lines to move up to the category of utility man or to get a "bench job" off the line. While the pay increase is small, the difference in work activities is large. The utility man escapes from the constant pressures of the line, only stepping in when one of the regular positions of the line is not covered. The man on the "bench job" sets his own pace. However, there are large numbers of regular line positions for every single off-line job so the line worker may have only one chance in 10 or one in 20 of moving up even one step. Such possibilities or limitations naturally have marked effects upon relations of workers to each other and to the company—matters that we will explore in later chapters.

What are the possibilities of a worker moving up into management? The official dividing line usually comes between the position of first-line supervisor or foreman and what is variously known as group leader, straw boss, or working foreman. A man called by one of these latter three terms is expected to divide his time between doing production work and directing the work of fellow workers, whereas the foreman is expected to devote himself entirely to planning, organizing, and directing the work.

In some plants, we find rather free movement of workers across the line into management so that foremen, general foremen, and even perhaps superintendent positions are manned by those who came up from the ranks. In other firms, a college degree seems to be the passport to appointment even at the first-line supervisory position so that workers can cross the line into management, in effect, only if they somehow manage to get a college education while at work or in periods of leaves of absence. In general, we would expect to find a relationship between the educational requirements of supervisory jobs and the level of technical and scientific development of the firm. The less the firm's production or process operations are based upon advanced technology and applied science, the more open we would expect it to be in providing promotional possibilities for noncollege men. Whether or not there is a ceiling blocking worker promotion into management may make a great deal of difference in the way workers regard management and each other, as we shall see in subsequent chapters.

The compensation system

Here we are concerned with financial rewards, but it is well to sort these into three categories: *membership rewards, positional rewards,* and *performance rewards.*

Membership rewards are those that an individual receives simply by virtue of being a member of the organization. Some "fringe benefits" are of this nature: For example, any worker may receive the same potential benefits in health insurance regardless of his position in the ranks. The pension may also be considered in this category because while the size of a man's pension generally varies in terms of his earnings over the years, the amount is not determined by a particular position he holds, but rather by his total experience with various positions in the company.

Positional rewards are those that are attached to a particular position. A man is paid a particular rate because that is the rate that has been established for the job which he holds.

Performance rewards are allocated according to managerial judgment of the individual's performance or according to some measurement of output. In the former case, we are talking of rate ranges and merit rating. In some plants, management establishes for each job not a single rate but a range of possible rates. The individual enters the job at a starting rate at or toward the bottom of the range. After a period of time (usually six months or a year) he becomes available for consideration of a rate increase, until he reaches the top of the range for his particular job. If progression up through the range is automatic, depending only upon time put in on the job, then clearly increases are not a function of the performance but should be considered positional rewards. If management proposes that increases shall only be granted in terms of improved or superior performance then these increases can be considered performance rewards. In these cases, management usually goes to some pains to evaluate the individual, so as to determine his "merit" in relation to a possible increase. Apart from human fallibilities of judgment regarding "merit," rate range increases are rarely based upon evaluation of merit alone. When workers know that they are eligible for consideration for an increase every six months or every year, they naturally come to count on it, and it easier for the foreman to recommend to the personnel department that the worker receive an increase than to justify to the worker why he should not be recommended for an increase. In effect, the foreman is considering length of service as well as merit. In fact, a mixing of these criteria is sometimes officially recognized: increases from the bottom to the middle of the range are expected to come well nigh automatically with the passage of time, but increases beyond the middle on up to the top are to be granted only on a merit basis.

Piece-rate incentive systems provide another common approach to performance rewards. Here the worker is rewarded, beyond his base pay, according to the number of units he produces, if he is working on an individual piece rate. There are also systems that provide rewards to the group, based upon the total output of the group. In a few cases, there are plantwide systems, where all of the workers are rewarded according to a formula that measures the performance of the plant against some base period. We will consider the problems and possibilities of these several approaches to incentives in later parts of this book.

A small, simple enterprise can get by with a compensation program based largely on custom and the personal requests, arguments, and counter arguments, that can be carried out among the participants on a face-to-face basis. With a large, complex, and changing organization, custom and informal adjustments will not suffice. Management needs to formalize its procedures and to set standards for the making of its personnel decisions. Management needs to develop a rational and predictable system to plan the placement and movement of personnel. Within this system, the individual position cannot be considered in isolation. A change in the rate paid for one position changes its relationship to the whole positional system, so that each proposed change must be considered in terms of the total pattern.

Union pressures also provide important forces toward formalization. Fifty years ago, if a worker questioned whether he was being paid an appropriate amount of money for the job he performed, he could be told that the determination of his rate was none of his business and that if he did not like it, he could go elsewhere to work. Where an active union exists—or where management is trying to prevent one from arising—such nonexplanatory reactions on the part of management are no longer accepted procedure. Management must proceed on the assumption that any of the rates it sets may be questioned, so management must be prepared to show that it has at least gone through certain sytsematic procedures to set rates and has not made its decisions on a capricious basis.

Describing and evaluating jobs

Establishment of a compensation system requires setting rates on the jobs in the system. Before jobs can be evaluated, they must be described. At first, we might think that this is a superfluous step. Does not anyone familiar with a given department know what all its jobs consist of? Research and experience both demonstrate that this is not the case. If we observe a worker over a period of time and then ask others around him or even the worker himself what his job consists of, we find wide discrepancies between the observational record and what we are first told. Certain elements of the job simply tend to be taken for granted, and the full record can only be developed if someone makes it his business to come in and question and cross-question and observe, to write a preliminary description, and then to check it with the worker and those familiar with his job.

Evaluation involves an application to these job descriptions of some system of points for the training that is required, level of skill, responsibility for equipment and so on. In general, the systems provide a point scoring scheme that is in accord with general evaluations of social desirability: higher skill rates more points than lower skill, responsibility for more valuable equipment rates more than responsibility for equipment of lesser value, and so on. On the other hand, management sometimes finds it necessary to award points for especially undesirable working conditions (extreme heat, exposure to danger, and so on.) If points were not so awarded, management might find it difficult or impossible to place workers in jobs that involved unpleasant working conditions and low point scores on other elements.

At best job evaluation is a systematic procedure and not a scientific procedure. It is unscientific in the sense that the points scored in each category are the product of subjective evaluations rather than objective measurements. It is systematic in that the personnel men carrying out these responsibilities seek to follow certain standardized procedures so that the decisions are not intended to be the result of individual biases. Especially when a union is involved with a complex organization, it is important that systematic procedures be followed. When complaints are raised, management seeks to examine them in terms of the procedures that were followed and in terms of the relationship of the job in question to other jobs that were evaluated by the same system. If management can demonstrate that this job was evaluated through the same standards and procedures applied to other jobs in the system, then the only really effective union counterargument is that the whole system is faulty and needs reorganization. While this kind of counterattack sometimes does indeed lead to a re-examination of the whole system and revision of the job evaluation standards, this is an enormously complex and time-consuming task that management and union leaders generally seek to avoid until the number of individual rate complaints becomes so large that it seems reasonable to assume that something is wrong with the system. In general, management finds it easier to defend a given rate in terms of its relation to the whole rate system than as an isolated problem.

Can there be a scientific system for job evaluation? In *Measurement of Responsibility*, Elliott Jaques[18] maintains that science can be applied if we accept the principle of what he calls "time-span of responsibility" (defined earlier in this chapter). Jaques claims that the time-span standard can be applied to measure small differences among jobs from level to level in the work ranks as well as in managerial positions. Further testing of the Jaques' approach may indeed reveal that it represents an important advance in the establishment of compensation systems, but as yet it has not been generally applied. For present purposes, we are concerned with the standards and procedures that management generally uses, so that we can then examine the reactions of workers and supervisors to those standards and procedures.

Rate setting for incentive systems

The decision to offer workers incentives for production is only the first step in a complicated series of procedures. These procedures are

---

[18] Jaques, *op. cit.*

generally administered by an industrial engineering department but sometimes may be carried out within a personnel department.

The effectiveness of an incentive system depends upon the setting of prices per unit produced high enough to stimulate worker efforts and not so high as to be unduly costly to management. For rate-setting purposes, management generally applies methods of time and motion study that were first developed within the school of scientific management.

Why motion study? If a rate were set on the basis of observing performance of workers, using any work methods they chose, then later the workers, through improvements in methods, could push earnings far above management's estimates. It is, therefore, thought to be important to study the motions of workers in performing the job and thus to arrive at the "one best method." The workers are then expected to be trained in the use of this method.

The time-study men are supposed to select a range of workers (fast, average, and slow) to observe and time. The rate to be set is not determined entirely by the observed times per unit of output. Certain conventional allowances are made for fatigue and for "personal time."

By now, so many time and motion studies have been done in American industry that it has become possible to build "synthetic rates" through motion study. The motions involved in the particular task are specified, and the analyst then checks the allowed times for each of these motions in a manual, and builds his rate-setting figures out of the book.

The aim of management is to set a rate so that the average worker, using the right method and not working so hard as to damage his health, through additional effort and diligence, should be able to increase his output (over what he would produce on a regularly hourly rate) by approximately 30 percent. The worker's base rate is guaranteed: that is, he gets his regular hourly pay regardless of his output. (Persistent low output can, of course, be cause for disciplinary action including discharge.) The time and motion study man then sets a price so that this assumed 30 percent increase in output will yield about 30 percent bonus over base pay. So as further to encourage the worker to produce as much as he can, management guarantees that when a rate has once been set, it will not be cut unless the nature of the job has been changed.

Incentives rates originally grew out of an individualistic economic logic. Management assumed that each worker would respond as an individual and would behave so as maximize his economic gains. In cases where rates are set on the performance of a group or total plant, different logics necessarily prevail.

Predictability and programming

A large and complex organization depends at least as much on coordination of human interactions as upon work efforts. Coordination requires establishing predictable sequences of activities and interactions. If B cannot perform task Y until A has performed X, then coordination involves seeing to it that A has performed X by the time B is ready to do Y.

The word "programming" is part of the modern language of data processing and computing. Since machines do not make independent judgments and decisions, the sequence of tasks to be performed by the computer must be specified before the computer is set into action. The same concept may well be applied to the planning of a sequence of human events: one, two, three, four . . . nine, etc., so that two regularly follows one, three follows two, and so on.

It will be useful to think in terms of Harvey's three types of programming, noted earlier: *role programming, output programming,* and *communication programming.* We have already discussed *output programming* under the general heading of "work flow": the sequence of work operations arranged in time and space. *Role programming,* in Harvey's sense, refers to the specification of operations to be performed and of the duties and responsibilities involved in carrying out the particular job. *Communication programming* involves the specification of who talks to whom, when and where, and what reports are prepared by whom and circulated to whom. Of course, organizations vary greatly in the extent to which either *role programming* or *communications programming* are specified, as Harvey already has noted.

While specification of what the worker is to do and to be held responsible for is an essential first step, the specification does not automatically get the job done. The gap between specification and performance is expected to be bridged by training. Workers are instructed in job operation and responsibilities and generally are given some supervised practice in these operations. The elaborateness of the program will depend in part upon the complexity of the operations to be learned, some craft skills involving months of training and some mass production operation involving less than a day of orientation and training.

Communications programming involves the structuring by management of relations among workers and between workers and managerial personnel, and within management. Here also we are dealing not only with the specification of communication but also with the training of supervisors and managers. Much of the popular training programs in human relations, supervisory leadership, and management development revolve around the programming of communication.

On the progress of scientific thinking

Besides setting the stage for the study of organizational behavior, this chapter has illustrated some important points regarding the development of scientific thinking concerning the structuring of the work environment. Let us make explicit the stages of thinking described here.

1. *The search for universal principles of formal organization structure.* The pioneers of the scientific management movement believed that it was possible to discover principles of organization that would be universally valid for any type of organization. They undertook to state some of these principles.

2. *Discovery of the conflict between facts and theory.* Joan Woodward and her associates set out to test some of these principles in a painstaking empirical study of 203 companies. Woodward concluded that her observed data were not in accord with the supposedly universal principles of scientific management theory.

Was this enough to destroy the old theory? Various historians of science have argued that scientific development does not take this form. A theory is never discarded in response to the discovery of facts that do not fit it. Human beings need to have some pattern to order their thinking. They go to extraordinary lengths to explain away discrepant facts in order to hang onto a theory to which they are accustomed. A poor theory only yields to a better theory. Better, in this case, means more in accord with known facts in the field.

These conclusions seem to fit the history of argumentation over scientific management. Woodward was not the first to point to discrepancies between facts and scientific management theories. For more than 40 years, various writers have been pointing to such discrepancies. To be sure, Woodward documented her case more impressively than any of her predecessors, but it seems highly unlikely that her superior disproofs would have laid to rest a body of theory that had survived all attacks for so many years. The interment of some of these time honored principles depended upon proceeding to the next stage of scientific thinking.

3. *Classification and systematic comparison.* Unable to find uniformities of formal organization structure with all companies lumped together, Woodward sought to classify her companies into types. She had the impression that certain differences in structure might be associated with certain characteristics of technology. She then proceeded to establish her typology on the basis of observable differences in technology that she assumed to be important.

How many types make up a good typology? No doubt Woodward could have proceeded to make much finer distinctions and thus propose far more types than the three she has presented to us. But, the larger the number of types specified, the smaller the number of cases falling under each type, and the greater the difficulty in drawing quantitative conclusions. Woodward wisely decided at this exploratory stage of research to limit herself to three types, with such a large number of cases falling in each as to permit quantitative comparisons.

When she had sorted out her cases into the three types and went on to make quantitative comparisons, she found uniformities within type and contrasts between types, which were not possible to discover when all the cases were lumped together.

4. *Establishment of concepts at a higher level of abstraction.* "Dimensional production" and the other names of Woodward's types are all concepts in the dictionary sense of being "abstract notions." The type stands for no particular plant but rather for certain selected aspects common to the plants so classified. Nevertheless, the types are at a relatively low level of abstraction, close to the concrete phenomena of machines and other physical objects. They enable us to make certain clearly important distinctions (between types), but they do not facilitate comparisons with work places that fall beyond the boundaries of this threefold classification.

When we posit such concepts as technical diffuseness-specificity (Harvey) or complexity (Bell), we take another step up the ladder of abstraction. If they indeed prove useful, such concepts can be applied across Woodward's range of technologies and to other types not studied by her. They can also be used to compare plants that fall within the same technological type.

This is not to say that the development of such concepts supercedes and renders obsolete the Woodward typology. It remains a question of important theoretical interest to determine empirically how types of technology relate to technical diffuseness-specificity or complexity. But we can only do that if we move on to the next stage.

5. *Expressing concepts in variable form.* A concept or "abstract notion" is not a variable. To express the concept in variable form, we need to specify operations that will indicate different quantities, more than or less than, or at least presence or absence. For complexity, for example, we need to specify those aspects of a job that will serve as indicators of high or low complexity, so that any job we study can be given a score on the variable of complexity.

6. *Back to generalization.* Scientific progress in this field required the abandonment of the search for universal principles or organization, along the route set forth by the early exponents of scientific management. We now seem to have come back to the search for universal principles, but the statements we hope to be able to make are quite different from those handed down to us a half century ago. The early theorists spoke in terms of relationships only implicitly as they asserted that *the* correct formal structure would yield better results than incorrect forms. The relationship implied is of such a global nature as to render it completely untestable. Modern theorists seek to generalize in terms of the relationships between or among variables: for example, the relationship between number of levels of authority and the degree of technical diffuseness-specificity.

I am not here suggesting that the concepts and variables proposed by Harvey and Bell now form part of the foundations of an evolving new theory of formal organization structure. Such a judgment would be premature. I am only using their work and that of Woodward to illustrate stages of scientific thinking in the hope that such an exposition will help the student to place the findings of research in this field in a more useful context.

On the implications of structuring

Let us review how far we have progressed to this point. We have presented organizational problems from the standpoint of those who design the organization and those who direct its activities. This has shown that the manager and even the first-line supervisor have rather complex jobs. Nevertheless, we have been able to present, in general terms, a straight forward account of the procedures taken by management in organizing and directing work operations. The relative simplicity of the presentation has been possible because we have abstracted out of the real world some of the major complicating elements of that world. We have indicated in general how management wants workers to behave and how management goes about structuring this behavior. We have said nothing about worker reactions to these management initiatives. We have spoken of management as if it were a unified collection of people all pursuing the same objectives in the ways specified by the top management of the organization. We have not considered the problems of personal rivalries, competing specialities, or any other aspects of internal management friction and conflict. Except for some incidental comments, we have described the organization as if a union did not exist within it. We have not entered into any of the problems that arise between management and union or within the union.

Succeeding chapters will explore these problem areas. Let us now simply anticipate briefly the problems that necessarily arise within the structures, systems, and procedures presented so far.

We have recognized the importance of organization structure, but these problems are just beginning to be faced in the research literature. In the cases to be examined as we go along, we will give special attention to the impact of the structuring of technology and organization structure.

We have noted the possible shifting of staffing policies from attempting to get the cream out of the labor market to attempting to make at least some contribution to the utilization and development of human resources of urban ghetto areas. But what happens when management brings into the plant a type of worker which, by color or by class background, management has not employed before?

We have noted the importance of lines of promotion, indicating to workers how they may progress as openings develop or what jobs they fall back to when contraction of the work force takes place. In the case of a new job, into which line of promotion should it be fitted? Suppose two work groups each claim the job, how is management to decide? And what problems does this present for the union?

We have noted that management tends to emphasize the criterion of ability for promotion. But how is ability determined? Can management persuade workers that it is recognizing superior ability in promotions? Or will workers think that supervisors are "playing favorites"? If the union presses for seniority as the main, if not exclusive, criterion for promotion (which is often the case), how is the ability-seniority issue to be resolved? And what consequences for management and the workers arise from the form that the resolution takes?

We have noted that some organizations offer wide possibilities for promotion through the worker ranks and some even are relatively open to crossing over of workers into management, whereas other organizations offer very restricted promotion possibilities. What difference does this make in the relations among workers, between workers and management, in worker satisfaction with the company, and in worker sentiments toward management or the union?

We have noted that, as industry becomes increasingly technical, a college education has become increasingly required for supervisory and managerial positions. Does this cleavage along educational lines accentuate problems of communication between workers and management?

The field of compensation offers us a host of problem questions, even when we are simply dealing with straight hourly rates. How shall rates and the distribution of money as between pay increases and fringe benefits be decided? By market competition or by group and union pressures? If the union plays an important role, how does this affect management procedures and decision making?

The installation of incentives opens a veritable Pandora's box. Motion study is based upon the assumption that there is a "one best way" to do a given job. Some engineers and behavioral scientists generally argue that this is not the case. They agree that there are better and worse methods for performing any given job, but they argue that individuals will have different styles of performance that will be best with them, so that a uniform standard is unrealistic. While we do not want to get into the technical complexities of the argument, we might use an analogy from the sports world. In any given sport, there will be standards of good form that are generally accepted, and yet we can readily cite examples of outstanding stars in one field or another who are unorthodox in some respect in their style of play. The manager is rarely foolish enough to try to retrain the man who has already proven himself a star performer. But if we assume such permissible individual variability in methods of work, what becomes of the supposedly objective standards of motion study?

The rate set also depends upon observation of workers when they are working at their "normal pace." Suppose the worker slows down while he is being timed, and the time-study man did not recognize what is happening, he will then set a rate that provides for excessively high earnings. But suppose he recognizes that the worker has slowed down so that he must make an adjustment for this slowing down: how much should he adjust?

What happens when the time-study man makes a mistake in setting a rate? It is generally agreed that, when the mistake is in the direction of setting the rate too low, management should be required to raise the price. The same logic might suggest that when an error leads to setting the rate too high, the price should be cut. But how is management to know that the rate is set too high if the workers restrict their output so as not to give the impression of gaining excessive earnings? And if the time-study man cuts the rate to compensate for his error, how can the workers believe in management's guarantee that rates will not be cut?

If the nature of the job changes, then rate changes are clearly justified. But will any job change justify a rate change? Or just a *major* change (as often specified in union contrasts)? And how shall it be determined what a major change is? And does it make any difference whether the improvement in method was contributed by management or invented by the workers themselves? If the workers develop the improvement, should they not get the advantage in increased earnings? In that case, this particular job will pay above management's expectations and will be out of line with the whole system of jobs.

Incentive rates often yield many grievances, slowdowns, and strikes. How are such conflicts to be resolved?

With a group incentive system, management somewhat reduces the complexity of setting the rates, and with a plantwide system the payoff depends upon a single formula which, however complex it may be, need only be calculated once and then perhaps be adjusted occasionally. Nevertheless, with a group rate management has weakened the relationship between individual effort and individual payoff, and with the plantwide system this connection has well nigh been eliminated altogether. If the individual's effort makes little or no difference in the rewards he receives, can such systems really function so as to stimulate productivity?

Technical training is beyond the scope of this book. With human relations programs we will be asking this question: can training actually improve performance in interpersonal and administrative relations in an organization? If so, are there some approaches that work better than others?

How shall we seek answers to such questions? There are two approaches we might take. Men holding leading roles in organization are constantly answering these and other questions like them, making decisions on the basis of wisdom and experience. Alternatively, we can seek to build a theoretical framework that will guide us toward the answers. In effect, we will use a combination of both approaches. We cannot rely entirely upon research findings, for there are some important questions on which research has not yet provided answers, and there are other issues on which the findings of research are still fragmentary and to some extent inconsistent. On the other hand, we cannot depend entirely upon management experience and wisdom. How does one determine who has the appropriate experience and the desired degree of wisdom? And what do you do when two men who appear to be equal in experience and wisdom arrive at contradictory answers?

In Parts II and III, which follow, we shall undertake to present a theoretical framework designed to improve our ability to get answers to such questions. The reader should not expect that the framework will deliver ready made answers. The best we can hope for at this point is that it will tell us what data we can safely disregard, what data to focus our attention on, and how to get the most out of the data. In later parts of the book we will explore questions raised in this chapter—and other questions related to them—in some detail, seeking as we go along to apply the theoretical framework to be presented in Parts II and III.

References

For the study of organization structure, two contrasting views:

Metcalf, H., and Urwick, L. (eds.). *Dynamic Administration.* New York: Harper and Bros., 1942. A collection of papers representing the scientific management approach.

Woodward, Joan. *Industrial Organization: Theory and Practice.* London: Oxford University Press, 1965. A full account of the research program summarized in this chapter.

For the best nontechnical account of job description, time-and-motion-study, and related matters, see:

Strauss, George and Sayles, Leonard. *Personnel.* Englewood Cliffs, N.J.: Prentice Hall, 1967.

Discussion questions

1. Select two work organizations known to you through experience and/or observation. Confine yourself to the plant level or departmental level. Describe for each one:

a) The main features of the technology.

b) Work flow within a given department and between that department and other departments or units outside the organization.

c) Its formal organization structure.

2. For each of the cases considered above, how appropriate is its formal organization structure to the existing technology and work flow? For each one present an alternative design of organization structure, without changing work flow or technology. What advantages and disadvantages do you find in these alternative forms, compared with the ones described in 1(*c*) above? (You are not required to design a *better* structure. The purpose of the task is simply to lead you further toward understanding of the relations among technology, work flow, and organization structure.)

3. Select two jobs in the same or different organizations known to you through experience and/or observation. Describe for each one:

a) Aspects of the technology utilized by the jobholder.

b) Position of the job in the work flow.

c) Position of the job in the formal organization structure and in a line of promotion (if any).

d) Forms and approximate amounts of compensation received by the jobholder. What relationships do you see between technology and work flow on the one hand and position of the job and compensation on the other?

Part II

FRAMEWORK
FOR ANALYSIS

In Part I, we have examined the historical development of our field of study, outlined the ways in which are gathered the data we shall be interpreting, and established the setting of technology, work flow, organization structure, and management systems and procedures within which organizational behavior takes place. We are now ready to examine that behavior itself.

To move in this direction, we need a conceptual scheme or theoretical framework. We do not start our exposition with a finished theory—which does not exist in any case. We use our framework for the sorting out of data and the focusing of attention. Behavior in complex organizations is so varied and subject to so many possible interpretations that we cannot hope to make progress through attempting to grasp the whole all at once.

Our theoretical framework is a set of abstractions. It directs us to abstract out of complex reality certain items of data (and not others) and it provides us with at least a preliminary statement of the possible interrelations among these items of data.

There seem to me five characteristics of a useful theoretical framework:

1. *Parsimony.* At least, we should begin with only the minimum number of concepts we find absolutely necessary. It will be easy enough to complicate our scheme later, as we find it necessary to do so. If we

begin with a highly complex and elaborate framework, we are likely to find ourselves entrapped by our own theorizing.

2. *Interrelatedness.* The concepts should be in some way related to each other. If they are not, we have only a miscellaneous set of categories into which to sort our data. When we have all our data sorted out into boxes, we will not know what to do next. (The nature of this necessary interrelatedness will be explored throughout this book.)

3. *Objectifiability.* The framework must point to data whose existence does not depend upon the particular personal philosophy or style of perception of a given investigator. That is, while two investigators with differing theoretical orientations may quite legitimately disagree in the way that they interpret a given body of data, they should be able to agree as to *how the data are to be described.* Here I am not referring to the particular words used in description. It is of no consequence if one man speaks of a couch while another refers to a sofa, providing they recognize that they are speaking of the same object.

4. *Measurability.* The framework should point to the specification of variables. Webster's dictionary defines a variable as "that which is subject to change" or "symbol that may have infinite number of values." The definitions combine the potentiality of change with the idea of measurement.

The measurability criterion does not require us to be able to make exact and finely calibrated measurements. If we say that phenomenon X was present in situation A and absent in situation B, we have made a quantitative statement—as if we were to say: let presence equal one and absence equal zero. Similarly, to say that there were more people at today's meeting than attended the meeting last week is also to make a quantitative statement, however crude it may be. Of course, we want to go beyond statements of presence or absence, more or less, toward more refined measurements. However, in the present state of our knowledge, we may well find that we progress more rapidly as we make rough measures of important phenomena than if we make refined measures of trivial phenomena.

5. *Modifiability.* The scientific value of a theoretical framework does not depend upon subsequent research "proving" that it is correct. If this were indeed a test, we would have to abandon all theorizing now. We can be certain that any theoretical framework we set up today will prove inadequate by future standards. The most we can ask of a theoretical framework is that it start us along a useful scientific road to travel and be so formulated as to allow for ready modification as we discover the phenomena that lie farther down the road.

The conditions of this fifth requirement will necessarily be met if all the preceding ones have also been met. A parsimonious set of concepts lends itself much more readily to modification and further development than an elaborate set. If we deal with unrelated concepts, then the data gathered under each heading will not guide us toward further theoretical development. If the concepts point toward interrelated data, then the study of those interrelationships must lead toward the modification and improvement of our concepts. If we deal with objectifiable data, we will inevitably find certain of those data which do not fit neatly into our framework and yet seem so real and important that they cannot be disregarded. Similarly, the specification and measurement of variables leads us to an examination of their interrelationships, and that process itself is bound to lead to some theoretical reformulations.

First, I present the key concepts we will be using in this book, and I also present some preliminary illustrations of their use. Later chapters will further demonstrate their uses as applied to other and more complex cases.

In Part II, we will begin on the individual level with our key concepts: interaction and activities, sentiments and symbols, and transactions. In Part III, we will move to the group level. We will continue to use the concepts defined and illustrated in Part II, but we will move on to certain distinctly group-level concepts such as *norms* and *cohesion*, which necessarily involve properties of groups.

It is important to note that we do not abandon one set of concepts for another as we move from individual to group level, nor will we do so from group to organizational level. While we need to add a few new concepts as we move from level to level, our scientific task is to understand the relation of individual to group and of group to organization. For this purpose, it is important to have tools that can be used at each level of our analysis.

We are dealing with concepts so interrelated that it is difficult to talk about one without also talking about the others. Nevertheless, for the sake of clarity of exposition, we will seek to take our concepts up one at a time, at least keeping others in the background as we focus on each concept.

Our concepts are more than interrelated; we consider them mutually dependent. That is, we are dealing with a social system made up of mutually dependent parts. For us the parts are interaction, activities, and sentiments. This means that if a change is introduced into one part, we can expect to observe changes in the other two. We are not dealing with a closed system. The individuals who are interacting and carrying on activities in plant or office are also interacting and carrying on activities outside of the workplace. Similarly, their sentiments regarding certain aspects of their working lives may be influenced by events outside of the social system—which have a symbolic impact upon the system.

When we talk about interactions, activities, and sentiments, we have not specified variables. We have simply pointed toward certain bodies of data, out of which we propose to abstract other variables. This task we begin in the next chapter.

What should the student get out of these chapters on our theoretical framework? While I shall present the framework as simply as I can, I do not expect students to grasp it on the first reading or even on several readings. I am presenting a way of thinking about organizational behavior. The meaning of this way of thinking can be fully grasped only as students seek to apply the framework to problems in organizational behavior. The chapters that follow after Parts II and III should give the student some exercise in following me through the process of applying the framework to cases. The student can only make the framework finally his own as he seeks to apply it himself either to cases in his own experience or cases that he encounters in field work.

4. Interactions and activities

INTERACTION refers to any interpersonal contact in which one individual can be observed acting and one or more other individuals responding to his action. Technically, interaction can take place when no words are spoken, as, for example, one man makes a hand signal to another man at some distance from him, and that other man then is observed to respond in some way (by a hand signal, a nod of the head, or change in physical activity). Most interactions involve oral communication, the speaking of words, accompanied by gestures and facial expressions. In practice, we will concentrate primarily on the interactions involving oral communication.

There are several aspects to interaction to which we shall give attention. First, following Eliot D. Chapple[1] and Conrad M. Arensberg, we may distinguish between *pair* and *set events*, a *pair event* involving interaction between two people, a *set event* involving interaction initiated by one person to two or more people. The distinction between two and three people in interactional studies is especially important in examining organizational life. Organizations and organizational leadership grow out of set events. If human beings could only interact in pair events, man would not be the organization-building animal that we are studying.

If we reflect upon our own experience, we will readily recognize individuals we have known whose natural pattern of social behavior is almost exclusively confined to pair events. Such an individual may find himself in a group situation from time to time, but, without thinking about it, he tends to withdraw from general conversation in order to fix his attention on one other individual and engage him in conversation. At the other extreme, we have all observed individuals who seem naturally to gravitate into group situations, where the conversation bounces back and forth among members of the group. We have put this illustration in

---

[1] Eliot D. Chapple, in collaboration with Conrad M. Arensberg, *Measuring Human Relations: An Introduction to the Study of the Interaction of Individuals*, Genetic Psychology Monograph No. 22 (Provincetown, Mass.: The Journal Press, 1940).

crude, common sense terms. If we are to deal with individuals who fall between these extremes, we will need to observe and measure.

For any individual or number of individuals, we can observe the frequency and duration of interactions in pair and set events over a given time period. For the individual under observation, we can also note which particular individuals he interacts with, how often, and for how long a time period during the time of our observation.

We are also concerned with who takes the initiative in interaction. We find some individuals who respond to others but almost never take the initiative; that is, they speak when spoken to but they do not initiate conversation. Others are frequent initiators and are observed to start most of the interactions in which they are involved.

When A and B are in physical proximity but inactive and A speaks first or gestures first toward B, then A has initiated interaction. When B comes physically to A (without previous order or invitation), we can say that B has initiated interaction when some interchange begins, even if A speaks first. (We assume that the physical movement of B into A's line of vision has triggered the speech of A.) In some work situations, interactions are so coordinated by the flow of work that it is impossible to determine who initiates, and it may be more realistic to speak of "situational interactions" in such cases.[2] In most cases of social intercourse, the observation of initiation of interaction in pair events is relatively simple.

When we consider set events, where we have the emergent phenomenon we call leadership, the observational problem is somewhat more complex. In a pair event, when we know who is speaking we automatically know to whom he is speaking, for only two people are involved. Set events involve discrimination of the interpersonal direction of interactions and the sequences that these interactions follow. Let us say that we observe an individual called Joe in a number of set events that follow this general form. Joe is the focal point of the conversation. That is, other members of the group do not address their remarks to the group in general. They speak to Joe. This can be observed when we see a member speaking and find that Joe is apparently not listening to him. When the member becomes aware that someone else has Joe's attention, he stops speaking and begins again when he has some cue that suggests that Joe is prepared to pay attention to him. Joe may be the only one in the group who addresses his remarks, from time to time, to the group as a whole.

Studies by R. Freed Bales[3] and his associates indicate that when a given discussion group is observed over a number of meetings, the individual who talks more than any other individual also tends to be that person who more frequently addresses the group as a whole. These phenomena seem

---

[2] Frank B. Miller, "Situational Interactions—a Worthwhile Concept?" *Human Organization*, Vol. 17, no. 4 (Winter, 1958–59), pp. 37–47.

[3] Robert F. Bales, Fred L. Stodtbeck, Theordore M. Mills, and Mary Roseborough, "Channels of Communication in Small Groups," *American Sociological Review*, Vol. 16, no. 4, (August, 1951), pp. 461–68.

to go together in pointing to our hypothetical Joe as the group leader. Joe may not appear to be a very talkative person, but if each individual addresses his remarks to Joe and Joe responds to most of what is said to him, Joe will naturally be talking more than any other single individual.

Micro-interaction and the cronograph

The observations described above can be readily handled in the field. The student need only keep his eyes and ears open and use an ordinary time piece or a stop watch if he desires more precision. If the observer wishes to go beyond the simple observation of who initiates the interaction and how long interaction continues following this initiation, he must utilize a more elaborate technology to measure the adjustment between subjects in interaction. The interaction chronograph, developed by Eliot D. Chapple,[4] provides the possibility of such more refined measurements. While the machine presently used is built to perform highly complex computations with the data, the essential step of putting observations into the machine is accomplished by an observer pressing buttons. When he observes A beginning to speak or gesture, he pushes down a button representing A. When A becomes inactive, he releases the A button. The same procedure is followed for B. This provides for refined measurements of adjustment within interactional sequences, giving us data on the following *sorts of questions:*

Who interrupts whom and how often? When an interruption occurs, does the interrupter keep talking while the speaker subsides, or does the man being interrupted keep talking until the interrupter subsides? If A interrupts B, how long must A continue speaking before B will fall silent? When B interrupts A, how long must B continue speaking before A falls silent?

When there is a pause in the conversation, who takes the initiative to pick up the interchange? When A begins to speak, how long does he keep talking? And similarly for B?

The extremes in interactional behavior are readily spotted without any measuring instruments. We have all had experience with the chronic interrupter, the person who is well nigh impossible to talk down when he is interrupted, the constant initiator who picks up the conversation out of any pause, and the nonstop talker who maintains his verbal flow for long periods of time. Similarly, at the other extreme, we can recognize the withdrawer who nearly always stops immediately upon being interrupted, the low initiator who almost never picks up the conversation following a pause, and the man of few words who responds only in short emissions.

Fortunately for the adjustment of human beings, most of us fall somewhere between these extremes. Where the patterns are not so ob-

---

[4] Eliot D. Chapple, "The Standard Experimental (Stress) Interview as Used in Interaction Chronograph Investigations," *Human Organization*, Vol. 12, no. 2 (Summer, 1953), pp. 23–32.

vious, we need systematic measurements to identify them. Furthermore, so that we can compare the pattern of one individual to another, it is highly desirable that we measure each individual under closely similar stimulus conditions. Chapple and his associates have accomplished this through training interviewers to standardize the form of their interaction, without attempting to standardize the content of the word spoken.

The standard interview[5] lasts for approximately 25 minutes, the exact time depending upon the response pattern of the subject. The interview consists of five periods, each of which marks a distinct change from the preceding period.

The first period, known as the adjustment period, lasts for approximately 10 minutes. The interviewer's effort here is to get the informant talking freely and comfortably. The interviewer opens with some general topic question. It may concern the individual's job experience, his family background, or any one of a number of topics that may appear to the informant to fit into the interviewing situation. When the informant has started talking, the interviewer avoids interruptions. He proceeds much in the manner of the nondirective interview described by Carl Rogers[6] or by F. J. Roethlisberger and W. J. Dickson.[7] There is only one marked difference; besides avoiding interruptions, the interviewer seeks to refrain from changes in facial expression, such as nods, smiles, and other expressive manifestations to which the informant might respond.

When the informant stops talking, the interviewer waits three seconds to make sure whether the informant is really finished or is just pausing momentarily. After this three-second pause the interviewer acts so as to encourage the informant to talk further. He may rephrase something that has been said or ask to know more about some subject that the informant has commented on. For each of the 12 times that the informant stops acting the interviewer waits a few seconds. After this has been done 12 times, if there is still time left in the adjustment period the interviewer speeds up his responses, allowing only a momentary pause.

The interviewer now moves on to the second period, where he systematically fails to respond to the informant. Each time the informant stops acting the interviewer remains silent and without change of expression or gesture for 15 seconds. If, at the end of 15 seconds the informant has not resumed acting on his own initiative, the interviewer finally responds by a general comment calling for further elaboration or detail from the informant.

The interviewer exhibits this failure of response 12 times in this period,

---

[5] This description of the Standard Experimental Interview is taken from my monograph, *Modern Methods in Social Research* (Washington, D.C.: Office of Naval Research, 1952).

[6] Carl Rogers, *Counseling and Psychotherapy* (Boston, Mass.: Houghton-Mifflin, 1942).

[7] F. J. Roethlisberger and W. J. Dickson, *Management and the Worker* (Cambridge, Mass.: Harvard University Press, 1939).

if that can be fitted in with the maximum time of 15 minutes allowed for the period. If all 12 of the 15-second failures to respond have been accomplished in less than 15 minutes, the period ends and the interviewer proceeds to the third period. This is an adjustment period just like the first, except that the time allowed is five minutes and the number of times the interviewer waits two or three seconds before responding is six instead of twelve.

The fourth period is known as the interruption period. Whatever the informant has to say, the interviewer allows him to talk for three or four seconds and then jumps in to interrupt. The interviewer speaks in a normal voice, but talks at the same time as the informant for a period of five seconds. If the informant continues talking throughout this five-second period, the interviewer then stops acting and allows the informant to continue unimpeded. When the informant finally stops talking, the interviewer makes a point of coming into the conversation immediately to stimulate further action on the part of the informant. Again, as soon as the informant has been in action for three or four seconds, the five-second interruption takes place. This process is repeated 12 times.

If the informant allows himself to be talked down by the interviewer and ceases acting before the end of the five-second interruption period, the interviewer completes his sentence as quickly as possible and then pauses for three seconds to see if the informant will resume acting within this period. If the informant continues inactive for more than three seconds, the interviewer begins acting again by rephrasing the topic or by expanding what was being said in order to stimulate the informant into another period of action and provide another opportunity for interruption.

Following 12 interruptions, the interviewer goes on to the final five-minute period, which is again an adjustment period just like the third.

This type of interview may be called a stress interview. It differs markedly from other types of interviews where the purpose is to put the informant at ease and, at the same time, get a full expression of his ideas and sentiments. Here, the interview is designed to test out the adjustment of the informant to a wide range of interaction situations, and do this in a standard manner so that his responses can be compared with those of others. While no individual would encounter such changes of pace within a half hour period of interaction with any other single individual in a natural situation, he can be expected to encounter people who interact in the several patterns that the interviewer assumes, and the purpose of the interview is to test how he responds to these different patterns. It also aims to test his flexibility in meeting these interaction changes.

What personality traits are measured by this chronograph interview? Chapple and his associates[8] have set forth types such as these:

[8] Eliot D. Chapple, Martha F. Chapple, and Judith A. Repp, "Behavioral Definitions of Personality and Temperament Characteristics," *Human Organization*, Vol. 13, no. 4 (Winter, 1955), pp. 34–9.

1. *Activity*. This concerns the individual's propensity for sustaining activity (speech, action, and responses to other people) over extended periods of time. Some individuals appear to be able to maintain interaction almost indefinitely, whereas at the other extreme are people who tend to subside after short periods of activity.

2. *Listening ability*. Some people are so prone to express themselves at all times that they rarely allow others uninterrupted use of the floor. Some are so silent that their conversational partners find them unresponsive and perhaps even inattentive. The good listener is able to be silent for extended periods and yet show sufficient activity (head noddings, changes of expression, etc.) as to appear responsive to his conversational partner.

3. *Flexibility*. How readily does the individual adapt his interactions according to differences in interaction patterns of his conversational partners? For example, a highly flexible person may be active for an extended period with a low activity partner and yet show listening ability when paired with a high activity partner. A low flexibility man who maintains activity for extended periods of time with a low activity partner would appear to be seeking to emit the same volume of verbal and gestural activity when matched with a high activity partner. He would show low listening ability in this situation and would also show signs of emotional stress over the conversational competition.

4. *Initiative*. How often does the individual start action after a period of inactivity? Some people characteristically break silences, whereas others characteristically have to have silences broken for them.

5. *Quickness: the speed with which a person takes the initiative.* While some people remain silent and inactive for long periods following a break in the conversational flow, others jump in so fast that the break is hardly perceptible to an observer—in fact, they take the initiative so rapidly that they are unable to observe whether other people are trying to speak. In between is the fellow who does not end a silence immediately but does take the initiative after short pauses.

6. *Dominance: the frequency with which a person takes over or maintains control in spite of the attempts of other people to assume control.* What happens when the person is interrupted? Some individuals immediately subside. Others keep talking until the interrupter subsides.

7. *Aggressiveness or overeagerness*. The individual doesn't wait for another person to stop but keeps coming in and responding or cutting him off before he is through.

8. *Hesitancy or inhibitedness*. An individual consistently is unable to respond immediately to another person's action. There is at least hesitation, and sometimes the individual appears to be in another world when approached.

In addition to the personality traits which we have presented in somewhat condensed form above, Chapple identifies "temperament traits" in terms of the individual's responses to certain specific situations provided by the standard interview: reaction on first meeting, when a person doesn't receive an immediate response; reaction following a period of unresponsiveness by another when there is a threat of competition; and reaction after the threat of competition is all over. We will not go into these aspects here because our purpose now is simply to make two general points:

1. Personality can be described in terms of observable and observed behavior of individuals in interaction.
2. The words used to describe personality traits can be based on quantitative interactional measures.

Words are simply an inexact statement regarding the interactional behavior of the subject. It seems best to define what is meant by a trait through illustrating with individual cases at opposite extremes. Of course, the human race provides all variations between extremes, but when we take up cases representing smaller differences, we need to think in terms of numbers rather than words.

Why measure interactions? Most research in sociology and psychology involving interaction has concentrated upon the meaning of the verbal content. It is hard for the behavioral scientist to accept the idea that there could be value in measuring the form of interaction, disregarding content. Those who measure interaction do not necessarily assume that the meaning of the verbal content is unimportant. They simply assume that the form of interaction is also important—and that is subject to precise measurements that enable us to test for significance.

The research of Chapple and associates has demonstrated that the pattern of interaction manifested by an adult individual in a standardized interview situation is a highly enduring characteristic of that individual. If he is chronographed at different times, each record will indeed be somewhat different from the others, but the variation tends to occur within rather narrow limits.

The statement that the same individual manifests highly similar interaction patterns in successive chronograph interviews does not indicate that he consistently interacts in his particular patterned fashion in all of the situations he faces at work and in the community. The chronic interrupter generally finds it possible to hold himself in check when he is in interaction with people substantially above his status. Similarly, the low initiative man of few words may give out with an extended statement when he is called upon to explain some situation of which he has knowledge and which he cannot cover in a few words. On the other hand, studies so far indicate that the individual who finds himself interacting for some time during the day outside of his "base rate" will feel somewhat disturbed if he does not have an opportunity to bring his interactions back into something approximating balance within the same 24-hour period. That is, the nonstop talker who finds himself in a situation where he cannot talk tends later to seek out situations where he talks even more than usual. Similarly, the man of few words who has had to emit many for a short period is thereafter likely to withdraw even more for a while and say even less than his "base rate" would indicate. On the other hand, a person high in flexibility is able to shift among situations with markedly different interactional requirements without the necessity of a compensatory adjustment period.

Personality and organization

Such interaction measurements may have a number of important uses. Of most concern to us is the relationship between personality and organization. Jobs in an organization differ along several important dimensions. We assume that one of the most important of these is interaction. Jobs differ markedly in regard to the amount of interaction they require; in some almost constant interaction is required, whereas in others the individual may work for long periods of time without interacting with anyone. Jobs also differ in the possibilities or limitations on nonrequired interaction. An individual who is naturally inclined to much interaction may adjust reasonably well to a job that requires little interaction, providing the work situation offers opportunities for interaction. If the same job is performed in an isolated situation, we would expect the individual to be much less satisfied with it.

The most impressive application of the chronograph so far has been in the field of department store selling. This has not been entirely accidental. If we want to test the effectiveness of a person in a job we naturally search for some sort of objective measure of performance. Sales people are particularly adapted to this sort of evaluation. While their volume of sales may not be the only criterion of their effectiveness for the organization, at least it is universally agreed that the sales record is a highly important factor. Therefore, with comparisons in sales records to relate to chronograph results, we can deal with objective measurements on both sides.

Chapple emphasizes here that the chronograph is not primarily a tool for the selection of salesmen. He feels that the chronograph will definitely weed out those who are not suited to selling of any sort, but that a large proportion of the population will be found adaptable to selling if the appropriate position can be provided.

There are marked differences in the interactions required in various departments of a large department store. For example, the bargain basement seems to require a person who is able to initiate interaction rapidly and handle very many brief contacts during the day. On the other hand, the salesman in the furniture department has to be able to proceed at a more leisurely pace, maintaining interaction with a single customer over an extended period of time. Chapple's chronograph work is full of instances of individuals who were exceedingly effective in selling in a department to which their interaction pattern appeared to be adapted, and were both ineffective and unhappy when transferred to another department where quite a different pattern of interaction was called for.

In field situations, where we do not have the chronograph at our disposal, we cannot make precise measurements, but we can spot interactional problems where particular job situations pose certain extreme interactional requirements. Let us consider several examples along this line.

Harrison Trice[9] found in his study of night watchmen in a large university that the job seemed to attract a particular type of personality. The men that he found on the job tended to have had relatively little interaction in their early experience and were quite accustomed to a degree of social isolation that men with other interactions patterns would have found intolerable. Trice also found among these men certain indications of paranoid tendencies. They tended to be suspicious of other people and to be concerned that others might be plotting against them. While more extreme paranoid tendencies could have led these men to mental hospitals, we have here an interesting case where what we would commonly regard as an 'abnormality" of personality appears to be quite functional to the job situation. Since the watchmen experience practically zero interaction while they are at work, it is important that they be men who have little need for interaction. While, in many other situations, the organization will function better with people who have a high degree of trust toward other people, it is clear that such trust is not functional in the watchman's job. The watchman who is suspicious that others are plotting against him is more likely to be on the alert for intruders or for evidences of unauthorized entry than is a person who is inclined to look at the world through rose-colored glasses.

The automotive assembly line presents one of the most oppressive work environments that has yet been devised by man. The physical movements of workers are controlled by the line; their interactions are also strictly limited by their positions on the line. While the assembly line job appears to be quite generally unpopular, as we look at its confining nature in terms of interactions, we might hypothesize that individuals with different interaction patterns would respond quite differently to the assembly line job situation.

Frank J. Jasinski[10] found an interesting relationship between reported need for interaction and sentiments toward the company and toward the immediate job. In response to the question, "Does the company do what it can for the workers?" almost two out of three of those who reported that

---

[9] Harrison Trice, "Night Watchman: A Study of an Isolated Occupation," *ILR Research*, Vol. X, no. 2 (1960) pp. 3–9.

[10] Frank J. Jasinski, "Technological Delimitation of Reciprocal Relationships: a Study of Interaction Patterns in Industry," *Human Organization*, Vol. 14, no. 2, (Summer, 1956), pp. 24–8.

they valued opportunities to talk on the job replied that the company did nothing for the workers. Of those who expressed indifference about talking on the job, less than one out of three reported that the company did nothing at all. In response to the question, "Is your job interesting?" those needing to talk showed the same tendency toward negative answers, but the contrast was not quite so marked in this case.

In Jasinski's sample, 125 men fell into the category of appreciating opportunities to talk, whereas only 49 fell into the category of indifference to conversational opportunities. This suggests what we might expect: that most workers do require interaction on the job and do feel deprived when it is not available to them.

In an oil company study, I observed another job that provided extreme interactional requirements. The engine operator worked all of his eight hours in and around the engine room in almost complete social isolation. Except when he brought his lunch up to the control room of the Hi-Test plant to eat with the control room operators, he experienced practically no interaction during the working day. Other jobs did not require any other workers to go into the engine room. If anyone did appear in the engine room, he found the noise of the six engines so loud as to make conversation practically impossible. Furthermore, the last three supervisors who had been in charge of the engine room and the Hi-Test plant together had all been chemical engineers who were concerned with the chemical processes and had little knowledge of or interest in engines.

Engineer Operator Borden described his work in this way:

I like that job of operating an engine. . . . Yes, the noise is bad, and it has hurt my hearing some, but I got so I didn't mind it. . . . No, there isn't much chance to talk with anybody down there. Supervisors never bother us much either.

Of the three engine operators I knew, Borden and one other had grown up on the family farm, isolated from the peer group interaction of town and city. Both of these farm boys expressed themselves as being quite contented with their jobs and having no interest in bidding on jobs that would take them out of the engine room, even when those jobs would pay more money. I classified the third man as "mixed farm-urban," because he had grown up on his grandfather's farm but had had much more urban experience than the other two operators. It seemed significant to me that he was the only one of the three who was trying to bid out of the engine room and move into the control room. While three cases are far too few to warrant any firm conclusions, they may be used as illustrating the possible interrelations of past and present interaction-activity-sentiment patterns. (From this point on, we will use IAS to denote interaction-activity-sentiment patterns.)

Note that here we are concentrating particularly upon past and present interactions. If we leave out the interactional aspects, the jobs of farmer and engine operator seem to have little in common. The farmer breathes fresh air and works in the solitude of nature, whereas the engine operator breathes the fumes of oil and gasoline, surrounded by the incessant explosions of his six large engines. Nevertheless, in interactional terms, the two jobs are highly similar. Note that even the noise, which most people would have found intolerable, seems just a minor problem to the engine operator, Borden. For a man who has little inclination to communicate with other people, damage to his hearing is a matter of little consequence.

Let us now turn to a job where a high frequency and complex organization of interactions are required: that of waiter or waitress.

While in any restaurant, waiting on tables necessarily involves a substantial amount of social interaction, the frequency and complexity of the interactions involved will vary with the size of the restaurant, the speed of the service anticipated, and the familiarity or unfamiliarity of the customers.

In a small restaurant, the waitress need only adjust to a simple social system, managing her interactions with customers and with a cook behind the counter. In such a situation, many of the customers are likely to be known to her, and she finds it easier to adjust to them than to a constant stream of strangers. She has to adjust to just one superior, who will often be the owner himself. In a large restaurant, she has to interact with a number of different people in the service pantry to get her food out and with bartenders for drinks. She is likely to have to adjust to a larger number of customers, and a higher proportion of these are likely to be strangers to her, so that she cannot anticipate their reactions. She is under the surveillance not only of the supervisor of the dining room, but she sees other management people around her, who may be checking up on what she is doing.

Volume of service is not entirely controlled by size of restaurant. It is also much influenced by the popularity of the restaurant and by the customary eating habits of the customers. A restaurant which provides a leisurely atmosphere that encourages customers to take time over their food and drinks builds up much less pressure on the waitresses than one where the "turnovers" are rapid.

To get down to cases in our examination of the fit between personality and interactional requirements, let us consider the case of Chandler's Restaurant, a large establishment serving meals on two floors, in the center of the main shopping district of one of our major cities. Here the pressure was particularly intense during the lunch period, when "turnovers" averaged little more than 20 minutes for the complete operation of taking orders, serving the customers, and getting them out to the cashier to make way for another set of customers. Each girl had several tables to manage during this period.

Our study was done in late 1944, at the height of the World War II labor shortage, so that the restaurant was operating with many inexperienced waitresses and there were often times when the restaurant was short-handed and girls would have to take on more work than would otherwise have been the case.

As we got acquainted with Chandler's Restaurant, it became evident that, although the girls generally had a high regard for the organization, they felt themselves under a great deal of nervous tension. It occurred to us that it would be of interest to examine the response to the pressures of the job on the part of waitresses, in order to try to account for the fact that some girls managed to handle these tensions with little difficulty, whereas others experienced very great difficulties. While we had no way of measuring internal manifestations of nervous tension, we did note one type of behavior that could be objectively examined and that varied substantially among the waitresses. Some would break down and cry and have to leave the floor and retreat to the locker room at fairly frequent intervals, whereas others never surrendered in this way to the pressures, and of course there were many girls distributed between these two extremes.

While we did not have the data to make fine measurements of the frequency of crying behavior for a large number of girls, we were able to identify a number of more or less frequent criers to compare with others who rarely, if ever, manifested the behavior. How to account for these differences?

Crying behavior was related to length of service: crying was much more frequent among the newer, less experienced waitresses than it was among the old-timers. This difference could be accounted for by two influences. A selective process was no doubt operating: those who often found themselves giving way to crying were likely to quite the job. There also seemed to be another influence at work: the experienced waitresses had ways of organizing their work to take the pressure off themselves. Here we are getting into an examination of the organization of interactions and activities in the workplace.

To visualize the pressures on service in Chandler's Restaurant, let us consider this statement by a 21-year-old girl, who had had a year of experience in this restaurant. She put it this way:[11]

You know, I was so mad! I finally broke down Tuesday and cried. That was really a terrible day. The guests were crabby, and I wasn't making any money, and we kept running out of food in the kitchen.

Once I went past one of my tables just when a new party was sitting down. One of the women picks up 50 cents and puts it in her pocket. She says, "Look, the people here must have forgot and left their money." I could have screamed, but what could I do?

---

[11] The description of the stresses in the waitress job is taken from my chapter, "When Waitresses and Customers Meet," in W. F. Whyte (ed.), *Industry and Society* (New York: McGraw-Hill Book Co., 1946), pp. 127–29.

Well the guests were yelling at me all day, trying to get my attention. Everybody had trouble. Sue cried too.

The waitress was asked if she could remember the particular incident that set the crying off.

Yes, it was like this. I was rushed, and I came in to the service pantry to get my hot plates. There were three hot plates standing up there on the counter, and, when I called my order in, the woman standing behind the counter just said, "Take them," so I put them on my tray and started out. I thought I was doing all right, but then Sue comes in. You see she had been stuck all day. She had orders for hot plates for her whole station all at once, and she couldn't carry it all out, so she left some of her hot plates at the counter and told the woman behind the counter to save them for her.

When she came back and saw the hot plates all gone with a long line of girls waiting to get them, she started to cry. Well, when I saw that the plates were really hers, I gave them right back to her, and a couple of other girls gave plates back to her, so she got her hot plates right back, and she didn't have to leave the floor.

But that upset me. You know, I was getting out of a hole with those hot plates, but then all of a sudden I had to give them up and get right at the end of a long line. I just started to bawl.

I had to go down to the rest room. Well, the way I am, I'm just getting over it when I think again what one of the guests said and the way they were acting, and then I get feeling sorry for myself some more, I start to cry all over again. It took me an hour to get back on the floor Tuesday.

Here we see that there is no one cause for crying. Rather it is a combination of pressures. This was a bad day in the coordination of production and service. The food was not ready when the waitresses needed it, and, when it did come up, there was a failure of adjustment between waitresses and counter people. Related to this problem, a number of the girls were having trouble in getting along with their customers.

The waitress brought up one important aspect of the customer relations problem: the matter of tipping. Her experience with customers pocketing the tip left by their predecessors was unusual. Her comment that on this particular bad day she was not making any money was a remark that we heard all the time. Even in high-quality restaurants there are always a certain number of "stiffs"—customers who don't tip.

Since it is well known that the waitress's income depends upon tips more than wages, we might be tempted to put down the "stiff" as an economic problem. However, when we get the girls to talk about the situation, it is clear that this is not the case. We asked one girl to explain how she felt when she was "stiffed." She said,

You think of all the work you've done and how you've tried to please those people, and it hurts when they don't leave anything for you. You think, so that's what they really think of me. . . . It's like an insult.

The waitress in this case said that she could have screamed. If she had screamed, probably she would not have had to cry. The relationship is well recognized by the waitresses themselves. As one of them said:[12]

The trouble is, when the guests get nasty with you, you can't tell them off. You have to keep it all inside you. That's what makes it so nerve-racking. It would be much easier for us if we could talk back.

The strength of this restraint depends very much upon the status of the clientele to which the restaurant caters. As one girl who worked in a lower class restaurant told us,

In this place, the customer is always wrong and he knows it, God bless him!

Since Chandler's Restaurant catered to middle and upper class people, management was constantly on the alert to see to it that the girls did not "tell the guests off," no matter how hard the customers made it for them. (In fact, the status difference in the two situations is illustrated by the use of the word "customers" in the lower class restaurant and "guests" in Chandler's.)

If the waitress cannot get the pressure off by "telling off" the customers (or guests) what can she do? We found that those waitresses who were able to handle their nervous tensions without breaking down did not submit passively to customers or other people in the work situation.[13]

The first question to ask when we look at the customer relationship is, "Does the waitress get the jump on the customer, or does the customer get the jump on the waitress?" The skilled waitress realizes the crucial nature of this question. One of them gave these instructions to a new girl:

Get a clean cover on the table, give them their water, take the order, and then leave them if necessary. Once they have a feeling that you have taken charge, they will be all right.

The skilled waitress tackles the customers with confidence and without hesitation. For example, she may find that a new customer has seated himself before she could clear off the dirty dishes and change the cloth. He is now leaning on the table, studying the menu. She greets him and says, "May I change the cover, please?" and without waiting for an answer, takes his menu away from him so that he moves back from the table, and she goes about her work. The relationship is handled politely but firmly, and there is never any question as to who is in charge. Most customers react favorably to this approach. While we have not interviewed them on the subject, it appears that it gives them a feeling of security when the waitress moves right in and shows that she knows how to handle her work.

---

[12] *Ibid.*, p. 130.

[13] Most of the rest of this section is taken in somewhat condensed form from Whyte, *Industry and Society*, pp. 132–37.

Getting the jump on customers involves not only such concrete moves as changing the tablecloth. It also involves giving the proper emotional tone to the relationship. This is a difficult matter on which to present objective data, but skilled waitresses know what they are doing and explain it along these lines:

The trouble with a lot of girls is that they're afraid of the guests. They wouldn't admit it, but they really are. You know, if you're timid, the guests can sense that, and I guess it's just human nature that people like to pick on you when you're timid. That way you get off on the wrong foot from the beginning, and you never get things right all day. I know how it is because I used to be afraid of people when I first started and I cried a few times the first month or two. But I've got more confidence now. I know there isn't any situation I can't handle.

A lot depends upon the way you approach the guest. I can tell it myself. If you go up to them as though you are afraid of them or as though you don't want to wait on them at all, they can sense that, and it makes them nervous and fussy. So I always go up to a guest as if I was happy to wait on the person. I try to make them feel comfortable and at ease to start with, and then I don't have any trouble.

While we need not accept the waitress's observation upon human nature, we can observe the behavior she describes. Apparently it is up to the waitress to seize the initiative in customer relations—to set the pattern for the relationship. This she does by the things she does, the things she says, the way she uses her voice, and the expression on her face. If she fails to seize the initiative in this manner, the customer senses her uncertainty and seems to feel uneasy himself. This is likely to lead to trouble.

While the waitress may get along well with the customer who seizes and maintains the initiative, that alone will not solve her problems. She must be able to lead those who want to be led and to get the jump on the uncertain and recalcitrant customers. She will always have difficult customers to deal with, but with this approach, she will find that there are not enough of them to upset her equilibrium.

This would lead us to expect that girls with some leadership experience —with some experience in taking the initiative in human relations—would make the best adjustment to waitress work. We found that this did prove to be an important factor.

In one of the restaurants studied, we were fortunate in finding two sets of twins. In both cases, one of the pair broke down on the job fairly often, while the other never or hardly ever cried. Being able to hold the age and experience factors constant, and taking the girls from the same general family and community environment, we should be able to explore individual differences in patterns of interaction.

The Swansons, Ruth and Sally, were identical twins, and both said that they had always been "very close," doing nearly everything together. While both girls were considered shy and quiet, we found in interviewing them that Sally was decidedly more articulate. We drew Sally out on their relationship, asking how they decided what they were going to do. "Well," she said, "sometimes we would have arguments about it, but we would always decide to do the same thing in the end." We asked who usually won out in the arguments. She smiled and said, "I guess I usually did." We asked for an example of the sort of arguments they had. She said:

Well, lots of times it would be about clothes. Ruth would want to wear one dress, and I'd want to wear another dress. We'd argue it out, and she would finally wear the dress I wanted her to wear.

Ruth was the girl who cried. Sally never cried.

The Careys, Rita and Lucille, were not identical. Both were quite attractive, talkative, and popular with the other waitresses, but in the matter of social initiative, there were striking differences. This may best be illustrated with part of an interview we had with both of them together:

RITA: Ever since I was little I had to take care of my small cousins and other kids in the neighborhood. I used to like to take care of kids. It never bothered me when they cried or got into some kind of trouble. I used to do a lot of running errands to the store for my mother, too, and I took care of a lot of things around the house. I always used to enjoy doing things like that.
INTERVIEWER: Did you both take care of your little cousins?
RITA: We both did, but I did it more than Lucille.
LUCILLE: They always liked Rita better than me. I don't know why it was, but it was always Rita first and then me. I guess Rita just had a way with kids. She always liked to take care of kids. Rita took care of me, too. (*She laughed.*) She fought my battles for me.
INTERVIEWER: How was that?
LUCILLE: Well, just to give you an example, sometimes we'd be out swimming, and some kid would duck me for no good reason at all. Rita would come up and give them hell. She'd tell them they couldn't get away with something like that on her sister.
RITA: You see, I was always bigger than Lucille. I was a regular tomboy. It wasn't that I had to fight very often. Most times I would just tell people, and they'd lay off Lucille.
LUCILLE: Yes, that's the way it was.
RITA (*sternly, to Lucille*): Don't bite your nails!
LUCILLE (*removes them quickly*): Well, I'm so nervous I have to do something.

It is hardly necessary to comment that in this case Lucille was the one who couldn't take it. In fact, she found the job so upsetting that she quit shortly after this interview, whereas Rita appeared always cheerful and in control of her situation.

In general, we found that it was those girls who had learned in the course of growing up to take the initiative in managing their relations

with other people who were able to structure the interpersonal relations
of the work situation in such a way that they did not break down. The
girls who grew up as followers tended to find that they had great
difficulty handling the tensions of the work situation. When we found
them reasonably well adjusted, we generally found that they were part of
an informal work group where other individuals were looking out for
them on the job and offering social support. Where we did find informal
leaders breaking down, we found other complications involved. We shall
turn to such a case in Part IV.

Foremen in interaction

While one first-line supervisory position may differ widely from another (and such differences will be examined in Chapter 12), research has
shown a characteristic interaction pattern for foreman jobs in two quite
different technologies: an automotive assembly line and a foundry. In
each case, we note a high proportion of the foreman's day devoted to
interaction, even though nearly all of the interactions are of exceedingly
short duration. On the assembly line studied,[14] 49.3 percent of the time of
the average foreman was spent on interaction, and the average duration of
each interaction ranged between 45 and 90 seconds for all except contacts
with the general foreman and superintendent (with whom contacts averaged 4 and 5 minutes).

In the foundry,[15] the 28 men observed spent 49 percent of the time
they were under observation in interaction, yet the average duration of
their interactions was only 79 seconds.

While there were, of course, variations among foremen in the proportion of time devoted to interaction and in the average duration of each
interaction, the figures for all of these men are sufficiently similar as to
suggest that the jobs the men are performing must require something
approximating the pattern we observed. Further study might show that
individual differences among the men could be accounted for in part by
differences in the interactional requirements from one foreman's position
to another, even in these technologies. But some of the variability must be
accounted for by the interaction pattern the individual brings into the job
situation. For example, in the foundry study, Schwartzbaum found a
correlation of .42 between rural-urban social origins and duration of
interaction, the foremen of rural origin having lower frequencies (the
difference being significant at the .05 level). Here again we see that the
individual is not free to vary his interactions at will. There is a necessary

---

[14] Charles R. Walker, Robert Guest, and Arthur N. Turner, *The Foreman on the
Assembly Line* (Cambridge, Mass.: Harvard University Press, 1956), p. 86.
[15] Allan M. Schwartzbaum, "Lateral Interaction and Effectiveness in Vertical
Organizations" (Ph.D. thesis, Cornell University, 1968), p. 55.

relationship between the interaction pattern experienced by the individual in his youth and that which he acts out in later life.

In these foremanship cases, the relationship between the individual's early interaction pattern and his pattern on the job is obscured by the fact that individuals who were unable to maintain something approximating the observed frequencies, durations, and proportions of time devoted to interactions would either not have been appointed to these jobs or else would have been dropped from the jobs. Suppose we were to select a foreman in such work situations and had in mind a highly skilled worker, who seemed to have all the technical qualifications. Suppose further that we observe him for some hours on the job and at rest breaks. We note that, compared to other workers, his frequencies of interaction are exceedingly low and that he rarely initiates interaction. These observations should be enough to convince us that this worker should not be considered further for the supervisory job.

I have presented an extreme case, where brief and even unsystematic observation should be enough to lead us to our conclusion. I assume that as we develop finer measures of the interactional requirements of jobs, combined with interactional measurements of individuals, we shall be able to make finer discriminations concerning the individual-job relationship.

While I have emphasized the importance of interactions in matching the individual with his job, I do not assume that having the appropriate interaction pattern is the only requirement for success in supervision. There are other requirements, which we shall consider in a later chapter. At this point, I am only concerned with showing that if the interaction pattern of the individual is markedly out of line with that required by the supervisory position, he will fail as a supervisor, no matter what other qualifications he may have.

Vertical or horizontal interactions

Earlier, we noted that the human being does not interact in a constant fashion throughout the day. What factors influence the variations exhibited by an individual from one time to the next? The physical environment has obvious effects: if the individual finds himself in a physical situation where other people are not present, he will not be interacting during the time spent in that place. Also important is relative status: whether the person interacting with ego is superior or inferior to him in social prestige or at the same level. We may assume that the individual has a "base rate" which is elicited when he finds himself interacting with peers—with people having more or less the same social prestige as he. This base rate is adjusted appropriately for interaction with superiors or with subordinates.

Let me take my own case as an example. While I have not been measured on the chronograph, from introspection and from comments of others, I have gathered a picture of certain aspects of my own interaction pattern. While I have no difficulty in talking for extended periods of time once I get started, I am a slow starter. In conversation with my peers, when a pause occurs, almost anybody else is more likely to take the initiative and fill it than I. I have found that if I want very much to get into the conversation, I have to prepare myself mentally for a relatively long time ahead (seconds to a minute or more) so as to be ready when the opening occurs. Observing conversations in the family, my wife informs me that sometimes she is aware of a low hum on my part for several seconds before I emit any words. It is as if I had to start the motor and warm it up for a while before I can be ready to put it into gear and take off.

Years ago, when I was a student among students, in any free wheeling discussion I often found myself at a disadvantage, being ready to speak only when the opening passed me by. Now, when I find myself in a discussion with students, I note that I no longer have these difficulties. When I am getting ready to say something, I almost invariably get to say it. I am rarely interrupted. When I interrupt someone else, I find the speaker falling silent so that the way is open for me to continue.

Has my interactional base rate changed in these last 30 years? I doubt it. What has obviously changed is the set of status relationships in the two situations I have described. I am now 30 years older and a full professor.

I am not suggesting that the students today, in discussion with me, make conscious adjustments in their interactions—that they say to themselves, "Because the professor has higher status than I in the university, I must take special pains to see that he gets to say what he wants to say and to avoid interrupting him." It is simply part of the socialization process that any normal person goes through that he learns intuitively to adjust his interactional behavior to the symbols that represent status in the interactional relationship.

A similar set of observations was made by F. L. W. Richardson, Jr.,[16] in an electronics firm. He was once consulted by a supervisor of an engineering department, who reported that he got along very well with the men he supervised but had almost constant difficulties in relations with fellow department heads. After some periods of observation and timing of the interactional behaviour of the engineering supervisor, Richardson came to the following conclusion. He noted that the engineering supervisor was slow to take the initiative and, furthermore, that upon finishing a given statement, he was inclined to fall silent for at least a two-minute period. It was as if his mental battery needed two minutes to recharge itself after every verbal output.

This pattern presented no difficulties to the engineering supervisor when he was engaged in discussions with his subordinates. When he was

---

[16] Personal communication.

ready to speak, other members of the discussion group tended to grant him the conversational right of way. He found the situation quite different in meetings with fellow department heads. There he was surrounded by faster initiators, who were not concerned with noticing when the engineering supervisor was warming himself up to make a verbal contribution. When the engineer finally did get to say something, such a long period had passed from one of his statements to the next that often he only got back into the conversation when other members had gone beyond the point that he wanted to take up. In this situation, naturally others were irritated with the engineering supervisor for delaying the progress of the discussion or getting it off the track.

We should also recognize that people differ in response to vertical or horizontal interactions according to the pattern of their preceding social experience. As we shall show later, when a union has become established in a plant, we can expect a pattern of dual loyalty—to both the company and the union—rather than an exclusive commitment to one or the other organization. When a campaign for union representation is in progress, men are forced to choose between vertical and horizontal orientation. Are they going to trust their fates primarily to the company, as represented by their organizational superiors, or are they going to throw their lot in with an organization of their peers?

We find that men view the union in quite different ways according to whether their earlier experiences have led them toward a vertical or horizontal orientation. The case to be discussed here involved a union representation election in 1943 among the workers in and around the Hi-Test plant of the Blank Oil Company. While the voting included a wider set of categories of workers, my own research was limited to the Hi-Test plant and immediately interrelated units.

Hi-Test plant operated continuously, 24 hours a day and seven days a week. On shift at any given time were the number one operator, or poly-operator (for polymerization), the hydro-stillman and the fractionator operator. In the engine room, about 100 yards away, an engine operator was on duty for each shift. There were also engine repairmen and other maintenance personnel involved in and around the plant.

Engine Operator Borden took this position on the union:

> I have a son and a nephew fighting in the Army. I don't think it right when they are fighting for freedom abroad for us to have a dictatorship here. That is what the union is to me—just a dictatorship. Maybe I am wrong, but they have to convince me. . . . No, I never attended any of their meetings. I didn't take no interest.

While the worker acknowledged that he might be wrong, he also made it very clear that he wasn't going to take any steps to let the union sympathizers persuade him of his error. He saw the union simply as an organization that could take away some of his freedom.

Other men had a diametrically opposed view. To them, a union was a democratic organization, working to get the men what they themselves wanted and deserved. They saw the dictatorship on the management side, particularly in the person of the general superintendent.

I found that even the most militant of the CIO sympathizers did not speak against the company, as such. They saw the union as a democratic organization which would limit the dictatorial powers of certain management people and permit the company to be as good an organization as they wanted it to be. One of them put it this way:

This has always been a good company to work for. They have taken care of their men. In the hard times, other companies have laid off a lot of men, but if you had been on the payroll with Blank Oil, you could practically be certain you had a steady job as long as you did the work.

How explain these individual differences?

I undertook no refined analysis of social background, but sought simply to distinguish three types of social situations which I called "pure farm," "mixed farm," and "urban-industrial." In the "pure farm" case, the farm on which the individual grew up was isolated from town or city, and the individual had had little interaction with boys his own age in the process of growing up. The individual's father was in control of the family and farm at least until the boy reached his late teens. (Some of these men set themselves up as independent farmers after leaving the parental homestead and only went into industry in their mid-twenties.) For example, this is the way Engine Operator Borden (previously quoted) described his early life:

We were 'way out in the country. There wasn't anybody living close to us. When I was growing up, we all worked 12 to 14 hours a day on that farm. We had to work hard to make it pay. The farm is just like a business. If you don't work hard to make it pay, you can't keep it going. Us kids just went to school maybe six to eight months of the year. . . . Yes, we went to church on Sunday. There wasn't much visiting between families where I lived. We just stayed on the farm, working all the time. . . . No, there wasn't much talking back and forth when we were on the farm doing our work. We had no time for that. My father told us what to do, and we just did our work.

Six of the "pure farm" types were in my sample, and five of these men were strongly anti-CIO and never attended a CIO meeting. In fact, they had never been active in the company union or in any grouping of men on the job. The sixth man was Mark Walling, Hi-Test poly-operator, whose personal background will be noted later.

Joe Logan, the Hi-Test hydro-stillman who was so active for the CIO, confirmed my impression about the difficulty of organizing the pure farmers.

They don't know nothing about working in an industry unless they have been in it for a long time. On the farm they are used to working 12 to 14 hours a day, so 8 hours don't mean a thing to them. I once worked on a construction gang with a bunch of farm boys. I grew up in the oil fields so I knew what a working day was supposed to be. But those men would turn out to work 15 or 20 minutes ahead of time and when it got to be 5 o'clock—quitting time—they would still want to load another truck. And you couldn't stop them. Now, I did as much work as any two of them, but when 5 o'clock came, I wanted to get off the job and get home. Another thing—those boys from the farm, when they get on a job, they think they are going to get ahead quick by getting on the right side of the supervisor. I seen that many times. They always want to do just anything the supervisor says so that they can get ahead.

While farmer Walling later underwent experiences (to be noted in Chapter 11) that made him more receptive to union appeals, his account of his earlier views clearly indicates the difficulties a union organizer faces with men from the farm.

Walling worked on his father's farm until his late teens. As he put it:

When I was growing up, I didn't think my father could do any wrong. I tried to do whatever he told me. When I went to work, I looked upon the foreman just like he was my father, and I tried to do everything just like he wanted it done. I didn't think the company could do any wrong.

I asked if other men had resented this attitude.

Yes, they did. I didn't realize it at the time, but I know now that they considered me_____ (subservient, and self-seeking). I didn't even know what that was then, but now that I look back on it, I can see that I didn't have any real friends among the men. I didn't know what the cause of it was. I was just doing the thing that I thought was right to do.

These "pure farm" men had had no experience in growing up with the frequent and regular interaction with boys their own age which often leads to group loyalties in opposition to formal authority. They had worked constantly under the direction of the formal authority in the family—the father—and now they seemed to accept authority from the foreman in industry just as if he were their father.

In "mixed farm" situations, although the individual was born on the farm and lived there during his early years, the full conditions of the pure farm had not been met. Several of these men had to leave the farm in their early teens due to the failure of the enterprise or to the death of the father. They then moved into farm labor or industrial jobs. In one case, the boy's father died when he was very young and the boy grew up on his grandfather's farm, but the grandfather had another man running the farm for him. Then there was the case of Frank Kendall, fractionator operator, who became the Hi-Test company union representative. He was brought up on a farm, but his father also operated a sawmill and cotton gin and had little time to supervise the farm work. Kendall left the farm for factory work when he was 15.

Four of the eight "mixed farm" men were for the CIO, three were against, and one I classified as undecided. It is interesting to note, however, that not a single one of the four men whom I identified as for the CIO played any active part in the organization drive.

Of those with urban and industrial backgrounds, four out of seven were for the CIO, two definitely against, and one doubtful. I had expected a larger proportion of CIO men among those of this background, but one should note that all the three not committed to the CIO enjoyed special ties with management men, the significance of which will be discussed later. It is interesting to note also that the four men for the CIO in this group were also the only men in my sample who worked actively for the organization. Consider their backgrounds. Joe Logan, Hi-Test hydro-stillman, was the son of an oil field worker, and his father was away at work much of the time that Joe was growing up. Joe started working in the petroleum industry while still in his teens. Another of the four was born on a farm, but his father began to follow the oil fields when he was a small boy. At the age of 15, this man went to work himself, holding several jobs before being hired by Blank Oil Company. The third man had grown up in a fair-sized town, coming of working age in the early depression years. For months he rode about the country in box cars, looking for work. When he got his first job, the work was not steady and he had to make several changes before he finally came to work for Blank Oil Company. The fourth man had gone to work at the age of nine in a southern textile mill. He had worked steadily since that time in a wide variety of jobs and had been in many conflicts with the supervisors.

Of the three men of urban-industrial background who were against or undecided about the CIO, Martin Shockley was the son of a Blank Company worker who had lost his life in a fire on the job. The owner of what was then a small company had then made annual payments from his personal bank account to the widow until Martin had finished school. As a young boy, Martin had even spent some time on several occasions on the owner's ranch. He told me that his mother always received a Christmas card and a birthday card from the owner, who by then had become head of a large corporation and a multimillionaire. Martin was a leading official in the union the company had organized to keep the CIO out. While other workers claimed that during a previous CIO drive, when Martin was particularly upset with his foreman, he had signed a union pledge card, Martin never acknowledged this to me, and there was no doubt about his anti-CIO sentiments when I knew him.

Andy Taylor was related to a member of management. He was also at one time company union representative for Hi-Test plant. While others had told me that few of the men in the Hi-Test control room had any use for the union and had elected Andy as a joke, still this position did involve him in interactions with management, not shared with other workers. In spite of these relationships, there was a time when, in reaction to a statement by a member of the home office management that was highly derogatory to the workers of his plant, Andy said to me, "I tell you a company-dominated union ain't worth a _____." Nevertheless, when I took my informal poll several weeks later, Andy had had several harmonious meetings with a management committee, and he had shifted back to his anti-CIO position:

> I think that the company union can do something for the men. Of course, I have been closely associated with the management in these discussions. I think that if the CIO came in, the company would just stick to the contract and would not deal with the man outside of that at all. In the company union we have a better chance to get things, I think.

Frank Kendall had for months been considered firmly in the CIO camp, but then he was elected company union representative for Hi-Test to succeed Andy Taylor. Frank had such a low opinion of the company union that he was inclined to refuse to serve, but Tom Lloyd, the popular foreman, persuaded him that he had nothing to lose and, in case the CIO did lose the representation election, the Hi-Test men would be at a disadvantage without someone to speak for them. Frank told me later that he did not enjoy the company union meetings with management, and yet he said that the discussions went smoothly, and the management people seemed a reasonable bunch. As the election approached, Frank was at least undecided and perhaps leaning toward a company union vote. Clearly he felt troubled by this change in his sentiments. Before he had expressed his pro-CIO views freely on the job, but at this point he sought to avoid discussions about the CIO with fellow workers.

Note that in all three of these cases, these men of urban-industrial backgrounds had been involved in interactions and activities with management people not shared in by other workers of similar background. Apparently the development of such special relationships can neutralize or even reverse the sentiments that might be expected to arise out of earlier life experiences.

The numbers of men involved here are too small to permit any firm scientific conclusion, but we may regard the cases as illustrative of the possible interrelations of personality and organizational behavior. We should regard the early IAS pattern as predisposing the individual to vote for or against the union, recognizing that the individual's subsequent experiences in the organization may either reinforce or counteract this predisposition.

Relating activities to interaction

Even as we have focused attention so far in this chapter on *interaction*, we have not been able to proceed without here and there dealing with *activities*—a concept hitherto undefined. By *activities* we mean simply the things that man does at work and at play.

At this point, we are seeking to show how interaction and activities relate together and yet are to be distinguished from each other.

All interaction is accompanied by activity: the men we observe may be engaged in conversation and/or working together. Most activities involve interaction, but not all do—the individual may be working by himself or playing solitaire.

We are interested both in the initiation of interaction and the initiation of activity. In one sense, the two phenomena coincide. For example, Tom comes up to Joe and says, "What do you want me to do now?" Joe replies, "I want you to run order XYZ now." Tom has initiated the interaction; he has initiated the activity (conversation). But we are also interested in what happens next: what activity *change* emerges out of the interaction. If we now observe Tom return to his work bench and start on order XYZ, we can say that Joe has initiated activity for Tom.

In informal group situations, where authority is not involved, we find that as the same individuals interact together over a period of time, a leadership structure inevitably emerges. We cannot observe this structure if we see only pair events. We may have the impression that Tom *asks* Joe to do something, whereas Joe *tells* Tom to do something, but our observations of the meanings of differences in tone of voice or words used are likely to be unreliable. It is when we observe set events that the pattern clearly emerges.

If we look at the content of the verbal interchange, we find that it is not necessarily Joe, the leader, who expresses most frequently his ideas of what the group ought to do. If we are correct in our conclusions regarding Joe's position in the group, we observe that a change in group activity takes place *either* when Joe suggests to the group what should be done next, *or* when another group member proposes an activity to Joe *and* Joe expresses agreement orally or with some gesture. We do *not* note a change in activity when another group member makes a proposal which is either ignored by Joe or to which he gives a negative reaction.

Leaders and followers

Note that we are trying to make statements about leadership, based upon direct observation. Discussions of leadership are often confused by questions of social or performance prominence. For example, we may hear of "one of the leading students in the school" and find out that the individual referred to is prominent because he is a good athlete or a good musician or because of his social background, and yet observation of this particular individual might indicate that he was an isolate or a follower. In focusing attention upon leadership, we are trying to separate the phenomenon from judgments about the value of individuals, concentrating attention only upon the way interactions and activities are organized.

As an indication of the fundamental importance of the leadership phenomenon, we should note that what are referred to as "pecking orders" or "dominance-submission patterns" appear to be universally found in animal societies. The term "pecking order" grows out of early studies of flocks of chickens. It has been found that if previously unacquainted chickens are put together, in a remarkably short time a stable order of pecking develops. Chicken A will peck all others and not be pecked back by any of them. Chicken B will unilaterally peck all except A and will be pecked by A—and so on down to the bottom fowl, which is pecked by all others and does not peck back. In animals, the leader generally maintains his position until weakened by advanced age or until he suffers some accident that prevents him from keeping the other group members in line.

Human groups may well display equal structural stability when we have small populations, with constant group membership, living in isolation from other groups and from larger institutions. Even in our complex and rapidly changing society, the durability of these structural patterns has been observed in many studies.

Leadership can be observed in its "purest" form in what are sometimes called "autonomous groups": sets of individuals who interact together with a high frequency and out of whose interactions a structure of leadership emerges without major interpersonal influences being imposed from outside the group. In this book, we will mainly be concerned with individuals and groups in organizations, where groups are not autonomous and where men are generally appointed to positions of power and influence, rather than emerging from the work group. This raises for us a number of important questions. For example, what happens when an individual who has been playing the role of informal leader finds himself in an organizational position allowing him little opportunity to act out his customary pattern of interaction and activities? What happens when management appoints as a foreman someone whose whole social experience has been as a follower in groups led by others? We will be exploring such questions in subsequent chapters.

Leadership and status

Dominance-submission patterns are related to (but not identical with) another universal human phenomenon, the status system. Even in a society like ours with a strong egalitarian ideology, differences in degrees of social prestige are universally recognized. While the word "status" is sometimes applied to indicate a leadership position—for example, "Joe has high status in that group"—it seems to us advisable to try to avoid confusing status with informal leadership. "Status" should rather be reserved for broad and general evaluations of the prestige of an individual or group in relation to the population of a community or organization. For example, we can say that Percival Vanderwater III has high status because he is a regularly participating member of a top prestige group in the community, even though observation of that group indicates that Percy is a follower who exercises minimal influence on the group's activities. On the other hand, an individual who exercises leadership in one group will generally be more widely known and respected outside the group than any of the followers, and he will thus enjoy a higher status than they—in reference to the larger society.

Status is important not only in the way the individual evaluates the position of others in society. The person also has a general idea of the status he himself holds in his community. Since he receives feedback about himself through his interactions with other members of the community, for a normal individual the conception he holds of his own social status is not likely to be far out of line with the status accorded to him by others around him. (Extreme discrepancies in perception are indicative of mental illness.)

In a simple society, we can think of social status in unitary terms: A man's community or tribe is his whole social world, so his status in the community applies wherever he goes. In a complex society like ours, that is not the case. A man may enjoy one level of status in his community and quite another one in his organization. Does it matter if his community status is markedly higher than the one he enjoys in the organization? We shall see that it does. The way that the individual evaluates the relation of these two statuses will be considered in the next chapter when we discuss Homans' idea of the rewards-investments balance.

Aspects of activities

Theories of scientific management appear to be based upon one fundamental assumption regarding human activities: that man is by nature a passive animal and needs to be rewarded and punished to become active. Our assumption, based upon considerable weight of social research, is that man is by nature an active animal. This does not mean necessarily that the worker wants to do what management wants him to do. The problem for management is not to elicit activity where none would otherwise take place, but rather to channel the activity along lines that will be rewarding to management. The individual, on his side, is naturally concerned with finding opportunities for activities that are rewarding to him. It is out of this interplay that many worker-management problems arise.

The activities in which human beings engage can be classified in a variety of ways. The classifications of most concern to us in studying organization will be three.

We can distinguish *degrees of complexity* in the activities performed and consequent differences in the levels of skill required to perform these activities. This is a somewhat oversimplified statement, for it implies that there is a single scale of complexity and skill levels, whereas we shall note important differences between those activities, depending upon the manual skills of the workers and those which depend upon the application of judgment based on observation of what is going on in the environment of the individual. These distinctions we shall explore later.

In the work situation, we note a number of different *social arrangements of work*. In some situations, individuals work alone at individual machines or work stations. When individuals work in association with others, there are several different types of activity patterns that may prevail. In some situations individual members of a work group are all carrying out the same activity. In others, the individual is a member of a task differentiated work group: the outcome depends upon the activity of each individual, but the activity of one individual is not the same as that of others; there is specialization of function within the group. There are also groups where individual activities are linked serially: the function of one individual is performed after the completion of the function of the previous individual, and the task being worked upon generally passes along between them.

We can also *distinguish between work and nonwork activities*. We can observe generally whether the individual is carrying out the activities required of his job or whether he is off the job in a coffee break or smoke break, at lunch, or engaged in some other social activity. Of course, there will be times when work and nonwork activities are combined—for example, when individuals engage in horseplay while working, and it is important to observe when this combination takes place.

Whatever our classifications of activities, we need to give special attention to the ways in which involvement in tasks tends to affect human behavior. There are four aspects of special concern to us:

1. *Tasks and degrees of "traction."*   We take this idea from W. Baldamus:[17]

> I have called (this satisfaction) "traction" because, in a sense, it is the opposite of "dis-traction." It is a feeling of being pulled along by the inertia inherent in a particular activity. The experience is pleasant and may therefore function as a relief from tedium. It usually appears to be associated, though not always, with a feeling of reduced effort, relative to actual or imagined situations where it is difficult to maintain continuity of performance.

To grasp the meaning of this term, try mowing a lawn according to two different patterns. In one, you mow one row and then double back, mowing the next immediately parallel to it, and so on. In the second case, follow a rectangular course, so that each time you complete the four sides the unmowed rectangle is reduced in size.

Suppose you were interrupted in each case before you could finish. In which case would you find it more difficult to stop? Judging from my

---

[17] W. Baldamus, *Efficiency and Effort: An Analysis of Industrial Administration* (London: Tavistock Publications, 1961).

experience, with the parallel line pattern, you would feel only the need to finish the line that you were on. The end of any line seems like a natural stopping place. With the rectangular pattern, the total task seems to induce much more traction. It seems to draw the mower toward the center with ever increasing force as the size of the unmowed part is reduced. As I complete each circuit, I estimate how many more it will take to complete the job, and I get pleasure in the thought that each circuit goes faster than the one before—because there is a little less ground to cover. While I cannot say that I have ever enjoyed mowing lawns, once I get well along into the rectangular pattern, I find it well nigh impossible to stop. I have been known to resist the most urgent calls to dinner until I could snuff out that last rectangle of grass.

Tasks vary greatly in the amount of traction they can induce. While there seem to be other factors involved, in general there appears to be a correlation between the complexity of the task and the traction it induces. A simple, repetitive task tends to induce little traction. At the other extreme, Vernon Buck's[18] study of tool and die makers shows them so involved in their work that supervisors were only needed to give them blueprints and handle other paper work. The progress of the task itself seemed to draw the worker on to the next stage. While a given assignment might take hundreds of hours, the worker would mentally divide it into meaningful parts and evaluate his performance as he moved through these parts.

A repetitive task which is normally without much traction may fit into a context that provides substantial traction. This is our interpretation of Donald Roy's[19] observation that on some incentive pay jobs where he found it possible to "make out" only if he really applied himself, he found himself playing a game against the clock. Let us say that 100 units per hour represented the maximum allowed by the norms of the work group. In this case, the endlessly repetitive work cycle is broken up in the worker's mind into 100 units per hour. He constantly measures his progress in the game as he checks output against the movement of the minute hand of the wall clock. If he has 52 done at the 30 minute mark, he can coast a little; if the count comes to only 48, he pitches in to catch up.

Of course, the worker is earning extra money as he "makes out" on such a rate, but we cannot say that the money incentive in itself creates traction. On jobs where Roy could "make out" easily he made just as much money as he did on the jobs where his best efforts were necessary for "making out." On the easy jobs, where he had to hold back so as not to violate group norms, Roy could not play the game against the clock, and he reported that it seemed as if the workday would never end. When

---

[18] Vernon E. Buck, "The Impact of Technology on the Social System: A Case Study of Tool and Die Makers" (Ph.D. thesis, Cornell University, 1960).

[19] Donald Roy, "Work Satisfaction and Social Reward in Quota Achievement," *American Sociological Review*, Vol. 18, no. 5 (Oct., 1953), pp. 507–14.

he was playing against the clock, the hours seemed to pass much more quickly. This seems to be a general relationship: With high traction jobs time seems to go faster than with low traction jobs.

2. *"Wholeness" of tasks.* Some tasks seem to present meaningful wholes to workers, whereas other tasks seem isolated fragments, without any inherent meaning. Even if the worker knows where his fragment fits into the total product, he finds it hard to feel involved with just a fragment to do.

In general, "whole" jobs seem to provide more traction than fragmentary jobs, but perhaps traction does not express all that is involved here. Workers whose tasks permit them to feel that they are creating or making a meaningful contribution to the whole tend to find greater satisfaction in their work than do those whose tasks provide no such feeling of wholeness.

Wholeness should not be taken as an all-or-nothing matter. The Walker-Guest[20] studies of the automotive assembly line show that the more operations a worker performs in completing his work cycle, the more satisfied he is with his job.

3. *Success or failure.* The human being has learned the meaning of success or failure in the performance of tasks long before he enters the work organization. This aspect is always present in any task, but tasks differ in the extent to which success or failure is defined by other human beings or by the task itself. For example, suppose the worker has the task of building a small engine. He knows very well when he has finished the task that the engine is supposed to run—and he also knows from experience how well the engine is supposed to run, at least during the time in which it is tested. If his engine does not run, no amount of praise will persuade him that he has successfully accomplished his task. Conversely, if the engine runs according to specifications, no one will be able to persuade him that he has failed to accomplish his task. (Of course, the supervisor may argue that he took too long to do it, but that is another issue.)

Many jobs do not provide such built-in standards of success or failure. There may be no question that the task has been completed, but success or failure will be defined by the quality inspector or by the supervisor.

In general, as man experiences success in task performance, his evaluation of himself will go up, as will his satisfaction with the job. We should add the qualifying condition that for this effect to be observed, the task must present some degree of "challenge." A routine job that anyone can perform does not provide this success effect. In general, as man experiences failure in task performance, his evaluation of himself will go down, as will his satisfaction with the task.

Note that these success-failure effects can be independent of any

---

[20] Charles R. Walker and Robert Guest, *The Man on the Assembly Line* (Cambridge, Mass.: Harvard University Press, 1952).

material rewards or penalties. We often observe individuals expressing satisfaction over a task successfully completed even when they go on to say that they know this will bring them no additional pay.

While we know of no research done on this matter, the distinction between inherent and people-imposed definitions of success and failure suggests an hypothesis regarding the relationship between worker and supervisor. The worker will show less concern for supervisory approval and less anxiety over supervisory disapproval on those tasks where success-failure is inherent in the nature of the task.

4. *Task performance and attitude (or sentiment) formation.* With our success-failure discussion, we have already considered certain ways in which task experience affects attitudes. Paul Breer and his associates have also shown the effects of task performance in forming attitudes (i.e., beliefs, preferences and values) on many attitude dimensions. The attitude dimension most frequently studied in this series of experiments was individualism-collectivism. Breer and Locke[21] investigated individualism-collectivism in three small group experiments; their work was replicated and extended in the laboratory and field investigations of Eustace Theodore.[22] In laboratory investigations of the individualism-collectivism dimension, the researchers asked undergraduate subjects to perform either a series of conjunctive or a series of disjunctive tasks. A conjunctive task is one which is performed more efficiently when people work together; a disjunctive task is one which can be performed more efficiently when each individual works alone. Subjects filled out a questionnaire dealing with individualism-collectivism before performing the experimental tasks, after performing the experimental tasks (some four hours later), and at a later date averaging 14 days following the experiment. In recent studies, this questionnaire was disguised as the work of a colleague in order to minimize the effect of the measuring instrument on the measures obtained. Randomly assigned experimental groups of six subjects were placed in either the collective or individual condition. Those in the collective condition were given conjunctive tasks to perform; those in the individual condition were given disjunctive tasks. Though groups were free to choose the manner in which they performed each task, almost all subjects chose to work together on conjunctive tasks and alone on disjunctive ones; being rational undergraduates they chose to work on their tasks in the most efficient way. The experimenters sought to show an attitude shift toward individualism as a result of working alone and a similar shift toward collectivism as a result of working together.

Laboratory results show that subjects in the conjunctive task treatment did shift their questionnaire responses toward collectivism by the end of

---

[21] Paul Breer and E. Locke, *Task Experience as a Source of Attitudes* (Homewood, Ill.: The Dorsey Press, 1965).

[22] Eustace Theodore, "Man's Beliefs, Preferences, and Values: A Search for the Source" (Ph.D. thesis, Cornell University, 1967).

the experiment, whereas those who received the disjunctive treatment shifted their attitudes in the individualism direction. Though diminished, some of this change in attitude position remained at statistically significant levels when assessed two weeks later. Questionnaire items tapped not only work-related attitudes but also remoter areas of concern such as family life, school activities, and neighborhood relations. Attitude changes in the predicted direction occurred on all of these attitude scales. In other words, task experience induced experimental subjects to generalize from work experience to individualism-collectivism attitudes far beyond the immediate task situation.

Subjects in most experiments were given pay for their performance on the experimental tasks. In addition, their scores were written on the board after each trial so they might compare their results with a standard the experimenter had set in advance. In most experiments, the standards were set so that all experimental groups would be rewarded by exceeding the standard. At no time during the experiments did the researchers try to persuade the subjects of the importance of working alone or together; the tasks themselves dictated performance. In fact, in Theodore's work[23] there is evidence to suggest that the rate of pay is less important than the involvement of the subjects in the experimental task. In this experiment, subjects in both the high- and low-pay groups, subjects who had their preconceived notions of pay violated, were more involved in task per-formance and showed greater attitude change than subjects from a medium-pay group.

This series of experiments demonstrates that tasks themselves and the way people perform tasks can have a significant effect upon attitudes. The researchers suggest that task experience may be one important *source* of what man believes, prefers and values.[24]

Summary and conclusions

Organizations are built upon the relations among their members. The student of organizations needs to have a systematic way of describing and analyzing these relations. We have introduced in this Chapter two of the fundamental elements in our approach to organizational analysis: interac-tions and activities. In discussing these concepts and illustrating their importance, we have encountered the concept of sentiments (or atti-tudes), which will receive full treatment in the next chapter.

We have distinguished between the observation and measurement of micro-interaction and macro-interaction. Micro-interactional studies in-volve the measurement with the chronograph of second-to-second adjust-

---

[23] Eustace Theodore, "An Exploration of Attitude Change as a Result of Task Experience" (Master's thesis, Cornell University, 1965).

[24] I am indebted to Eustace Theodore for this interpretation of the experiments of Breer and associates.

ments of two individuals engaged in a conversation or interview. In order to establish in quantitative terms the personality of the subject, he is subjected to the standard interview, which involves systematically controlled periods of change in interviewer behavior. Such measurements make possible the description of the subject's personality in terms of activity level, listening ability, flexibility, initiative, dominance, and so on. Repeated measurements of adult subjects over widely spaced time intervals indicate that adult personality, as described and measured by the chronograph, varies only within narrow limits. (We should note, however, that one of the traits so described and measured is *flexibility*. An individual who scores high on flexibility at one time period will also score high at a later period, meaning that in both periods he will be able to adjust successfully to a wide range of interactional situations.)

Since dealing with the chronograph and its measurements takes us in a highly specialized direction, we will not pursue this subject much beyond the present chapter. Why then do we introduce it here? Since personality is so often dealt with in such vague and artistic terms, we think it important for the student to grasp the possibility of an observational quantitative approach to personality. Furthermore, the types of micro-interactional measures developed by Chapple are closely related to macro-interaction, which we shall deal with extensively throughout this book (calling it simply "interaction").

Cruder but yet highly useful measures of interaction can be made in field observation. We distinguish first between pair and set events (two-person and more than two-person interactions). While in the ordinary course of organizational life set events are far less frequent than pair events, it is observation of sets which enables us to determine leadership. We can also observe and measure frequencies and durations of interactions and note, for an observed pair, how often A initiates interaction with B compared to how often B takes the initiative (which closely parallel's the initiative measures in micro-interaction). Data on interactional frequencies can also be elicited through interviewing. The informant says, "I used to see Joe every day, but for the last month or so I have only seen him a couple of times." Such a statement is only a rough estimation, but the difference in frequencies is so great that we can safely assume a marked reduction in interaction between the informant and Joe within the past several weeks. If we need more precise measures, we must rely upon observation.

Much of the analysis in this book will be based upon interaction. While this chapter has been mainly devoted to exposition, we have already illustrated two problem areas which we can usefully approach through interaction: personality and job adjustment, leadership and supervision.

We have illustrated the personality-job adjustment problem with three jobs which are extreme in the restrictions they place upon interaction: night watchman, engine operator, and automotive assembly line worker.

When we have more data upon the interactional requirements and limitations involved in a variety of jobs, we shall be able to assess the personality-job relationships with individuals and jobs which do not show such extreme patterns.

Looking at waitresses and foremen, we see two jobs which (in the work situations studied) require a very high frequency of interaction, while very few of the interactions last more than a minute. For such jobs, we must combine our personality-job focus with an examination of leadership. Superficially, the waitress does not appear to play a leadership role in the organization, but we have noted that the girls who in the past had been informal leaders were better able to manage the complex and rapid flow of interactions of a large and busy restaurant than those who had played follower roles.

We examine leadership through both interaction and activities. In group situations, the leader is the central person in the flow of interaction. That is, we observe others addressing their remarks to him and cutting off their own statements when they observe he is not paying attention. He addresses the group as a whole more than any other member, and he is interrupted less often than others.

In examining leadership, we need to distinguish between initiation of interaction and initiation of activity changes. In set events, any member may propose a change in activity, but changes take place only as the leader endorses what is proposed or makes his own proposal.

We have suggested distinguishing between status and position in the group. Here we will use status to mean social prestige. We have noted that an individual may hold high social prestige (or status) and yet exert little influence within a particular group.

Formal position in an organization (one of the principal indicators of status) does indeed tend to influence the flow of interactions when those interacting hold positions at different levels. In micro-interaction terms, we can expect an individual who measures high in dominance to show less dominating behavior when with his boss than with subordinates.

We have also noted that past interactional experience tends to influence the individual toward a vertical or horizontal conception of organizational life. Those who grew up with active peer group experience are more likely to respond to union organizing drives than those who grew up under strong parental controls and with little peer group experience.

Since we argue that interactions, activities, and sentiments are interrelated, it has been impossible to discuss the first two without some reference to sentiments. Let us review how sentiments have already entered our consideration.

We have been concerned with how the fit (or lack of fit) of the personality to the job affects the individual's sentiments toward his job. We have argued that (other things being equal) the individual will be better satisfied with a job that fits well with his interaction pattern than with one that fits poorly. (We say "other things being equal," because clearly the interactional fit is not the only factor influencing job satisfaction. Other factors will be considered later.) We have also suggested how interactions, past and present, influence the individual's sentiments toward the union.

In examining activities, we have noted how the degree of possible task involvement and success experience available in a given job may influence the worker's sentiments toward the job. We have also noted how experience with a conjunctive task (one better performed by a group) tends to raise the individual's estimation of the value of collective efforts, whereas experience with a disjunctive task (one better performed alone) tends to lead toward a greater appreciation of individualistic efforts.

Social implications

Those of us in this field used to be charged with "trying to adjust men to machines." Anyone making such a charge has a greatly exaggerated conception of the possibilities of changing adult human personalities. As Chapple and others have pointed out, it is a great deal easier to change machines than to change adult personalities.

In considering the adjustment of personality to job, we have compared the interaction pattern the individual brings to the job with the interactional requirements and limitations of the job. We assume that the individual is born with certain genetic characteristics that influence the interaction pattern he develops. The nature and extent of genetic influence is beyond the scope of this book. In any case, we assume that the adult pattern is shaped in considerable measure by the social experiences the individual has in growing up. By the time he reaches maturity, the individual's interaction pattern displays marked stability over long periods of time.

If that is the case, how can we achieve a better fit between personalities and jobs? One strategy is that of matching: we seek to select individuals whose interaction patterns will be reasonably compatible with the jobs they are to hold.

While this strategy offers some possibilities, its application is clearly limited in scope. Consider Jasinski's finding that individuals who expressed little interest in interaction on the job are more satisfied with assembly line work than those who express the need for interaction. Suppose we then select for such assembly line jobs those individuals who fall at the low end of the scale in their need for interaction. But Jasinski has also pointed out that individuals having such a low need for interaction make up only a small proportion of the factory work force. Clearly there are not enough unsocial individuals around to man the assembly lines.

Job progression ladders also limit the application of this strategy. The various jobs in a line of promotion may have quite different requirements for, and limitations on, interaction. Union leaders would hardly look with favor on any scheme that made promotion dependent upon the candidate's interaction pattern in preference to seniority, nor could we expect such a criterion to win favor with workers or supervisors.

This approach to selection and matching may offer much more promise at supervisority and executive levels. At the work level, the best we can do is recognize some of the consequences of a bad personality-job fit and raise questions particularly about jobs which have such extreme interactional requirements or limitations that very few individuals fit them.

The automotive assembly line falls in this category of extreme interactional limitations. While we can hardly expect the automotive companies to abandon this form of organization because of interaction considerations, we should point out that this technology is actually on the decline in the United States, for other reasons. While the popular view of the automotive assembly line representing the typical mass production technology was always a gross caricature of the actual situation, in recent years many companies have been converting such assembly lines to more automated technologies, which free workers from the most direct pressures of automotive assembly lines.

Up to this time, such technological changes have been carried out without any consideration of the requirements and limitations on interaction of the modified or newly created jobs. If the point of view expressed here is given serious consideration by managements in future planning of technological change, this certainly does not mean substituting social and psychological for economic considerations. It should mean that managements will seek to integrate social and psychological with economic considerations in future technology planning.

In this section, we are not attempting any final answer to the problems of man's relations to technology. We simply explore some of the complexities of this problem in order to indicate that if anyone believes that we shall be able to "adjust men to machines" he seriously overestimates both the plasticity of the adult personality and the powers of behavioral scientists.

References

On interaction:

Chapple, Eliot D. in collaboration with Arensberg, Conrad M. *Measuring Human Relations: An Introduction to the Study of the Interaction of Individuals.* Genetic Psychology Monograph No. 22. Provincetown, Mass.: The Journal Press, 1940. A rather technical first statement.

Chapple, Eliot D. "The Standard Experimental (Stress) Interview as Used in Interaction Chronograph Investigations," *Human Organization*, Vol. 12, no. 2 (Summer, 1953), pp. 23–32. A description of a method of measuring interaction.

Chapple, Eliot D., Chapple, Martha F., and Repp, Judith A. "Behavioral Definitions of Personality and Temperament Characteristics," *Human Organization*, Vol. 13, no. 4 (Winter, 1955), pp. 34–9. Translates quantitative chronograph measures into personality and temperament descriptions.

Bales, Robert F. *Interaction Process Analysis*. Cambridge, Mass.: Addison-Wesley Press, 1950. An introduction to Bales' method of coding interaction in terms of content categories.

Walker, Charles R., Guest, Robert, and Turner, Arthur N. *The Foreman on the Assembly Line*. Cambridge, Mass.: Harvard University Press, 1956. Presents quantitative data on foreman interactions, based upon field observation.

On the nature of work activities:

Baldamus, W. *Efficiency and Effort: An Analysis of Industrial Administration*. London: Tavistock Publications, 1961. Reviews the literature and develops the author's own notions regarding traction.

Discussion questions

1. Describe your own characteristic interaction pattern in terms of the approach taken by Chapple. You will find it useful to make a preliminary description and check it with two or more people who know you well.

Note: Without the chronograph, you cannot be expected to be entirely clear on your own or on the pattern of another person. The purpose of this question (and of number 2) is to help you gain some familiarity with this way of viewing personality. For further background on interaction measurement and description, read Eliot D. Chapple, Martha F. Chapple, and Judith A. Repp, "Behavioral Definitions of Personality and Temperament Characteristics," *Human Organization*, Vol. 3, no. 4 (Winter, 1955), pp. 34–9.

2. Describe the interaction pattern of another person. You may select someone you know well, but do not rely entirely upon impressions from your memory. Observe that person several times in pair events (two individuals) and in set events (three or more individuals). Try checking your description with the person observed.

3. Select two jobs which appear to have different interactional requirements and different opportunities and/or restrictions on interaction. Describe the jobs in terms of these interactional aspects. What do these descriptions suggest regarding the personalities of individuals who can adjust well to one job or the other?

4. Select two jobs in the same or different organizations known to you through experience and/or observation. For each job, consider what it offers the jobholder in:

 a) Freedom or restriction of physical movement.
 b) Opportunities for interaction.
 c) Traction.
 d) Success experiences.

5. How do the four aspects (above) of these particular jobs affect the job satisfaction of the jobholders?

5. Sentiments and symbols

MAN NOT ONLY INTERACTS and carries on activities. He has "feelings" about those activities, about those with whom he interacts, and about the world within which these behaviors take place. There are two commonly used terms to refer to what we have in mind: attitudes or sentiments. I shall not distinguish between them. While "attitudes" is the term more frequently used in the literature, I am more accustomed to use "sentiments" and shall stick to this term throughout this book. The student may speak of "attitudes" if he wishes. There will be no confusion as long as we are both clear that we are talking about the same things.

The nature of sentiments

Sentiments refer to the mental and emotional reactions we have to people and physical objects. Sentiments have the following three elements:

1. An idea about something or somebody—that is, a cognitive element.
2. Emotional content or affect.
3. A tendency to recur upon presentation of the same symbols that have been associated with it in the past.[1]

I regard sentiments as a personal frame of reference, through which the individual perceives, interprets, and evaluates the world around him and his place in it. Many schemes of classification of sentiments are possible. For our purposes, I find it useful to set up these categories:

1. Self-concept.
2. Evaluation of activities.
3. Personal identification.
4. Ranking.

We shall be concerned primarily with these three aspects of the

---

[1] I am indebted to discussions with Alexander Leighton for this approach to sentiments. See particularly Chapter VII and Appendix A (with Jane M. and Charles C. Hughes) in his *My Name is Legion* (New York: Basic Books, Inc., 1959).

self-concept: status, personal worth, and level of aspiration. Status involves the individual's own conception of his prestige position in society. As he begins work, this self-evaluation is likely to be strongly influenced by the status of his parents in the community and by the status of those with whom he is customarily associated outside of the workplace. Perhaps his father is a skilled worker, and he is inclined to think of himself as at least a slight cut above those who come from families where the father was unskilled and perhaps only sporadically employed.

Personal worth involves the individual's own evaluations of what he is good at and what he is not good at. For example, he may consider himself one of the most skilled men on his particular job, and may also take pride in his tinkering at home.

Level of aspiration refers to the objectives the individual hopes to reach. These hopes tend to be limited by what he thinks is—or should be —possible, providing he is a normal individual. That is, if you ask him whether he would like to have a million dollars, he will give an affirmative answer, but he does not expect to have a million dollars and is not going to be frustrated by his inability to acquire this fortune. On the other hand, if you ask him whether he would like to have the job immediately above him in the line of promotion, his response will be more closely related to reality. Perhaps he not only expresses an interest in having that job, but says that he will be seriously disappointed if he does not have the opportunity of moving up within the next year. He may go on to say that he would like to become a foreman, even though he recognizes that most foremen in his company are college graduates and he has not had a college education. In that case, he recognizes that he probably won't be able to achieve his ambition, and yet the job is so close to his present experience that he can't help aspiring to it and feeling frustrated at his lack of progress.

Status, personal worth, and level of aspiration tend to be related to each other, but may also vary independently of each other. For example, the man who thinks of himself as having high status is likely also to place a high evaluation upon his personal worth, but this may not always be the case. He may recognize that his family and friends have high status and yet still lack confidence in his own abilities. Similarly, a man who considers himself very good at his work is likely to aspire to promotion, but we do encounter individuals who tell us, in effect, "Sure, I am good at this job, but this is a job I like to do, so why should I want to move up?" In this book, we will be concerned with each of the three aspects of the self-concept and with the ways in which they move together or move independently.

Evaluation of activities involves the individual's judgment about which activities are good or bad, right or wrong. For example, Joe may believe that 100 units a day is a "day's work" in his job. He could produce more and is sometimes tempted to do so, but he feels that this would not be the right thing to do. He may believe that it is good to swap jobs with fellow workers to break the monotony, even though this is against management rules. He may believe that the activities of the time study man are bad and that any worker who gives him accurate information is doing the wrong thing.

The reader may be familiar with the concept of "norms" and feel that this is what we are talking about. That is not the case. At this point, we are considering the evaluations that an individual makes. Norms will be discussed in Chapter 8.

Personal identification involves the individual's feelings as to who are his friends and who are his enemies. He may consider all members of his work group friends, but even in that case he will probably acknowledge that he is "closer" to some than to others. Or we may find the work group seriously divided, so that he considers only some of them for him and with him, whereas others he feels are against him. He makes similar evaluations of management people.

On the individual level, it is probably not enough to speak simply of liking or disliking. We often hear people distinguishing between liking and respecting. I assume that liking and respecting go together more often than not, but we should be alert for situations in which they do not; therefore, we should keep our eyes open to both aspects of interpersonal sentiment.

We can also speak of personal identification at the level of group, department, and organization. Does Joe feel really a member of his work group? Does he feel that his is a good department to work in? How does he feel about the company? We will be concerned with all of these aspects of personal identification as we proceed in this book.

Ranking involves the individual's evaluation of the relative prestige of those he sees around him. Within Joe's department, we find both formal and informal ranking among workers. Formal ranking is determined by the job classification scheme in effect in the department. Everyone knows that job A is a better job than job B, so that we may say that the man who works on job A has a higher rank than the man who works on job B. This formal ranking generally has a strong influence on the informal rankings accorded to departmental members by their fellows. Informal group leadership within the department tends to be assumed by workers holding high formal rankings. However, this is not uniformly true, so we must always be concerned with the personal evaluations of rank that are given fellow workers by the other members of the department.

While we speak of ranking again on an individual basis, it has been shown that there tends to be a high degree of agreement among people in the same community or organization about the relative prestige ranking of their fellows.[2] While workers do not talk explicitly about ranking,

[2] W. Lloyd Warner, Kenneth Eells, and Marcia Meeker, *Social Class in America* (Chicago: Science Research Associates, 1948); also Joseph Kahl, *The American Class Structure* (New York: Rinehart & Co., 1957).

their conversation is interspersed with casual or pointed comments that express approval or disapproval, a liking or disliking, of individuals around them. As the expression of these sentiments is exchanged among members, a collective ranking arises.

The individual also ranks members of management. Here the formal titles play a role perhaps even more important than at the work level. But again, they do not completely determine the way members of management are ranked. For example, the worker may feel that his own foreman does not "carry much weight" with higher management, whereas the foreman of an adjoining department "carries a lot of weight." In effect, he is saying that he ranks the other foreman above his own.

When we think of sentiments, as when we think of interactions and activities, we need to think in terms of patterns. We can describe units in isolation, speaking of the sentiment or attitude of one individual toward another or toward a particular job or type of work. For the normal individual, we assume that such sentiments do not exist in isolation. Out of the whole course of his social experience, the individual builds up a pattern of sentiments, a characteristic framework through which he interprets himself and the world around him.

Here we have another clue to the forces that tend to induce attitude or sentiment change: the principle of *cognitive dissonance*.[3] When the individual experiences a situation that produces for him cues that do not fit with his prevailing pattern of sentiments, he finds this dissonance uncomfortable. There are two ways of resolving the dissonance. He can rationalize in an effort to find some way of convincing himself that these new cues after all do fit with his pattern of sentiments. Or he can change the pre-existing pattern of sentiments to accommodate it to his new experiences. As yet we know little about the conditions under which the individual will rationalize or will change his sentiments, but at least we can say that when dissonance occurs the individual is more likely to change than when he faces no dissonance. We should be alert to note instances of dissonance—and some of these will be examined in this book.

The framework of time

More than any other animal, the human being is oriented toward time. This means that his sentiments toward people, activities, and objects are established in relation to past and future as well as to present time. His present position may not look imposing to the outsider, but if the individual has occupied more humble positions in the past, he is likely to feel that he has a "good job" now. Similarly, a given job may be judged as satisfactory or unsatisfactory according to the prospects it offers for the future. If the individual sees it as a "dead end job," he is more likely to be dissatisfied than if he sees it as a stepping stone to more desirable jobs.

---

[3] Leon Festinger, *A Theory of Cognitive Dissonance* (Evanston, Ill.: Row, Peterson, 1957).

While there will be variations in the way a given job is evaluated by the jobholder, whoever does the evaluation, he will not think solely in present-time terms. He tends to evaluate his present situation in terms of his past and in terms of his estimate of his future.

While everyone thinks of himself in terms of past, present, and future, there are wide individual differences in emphasis placed upon these different segments of the time continuum. When we say of a man, "he is living in the past," we mean that he seems to be orienting his behavior to aspects of his past experiences, with little regard to the changing times.

Similarly, there are individuals who are heavily present-time oriented. They appear to be seeking immediate gratifications, without regard to long-run consequences. And there are individuals who are future oriented, who are willing to defer present gratifications in the hope of one day experiencing what (to them) are more important gratifications.

Individual differences in time orientation are more properly the subject matter of individual psychology and thus will not occupy us at length here. We are more concerned with general social influences. Here we should note social class influences in time orientation. Various studies have indicated that in the United States it is particularly members of the upper middle class who are oriented toward a long future time span. Persons of lower class origin are less likely to defer immediate gratifications in striving toward long-range goals.

Such social class differences are, of course, matters of averages of perceptions and behavior. We will find individuals of upper middle-class origin who are highly oriented toward short-run gratifications, and we will find persons of lower class backgrounds who are strongly oriented toward long-range goals. Whatever the social class or personality characteristics of the individual, he always evaluates his present situation *to some extent* in terms of his past experience and his anticipation of future developments. His sentiments must therefore be interpreted in this time context.

The investment-rewards relationship

There are other comparisons that the individual tends to make in judging the acceptability of his present situation. George Homans speaks of the principle of distributive justice,[4] involving the balance between the individual's rewards and his investments. Homans and his associates claim that implicit with all human beings in judging the adequacy of their position is their estimate of the balance between the rewards they are receiving in that position and the investments they have made in reaching

---

[4] A. Zaleznik, C. R. Christensen, F. J. Roethlisberger, with the assistance and collaboration of G. C. Homans, *The Motivation, Productivity and Satisfaction of Workers: A Prediction Study* (Boston: Harvard University Graduate School of Business Administration, 1958).

that position. If the individual feels that he has invested more than the sum of the rewards he is receiving, he feels aggrieved, expresses concern about getting a better job and/or is inclined to reduce his investment in the present job (through reducing the effort he puts into it). If the individual feels that the rewards he is receiving are greater than the investments he has made, he is inclined to feel that he is especially favored and that he owes the organization an extra measure of effort and loyalty.

What elements figure into the calculation of investments and rewards? Education and training are major items on the investment side. The effort and ingenuity the individual is putting into his job and the skill he has acquired are other investment items that are to some extent under the control of the individual. There are items over which the individual has no control, but which nevertheless he considers as investments: for example, the social class position of his family and his ethnic group identification. The individual from a middle-class family is less likely to consider a low-level job appropriate to himself than is the individual from a lower class family. Similarly, in many industrial situations there have arisen informal understandings that the better jobs belong to the Irish Americans rather than the Italian Americans, to the Swedish Americans rather than to some other group, and so on. We will consider several cases of this nature. In such cases, membership in the preferred group is viewed by the individual as if it were a personal investment. Seniority is also an important element: the more time given the firm, the greater the investment.

On the rewards side, the earnings that go with the job are the most obvious item, but also very important are such iems affecting the desirability of the job as its title and associated status characteristics, the freedom of the individual to move about physically, and the measure of independence that he enjoys on the job.

When workers talk about their jobs, we often find them verbalizing in terms of this investment-rewards relationship (IRR): "Of course, this isn't one of the top jobs in the plant, but for a fellow with my education, I am doing pretty good." Or, "With my education and the skill I have and what I produce on this job, I ought to be doing a lot better than I am."

Social relativity

The human being also evaluates his job in terms of social relativity. To be sure, if his wage is so low in relation to his family needs that he cannot meet the minimum food and clothing bills at home, he will be unhappy even though there are many others in his situation. Few workers in the United States today who are regularly employed in industrial or governmental organizations are at this minimum subsistence level. Those above the minimum tend to think of their position in relative, more than in absolute terms. Whether the rewards the individual receives are perceived as adequate to him depends not only upon the investments he has made. In fact, his conception of what rewards should balance what investments is strongly conditioned by his observation of how those with whom he compares himself are faring.

Sociologists speak of those with whom the individual compares himself as his "reference group." Within the organization, the most available reference groups are those workers who are on the same or similar jobs, especially when their work stations are near enough to that of the individual concerned so that he can be thoroughly aware of how they are faring in relation to himself. While most individuals will make their most important comparisons with fellow workers in the same plant, there are some whose most salient comparisons will be made outside. The craftsman will be just as concerned with how his pay compares with men in his own craft in other organizations in the same area as he is with the internal plant comparisons. Then there will always be some individuals who feel that they basically do not belong in the work situation where they are employed and tend to compare themselves with individuals in other and higher status occupations outside of the plant.

While collective bargaining of plant and companywide increases in pay receives the primary attention of reporters and commentators, anyone who has observed negotiations and the handling of grievances can testify to the frequency and importance of "inequity" issues. An inequity is an instance of our social comparison process. The argument is not over the adequacy of the wage rate in an absolute sense. The parties are arguing as to whether the rate in question is "in line" with what certain comparison groups are receiving. Furthermore, as the parties make these comparisons, they are also speaking about the IRR. Let us say that the union negotiators compare job B with job A, claiming that the investments of the workers in question are approximately equal. If those on job B are receiving more pay, then it follows that management should correct the inequity by raising the pay of the men on job A. While it might appear that the alleged inequity could equally well be corrected by reducing the pay of the men on job B, in practice it almost never seems possible to do it this way. In Chapter 8, "Groups: Offense and Defense," we will attempt to grapple with such inequity cases.

Other ways of dealing with sentiments

Up to this point, I have concentrated upon my own approach to sentiments and symbols. Whether or not the student is satisfied with this approach, he should be aware that other people have pursued different approaches. While it is far beyond the scope of this book to undertake a comprehensive review of the literature in this complex field, at least I shall undertake to relate my approach to two important lines of thought: the Maslow "structure of needs" approach and the Herzberg "two-factor theory of job satisfaction and motivation."

Psychologists think in terms of human needs and of the striving of individuals to satisfy these needs. Many different needs may be posited, with different lists being used by different writers, leaving the whole field somewhat confused. One ordering of needs developed by A. H. Maslow[5] has been widely used by students in industry. Maslow postulates five orders of needs: physiological needs, safety needs, belonging and love needs, esteem needs, and the need for self-actualization. Maslow sees these five in terms of a hierarchy such that man does not become concerned with (or become motivated toward) fulfilling a given higher order need until he has satisfied the lower orders. For example, until the person can count on satisfying his physiological needs for food, drink, sleep, and sex, he does not become concerned with higher order needs. It is only when the individual feels his physiological needs satisfied, experiences a feeling of security in his environment, feels some warmth of personal association, and has won some respect from others, that he becomes concerned with self-actualization—with developing his abilities and talents to the utmost.

A modified scheme which seems better adapted to our examination of men at work is that recently presented by Dickson and Roethlisberger.[6] While accepting the importance of physiological needs, the authors proceed on the assumption that these needs are satisfied outside of the organization. They then concern themselves with the following five areas of needs:

1. *Safety needs:* securing, holding on to, protecting, and conserving the job as a source of a livelihood.
2. *Friendship and belonging needs:* satisfactory relations with fellow workers and supervision, commonly expressed as the need for belonging.
3. *Needs for justice and fair treatment:* adequate rewards for contributions in comparisons with others.
4. *Dependence-independence:* treatment as a responsible adult in whom needs for both dependence and independence are recognized.
5. *Needs for achievement:* opportunity to develop in one's job, to become what one has the potentiality of becoming.

We note that 1, 2, and 5 are closely matched with three of the needs in the Maslow hierarchy; 3 and 4, *Needs for justice and fair treatment, and Dependence-independence,* represent modifications in the Maslow system.

How does this modified framework of needs relate to our framework? The first category, safety needs, we have not discussed, though we must accept this as a fundamental requirement that must be met if the individual is to be satisfied with his position in the organization. Friendship and

---

[5] A. H. Maslow, *Motivation and Personality* (New York: Harper & Bros., 1954).

[6] William J. Dickson and F. J. Roethlisberger, *Counselling in an Organization: A Sequel to the Hawthorne Researches* (Boston: Harvard University Graduate School of Business Administration), pp. 79–80.

belonging needs provide another way of speaking about the requirements of the individual to develop and maintain a pattern of interaction. Dependence-independence refers to the individual's responses to the authority situation. Dickson and Roethlisberger argue that all individuals have certain dependence needs and certain independence needs—on the one hand, we want to be taken care of to some extent; on the other hand, we want to assert our independence.

We have expressed this by pointing out that the individual develops a pattern of initiating activity for some individuals and responding to others. As noted in the last chapter, individuals differ in this regard with some individuals responding passively to their social environment and others taking considerable initiative. We can speak of the individual's characteristic pattern of interaction in terms of psychological needs, for we observe that when the individual is unable to continue interacting in the manner to which he has become accustomed he becomes disturbed.

Needs for justice and fair treatment represent a psychological orientation to what we have been discussing in terms of IRR and the social comparison process. To some extent, we have already dealt with needs for achievement in considering the relationship between the individual's social background and his position in the plant. We assume that the need for achievement may be activated or suppressed in the individual's experience in home and family, but in general we will leave to others the examination of this important area of human development. As we go on, we will find instances indicating how the individual's experience in the plant may satisfy or thwart his need for achievement.

Another currently popular approach to the study of sentiments con-concerning work is that of Frederick Herzberg and his associates.[7] Their dual-factor theory of job satisfaction and motivation grew out of a study of 200 engineers and accountants which they carried out with a novel approach. Instead of surveying respondent reactions to a wide variety of items presumably related to satisfaction-dissatisfaction, the Herzberg group asked each subject first to recall a time when he had felt exceptionally good about his job. The investigators then questioned the subject further to seek the elements responsible for this high satisfaction and to probe for possible effects upon the subject's job performance. In a second interview, they followed the same procedure following a request for information regarding a time when the subject's feelings about his job were exceptionally negative.

Examination of the factors apparently producing satisfaction and of those producing dissatisfaction indicated that they did not fall at opposite

---

[7] F. Herzberg, B. Mausner and B. Snyderman, *The Motivation to Work* (2nd ed.; New York: John Wiley & Sons, 1959). The opposing viewpoints are well stated in *Personnel Psychology* (Winter, 1967). See Robert J. House and L. A. Wigdor, "Herzberg's Dual-Factor Theory of Job Satisfaction & Motivation: A Review of the Evidence and a Criticism," and D. A. Whitsett & E. K. Winslow, "An Analysis of Studies Critical of the Motivator-Hygiene Theory."

ends of the same continuum. In other words, the absence of the "satis-fiers" did not produce dissatisfaction, and the absence of the "dissatisfiers" did not produce satisfaction.

According to the theory, the "satisfiers" are related to the nature of the work itself and to the rewards growing directly out of work perform-ance. These are intrinsic factors such as sense of achievement, recognition, interest in the work itself, and advancement.

The "dissatisfiers" are associated with the individual's relationship to the context or environment in which he does his work. Company policies and ineffective administration rank highest in this dimension, followed closely by incompetent technical supervision. Also involved are items such as working conditions, salary, and interpersonal relations with super-visors.

Herzberg was particularly interested in using analysis of satisfaction-dissatisfaction to get at motivation. He argues on the basis of his research findings that the presence of "satisfiers" tends to motivate people toward greater effort and improved performance, whereas the absence of "dissat-isfiers" has no effect upon motivation.

Relating Maslow and Herzberg to our framework

Before evaluating the Maslow and Herzberg theories, let us seek to relate them to the framework we are developing in this book. It is important to recognize that Maslow, Herzberg, and Whyte (in this particular chapter) have three quite different objectives. The differences may be visualized in the following diagram:

Maslow is primarily concerned with *Needs* (1) and considers 2 through 5 only as they relate to 1. Herzberg is primarily concerned with *Motivation* (4) and examines 2, 3, and 5 as they relate to 4. Herzberg makes no assumptions regarding 1.

Both Maslow and Herzberg are attempting to support theoretical propositions concerning the nature of the relations among several of these factors. I have no such purpose in mind in my discussion of "sentiments" in this chapter. I am here concerned with "sentiments" primarily as a conceptual category with a wider range than those treated by Herzberg. We can use the rest of the book to explore the ways in which sentiments are related to other aspects of organizational behavior.

Within this general context, let us attempt a preliminary evaluation of the Maslow and Herzberg approaches. Some have argued against Maslow's assumption that the higher level needs are not activated until the lower level ones are satisfied—and Dickson and Roethlisberger make no such assumption. Given this qualification, how useful are such schema?

When an individual quits his job, we can readily infer which needs were not satisfied and therefore why he made his decision. But that is an after-the-fact judgment. Will the needs approach enable us to predict or control behavior? My judgment is that such schema are so broad and general that—except in extreme cases—they have little predictive value. To be sure, if we find an individual in a job where he is constantly exposed to severe physical threats and discomforts, we can predict that he will leave that job if he is physically able to do so, but we hardly need a psychological theory to reach such a common sense conclusion. When conditions are such as to more or less satisfy a wide range of needs—and many situations are like that—then a needs schema offers little predictive or explanatory value.

Can the same criticism be leveled at our *sentiments* approach? If you know a man is dissatisfied, you can always find some factors to blame for that dissatisfaction, but can you predict satisfaction-dissatisfaction from knowledge of these factors? While I have not been primarily concerned with theoretical propositions in this chapter, I have already indicated certain predictive possibilities for sentiments that are not found in the Maslow or Herzberg approaches. The approach to prediction is through examination of the IRR and the notion of social relativity. For the members of a given organization, we can devise rough measures of investments made and of rewards received. We can examine this relationship in terms of the IRR prevailing in other social units to which the members of our unit are likely to compare themselves. With these data, we can then predict job satisfaction of our individual subjects. The predictions will be far from 100 percent in accuracy, but we can expect to do much better than chance. This approach is described in Chapter 7, "Groups: Membership and Structure."

The main argument against a needs schema is not that it is wrong; it is that it offers us little if anything beyond the conceptual tools we already have presented. The student should withhold judgment until he has learned to use these tools and tested their utility. If he then finds them useful and finds that adding the needs approach makes little or no additional contribution, the principle of *parsimony* suggests that he should not clutter up his mind with terms which do not increase the power of his analysis.

The Herzberg theory has attracted wide attention and stirred up vigorous debate. Some critical fire has been directed at the particular method used. As Victor Vroom[8] has commented:

---

[8] Victor Vroom, "Some Observations Regarding Herzberg's Two-Factory Theory," presented at the American Psychological Association Convention, New York, 1966 (also cited in House and Wigdor [see fn. 7] pp. 7–8, 10).

People tend to take the credit when things go well, and enhance their own feeling of self-worth, but protect their self-concept when things go poorly by blaming their failure on the environment. . . . If you grant the assumption about the way in which biases operate, it follows that the story-telling methods may have very little bearing on managerial practices.

Do other methods yield the same general results? That question yields no simple answer, for some subsequent studies tend to support Herzberg, while others bring forth contradictory evidence. Furthermore, supporters of Herzberg argue that studies yielding contradictory evidence were not designed so as to effect reasonable tests of the theory.

This is not the place to attempt to resolve the complex scientific questions involved in this case. For present purposes, the safest course is to assume that the final answers are not yet in. We are at least justified in considering the potential usefulness of the Herzberg approach while withholding final judgments.

It should be recognized that neither acceptance nor rejection of the Herzberg formulations is incompatible with the framework of this book. We can say that Herzberg has produced a particular way of sorting out the sentiments involved in satisfaction or dissatisfaction toward work.

I prefer to think in terms of three rather than two aspects of job satisfaction: extrinsic, intrinsic, and social. Such a sorting fits better with the IAS schema. Under extrinsic, I count some but not all of the "hygiene" factors. Under intrinsic I list all that Herzberg puts under the "motivator" (or "satisfier") label except "recognition," which seems to me to belong more properly in the social category. My category of "social" draws from both sets of Herzberg variables. Further breakdowns should be made to distinguish between satisfactions from management and satisfactions from fellow workers, since these two types often do not go together. The following diagram indicates how our two approaches compare.

	Whyte		
Herzberg	Intrinsic	Extrinsic	Social
Motivator	Work itself, job responsibility, advancement		Recognition from superiors, from peers
Hygiene		Pay, working conditions, company policies	Interpersonal relations with superiors, lack of recognition from superiors, lack of recognition from peers, incompetent supervision

What schema for sorting out job-satisfaction variables is most useful depends in part upon the purposes for which we are trying to use it. My judgment is that my sorting is superior for my purposes. There is, however, a still more important standard of judgment: statistical measurements indicating which variables fit most closely related. On this score, the Herzberg formulation—or some future contender—may prove superior to my very tentative mapping of the job-satisfaction area. I simply suggest that the student should be aware of the major lines of work in this area and make his own judgments.

On the importance of structural effects

One basic problem with the Maslow and Herzberg formulations is that they address themselves to the *individual* or to *aggregates* of individuals, without regard to the structural context within which behavior takes place and sentiments are formed.

For some purposes, it may be useful to sort jobs out in terms of certain criteria, regardless of their places in the social system; for other purposes, we need to recognize that each job has a particular place in the social system of the plant. The nature of that place has powerful effects upon the jobholder. It conditions the satisfactions available to him.

The individual's sentiments regarding achievement, advancement, and recognition cannot be understood without locating his job within the framework of jobs and the lines of promotion in the social system. Clearly, it makes a good deal of difference whether the individual is in a dead-end job or in an equally low-ranked job which fits into a long line of promotion.

How much does man like money, compared to other values to be had in his job? That seems like a straightforward question which should have a straightforward answer—you just give informants a list of values, including money, and ask them to rank the values in the order of importance. Indeed, that has been done in surveys, and respondents have been able to make such rankings, and yet we must remain skeptical as to what the responses mean. In the real world, money is not offered man in this neat and abstract form. Nor is money the simple stimulus that meat was to Pavlov's dogs, who responded to the sound of a bell or to a simple visual image.

In an hourly rated job, the amount of money earned is only remotely related to worker effort. On an incentive job, the connection is closer, yet even here the reward and response are imbedded in a complex structure. Management first has to establish a price, and that crucial operation is strongly influenced by the existing pattern of worker-management and union-management relations. How workers in general respond to that price depends upon the sentiments workers have concerning what is a "fair day's work for a fair day's pay" and upon the ways sanctions are brought to bear upon those not inclined to submit to the group norms.

For individual workers, we need to see responses to the incentive in terms of differential experiences in plant and community.

Wherever there are incentive rates, we can safely assume that money is an important concern to workers. But the degree of that concern will not be expressed simply in the degree of work effort the individual commits to the job. In some situations, the incentive also stimulates group pressures to hold down production and to protest to management. Such cases will be examined in Chapter 8.

It is structural effects such as these—effects of established patterns of relationships and the application of the programmed behavior of management systems and procedures—that need to be taken into account if we are to control and/or predict behavior in complex organizations. Theories like those of Maslow and Herzberg, which omit these structural effects, can at best only account for a small fraction of the variability of behavior that is to be observed. In this book, we are trying to develop a framework of analysis that will take these structural effects into account.

Symbols

Up to this point, we have been talking about the way the pattern of sentiments acquired by the individual affects his perceptions of objects and people around him. Let us now look outside him at those objects and people who make up his environment. The first thing to note is that the individual does not perceive all aspects of the object or person at the same level of attention and concern. In the case of a job he is to perform, for example, he sees a machine and materials, but beyond that he selects particular cues which enable him to evaluate the job from his own point of view. For example, he may observe that the machine is larger and more complex than the one on which he has been working. The cues of size and complexity may communicate to him that this is a higher prestige or status job than the one he has been on. Or he may perceive that in doing this job he would get much dirtier than he has been getting on his current job, and the cues that suggest dirt communicate to him that this is a lower prestige and hence less-desirable job.

Such cues I shall call *symbols. Symbols are words, objects, conditions, acts, or characteristics of persons which refer to (or stand for) the relations among men, and between men and their environment.*

Men use verbal symbols to express their sentiments. Other men respond to these symbols in terms of the pattern of their own sentiments. This perception of symbols activates or reinforces certain sentiments for the individual. Symbols may also serve to trigger certain activities and interactions, without any prior impact upon sentiments.

There are symbols related to territoriality, the use of physical space and the possession of physical objects. Most species of animals have definite attachments to particular territories. This can be determined by observing that the animal acts quite differently in his own territory from the way he acts when he is in the territory of another member of his species. The animal in his own territory will be much more aggressive toward other animals and his aggression will be much more effective than is the case when he is interacting with another animal of his species in that animal's territory.

Human beings appear to have similar attachments to territories, ranging from the boundaries of the national state to the individual's home. In the plant, individuals behave as if they owned certain work places, machines, and tools, even when all of these assets are the legal property of the company. The individual learns to recognize certain symbols indicating his own territory and distinguishing it from territories of others.

Even when two people come together who have never met before, they do not start from a blank slate. Each person has categories into which he places other people, most of these categories being shared with others in his community.

Sex is an obvious and universally recognized symbol. When A recognizes that B is a female, he immediately recognizes (without conscious thought) that certain behavior is appropriate and certain other behavior is not appropriate, the appropriateness or inappropriateness of a given unit of behavior being further influenced by other symbols, such as the time and place of their encounter and the social definitions he has learned regarding behavior. For example, an encounter with a female in a church service is different from an encounter with the same female in the corner bar.

Age is also another universally recognized symbol. While our society in general does not sort out behavior in terms of age differences as sharply as is the case in many other societies, nevertheless the individual intuitively recognizes that it makes a difference regarding appropriate behavior whether his encounter is with an older or with a younger person.

We do not need to see a person's birth certificate in order to make a judgment regarding his age. There is another age symbol that cannot be judged so readily at a glance: The individual's seniority with the organization or department—that is, the length of time of continuous service that he has accumulated with the organizational unit in question. Before the individual has been on the job long, he will have learned the seniority standing of those around him, and this set of symbols will influence his own conception of what he and they should be able to expect from the organization.

Ethnic and community status differences may also have an impact upon the work place. People are identified as Irish, Polish, Italian, Jewish, or Negro, according to characteristics of the name, facial features, hair color, skin color, and so on. On occasion, ethnic membership may serve to draw people together and differences in ethnic identification may stir rivalries.

Differences in status in the community are not so readily identified in the plant, and yet there may be behavior that suggests that difference. There tends also to be an associated characteristic: education. Organization members tend to learn how much education a given individual has had and to respond to him to some extent in terms of that degree of education.

Actions can also symbolize the relations among people. While the shaking of hands may be such a routine gesture as to evoke little reaction from the participants, the refusal of one party to shake hands when the gesture is expected is a symbol of hostility. Similarly, when two individuals have been in conflict with each other, and one of them proffers his hand, this is generally taken to be symbolic of friendlier sentiments.

Symbols are also associated with objects, activities, and conditions of work. For example, one highly skilled and well-paid woman in a large restaurant kitchen was very unhappy because she was referred to as the "fish woman," and she resented it bitterly when people walking by her station would sniff, wrinkle up their noses, and make unpleasant faces. She insisted that her proper title was "Sea Food Station Supervisor."[9]

Summary and conclusions

This chapter presents an approach to the problem of dealing with the subjective aspects of human relations. We not only interact and carry on activities; we also have feelings about what we are doing, about the people with whom we are associating, and about the world around us. We call "sentiments" those feelings of particular concern to us.

Sentiments are composed of the following three elements:

1. An idea about something or somebody; that is, a cognitive element.
2. Emotional content or affect.
3. A tendency to recur, upon presentation of the same symbols that have been associated with it in the past.

An important cluster of sentiments is that which make up the individual's *self-concept*. Within this cluster, we distinguish three elements: *status*, *personal worth*, and *level of aspiration*. Status involves the individual's evaluation of where he himself fits on a scale of social prestige. Personal worth involves the individual's judgment of how good a person he is, of what abilities he has and what he lacks. Level of aspiration points to how far the individual wishes to advance in his career.

The individual is also involved in the *evaluation of activities*, what

[9] W. F. Whyte, "Status in the Kitchen," *Human Relations in the Restaurant Industry* (New York: McGraw-Hill Book Co., 1948), Chap. 4, pp. 33–46.

things are good to do and what are bad, what activities have high prestige and what are looked down upon.

Every individual has his own sentiments of *personal identification*. He tends to feel that certain people are "for" him, while others are "against" him. Even among those he considers "for" him, he feels that some are close to him and others are more distant. He respects some people and does not respect others.

The individual also tends to look upon others in a vertical dimension, how high up they are in his subjective scale of social prestige. This we call *ranking*.

We do not directly observe sentiments. How then do we know what they are, and how can we tell whether Joe Jones indeed has a sentiment we attribute to him? Either in a standardized set of survey questions or in a less structured interview, we ask him how he feels, and he reports to us on his feelings. Or we observe him in action and from this infer something about his sentiments. Neither through questionnaires, interviews, nor observations can we be sure we are getting a true record of Joe's real sentiments. We make the best inferences we can, and we seek then to relate the sentiments we infer to the interactions and activities on which we are also getting data.

We have placed our interpretation of sentiments into three interrelated contexts:

1. *Time:* The individual is always judging his present situation in terms of his past and anticipated future experience.
2. *IRR:* The individual tends to balance his investments against the rewards he is getting. A negative or positive balance affects his sentiments correspondingly in regard to the situation for which he is making the judgment.
3. *Social relativity:* The individual evaluates the rewards or penalties he is receiving in relation to those being received by others with whom he tends to compare himself. (Factors determining the reference or comparison group will be discussed later, particularly as we deal with "inequities.")

We have also examined alternative ways of looking at sentiments—or at concepts closely related to sentiments. Maslow is particularly concerned with establishing a hierarchy of needs. In his approach, the manner in which the job situation satisfies or fails to satisfy these presumed basic human needs will determine the sentiments the individual holds toward his job. While we have tried to relate the Maslow needs approach, particularly as modified by Dickson and Roethlisberger, to our own framework, we have argued that the needs approach is so broad and general as to have little predictive value.

We have found the Herzberg two-factor theory of job satisfaction and motivation provocative and possibly useful. It seems to us fruitful to expand the intrinsic-extrinsic factors by adding a distinct category of social factors directly involving interpersonal relations. Furthermore, since individuals often have quite different sentiments toward their peers from those toward their superiors, the social factors might well be broken into two types.

The proposed distinction between relations with superiors and relations with peers is one aspect of our general criticism of both Maslow and Herzberg: their neglect of structural elements. Both men are concerned with the individual in general or with aggregates of individuals. In this book, we are trying to understand behavior in an organizational context.

The person orients himself to the world around him through cues he receives from his environment. We are particularly concerned with his social environment and with the cues we call symbols: words, objects, conditions, acts, or characteristics of persons which refer to (or stand for) the relations among men, and between men and their environment.

Symbols may indicate that a job or an office has high or low status, that a person or organization is friendly or hostile, that a given action is appropriate or inappropriate. Symbols affect sentiments and also may trigger changes in interactions and activities. At various points throughout this book, we will be pointing out how the appearance of a given symbol served to initiate changes in organizational behavior.

References

On social class and status symbols:

Warner, W. Lloyd, Eells, Kenneth, and Meeker, Marcia. *Social Class in America*. Chicago: Science Research Associates, 1948. Warner has been the most influential figure for several decades of anthropological and sociological research into social class in the United States.

Kahl, Joseph. *The American Class Structure*. New York: Rhinehart & Co., 1957. An analysis of several different approaches to the study of social class, indicating the extent to which different methods yield different conclusions.

On sentiments, IRR, and social relativity:

Zaleznik, A., Christensen, C. R., and Roethlisberger, F. J., with the assistance and collaboration of Homans, G. C. *The Motivation, Productivity and Satisfaction of Workers: A Prediction Study*. Boston: Harvard University Graduate School of Business Administration, 1958. A good statement of ideas particularly developed by Homans on IRR and social relativity.

On alternative approaches to the study of subjective life:

Maslow, A. *Motivation and Personality*. New York: Harper & Bros., 1954. A full presentation of Maslow's needs hierarchy schema.

Herzberg, F., Mausner, B., and Snyderman, B. *The Motivation to Work*, 2nd ed., New York: John Wiley & Sons, 1959. The basic book for the exposition of the Herzberg two-factor theory. For arguments pro and con, see the footnoted articles by House and Wigdor, and by Whitsett and Winslow. *Personnel Psychology*. Winter, 1967.

Discussion questions

1. Pick out a time when you felt particularly happy about a job you held. Describe the situation which gave rise to this high degree of satisfaction. Pick out a time when you felt particularly unhappy about a job you held. Describe the situation which gave rise to this extreme dissatisfaction.

Examine these two descriptions in terms of:

a) Maslow's "needs" schema.

b) Herzberg's "two-factor" theory.

c) Whyte's classification of sentiments in relation to IRR and social relativity.

On the basis of this exercise, what problems do you have in applying each schema? What tentative evaluations do you make of the possibilities and limitations of each schema? (Of course, you should not reach any firm conclusion on the basis of a single case. The problem is designed simply to give you experience in applying several theoretical frameworks to your own social world.)

2. Do the same exercise on the basis of *interviewing* someone who has had substantial job experience.

3. What are the significant *symbols* in your organization (factory or office, fraternity, or social club)? Select one for analysis. For each symbol cited, answer these two questions: How do you know it is significant or important? How do you know what it means?

6. Transactions

In my earlier book titled *Men at Work*, I rested my theoretical case almost entirely upon three fundamental concepts: interaction, activities, and sentiments. Useful as these concepts are, I have now come to the conclusion that they are not sufficient for our purposes.

Why do human beings engage in the particular patterns of interactions and activities that we observe? The last two chapters have only partly answered this question, with the discussion of satisfactions in our chapter on sentiments and symbols.

We confined our attention almost entirely to what we call intrinsic satisfactions: those that arise directly out of the interactions and activities of the job. These aspects are certainly important. If the individual does not have a job which permits him to interact in something approximating his customary pattern, we can expect him to show signs of strain and dissatisfaction, no matter what extrinsic rewards are offered on the job. Our examination of activities has also revealed certain intrinsic sources of satisfaction involved in traction and success in job performance.

While we urge the importance of intrinsic aspects, we can hardly claim that men and women seek employment simply to find an appropriate setting to act out their interaction patterns and to enjoy the gratification of absorbing work, successfully performed. We must recognize the important extrinsic aspects of work situations such as wages and fringe benefits and working conditions.

Departing from the Herzberg scheme, we have proposed a separate category of satisfaction-dissatisfaction: the social aspects of the job—the relations the jobholder has with others at his same level and above and below him. In this book we will be exploring some important aspects of these social relations. We need to broaden our framework still further. When we ask ourselves what the jobholder gets out of his job, we find ourselves thinking in terms of rewards and penalties. We begin with this common sense assumption: man continues doing that which is rewarded and stops doing that which is penalized. While research psychologists make all sorts of qualifications on this simple-minded statement to take

147

into account the nature of the rewards and penalties and the behavior emitted, etc., this general line of thinking is indeed supported by psychological experimentation.

We are now talking about what is known in psychology as *reinforcement theory*. If man is rewarded following the emission of a particular unit of behavior, he tends to emit further units of that behavior. If man is punished following the emission of a particular unit of behavior, then he tends to reduce the frequency of this kind of behavior.

Up to this point in our discussion of reinforcement theory, we have been dealing with the psychology of the individual. From Ivan Pavlov to B. F. Skinner, the great men in psychological experimentation upon animals have focused upon the behavior of the experimental *subject*, whether he be dog, monkey, or pigeon. They have not been concerned with examining the behavior and motivation of the human *experimenter* who produces the conditions to which the individual subject is reacting.

This is the crucial difference between our approach and that of the experimental psychologists. We recognize that among human beings most of the rewards and punishments experienced by the individual are offered him or imposed upon him by other human beings, directly or indirectly. We are concerned with both sides of this relationship: with the giver as well as the receiver of rewards and penalties. We shall call *transactions* those events involving the giving-receiving of rewards or penalties. Since we are dealing with both sides of the relationship, we shall have more types of events to examine than would be found by experimenters who are concerned only with a given experimental subject, be he lower animal or human being.

How explore this field of transactions? We began by examining the literature, both theoretical and substantive. On the theoretical side, we started with exchange theory, which has formed the basis of much of the theorizing to be presented below. On the substantive side, we reviewed various studies of the behavior of men in organizations and communities to see to what extent the recurring types of interpersonal events could be reinterpreted in terms of our evolving theory of transactions.

We then asked ourselves whether the behaviors that we were now inclined to see as transactions could be classified into a number of types so that we could deal with them in a more orderly fashion. To develop this scheme of classification, we have looked particularly at the values involved in each transaction, as perceived by the parties receiving the rewards or penalties. We have also been concerned with the temporal form of the transaction: whether it is accomplished simultaneously by both parties or by the parties alternating in their performance, whether the relationships involved tend to be continuing or not. We ask whether the relationships described tend to be governed by customary understandings or worked out through rational calculation. We might also ask whether the sources of the rewards and penalties are found directly among the participants in a given type of transaction or whether they are brought in from outside social units. Finally, we might distinguish in terms of simplicity-complexity.

The following table presents seven types of transactions. The table is constructed primarily in terms of the values involved and the temporal form in each transaction. The other characteristics will be considered in the discussion of each type.

Types, Forms and Values of Transactions

	Net Value Balance		
Type	For A	For B	Temporal Form
1. Positive exchange.......................+		+	Alternating
2. Trading................................+		+	Simultaneous
3. Joint payoff............................+		+	Simultaneous, continuing
4. Competitive...........................$\genfrac{}{}{0pt}{}{+}{-}$ or		$\genfrac{}{}{0pt}{}{-}{-}$	Simultaneous
5. Negative exchange.....................−		−	Alternating
6. Open conflict..........................−		−	Simultaneous, continuing
7. Bargaining............................−		−	Simultaneous, continuing
	+	−	
	−	+	
	+	+	

1. Positive exchange

Examination of this type of transaction has led to the development of exchange theory by sociologists such as George C. Homans,[1] Peter Blau,[2] and Alvin Gouldner.[3] The theory is based in large measure upon the pioneering study of the French anthropologist, Marcel Mauss.[4] Analysis of many ethnological studies led Mauss to the statement of the principle of reciprocity. If A gives a gift to B, or performs some valuable service for him, this action creates in B the sentiment of being obligated to A and the need to cancel this obligation in the future by means of a gift or service of like value.

---

[1] George C. Homans, *Social Behavior: Its Elementary Forms* (New York: Harcourt, Brace & World, 1961). Note however that Homans does not wish to be known as an exchange theorist. Commenting on an earlier version of this chapter, he wrote me, "Nor do I like to have the kind of theory I developed in *Social Behavior* be called an exchange theory. It is in fact a psychological theory. The basic propositions it uses are all psychological."

[2] Peter Blau, *Exchange and Power in Social Life* (New York: John Wiley & Sons, 1964).

[3] Alvin Gouldner, "The Norm of Reciprocity," *American Sociological Review*, Vol. 25, no. 2, (April, 1960), pp. 161–78.

[4] Marcel Mauss, *The Gift* (Glencoe, Ill.: The Free Press, 1954).

Mauss claimed that this principle is universal. While it is found in all cultures, it is the culture which determines the value of the gifts or services and specifies the forms and norms of exchange.

The relationship among the values being exchanged is not explicitly discussed, though both parties implicitly recognize the nature of the social bonds and obligations created and met. This type is alternating in temporal form. That is, A does something for B and B reciprocates only at some future time. B cannot postpone his reciprocation indefinitely without damaging his relationship to A, but neither is he expected to pay back the favor immediately.

We may distinguish between balanced and unbalanced exchange relationships, which have quite different correlates in the development of organization structure. In the balanced exchange, we have a reciprocal relationship between A and B. B reciprocates by giving to A at some later time goods or services that are of approximately equal value to those received. As such transactions continue, they tend to build or support favorable sentiments between the two men: they like each other. They also tend to promote the continuation of interaction between A and B and participation in joint activities.

The unbalanced exchange is one in which A provides B with goods or services that B needs and values, and B is not in a position to return the favor with like values. Peter Blau[5] examined cases of this subtype in his study of a government agency whose chief employees had the assignment of carrying out factory inspections. Blau found in this agency that there was a small number of individuals with prestige coming from expert knowledge and good judgment. When the average agent had a particularly perplexing problem, he would seek out one of these experts and ask for advice. The expert would, in effect, give him his time for the discussion of the problem and the service of the advice as to how to handle the problem. The expert agent did not in turn consult any average agent regarding his problems, and therefore the average agent was not able to balance accounts by giving as well as receiving advice. In such a case, the correlates in interactions, activities, and sentiments are different from those prevailing in balanced exchange. B may continue to go to A on a particularly difficult problem, but, recognizing his inability to reciprocate with advice, he tries to keep the interactions and activities involved in seeking advice from A at a minimum. In other words, in view of the unbalanced nature of the relationship, he tries not to ask too much and too often from A.

The unbalanced exchange also tends to generate positive sentiments from B to A, but here it seems more appropriate to describe the sentiments as respect rather than liking. In contrast to the balanced exchange,

---

[5] Peter Blau, *The Dynamics of Bureaucracy* (2nd ed.; Chicago: University of Chicago Press, 1963).

the unbalanced exchange tends to give rise to a differential in power between the two individuals. If A does more for B than B does for A, and B continues in this relationship, we may say that A has power over B. But what we mean by *power* is an important enough question to be treated in a later section of this chapter.

2. Trading

This type of transaction appears in several forms. The buying-selling relationship relates various parts of the organization to the outside world. In more primitive situations, the transaction can be carried out on a barter basis, one type of goods being exchanged for another. Within the organization, money can be involved in an accounting sense, credits or debits being transferred from one subunit to another. Trading does not need to be limited to transactions involving the transfer of money or other concrete resources. Services may be performed by the parties for each other without resources being transferred.

Trading is like positive exchange in that it produces plus values for both parties. It differs in three respects:

1. This type of transaction is simultaneous in temporal form instead of alternating. That is, the parties arrive at the same time at an agreement as to what each is to do for the other or give to the other, although the actual performance of the services or transfer of the resources may take place at different times in the future.
2. The values to be transferred are stated explicitly, at least in major part. That is, while the parties presumably make no attempt to discuss the intrinsic satisfactions they are going to get out of the transaction, they do make explicit the extrinsic values that are to be transferred.
3. In trading, the values that are transferred are always different. That is, in a trading transaction, A may agree to give B $200 for a typewriter, but A does not agree to give B $200 in order to have B give him $200. While positive exchange sometimes involves transfers of different types of values, positive exchange often involves the passing back and forth of the same type of value: A gives a gift to B and later B reciprocates by giving a gift of similar value to A; A buys a drink for B and later B buys a drink for A, and so on.

How does this type of transaction affect sentiments? We formulate our answer in terms of two assumptions: (1) this is not an isolated event and A and B become involved in a continuing series of trading relationships, and (2) each party is equally free to make the transaction with this particular partner or to refrain from making it.

The first assumption is important because we cannot expect to observe much effect upon the sentiments of the two parties through a single trading transaction—unless the outcome of this particular transaction proves to be extraordinarily disadvantageous or advantageous to one or both of the parties. If you observe a man entering into a store where he has never been before and buying an object from a salesman that he has never before encountered and then you ask him later how he feels about that salesman, the chances are that he will find this a meaningless question —unless the transaction involved a long period of interaction. On the other hand, if two individuals engage in a continuing series of trading relationships, we can assume that they are deriving satisfaction out of these transactions, and we can also assume that this satisfaction with the transactions will have a favorable effect upon sentiments toward the partner in the transactions.

Both of the foregoing assumptions regarding sentiments depend upon the assumption stated earlier that the trading transaction takes place under free market conditions: A and B are equally free to engage in or to decline to enter into the transaction. Under such conditions, we can assume that A and B each give up what they need less in order to receive what they need more, and thus both make a profit. Out of such profitable transactions favorable interpersonal sentiments grow.

Under monopoly conditions we make no such assumptions regarding sentiments. The case of the company store in the company town illustrates this monopoly condition. In this situation, the worker would continue to do his buying in the store simply because he had no other alternative, but we would not expect the interactions and activities involved in company-store buying to lead to favorable sentiments of the worker either toward the storekeeper or toward the company that owned the store.

The same point regarding monopoly conditions can be made regarding relations internal to the company organization and for transactions where money is not involved. Let us say that we are dealing with a trading of two forms of activity: what A does for B and what B does for A. If B can get what he needs only from A, whereas A can get what he needs from B, C, D, E, etc., we recognize a condition analogous to the economic monopoly position of the company store. Sometimes we describe this imbalance by saying that in relation to A, "B has a poor bargaining position."

What happens under such monopoly or imbalance conditions? Let us illustrate with two extreme examples:

1. In spite of his superior bargaining position, A is willing to trade with B on something approximating the terms proposed by B. This tends to generate positive sentiments on the part of B toward A, and it also increases the probability that A will be able to initiate activity for B in the future (outside of the trading relationships). For example, A gets B to support him in an effort to increase the budget for A's department.
2. A takes advantage of his superior bargaining position to delay his

compliance with B's wishes and to exact from B a much larger contribution than B would be willing to give if B could get what he needs from alternative sources. This condition leads B to feel that he is being treated unfairly and to generate negative sentiments toward A. As long as B has no alternatives available, he will continue trading with A, but he will look for ways of redressing the imbalance. He may oppose something that A wants to get done (outside of the trading relationship), or he may appeal to a mutual superior to penalize A.

3.   Joint payoff

This type is similar to the two before in that positive values are involved for both parties. It is like trading (but not like positive exchange) in that the values sought tend to be stated explicitly and the activities to be carried out simultaneously. It differs from both in that the sources of the extrinsic rewards are outside of the parties engaged in the joint activities. That is, success or failure in the activities engaged in by the parties determines the rewards-penalties in which they share, and these rewards-penalties are provided by individuals, groups, or organizations outside of the immediate joint payoff relationship.

In business management, the formation of a partnership puts in legal form the intention of the partners to engage in joint payoff activities. Note here that the nature of the extrinsic rewards-penalties is explicitly worked out in the formation of the partnership, but the intrinsic and the social rewards tend to remain on an implicit level. In fact, we may hypothesize that if the parties in interactions and activities do not experience intrinsic and social satisfactions through working together, the joint payoff activities will not long continue. Nevertheless, the joint payoff activities tend to be focused upon gaining extrinsic rewards from the environment around the participants.

In the manufacturing plant situation, individuals who are engaged in jobs that are compensated for with a group piece rate are in effect engaged in joint payoff transactions among the members of this group. That is, the money rewards of each individual depend upon the performance of all the other individuals in the work group together. A superior performance by the group brings higher than ordinary rewards to all members of the group, whereas an inferior performance penalizes them all alike. Of course, we do not assume that workers on a group piece rate are engaged in only one type of transaction: the joint payoff. Pointing to the transaction in this case simply means that the job situation is so structured that the individual's rewards or penalties depend upon the performance of the group of which he is a part. There are, of course, other rewards and penalties experienced by the workers quite apart from those that come directly through membership in a particular pay system.

Can we conceive of joint payoff transactions involving units larger than a work group? If a formula is devised whereby extra compensation is paid to all members of the work force of a plant on the basis of certain measures of plantwide performance, then, at least as far as this formula and this extra compensation are concerned, the workers involved are engaged in a joint payoff situation. This is what we find in the Scanlon Plan[6] and similar arrangements that are designed to establish joint payoffs on a plantwide basis.

4. Competitive

At first I was inclined to call this type "competitive zero sum," but I now feel that the addition of the terms, "zero sum," make the concept too restrictive. Zero sum applies to one subtype of situation where A and B are in direct competition and what A wins B loses, and vice versa.

We have an apparently pure case of zero sum in games or sports contests. If Teams A and B are playing against each other, then if A wins, B necessarily loses, and vice versa. Excluding ties, if there is a winner, there must also be a loser. Nevertheless, even in this apparently pure case, if we look at the values as *perceived* by the participants, we do not necessarily come out with a zero sum. Let us assume that team A is expected to defeat team B easily. A does indeed win but only after withstanding a much more severe challenge than was expected. The members of team A are happy that they have won—they may even derive additional satisfactions through having thrown back a severe test rather than gaining an easy victory. The members of team B, while they would have been still happier if they had pulled off the upset, can now get the satisfaction of claiming a "moral victory." In other words, if we take the expectations of the parties into account, even in the apparently pure case of an athletic contest, it does not follow that the gains of one party are exactly equal to the losses of the other.

Within organizations, gains and losses are neither so readily calcuable nor so easy to balance as they are in games or sports. Nevertheless, relations often do seem to be structured in a competitive fashion, so that party A gains its rewards through actions which tend to penalize party B. We find this, for example, in the classic friction between the inspection and production departments. Inspectors gain their rewards through finding deficiencies in the performance of the production departments, and workers and especially their supervisors in production tend to be penalized through the points that are scored against them in inspection. While few organizational units are in such a built-in plus-minus relationship, we frequently observe competitive struggles between production and sales, production and engineering, and so on. Specific issues often arise in such a way that they are perceived in a win-lose format.

---

[6] W. F. Whyte *et al.*, *Money and Motivation* (New York: Harper & Bros., 1955), pp. 166–88.

In competitive situations, the relative outcome may be more important than the absolute outcome in affecting the future sentiments and interactions and activities of the competitors. Let us say that Jones and Smith are in competition for the same position in the organization. Jones gets the promotion, and Smith gets a small salary increase. In absolute terms, we can say that Smith has gained something, but in this type of situation Smith will no doubt feel that he has lost and he will react accordingly.

Competitive relations among individuals and between groups are likely to stimulate the participants to increased efforts, and they tend to create or intensify negative sentiments from competitor to competitor. If individuals A and B or groups A and B, which have been and continue to be in competition with each other, as seen by the participants, are asked or ordered by an organizational superior to "cooperate," we can expect to observe difficulties of participants in arriving at any stable pattern of interactions and activities, and we can expect to hear expressions of negative sentiments—with each individual blaming his competitor or each group blaming the other group for poor performance.

If the competitive transactions are on the level of intergroup relations, we can expect to observe increased cohesion among the members of each group and increasingly hostile sentiments toward the opposite group. If there turns out to be a clear loser in this intergroup competition, the loss is likely to have the effect of stirring dissension within the group, with some individuals blaming the others for the defeat. A case along this line will be described in the next part as we deal with group and intergroup level problems.

Before finishing our discussion of competition, we need to introduce a note of conceptual clarification. We have given a good deal of emphasis to the negative effects of competitive transactions. This seems to be at odds with prevailing American beliefs regarding the positive values of competition. While we have no wish to become involved in an argument about the total effects of competition in the economy and society of the United States, it is important to point out that such arguments tend to arise out of a failure to distinguish among types of competitive situations. For our purposes, we need to distinguish between the two extremes of *pure win-lose* and *pure independence*.

In the pure win-lose situation, one competitor can only win by imposing a defeat on the other. At the other extreme, the two competitors are completely independent of each other. For example, let us say that there are two research groups in a company research and development department. The groups are working on two different problems and are not sharing the same work space or equipment. In such a situation, each group may be stimulated by the presence of the other and by knowledge of the progress of the other group. Members may respond as if by saying to themselves, "Let's see if we can solve our problem better and faster than they can solve theirs." At the same time, in our hypothetical case, since neither group can prevent the other from doing its job, the situation is not likely to provoke the intense negative sentiments between groups we find under pure win-lose conditions.

In presenting these two types of competitive situations, we have of course greatly oversimplified. In life there are many situations which fall somewhere between pure win-lose and pure independence—where the success of one competitor is neither completely independent of, nor completely dependent upon, the failure of the other competitor. For example, the research laboratory situation imagined above may easily include features that compromise its pure independence. It may be that the two groups are in competition for scarce work space and that the group which wins the competition is able to establish more favorable conditions for the solutions of its own problems than are now open to the other group. It may be that the two groups are in competition for scarce items of equipment and for differing amounts of the departmental research budget. Furthermore, naturally the participants will assume that the success or failure of their particular project, compared to the other project, will help to determine who gets promotions, increased budgets, and other advantages in the future. But even when we introduce these complications, we still must recognize that team A cannot directly prevent team B from succeeding or vice versa, as in the case of pure win-lose situations.

In this book we will be particularly concerned with competitive transactions that are perceived as toward the pure win-lose end of the continuum. However, especially as we consider in our chapters on research and development what is meant by the creation of a climate that stimulates creativity, we will need to give attention to conditions which promote competitive transactions that tend toward the other end of the continuum toward independence.

5.   Negative exchange

This is the obverse of positive exchange: the values involved are negative, but the form is also alternating. A tries to do some damage to B and later B tries to do some damage to A. This is a very common type and tends to be explicitly recognized in conversation. We often hear one person saying that he needs to "get even" with another or wants to "pay him back," thus making clear the balanced nature of the transaction.

In cases of negative reciprocity (an exchange of more or less equal negative values), we observe the creation or maintenance of sentiments of mutual hostility. This situation tends to be unstable. When A and B are not obligated to maintain the interactions and activities in question, there is a tendency (1) to break off relations altogether, or (2) to escalate the hostilities to the type next to be discussed.

In an unbalanced relationship (where A can impose much more damage on B than B can impose upon A directly), we observe the following tendencies: (1) If B can do so without suffering greater losses than A imposes on him, he will terminate the relationship with A. (2) If B is not in the situation where he can terminate the relationship, we observe him continuing to respond to the initiatives of A. At the same time, B tries to do damage to A in such a concealed manner as to escape punishment. This situation also tends to lead B to look to others in a similar position so that they can somehow join forces against A.

This sort of unbalanced relationship is frequently observed in supervisor-subordinate relations. The superior is in the position to penalize his subordinate directly, whereas the individual subordinate cannot directly impose negative values upon the superior. In this situation, the subordinate has two general alternative courses of action (which he sometimes pursues simultaneously). The subordinate seeks to follow the orders of his superior, but to perform in such a way as to penalize the superior without incurring additional penalties himself. We often hear of this strategy being used as workers begin following management directives and supervisory orders in such a slavish fashion that productivity is markedly reduced. In almost any work situation we will find that there has accumulated over the years a set of detailed rules and regulations designed to meet particular types of problems. In other situations, workers will tend to ignore those rules and regulations which, in their judgment, do not apply to the situation in hand, and supervisors will encourage them to do so. The strategy of legalism tends to put the superior in an awkward position. He can hardly tell a subordinate to go ahead and violate certain rules, and he will also find it difficult to penalize the subordinate directly for obeying the rules. The subordinate may thus be able to "get even" with his superior without escalating the conflict.

The slavish rule-following strategy is more likely to be a collective than an individual response. If the subordinate is a worker and this is a unionized situation, he may take another pathway that tends to transform the individual problem into a collective problem. He may submit a grievance against his foreman and seek to get union officials involved in pushing this grievance.

In our section on union-management relations, we will undertake some detailed exploration of negative exchange transactions.

6. Open conflict

This resembles negative exchange in that negative values are involved for both parties but differs in that the temporal form is not alternating, but rather simultaneous and continuing. On a group or organizational basis, this represents strikes, or physical conflicts between groups or communities or nations. Of course, this type of transaction tends to reinforce negative sentiments between persons, groups, organizations, communities, or nations. As in Type 5, we must distinguish between the extrinsic losses suffered by both sides and the satisfactions (sentiments) enjoyed by each in damaging the other.[7]

7.   Bargaining

Bargaining is a complex set of transactions. It can and often does include transactions of each of the types previously discussed, with one exception. Positive exchange is unlikely to be involved, because the parties are seeking to make very explicit what the terms of the agreement are to be. An exchange of personal favors may be important between union and management in the day-to-day life of a plant, but in the bargaining process itself, what each party is to get and what each party is to give up tend to be openly discussed and finally reduced to writing.

Bargaining differs from trading in two important respects. Trading simply involves the working out of the conditions for an exchange of positive values, whereas in bargaining negative values are prominently involved. We may have trading transactions between two individuals where each is free to make a trade or not to trade, whereas what we call bargaining also arises in such situations where two parties are so inter-locked in each others' affairs that they are not free to withdraw from the relationship. Finally, while we can imagine bargaining taking place be-tween two individuals who represent no one but themselves, we find that bargaining nearly always is a collective phenomenon. The bargainers speak as representatives of others, and indeed bargaining sessions are very rarely limited to two individuals, one representing each party.

The process of bargaining does not in itself involve the distribution of values indicated in the chart, but rather the parties talk about what they want or intend to do in ways that symbolize these values.

For example, a union leader says that unless management concedes such and such a demand, the workers will go out on strike (negative values for both parties, with workers losing their pay while management loses the

---

[7] Eustace Theodore has proposed an additional type: "totalitarian exchange." In the concentration camp or traditional prison, A, the superior, has practically com-plete control over B, the subordinate. A can thus take actions that are perceived as negative to B and yet have B respond with actions gratifying to A. This is a plus-minus transaction but differs from the competitive plus-minus in that in the competitive transaction the participants do not know in advance which one will get the plus and which one the minus. In the totalitarian situation, it is always A who gets the plus and B the minus. For the sake of logical completeness, perhaps the totalitarian type should be included. On the other hand, the most common and also the most important problems to students of organizational behavior are those where behavior is not completely physically coerced and at least some small element of voluntarism is open to both parties. We do not need to ask why B obeys A when A has power of life and death, or of extreme physical coercion over him. In this book we shall be concerned with relationships where power is not *absolute*. Therefore, while acknowledging the existence of "totalitarian exchange," we will not discuss it further in this book.

production). Or the discussion takes the form of simply determining how much of management's resources it is going to turn over to workers— competitive in form because the gains achieved by the union will be directly at the expense of management. Or the parties may discuss how they are going to resolve some problem that is of concern to both parties—plus values being sought on both sides simultaneously.

It should be noted that a strike does not necessarily impose equal negative values on both sides. There can be situations where business is slack and the company has a high inventory so that a strike will impose little if any loss on management unless it carries on for an extended period of time. In such a case, the union leaders may not be able to assume an equal desire on the part of management people to avoid a strike. Similarly, there are sometimes cases (as in newspaper strikes in New York City) where the unions are in the position to pay such high strike benefits as to almost approximate regular wages, so that management cannot assume that union leaders and workers have an equally vital stake in avoiding or ending a strike.

I assume that bargaining rarely if ever consists of a sole type of transaction. We can nevertheless examine the distribution among types of transactions involved in the bargaining and on this basis predict the interpersonal and intergroup sentiments that will be observed following the conclusion of the bargaining. If minus-minus or plus-minus transactions have predominated, we can expect negative sentiments to prevail. If there have been instances of plus-plus transactions also involved, we can expect more positive sentiments to emerge.

We shall seek to apply this framework on bargaining to our discussion of union-management relations in Part VI.

Dynamic tendencies

These transactions appear to differ in degrees of stability–instability: the tendency in a given interpersonal or intergroup relationship for the same transaction to keep recurring.

I assume that Types 4 and 5 (competitive and negative exchange) are inherently unstable. Parties that engage in such transactions frequently are likely to find their negative sentiments so increased as to escalate the interchange to Type 6 (open conflict).

Unfortunately for mankind, Type 6 (open conflict) tends to be a good deal more stable than Types 4 or 5. As A punishes B, the punishment he receives from B tends to reinforce in A the desire to punish B further and perhaps more severely. The forms of conflict may "escalate," but the transaction type remains basically minus for minus values. From union-management relations to the Vietnam war, men have shown impressive (and depressing) capacities to endure punishment and come back for more.

I assume that Type 1 (positive exchange) may have great stability in a small closed society. In a larger more open community, when A has a positive exchange with B, we need to take into account that B is also engaged in positive transactions with C, D, and perhaps others. Thus, after receiving a favor from A, B may find himself so involved with C, D, and others that it becomes too costly for him to balance his accounts with A.

Similarly, Types 2 and 3 (trading and joint payoff) seem to me to have no intrinsic tendencies to instability, but we must always bear in mind that the partners in these transactions may also be engaging in transactions with other individuals or groups. We might assume that the greater the frequency of interactions and activities that the partners in a given set of transactions have with individuals and groups outside of this particular transactional relationship, compared to the interactions and activities within a transactional relationship, the greater will be the tendency for these positive transactions to break down. In other words, the maintenance of these positive transactions may depend upon building up the frequency and duration of interactions and activities between the partners in the transaction.

How are transactional values determined?

We are talking about values as perceived by the participants in particular types of transactions. At this point, Peter Blau has pointed to an apparent ambiguity in our schema. Commenting on negative exchange and open conflict types, he writes (personal letter):

. . . is there no concealed gain in "getting even"? In both types 5 and 6, what induces either party to continue, if it is not some hidden gain from hurting the other?

Blau is of course correct; in the types he notes, A does get satisfactions from imposing penalties on B and vice versa. Nevertheless, if we followed this line of reasoning to its logical conclusion, the distinctions among our types of transactions would be hopelessly blurred. We would simply be saying that all conscious behavior is motivated, which means that the actor seeks to get some positive value out of the behavior in question. Thus, in all transactions involving negative values, we would have to show positive values appearing also. To further complicate our problem, we could argue that all transactions involving positive values also necessarily involve some negative values. For example, when A does a favor for B, A is giving up time, valued resources, or effort or a combination of all of these.

Such an argument leads us to the conclusion that all transactions involve positive and negative values on both sides—which makes all transactions similar and destroys our typology. To escape from such a dead end generalization, we must distinguish between the *giver* and the *receiver* of the value in question in each type of transaction.

Plus or minus values are assigned to each party in each transaction type *solely on the basis of the values perceived by the receiver*. For example, in the case of negative exchange, we place a minus in the A column to indicate that A is *receiving* negative values from B and also a minus in the B column to indicate that B is receiving negative values from A. For purposes of our classification schema, we are solely concerned with the perceptions of the *receiver*. For the moment we are not concerned with how A feels about the damage he is doing to B.

When we consider the *sentiments* of each party to the transaction, at that point we are indeed concerned with the feelings of the *giver* as well as of the *receiver*. We simply did not take the *giver* into account in setting up our plus and minus signs in the transactional diagram.

In separating elements that in common sense terms may seem to belong together, are we not being arbitrary? I would argue that such a separation is essential in order to advance our analysis. We may have a feeling that X and Y belong together, but if we are interested in the relations between X and Y, we need to separate them conceptually before we can examine the relations between them. We follow the same logic here. We set up our transactional typology solely upon the values perceived by the receiver. We then ask how participation in a given transactional type affects the sentiments *of both parties*.

We are now ready to answer the question: What influences the perceptions of values on the part of the receiver? The following points seem important to us:

1. *Concrete measurable units or structural conditions generally recognized in the society as a whole.* To illustrate the influence of a concrete and measurable value, let us say that A offers B $5 for a pig when the current market price for this size and quality of pig is $10. While we may not be able to predict how strongly B will feel about this offer, we can predict that unless B is feebleminded, insane, or unaware of market prices, he will consider the proposed transaction unfair and will react negatively to it and to the proposer.

An athletic contest is an example of a situation that is clearly structured and so universally recognized that the participants cannot vary much in their perception of the distribution of the values. At least they will recognize that where there is a winner, there will also be a loser (subject to the qualifications noted earlier.)

2. *To some extent the magnitude of values is perceived in terms of the culture in which the perceiver is a member.* That is, it is apparently a universal phenomenon that if A does something for B, B will feel obligated to do something for A. The value of what A does for B and the value therefore of what B should do in return are in part culturally determined. That is, a big favor given deserves a big favor in return, but

the determination of what is meant by bigness depends in part upon the definitions given by the common understandings arising in the culture of society in general or of that particular organization.

3. *Investment-rewards relationship and social comparison process.* Suppose we know that in a given joint payoff transaction A gains three times as much as B. This fact alone would lead us to assume that B would consider the transaction inequitable and would react negatively toward his partner. But suppose we also know that A has invested approximately three times as much as B in time, effort, and resources. In that case, the rewards of the two parties will be proportional to their investments. If A and B both perceive the investment-rewards relationship in the same fashion, B may be quite satisfied with the transaction and willing to continue, manifesting the same positive sentiments toward A.

Here we are applying Homans' notions about the IRR in order to estimate the values that each party is getting out of the transaction. We are saying that human beings react as if they felt that the rewards they get should be proportionate to their investments.

Human beings also evaluate their rewards or the penalties they suffer in terms of the experience of those around them. Thus, a particular transaction that promises to offer Smith a net positive value balance in his IRR may still be rejected if Smith feels that others in positions similar to his have entered into similar transactions and have been much more highly rewarded than he is to be.

4. *The personality, as a product of social experience.* As the individual grows up and continues to live in society, he experiences an endless series of transactions. If his experience has been predominantly with a particular type of transaction, he is likely to perceive each new situation as representing that type of transaction. For example, let us say that the individual has had most of his experience with competitive transactions or with negative exchange. This sort of experience has shaped his orientation to the world so that he is likely to assume that each new situation represents a plus-minus or minus-minus transaction. Thus, if someone appears to be offering him a plus-plus transaction, the individual is first likely to assume that there must be some trick to it.

We must not assume that the individual's style of perception is all-important in defining the nature of a given transaction. Some transactions will appear to be so clear and unambiguous as to be perceived in approximately the same way by all who experience them. On the other hand, there are situations where the transaction offered appears to be ambiguous and also situations presenting more than one type of transaction at the same time. It is in situations like these where there is ambiguity as to the type of transaction or where more than one type is involved that the individual's style of perception is particularly important.

In the determination of transactional values, as perceived by the participants, we are examining perceptions of the transactions before they are acted out. That is, A and B may enter into a joint payoff transaction where it turns out that A gains the major share of the rewards and B is not rewarded nearly in proportion to his contribution to the transaction. Whether or not it was planned in this way, the outcome is likely to persuade B that future transactions with A are more likely to be of the competitive than of the joint payoff type.

5. *The nature of the social structure and of the positions of A and B in it.* Large disparities in power between A and B tend to perpetuate an exchange rate that is apparently disadvantageous to B, who holds the inferior position. We must distinguish between *acceptance of* and *satisfaction with* the exchange rate between A and B. If B sees no possibility of changing the situation, he continues to deal with A, but he still may not be satisfied with this relationship. Before going farther with this point, we need to ask what we mean by *power* and how power relates to IAS as well as to transactions.

What is power?

What is power? Can we give a behavioral science answer to a question that is usually discussed in philosophical or even metaphysical terms?

First we need to divide that question into two questions:

1. How can we observe power being exercised?
2. Upon what elements is the exercise of power based? In other words, what determines how power is distributed between A and B and others in the same situation?

We observe the exercise of power in the initiation of changes in activities, particularly in *set events*. In events involving A, B, C, and D, if A is the one who characteristically initiates changes in activities for B, C, and D, we can say that A has more power than B, C, and D. "Characteristically" implies quantification. We can observe and count *set events*.

Note that so far we have done nothing more than give a name to a set of observations. We have defined power in terms of observable behavior. We have said nothing about how A acquires power over B, C, and D.

Power relations arise out of unbalanced exchanges, both positive and negative, and also out of unbalanced trading transactions and open conflict. When A and B are engaged in reciprocal positive exchange transactions, such behavior provides no evidence of a power differential between them. It is only as A does more for B than B is able to do in return that a power differential in favor of A arises. We noted in the Blau study that the expert agents helped the rank and file by offering information and advice. They were not paid back through information and advice from the lower status agents. But when group activities were organized, it was regularly the expert agents who either took the initiative or endorsed a suggestion of one of the rank and file. It was only the expert agents who were able to initiate activity changes for two or more other individuals.

In trading transactions, building of power depends upon one of the two parties holding a monopolistic advantage: A can get what he wants from B, C, D, etc., whereas B can only get what he wants from A. In this situation, A can increase his power over B, outside of the trading relationship, through declining to exploit fully his monopolistic advantage. That is, he responds to B's requests and proposals on terms more favorable to B than B could get if A chose to exercise his monopolistic advantage to the fullest extent. As noted earlier, this sort of response by A generates or reinforces in B favorable sentiments toward A, and it also increases the likelihood that A will be able to initiate activity for B (outside of the trading relationship).

If A chooses to exercise fully his monopolistic advantage, we can describe this as an exercise of power by A, but this action involves a spending rather than an accumulating of power. By acting in this manner, A tends to provoke or reinforce B's negative sentiments toward him, which leads B to more active searching for ways of getting what he wants without dealing with A or of getting other people to penalize A.

If he wishes to exploit his monopolistic advantage and still maintain (or increase) his power over B, A must resort to other types of transactions. He may engage in unbalanced negative exchanges in which he is able (directly) to penalize B more heavily that B can penalize him (directly). We add the word "directly" to suggest that in organizations the man holding the superior formal position usually has greater opportunities to penalize a subordinate than the subordinate can apply directly to him, but we have already indicated that subordinates often find ways to penalize their superiors indirectly.

As a last resort, A may engage in open conflict with B. In effect, this indicates that the distribution of power between the two men is in some doubt. If such an open conflict does arise, it is only through winning it that A is able to consolidate or re-establish his power and thus his favored position in the control of resources.

Underlying all this discussion of power is the question of alternatives. We defined A's monopolistic advantage over B in terms of A's ability to get what he wants from others as well as B, whereas B can only get what he wants from A. To the extent that B can find others who are able and willing to supply him with what he has been wanting to get from A, B will have decreased A's power over him. In that case, B can withdraw wholly or in part from his relationship with A, or else demand from A terms more favorable to B in future trading transactions.

This note on alternatives suggests a relationship between the distribution of power and interpersonal exchange rates. Let us say that there are extreme differences in power between A and B. B is highly dependent upon A for much of what he wants out of life and has no alternative sources for the satisfaction of his needs, whereas A can get what he wants from many others beyond B. A can penalize B much more heavily than B can penalize A. In this situation, B may not be happy over his exchange rate with A, but he will accept it at least in the sense of not protesting openly. In fact, if A then does not exploit his power advantage to its fullest extent, B may be grateful for what an outside observer would consider very small favors.

If the power differential between A and B becomes narrowed, B will no longer accept the exchange rate that formerly prevailed between A and B. He will demand more favorable terms.

On identifying transactional types and measuring values

We have classified transactions in terms of the way they are perceived by participants. Can we now objectify this area of study, putting ourselves in the role of observer instead of perceiver?

As noted before, perceptions are by no means divorced from realities. We certainly do not assume that how a given transaction is perceived is entirely dependent upon the personality of the perceiver. Through observation and interviews, we can note that certain situations tend to be perceived in characteristic ways. Such observations should enable us to increase the predictability of behavior through transactional analysis.

Can we measure the values involved in transactions? Some aspects of these values are concrete and subject to observation—for example, money and the time spent on a certain activity.

The economist bases his analysis primarily (but not exclusively) upon these concrete values. We recognize the importance of subjective aspects: the values that the individual seeks which cannot readily be expressed either in money or in other concrete terms. At first thought, it might seem that it would be impossible to measure these subjective aspects, but in fact this is what behavioral scientists are doing all the time when they deal with surveys including attitudes and values. We do not claim to be able to measure exactly how Jones and Smith feel about each other, but we can ask them questions designed to elicit these interpersonal attitudes, and we assume that there is some relationship between the attitudes thus expressed and the unmeasurable feelings possessed by the respondents. It seems to me, therefore, that the task of measuring the values involved in a given transaction or in a series of transactions is not inherently any more difficult than many other tasks we set ourselves in attitude surveys. We would simply have to change the questions we customarily ask in order to fit questions and answers into our transactional framework.

Up to this point we have attempted no measurement of transactional values beyond the simple allocation of plus or minus signs. We assume that a large plus experience will affect the individual more than a small plus experience, and similarly with negative experiences, but now we are simply at the point of discriminating between plus and minus signs and noting the common combinations of these signs which arise when two parties are involved in transactions with each other. If we can draw some useful conclusions out of this very crude sorting out of social experience, then it will pay us to bend our efforts toward finer discriminations and greater quantification.

We can make the most precise and best controlled studies of transactions in laboratory situations. There we can exercise control over the situation so that the experimental subjects only experience the type of transaction to which we wish to expose them. Real life situations outside of the laboratory may present rather few cases of situations where only one type of transaction is involved. Most situations in organizations involve a mix of types, but we would not expect the mix to be indiscriminate. We should expect to find that among individuals at certain specified positions in a given organization, there is a characteristic distribution of transactions being experienced. We should be able at least to make crude discriminations among the major types of transactions observed and to note changes in frequencies of given types—an operation whose theoretical and practical importance will be discussed at the conclusion of this chapter.

It is important to examine transactions in terms of the particular human relationships involved. The need for such a viewpoint becomes especially clear as we examine situations where two or more types of transactions seem to be taking place. For example, we may have a group of workers regulating their own behavior in such a way as to indicate their perception of the work situation in terms of a joint payoff transaction among the workers—each one shares payoffs with all the others. At the same time and in the same situation, we may observe that workers are responding to management in terms of a negative exchange transaction, feeling penalized by the supervisor and seeking to "get back" at him. In order to keep our thinking clear, therefore, *we must always specify the particular relationships involved in any given transaction.*

Level of analysis

We have illustrated this approach mainly at the individual level. The scheme should also be applicable at the group and organizational level.

To make such higher level applications, we need again to specify the relationships involved. Is a given plant-level union-management relationship characterized by predominantly negative or predominantly positive transactions? To answer that question, we need to examine not only the transactions between leaders of both organizations but also between leaders and the rank and file. For example, let us say that A (for management) and B (for the union) see themselves as developing positive exchange and trading transactions, and perhaps even engaging in certain joint payoff transactions. They appear before university and other public industrial relations meetings to explain how it is that the union and management are able to get along so well together, and these appearances give each of them a good deal of personal satisfaction.

In this situation, will the union rank and file view the union-management relationship in the favorable light seen by their leader? They will not, unless they also see themselves as participating in positive exchange, trading, and perhaps even joint payoff relationships with the union leader and with members of management. In other words, the sentiments of lower levels of an organization cannot be predicted simply on the basis of examining the transactions engaged in by organizational leaders.

Transactions in relation to IAS

I have used the concepts of interaction, activities, and sentiments in the process of defining and explaining transactional types. At this point, let me state what I conceive to be the relationship between the concept of transactions and IAS.

Each type of transaction represents a particular combination of IAS. That is, in discussing and carrying out a given transaction, the parties are engaged in interactions and activities. They express their sentiments in discussion of a given transaction, and the nature of that transaction and the outcome of that transaction have effects upon their sentiments.

In previous chapters, I have emphasized that changes in IAS can and do come about through changes in technology, workflow and organization structure. This is true whether or not the planners of the changes intend to affect the IAS of the people involved. But do IAS changes only come about through changes in technology, workflow, and formal organization structure? Important as those changes are, I would argue that changes are also introduced into IAS through the transactional route.

I assume that a given IAS pattern in an organization is associated with a certain distribution in the frequencies of the various types of transactions. If we observe IAS changing, we are likely to find that the distribution of types of transactions in the organization has also changed. If we wish to introduce IAS changes, we may do so by changing the frequency of the types of transactions being experienced by the organizational members.

For example, let us say that a given plant-level union-management relationship has been marked by friction and conflict, frequent interruptions of production, and generally a low level of productivity. If we want to resolve the conflict and get union and management working effectively together, we need to reduce the frequency of transaction Types 4, 5, and 6, and increase the frequency of Types 1, 2, and 3. Note that this apparently simple prescription does not tell the union or management leader "how to do it." It does provide a theoretical framework upon which to build a strategy of action. In our chapters on union-management relations, we will further explore the theoretical bases and the practical implications of the transaction framework.

This framework does *not* depend upon the assumption that the transactions we observe are rationally planned by the participants to achieve their particular objectives. Even in the most highly organized social unit, the individual will frequently confront situations that were not planned for at all by any organizational participant. He will also encounter transactions that were intended by the planners to yield plus values for the participants and yet which turned out in practice to yield minus values. However, the fact that many of the situations facing us in life are not the result of any conscious planning does not prevent us from examining the transactions that actually occur. Nor does it prevent us from using our transactional analysis to achieve better control over the flow of organizational life.

Summary and conclusions

With *transactions*, we complete our discussion of the basic concepts we shall use throughout this book in examining problems at the individual, group, and organizational level.

Here we are dealing with types of interpersonal (intergroup or interorganizational) events that are perceived as rewarding or penalizing the parties involved. If we set up our typology solely in terms of the distribution of positive or negative values, we would only have three types: plus for both A and B, minus for both A and B, and plus for A and minus for B (or vice versa). When we introduce the temporal form of the events, the source of rewards, calculation versus customary understandings, and combinations of these events, we come out with the following seven transactional types:

1. *Positive exchange.* Here the temporal form is alternating, the values involved remain implicit, and the same object or activity *may* be exchanged.

2. *Trading.* Here both parties act simultaneously, there is explicit discussion of the values being exchanged, and different objects or activities are always involved on the two sides.

3. *Joint payoff.* As in the first two, plus values are sought by the two parties. Actions are more or less simultaneous and tend to be continuing, as a momentary event of this nature is not likely to produce much of a reward. In contrast to all the other types, here the main extrinsic rewards are sought from outside of the two parties.

4. *Competitive.* Here the parties seek the same value in situations in which A wins and B loses or A gains more than B. We have further distinguished between the extremes of zero sum, where what A wins is exactly what B loses and complete independence where success for one

party does not depend upon failure for the other. Actions are carried out simultaneously.

5. *Negative exchange.* This is the obverse of type one, the parties alternating in penalizing each other.

6. *Open conflict.* Here also negative values are found on both sides, but six differs from five in that the actions are simultaneous and the values struggled over are explicitly stated.

7. *Bargaining.* This is a complex combination which may include all other types, with the possible exception of *Positive exchange.*

How do we determine the values involved in each transaction? We have classified transactions in terms of the *values received by each party from the other.* We ask what values the *receiver* perceives.

Perceptions of transactional values are affected by the following influences:

1. Measurable units or structural conditions commonly recognized by all participants. In such situations, perception of the nature of the values is not likely to be affected by individual differences in perception.
2. The culture provides cues that help to distinguish between large and small rewards and large and small punishments.
3. The IRR of each participant influences his perception of the adequacy of expected rewards. He also compares what he expects to get with what others in like circumstances are getting.
4. The personality as a product of social experience. If the individual's experience has been very largely limited to one or two types of transactions, he is predisposed to see each proposed transaction in terms of that limited experience.
5. The nature of the social structure and of the positions of A and B to a large extent determines what each can expect to get from the other.

This last point brings us to a consideration of power. We recognize power in action through observing A characteristically initiate activity changes for B, C, and D—in other words, through the observation of set events. This does not tell us how power arises.

The power of A over B arises out of unbalanced positive and negative exchange relations and, in the extreme case, out of open conflict. When B can neither directly reciprocate the favors he gets from A or "get even" with A for the penalties he receives, then B must subordinate himself to A —unless B is able to withdraw from interactions and activities with B. If B can find alternative sources of the rewards he has been getting from A, he can thereby reduce the power differential between them and improve his exchange rate with A.

We see here the linking of power with the interpersonal (or intergroup or interorganizational) exchange rate. Changes in power relations are reflected in changes in the exchange rate and vice versa.

While most of our illustrations have been at the individual level, the schema should apply also at the group and organizational levels. At these higher levels, we simply have a more complex network of transactions to examine and sort out in terms of the interpersonal relations involved.

How are transactions related to IAS? Each transactional type represents a particular combination of interactions, activities, and sentiments. We assume that if individuals are experiencing the same pattern of interactions and activities over time, they will also be involved in the same distribution of transactional types. If this is true, then a participant who wishes to change the interactions, activities, and sentiments of other individuals or of groups should see to it that they experience changes in the types of transactions they are experiencing. Of course, we earlier noted that IAS can be and frequently are changed through introducing changes in technology, work flow, and formal organization structure. Transactions provide another important element of leverage in introducing changes into the social system.

References

Blau, Peter. *Exchange and Power in Social Life*. New York: John Wiley & Sons, 1964. Also *The Dynamics of Bureaucracy*, 2nd ed. Chicago: The University of Chicago Press, 1963.

Gouldner, Alvin. "The Norm of Reciprocity," *American Sociological Review*, Vol. 25, no. 2 (April, 1960) pp. 161–78.

Homans, George C. *Social Behavior: Its Elementary Forms*. New York: Harcourt, Brace and World, 1961.

Mauss, Marcel. *The Gift*. Glencoe, Ill.: The Free Press, 1954.

Discussion questions

1. Select an organization to which you belong or have belonged. Describe the transactions among members and between members and nonmembers. Describe the interactions, activities, and sentiments among members and between members and nonmembers. Did you observe IAS changes during the period of your membership? If so, were these accompanied by changes in the distribution of types of transactions?

2. Apply the concept of transactions to the professor-student and student-student relationships. To what extent is the distribution of types of transactions "built into" the differences in status and formal organizational position of professor and student? To what extent can the professor change the distribution of types of transactions through changing his methods of teaching?

Part III

GROUPS AND
INTERGROUP RELATIONS

PART II PRESENTED the key concepts we shall be using for analysis of behavior at the individual level throughout this book. When we move up to the group level, we continue to apply the same concepts already presented, but we add several important concepts that are only applicable at the group level.

There are two approaches we shall take in examining groups: internal and external. In Chapter 7 we shall take the internal view, examining groups in terms of membership and structure. In Chapter 8 we shall take the external view, considering groups as offensive and defensive social units in relation to other groups or segments of organizations. Anyone who studies a group must deal with both external and internal aspects. The internal structure can not be fully explained without taking into account the group's external relations, nor can the group's response to external relations be explained without taking into account its internal structure. Nevertheless, for purposes of exposition it will be useful to treat the internal and the external in separate chapters.

The groups of concern to us are those found within an organizational framework. Since much of the research on small groups had focused on the "autonomous group," we will begin in both chapters with examination of such groups. We will then proceed to show what remains constant and what changes as we move to an analysis of the group within the organizational context.

7. Groups: membership and structure

EACH OF US has his own common sense definition of what is a group, but the language of common sense is not good enough when we must go beyond the broadest discriminations. If we think of any group that we have known well, we immediately think of certain individuals who were clearly identified in everyone's minds with that group. But then we recognize that the boundaries of most groups are not clear-cut. While certain individuals are definitely in the group and innumerable numbers of other individuals are definitely outside of it, there appear to be some who may be described as "on the fringes of the group" or as "peripheral members."

What do we mean by these vague phrases? If we examine the bases of our judgments, we will find that we have been classifying in terms of frequency of participation. The core members are nearly always together when some group activity is taking place, whereas those individuals "on the fringes" are not so frequently present and may be left out of a number of activities.

If that is indeed the basis of our judgment, let us make it explicit and systematic: let us observe individuals in interaction over a period of time, noting the frequency and duration of those interactions, and determine group membership or degree of membership on this quantitative basis. With this kind of information, we need no longer be concerned with arbitrary judgments as to which individuals are members of the group and which are outsiders. In this way, we shall be able to compare the frequency of participation in group activities among the men who come within our field of observation.

There is another method commonly used for the determination of group memberships: sociometry. Here the approach is taken through the interviewing or questionnaire method, the respondent being asked to choose a number of individuals with whom he would most like to spend leisure time, or he may be asked to indicate those that he would like to have with him as members of a work team. He may be asked which members are contributing most to getting the group ahead, and so on.

Subjects also may be asked for negative choices: the people that they do not want to associate with socially or do not want to work with. This type of question is less frequently put because subjects are naturally more hesitant to reveal data about their antagonisms.

Sociometric data provide readily quantified material that can be used to develop a number of patterns of social data. The simplest form is that which gives us simply a ranking of individuals in terms of frequency of

Figure 7–1a. End of stage II, in-group formation.

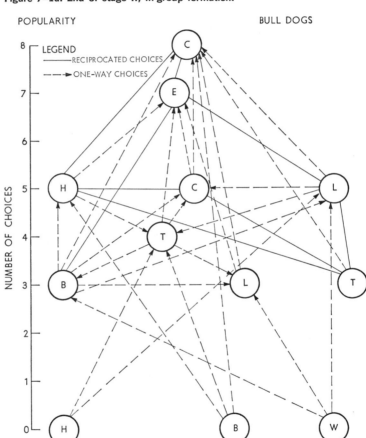

choice by others. (Similarly, we can check negative choices.) As we examine who chooses whom, we observe that there are a number of mutual choices and other nonreciprocal choices. We can map out this information, linking individuals together to show how the most chosen ones are related to each other in their choice pattern, with the less chosen and unchosen on the periphery or at the bottom of our diagram. For examples of this approach, let us consider the sociometric structures of two groups of 12-year-old boys, the Bull Dogs and the Red Devils—cases which we shall examine in detail in the next chapter.[1]

How do the sociometric diagrams shown in Figures 7–1a and 7–1b correspond to structures that would be drawn to represent leadership in organizing group activities? In the case of the Bull Dogs, there appears to be a close correspondence. The most chosen boy, C, was also the group

Figure 7–1b. End of stage II, in-group formation.

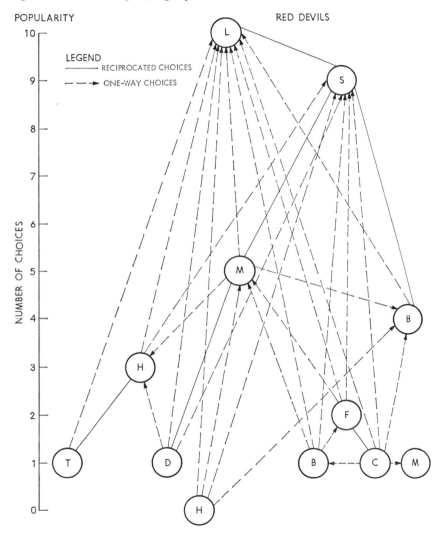

[1] Muzafer Sherif, "A Preliminary Experimental Study of Inter-Group Relations," in John H. Rohrer and Muzafer Sherif (eds.), *Social Psychology at the Crossroads* (New York: Harper & Bros., 1951), pp. 408–9.

leader, working particularly through lieutenants H and E. Sherif describes the leadership pattern in this way:[2]

The Bull Dog group was, then, focalized around C's leadership. However, he did not lead in every situation. For example, he was not as good in athletic events or those requiring muscular skill as a boy named H. H took over the lead in such situations with C's approval. However, C would occasionally overrule a decision of H's in such a situation, telling him, for example, not to put in a substitute player in a game, and H would comply. A third popular boy, E, was delegated authority by C in other tasks, such as camping or hiking.

The correspondence was not so close for the Red Devils. The dominant boys, S, received one less popularity choice than L, and if negative reactions to S by low ranking members had been taken into account, the discrepancy in popularity would have even been greater. Sherif describes the structure in this way:[3]

. . . . the boy who became recognized as leader of the Red Devils, S, won his position chiefly by virtue of his daring, athletic skill, and "toughness." He was noted as successfully leading the group in games and in daring expeditions. He was overtly recognized as the "captain" by other Red Devils. Yet S tended to be "cliquish," confining his favors and most of his attention on the whole to a few other boys high in status, and preferring to be with them. He sometimes enforced his decisions by threats or actual physical encounters. On some later occasion, he even encouraged and participated in an attack on two members low in status in his own group.

The observers noted that the leadership position of S depended in part upon his mutual bond with L, who ranked higher in popular choices and might have contended with S for power over the group but preferred to support him.

Examination of these diagrams reveals an interesting difference: popular choices were more widely distributed among the Bull Dogs, more centralized among the Red Devils. While the Bull Dogs had three unchosen members, each of the other nine received three or more choices. Half of the Red Devils were in the zero or one category. The significance of this structural difference will become clear in the next chapter when we consider intergroup relations.

In Chapter 4 on "Interactions and Activities," we pointed out that patterns of dominance and submission are universal in human and other animal societies. We are now considering how the positions individuals hold in the "pecking order" form a structural pattern.

First, we need to make an essential distinction between leadership and popularity. Popularity is a concept that usually refers to the frequency

---

[2] *Ibid.*, pp. 407–8.
[3] *Ibid.*, pp. 408–9.

with which an individual is chosen by others in some form of human association. Leadership (in the sense used here) involves the frequency of initiation of changes in group activity.

The distinction can be made to some extent, even in the sociometric approach, according to the type of question which is asked. If subjects are asked to name those with whom they would like to associate in leisure time activities, the choice pattern may be said to reflect popularity. If subjects are asked which individuals have made the greatest contribution to getting the group ahead in its chosen activities, the choice pattern may be taken to indicate leadership or influence.

The patterns emerging from these two types of questions are not necessarily similar. In fact, they are likely to show wide discrepancies. For example, in a 20-person discussion group that I observed over a two-week period at the National Training Laboratory in Bethel, Maine, I found that the most highly chosen individual for leisure time pursuits was not chosen at all among those contributing to get the group ahead. This sociometric finding coincided very well with my own observational data. The individual in question was, in everybody's opinion, a "nice guy." He was pleasant to everyone. But he never suggested what the group should do, nor did he give strong vocal support to any position stated by any other member of the group.

We should not assume that leaders are unpopular—that is, unchosen for leisure time activities. In this case, as in others, those who emerged sociometrically as contributing the most to the group's progress were found in the moderate to high-choice positions in leisure time activities.

The relationship between influence and popularity has been further explored by R. Freed Bales[4] and his associates. The Bales work to be noted here involved observational studies of discussion groups, composed of individuals who did not know each other before they were brought into the experimental sessions. In addition to observational data, the researchers had the subjects fill out sociometric questionnaires after each session. In the first meeting, there was a marked tendency for the same individual to be most highly chosen both as most influential and as most popular. As the meetings proceeded, this correspondence between popularity and influence tended to break down so that it became increasingly rare for the same individual to be most highly chosen on both criteria.

Bales and associates interpreted these trends in this way. They referred to the person voted the most influential as the "task leader" and to the person getting the highest number of leisure time choices as the "social-emotional leader." Why does the task leader tend to lose his top popularity ranking as the meetings proceed? The researchers argued that it is the task leader who tends to make or ratify decisions for the group, and in this role he uses his influence in favor of certain ideas proposed by other

---

[4] R. Freed Bales *et al.*, "The Equilibrium Problem in Small Groups" in Paul Hare, E. F. Borgatta, and R. F. Bales (eds.), *Small Groups: Studies in Social Interaction* (New York: Alfred A. Knopf, 1955).

members and against certain ideas. When the group is faced with the necessity of making a decision and no consensus emerges, it falls to the task leader to resolve the impasse by pushing in one direction or the other. Such actions on his part have mixed values for members of the group. For the group as a whole, the task leader may win some favorable recognition as being able to bring forth a group decision even when unamimity is lacking. All of the members recognize that decisions have to be made if the group is to move ahead on its tasks. Those who support the idea of the task leader naturally respond favorably to him, but those whose ideas he opposes can hardly be expected to respond so favorably.

The social-emotional leader appears less ready to take positions in arguments. He may be more sensitive to the feelings of others. He can make a really important contribution to the group by smoothing over ruffled feelings after the strain of decision making. In other words, it may be useful to the development and maintenance of the group to have the task leadership and social-emotional leadership role separated, thus providing some balance between task progress and group maintenance.

These general observations will become more meaningful as we focus our attention on the structures, interactions, and activities of particular groups. To simplify our analysis, we shall begin on an autonomous group, the Nortons. We call this group autonomous because it does not form part of the structure of any larger organization. We can therefore direct our attention primarily at internal relations, even though we must take certain external influences into account.

We will then turn to a work group in industry, undertaking to look at internal structure in relation to job and social activities and to the larger company organizations.

The Nortons

The Nortons were a group of 13 men between the ages of 22 and 29 who "hung around" on what they called a "corner," though its location was in the middle of the block on Norton Street. This was "Cornerville," an Italian-American slum district of a large city. In the period of several months when participation was at its height, the group's schedule of activities was highly predictable (barring rain, snow, or extreme cold). Sometimes in the late afternoons, but always in the early evenings, the members would gather at the corner. Usually by eight o'clock all those who were going to show up were present, and the members engaged in conversation while figuring out what—if anything else—they might do in the next two hours.

Corner activities consisted largely of conversation within the group punctuated with interchanges with those outsiders who passed by. Occasionally pairs of the men would get into "la morra," the Italian finger-throwing game.

Sometimes the men would take a walk into a neighboring district, and there were occasional excursions on foot to a movie theater in the central commercial district. Whenever the men were on the corner as 10 o'clock approached, they would set off for "coffee-ands" in a cafeteria on the edge of Cornerville. It was always the same cafeteria and the members always undertook to sit at the same tables. Since the cafeteria was open to the general public, the Nortons occasionally found their tables taken. While they had no formal grounds for complaint, the necessity of sitting elsewhere always provoked grumbling and hostile stares at the intruders. Several other corner "gangs" from Cornerville also frequented the cafeteria at about the same time, but the Nortons had no problems with them. Each group respected the other's territory within the cafeteria—as on the streets of Cornerville.

From early fall until late spring, the high point of the week came regularly every Saturday night. When the Nortons were assembled as usual on the corner, the group would set out for an evening at the bowling alleys. The group always went to the same establishment and always bowled on the same two alleys, which were reserved by the Nortons.

Out of the regular pattern of interactions and activities in the fall, winter, and spring (1937–38), there emerged a sharply defined group structure. I have diagrammed it as shown in Figure 7–2.[5] The chart is

Figure 7–2. The Nortons—Spring and Summer, 1937

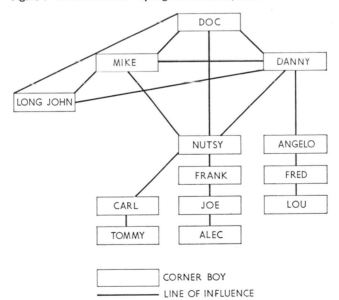

[5] W. F. Whyte, *Street Corner Society* (enlarged ed.; Chicago: University of Chicago Press, 1955), p. 49.

designed to indicate composition of subgroupings, relative ranking, and lines of influence.

We see that the 13 men were observed to form four subgroupings: the leadership group consisting of Doc, Mike, Danny, and Long John; Nutsy's group, including Frank, Joe, and Alec; Angelo's group, including Fred, and Lou; and the pair, Carl and Tommy.

These subgroups are based upon frequency observations. I often saw Carl and Tommy together when no one else was present, and I rarely saw Carl or Tommy with any member of the Nortons when the other member of the pair was not present. Similarly, I often saw Doc, Mike, Danny and Long John together when other members of the group were not present. I saw either Mike, Danny, or Long John with lower ranking members of the group much less often when Doc was not present. I observed Doc more frequently in interaction with lower ranking men than I did the other three members of the leadership subgroup. Similarly, the members of Nutsy's subgroup and the members of Angelo's subgroup were each observed more frequently interacting among fellow members of their subgroup than they were with any other individuals when other members of their subgroup were not present.

The ranking charted here is based upon two types of observation. The flow of interaction in conversation clearly indicated the central position of Doc. When I arrived on the street corner before Doc had appeared, I generally found those present divided up into two or three subgroups, with all interaction channeled within subgroups. When Doc would appear, these spatial positions of members of the gang would immediately assume a new formation. In fact, while the group hung out on the sidewalk in the middle of a block, physical movements would be observed as soon as Doc appeared around the corner and well before he had reached the group. Upon his arrival, all conversation would be channeled through him, and what had been two or three separate conversations would become one large group conversation. The central position of Doc could be observed further by noting who spoke to the group and what happened when other individuals addressed remarks to Doc. When other members of the leadership subgroup were not present, Doc was the only individual who would frequently address the group as a whole. The lower members of the group would address their remarks to Doc far more frequently than to any other group member. In fact, it was only through communicating with Doc that lower ranking man could have the attention of the whole group. I often observed one of the followers start to say something, only to find that Doc was not paying attention to him. The follower would then stop and wait until he found another opportunity to try to gain Doc's attention.

Occasionally, when either Mike or Danny was present on the corner without Doc, either of them could play this focal position in conversation. Such was not the case with Long John.

The structure was also acted out in changes of group activity. Doc was by no means the only one to make proposals for changes in activity, but I never observed any such change in group activity take place unless he gave the proposal his endorsement. In other words, changes in group activity arose either directly from proposals by Doc or from proposals by other members that were accepted by Doc. When other members proposed an activity, and Doc ignored the proposal or expressed disapproval, I never observed the conversational activity changing to the activity proposed by the other member.

Doc did not treat the other members as an undifferentiated group. When Mike and Danny were present, he regularly consulted them about what was to be done. He was also much more likely to respond to their proposals than he was to those of other members.

The same hierarchical characteristics were exhibited in the other subgroups. Within Nutsy's group, proposals for activities were either made or endorsed by Nutsy if they were to be carried out, and Angelo occupied the same focal position in his subgroup.

The chart illustrates the ambiguous position of Long John: high ranking, low influence. Unlike the other members, Long John had not grown up on Norton Street. He had come into the group through frequent participation in a crap game run by Mike and Danny on an adjoining playground. The lower ranking group members did not participate in these crap games and regarded those who did as "suckers." No moral judgment was involved, for the entrepreneurs who ran the game and managed relations with local police officers held a respected position in the group. Through his close association with Mike and Danny, Long John became friendly with Doc and came to participate actively in the leadership subgroup, but he was never fully accepted by lower ranking members. In fact, on those occasions when he appeared on the corner unaccompanied by members of the leadership subgroup, the other men frequently picked on him. It was as if they were telling him that his high ranking was due exclusively to the protection of Doc, Mike, and Danny, that he did not deserve it on his own merits.

Positive exchange transactions also followed the lines of group structure. While it was one of the *norms* of the group that each man should help any other member when help was needed, the exchange of favors took place predominantly among members in closely linked positions in the group structure. When favors were exchanged among members of markedly different ranks, the higher ranking member behaved so as to remain on the credit side of the ledger. While Doc had very little money throughout the months of my observation of the group, and frequently borrowed from Mike or Danny and accepted treats from them, he avoided accepting favors from lower ranking members so as not to put himself under obligations to them. In fact, when he had no money at all, he tended to stay away from the group so that he would not be in the position of having others pay for his share of whatever activity was undertaken.

I found a relationship between ranking in the group and living up to group norms. Doc, Mike, and Danny could be counted on to live up to their obligations to other group members. Joe and Alex were often criticized for their tendency to break commitments to group members when they had a chance to make dates with girls. Frank once condemned them in these words: "A girl you can meet any time; it takes years to make a real friend." The low ranking men had no rank to lose through failure to observe group norms; the only sanction left to the group would have been expulsion, and no one wished to go this far.

I observed a relationship between rank in the group and performance in activities important to the group. While group members turned up at the bowling alleys every Saturday night over a period of months, and there were many good-natured arguments about relative bowling abilities, when it came to an important competition—such as when the owners of the alleys offered a small pot of prize money to the group at the end of the season—the members of the leadership group could be counted on to outscore the followers. This pattern seemed neither accidental nor correlated with the "natural ability" of group members. While there was much heckling and good-natured razzing of individuals at the alleys, I observed differences in expression and tone of voice, that were related to ranking in the group. When a low-ranking man was performing well, members of the leadership subgroup and followers on the team opposing him would "get on him" to let him know that he was "bowling over his head." When one of the high-ranking members began making errors, he would hear, "You are really off form tonight," "You're not the man you used to be" and other remarks which, while apparently directed against him, at the same time gave recognition to the high ranking he held.

That differences in natural ability did not account for this ranking of bowling performance is best demonstrated by the case of Frank, who, on his record outside the group, could have been considered the best natural athlete. He wanted to become a professional baseball player. When the major league baseball team in the city held open tryouts for all comers, Frank turned up at the ball park along with more than 1,000 other young men. In the first step of the elimination contest, each young man had a chance to take several swings at bat, and the infield candidates had to field three ground balls and make the throws to first base. Under this extreme pressure, where one mistake could have blasted all his hopes, Frank performed so well that he survived all eliminations and was one of seven young men who were promised opportunities with a minor league club.

On the basis of this record, one would think that Frank must outshine us all in a neighborhood game, but when our Norton Street gang played a group of younger men from the same street, Frank was a great disappointment. He struck out with long graceful swings. In the field, I performed my most useful service for our team in the outfield by stopping the grounders that got past Frank. When it was all over, he shook his head and said to me, "It's a funny thing, but I can never play good when I am with my own gang."

When among strangers, Frank did as well as his natural talent permitted. When with his own gang, his performance corresponded with his social ranking.

I also found that rank and the patterns of interactions and activities going with such rank were associated with the mental health problems of group members. On several occasions before I knew him and on one occasion when I was with the Nortons, Doc was subject to dizzy spells that interfered with his social participation. He would accept some social invitation and plan to go, but at the last minute a dizzy spell would make it impossible for him to go out. The spells arose only in those periods when Doc was both out of work and without any money at all. To have gone out at such times would have meant being completely dependent on others even for buying a cup of coffee. The dizzy spells, during my period with the gang, terminated abruptly when Doc got a part-time job. As soon as he had even small change in his pocket necessary both to participate and to maintain his group ranking in the exchange of favors, the dizzy spells were a problem of the past.

Before we leave the Nortons, we should ask to what extent we can use that gang as a model for all autonomous groups. While no definitive answers can be given to such a question, let us note some ways in which the Nortons may be similar to other autonomous groups and different from still others. On the side of similarity, I would argue that any group that comes together and remains together beyond a few days necessarily develops a structure which can be charted on the basis of the observations I have given. Groups will differ in the frequency and duration of the interactions of their members through time and also in the proportion of group activities of members that are concentrated in this particular group. The Nortons represent an extreme case in these respects. When the group was intact, most of these men regularly spent from two to four hours a day in each other's company. Furthermore, for all of them and particularly for the low-ranking men, there was very little exposure by individual members to participation in other group situations.

I believe this concentration of activities and interactions within this particular group accounts for the close correspondence between bowling performance and group structure and for the vulnerability of group members to changes in their interactions and activity patterns. In other words, when I find a group of men interacting together with high frequencies and long durations and confining their group activities largely to this particular group, I would expect to find a marked correlation between position in the group structure and performance in any competitive activity of importance to the group. On the other hand, in the case of men who bowl together once a week over a period of months, but who have little or nothing to do with each other between bowling nights and who participate in other groups between these bowling alley sessions, I would not expect to find a marked relationship between bowling scores and position in the group.

On similar grounds, while I would expect any individual to find it emotionally disturbing to lose his position in the group, this problem would be especially disturbing only for those whose participation is very highly concentrated in that group. Many individuals participate more or less regularly in a number of different groups. We also have some experience in moving from one group to another. Therefore, when the individual loses his position in a particular group, he may still be able to act out a pattern of interactions and activities that is comfortable to him by reducing his interactions and activities in the group where he has suffered his loss and increasing his interactions and activities in other groups.

We have been examining what is often called an "autonomous group," a social unit that does not have an established position in any larger structure. In such situations we see group processes in "pure" form. To be sure, the members of the group do interact with outsiders and are influenced by the physical and social environment, but they do not act under the authority of any outside organization, and they are free to participate in or abstain from group activity.

Let us now move inside the industrial organization to see what group processes look like in this institutional setting.

"Banana time"

We will begin with a classic case described by Donald Roy,[6] out of his experiences and observations as participant observer on the clicking machines. Here we have as close to an autonomous group as we are likely to find inside a work organization. Four men were working together in a space physically separated from the rest of the plant and they had minimum contacts with other plant personnel. While they were socially isolated, the organization provided the machines and materials that served to fix them in physical space and prescribe the most persistent activity of the day: work.

The machines were lined up in a row. The operation was simple and completely routine. The operator would place strips of plastic under the head of the clicking machine. The operator would start the head of the

---

[6] Donald Roy, "Banana Time: Job Satisfaction and Informal Interaction," *Human Organization*, Vol. 18, no. 4 (Winter, 1959–60), pp. 156–68.

machine down manually, and electric power would take over to bring the head down with a sharp punching action that cut the plastic according to the pattern of the die placed in the head. Except for occasional pauses to scrape the block clear of residue, the operation was completely uniform in a physical sense. The only variety was introduced by differences in the color of the plastic on which the operator worked. At this time, demand was such that the men were all working overtime, Roy himself putting in a 12-hour day.

Roy describes his clicking machine workers in the following way:

George, a stocky fellow in his late fifties, operated the machine at the opposite end of the line; he, I later discovered, had emigrated in early youth from a country in Southeastern Europe. Ike, stationed at George's left, was tall, slender, in his early fifties, and Jewish; he had come from Eastern Europe in his youth. Sammy, number three man in the line, and my neighbor, was heavy set, in his late fifties, and Jewish; he had escaped from a country in Eastern Europe just before Hitler's legions had moved in. All three men had been downwardly mobile as to occupation in recent years. George and Sammy had been proprietors of small businesses; the former had been "wiped out" when his uninsured establishment burned down; the latter had been entrepreneuring on a small scale before he left all behind him to flee the Germans. According to his account, Ike had left a highly skilled trade which he had practiced for years in Chicago.

Roy found out that the way the men were positioned along the row of machines, from George down to himself, represented a system of social ranking. George had top seniority, received five cents more per hour than the others, and had daily contact with the plant superintendent. However, George was not formally described as a group leader, and often instructions were given to the men as a group over the public address system.

Roy describes in this way his first experiences with the clicking machine:

It was evident to me, before my first workday drew to a weary close, that my clicking machine career was going to be a grim process of fighting the clock, the particular timepiece in this situation being an old-fashioned alarm clock which ticked away on a shelf near George's machine. I had struggled through many dreary rounds with the minutes and hours during the various phases of my industrial experience, but never had I been confronted with such a dismal combination of working conditions as the extra-long workday, the infinitesimal cerebral excitation, and the extreme limitation of physical movement. The contrast with a recent stint in the California oil fields was striking. This was no eight-hour day of racing hither and yon over desert and foothills with a rollicking crew of "roustabouts" on a variety of repair missions at oil wells, pipe lines, and storage tanks. Here there were no afternoon dallyings to search the sands for horned toads, tarantulas, and rattlesnakes, or to climb old wooden derricks for raven's nests, with an eye out, of course, for the telltale streak of dust in the distance which gave ample warning of the approach of the boss. This was standing all day in one spot beside three old codgers in a dingy room looking out through barred windows at the bare walls of a brick warehouse, leg movements largely restricted to the shifting of body weight from foot to the other, hand and arm movements confined, for the most part, to a simple repetitive sequence of place the die, punch the clicker, place the die, punch the clicker, and intellectual activity reduced to computing the hours to quitting time. It is true that from time to time a fresh stack of sheets would have to be substituted for the clicked-out old one; but the stack would have been prepared by someone else, and the exchange would be only a minute or two in the making. Now and then a box of finished work would have to be moved back out of the way, and an empty box brought up; but the moving back and the bringing up involved only a step or two. And there was the half hour for lunch, and occasional trips to the lavoratory or the drinking fountain to break up the day into digestible parts. But after each momentary respite, hammer and die were moving again: click, move die, click, move die.

Before the end of the first day, Monotony was joined by his twin brother, Fatigue. I got tired. My legs ached, and my feet hurt. Early in the afternoon I discovered a tall stool and moved it up to my machine to "take the load off my feet." But the superintendent dropped in to see how I was "doing" and promptly informed me that "we don't sit down on this job." My reverie toyed with the idea of quitting the job and looking for other work.

The next day was the same: the monotony of the work, the tired legs and sore feet and thoughts of quitting.

In his previous work experiences, Roy had learned how to find interest in a repetitive job. If it was a piece-work job, he could make a game of racing the clock—at least on those jobs where his maximum possible production fell within the limits of the work group's norms. Where there was conflict between workers and management, workers could get satisfaction from talking about past or presumed future management strategies and tactics and the maneuvers that workers had used or should use to frustrate management. But here, says Roy:

There was no piece work, so no piece work game. There was no conflict with management so no war game.

Roy managed to break up the long working day by establishing his own subgoals in the form of activity changes:

If, for example, production scheduled for the day featured small, rectangular strips in three colors, the game might go: "As soon as I finish a thousand green ones, I'll click some brown ones." And with success in obtaining the objective of working with brown materials, a new goal of "I'll get to do the white ones" might be set. Or the new goal might involve switching dies.

Still, Roy cautions against assuming that these simple intellectual structurings of the situation made 12 hours at the clicking machine into fun. Before the end of the first week, he was discovering much more potent sources of interest in the work place: the social activities and interactions on the job. At first these interactions and activities seemed to Roy no more than random bits of communication which were often nonsensical in character. Gradually he came to realize that the events actually were highly structured.

What Roy calls "times" broke up the day into regular, highly predictable units. Besides those formally recognized—such as coffee break, coke break, cigarette break, and lunch time—the other three men had developed their own elaborate pattern. Roy describes in this way the "times" of the first half of the working day:

My attention was first drawn to this "times" business during my first week of employment when I was encouraged to join in the sharing of two peaches. It was Sammy who provided the peaches; he drew them from his lunch box after making the announcement, "Peach time!" On this first occasion I refused the proffered fruit, but thereafter regularly consumed my half peach. Sammy continued to provide the peaches and to make the "Peach time!" announcement, although there were days when Ike would remind him that it was peach time, urging him to hurry up with the mid-morning snack. Ike invariably complained about the quality of the fruit, and his complaints fed the fires of continued banter between peach donor and critical recipient. I did find the fruit a bit on the scrubby side, but felt, before I achieved insight into the function of peach time, that Ike was showing poor manners by looking a gift horse in the mouth. I wondered why Sammy continued to share his peaches with such an ingrate.

Banana time followed peach time by approximately an hour. Sammy again provided the refreshments, namely, one banana. There was, however, no four-way sharing of Sammy's banana. Ike would gulp it down by himself after surreptitiously extracting it from Sammy's lunch box, kept on a shelf behind Sammy's work station. Each morning, after making the snatch, Ike would call out, "Banana time!" and proceed to down his prize while Sammy made futile protests and denunciations. George would join in with mild remonstrances, sometimes scolding Sammy for making so much fuss. The banana was one which Sammy brought for his own consumption at lunch time; he never did get to eat his banana, but kept bringing one for his lunch. At first this daily theft startled and amazed me. Then I grew to look forward to the daily seizure and the verbal interaction which followed.

Window time came next. It followed banana time as a regular consequence of Ike's castigation by the indignant Sammy. After "taking" repeated references to himself as a person badly lacking in morality and character, Ike would "finally" retaliate by opening the window which faced Sammy's machine, to let the "cold air" blow in on Sammy. The slandering which would, in its echolalic repetition, wear down Ike's patience and forbearance usually took the form of the invidious comparison: "George is a good daddy! Ike is a bad man! A very bad man!" Opening the window would take a little time to accomplish and would involve a great deal of verbal interplay between Ike and Sammy, both before and after the event. Ike would threaten, make feints toward the window, then finally open it. Sammy would protest, argue, and make claims that the air blowing in on him would give him a cold; he would eventually have to leave his machine to close the window. Sometimes the weather was slightly chilly, and the draft from the window unpleasant; but cool or hot, windy or still, window time arrived each day. (I assume that it was originally a cold season development.) George's part in this interplay, in spite of the "good daddy" laudations, was to encourage Ike in his window work. He would stress the tonic values of fresh air and chide Sammy for his unappreciativeness.

Following window time came lunch time, a formally designated half-hour for the midday repast and rest break. At this time, informal interaction would feature exchanges between Ike and George. The former would start eating his lunch a few minutes before noon, and the latter, in his role as straw boss, would censure him for malobservance of the rules. Ike's off-beat luncheon usually involved a previous tampering with George's alarm clock. Ike would set the clock ahead a few minutes in order to maintain his eating schedule without detection, and George would discover these small daylight-saving changes.

There were also "themes" described in this way:

To put flesh, so to speak, on this interactional frame of "times," my work group had developed various "themes" of verbal interplay which had become standardized in their repetition. These topics of conversation ranged in quality from an extreme of nonsensical chatter to another extreme of serious discourse. Unlike the times, these themes flowed one into the other in no particular sequence of predictability. Serious conversation could suddenly melt into horseplay, and vice versa. In the middle of a serious discussion on the high cost of living, Ike might drop a weight behind the easily startled Sammy, or hit him over the head with a dusty paper sack. Interaction would immediately drop to a low comedy exchange of slaps, threats, guffaws, and disapprobations which would invariably include a 10-minute echolalia of "Ike is a bad man, a very bad man! George is a good daddy, a very fine man!" Or, on the other hand, a stream of such invidious comparisons as followed a surreptitious switching-off of Sammy's machine by the playful Ike might merge suddenly into a discussion of the pros and cons of saving for one's funeral.

Sammy was usually the butt of these kidding themes, with George or Ike taking the initiative. Sometimes Ike was the target, rarely George himself.

Roy was target or chief character in four of the themes. Ike's favorite question: "How many times did you go poom-poom last night?" was addressed to others as well, but they begged off on the grounds of being too old, thus leaving Roy in an exposed position. Once, in a serious discussion of property ownership and taxes, Roy remarked that he owned two acres of land in a western state.

. . . and from then on I had to listen to questions, advice, and general nonsensical comment in regard to "Dannelly's farm." This "farm" soon became stocked with horses, cows, pigs, chickens, ducks, and the various and sundry domesticated beasts so tunefully listed in "Old MacDonald had a Farm."

The other Roy themes he describes as "helping Dannelly find a cheaper apartment" and "getting Dannelly a better job." Lack of success with either mission did not diminish the volume of conversation on these themes.

There was one theme of especially solemn import, the "professor theme." This theme might also be termed "George's daughter's marriage theme"; for the recent marriage of George's only child was inextricably bound up with George's connection with higher learning. The daughter had married the son of a professor who instructed in one of the local colleges. This professor theme was not in the strictest sense a conversation piece; when the subject came up, George did all the talking. The two Jewish operatives remained silent as they listened with deep respect, if not actual awe, to George's account of the Big Wedding which, including the wedding pictures, entailed an expense of $1,000. It was monologue, but there was listening, there was communication, the sacred communication of a temple, when George told of going for Sunday afternoon walks on the Midway with the professor, or of joining the professor for a Sunday dinner. Whenever he spoke of the professor, his daughter, the wedding, or even of the new son-in-law, who remained for the most part in the background, a sort of incidental like the wedding cake, George was complete master of the interaction. His manner, in speaking to the rank-and-file of clicker operators, was indeed that of master deigning to notice his underlings. I came to the conclusion that it was the professor connection, not the strawboss-ship or the extra nickel an hour, which provided the fount of George's superior status in the group.

At the other extreme from the serious topics were what Roy calls the "chatter themes." There were individual sayings such as Sammy's often repeated statement that "George is a good daddy, a very fine man! Ike is a bad man, a very bad man!" Then there were chatterings that the other three operators would pick up in a sort of a chorus, their favorite being, "Are you a man or a mouse? I ask you, are you a man or a mouse?"

The pattern repeated itself day after day until Roy had an idea for introducing a modification of one theme. It happened on a day that was ordinary in every way, except that Sammy was away on vacation so that Roy was at his machine. Roy suggested to Ike that he kid George by saying that he had seen "the professor" instructing in a barber college in the "lower reaches of Hobohemia" in the center of the city. Ike liked the idea and a few moments later tried it out on George.

When George said nothing in response to this announcement, it fell to Roy to bring out the details in questioning. Still no reaction from George, who got red in the face and slammed into his clicking with increased vigor. Ike whispered to Roy, "George is sore!"

George was indeed sore. He didn't say another word the rest of the morning. There was no conversation at lunchtime, nor was there any after lunch. A pall of silence had fallen over the clicker room. Fish time fell a casualty. George did not touch the coke I bought for him. A very long, very dreary afternoon dragged on. Finally, after Ike left for home, George broke the silence to reveal his feelings to me:

"Ike acts like a five-year-old, not a man! He doesn't even have the respect of the niggers. But he's got to act like a man around here! He's always fooling around! I'm going to stop that! I'm going to show him his place!"

". . . Jews will ruin you, if you let them. I don't care if he sings, but the first time he mentions my name, I'm going to shut him up! It's always "Meet Mr. Papeatis! George is a good daddy!" And all that. He's paid to work! If he doesn't work, I'm going to tell Joe (the superintendent)."

For the next 12 days, the pattern of times and themes was completely eliminated, the only communication out of George being completely work-oriented. George emphasized his quasi-supervisory status, saying that the shop was going to be on a "strictly business" basis, and that the men would have to raise their level of output. To make this point, George got to talking about the poor work performance of the still-absent Sammy. Ike would reply by defending Sammy's abilities, and Roy would do his best to keep out of the argument.

The breaking of the pattern transformed the working day not only in a psychological, but even in a physical sense. Let us note two statements of Roy, regarding the situation before and after the barber college incident:

So my initial discouragement with the meagerness of social interaction I now recognized as due to lack of observation. The interaction was there, in constant flow. It captured attention and held interest to make the long day pass. The 12 hours of "click, move die, click, move die" became as easy to endure as 8 hours of varied activity in the oil fields or 8 hours of playing the piecework game in a machine shop. The "beast of boredom" was gentled to the harmlessness of a kitten.

. . . . .

Twelve-hour days were creeping again at snail's pace. The strictly business communications were of no help, and the sporadic bursts of distaste or enthusiasm for Sammy's clicking ability helped very little. With the return of boredom, came a return of fatigue. My legs tired as the afternoons dragged on, and I became engaged in conscious efforts to rest one by shifting the weight to the other. I would pause in my work to stare through the barred windows at the grimy brick wall across the alley; and, turning my head, I would notice that Ike was staring at the wall, too. George would do very little work after Ike left the shop at night. He would sit in a chair and complain of weariness and sore feet.

On the 13th day, communication between Ike and Sammy was tentatively re-established, and in a few days their old times and themes had taken their customary places. But there was one exception: George never again mentioned his Sunday walks on the Midway with the professor.

What meanings can we draw from this case?

The case suggests a conclusion regarding intrinsic satisfactions in the work. Some jobs may appear to be interesting and challenging and thus provide such rich satisfactions that workers can find their satisfactions primarily in the work itself. In jobs of extreme routinization, the work itself provides neither interest nor the structuring of the working day. In such situations, workers are likely to develop a pattern of interactions and activities that relieves the boredom and makes the time seem to pass faster. Development of this pattern even serves to relieve physical fatigue.

Does such a pattern have effects upon productivity? On this point, Roy says he has no clear evidence. There was a clear and important effect upon satisfaction, and that in turn had its effect upon labor turnover. Roy reports that he could not have stood the job for long without the "times" and "themes." As it was, it took a research fellowship at the University of Chicago to get him off the clicking machine. Roy's observations of the other workers during the period immediately after the barber college incident suggests that Roy was not the only one to find the job hard to stand in the absence of a social pattern.

It is interesting to note the direction of causality in the barber college incident. In general, we can expect a change in the IAS patterns to enter through a change in interaction and/or activities. In this case we see the entry point in sentiments. George's association with "the professor" had a great symbolic meaning to him, and the sudden association of that symbol with "barber college" had an explosive effect upon the small social system. It should be noted that the effect was determined in part by George's position in the social system and the role he had been playing in the kidding. He was the informal leader, and he was not accustomed to taking much kidding from the others. On the rare occasions when they did kid him, it had never been on such a sensitive point.

One department, many groups

We now turn from the pure simplicity of a small work group that in itself constituted a department to the greater complexity and variety of groups found in a larger department of a different organization.[7]

The department in question consisted of 47 men and women, distributed spatially in four subsystems of work areas. The accompanying diagram is the physical layout of the department.

Among the 47 workers were group leaders, grinders, lathe operators, dynamic balancers, paint sprayers, drill press operators, assemblers, light machinists and inspectors. In a plant with labor grades from 1 to 10, the workers in this department were spread over grades from 3 through 8.

---

[7] A. Zaleznik, C. R. Christensen, F. J. Roethlisberger, with the assistance and collaboration of G. C. Homans, *The Motivation, Productivity, and Satisfaction of Workers: A Prediction Study* (Boston: Harvard University Graduate School of Business Administration, 1958).

Hourly pay ranged from $1.63 to $2 (in 1955). No workers were on incentive rates.

Compared with the clicking machine group, we have here many more and more varied interactions available. The work also was much more varied and more intrinsically interesting. Even so, workers had developed an elaborate pattern of interactions and activities beyond those necessary to get the work done.

The accompanying table shows the number and variety of activities involved. The authors used the terms "extended non-work activities" for the activities observed daily and "limited non-work activities" for those which took place once a week or at irregular intervals.

The Physical Layout of the Department

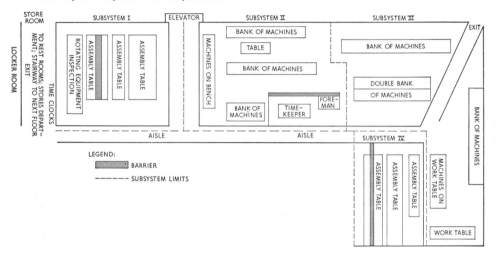

The Major Nonwork Activities

Limited Nonwork Activities	*Extended Nonwork Activities*
Number Pools	Coffee Groups
$155 Number Pool	Coffee IIIa
50-cent Number Pool	Coffee IIIb
Wednesday Night Fight	Coffee IIIc
Pool	Intersystem Coffee
50-cent Draw Pool	Coffee IV
Savings & Merchandise	Games
Clubs	
$11 Savings Club	Cribbage
$20 Savings Club	Whist
$10 Savings Club	500 Rummy
Better Homes &	
Gardens Club	
Christmas Club Savings	
Vacation Club Savings	
Collections	

The men were more involved in the pools, the women in the savings clubs. Some of these limited non-work activities involved elaborate organization and procedures, such as having one person serve as collector, and another as treasurer (to hold the money), and another as record keeper.

Collections were an extended form of positive exchange transactions, a sort of group insurance against loss or adversities. Collections were taken up in the case of extended illness of a member, death in a member's family, or marriage or birth of a child. In each case, a close friend of the person affected would assume the responsibility to take up the collection and pass around a cardboard box with a hole punched in the top. While the form of collection was designed to assure some privacy as to the amounts contributed by individuals, there was nonetheless a general understanding as to what amounts were appropriate for each situation, and those who were thought not to contribute up to standard were known unfavorably throughout the department. While members did not calculate that they would get back exactly what they put in collection, the research men heard a number of comments about what a feeling of security it gave a worker to know that fellow workers would come to his aid when he needed them.

The games were not played indiscriminately by all. In each case, the entry of players was limited, and there was a distinct social ranking of games, cribbage having the highest social standing, whist next, and 500 rummy ranking at the bottom. These rankings were determined by observation: the observers noted numerous cases where outsiders tried to get into the cribbage game and were rejected, while they saw no comparable cases of cribbage players trying to get into the whist game.

To supplement the observational data, the research men determined friendship ties through interviews. This gave them data upon social interaction outside of the workplace and upon special mutual aid relations that might not be observable in the plant.

The authors noted eight social groups. The membership of these groups was determined by examining the following types of data: social activities while at work, participation in the same in-plant nonwork activities, higher percentage of friendship choices within the group, high percentage of interaction during work within the group, common social activities outside of the plant, and common interests (as determined by interviewing).

The authors make a further distinction between "regular groups" and "deviant groups," regular groups centering their participation around the higher prestige activities. Members of these groups were often mentioned as friendship choices by members of deviant groups, but choices rarely went the other way. In observed interaction, members of deviant groups would tend to initiate interaction more with the regulars than occurred in the other direction. The informal leaders in the department, those who organized activities, were, with one exception, all members of regular groups. This one exception was not closely involved with any group but performed a linking function with all of them.

For the eight groups listed below, the first five were described as regular groups, while the others were described as deviant groups. We present the following brief summary of the characteristics of each group:

1. *"The men": four older married men.* In this group, 49 percent of their observed interactions during work were among themselves. Of their 33 friendship choices, 12 were also within the group. In effect, this meant that each member chose the other three as friends and yet they considered that they had many friends outside of their own group.

2. *"The Boys": five unmarried men.* In this group, 40 percent of their observed interaction during work were within the group. Out of 38 friendship choices, 20 were also within the group, which means again, in effect, that each member chose the other four as a friend and yet they had many friends outside. (The authors report them as making 22 internal group choices, but this must be an error because if each man chose all of the remaining members of the group, the total would only come to 20.)

3. *"The Old Girls": four older women.* They worked at separate places so that their interactions during work were low, but they were high in mutual friendship choices and reported frequent out-of-work association.

4. *"The Women": a three-person group, two of them being relatives.* They regularly had coffee together and participated in many activities outside of the plant.

5. *"The Old Men": a three-person group.* They had a high rate of interaction at work and much sharing of work activities. They were also active in mutual aid outside of the plant.

6. *"The Deviant Men": a five-man group.* The men were observed more frequently in interaction with "The Boys" than within their own group. They had no friendship choices within the group, giving their choices primarily to "The Men."

7. *"The Deviant Girls": a four-person group.* Members were separated at work, but they gave 12 out of 27 friendship choices within their own group, thus in effect having each girl choose the other three. (Here the authors report 16 internal choices, which is impossible with a four-person group.) The deviant girls also engaged in some non-work activities in the plant.

8. *"The New Girls": a four-person group.* They were high in mutual friendship choices and engaged in outside social activities together, but within the plant they were observed in interaction with "The Women" (28 percent) more than with their own membership (19 percent).

It should be noted that the titles of these groups were conferred by the authors, to make it easier to talk about them.

The remaining 14 workers in the department were characterized as isolates. They were so identified in terms of the following four criteria: no participation in extended nonwork activities, low participation in limited nonwork activities, low number of friendship choices received, and low interaction rate with other members of the department. The authors note that four of the isolates were not simply rejected by other members of the department but they themselves actively rejected these potential social associates—that is, in interviews they expressed strong disapproval of their fellow workers and a desire to avoid having anything to do with them. Two of these four even refused to participate in the collections.

What factors determined group membership and particularly membership in the preferred "regular groups"? After examining a number of factors, the authors concluded that the characteristic more important than any other was ethnicity. Of the 47 workers, 23 were Irish Americans. Out of 20 members of regular groups, 16 (80 percent) were Irish, compared to 4 out of 13 members of deviant groups and 3 out of 14 isolates. Clearly, being Irish was a most important key to acceptance in the leading social circles of the department.

Were any other factors involved? The authors examined status and status congruence. They indexed status in terms of six variables: pay, age, seniority, education, ethnicity, and sex. In the first four items, the authors constructed indices based simply upon increasing amounts of pay, age, seniority, and education. In the case of ethnicity, they applied the values which may reflect the evaluations prevalent in New England where the plant was located: at the top were Yankees or North or West Europeans, those with a background of several generations in the United States and Protestants; next were Northern and Western European Catholics; next, Southern Europeans and French Canadians, also Catholics; and lowest, Eastern Europeans and other adult immigrants to the U.S., Jewish and Greek Orthodox (non-Catholic) employees. In the case of sex they followed prevailing values, giving males more points than females (although, as we shall note later, the most influential leader in the department was a woman).

On the basis of the scores of each individual on the six indices of status, the authors developed two types of measures. By adding the scores on each of the six indices for each individual, they arrive at an overall measure of status. By examining the *discrepancies* for each individual among his scores on the six status indices, they arrive at a measure of "status congruence." These two types of measures are not completely independent of each other, particularly at the highest and lowest extremes of status. That is, the people who have the highest level of general status must have all of their six status factors at a reasonably high level in order to occupy this position, and similarly those who are at the lowest overall level in status must have all of their status factors on the lower end of the score in order to come out at or near the bottom in total status. In other words, at the extremes of overall status we would expect to have a high status, high status congruent people and low status, high status congruent people. Between these two extremes, other combinations are possible. Thus we may have high status, low status congruent people and low status, low status congruent people.

What difference does congruence or noncongruence make? While, for some purposes, it may be useful to think of the individual's status in his society in terms of a general, overall prestige ranking, we find that people do evaluate each other in terms of a variety of status factors such as those discussed here: education, seniority, pay, and so on. When we recognize that individuals may not "score" at the same level on all of the relevant factors tending to establish their prestige in their social environment, we naturally wonder whether status congruence or lack of it make a difference in attitudes and behavior. Other writers have theorized that degrees of status congruence do make important differences in the way the individual views himself and those around him and the way others react to him.[8]

The investigators devote a good deal of analysis of group formation to status and status congruence. Those interested in methods of measuring status congruence are referred to their book (especially pages 56–76). For our purposes, it will be sufficient to have a general idea of the nature of the approach and the conclusions they are able to draw from it.

The authors found that the high status, high status congruent people tended to be regular group members. The high status, low status congruent people tended to be isolates. It was as if, being unable to place themselves or to be placed by others, they simply remained outside of the system. The low status, high status congruent people tended to be deviant group members. The fourth possible combination (low status, low status congruent) produced indeterminate results. That is, knowing that the individual was low status, low status congruent, did not enable one to make an improvement in the prediction of membership and participation beyond a chance basis.

What factors determined social leadership in the department? The four group leaders were, in effect, designated as leaders by management, but two of these were observed to be social isolates. The other two were members of regular groups, but only one of these was an informal social leader in the department.

On the basis of observations and interviews, the investigators identified five social leaders in the department. The most prominent and influential one designated as "the queen bee" by the investigators, was a large Irish woman, a grinder, who was also a union officer. She did not participate in

---

[8] See Stuart N. Adams, "Status Congruence as a Variable in Small Group Performance," *Social Forces*, Vol. 32, no. 1 (Oct., 1953), pp. 16–22; and Gerhardt Lenski, "Status Crystallization: A Non-Vertical Dimension of Status," *American Sociological Review*, Vol. 19, no. 4 (August, 1954), pp. 405–13.

any of the informal groups of the department, but she was anything but an isolate. Individuals from all groups in the department came often to her workplace to consult her, to talk informally with her, to bring her a cup of coffee, and so on. On interpersonal, intergroup, or worker-management problems, she was not only consulted but was generally looked upon as the one who should work out the problems. She enjoyed a good relationship with the foreman, often consulting with him or being consulted by him. He, too, was Irish. While her social participation was spread widely among department members, she chose many friends and was chosen by many as a friend.

Of the other four social leaders, two were men and two were women. All were Irish and members of regular groups. The researchers noted that the deviant groups showed no clear-cut leadership pattern and appeared to be markedly less cohesive than the regular groups.

What difference did it make whether a worker of this department was a regular or a deviant group member, or was an isolate? The authors examined the relationships between group membership and productivity and group membership and satisfaction.

In productivity, the investigators were interested not only in amount produced, but in the relationship between this amount and the informal group *norms* that existed in this department, as in so many others, as to what constituted "a good days work." In general, they found that regular group members tended to produce "on the line" in relation to group norms. Deviant group members tended to produce somewhat higher, while isolates tended to produce below the norms.

Satisfaction scores were derived through interviews covering six possible areas of satisfaction-dissatisfaction: intrinsic aspects of the job, extrinsic aspects, the supervisor, work associates, the company, and the union. In general, the investigators found that the females were more satisfied than the males, the Irish more satisfied than the non-Irish, and regular group members more satisfied than any others. The isolates turned out to be least satisfied in five of the six categories. In their evaluation of a highly popular supervisor, they did not differ from other workers.

This study is impressive in showing the extent to which social participation is related to status factors, and social participation in turn is related to productivity and satisfaction. At the same time, we must recognize that we are speaking in terms of statistical relationships. This does not mean that if we have data on the spatial position of workers and on the status factors, we can then predict with full confidence group membership and the individual or group characteristics in terms of productivity and satisfaction. It simply means that these data improve our predictions over what we would get on a chance basis.

With all due caution, we must nevertheless recognize the great importance of ethnicity. We have noted that 16 out of 20 of the members of regular groups were Irish and that all five of the social leaders of the department were Irish. While the two group leaders who were members of regular groups were Irish, the two group-leader isolates both fell in the bottom ethnic status category.

We should also note that there were nine workers who fell in the top ethnic status category: Yankee or Northern Western European, a history of several generations in U.S., Protestant. Five of these nine were classified as social isolates. In other words, a Yankee had a 55 percent chance of being a social isolate, compared to the departmental average of just under 30 percent. Furthermore, the only two who refused to contribute to collections were Yankees.

What is going on here? We should note the discrepancy between the factory and the larger society on this point. While these Yankees did indeed enjoy an ethnic identification of higher prestige in the society as a whole, this department was clearly dominated by the Irish. It was as if the Yankees, finding that in this particular setting they were not going to get the respect due their ethnic identification in the larger society, resolved to have nothing to do with the social system of the plant.

Ethnicity and group pressures

The previous study shows the great importance of ethnicity in group formation and leadership in one industrial department. Is this an unusual situation? Let us look farther.

Orvis Collins[9] earlier presented another case from New England. He states his thesis in this way:

In this factory, individuals must be ethically qualified to hold certain jobs, a circumstance which has resulted in the development of ethnic job expectations, sponsorship and rejection.

The president and all the vice presidents were Yankees. Seven out of eight of the superintendents were Yankees, the other being a testing engineer. Seven out of eight members of the personnel department were Yankees, the other being "a young Italian who does safety cartoons and acts as a general errand boy." Of the 22 foremen on which Collins had ethnic information, 19 were Irish Americans.

The work force ran between 1,800 and 2,000 and was heterogenous in composition, there being large numbers of Italian Americans, Polish Americans, and other ethnic groups as well as Irish Americans. Thus there were ample numbers of potential non-Irish candidates for foremanship positions, but Collins reports the implicit understanding of leaders of the work force that the foreman's job belonged to the Irish.

---

[9] Orvis Collins, "Ethnic Behavior in Industry: Sponsorship and Rejection in a New England Factory," *American Journal of Sociology*, Vol. 51, no. 4 (January, 1946), pp. 293–98. Reprinted in Robert Dubin, *Human Relations in Administration* (Englewood Cliffs, N.J.: Prentice Hall, Inc., 1951) pp. 243–49.

When subforeman Sullivan left the plant to go into World War II, management appointed a Yankee by the name of Peters to take his place. Peters had long seniority and previously had seemed to be well liked by the other men. The announcement of the appointment was shortly followed by a walkout in the department in support of a man named Donovan.

The union president announced that this was a wildcat strike and not supported by the union, but he let it be known within the department that the union would remain neutral. The work group filed a grievance. Collins points out that such a grievance had no legal standing because the contract gave the union no right to challenge managerial appointments. Nevertheless, the filing of the grievance did give the men an excuse to go back to work while still keeping the pressure on management.

Throughout arguments over the issue, no mention was made of the implicit qualification for foremanship of Irishness. The workers simply claimed that in the past foremen had always chosen the subforemen, and now management had violated this right by appointing Peters without consulting the foreman (Connor). But note that since the contract gave no legal right to the union to have a say in supervisory appointments, this claim also had no legal standing.

Shortly after the walkout, Peters remained at home "sick." When it became evident that he was not going to return, management appointed a man named Murphy to the position. There were no further complaints on the part of the work group.

Collins provides this interpretation:

The group rationalization seems to have been: it has always been the duty of the foreman to help choose his subforeman, but management appointed a subforeman, a Yankee, without consulting the foreman under whom he was to work. If Connor had not been cheated of this privilege, he would have insisted upon an Irish assistant. Donovan is Irish and leader of a gang; therefore, it is up to us to see that Donovan gets the job by inducing the Yankee, Peters, to leave. But if Murphy gets the job, that's all right because he is Irish, too.

Collins notes that Murphy and Donovan had been good friends before the issue arose, and they remained good friends after Murphy's appointment. Since management had now done "the right thing" by appointing an Irishman, Donovan could hardly hold this result against his friend.

A somewhat similar issue arose when management decided to consolidate its cleanup services and appoint a "janitor foreman." The union's safety and health subcommittee of the labor-management committee demanded the right to choose the new foreman. Management stood firm on its prerogatives, but agreed to consider nominations proposed by the union. All but one of these nominees were Irish.

Management rejected them all, reclassified the position as "sanitation engineer" and appointed Roundtree, a Yankee and plant guard. There were indeed complaints, but neither the union nor the work group took drastic action. By well-established custom, administrative positions belonged to Yankees. By calling the job "sanitation engineer," management effectively removed it from the jurisdiction of the union and the work force.

Is it only the Irish who "stick together"? In the Benton Glass Works plant, we observed a case of Swedish dominance. The first glass blowers had been Swedish immigrants, and it was assumed in this shop that only the Swedes really knew how to blow glass. When the sons of the Swedish craftsmen did not follow them into the shop, management had to bring workers with other ethnic backgrounds in at the bottom. As the Swedes grew old, died or retired, it became necessary to move workers of other ethnic groups up until they eventually took over the top positions. The first non-Swedes to push their way up were eloquent in describing the way the old Swedes stuck together—even talking in Swedish while on the job. The Swedes were notably uncooperative in teaching members of other ethnic groups the trade and saw to it that these men got no time to practice with the irons, even on the lunch hour.

In some lines of work, ethnic divisions are even officially recognized, as in the Jewish or Italian locals of the International Ladies Garment Worker's Union. Where the work force is made up of members of a number of different ethnic groups, we can expect that it will be an important (although unvoiced) issue in elections to union office whether the candidates are Irish, Italian, Polish, Jewish, Afro-American, Puerto Rican, and so on. This is hardly surprising if we remind ourselves that these ethnic group identifications to this day are important factors in political elections to local, state and national bodies.

This situation suggests certain implications for the integration and upgrading of Afro-Americans in the work force. The social barriers the Afro-American faces are not new. A man's ethnic group membership has always been a matter of consequence in placing him in the work situation—or excluding him from it. On the other hand, the sentiments upholding these social barriers are no doubt stronger than in the case of the Irish versus the Italians or any other ethnic group divisions.

If workers in a department where no Afro-American has worked before were asked to vote as to whether Afro-Americans should be introduced, the chances are that they would vote the proposition down. However, we must recognize that in the past management has not been inclined to consult workers about whom to hire. There is no reason that management should ask permission of presently employed workers now.

On the other hand, management should recognize not only that the introduction of any new ethnic group into the organization presents problems, management should also recognize that the internal social structure of the work force makes a great deal of difference in the potential ease or difficulty of introducing representatives of a new ethnic group. In a small department with a tightly knit structure, the introduction of any "different" person will be difficult. In a larger department, with more loosely knit structure, entry should be much easier. To be sure, the "different" person may have to put up with some degree of social isolation in the early stages, but he is not likely to encounter the severe social pressures developed within a small and cohesive department.

But the success of introduction of "different" people depends not alone upon the social structure of the workplace. Success is influenced very strongly by the actions taken by union and management leaders. This puts the problem in a broader context which we will need to consider as we deal later with these larger structures.

Summary and conclusions

A group consists of a number of individuals who interact with each other and engage in common activities. In this book we are not concerned with groups which come together on just one occasion. We shall be dealing with groups which carry on a pattern of interaction and activities over a period of time.

We can determine group membership observationally in terms of the frequency of interaction among individuals. We can also make a determination through interviewing, asking each individual to give us a list of those he considers members. Generally, the two types of data will lead us to the same conclusions. Where we find discrepancies, these are likely to point to individuals who hold marginal positions in the group.

Whenever three or more individuals interact together over a period of time, the group tends to develop a structure. We have noted two ways of delineating the structure.

Through an observational approach, we determine leadership by noting which member tends to initiate changes in activities for the other members. In a group in existence long enough to have a crystallized structure, we find that there is one person who either directly initiates activity changes or who endorses proposals by others; without his initiation or endorsement, activity changes do not take place. The leader is also the focal point in conversation: he addresses the group more than does any other, remarks are addressed to him more than to any other, and we see members cutting short their own remarks when they observe that the leader is not paying attention to them.

Through a sociometric approach, we establish structure in terms of the choices members make of other members. The structure we draw depends to a large extent upon the type of question we ask. If we ask for personal preferences for spending leisure time together, the sociometric network reflects popularity. If we ask which members contribute the most to getting the group ahead in whatever it is doing, then we are likely to come out with a leadership structure similar to that which we would draw on the basis of observation of initiation of changes in activities.

It is important not to confuse popularity with leadership. The leader, as determined by observation of set events or by a sociometric question focused on personal influence, will not be unpopular, but often we will find that he is not the most popular individual in the group. Furthermore, we often find that the most popular individual has little influence in the initiation of activity changes.

We should also distinguish our definition of leadership from status or talent. The person of high social prestige is more likely than the person of low social prestige to be observed initiating activity changes for others, but the correlation is far from perfect. We can all think of cases of individuals of high social prestige who have had little influence on group activities. While we often hear it said that Joe Jones is a leader because he is a football star, an outstanding student, or a skilled debater, Jones is not a leader in our terms unless we find him frequently initiating changes in activities for other students.

Our first purpose in presenting the Nortons was to show what we mean by group structure and to indicate the evidence upon which such a structure was based. We noted that the organization of group activities could only be understood in terms of the group structure. We then went on to show that this structure had effects upon the mental health and performance of its members. When a member (Doc) was prevented from playing the role to which his position in the group had accustomed him, he experienced dizzy spells. When a member (Frank) who had demonstrated exceptional skill in baseball, played on a team made up of group members, his performance conformed to his low ranking in the group.

In "Banana Time" we examined a four-man group which, while in the factory, appeared to be little affected by interpersonal relations outside of its small department. The life of the group was dominated by the simple repetitive production activities and by efforts of the members to cope with tedium and fatigue. The satisfactions the men found in the work place were highly dependent upon the pattern of interactions and activities they developed to break the long and monotonous day up into meaningful subunits. When Roy provoked the "barber college" crisis and the pattern of interactions and activities fell apart, the social satisfactions of work were lost, and the monotony and fatigue of the job became almost unendurable.

When we consider a department made up of a single small work group, questions of membership and structure are simple and clear cut. As we increase the level of complexity with the Harvard study of a department of 47 workers, we find not one but various work groups and neither membership nor structure are immediately apparent. By observation and interviewing, the researchers delineated six groups and also found that 30 percent of the workers belonged to no group. They identified the leaders of each group and also found status differences among groups.

In this particular factory, ethnic identification (being Irish) proved to be the most important factor in group membership and leadership, and it also strongly influenced work satisfaction. In the Collins study of "Ethnic Behavior in Industry," we found that ethnic identification was also important in determining who "belonged" at the supervisory level. That study provides us with a bridge to our next chapter, for we have been unable to examine membership and leadership in this case without considering also intergroup relations.

In this chapter, we have introduced three new concepts: *status congruence, norms,* and *cohesion.*

Status is often viewed in global terms. We can seek to determine the general level of social prestige occupied by an individual in an organization or community. But if we ask what characteristics of the individual lead others to accord him a given status, we are posing quite a different question. We know from experience as well as from research that status evaluations tend to be based upon such criteria as education, skill, age, seniority, ethnic background, earnings, and sex. When we recognize that, as perceived by others, the status of an individual is a reflection of not one but of various characteristics, we see at once that individuals are not necessarily uniformly high or uniformly low on these status characteristics. We are then led to ask: Does it make a difference in the behavior of the individual and in the reactions of others to him whether his status characteristics are "in line" or whether they are incongruent? The Harvard study presents evidence to indicate that the concept of *status congruence* provides us with a useful analytical tool for the understanding and prediction of behavior.

By *norms* we mean those beliefs strongly held in common by group members as to what behavior is right and what is wrong for members in the course of group activities. We use the word "strongly" to indicate that when norms are violated by one individual, the other members are not indifferent to his behavior, but rather seek to penalize him in some way.

Cohesion in terms of sentiments refers to the degree to which the members prefer to be together and act together in preference to participating in some other group. Behaviorally, *cohesion* refers to the degree to which the members "stick together" and follow a common line of action, particularly when confronting outside forces. We find that some groups show a high degree of "stick-togetherness," whereas others seem unable to act together when faced with the slightest opposition. In this book we will seek to explain some of the factors that lead to these differences.

Norms and *cohesion* can best be understood in a context of intergroup relations. The norms most strongly held by group members are likely to be those whose violation would expose the group to some outside threat. We often find that the most cohesive groups are those which find themselves in competition or conflict with other groups. Thus both concepts should take on more meaning for us as we proceed in the next chapter to examine intergroup relations.

References

Homas, George C. *The Human Group.* New York: Harcourt, Brace and World, 1950. This is one of the classics of small group research. Of the five groups analyzed, three are particularly relevant to our purposes: the Nortons, the Bank Wiring Room of the Western Electric Company, and the Electrical Equipment Company (which we will discuss in a later chapter).

Hare, Paul, Borgatta, E. F., and Bales, R. F. (eds.). *Small Groups: Studies in Social Interaction.* New York: Alfred A. Knopf., 1955. A useful collection of small group studies.

Roy, Donald. "Banana Time: Job Satisfaction and Informal Interaction," *Human Organization,* Vol. 18, no. 4 (winter, 1959–60), pp. 156–68.

The full presentation of one of the cases summarized in this chapter may be found in:

Zaleznik, A., Christensen, C. R., Roethlisberger, F. J., with the assistance and collaboration of Homans, G. C. *The Motivation, Productivity and Satisfaction of Workers: A Prediction Study.* Boston: Harvard University Graduate School of Business Administration, 1958. One of the best case studies of work groups. Also important for its theoretical contribution.

Discussion questions

1. Select a group known to you through experience and/or observation.

a) Chart its leadership structure. Present samples of the evidence you use in determining this structure.

b) What characteristics do the members have in common? If there are individuals who are on the margin of the group, what distinguishes them from the core members?

c) State one or more norms of the group. How do you know that your examples are norms?

d) Would you say that this was a group with high or low cohesion? On what evidence do you base your conclusions?

Note: in presenting a case from memory, you cannot be expected to marshall sufficient evidence to "prove" your points. Think rather in terms of samples of the types of data you would look for *now* if you were to undertake a new field study of such a group.

8. Groups: offense and defense

UNTIL RECENT YEARS, behavioral scientists have concentrated much more attention on study of interpersonal relations and upon the study of groups than they have upon intergroup relations. We are now coming to recognize that we will be severely handicapped in our efforts to predict individual and group behavior unless we also have systematic information on the relations between this group and others with which it comes into contact. Many of the problems that we shall deal with in later chapters will have important intergroup aspects. Let us prepare ourselves for these more complex problems by beginning on a simple level.

We will begin with a field experiment in which two groups of boys interacted together, isolated from all other contacts except for several adults responsible for the program. We will take a step toward the study of intergroup relations in organizations by examining laboratory experiments performed on members of management of an industrial company. We will then present some brief examples of typical intergroup problems that arise in the ordinary course of events in industry. Finally, we will see what preliminary generalizations we can make across this wide range of cases.

1. Bulldogs versus Red Devils

We present first a brief summary of the boys camp experiment conducted by Muzafer Sherif.[1] The experiment was remarkable in several respects. It was carried out under "natural" field conditions. The subjects were unaware that they were participating in an experiment, and yet their behavior was systematically observed, and the data were further enriched by informal interviews. Furthermore, in spite of the apparent naturalness

---

[1] This is taken from "A Preliminary Study of Intergroup Relations," by Muzafer Sherif, in J. H. Rohrer and Muzafer Sherif (eds.), *Social Psychology at the Crossroads* (New York: Harper & Bros., 1951). The experiment has been reported more fully in M. Sherif and C. W. Sherif, *Groups in Harmony and Tension* (New York: Harper & Bros., 1953).

of the conditions and the freedom of action of the subjects, the experimenter and his staff exercised a high degree of control both in the selection of subjects and in the production of the effects that they wished to observe.[2]

Sherif selected 24 boys as his subjects. His aim was to pick individuals who would be as homogeneous as possible in their background characteristics in order that the differences in behavior shown in camp could not be attributed to these factors. The boys selected were all 12 years old. They were of native American stock, and Protestant in religion, with 19 of them belonging to one church and five belonging to a closely similar church. Their parents were all judged to be lower middle class. Psychological interviews with the boys and their parents indicated that the boys were all normal in personality, at least to the extent that there was no case of a recognized behavior problem. They all had approximately average IQ's.

The parents of the boys were asked to pay a nominal fee for the camping period, and the boys and their parents were told that this was an experiment that Yale University was conducting in order to discover improved methods of camping. They were not told the main purpose of the experiment: to learn more about intergroup relations.

The experiment covered a period of 18 days and it was organized in three stages.

Stage one, three days in length, provided a maximum opportunity for all 24 boys to mix and play together, with each boy seeking out the associations he wished. During this period they were closely observed by the research staff, which was acting in its dual capacity of camp staff. Sherif was assisted by two graduate students who acted as counselors. Theirs was primarily a research responsibility and they were assisted by two junior counselors who had had a good deal of previous camping experience. Sherif, himself, posed as Mr. Musee, the camp caretaker. This role allowed him to be with the boys throughout their activities, carrying things, helping with the equipment, and indulging in other activities which might fit in with the caretaker role and at the same time provide him with an opportunity for observing.

Toward the end of the first stage the counselors informally interviewed the boys to get their preferences as to the activities they particularly enjoyed and the boys that they particularly wanted to have in their group. This process was explained to the boys as being simply an aid in providing the camp staff with a better idea of how to organize pleasant and profitable activities for the campers.

The observers did not take notes while the activities were going on. At the end of the camping day they retired to their own quarters and

[2] The following summary of the case is taken from W. F. Whyte, *Modern Methods in Social Research* (Washington, D.C.: Office of Naval Research, 1951), pp. 75–78.

worked long hours to record as fully as possible the significant interpersonal events that they had observed.

Stage two, lasting five days, began with the division of the 24 boys into two groups of 12. In making this division the camp staff considered strength and athletic ability so as to make the two groups as evenly matched as possible for later contests. However, the primary criterion for placing boys in groups was a sociometric one. The staff carefully examined the friendship choices of each boy and then sought to place him in the group which would have the *fewest* possible of such choices.

This unusual step was an important part of the experimental plan. Sherif wished to test the effects of frequent interaction within a group upon the sentiments of the members toward their group and toward an out-group. In order to do this he wished to minimize the effects of any affinities of personality that might exist. He arranged the division so that the members had indicated that approximately 65 percent of their best friends were in the other group.

As soon as the division was made, the two groups were separated with a counselor and junior counselor going with each group. The activities of the second stage consisted of hikes, cook-outs, swimming, and other activities that had been indicated as popular ones by the boys. All of these activities were planned and executed by the boys themselves. The counselors were present only to see to the physical safety of the boys and to provide necessary supplies and equipment.

As was to be expected, leadership structures emerged in both groups. The activities of the second stage also served to bring about a drastic reversal of the friendship choices so that now the research staff found that nearly all choices made were within the group.

As each group established its separate identity in isolation from the other, the boys gave their group its own name. Instead of just having two groups of 12 boys, we have the Red Devils and the Bulldogs.

As the boys interacted more frequently together, they developed great pride in their own group and, toward the end of this stage, members of each group began to demand competitive activities with the other. This fitted in with the experimental plan.

Stage three, consisting again of five days, was marked by the organization of intergroup competition. The Bulldogs and the Red Devils competed with each other in tugs-of-war, baseball, and other contests. The camp staff assigned a point score for victory in each of the contests and announced that there would be a prize for each member of the winning group at the end of the series.

At the same time the camp staff announced that there would be points awarded for the performance of camp duties such as the cleaning up of the group's living quarters (each group now had a separate bunkhouse), for K.P. duty, for waiting on tables, and so on. Here, the judgments for the awarding of points were in a large measure subjective, and it was for this reason that they were introduced. The camp staff wished to be able to manipulate the number of points awarded to each group so as to avoid a situation in which one group might so far outstrip the other in athletic contests as to destroy the competition before it had run its course. This manipulation of points kept the Red Devils within reach of the Bulldogs throughout the period, even though the Bulldogs proved themselves more effective in the athletic contests.

Observations on this period threw some interesting light upon leadership and group structure, for there is considerable evidence that the athletic victories of the Bulldogs were due to more effective organization. The diagrams and the discussion in the previous chapter indicate that influence and popularity choices were more widely shared among the Bulldogs.

As the contests proceeded with still a complete separation between the two groups outside of the contests, hostile feelings between them steadily increased. The Red Devils, who were losing the athletic contests, claimed that their opponents were very dirty players. The observers noted that the most aggressive sentiments manifested against the other group came from boys who had low standing in their own groups.

The Bulldogs' final victory was celebrated by the presentation of a pocket knife to each member of the group. Then the staff organized a party ostensibly to celebrate the finish of these contests. The aim here was to make it appear that one group was frustrating the other and to avoid any suspicion that the frustration had been arranged by the staff.

The frustration was arranged in the following manner. All of the boys were invited to the dining hall for an ice cream and cake party. Before the scheduled time, 24 plates of ice cream and 24 pieces of cake were set out. Staff members then messed up 12 of these pieces of cake and of ice cream so that there appeared to be two qualities of fare provided. One of the counselors arranged to delay the Bulldogs for a few minutes so that the Red Devils would be first to arrive in the dining hall. When the Red Devils came in they were told simply to help themselves. Naturally they needed only a quick survey of the scene to point out to them the beautiful pieces of cake and ice cream and to leave the mashed portions to the latecomers. When the Bulldogs came in, they immediately observed what had happened and began hurling insults at the Red Devils. The Red Devils replied simply, "First come, first served," and hurled the insults back.

This incident seemed to touch the fuse to the explosive relations between the two groups. Individual fights began to break out so that the counselors had to intervene. The boys also stored up baskets of green apples and sought to stage midnight raids upon the other group. Only the fact that the boys were unable to assemble their forces and get out of the bunkhouse with their ammunition without waking their counselors prevented the outbreak of open green-apple warfare.

In the final days at the camp the staff members sought actively to compose the differences between the two groups. The experimental period was now over and the staff was simply trying to patch up the situation. Since this was not part of the experiment we need not recount the events here.

The experiment is certainly remarkable from a number of points of view. Note particularly the care with which each step was designed and executed. Note also the steps taken to assure that the observers were going to observe what was planned instead of extraneous influences.

Here we see the most bitter signs of intergroup conflict created, apparently out of nothing. The experiment demonstrates very vividly the effects of building up a high frequency of interaction within each group and then producing competitive transactions between groups.

2.   The Esso intergroup experiments

The case to be reported now brings us a step closer to organizational life, for it concerns supervisors and executives of Esso Standard Oil Company meeting together in a training program where some of the content of their discussions involved the problems they faced in their jobs in the plant and office. These men met together, isolated from the plant situation, over a period of one week to two weeks. Their training involved participation in group discussions, but these discussions had certain unusual aspects which are of particular concern to us here.[3]

The laboratory experiment consisted typically of two eight-man groups. Each group constituted a "vertical slice of the organization" (including a considerable range of status from first-line supervisor up to high levels), but no man was in the same group with either his boss or with anyone who was directly subordinate to him. The experimenters thus built in the problems of handling status differences that are common to industrial hierarchies, but the composition of the group was quite different from groups normally meeting within a given department of the plant where a superior would discuss problems with his direct subordinates.

The group members spent from two to four hours each day in these group discussions. The groups were isolated from each other for three or four days, each meeting separately for approximately 10 hours. This provided each group with an opportunity to have its members become familiar with each other, to develop a stable pattern of interpersonal relations, and to try out certain problem solving discussion approaches. The members also got accustomed to having their group discussion used for research purposes. After each meeting, each member filled out a post-meeting reaction form, rating the value of the meeting and also

---

[3] Robert R. Blake, "Typical Laboratory Procedures and Experiments," in *An Action Research Program for Organization Improvement in Esso Standard Oil Company* (Ann Arbor, Mich.: Foundation for Research on Human Behavior, 1960).

providing certain data on interpersonal relations such as individual evaluations of the influence exerted by other group members. Summaries of these data were fed back to group members from time to time.

Now that each group had established an identity in the minds of its members and built up cohesion, the laboratory directors introduced the intergroup phase of the program. Robert Blake describes the process in this way:[4]

At this point, conflict is introduced in the following manner: It is suggested to the groups that they have now had a good opportunity to work together within their groups, and time for each to study its difficulties of working as a decision-making group. Therefore, an appropriate point may have been reached for introducing a problem that will permit each group to evaluate its own skill in dealing with a problem—a problem on which one group will win and the other will lose. No group ever rejects this proposal. The very idea of competition in a laboratory situation like this makes the fingers tingle.

As for the content of the problem, it might, for example, be "What are the conditions causing friction between management and labor in the refinery and what constructive steps might be taken to resolve these points of friction?" This is a down-to-earth, concrete problem on which each member has had some experience. Usually a labor-management issue is used, because this in itself represents two groups, fighting it out.

Each group is presented with the problem, and each group gets right to work, spends about two hours reacting to the problem, and in each case the problem results in something like a two-page typewritten report. This is the first phase of the intergroup competition.

In the second phase, each group receives the other group's solution as well as its own. Meanwhile, all along the way, all members in both groups are making data reports on how good they feel about their own groups, how they feel about the other group, how adequate they think their own solutions are, how inadequate, or adequate, they think the other group's solution is, and so on, all on nine-point scales. If the first phase was developing a solution, the second is comparing solutions on an ingroup basis, and this serves to intensify the intergroup competition. Neither group sees the other, but each sees the other's product. The sessions at this stage are fascinating to observe. A group will disparage another group's solution, disregard this and that, say "What a ridiculous thing this is," or "This is absolutely lousy."

In the third phase, each group selects a representative so that the two representatives may come together to evaluate the two solutions. The groups are now brought together and the representatives meet in the presence of everyone. Members of each group sit together, but the groups are separated. It is important that further communication take place, but undesirable that people speak out or wade in verbally, so they pass notes to their representatives. Here we have seen what brilliant skills people bring to the fore in intergroup representation of a win-lose basis. They throw each other off balance, use innuendo and slur, occasionally move in the direction even of slander.

---

[4] *Ibid.*, pp. 19–20.

In the in-group interaction stage, the observers noted the tendency toward equalization of influence among high- and low-status participants. This is hardly surprising, given the knowledge participants must have had regarding the philosophy behind such discussion groups, with their emphasis upon freedom of expression and democratic values.

When the intergroup competitive phase began, the observers noted a marked change in the pattern of participation of group members. Those who had high status in the organization tended to become more dominant in group discussions, and this was recognized by the members themselves in their evaluations of member influence. It was as if the high-status individuals interpreted the competition with another group as an emergency which called for them to take over leadership, as they would have done in the plant situation.

Blake has reported upon the emotional commitment expressed by group members toward the solution of their own group and against the solution of the other group. The social participation pattern and resulting commitment to the group have a measurable effect upon knowledge of the facts regarding solutions proposed. On the basis of an examination of the points covered in the solution of each group, the experimenters drew up a test of 40 items, with each subject being required to check those items that were found exclusively in the solution of his own group, those found exclusively in the solution of the other group, those found in common in both solutions, and those present in neither solution. The test provided for 10 items in each of the four categories. Eighteen out of the 20 groups studied in this experimental situation showed a greater tendency to claim common items as belonging to their own group than to credit them to the other group. Another exercise tested for knowledge of the points covered in the solution of each group. All of these 20 groups performed on the test in such a way as to indicate that they knew their own group solution better than that of the other group, even though they had spent much time examining the other group's solution.

As we have described the experiments so far, it was impossible to reach an outcome in the competition. The predictable result was an impasse, with each group upholding the superiority of its own solution and each representative refusing to be persuaded that the other group had a better solution.

So as to study the impact of victory and defeat, the experimenters introduced an additional step. They selected an impartial person, unconnected with either group, to study the two solutions carefully and then render his judgment as to which group had won. The judge's verdict would be delivered in a meeting with both groups assembled, and the event was naturally anticipated with a great deal of tension and interest.

When the judge delivered his decision, the experimenters observed typical reactions on the part of the winning group and the losing group. The winners would greet the announcement with jubilation that they made no effort to conceal. They were also lavish in their praise of the judge who had shown such good judgment in appreciating the fine points of their solution and seeing through the loopholes in the solution proposed by their opponents. The decision would be rendered at the end of a working day, and this would set the winning group off into a pattern of celebration. The evening would be spent drinking, singing, joking, and otherwise expressing their enthusiasm about each other and their group.

The reactions of the losers were drastically different. After a brief period of stunned silence, they would begin to react against the decision. The reaction would take the general form often expressed among groups of boys as "we wuz robbed." Of course, this sense of outrage would be expressed in more sophisticated terms. Members would say that they were disappointed that the judge did not have either the intelligence or the sense of good judgment that they had been led to expect from him. How could any well-qualified person fail to appreciate the superior merits of their own solution and fail to note the transparent absurdities in the solution of their opponents?

After a period of venting their antagonisms toward the judge, the losers would then turn their frustrations toward certain members of their own group. Typically, one of the men who held low status in the company hierarchy would say something like this: "Do you remember that point in our solution that the judge criticized? Well, I never did like that myself, and I had another idea, but you wouldn't listen to me." There would follow some argumentation as to who—besides the judge—might have been responsible for the group's losing the contest.

The experimenters further observed that win and lose outcomes had quite different effects upon the subsequent learning ability of members in these group discussions. The members of the winning group were so satisfied with public recognition of their excellence that it was difficult to get them to give serious thought to any problem that might have existed in the way the group worked through problems presented to it. It was as if the members had concluded that, since the group had won, it naturally followed that the group was an excellent group that had no problems.

The further progress of the losing group depended upon which of two possible pathways it took after going through the two stages of blaming the judge and then arguing over the way the group had been run. The argumentation might bring to the surface such feelings that it was difficult for the group to pull itself together and handle its interpersonal problems so that a meaningful group discussion could be continued. The other pathway found the group members transforming their frustration and disappointment into a thoughtful re-examination of the problems of their group and of ways in which the group might perform better. The experimenters felt that when a losing group was able to reach this pathway, its members learned more in subsequent sessions than was the case with members of the winning group, who were so satisfied with their success that they were unable to consider ways of improving their performance.

Note the striking parallels in the intensity of in-group commitment and intergroup rivalries found both among the 12-year-olds and among the industrial management people. The reader might ask: How could grown men with responsible positions in a leading company become so involved in an artificial and temporary situation? The answer is hard to comprehend by anyone who has not had an intensive and prolonged experience in a discussion group.

The case recalls my own experience in observing a discussion group that met for two hours every afternoon for a three-week period in a program of the National Training Laboratory for Group Development in Bethel, Maine. The participants in the discussion were all adults, and many of them had responsible positions in a variety of organizations. In general, they were upper middle-class people, who, under ordinary circumstances, could have been expected to display a lively interest in world affairs. The Training Laboratory program was carried on in the summer of 1950, just as the time when the Korean War was getting underway. While we were all aware that something important was happening far away, in conversations outside of the regular group meetings, the Korean War received scant attention. We were too much concerned with thrashing out what was happening in our particular discussion group.

I therefore conclude that the phenomena observed in the Esso Training Lab and the Bethel discussion groups were normal in the sense that they could be expected regularly to occur under the conditions of high frequency and long durations of interactions among a limited group of people. Under those circumstances, the normal individual develops an intensity of commitment to the group and its activities that an outsider finds difficult to comprehend. The same individual may look back on the events of this discussion some months later and ask himself, "How did I ever get so deeply involved in such trivial issues?" But note that he is asking the question when he is no longer involved in the interactions and activities that built the emotional commitment.

3.   The work group versus management

Much of the life of any complex organization is to be understood in intergroup relations terms. In the factory, lines tend to be drawn between workers and management. As we shall note later, when we study management, we are not dealing generally with a unified group but rather with a number of groups in competitive or collaborative relations with each other. In many plants, competitive relations within management are either not perceived by workers or else are submerged under the global perception of management as *the* out-group. Workers then react to individual members of management as representing this out-group.

Workers tend to see issues as we-against-them. This is not to say that hostile sentiments will inevitably prevail between workers and management. We are simply saying that the differences in organizational position are likely to lead to mutual perceptions that the parties are engaging in competitive transactions and negative exchanges. Here we will illustrate some of the forms that these transactions tend to take. Elsewhere we shall explore possibilities of promoting positive exchange and joint payoff transactions between workers and management.

Individual piece-rate systems provide an ideal setting for examining competitive transactions between workers and management, for piece-rate systems seem to make the perceptions of these transactions very salient for all parties concerned. This pattern of perception tends to arise at the very outset of the experience of the new worker. Management representatives picture the organization as "one big happy family." They suggest that the worker's cooperation with management involves joint payoff transactions for him and for management. Older workers seek to orient the new man in quite a different way. They suggest that joint payoffs are to be experienced by the new worker only in his transactions with other workers. They define transactions between the work group and management as of the competitive type.

In the following scene, we observe these conflicting orientations being brought to bear upon a new worker, Orvis Collins (who in this case served as participant observer). Collins had just returned from the talk regularly given to new employees by Mr. Heinzer, the factory superintendent, when an experienced worker presented him with this conflicting definition of the situation:[5]

JOE: Well, I suppose you've been up to see Heinzer. Gosh! I remember when I went up to see him.

COLLINS: What did you talk about?

JOE: It was a hot August afternoon and we all sat around there in a big circle. Heinzer did the talking. He just went on and on about the company, and what a good place the company is to work at, and how democratic it is here, and how everybody can talk to anybody they please about any gripe, and how he wanted to hear about it if there was anything we didn't like. He just went on and on.

COLLINS: What else?

JOE: He told us about how the piecework system was set up so that nobody could hang on anybody else's shirttail. He said it was every man for himself. He said, "You've got your friends. Sure! But you're not going to give them anything unless they give you something in the bargain in return." He went on this way:

"Now say that you want to buy a suit and you have a friend who is in the clothing business, you might go in and say, 'Look here, Joe, I'm looking for a suit and I want to pay about $25 for it. What have you got?' Joe shows you what he has in stock and you're pretty well satisfied with one and you say, 'I'll come in Monday with the money, Joe.' And you go out, but while you're

---

[5] W. F. Whyte, *Money and Motivation* (New York: Harper & Bros., 1955), pp. 11–12.

walking down the street you see this other suit in the window. Just the same suit Joe offered you for $30, but this outfit only wants $25. All right, young man, which suit do you buy?"

Heinzer looked right at me, and I knew what he was getting at. So I thought for a minute and I said, "I'll buy the $30 suit and lose the extra $5 if I can help a friend out."

Heinzer didn't know what to say. He took off his hat and wiped for forehead with his handkerchief. Then he said, "But that isn't good business, young man."

I said, "When it comes to buying a suit from a friend or from some other fellow, I'll buy from a friend, and I don't care about business." (We knew we were both talking about piecework.)

Heinzer thought for a long time and then he said, "But that's not the way the world is run. Now what would you do if you were walking down the street with your wife and met another friend, and this fellow was wearing the identical suit with the one you had on and your wife was with you and his wife was with him, and your wife said to this fellow, 'Why, that's just like Joe's suit, how much did you pay for it?' And the fellow said, 'I paid $25 for it at such and such a store and bought my wife a new hat with the $5 I saved by not trading at our mutual friend's store.' (He had fancy names for all these people worked out and everything and you could tell that he had been working up this story for a long time but I'll bet this is the first time he had to use it this way.)

I said to Heinzer, "Whoa, just a minute! My wife wouldn't say such a thing. My wife isn't selfish. She would want me to do the right thing by my friend." That ended Heinzer's talk.

He just said, "I guess that'll be all for today, boys." As we walked out, he said to me, "That's all right, son. I like a man who can give a straight answer." Like hell he does.

What was going on here? Heinzer was expressing the scientific management view of motivation: man reacts as an isolated individual; he should be interested only in working hard to get himself ahead. The only relationship Heinzer had in mind was that between the individual worker and management. The experienced worker not only argued for a collective orientation; he drew a line with the work group on one side and the management on the other.

The orientation Joe gave to Collins was only general in nature. The fable of the $25 or $30 suit told Collins how he was supposed to feel and what he was supposed to believe. It did not tell him how to behave on the job.

Experienced workers are not backward in giving new men specific behavioral advice. In the following report (from participant observer Donald Roy), Starkey, the experienced worker, is telling Tennessee how to cope with the time study man:[6]

---

[6] *Ibid.*, p. 15.

"If you expect to get any kind of a price, you got to outwit that son-of-a-bitch! You got to use your noodle while you're working, and think your work out ahead as you go along! You got to add in movements you know you ain't going to make when you're running the job! Remember, if you don't screw them, they're going to screw you! . . . Every movement counts!"

"Another thing," said Starkey, "You were running that job too damn fast before they timed you on it! I was watching you yesterday. If you don't run a job slow before you get timed, you won't get a good price. They'll look at the record of what you do before they come around and compare it with the timing speed. Those time-study men are sharp!"

"I wasn't going very fast yesterday," exclaimed Tennessee. "Hell, I was going as slow as I could without wearing myself out slowing down."

"Well, maybe it just looked fast, because you were going so steady at it," said Starkey.

"I don't see how I could of run it any slower," said Tennessee, "I stood there like I was practically paralyzed!"

"Remember those bastards are paid to screw you," said Starkey. "And that's all they got to think about. They'll stay up half the night figuring out how to beat you out of a dime. They figure you're going to try to fool them, so they make allowances for that. They set the prices low enough to allow for what you do."

"Well, then, what the hell chance have I got?" asked Tennessee.

"It's up to you to figure out how to fool them more than they allow for," said Starkey.

"The trouble with me is I get nervous with that guy standing in back of me, and I can't think," said Tennessee.

"You just haven't had enough experience yet," said Starkey. "Wait until you have been here a couple of years and you'll do your best thinking when those guys are standing behind you."

As this conversation continued, Starkey went on to give Tennessee even more specific instructions. If he expected to run the job at a speed of 610 r.p.m., when he was being observed by the time study man, he should start running it at 180. The time study man would make him speed up, of course, but starting at 180, he would have a good chance of settling for 445. If he started at 445, he could be sure the time study man would push him up to 610, and then he—and everybody else—would be stuck with a tight rate.

If the time study man demanded that he set the speed beyond his desired rate, then he should speed up and demonstrate how excessive speed would break the drill. How could you break a drill to prove your point?[7]

It's in the way you grind the drill. . . . The wrong kind of grind will burn up a drill at a lower speed than the drill will take if it's ground right for the job. . . .

---

[7] *Ibid.*, p. 17.

While the tools and techniques used by the work group in its contest with management will vary from plant to plant and job to job, note how Starkey clearly states his perception of the situation in terms of a competitive transaction: "It's up to you to figure out how to fool them more than they allow for." If the worker outplays management, he wins —and so does his work group. If the management man outplays the worker, then management wins and the worker loses—and so does his work group.

When rates are once set, the apparent tightness or looseness of a given rate leads to two different patterns of worker response. In the tight case, the workers seek to persuade management that the rate really is unfair. If individual complaints or formal grievances do not bring redress, then collective action is called for. Let us say that, through working as hard as they can, workers could make 110 percent of the base rate on this particular job. They feel that a 10 percent bonus is not enough for the additional effort. Rather than producing at somewhere between 100 percent and 110 percent, which would be acceptable (but not ideal) to management, they hold themselves down to 70 to 80 percent, which is punishing to management. Here the workers do not penalize themselves because they are paid their regular base rate while only "earning" 70 to 80 percent of that base. Since they feel that the possible 10 percent bonus is not worth the extra effort, they are not giving up anything of value in holding production below 100 percent.

Here we have an instance of negative exchange, the workers imposing the minus on management. Management representatives might like to balance the exchange by retaliating, but how can they do it? If one or two of the workers produce at around 110 percent, while the others hold down to 70 to 80 percent, then management has the necessary opening. The supervisor can argue that since one or two men are making 110 percent, with more experience and more effort, all would be able to make a reasonable bonus (120 to 130 percent). This proves that the rate is fair and that therefore management should not be pressured into loosening it. Besides, it proves that the other men are soldiering on the job, which is against the rules. The supervisor can threaten them with punishment and even carry out his threat on one or another of the men.

As long as the men maintained a united front at 70 to 80 percent and claim they are doing the best they can, it is very difficult for the supervisor to retaliate. He may be convinced that he is facing a slowdown, but does he dare act against the whole group? It is therefore very important for the group to prevent any of its members from "getting out of line."

Suppose the rate turns out to be loose, so that the men, with diligence and skill, could produce at 200 percent. Do they go all out for this payoff? Such lack of restraint is seldom observed. The men well know that the time study man did not intend the job to pay more than approximately 130 percent. If they should produce at 200 percent, they fear that the rate would be cut, so that they would have to work harder for less money.

If management has guaranteed that rates will not be cut, how explain this fear of rate cutting? It does evidence a distrust of management, but the problem is more complicated than a question of belief-disbelief. Earnings around 200 percent demonstrate to the time study man that he has lost the game to the workers in setting this particular rate. Can the time study man initiate another game in the hope of squaring accounts? In order to produce at far beyond the anticipated ceiling, the workers may well have discovered short-cuts in job methods. The time study man can argue that a "major" change has been introduced into the job and that therefore he has the right to restudy the job, as performed with these new methods. While the workers may be outraged at the thought that they are to be penalized for their inventiveness, the changed methods do in fact provide the time study man the argument he needs to reopen the case and start a new game that the workers are bound to lose.

If the time study man cannot prove that different methods are being used, there is still another option open to management: the job can be "reengineered." While the workers may feel that this move is only a disguised rate cut, if management does in fact introduce substantial changes in equipment, tools, and methods, then the action is clearly legal —whatever the motivation.

This analysis suggests that worker restriction of output on guaranteed incentive rates is not as irrational as it has often been considered. If production at around 200 percent clearly invites a threat of retaliation, then it is better for the group to hold back at some lower figure. What is a safe figure? The worker ceiling may come to be about 150 percent. If this is more than what management ideally would like to pay, it is not enough more to make it worthwhile for management to undertake the retaliation, which would provoke further retaliatory moves on the part of workers.

If 150 percent becomes the accepted ceiling by workers, we call this a work group norm: It is wrong to produce more than 150 percent. We can determine if, in fact, this is a norm by observing what happens when a member shows signs of going beyond 150 percent. Other workers tell him that he is doing wrong. If he persists, more serious sanctions may be brought to bear. The "rate buster" becomes a social isolate.

The norms regulating group member behavior are likely to arise particularly in intergroup situations: it is felt that the members must abide by the *norm* in order to protect the position of the group in relation to other groups.

Norms should not be considered an all-or-nothing proposition: unless everyone obeys the norm, the norm does not exist. For any group, we need to ask how closely behavior important to the group is regulated. Here we introduce the concept of *cohesion*. Nonconformity may be considered a phenomenon of the individual personality, but we may also approach the problem from the group side, asking to what extent group members "stick together." We recognize that groups differ widely in *cohesiveness* (in this sticking together sense). While we shall consider *cohesion* more systematically later (in Chapter 21), we will now turn to a case where a series of competitive transactions broke a department into groups at war with each other.

4.   The problem of the grinders[8]

The case of the grinders represents a very common situation in which a change introduced in one part of a department disturbs the social equilibrium of that department and leads to intergroup conflict. The grinders constituted one department of a steel mill studied by Leonard Sayles. There were three stages of operations in that department. First came rough grinding and then finish grinding, both of these operations being performed on all materials flowing through the department. From finish grinding, much of the material went directly to shipping, but some of it was routed through a small group of fine grinders who put on an extra polish.

In status, the finish grinders held a marked superiority over the rough grinders. The fine grinders held the same pay classification as the finish grinders, but they were much fewer than the finish grinders and did not occupy as important a place in the social structure of the department.

The finish grinders worked on what Sayles has called the Bell machines. Their jobs were thought to be the easiest and most prestigeous in the department. As a natural consequence of this desirable position in the job structure, the finish grinders were men with top seniority in the department. They had also come to exercise informal leadership in the department, and they spoke for the department in union affairs.

All was well as far as the finish grinders were concerned until management decided that it had to get more production out of the finishing operation and introduced the Scott-Winston machines, which were capable of speeding up the work substantially. Management opened the jobs on the Scott-Winstons to bid by members of the department. The men on the Bell machines, with their top seniority, could have taken over the Scott-Winston jobs, but at this time they saw no advantage in doing so. In the past, members in the department had stood firm against the introduction of incentive rates. The new Scott-Winston jobs paid the same hourly rates as could be had on the Bell machines. Thus, the Bell operators allowed the lower seniority men in the department to take over the Scott-Winston positions.

Management had decided that the potential gains in productivity on the Scott-Winston machines could only be realized if incentive piece rates

---

[8] *Ibid.;* case summarized from pp. 67–76.

were introduced. Had members of the department maintained a united front against piece rates, it might have been impossible for management to put over the change. Two influences swung the balance in favor of management's new program. Management people argued that costs in the grinding department were so high that management would either have to increase output in that department or else transfer most of its grinding operations to another plant. To lend an air of realism to his threat, management left some of the new Scott-Winston machines in their crates in the department, so they could be readily moved to a different location.

The other influence was a division within the department. While the Bell grinders remained firm against incentives, a number of men on the Scott-Winston machines were attracted by the possibility of increasing their earnings and were more inclined to use group pressures to gain attractive rates than to resist the introduction of incentives at all.

As the men got used to the Scott-Winston machines and discovered that they could indeed boost their earnings through the incentive rates, they began producing at a rate that gave them a substantial financial advantage over the men on the Bell machines. This development led to long and bitter friction within the department. The men on the Bell machines argued that the Scott-Winston men had sold out their union brothers in going along with the incentives and thus enabling management to profit disproportionately from the increased production. They also argued that the Scott-Winston men were producing so much as to invite management to cut the rates in the future, so that everybody would have to work harder to make the same income. The Scott-Winston men replied, in effect, that they saw no reason why they should sacrifice their own interests to those of the Bell grinders, who had mainly looked out for themselves in the past anyway.

When the men on the Bell Grinders saw the Scott-Winston operators, now on incentive, making far more than they did, they overcame their scruples regarding the iniquities of piece rates. Now they demanded the right to exercise their superior seniority and "bump" the Scott-Winston operators off of these positions.

What had been a unified department was now sharply divided. The rough grinders found themselves in the middle of the dispute between the Bell and the Scott-Winston men. Since they had the heaviest and dirtiest jobs in the department and received the same hourly pay as the other grinders, as long as incentives were not generally introduced, their position was low but secure. But now it became apparent that management was determined to introduce incentives for the rough grinders also. The rough grinders were not sympathetic to the men on the Scott-Winston machines, for they felt they were producing so much and getting such high earnings as to convince management that it had set too loose a rate. Management could then be expected to aim for a tighter rate on the rough grinders. On the other hand, the rough grinders were afraid that if they got a good rate on their job, the Bell machine operators might try to bump them out of those jobs. The ambiguous situation they found themselves in in the course of this dispute was illustrated by the fact that several self-contradictory grievances were submitted by rough grinders during this period.

The department steward, a Bell grinder, resigned because he said, "All the men in the department aren't behind me." A department meeting, dominated by the older finish grinders, passed the motion that would give them the right to take the lucrative positions on the Scott-Winstons. However, the bargaining committee on the union refused to recognize this decision.

In the course of this dispute, both management and the union leaders were neutral. They would have been satisfied with any decision that was acceptable to the department. As the informal organization of the department broke up into competing and conflicting groups, no generally acceptable solution was possible.

All these grievances and countergrievances, meetings and threats had had their effect on departmental unity. The coexistence of two incentive plans and men working on similar machines on a nonincentive basis were destructive of the informal organization that normally governed the workers' affairs.

The best example of this is an incident that took place early in 1951. The company, anxious to expand output, offered to schedule a regular sixth day of work for the entire department. Management had made this offer only after substantial pressure from the union. This reflected what had been a serious inequity in the eyes of the rank and file. The grinding department was the only unit in the plant that had not been working six days a week because of its fourth shift. Union leaders had implied that they could not be responsible if a walkout took place in the grinding department unless substantially more overtime was granted.

The only barrier to implementing the company's proposal was agreement within the department on a new work schedule to facilitate the additional day of work, the major problem being that everyone could not have his day of rest within the weekend period (with four shifts operating).

Under normal circumstances, the men themselves, through their own informal organization, would have arrived at some arrangement to schedule days off. Now they were unable to do so. The turmoil was so great that when the company called for a vote on the plan for implementing the overtime agreement the proposal was defeated. This was catastrophic to the hopes of most of the men, who wanted an extra day of work to catch up with the steadily rising cost of living. When some weeks later the company offered men in the department overtime work at a lower hourly rate in another part of the plant, a majority of the men accepted. Here they had no voice in the selection of their day off, the work was harder, less well paid and much more inconvenient than would have been their assignment in their own department.

Let us apply the transactional framework to this case. Management opened with a positive exchange transaction with the intermediate seniority workers, who grasped the opportunity, that the top seniority men let slip, to take over the new Scott-Winston machines. In order to put over the incentive rates, management now applied simultaneously a two-transaction strategy. To the Scott-Winston men, who had already reaped the rewards of one positive exchange, management now offered a trading transaction: You agree to the establishment of piece rates, and we will see to it that you get attractive rates. At the same time, management moved against the department as a whole by threatening to initiate a negative exchange: If you do not agree to the establishment of piece rates, we will move the production to another plant, and many jobs will be eliminated.

This dual strategy broke the united front in the department. No longer do we see intergroup conflict dividing workers from management. The lineup shifted to Bell grinders versus Scott-Winston men, with the rough grinders fluctuating in their allegiance. So hostile did these intergroup sentiments become that the members were unable to agree upon a joint payoff transaction (an overtime day for everyone) because some individuals would get more payoff (in preferred day off) than others.

5.   The case of the steel containers[9]

The men in department X were engaged in assembling and welding large steel containers for the armed forces. The work was considered of relative low skilled, and the department contained some of the lowest rated jobs in the plant. However, there was an urgent demand for the product, and management was much concerned when it could not get more than five or six units out of the department in an eight-hour day.

The union president urged management to offer the department an incentive rate. Management agreed, but somewhat reluctantly, since the group operation presented especial difficulties from a time study standpoint.

As the time studies proceeded, the union president himself spent a good deal of time in the department. Being a welder, he considered himself qualified to pass judgment upon time study estimates. He also thought he was on good terms with the workers in the department, so that they would talk to him freely and frankly. On the basis of these observations and conversations, the president became convinced that eight units a day would be about the maximum possible production for an eight-hour day. After considerable argument with time study men and production management, the president finally persuaded management to offer a rate figured in terms of maximum production of eight units.

_____

[9] *Ibid.;* case summarized from pp. 88–89.

No sooner had the rate been established than the workers began to do the impossible. Perhaps it was because they were short-service employees, not yet used to the ways of restriction of output, or perhaps it was because the defense order was considered a temporary run. Whatever the reasons, the workers cut loose. Within a few days production was up to 12 units, and it leveled off at 16 per day.

Presumably the defense department was happy with this outcome, but all hell broke loose within the plant.

Long-service employees were bristling that young men who had been in the plant for less than a year were earning substantially more than they. One worker, a former union officer, summed up their sentiments:

Can you imagine how I feel walking into a bar and getting my check cashed next to some youngster who has only been in the plant a few months? He maybe gets $30 more than I do and I've been around here for 15 years.

Throughout the plant there were demands that all incentive rates be renegotiated. At the time the company was attempting to establish a new system that would provide better cost control. For many months their efforts to gain union acceptance were fruitless; the men refused to cooperate in the new program.

Of course, there were also rank-and-file pressures on union officers to permit the older men to leave their regular jobs and bump some of the young men with the exceptional earnings. In fact, the union faced a whole series of internal squabbles on seniority questions related to such moves as men competed with one another for the right to move into that department. This, in turn, threatened the company with the loss of many experienced workers who were requesting transfers from other departments.

The union president now occupied a most awkward position. He had gone out on a limb to get an incentive for this department, and his beneficiaries had chopped the limb right off. Workers in other departments thought he had been played for a sucker and demanded that he go right back and get that rate cut. But who ever heard of a union demanding that management cut a rate?

Finally, the president and his grievance committee went to management with demands that management loosen certain tight rates in other parts of the plant. Management responded with a demand that it be allowed to cut the rate in department X. When management agreed to loosen certain of the tight rates, the union committee men found no difficulty at all in agreeing to the rate cut.

This decision was greeted with indignation in department X. The workers protested loudly that the union—and particularly the union president—had sold them out.

Several months later the plant was shut down by an unexpected month-long strike. The issues presumably concerned a general wage increase under a contract reopening clause. However, the conflicts within the union may well have been a factor in precipitating the strike and building up bitter feelings that accompanied it. The desirability of a general wage increase seemed to be the only point on which the various factions of the union could agree.

In an election of officers several months after the strike, the union president was defeated. In the earlier period he had seemed to be highly popular with the members. Was the department X case his downfall? Such an overturn cannot be accounted for by any single factor. No doubt many factors influenced the election. However, can it be only a coincidence that the man who defeated the president had once worked in department X and had remained close to the workers there?

The Steel Container Case opens with a demand from workers in department X for a joint payoff transaction: establishment of a group piece rate. They even persuaded the union president and management that the transaction could be inclusive enough to include them all: the president would get the credit for solving the key problem of this department, and management would get out the production.

Transactions often do not turn out in the way some of the participants have anticipated. In this case, the department X workers profited far more handsomely than even they themselves had imagined. Management greeted the outcome with mixed feelings, happy with the production but worried over the outburst of conflicts within the social system. The union president had been so successful in department X as to disturb his relations with other departments throughout the plant.

Why should other workers have been disturbed? In a concrete sense, while the X men had gained heavily, no one had lost anything. In a relative sense, all the other departments had indeed lost ground when this low-status department came out with top earnings. The outcome upset the investment-rewards equation and deeply offended the values especially of the older, longer seniority, and more highly skilled workers. They felt it was just plain wrong for men with a minimal investment in the system to reap the maximum rewards.

These sentiments converted a union-management problem into an internal union conflict, with other groups openly seeking to put department X back into its place. With these groups behind him, the union president now inflicted a defeat on department X. The workers of department X could not restore their lost earnings, but they retaliated as best they could, helping to defeat the union president in his campaign for re-election.

Summary and conclusions

We have begun with analysis of intergroup conflict between two autonomous groups, Sherif's 12-year-old boys and the Esso training groups. In both situations the experimenters created the following conditions:

1. Isolation of each group from the other for an extended period of time.
2. A high frequency and long duration of interaction around common activities within each group.
3. A competitive transaction or series of transactions (in the extreme zero sum form) between the groups.
4. High cohesion within each group and extremely negative sentiments toward the out-group, while the competition was going on.

George C. Homans has proposed this regularity of social behavior: Up to some maximum point "the more frequently persons interact with one another, the stronger their sentiments of friendship for one another are apt to be."[10] Simple-minded as it appears, this is an important proposition. But then Homans adds the qualifying phrase, "other things being equal." In other words, the proposition holds under certain conditions and not under others.

The present chapter enables us to say something about those conditions. A high frequency of interaction within the group does indeed produce the favorable interpersonal sentiments predicted by Homans. Indeed the intensity of those sentiments among managers as well as among young boys has been most impressive. But when we involve the subjects in competitive transactions between groups, increasing the interactions produces quite a different result. The relationship between frequency of interaction and *intensity* of sentiments still holds but the direction of the sentiments is reversed: we get intense negative sentiments toward the out-group.

It is important to know not only whether A has favorable or unfavorable sentiments toward B, but also whether these sentiments are deeply felt. This leads us to restate Homans' proposition in the following form: *The more frequently persons interact with one another, the more intense their sentiments are apt to be.* We would then need further propositions to predict the positive or negative direction of these sentiments.

Our framework suggests two hypotheses on direction (now holding frequency of interaction constant):

1. If the persons are engaged in joint payoff or positive exchange transactions, their sentiments toward each other will be positive.
2. If the persons are engaged in competitive, negative exchange, or open conflict transactions, their sentiments toward each other will be negative.

If we wish to predict both the intensity and the direction of sentiments, we must know (at least in rough form) the frequency of interactions and the types of transactions in which the persons are

---

[10] George C. Homans, *The Human Group* (New York: Harcourt Brace; 1950), p. 133.

engaged. I hasten to add that as yet we have no good measures of intensity of sentiments. Nevertheless, large differences in intensity can be readily identified. We have noted, both for the boys and the managers, the high buildup of intensity of sentiments among individuals who, previous to the experiments, either did not know each other or else were only casual acquaintances.

When we move from experiments into the daily life of the organization, we go from situations that can be created in relatively "pure" form to more complex situations containing a greater variety of elements. We have tried to apply the same IAS and transactional framework to these nonexperimental situations.

In many factories the most salient in-group, out-group cleavage is that between the work group and management. The new worker is socialized into the plant social system primarily by fellow workers. They let him know where his loyalties are supposed to lie, and they seek to enforce compliance with the norms of the group. Nearly always one of the important norms will involve the amount of production considered appropriate for each job.

We have used the piece rate system to illustrate some of the common types of intergroup transactions seen in the factory. Rate-setting often comes to be perceived as a competitive transaction. If the worker fools the time study man more than the time study man allows for, then the worker wins and the management man loses. If the time study man correctly estimates the amount he is being fooled, then he wins for management and the work group loses.

The challenging of a rate involves the work group first in a negative exchange: holding back production to pressure management to loosen the rate. Management then tries to balance accounts by finding some way to retaliate. We have seen cases where worker-management relations were primarily made up of a continuing series of negative exchanges. The workers would devise ingenious tactics in order to punish management without incurring severe penalties themselves, while managers would scheme to devise new rules and new systems of control so as to be able to retaliate. Such a series of transactions often escalates into open conflict.

So much public attention has been given to worker-management and union-management conflict that we are inclined to forget that conflicts can and do arise between groups of workers. The cases of the grinders and the welders of the steel containers have illustrated breakdowns of solidarity among workers. Here we see a trading transaction between management and one group of workers (setting an incentive rate for the Scott-Winston men or for the container welders) provoking intergroup hostilities at the worker level. We have also related our transactional analysis to Homans' IR ratio and the disruption of the status system. In both cases a transaction with management enabled one group of workers to surpass in earnings workers who held higher status and had made greater investments in the system. While the status differences and the shifts in earnings were much greater in the steel container case, the same forces were operating in both cases.

In this chapter, we introduced two new concepts: *norms* and *cohesion*. Norms are particularly relevant to the understanding of intergroup relations, for the norms most strongly felt by group members are likely to be those whose violation would expose them to some loss in relation to some other group. We have also seen how competitive transactions between groups tend to increase in-group cohesion—at least to the point where victory or defeat is decided. Similarly, the increase of intergroup competitive transactions at the worker level leads to a decrease in cohesion within the larger unit of which the competing groups form parts. Forces leading to the increase or decrease of cohesion will be examined more fully in Chapter 21.

References

Homans, George C. *The Human Group*. New York: Harcourt Brace and World, 1950. A basic book for the analysis of small groups. Chapters 3–6 deal with the Bank Wiring Room of the Western Electric study. See these parts especially for analysis of norms and social control.

Roethlisberger, F. J., and Dickson, W. J. *Management and the Worker*. Cambridge, Mass.: Harvard University Press, 1939. See especially part IV dealing with the Bank Wiring Observation Room.

Whyte, W. F. *Money and Motivation*. New York: Harper & Bros., 1955. Part I deals with "The Worker and his Work Group." Part II deals with "Intergroup Relations."

Discussion questions

1. It might be said that the propositions regarding interactions and transactions stated in the Summary and Conclusions of this chapter are "obvious" or just matters of "common sense." To what extent is that an accurate statement? Do the points raised go beyond "common sense" in any useful way?

2. In his discussion of the Bank Wiring Case (see References), Homans applies an IAS approach similar to that used in this book, but he does not use the concept of *transactions*. Re-examine the case from the transactional point of view. Does this new concept add anything to the analysis presented by Homans? Or does it just clutter up the scene with additional complications?

3. Read the case presented in Chapter 10 of *Money and Motivation* (see References) on "Group Dynamics and Intergroup Relations." Re-examine the case, describing systematically the changes that took place in IAS and in types of transactions. Does this re-examination add anything to the author's analysis. Why or why not?

4. Select for analysis a group of which you have been a member. Focus particularly upon this group's relations with outside individuals, groups or organizations. Can you show how changes in this group's relations with the outside social world affected the internal structure of the group, its cohesion, and member compliance with group norms?

Part IV

INDIVIDUAL AND GROUP IN THE ORGANIZATIONAL CONTEXT

AFTER SETTING THE STAGE in Part I, we have proceded to present a framework for the analysis of behavior of individuals (Part II) and of groups (Part III). The purpose of Part IV is to begin the application of this theoretical framework on cases of individuals and groups and to place each of these units within the larger organizational context.

Chapter 9 deals with the conflict between a waitress and a restaurant supervisor and examines the impact of this conflict not only upon the waitress, but also upon her work group. Chapter 10 focuses upon a group leader or working supervisor in relation to his work group of craftsmen and to management. Chapter 11 deals with the man-group-organization relationships in a chemical process technology.

Part IV also aims to demonstrate how the personal history of the individual can be fitted into the analysis of his behavior in a current organizational situation. While the personal history record is only sketchy for Chapter 11, we have rather full accounts along this line for Chapters 9 and 10.

9. Supervisor, waitress, and the work group

THIS IS THE STORY of Ellen Geiger, Ann Lindstrom, and Ann's work group in Chandler's Restaurant. At the time of our study, Miss Geiger was directress of service, and Ann Lindstrom was an informal leader among the newer waitresses who worked on the second floor. While there were two levels of authority (assistant directress and hostess) between the two women, Ann Lindstrom looked upon Miss Geiger as her principal problem in Chandler's and Miss Geiger looked upon Ann as a serious problem.

In Chapter 4 we encountered Chandler's: a large restaurant operating on two floors in the central business district of a major city. There we emphasized the high pressure of the operation: high "turnovers" and often difficult problems of coordination. Before we put our principal characters on the scene, we need to fill in one further element: the status characteristics of the restaurant.

Status and mobility opportunities

As management people told the employees, the atmosphere of Chandler's was one of "refinement"—and we found the waitresses using that word in describing the restaurant to us. Strict standards of cleanliness and grooming were enforced upon the girls. There were rules regarding makeup, the wearing of stockings, and other matters of appearance, and these rules were enforced daily through an inspection held before the girls went on the floors to begin work.

Chandler's recruited its waitresses, to a large extent, from country girls who were in the big city for the first time and from lower class city girls. Many of them saw Chandler's as opening the door to upward social mobility. For example, Mary Collins had grown up on the farm and had had only a high school education when she came to the city to work at Chandler's. After several years at the restaurant, she married a college graduate who was an accountant. She continued to work while he was in the Navy. Of her husband's social group, she says:

231

Most of my husband's friends have married girls who went through college. I am good friends with them, and we write back and forth. I don't think they think any the less of me because I didn't have the opportunity.[1]

Mary Collins was our authority on what happened to the country girl who came to the city to work in a "refined" restaurant:

Well, the first thing is that she has to make some friends where she works. Then lots of times she'll move in and live with some of the waitresses (in hotels and apartments). Most of the girls do that. She can learn a lot from her friends.

You know, you really should be a little mouse and hang around in the dressing room. That's where it all goes on, when the girls are getting undressed and dressed. You get a lot of suggestions that way. I even got a good suggestion the other day about a new way of putting on my lipstick. I tried it out, and I like it better.

You know, some girls just don't know how to dress. They wear the wrong color schemes, and they have the wrong foundation garments.

Well, we just take them in hand and try to help them on those things. Lots of times they'll ask for it themselves. They'll say, "Where did you get those foundation garments? Where did you get that dress? Where did you get that coat?" Well, maybe I'll say that I happened to get this coat in New York, but I can take them to a place where you get the same thing here in Chicago.

Lots of times we'll take a girl out to this store for the first time. You know, there are some girls that are kind of timid, and if a saleswoman tells them that a certain garment looks wonderful on them, they'll buy it even if it looks terrible. You have to go along with a girl and make sure she gets the right thing. Now you take Alice and me. She wore entirely the wrong color scheme. She wore all dark colors except for pink. She never wore red. Well, those colors just didn't do anything for her. I got her to change to bright print colors, and she really looks 100 percent better. Then I took her out to a store once to get her a wool skirt. She said it was too tight at the hips. Now, I said, "You take that and get rid of that spare tire around your middle. You don't need it." I told her that she would have to take an inch off her waist. She took two inches off, and she looked a whole lot better.

Most of the girls appreciate it when you try to help them, and they catch on fast. A girl may not know how to dress at all when she comes here, and in a month or two she'll go out looking very nice. Sometimes I wish you would stand out on the sidewalk at about the time that the girls are coming out at night, and I think you wouldn't find a better dressed lot of girls anywhere in Chicago.

We asked Mary how a girl could get started in her contacts with men.

A girl can come in here without any contacts in Chicago at all and not have any trouble if she does it right. Soon she gets to know some of the girls here that she works with. That isn't hard if she is at all friendly, because the

---

[1] W. F. Whyte, *Human Relations in the Restaurant Industry* (New York: McGraw-Hill Book Co., 1948), pp. 153–56.

girls here are glad to help out. Well, one afternoon a girl she works with might say to her that she has a date that night and her boy friend has a man that he wants to get a girl for. If she wants to take a chance on a blind date, she can go out. In that way she gets started. She goes out on a double date and naturally she goes where other people are, and she meets other people too. Pretty soon she can make her own contacts.

You know, waitresses work hard and they also play hard. You'll find some girls go in for riding and other sports. Their wardrobes run mostly to sports. Then other girls like to step out at night, and their wardrobes run mostly to evening clothes.

There are lots of places where you can meet men even if you haven't been introduced. I always say that you meet your husband at play, not at work. That's the way it happens with most girls. When you go out riding, you get to know the people that ride. That way I've met some very nice people. I've met a man who has his own horses, and I've been invited to parties with him and his friends. It's not hard for a girl if she has a good personality.

Ellen Geiger's story

Ellen Geiger fitted in very well with the "refined" atmosphere of Chandler's. While of rural farm background herself, she dressed in the best of urban middle-class taste and always kept herself well groomed. She was blond with classic features.

I approached Miss Geiger for her story with some apprehension. While she had always been polite to me in the three months I had spent in the restaurant, only once did I detect the slightest sign of expression of an emotion. I had asked her a question, which she apparently found awkward, for I noticed a slight quiver to her throat as she swallowed—but nothing more. I had felt that she was always giving me the correct management answers to any question I posed.

My request for the story suddenly changed her whole manner. She relaxed, smiled, and even laughed once or twice as she told me about her early life with obvious pleasure.

I can say that I had a very happy home life. Of course, we had difficulty, but we were a happy family. My parents were strictly religious. I had a religious training all the way through.

Since my mother was sick for a good many years, she had to have her children do most of the work in the house. She had to have it organized in a good system or else the work wouldn't have gotten done at all. There were three of us girls to take care of the house and at the start of each day she would lay out the work for each one of us. She tried to make it like a game so that we wouldn't mind the work, but it had to be done. If we didn't finish with our task in the morning we had to stay in in the afternoon until the work was done before we could go out for our leisure or to play. My mother was a good manager. When she went to school she studied things like that so she would be able to take care of her home when she got married. I attribute a lot of my success to the training I got from my mother.

She got us to take a lot of interest in our work around the house. We would try to outdo our older sister and she would try to keep ahead of us. It was like a game.

I asked her how her mother had stimulated such competition.

She'd tell us, "Now, you don't want your older sister to do a better job than you, do you?" And she'd tell our older sister, "Now, you're older than they are so it's up to you to set a good example." She was supposed to help us in our work too.

I asked how her mother had enforced her orders.

We weren't punished very much. You know, I think it's because my mother was sick and had to depend on us and because of religious training; we had such a respect and consideration for my mother that it would have seemed a terrible thing not to obey her.

You know, my father often threatened to whip us, but he never did. Still we were always afraid that sometime he would. My father was a stern person. When we did things we weren't supposed to do, he'd remember it. Maybe a couple of weeks later, we'd go to him and ask him for money for something we wanted to buy and he'd remember something we'd done not long ago and wouldn't give it to us. I remember one time I threw a stone at a girl and hit her on the ankle. That was when I was about 11 years old. I didn't mean to hit the girl. I only wanted to scare her. I wanted to be friends with her, and after that, she'd have nothing to do with me. She wasn't badly hurt. Her ankle was sore for a couple of days, and I felt terrible about it. A little while after that, we went to the fair and I asked my father for some money to buy some ice cream. He said that he'd give me 10 cents if I'd spend five of it for that girl. I refused to do it, so he didn't give me the money. Yes, I remember I thought that that was terribly unfair. I thought that other girls were a lot lucker than I was in their fathers. But then at other times, I'd look at it differently and think that it was wonderful to have a father like ours.

I asked what occasions would give rise to those sentiments.

Well, he'd play with us sometimes, and then, you know, we had a horse and buggy to ride to town in. Sometimes he'd sit up with us but let us do the driving. We had a lot of fun that way.

I asked her whether she confided much in her father and mother.

Not so much in my father as I did in my mother. We girls were much closer to our mother than we were to our father. I think that's the way it usually is, so we would take things up with her whenever we had anything that worried us. Whenever we had done anything wrong, we'd go and tell my mother first and let her tell Father about it. We knew that my father would find out about it sooner or later, but we thought that we'd get off easier if we spoke to my mother first. As I look back on it, it seems that my mother did most of the disciplining in our family.

I asked whether she would confide to her mother any problems that she might have with boys she thought of dating.

No, my parents really selected the boys we could go with. We used to have parties at home.

I asked her to tell me about her friends and the group in which she played in growing up.

We lived in a little town. There were no big cities near where we grew up in southern Illinois. All the people in town knew each other and most of them were related in one way or another. They were cousins and friends from the old country, yes, Germany. I did have four girl friends that I knew pretty well; they were all classmates of mine. But the really biggest activities that we had there were the church socials and the church clubs. We'd get together to make patchwork quilts and bake cakes—things like that to be sold or raffled off for the church—and then we'd have big parties in the church. There were four or five older women in the club that conducted our meeting and got us organized. No, you couldn't take a leading part in a club like that until you were middle-aged.

I asked her to tell me about her religious training. She said that she had belonged to the Lutheran Church.

We went to church and Sunday school in the morning and then after lunch, we'd sit around and then my father would read the Bible to us. We were taught how to behave out of the Bible. That we should respect the old and the sick, that we should not hate people, but instead forgive them even when they had done wrong.

Ann Lindstrom's story

Ann was of Norwegian extraction, her grandfather having come to this country and settled in the city where Chandler's was located. Ann's father had conducted a successful real estate business until he was ruined by the depression of the 1930's. At the time I knew Ann, her father was working in a factory.

Ann has an older brother and an older sister.

When I came along, my parents were very much disappointed. I know they wanted another boy. My mother always disapproved of me. You see, I grew up to be a tomboy, and she was always telling me, "Why can't you act like a lady."

Apparently she was continually at odds with her parents, although they were not severe in their discipline. Instead of spanking her, they would talk to her and make her feel very guilty. She had great difficulty in avoiding parental discipline.

It seemed like when I did something wrong, I always got punished by God. They said that God saw to it.

I asked her whether she had run around with any group of children in growing up.

Oh, we had a gang all right. There was a bunch of boys and me and another girl. We used to get in a lot of mischief together. We never did anybody any harm on purpose, but there were a lot of little things we would think up to do.

I asked who had the ideas. She laughed.

Mr. Whyte, don't you look at me that way. Yes, I generally had the ideas. It was a very active kid.

I asked if she ever had cried when she was growing up.

No, I never did. I couldn't cry and be with a bunch of boys like that, could I? I had to show them I could do anything they could do.

I went with a crowd of Swedish fellows even after I got married. I always get along better with men. We go out hunting and hiking and stuff like that. When I'd fall down nobody would pick me up. They'd talk about me as just another fellow, and we'd all have good fun together.

I asked about her husband.

My family disapproved of having me marry him. You see, he was a foreigner. That is, not that he spoke with an accent, but he had come over from Sweden when he was a kid. People around my neighborhood would say to my mother, "Couldn't she do any better for herself than that?" I heard about it, and that hurt me. I'm the type; I don't forget. I get back at them. This one woman that said she didn't like it because she thought I should marry her son.

Well, a little while after that he got married because he had to get married. We were together at tea one day, and I said to her, "Well, at least I didn't have to get married." My mother was furious. She wanted me to apologize, but I never would.

After her marriage, she and her husband continued to lead a very active social life. Their house became headquarters for the gang, and they got together every night. She was working at the time and so got little rest.

You know how thin I am now. Well, I weigh around 95 pounds. I had got so that I was down to 79 pounds, and I'd wake up at night in a cold sweat having nightmares. . . . Yes, I remember it very well. I always had the same nightmare. I would be being run down by a streetcar and Frank, my husband, and the other fellows would be standing around. I'd call out to them to help me, and they wouldn't do anything about it.

That went on for some time. I had to quit my job and stay home, and we had to cut out the parties. I will say for Frank that he was very good to me then. He'd hold me to him and he'd take out the towel and dry me off because I always got into a terrible sweat with those nightmares. We just had to cut out those parties until I got back on my feet, and then I wasn't working any more.

I asked about her divorce.

Well, you might just lay it to the war. We had good times together. We got along all right, and it lasted seven years. . . . No, I don't really regret it at all. I don't think it bothers me now. I waited three months after we separated before I came to work here. The divorce was granted just about a month ago (when she had been at Chandler's about three months). I still live in the house where I lived with my husband. I have all the furniture there, and I don't want to go home to my parents. Oh, I don't deny that it was a great shock to me, but I've got adjusted to it now.

In my first interview with Ann, she began talking about her work by saying, "This is definitely not my type of work." She had had a white-collar job in the credit department of a large firm until she was involved in a train accident which injured her eyes and prevented her from continuing with such close work. It was this which pushed her into waitress work.

Ann's initial adjustment to Chandler's

Ann entered Chandler's at a time when a series of changes was in progress within the management ranks. Shortly before her entry, the restaurant manager, Mr. Potter, had resigned to take a bigger job in another restaurant and had been succeeded by Mr. Stanton.

This change from Potter to Stanton will be examined in a later chapter on "Managerial Succession." Under Mr. Potter, Miss Ellis had served as directress of service, Miss Schulz as assistant directress, and Mrs. Loomis as hostess supervising the section of the second floor where Ann Lindstrom worked with other waitresses of low seniority. In this period, Miss Geiger had served in a staff position in charge of training of new waitresses. Over the first few weeks of Ann Lindstrom's tenure, Miss Ellis, Miss Schulz and then Mrs. Loomis all quit their jobs. Mr. Stanton eliminated the training position and moved Miss Geiger over to take Miss Ellis' place as directress of service, and he made other replacements at the assistant directress and hostess levels. This series of personnel changes had widespread impacts throughout the organization. Here we will concern ourselves only with those affecting Ann Lindstrom and her informal group.

Ann Lindstrom spoke in this way about her former directress of service, assistant directress, and hostess:

Miss Ellis was very popular with the girls. As busy as she was, she would always listen to you when you wanted to talk to her. You could go up to her anytime and she'd sit down and let you talk over the problem with her. You know, we were very shorthanded when she was here, but even so if you didn't feel right when you called in in the morning and told her you couldn't make it that day, she'd want to know how you felt and wouldn't try to persuade you to come in. She'd just ask you if you were going to be able to make it tomorrow, because she wanted to make up her schedule for the next day. Suppose you called in in the morning and you said you had a bad headache and you couldn't make it that morning, but you could get in for dinner. Just as soon as you got in and dressed, she'd be down in the dressing room asking you how you felt, and if you were sure you were all right to go on the floor.

I didn't like Miss Schulz at first. She has that sarcastic exterior. She tries to be hard, but she's really all "moosh" inside. I've seen her talking to the girls when she had tears in her eyes.

I asked how Miss Schulz tried to be hard and sarcastic.

Oh, when we made noise in the kitchen, she'd call us down about it at lineup and say that if we couldn't be grownup girls, she'd have to treat us like babies. Things like that the girls didn't like.

When you got to know her, it was different. I remember one day I had something I wanted to ask her about. I went up to her, and she asked me to sit down. Well, we talked for a long time. We talked about things outside the store too, and after that I got to like her very much. You know, she's a very thoughtful person. In that time just before she left Chandler's, she was really sick. She shouldn't have been working at all. One time I met her in the station waiting for a train. She really looked terribly sick. You wouldn't have thought that she could even stand up any more. I went up to her and said, "Let me get you a coke or something." "Oh, no," she said, "I know how hard you waitresses have to work. You're on your feet all day. Let me get it for you." And she went and did it. All the girls that got to know her liked her a lot. The girls who didn't get to know her didn't like her.

Of Mrs. Loomis, Ann said:

I can't think of any time I ever heard of anybody saying anything against her. She was a lovely person. You just couldn't turn her down when she asked you to do something. It was the way she put it. You know, she wouldn't give you an order, she'd just ask you to help her out, and you couldn't refuse her. Yes, on things like closing downstairs and working tea, we were supposed to do those things one week out of three taking our turns and it worked very well when she was there.

Sometime after they had both left Chandler's, I called upon Miss Schulz and Mrs. Loomis, who were living together. They gave me this picture of their relations with Ann Lindstrom and observations of her:

Loomis: Yes, I knew Ann quite well. At first, I didn't have much time to give her because as closing hostess I had to cover the whole floor. I noticed her from the start. It seemed that in the beginning she was a little on the defensive, and she had that sarcastic way about her. When I got to know her better, though, we got along very well. She was a good little waitress. You know, she isn't very strong. But when we gave her that station near the doorway, she was perfectly satisfied. I think she worked out her problems pretty well, and I felt that she was reasonably happy. I could always call on Ann to do anything for me in a pinch. She was very good about that. I knew that the girls got to like her a great deal too. You know, she was quite a bright girl.

SCHULZ: Did you know that she writes very well? Yes, she's showed me a couple of her things. . . . Now, I can tell you a story about Ann Lindstrom that might interest you. You know, Ann is rather outspoken. Well, it happened that time when they put in that new system in the kitchen. That was terribly hard for the girls. They complained about it and complained about it, but it seemed that no one would pay any attention to them. Finally Ann decided to write in a suggestion and put it in the suggestion box. She didn't sign her name to it, but I guess they checked up on her handwriting in the office—you know, on her employment card and when she signed her pay check. She worded it pretty sharply. It went something like this: "We've complained and complained about the new system in the kitchen, but it looks like management is just taking care of their own interest and doesn't care how the girls feel. Maybe if this is put down in black and white somebody might pay some attention to it."

Now, you know the way Mr. Stanton is. He'll just take a dislike to somebody and right away he wants to get that person fired. He called Miss Ellis and me into the office and said, "Miss Ellis, Miss Schulz, I want you to fire Ann Lindstrom within the next 24 hours. I don't want to see her around here anymore. Get rid of that girl." He just sat there with that grim expression on his face, and we knew there was nothing we could say to him about it. Frances and I just looked at each other, and then we went out of the office. Well, we decided just to forget about it at present, so we didn't fire Ann. I guess Mr. Stanton forgot about it too.

Up to that time, I didn't really know Ann, but I took her aside and I didn't tell her about what had happened in the office, but I said to her, "Ann I want to give you some advice. After this, if you have some complaints, don't put them in where you'll get into trouble. Just come talk to me about them and you'll be better off." She responded to that right away, and we were on a friendly basis from that time on. This was the last time she put a suggestion into the box.

Fellow waitresses also noticed the defensive attitude that Ann Lindstrom manifested when she first came into the restaurant. Rita Carey told me:

You know, at first I didn't like Ann at all. I couldn't stand her. We're working together, and she says to me "I'll close tonight; you close this noon." I says to her, "I'm going out this afternoon so I have to get off early." I says, "Since I'm the older girl here, I think you might do it." She says, "I don't care. I don't want to do it." "Well, then," I says, "the dishes will just lay there all afternoon." "All right," she says, "let them lay there."

Well, that burns me up because I came here long before she did, but I'm good-hearted, I guess. I didn't want to leave things in a mess, so I cleaned up for her. But after that I asked Miss Geiger to transfer her to another section. We didn't work together for a while, but then I guess it turns out that Ann is a good waitress so she puts her back in my section. I didn't think I was going to like it at all. The first day she comes to me, she says, "I'm closing this noon if you can close tonight." Well, I had no place to go so that was all right with me. But then she says, "Tomorrow I'll close at night, and you can close at noon." Well, I says to myself, that sounds all right. That's a fair exchange. So ever since then we've been working together and now we get on real good.

What became known as the "Chandler Nut Club" became the center of social life for the girls working on the second floor, and Ann Lindstrom became the leader of the group. The regular members of the group were Ann Lindstrom, Rita Carey, her twin sister, Lucille, Marie Pappas and several other waitresses. Two bartenders and an assistant maintenance man often ate lunch with the girls. The girls often went out together after they had finished work.

Ann and her friends under pressure

By the time I became acquainted with the Chandler Nut Club, I found they were beginning to have trouble with Miss Geiger, who had recently taken over as directress of service. My first indication of this trouble was a comment from Rita Carey that she and her twin sister were quitting the job. Rita began by complaining that the hours upset their social life, and she went on in this way:

Well, Miss Geiger knows that this job is getting on Lucille's nerves, but she doesn't see why I can't stay. I says to her, "Miss Geiger, Lou and me have always worked together, and that's the way we want it to be." She says to me, "Why do you have to do everything your sister does?" "Well," I says, "I think it's nice to be so close. We always work together." You know, when we go to work or when we come back from work, we have somebody to go with. Then like one time I had an accident on a job and Lucille was there to come home with me. That was nice. I think it's a wonderful thing to have a twin. It's much closer than just sisters. You really have more love for a twin. But Miss Geiger is always trying to bust us up.

One time there when they had the meeting on the insurance, she passed around the cards to sign up. Then she came around and tried to collect mine from me. I hadn't signed yet. I says to her, "Miss Geiger, I want to consult my sister on this." She says, "Why can't you make up your own mind?" I says, "I can make up my own mind. I got a mind of my own, but I always like to talk things over with my sister. It ain't inconveniencing you any, is it? I can get the card in tomorrow, but I always like to talk to my sister first on things like this. I'll get together with her and see what's what, and then I'll let you know."

Rita and Lucille then went on to discuss whether they should quit Friday night or stay through Saturday, as Miss Geiger had asked them to do.

RITA: Miss Geiger says she thinks we owe it to her to stay and work Saturday. Well, I don't see that. I don't see that we owe her a thing. Now I think Miss Geiger is all right. I don't agree with some of the girls on that. If you do something for her, she'll do it back for you. But Miss Geiger, she always figures whether you owe her something or not. She'll never do anything for you and not expect to get it back. Mrs. Loomis was different that way.

The next day Rita had changed her mind.

I'm staying. They talked me into it. Lucille's quitting, but I'm going to stay awhile. Yes, it was the girls, Ann and the rest of them, they went to work on me. They told me I was foolish to quit. Well, I thought it over, and I thought after all I'll never have such a good bunch of kids to work with. I've been here eight months so I might as well stay another four and make it an even year.

I got Ann aside and asked her what part she had played in getting Rita to change her mind. She grinned.

I gave her the old sob stuff. I told her, "What am I going to do with all these clucks if you leave me? I'll have to quit myself, and this is the only kind of work I can do now."

Then that night Rita got sick. They took her downstairs and gave her some kind of pills. Well, the pills didn't work. They made her hysterical, and she couldn't move her legs at all, and she felt real bad. When the girls heard about it, they all gathered around, got her hot tea and stayed with her, and I guess she decided that she'd never find a group of girls like that anywhere else, so she stayed.

The Chandler Nut Club lost Lucille, but Rita was the dominant member of the pair and a very important part of the gang. As she stayed, the gang was able to continue with its lunch meetings and parties once or twice a week after work in a nearby cocktail lounge.

Ann prepares to quit

Soon after that I began to hear that Ann was becoming very dissatisfied with her job.

I feel like quitting this job. It's really getting me down. It's just one crying jag after another.

This work is getting me down. I think one of the causes is that I resent doing this kind of work. I don't think it's for me. I don't like to take orders from people.

It isn't that I don't like to do things for people. It's just the way they approach me. Now suppose someone came in from the service pantry and said to me, "You go out and take the mop and clean the floor." The chances are I'd take the mop and wrap it around their neck, but if they ask me, "Would you please mind giving us a hand and help us with the floor," I'd be only too glad to do it.

Then it's so hard to get a rest here. You go to Miss Geiger for a day or two off, and she just won't give it to you. You have to be actually sick on the floor before she'll let you go home. She just says to you that she needs you. A girl can go just so long and then she needs to take a day or two off and get herself straightened out.

Less than two weeks later, I heard this from Rita Carey:

Ann's going to quit. That's what she told Miss Geiger. Miss Geiger talked to her the other night about talking back to the guests and other things, and now she's going to leave. Isn't that terrible? Here she got me to stay and now she's going to quit. A lot of girls are getting it these days. Martha and Sue got caught the other night for not wearing stockings. Would you believe it? They didn't even have leg makeup on. Now I got away with it once, but I had leg makeup on.

I sought out Ann and got her talking on her problems:

Well, last night I was just getting ready to go home when Miss Geiger opened the door and called down the stairs, "Ann, I want to see you." Well, can you imagine that? Just when I was on my way home. The trouble with Miss Geiger is that she doesn't know how to talk with the girls. Oh, she had a lot of things on her mind. She had an idea that I'd been talking back to the guests. I don't recall anything like that. I try to treat them all the same no matter how they treat me.

Another thing, you know they tell us around here, if you don't get along with a girl in your section, ask either to have her transferred or have yourself transferred. Rita and I always get along together, and this was the only time it ever happened. We just couldn't get along with this girl, and I spoke to Miss Taylor to get her transferred. Well, Miss Geiger held that against me. She said she didn't like to have girls that didn't get along with some of the other girls. Now, can you imagine that! First they tell us if you don't get along with a girl, we should complain; and then when we do complain, they hold it against us.

She said to me, "Ann, I don't believe you look upon waitress work as a career." I said, "Miss Geiger, you're right there. I certainly do not. I don't care for this work. There's no advancement in it." Well, she said to me that some of the girls here have worked for seven or eight years and are just working for their 10-year pin. I said, "That's all right for them but not for me. I don't look upon it as a career." Well, she didn't like that at all. She said to me, "If you don't like it here, why don't you quit?" "All right," I said, "I think I will quit." I didn't tell her when. I'm going to tell her that later.

You know one thing she didn't like. She told me she thought I was a disturbing influence among the girls. I said to her, "Miss Geiger, you don't have any idea how many girls were going to quit that I persuaded to stay here." She didn't like that at all.

Rita Carey: Ann, stop talking about quitting. Cut out that nonsense. You got me to stay, and now it's not fair for you to get out.

Marie Pappas: If you quit, I'll quit too. I really mean it.

Rita: I used to like Miss Geiger. I used to think she was all right, but now I don't like her any more.

Marie: Miss Geiger is two-faced. She comes up and fusses around you, straightens your collar, and smiles at you, and then she tells you something.

Something real sarcastic. I'd give anything in the world to have Miss Ellis back. She was really good. She'd tell you straight from the shoulder, but you could talk to her. You can't talk to Miss Geiger. She isn't interested. She just wants to tell you.

Three days later I encountered Ann and Marie at a table in the upstairs dining room. Ann said she would not be at work the following Monday.

ANN: Miss Geiger says I should make this my career. (*She laughed.*) You know, I really think she wants me to quit.

MARIE: That's just why you should stay here.

ANN (*Shakes her head*): I think she thinks I'm a disturbing influence. She doesn't realize that I've had to smooth out a lot of troubles. Why, this friend of mine, she wanted to get up a petition to have Miss Geiger taken away from here. I told her not to do it. I told her that if she did that she'd be blackballed from every restaurant in Chicago.

WHYTE (*to Marie*): Were you really serious about that?

MARIE: I sure was.

ANN: What I don't like is this Gestapo system. When I just think about it, it positively nauseates me. The idea of a girl squealing on another girl. Now yesterday 12 girls were caught for picking food in the service bar. You know yourself that Miss Geiger couldn't have seen that. It must have been somebody squealing on them. Now I've kept my eyes open, and I've looked around, and I've got a pretty good idea of what goes on here. Rachel, the rest room matron, she used to be part of that Gestapo system. I didn't want to say that to any of the girls because they mostly all loved her, but I knew it. One afternoon she asked me, "Ann, how is your marital situation coming along?" Well, I looked at her and I says, "My marital situation is strictly my own business." Whew! Can you beat that? What a nerve. After that I began to watch her to find out what she was doing. I heard her pumping different girls about their personal lives. She asked a lot of things she wouldn't have to know if she wasn't giving information. Jane Jones [ex-waitress, hostess] used to do that, and she still does it.

WHYTE: You feel that Miss Geiger knows things about you that she couldn't have learned by herself.

ANN: That's right. Now, take this case. When she was talking to me the other day, she said, "Ann, some of the girls here save their money." Now you can easily tell what she meant by that. She didn't think I was saving my money, and how did she know? She was talking about us going to the lounge. Maybe once or twice a week I get together with the other girls, and we go over and have some beers there. That's what we do. But how would she know about it if somebody hadn't told on me.

MARIE: I think what we do outside of the restaurant is strictly our own business. I don't think they've got any right to pry into your personal affairs.

ANN: Another thing Miss Geiger said to me—she criticized me for telling one of the guests that her selection of food was a crazy combination. Now when she first said that I didn't have any idea what she was talking about. Then I began to think about it, and finally I remembered what had happened. I was waiting on this girl toward the end of lunch hour. She ordered ice cream for desert. I found out that we were all out of ice cream; we only had chocolate ice cream and chocolate sauce. She said to me, "That sounds like a disgusting idea." I said, "Yes, if you ask me, it's a crazy combination, but that's all we have left." Now I remember as I was saying that one of the girls went past. I didn't think anything about it at the time, but now I know she must have squealed on me. If she was going to do something like that, why didn't she hear the whole conversation?

WHYTE: Could it possibly be that the guest complained about what you said?

ANN (*Shakes her head*): What would she have to complain about? I was just agreeing with her.

The following week Ann did not work. She told me that she had spent her time getting a rest and looking around for a new apartment, since she wanted to move. Having been unable to find what she wanted, she came back for just one more week, and I was able to interview her again on the job. After telling me that she still planned to quit, she went on:

I called into the office every morning last week. You know, you have to do that or you are automatically fired. I would give the message, and they would say, "Just a minute. I'll connect you with Miss Geiger." I'd say, "Oh, no, I don't want to talk with Miss Geiger. That's all."

Wednesday morning when I called, that pipsqueak in the office said, "Are you still sick?" I said, "Sure I'm still sick." She said, "Did you see a doctor?" I said, "Sure, I saw a doctor." She said, "What did the doctor advise?" I said, "That's none of your business." Why should I tell them in the office?

Friday afternoon Miss Geiger called me. She wanted to know if I'm quitting. I tell her that I think I'm going to quit some time, but I don't want to quit right now. She wants to know then if I'm going to work Saturday. I tell her I'm not. Well, she asked me what seems to be the trouble. I tell her, "Miss Geiger, you ought to know that better than anybody else." Why should I be afraid of her. She said she was making up a schedule for this week and would I come in Monday. I told her I would come in and here I am.

At the end of this week, Ann quit for good, but she was in the following Wednesday to pick up her paycheck. All her clique members gathered around her to greet her warmly, and the other girls on the floor all smiled and said hello as they passed or stopped to talk with her. She greeted them all with a "Hello, jail bird," and as some of them pleaded with her to come back, she said, "No, I'm a free woman now."

Ann told me:

It was convenient to come in today. I had to be in town anyway to go to court. You know, Miss Geiger asked me if I would be able to pick up my pay check, and I told her why I was coming to town. "Oh," she said, "isn't your divorce final yet? I thought that was taken care of long ago." I told her it was taken care of. Can you beat that? What right has she got snooping into my business?

Aftermath of Ann's departure

Ann Lindstrom's departure seemed to let loose a torrent of griping on the second floor. The whole social atmosphere changed. Instead of waitresses and bartenders sitting together, joking and laughing, they generally wore sullen expressions and there was little lighthearted conversation. Once I sat down beside Rita Carey, and I only had to ask her how things were going to get her started on a half-hour's tirade against Miss Geiger and Chandler's. Rita was generally the gayest one of all, but this time she was deadly serious, talking with a tense expression, speaking much faster than usual, and throwing in one grievance right after another without stopping for breath. She said she was thinking of quitting herself.

Marie said:

Ann really had a nerve. I admire her for what she did. If the rest of us were like her, we'd just go up to Miss Geiger and tell her that we're going to quit. You know, one reason I'm not quitting right now is because I have some bills to pay off. I want to get myself a few things, and I'll have to keep on working for a few weeks until I can shop. But then I'll surely quit. There are at least six other girls around here I can name that are going to quit, too. They're all disgusted with the place.

I commented that she seemed to feel differently about Chandler's than she had when I first talked to her.

I sure do. I thought it was a wonderful place to work in, but there's been so many changes. You know, a new manager, and then this place lost three of the best hostesses they've ever had (Miss Ellis, Miss Schulz, and Mrs. Loomis).

Reactions to changes in supervision even affected memories of past experiences. When I first talked with Marie, she compared the restaurant where she previously had worked with Chandler's in order to tell me how much better Chandler's was. Among other things, she said:

At Blank's, they specialize on sizzling steaks. But for the ones who work there they only have a fish dish at noon and a meat dish at night—no choice at all. It isn't like here where you can get anything that is served to the guests.

One day after Ann had quit, I was telling Marie that I was planning to move on to another restaurant.

MARIE: You ought to go to Blank's. They have wonderful food.

WHYTE: I thought you waitresses didn't get a chance to sample much of that good food.

MARIE: Oh, yes, we did. There was one month there after rationing came in when it was pretty monotonous. We had one fish meal and vegetable plate the next, but except for that month, we had a chance to eat pretty much what the guests ate. It's just like in here, and the food was much better.

The clash with Miss Geiger also had an effect upon unexcused absences of the waitresses. Ann Lindstrom expressed the general feeling on this point when she said:

Miss Geiger is entirely different from Miss Ellis. You call her on the phone and tell her you're sick and she just won't listen to you. She'll say she can't spare you, and you'll have to come in. Why she tries to drag you right through that telephone wire and in to work.

The girls had to find some way around this pressure. One afternoon I was talking with Ann Lindstrom several days before she left when Rita Carey came up to us.

RITA: Ann, will you go up and talk to Miss Taylor [assistant directess] for me, and tell her to go easy on me because I'm not feeling very well? I want you to get them ready for it when I don't come in tomorrow and Saturday.
ANN: You go and do it yourself.
RITA: Well, do you think a stomach ache would be a good thing to have?
ANN: Whatever it is, you'd better begin feeling sick pretty soon.

Later I encountered Rita, looking very pleased with herself.

RITA: I've decided what I'm going to do. I'll call in and tell them I sprained my ankle. How does that sound to you? Do you think I'll get away with it?
WHYTE: Well, how has that story worked out in the past?
RITA: Nobody ever used it before. That's why I think it's pretty good, don't you? I could have sprained my ankle and then I wouldn't be able to come in. Sure, it would be all right by Monday when I want to come back. Of course, if I don't get away with this, it means my job, but I don't see why I should be worried about that anyway. I was going to quit two weeks ago and Miss Geiger called me into the office and talked to me. You might think she wanted me to stay. I think it's just the help shortage and all. That's all that bothers her.

Rita's "sprained ankle" kept her away from work Friday and Saturday, and Monday she was still so tired from her weekend that she called in and said that she still couldn't walk on it very well. By Tuesday, when she was back at work, the ankle appeared to be as good as new.

Later, in talking this case over with Ann, I asked her if she recalled cases in which girls had made up spurious excuses while Miss Ellis was in charge. She said emphatically:

No, they never did. At least I never heard of it in all the time I was there under Miss Ellis. I never heard a girl say that she had called in when she wasn't really sick. We didn't want to let Miss Ellis down.

Rita Carey told me this story:

Did you hear about Mary and Miss Geiger? Well, a week ago, Mary asked for a half day off. Miss Geiger said that she would fix it up for her. Well, the day before this half day off, Mary asks Miss Geiger if she could have the whole day off. Miss Geiger goes right up into the air. She says to her, "I nearly broke my neck so that you could have a half day. I think you could have a little consideration for us." Well, Mary talked right back to her. She says, "I think you could have a little more consideration for the waitresses." Now, it would be all right if Miss Geiger had said no, she's sorry but she can't arrange it, but she has to tell the girl off, and when Mary talks back, she says to her that she'll never give her another day off. "All right," Mary says, "I'll never ask for another day off from you. I'll just take it, and if you want to fire me, go ahead and fire me."

Oh, a lot of the girls are getting fed up with this place. I think a lot of them are going to quit. Mary and Ethel won't stay long. They've been fed up for a long time, so they're going to quit, and they're not going to give any notice. Just to get back at Miss Geiger.

It is difficult to obtain any quantitative conclusions on this matter, but at about this time Miss Geiger felt that waitresses were talking back to customers with increasing frequency, and she was very much concerned over the matter. She did not, of course, connect it with the increasing pressure she was putting on the girls, but in some cases the two factors seem to have been tied together. For example, she told me of a woman who bounced up to Ann Lindstrom's table in a jolly manner and said, "How *do* you do?" Ann replied coldly, "As I please." This seems to have spoiled the atmosphere for the customer, and afterwards she mentioned the incident to Miss Geiger without giving the girl's name. Miss Geiger followed the customer to the cashier and got from her the number on the waitress' check, thus identifying Ann. Later she called Ann aside and told her that she would make better tips if she would be more pleasant. This occurred shortly before Ann left, at a time when she felt under great pressure not only from customers but also from Miss Geiger. Talking back to customers seems to have been one reaction to this dual pressure.

In a restaurant such as Chandler's there is frequently a necessity of calling on waitresses for an extra measure of effort to meet emergencies. During Miss Ellis' regime, Marie Pappas had been the most dependable workhorse on the floor, and Miss Ellis, Miss Schulz, and Mrs. Loomis had always been able to count on her when a special effort was needed. However, after Ann left, Marie said to me:

In another week (when the college-girl waitresses and service bar girls leave) it's going to be hell around here, and if they think we're going to take over extra tables like we did before, they have another think coming. I just won't do it.

There was another way in which the girls showed their resistance to Miss Geiger. In writing up her experiences at Chandler's, Ann Lindstrom put it this way:

To aggravate Miss Geiger and to display their dislike and lack of respect, the girls constantly stole restricted foods, sat down at every opportunity, sang and danced in the kitchen, etc. this became almost a game with them to see just how much they could get away with before getting caught by her.

Analysis of the case

We shall analyze the case first by interpreting the clash between Ellen Geiger and Ann Lindstrom in terms of their personal IAS backgrounds and transactional experience.

Miss Geiger's story is noteworthy in the dominance of vertical interactions and organization of activities and in the extreme scarcity of her experience with horizontal interactions and with activities organized within a group of her peers. The only group activities she reported outside of her family were directed by the older women of her church.

Miss Geiger could not even come to feel part of a group with her sisters. Her mother promoted competitive transactions, sister against sister. All rewards and punishments were in the hands of the parents, and Ellen Geiger won or lost according to her particular relationship with the authorities. From her parents and the church, she took on a highly individualistic and moralistic view of the world.

This early orientation clearly carried over into the leadership style Miss Geiger displayed in Chandler's. There she saw the world entirely in vertical terms. Those who had worked with her in supervision reported that she had no close friends and appeared to live for her work. She was extremely responsive to her boss, Mr. Stanton, and personally identified with the company. She was proud of the position she had achieved in the big city.

Miss Geiger's individualistic outlook showed itself in the anxiety she showed in the face of informal groups or indeed any interpersonal loyalties. Note how she sought to persuade Rita Carey that what her twin sister did should be of no importance to her. Miss Geiger saw Ann Lindstrom as an individual troublemaker, not as the informal leader of a group and as a potential stabilizing influence for that group.

Miss Geiger had had little experience with positive exchange transactions. She tended to calculate what was owed her, which destroyed the basis of possible exchanges of favors. She saw the world in terms of absolute standards, with penalties to be imposed when individuals did not measure up to those standards.

Ann Lindstrom grew up with a strong (horizontal) orientation toward her peer group. Her record shows a resistance to authority that she manifested early and consistently.

While girls from the country or from lower class backgrounds looked upon Chandler's as an opportunity to move up in the world, for Ann the job represented a step down. She felt she was where she did not belong.

Downward mobility and resistance to authority seem to account for the "chip-on-the-shoulder" manner that was noted both by supervisors and friends as they commented on their first impressions of Ann. How did she reach her early adjustment? After a brief period of friction with coworkers, she established the pattern of informal leadership that was characteristic of her growing up period. She also appears to have received special attention from her superiors in the organization. Here the frequency and duration of interaction was important. Miss Schulz could hardly have learned about Ann's writing talents and interests if she had not spent a good deal of time talking to her.

We also see the growth of positive exchange transactions between Ann and the members of the Chandler Nut Club and between Ann and the supervisors. Note that Rita Carey first reacted against Ann's announcement of who was going to work at what times, but then warmed up to her when next time Ann took over the undesirable hours for herself. The Chandler Nut Club became a tightly knit group marked by high frequency and duration of interactions and by a network of positive exchange transactions. Ann also developed positive exchanges with her superiors. About the directress of service, the assistant directress, or her hostess, Ann commented, "She was always ready to do a favor for you." Ann's friends spoke in the same manner, suggesting that the presence or absence of positive exchange transactions between workers and supervisors in this case strongly influenced the sentiments of workers toward supervisors.

Personnel changes in management brought about a drastic alteration in Ann's social situation. Her interactions with her superiors were sharply reduced—she received no special attention from the new hostess or the new assistant directress of service. Her interactions with the directress were nearly all initiated by Miss Geiger, and they led in each case to a negative experience. Ann and her friends found that Miss Geiger would make no adjustment to them until they had met the standard of performance and behavior she set for them. The positive exchanges with previous supervisors now gave way to a pattern of negative exchanges.

As Ann lost the supporting relations with superiors, she found herself for the first time breaking down in tears on the job. Miss Geiger also claimed to find increasingly frequent instances where Ann had talked back to customers. While Ann denied this sort of behavior, it seems likely that the increasing tensions she felt found some outlet in this direction.

Within a few weeks of Ann's resignation, all members of the Chandler Nut Club had left the restaurant except Marie—the one who had had the longest previous experience as a waitress. Ann talked Rita Carey into staying even when her twin sister left, but when Ann left, the others left also. A leaderless group was not enough to keep them on the job.

Summary and conclusions

Let us review the steps of our analysis. For Ellen Geiger and Ann Lindstrom, we established the IAS pattern developed in childhood and youth that each brought into the restaurant. We noted the marked vertical orientation of Miss Geiger and her tendency to seek rewards only from her organizational superiors. We noted Ann Lindstrom's strong horizontal orientation and resistance to authority. These observations could have enabled us to predict that if the two women had much contact with each other there would be friction between them.

We also noted two diametrically opposing conceptions of social groups. To Ann, the group was what made life livable in the restaurant, and her leadership position in it was a natural outgrowth of her early experience. To the highly individualistically oriented superior, each individual should stand alone and any group was likely to be seen as a violation of the moral order. Miss Geiger probably felt threatened by the group in this case, and she took steps to get rid of it.

In this chapter, we are examining the links between personality and organization. We have not attempted an in-depth analysis of the personalities of our two chief characters. From the standpoint of intensive personality studies, there is much we have left out or have failed to explain. For example, Ann provides us with information pointing to rather severe emotional disturbances at certain points in her life, but these we have not sought to explore. Similarly, Miss Ellis and Miss Schulz both depicted Miss Geiger as a very lonely and unhappy person, and Miss Schultz reported that Miss Geiger had once sought psychiatric care. Whether or not these reports were true, we are not concerned with them here. We are not trying to explain the happiness or unhappiness of Ellen Geiger or Ann Lindstrom. We are only trying to explain the behavior of the individual in the group and organizational context.

References

Whyte, W. F. *Human Relations in the Restaurant Industry.* New York: McGraw-Hill Book Co., 1948. A discussion with many case illustrations of some of the human problems of the industry.

Whyte, W. F., and Hamilton, Edith Lentz. *Action Research for Management.* Homewood, Ill.: Richard D. Irwin, Inc., and the Dorsey Press. A report on a program to improve the management of a hotel through a research project. Chapters 4, 7, and 9 deal primarily with restaurant personnel and problems.

Whyte, W. F. "The Social Structure of the Restaurant," American Journal of Sociology, Vol. LIV (January, 1949). Also available in The Bobbs-Merrill Reprint Series in the Social Sciences, number 314. A discussion of restaurant structures, of different size units, and of problems of coordination and collaboration in both horizontal and vertical dimensions.

Discussion questions

1. In this chapter, we try to distinguish between the information needed for a personality study and for a personality-in-organization study. Is this a valid and useful distinction?

2. From the literature of psychology or psychiatry, select a case study of a personality. Now try to utilize the information given to explain the behavior of that person in some group or organization. Does the case study fail to provide information that you would need for a personality-in-organization study? Does the case study provide items of information of the type that would be useful to a personality-in-organization study, but which are not presented in our study of Ellen Geiger, Ann Lindstrom, and Chandler's Restaurant?

3. The waitress said of supervisors they liked, "She is always ready to do you a favor." Some people say that this kind of responsiveness involves favoritism and an undermining of good discipline. Do you agree or disagree?

4. Think back on your own organizational experience. If you had a supervisor who was "always ready to do you a favor," what were the consequences of this behavior? If you had a supervisor who refused to do favors, what were the consequences of this behavior?

10. Group leader, work group, and management

THIS IS THE STORY of Jack Carter and his work group in relation to management of the Benton Blowing Room of the Shawcross Corporation.

In the terminology of the glass industry, Jack Carter was a gaffer, which means he was in charge of a small work team or "shop" as it was called at Benton. Like other positions known in industry as "straw boss," working foreman, or group leader, gaffer was an ambiguous one. The gaffer was a full-time worker in the glassmaking process, yet at the same time he had certain supervisory responsibilities, since he was responsible for the work of his shop.

The case of Jack Carter is of special interest because he was not only a group leader by management appointment; he was also an informal leader. Under changing and difficult conditions that tended to undermine the leadership of other gaffers, Jack developed a leadership style that was highly effective in solving both technical and social problems.

Before bringing Jack Carter on the scene, we shall set the stage by presenting historical background, a description of the work process, and an account of the general state of worker-management relations. We shall then focus on Jack Carter, his work satisfactions and particularly his leadership style. Finally, in an attempt to answer the question: "How did Jack get that way?" we shall link up his early social experiences with the leadership pattern we observed in the blowing room. The case is based primarily upon field work carried out by Frank B. Miller, Jr., and me in 1952–53.

Historical perspective

An historical review in most factories would give major emphasis to technological and process changes. Not so here. While all of the knowledge and skills of chemical engineering have been brought to bear upon production of an absolutely clear crystal glass and the development of rigid temperature controls over the gas furnaces, the basic material is still fabricated according to methods that are centuries old. There has been only one technological change of any significance in recent years. In the old days, the gatherer had to make his gather out of a large pot of molten glass, so that he had to estimate the amount of material that he would be using. Today, the molten glass is provided him by the gob machine. At this machine, a constant stream of molten glass flows at a uniformly controlled rate so that the number of seconds of flow determines the weight and volume of the glass. The gatherer now calls into a public address system "40 seconds"—or whatever amount required. When this amount is provided him in a metal mold, he simply sticks his iron in, rotates it, and pulls the glass out. This assures that a uniform amount of glass will be used on each piece. Beyond this point the blowing, shaping, shearing, and ornamentation are all done by hand.

Although there has been very little technological change, there have been tremendous changes in the social organization of the blowing room. Years ago, the craftsmanship of Benton glassmaking was almost entirely a Swedish monopoly. It was widely believed that only the Swedes had the skill and artistic sense to reach the top in this difficult craft. Naturally, the men of Swedish extraction supported this view. In general, they offered no help to young Italian-Americans or indeed to young workers of any other than Swedish stock. In fact, some of the glassworkers today speak of how the old Swedes used to get together and talk in Swedish so that the non-Swedes were completely shut out of their conversations.

While today a man may be encouraged to "frig" (experiment with the different phases of glassmaking) during his lunch hour or at odd times when he is not needed on production, in the old days the controlling Swedes would not allow any of the younger glassworkers to perform any operation that was not strictly part of the job.

The Swedish gaffer in those days was a man of great prestige in the community as well as in the factory. The old-timers today say that you used to tip your hat to the gaffer when you met him on the street.

Within the factory, the control of the old gaffer was well-nigh absolute. Discipline was sometimes enforced physically—a kick in the pants to one of the young men seemed part of the accepted way of doing things.

The gaffer had almost complete control over the membership of his work team. While the assignments and promotions were made officially by management, every effort was made to give the gaffer the people he wanted to work with, and we have never heard of instances where a gaffer was forced to accept a man that he did not want. Thus, a man could be refused an increase in pay or a promotion if the gaffer who had the vacancy on his shop did not want that particular individual.

Since the Swedes in Benton started at a very early age and displayed remarkable longevity, the progress of younger men was very slow. Many shops worked together for years without any changes in personnel. Thus, a very settled social system developed.

When the situation in the blowing room did change at last, it seemed that everything was changing at once and with extraordinary rapidity. The old Swedes began to die or retire. Their sons did not succeed to their positions as might have been the case in Sweden, for in this country the sons of the craftsmen went on with their education and advanced into technical, professional, and managerial positions.

The new generation of non-Swedish glassworkers rose rapidly to positions of control. However, as these new men rose to the top, they discovered that they did not have the control that had been exercised by the old Swedes. There seemed to be several factors responsible for this change.

A union came into Shawcross in 1943. While the Benton workers had taken little, if any, part in the organization process, they were included in a union shop contract. Until the union came in, the gaffer at Benton regarded the organization of the factory as having a step-by-step series of gradual gradations of prestige and authority from shop boy up through gaffer, foreman, plant manager, and so on. The gaffer did not have to decide whether he was a worker or a member of management, and no one decided it for him. The coming of the union drew a horizontal line through the factory. You were either a worker and union member, or a member of management. This did not mean that the two groups were necessarily in conflict; it did mean that you could belong to only one group. So far as the union was concerned, the gaffer became a glassworker like other glassworkers. He might even be represented before management by someone lower than himself in pay and prestige.

The entrance of the union also meant that seniority became the dominant factor in promotions. Thus today the gaffer may want a certain individual on his shop, but if the man does not have the requisite seniority, there is nothing that management can do in acceding to the gaffer's wishes. Furthermore, when the gaffer does not want a certain individual on the shop, management will seek to take his preferences into account. Nevertheless, the man may have the seniority that entitles him to a chance to make good on this shop and the gaffer may have to accept him.

Team composition and work operations

The work of the team (or shop, as it is called in this industry) is carried on around a circular furnace, which has four circular openings, or "glory holes." Four work benches are attached to the furnace extending out in the spaces between the glory holes. A metal bar protrudes parallel to the work bench, to provide support for the glassworker as he rolls and manipulates the iron holding the glass.

The Benton plant has five furnaces, arranged in the pattern of the number five on a pair of dice. In some cases all members of the same team work around the same furnace, but in other cases a team may be divided between two adjoining furnaces. Thus it is possible to have six work teams or shops working on the five furnaces.

From the top down, in the order of skill, pay, and prestige, the teams consist of gaffer, servitor, gatherer, bit gatherer, stick-up boy and carry-in boy. Some shops may contain seven or eight members, since some pieces may require an additional bit gatherer or an additional servitor or gatherer.

The work cycle begins when the gatherer goes to pick up a piece of molten glass on the end of a hollow blow iron. He may rotate or "marver" the piece on a smooth metal stand, he may "block" it in a cupshaped wooden tool, and he may begin the process of blowing it up. While he works, he is likely to push the piece through his door of the warming furnace, or glory hole, in order to maintain the proper temperature for working the glass. As he finishes his part of the work, he carries the piece around to the servitor and generally reheats it so that it is ready for the servitor. The servitor brings the piece closer to its final shape by blowing and by the use of hand tools. When the piece has reached the basic shape of the final product, except for ornamentation and the finishing of its top, the stick-up boy steps forward with a solid metal rod with a piece of molten glass at the end and fixes the rod to the bowl at the opposite end of the servitor's blow iron. The servitor then breaks off the bowl at the end of his blow iron, leaving the bowl open at the end where it has been broken from the iron. The glass, firmly cemented to the solid rod, is taken by the stick-up boy to the gaffer's bench. The gaffer then opens up the bowl, shears it, and shapes it with iron tools, assisted by the carry-in boy, who sometimes holds a wooden paddle against the piece. If the design requires smaller pieces of glass for handles or ornamentation, the bit gatherer brings them to the gaffer and puts them on the bowl under his direction. When the gaffer completes the piece, the carry-in boy slips an asbestos-covered fork under it and the gaffer cracks it off of the iron rod, whereupon the carry-in boy carries it to the kiln or lehr where it goes through a gradual annealing process.

The work process goes on, so that at any one time there may be two or more pieces in various stages of production. The work sequence outlined here would not hold for all pieces, since there are some large pieces on which the servitor, instead of the gaffer, affixes the bits. Furthermore, in the production of stemware (wine glasses), the gatherer performs the servitor functions observed on other shops, and the servitor attaches the stem and foot with bits furnished him by the bit gatherer.

Work flow problems

The performance of a shop depends not only upon the technical skills of each of its members. It depends also upon the organization of a smooth flow of work so that the piece of glass arrives at the right place at the right time. The work flow is complicated by the chemistry of the glass. It can only be worked effectively within a certain temperature range. If it is worked when too cold, imperfections will show up in the annealing process, and the piece will have to be discarded. Even with the most efficient work flow, the glass will have to be warmed-in in the furnace several times in the course of operations. If the work is not well coordinated, additional warmings-in will have to be added, which means extra work for certain members of the team for the same amount of finished production. When the pieces are heavy, this extra work becomes particularly onerous.

The work flow has its psychological effects also. When the work is running in a smooth and well-coordinated fashion, each worker can develop his own rhythm of work. When coordination breaks down, work rhythms are destroyed, and this is likely to lead to technical as well as emotional difficulties.

We tend to take work flow coordination for granted, but its importance becomes apparent when it breaks down. We observed one striking incident of this nature between a servitor and a bit gatherer. It involved a large and rather heavy piece on which the servitor had to affix a series of bits brought to him by the bit gatherer. The servitor noted that he was having to lift up the heavy piece to warm it in after each bit, whereas he could get at least two bits on before the warming in became necessary if the bit gatherer would move faster.

The servitor told the bit gatherer to bring the bits in faster. The bit gatherer replied that he was working just as fast as he cared to. The servitor insisted with increasing vehemence, and the bit gatherer replied equally heatedly that the servitor was not going to make him move any faster. Finally, the servitor passed the piece on to the gaffer and slugged the bit gatherer.

This was an extreme case of incoordination and conflict. It was the only fight we observed or heard about during the 18 months of our study. However, it illustrates the tensions that can and do arise along the line of the work flow.

Atypical as it is, the case nevertheless illustrates other points we have been making regarding the changing nature of shop leadership. In the old days, it would have been unthinkable for a bit gatherer to resist the directives of a servitor. If the servitor had been less than satisfied with the cooperation he was receiving, he probably would have taken the matter to his gaffer. The gaffer could then have told the bit gatherer that he would either have to cooperate, or else the gaffer would have him taken off the shop. In this case, it would have been no help for the servitor to appeal to the gaffer because the gaffer was one of those who just could not bring himself to make a criticism directly to a subordinate.

In most cases coordination of work activity is achieved without argument—and even without verbal or gestural communication. Making a quantitative study of interactions on four Benton shops, Frank Miller started with the assumption that, for each interaction, there must be an originator and a responder—that is, for each pair interaction, one man acts first and the other responds to him. Whenever the interaction involved words or gestures (such as hand signals or head nods), one could readily observe who acted first. However, Miller noted large numbers of interactions in which no such communication took place. Apparently two men came together and acted together in response to their observation of the condition of the glass and the stage reached in the manufacturing cycle. On any design that was a familiar part of the shop repertoire, such interactions labeled "situational" by Miller outnumbered those in which verbal or gestural communication was involved.[1]

While we do not have sufficient quantitative data on this point, observations might be expected to show a pattern of relations between situational and "free" contacts when the work and personal relations are going smoothly. When the shop is getting "on the hog" (getting into a rut where nothing seems to go right), we might expect to see changes in the pattern of free interactions and a marked increase in the proportion of free interactions in relation to situational ones.

There is another aspect of the work flow that is important to the emotional equilibrium of the men. Individuals reported to us most satisfaction with a flow in which they could "get ahead" and have free time for relaxation before the next operation, or in which the next piece of glass arrived at their station momentarily after they had passed on the preceding piece. Individual tastes differed as to whether it was better to get ahead and relax or to work in a continuous flow. On the undesirable conditions, there was general agreement. The worker felt under pressure when the next piece arrived before he had completed work on the preceding one. This did not mean that a piece would be offered to him before he could take it. It meant that, as he was trying to finish a piece, he could see out of the corner of his eye his predecessor in the work flow holding the next piece in readiness or warming it in again to keep it ready. While many men welcomed the free time that came with getting ahead, time in which you had to wait for a coworker while you had your iron in your hand was definitely not welcomed. This kind of waiting time meant additional labor in warming-in, as we have noted in the fight between servitor and bit gatherer.

Since one man being ahead often means that he is crowding the pace for the next man, it is not an easy task to smooth the work flow on a shop. The pace is influenced in large measure by the nature of the piece being produced. On one piece an individual may have little to do and often find himself ahead. On another he may have a much longer work cycle and

---

[1] Frank B. Miller, Jr., "Situational Interactions: A Worthwhile Concept?" *Human Organization*, Vol. XVII, no. 4 (Winter, 1958–59).

may drop behind. Since different pieces exert pressures at different places on the shop, the reactions of shop members to the same piece may be quite varied.

These work flow problems present delicate tasks of coordination, particularly for the gaffers. They also present problems for the foremen who need to note chronic cases of incoordination, so as to transfer men in the hope of building more compatible teams.

Management-worker relations

The nature of the work in the blowing room made it difficult, if not impossible, for management to exercise the control that is possible in other work situations. A man with training in industrial engineering naturally thinks of production problems in terms of discovering the best job operations and then standardizing their use for the whole department. This calls for time and motion studies. In his early period at Benton, Assistant Production Manager Dayton did indeed toy with the idea of having such studies made, but he either abandoned the idea of his own volition or was warned off by higher management.

Time and motion studies in the blowing room would have encountered two problems. In the first place, they would have created an issue with a homogeneous impact upon all of the men in the blowing room, and united resistance could have been expected. In the second place, time and motion studies in the blowing room would have faced unusual technical problems. The industrial engineer could observe and time each movement made, but how could he determine how many movements were necessary? This applied to the movements a man made in working the glass, and even more, to the warming-in periods. An additional warming in or two could add markedly to the duration of the work cycle, and yet how could the industrial engineer say just how many times a piece needed to be warmed in? The servitor or gaffer made this judgment by the appearance and feel of the glass, based on long years of experience. If the men were required to speed up their pace, they could spoil piece after piece, and it would be impossible for management to prove that it had been done on purpose.

Management did try to establish control over the work pace through setting production standards: so many pieces per hour for a given design. Without observing the same situation with production standards removed, it was impossible to say what the effects of these standards were. Perhaps on balance they brought forth more production, but on some individual jobs they seemed to raise production, and on others to depress it.

At one time in our study, Dayton reported that production was averaging about 70 percent of production standards. The range was around 40 percent to 100 percent, with a shop going over 100 percent only very occasionally.

Acknowledging the difficulties of making accurate estimates of production possibilities, management people reported that they would have been quite happy for the workers to be under 100 percent on some pieces and over on others. The workers interpreted the standards quite differently. When they were making 100 percent or close to it, they would tell us that they were doing all that management had asked them to do. Why do any more? On jobs that ran well below 100 percent, they would complain that the production standards were ridiculously high and that it was impossible to meet them.

Management considered the possibility of revising downward those production standards where workers fell far short, but this was not done. There seemed to be two main reasons for such a decision. In some cases, management could argue that failure to approach the production standard was due to deficiencies in skill and experience of members of the shop. Hopefully, they would be able to come closer in the future. In a few cases, management could show that the old Swedes years ago had met the production standard. This was not possible to demonstrate in most cases because new designs were added twice a year and very few pieces remained in the line year after year. Furthermore, since 100 percent was interpreted by the men as the maximum they should produce, management people were afraid to drop any of the standards for fear that this would limit possibilities of improvement.

Even when the men looked upon a particular production standard as unrealistically high, they could not afford to ignore it altogether. Pay increases within a given classification were not automatic at Benton. A man became eligible for "consideration" for a merit increase every six months until he reached the top of his classification, but these increases did not come automatically. A man had to persuade his foreman that he was showing progress. While promotions to higher classifications were restricted by seniority, a man also had to show that he could do the work, and he might fear to take on a higher job if he had not been able to persuade management that he was doing well at his current job.

The task of determining merit is difficult in any case and especially in a work team. A good man may be working on an inferior team or a poor man may be carried along on a good team. How is the foreman to assess the contributions each man is making to his team? This was an issue continually arising between individuals and the foreman.

The task of evaluating quality of work presented special difficulties in the blowing room. While relations between production and inspection are likely to be strained in any factory, in many situations there are tests or measurements that inspectors perform as an aid in reaching their decisions, and these concrete operations can be referred to as a means of making the decisions understandable to people in production. Such was not the case in the blowing room. On the one hand, since all the objects were produced by hand, no two would be exactly alike and no piece would match the design perfectly in every detail. Therefore, some deviation from design standards had to be accepted, but how much was permissible? That question was a constant source of friction between the glassworkers and the inspectors. The workers claimed that the inspectors rejected objects for slight defects or variations that no potential customer would notice. Jack Carter reported that a fellow gaffer had once provoked the resident designer and chief inspector by saying, "I challenge you to draw a perfect circle on a piece of paper 15 times freehand. That's what you are demanding of us." Carter reported that the designer-inspector got red in the face and declined to accept the challenge —but this did not lead him to relax his inspection standards.

The gaffers claimed that there were wide fluctuations in inspection standards, with "selections" (pieces accepted) being 80 percent one week and 40 percent the next, and the differences being chargeable more to changes in inspection personnel and standards than to changes in worker performance. The time lag between production and inspection decisions also presented problems to the workers. Jack Carter said that in another Shawcross Plant producing a different type of glassware, the pieces would cool in an hour or two, and "the inspectors could let you know almost right away what kind of quality you were getting so you could make adjustments." In Benton the cooling time was so long that the workers could not check the quality of their production until the following day. By that time generally all but a few samples of the rejects had been thrown away, and the gaffer had to interpret a sheet of paper that summarized deficiencies in such general terms that it was exceedingly difficult for him to visualize what had been done wrong. This communications problem was frustrating for the gaffers, and it also meant that management was not providing the type of informational feedback that would have been useful to improve performance.

Since the rejection of pieces in inspection did not affect the pay of the glassworkers, why were they upset by losses in inspection? Jack Carter commented:

You like to think you are doing a good day's work for what you get paid. It hurts your pride if they throw away the pieces you put so much work into.

The foremen we observed had risen through the ranks in other plants of the company, so they had had no direct experience with the kind of craftsmanship being practiced in Benton. This meant that they were severely limited either in training men on the job or in criticizing the work done, because they could neither speak from experience nor demonstrate the operations.

The foremen made up the work schedules and assigned the designs to be made by each shop, within the general production plans presented them by the assistant production manager. They had to bring the gaffers reports on imperfect work done, but they had to be quite tentative in suggesting the sources of the difficulties. When the gaffer's control over his own men broke down, the foreman had to intervene, but he was never sure as to how much initiative he should take with subordinates on the shop and how much he should work directly with the gaffer. He had to learn to vary his approach with each gaffer.

The foremen spent some of their time out on the floor observing the men and their work, but given limitations of craft knowledge, just what they should do on the basis of these observations was not an easy question to answer. At one time, Assistant Production Manager Dayton, believing that the men would work harder if the foremen were on the floor more often, moved the foremen's desk and telephone out of the room next to the blowing room and placed them right out in the open, on the edge of the blowing room itself. This was looked upon by the foremen as a blow to their status. It provided further practical difficulties, since the desk was located in a dirty and noisy area where the foremen had trouble understanding telephone conversations, could not keep their records clean, and could not carry on a conversation that would not be observed by everyone in the blowing room. This move was likewise resented by the workers, who knew at once why it had been made. Within a short time the foremen had their own office back, but were still under pressure to spend more time on the blowing room floor.

Just what effect, if any, the foremen's presence had on productivity seemed a highly dubious point to us. On the other hand, opportunities to observe and interact with the men made possible two important functions. The performance of a shop depended upon teamwork. As the foremen got to know the men, they learned to spot friction points and to transfer individuals from one shop to another. All three foremen prided themselves on utilizing their knowledge of the workers in this way.

Observation also enabled the foremen to offer technical assistance in some exceptional cases. At first we did not see this as a possibility, and indeed there seemed to be only one foreman who had both sufficient observational skill and skill in relating himself to the workers to be of real help. The foreman demonstrated this at a critical point in the work career of Jack Carter.

Early in Carter's tenure as a gaffer, his shop was working on a design that had been handled by the top-prestige Campisi shop. This design was more difficult than anything Carter and his shop had done heretofore. After a promising start, Carter ran into trouble. For two days, nearly every piece his shop made was rejected in inspection. Carter and his shopmates were exceedingly worried and nervous; when things went wrong in this way, there was always the danger that the men would lose confidence in their ability to do a job. Carter knew that the old-timers had been saying he would never be able to master this design. Carter was not inclined to give up, but he felt himself blocked at every point.

It was at this time that one of the foremen spent two hours observing him and talking with him. On the basis of his observations on this shop and others involving this and similar pieces, plus his observations of

Carter's technique, the foreman suggested several changes in technique to Carter. Some of these were entirely the foreman's ideas, while some evolved from the discussion between the two men. As Carter put these new ideas into practice, he found the work smoothing out almost immediately. Rejects in inspection dropped rapidly, and within a few days the Carter shop had mastered this particular piece.

In this case, the technical points contributed by the foreman were certainly of significance, but perhaps equally important was the emotional support that he gave Carter in the crisis situation. It helped Carter to feel that there was someone working with him, sympathetic to him, and trying to help him at every step. He always spoke warmly of that particular foreman.

Working conditions and the job itself

The workers' relations with foremen and other management people are always of some importance in building the sentiments attached to the job, but they are not the whole story. How do these men feel about the conditions of their work and about the actual job activities? Their sentiments toward working conditions can be summarized in simple terms because they were highly uniform. Compared with all of their previous experiences in the old Benton plant or elsewhere, this new plant offered ideal working conditions. It was light and clean and well-ventilated—an important point when men have to work around furnaces.

The men who had worked in other types of glass manufacturing were particularly enthusiastic about working conditions. They spoke of their earlier jobs as being hot and heavy, whereas they recognized the jobs in the blowing room to be physically light and relatively clean work.

They considered the pay good, particularly in the top brackets. The period of rapid expansion had been particularly rewarding economically to the younger men, who had moved up in classification and pay.

But what did it mean to these men to become craftsmen in a mass-production world?

When we tried to get at worker reactions to the mental and physical processes involved in the work itself, we had great difficulty in getting any meaningful answers. For example, we wondered whether the men experienced esthetic satisfactions—had feelings of creativity—in their work. We found we could not tackle this question directly without embarrassing ourselves and the workers. Such matters are not easy to talk about in the factory.

The card-ranking method

Frustrated at our direct approach, we devised an indirect approach through asking the gaffer or the servitor to arrange a set of cards, each one representing a job his team performed, in order of preference. (We are indebted to Assistant Production Manager Dayton for the suggestion that cards might be used in this matter.) When the glassworker had placed the cards in order of preference, we asked him to explain why he ranked them the way he did.

We found that we got no data of any particular value out of the ranking itself, but when the men were called upon to explain their rankings, most of them talked in a manner that revealed much more of their feelings about the work process itself than we had been able to elicit in the ordinary type of interview.

The most noteworthy finding in response to the cards was the wide variety of reactions. In a mass-production situation, we expect to find only a small range of variety in worker responses to the job itself. Here at Benton the work itself apparently had many possible meanings. Some gaffers responded in terms of creativity: "When you get done, you've got a nice piece of work there. . . . it really looks like something. . . . when I can say I made that piece, I really swell with pride." Others responded in terms of achievement: "showing you could make a piece considered especially difficult." Many responded in terms of the amount and pace of work involved, expressing preferences for pieces where the physical labor was not too heavy or where the work flow was paced so as not to put them under pressure. Variety appealed especially to some men; they ranked high pieces that were different from their more common production items. One man emphasized the *contribution* he was making to the company; an old man of low prestige among his fellows and limited to a simple repetoire, he took pride in his claim that the item he most frequently worked on was the biggest seller in the company's line.[2]

Jack Carter's card sort

Jack Carter evaluated his first four choices in the following way:

1. Gustafson (high-prestige gaffer, then retired) said that this was a son-of-a-bitch. Sometimes he refused to make it and would put it off until another week. He said it would take anybody a year to learn how to make it. (Carter said he made a few of the right quality the first time and that he was finding it going very well.)
2. The fellow that used to make this (Campisi) said that nobody else could make it. . . . Well, I proved I could make it. I got a few the first time and I'm doing better now.
3. Jessup (old gaffer, not of the highest prestige) said it would take at least three months to learn how to make this. (Carter added that he had been able to make it almost from the very start.)

---

[2] This discussion is based on William F. Whyte, "On Asking Indirect Questions," *Human Organization*, Vol. XV, no. 4 (Winter, 1957–58).

4. This was supposed to be hard to make. The first time I made it, I found out later that some of the young fellows had bets on that I wouldn't get one out of the first three that I tried. Well, I found that I could make it all right.

It is interesting to note that in Carter's case his pride in achievement and his competitive rivalry with the older men dominated his feelings regarding the work.

Carter had entered the Benton plant only eight years earlier, but he had brought with him seniority from another Shawcross plant in the same city. Since citywide seniority prevailed at Shawcross, Carter was able to utilize his total seniority to move up rapidly as positions opened. He was not accepted as a real craftsmen by the few remaining old-timers. Nor had he yet achieved management recognition as the best of the younger gaffers. Leaving aside the stemware shop, a specialized operation to which Carter did not aspire, he was perhaps number three or four in management's evaluation of gaffer skills. First was Campisi, now in his fifties, the first non-Swede to get to the top and the special protege of the greatest of the old Swedish craftsmen. Management seemed to be grooming Ed Pecci, who was Carter's age, to take over the high prestige exhibition pieces as Campisi approached retirement. Jack Carter was determined to demonstrate that he could do as well as Pecci—and even as well as Campisi.

Quantitative measures of leadership

As Frank Miller and I observed the blowing room, we had the impression that Jack Carter was displaying an unusual style of leadership in his shop and also that he was the informal leader among the younger men of the blowing room. Could we test these notions by quantitative measures? The measures to be reported here were based upon systematic observations by Frank Miller.[3]

He observed four shops in samples of 20-minute periods, totaling four hours each on two pieces, or eight hours of observation time per shop. Only four out of the 12 shops had their men located so that Miller could observe all shop members simultaneously, which meant that some interesting shops had to be left out of this phase of the research. The sample did not include Campisi, the top status man among the old-timers. Three lesser status gaffers, Kurt Larson, Gus Pinelli, and Carl Schultz were included. The sample included only one of the young gaffers, but that was Jack Carter, with whom we are already well-acquainted. These data covered a total of 23 men on the four shops.

For each man, Miller noted the number of situational interactions (S), interactions originated (O), and interactions responded to (R) within the

---

[3] Miller, op. cit.

shop. For interactions with men outside of his own shop, originations and responses were also noted. (There were, of course, no situational interactions between men on different shops, since the work flow was confined to a single shop.)

For interactions originated within one's own shop, Carter had the highest number of all of the 23 men; 160 in eight hours, or 20 per hour. He totaled 103 responses, tying for fourth place among all 23 men, but placing first among the four gaffers. His situational interactions (213) were lowest of the four gaffers observed. (Since situational interactions vary greatly with work classification, it would not be meaningful to compare Carter with men in other classifications.)

These figures for Carter seem to result from a combination of task, skill, and personality factors. The particular designs observed gave him some free time to move around—and originate interaction. The designs were relatively new to the shop, and the men were relatively inexperienced; this tended to raise the proportion of free, as against situational, interactions. And finally, Carter was an exceedingly active person socially. He made the most of the interactional opportunities offered by the work.

Gus Pinelli presented an extreme contrast to Carter. His designs of ash trays and plates presented few technical problems and moved very fast. This gave him the highest number of situational interactions (433) of all the gaffers. It also served to pin him down to his bench most of the time, thus limiting his free interactions. Only the servitor came in contact with him in situational interactions. They could have talked together, but seldom did. For interaction with other men, they would have had to seek these men out—and generally they did not. For eight hours, Pinelli had 33 originations and 14 responses. (Compare this with 160 and 103, respectively, for Carter.)

These quantities fitted in well with the sentiments we heard expressed toward Pinelli. He was accorded little respect as a workman. He was thought unimportant in the informal organization of the department. He was considered a disagreeable fellow to work for; you avoided contact with him when you could.

The quantities do not tell us such a clear story for gaffers Larson and Schultz. In this early stage of such quantitative studies, we might expect the figures to be more revealing at the high and low extremes. Further research might give us comparative data that would enable us to make more of the Larson and Schultz figures.

Jack Carter, the top originator of in-shop contacts, was also top man in originating and responding to out-of-shop contacts. Gus Pinelli ranked at the very bottom in originating and responding to out-of-shop contacts, reflecting again the sentiments held toward him in the department as a whole. For the four teams, Miller found that the individual's rank in originations within his team correlated at .98 with rank in out-of-team contacts (originations plus responses). The very close correspondence between interaction counts in-shop and out-of-shop suggests that individuals have characteristic patterns of interaction. The active man on the shop is also active outside.

In spite of his strained relations with the older gaffers, Carter was the only Benton worker capable of mobilizing blowing room support on an issue involving the union. The frequencies were too small to support quantitative conclusions, but it seems significant that in the two cases that arose during our two-year study, it was Jack Carter in each case who defined the issue for his fellow workers and brought the union in. Those cases will be described in Chapter 21.

Now let us move from quantities into the content of Carter's leadership style, concentrating on his own shop.

Team leadership, Carter style

The entrance of new people, the rapid changes in shop composition, and the promotions of relatively inexperienced men had changed the social system, so that the gaffer faced problems of leadership and control far different from those experienced by his predecessors. At the same time, he faced younger people who had grown up in an environment where authority was questioned far more than it was many years ago. This seems to be true throughout our society. Children at the dinner table are no longer expected to speak only when they are spoken to by adults. And in many ways the strict controls over the young have been relaxed year by year. There has arisen a generation of workers which is no longer conditioned to give automatic response to authority.

Against this background we can see that the gaffer had an extraordinarily difficult leadership job. At one time, the old-timers who were now at the top had to submit passively to the very heavy subordination that was required of them over the years by the old-time Swedish craftsmen. Now, they themselves were at the top, and they recognized that it was not possible for them to exercise authority as it was exercised upon them. They were not bitter about this. In fact, we found them quite openly critical of the strict controls that were exercised. They recognized that times had changed and they felt that times should have changed, although they wondered whether the pendulum has not swung too far against authority. But even as they accepted the changes intellectually, they were in an uneasy and uncertain position. The knew that the leadership that was exercised upon them could no longer be practiced, but they had had no experience in any other approach.

The young men never served under the old system of tight control, so they were perhaps more free to devise new ways for meeting a changed situation. At the same time, their task was not an easy one either technically or socially. On the technical side, they had had to learn the skills of the craft much faster than was ever before thought possible. At the same time, they had to find a place for themselves socially among the older gaffers who had always believed that it took 20 to 30 years in the trade to become a really skilled craftsman. In a sense, as the young man proved that he could do an adequate job in working up to be a gaffer in five years, he was demonstrating that the craft was not as difficult and exalted as the old men had claimed it to be. In this situation, it was hardly surprising that the young gaffer received little advice and encouragement from the older men whose technical skills and experience could save him countless mistakes.

The gaffer of old had his control of the shop built into the legal environment. Now he found himself in the ambiguous position of many of his counterparts elsewhere—group leaders, straw bosses, or working foremen, as the position is variously known. He had responsibility for the performance of his shop, and yet lacked formal authority to run the shop.

There are effective ways of meeting this situation, as we will see in the case of Jack Carter. In effect, Carter had built a social leadership to take the place of the technical-legal system which supported earlier gaffers. This was evident in his handling of both technical and disciplinary problems.

In the old days, when a technical difficulty arose in the shop and the gaffer could not correct it in words, he would "go back" and demonstrate to the servitor, gatherer, or bit gatherer how he wanted the work done. During the period of our study, even the older gaffers seemed reluctant to do this. Lacking the formal supports of the old system, they seemed also to lack confidence in themselves. It might have been years since the gaffer had done any gathering. Was he sure now that he could do it just right? Furthermore, particularly in this type of work, there is no "one best way" of handling the job. Different men can perform the same operation in different ways and get equally good results. The old-time gaffer would have had the confidence to insist that his way was the best way, but if some of the old gaffers we observed had sought to demonstrate an operation, they might have been greeted by a comment from a subordinate to the effect that "Johnny Jensen used to do it different." Jensen, who had retired shortly before the beginning of our study, held the highest prestige of the old-time Swedish gaffers.

For the younger gaffers, there was just no possibility of demonstrating the way the work should be done by the servitor, gatherer, or bit gatherer. They had moved up through these positions so rapidly that they just did not have the requisite skills.

Jack Carter met these technical problems through directing a group discussion among the members of his shop. Whenever any new problem came up, he would call the group together for a pooling of ideas. Although the men under him all had less experience than he, their experience spread throughout the blowing room. Some of the shop members had worked under old-time Swedish gaffers and had observed how things were done by these master craftsmen. Even if he was not performing the operation himself, an alert worker could learn a great deal from observing a skilled man. In this situation, Jack Carter directed the discussion and made the final decision, but there was a vigorous sharing of ideas before the gaffer made the decision.

We never observed anything like this with the older gaffers. They took as their model the old-time Swedish gaffers, for whom it would have been inconceivable to ask for technical opinions from subordinates.

How does the gaffer handle criticisms to his own subordinates? In the old days, when the gaffer was the acknowledged boss, this seems to have been much easier to do. Now, when the gaffer had no formal authority and still worked so closely with his men, he often seemed to be so concerned about being accepted by them that he found it difficult to address criticisms to them. But refraining from these criticisms did not solve the interpersonal problems any more than it solved the technical problems, as the following case indicates.

As the foreman was observing the shop, he noticed that the men seemed to be having difficulty and that the gaffer was getting very upset. The foreman approached the gaffer and asked for an explanation. The gaffer shook his head and said, referring to his gatherer, "Joe isn't blowing it up straight."

The foreman looked at the piece and noted that the observation was correct. But then he asked, "Have you spoken to Joe about it?"

The gaffer again shook his head and said, "No, that wouldn't do any good. He just can't get it right."

The foreman now started around the glory hole to speak to the gatherer, but he had only taken two or three steps when the gatherer approached him and said, "What's *he* complaining about now?"

The foreman explained. The gatherer grunted and went back to the next piece. This particular piece came out perfectly straight, so the foreman was hopeful that the immediate problem had been solved. However, when he returned to talk to the gaffer, he was met with a request to change the job assignment to another piece. The gaffer said that things just weren't going right. Knowing from past experience that this particular gaffer was likely to get "on the hog" and then to "fire over" with his shop (go home in the middle of a shift), the foreman reluctantly agreed to the change.

The gaffer in this case was a young man of a good deal of promise. He was thought by management people to have the technical possibilities which would make him as good at the gaffering operations as the best of the oldtime Swedes. His inability to handle interpersonal problems directly on his shop slowed down even his technical progress and made it difficult for him to resolve his nervous tension.

Jack Carter handled a similar situation quite differently. He sought to take direct action before the foreman noticed that anything was wrong. If the foreman did find something wrong, Carter insisted that the matter be brought to his attention first. Then he would take direct action. It was not always easy.

Consider the case of Don, the obstreperous bit gatherer. He had a reputation for being a wise guy who would not let anyone tell him what to do and who would do as little work as possible. He had been moved from shop to shop because of complaints lodged against him. When Don was moved into Jack's shop there was trouble again, but this time it was short-lived. Within a week after the transfer the gaffer gave me this account:

We're getting along all right now. I had it out with him on the first day. I would tell him how I wanted things done, and he was always giving me an argument about it. It seemed that every time I would say something to him he would take it as a personal criticism.

So finally I had it out with him. I told him: "Don, when I tell you I want you to do things different, that's no personal criticism. I'm just telling you the way I work best. Now, I don't want an argument every time I tell you what to do. I want you to do it my way even if I'm wrong."

Well, at first he didn't like it. He went around sulking and saying that he was going to put in for a transfer to another shop. Then he comes up to me and says: "You've never heard anybody else complain about my work, have you?" That's what gave me the opening to lay it on the line for him. I said to him: "Good God yes. I've heard everybody talking against you. Why do you think you've been transferred around here so much?"

Well, that really set him back. He was really surprised. He said to me, "Nobody's ever told me about it." I told him, "That's what I mean. Some fellows around here will complain about you to each other and they'll talk against you to the foreman, and they will never tell you anything to your face. Now, if I've got something against you, I'll tell it to you right to your face and I won't go around talking against you. The way I feel about it, what you do in this shop is between you and me and shouldn't concern anybody else, and if I have anything against you I'm not running to the foreman. I'll take it right to you and we'll straighten it out that way. That way it'll be better for you and better for me too."

Well, he said he'd think it over. I guess he's changed his mind now. It took him just a couple of days. Yesterday he came to me and said: "Jack, if I tell you I won't ask for a transfer, will you ask them to keep me on this shop?" I told him I wasn't going to ask anybody for anything. I told him that I didn't want him to be obligated to me or me be obligated to him. It was all right for him to work on this shop as far as I was concerned, but it didn't need to go beyond that.

A few days later I had a chance to get the reaction of the bit gatherer. He put it this way:

I like this shop all right. I really think this is the only good shop in the place. When you're doing something wrong here, Jack or Tom (servitor) will tell you to your face and they keep it right on the shop. This is the only shop where they treat you like a human being. When they take it to you that way, they make you feel like you're part of the team.

Very occasionally, there were problems that Jack Carter could not resolve directly—that called for an appeal to the foreman. However, in such cases, he always insisted that the subordinate in question go into the foreman's office with him so that they could put the case to the foreman together. No one enjoyed going into the foreman's office in this way, but the men valued the assurance that Carter would never complain to the foreman about them "behind our backs." On Jack Carter's shop, you always knew where you stood with the gaffer.

Taking action on mistakes is difficult enough to handle when the responsibility for a particular mistake is clear. The problem becomes much more difficult on those frequent occasions when responsibility is not clear. As he spends most of his time at his own bench, the gaffer has limited opportunity to observe the performance of subordinates and to check on questions where there may be doubt as to responsibility.

Under these circumstances, what can the gaffer do? He may wait until he has accumulated enough evidence to make sure of the nature of the difficulty. This is certainly better than jumping to conclusions, but the process may take considerable time and it may be a source of annoyance to the gaffer as he deals with imperfect pieces to such an extent that it upsets his own emotional equilibrium.

There is still another alternative: to present the difficulty to other members of the shop as a problem to be solved. Consider this example from the Carter shop. The shop had been having trouble with what are called mold marks—marks left on the glass by the mold used in blowing up the piece. We asked the gaffer for the source of the difficulty. He said he thought that the shop boy had not been holding the mold tight as his servitor blew up the piece. Immediately after giving me this explanation, Carter walked over to show the imperfect piece to the shop boy. They conversed for perhaps two minutes in a good-natured fashion. The shop boy asked the gaffer what he thought was the source of the difficulty. The gaffer said that there were several possibilities, that he was not sure, but one possibility was that the shop boy was not holding the mold tightly shut. The shop boy responded by saying that that was a possibility, but he had the impression that he had been keeping it tightly shut. At this point, the servitor joined in the conversation. After he had looked at the piece in question, he said that it was entirely his own responsibility. He had been blowing the piece up too fast.

There are several interesting aspects to this incident. In the first place, the gaffer thought he knew what the trouble was, but he happened to be mistaken. If he had acted directly on his mistaken impression, he would only have upset his relations with the stick-up boy and stirred up a very defensive reaction.

Instead of telling the worker that he was wrong, the gaffer simply listed various possibilities. It was noteworthy that, although the stick-up boy did not think he was at fault, he nevertheless seemed to be willing to consider that possibility calmly without being defensive about it. And finally, the servitor was perfectly willing to take over the responsibility himself. In approaching the problem this way, the gaffer avoided defensive reactions and made it possible for his men to look upon the problem objectively. As they handled it harmoniously, they also strengthened themselves technically.

By his own leadership skill, Jack Carter built high morale on his shop. The men took pride in their team membership. They wanted to work with Jack. So strong was this effect that the servitor, who had seemed to us an ambitious young man, turned down a promotion that would have increased his pay by $8 a week, because it would have meant moving to another shop. As he explained it:

Well, I've been working for Jack for five years now and we have always got along good together. I just didn't want to make the change. I remember how it was when I was working for this other fellow. I was on edge all the time. Then when I would go home at night I would get in arguments with the wife and kids. It's different today. I get along good on the job and I get along good at home. It isn't worth $8 to me to make that change.

Carter's experience suggests that, even without the formal supports of authority, it is possible for a gaffer to become a strong team leader. However, his case was exceptional. We can say that the situation allowed such leadership to arise, but we cannot say that it provided any formal supports for such leadership.

How did Jack Carter get that way?

The chapter so far is based almost entirely upon data gathered in 1952–53. As I began work on this book, I became increasingly interested in relating the observed behavior of the worker on the job with the history of his social experience in family, school, community, and previous jobs. I knew next to nothing of Jack Carter's personal history. Could I go back to him after 15 years and get him to fill in the story?

I sent Carter a copy of *Men at Work*, and asked him to reread the chapter on "Teams of Artisans," which he had seen in draft form before publication. We then spent an afternoon together going over the story.

I found Carter now one of the older gaffers, no longer straining to gain acceptance as a superior craftsman. Campisi had long since retired, and Pecci, his particular protegé among the then younger men, had suddenly dropped dead a few years before our conversation. Even before that event, Carter had persuaded management that it was not good policy to concentrate the exhibition pieces on one shop and thus become so dependent upon a single gaffer. Carter now gets his share of the highest prestige pieces.

Jack Carter was born into a family with two older sisters and an older brother. He does not recall his father, who deserted the family when Jack was nine months old. A little later, his mother married again, and Jack got a stepfather who was "real mean—like those stepfathers you read about in books."

Jack has vivid memories of his stepfather's style of discipline:

Anything you did he didn't like, right away he'd pull out a strap and let you have it. I remember one night when my brother and I were in bed together and got talking and giggling the way kids will, my stepfather came in and told us to shut up. After he left, we shut up for a while, but then I shoved him or he shoved me, and we started giggling again. This time my stepfather came in and said he would beat the tar out of us if we didn't keep quiet. We kept quiet for a longer time, but then sure enough we got started giggling again.

When he came in, I slipped off the bed, and he caught only my brother under the covers. He gave him one hell of a beating all over his body. I can still hear my brother's screams. The next morning when he came to breakfast, my brother's face was so puffed up, he could hardly see, and he said he didn't think he could go to school. My stepfather told him he had to go. My brother asked him what he should tell the teacher. My stepfather said, "You tell him that you fell into a barn door. Make sure that's all you tell him." He warned me that I had to stick to the same story.

Believe me, we both told that to the teacher. The teacher naturally didn't believe it, but he couldn't get anything different out of us, because we were scared to death of my stepfather.

Jack's early years were spent in an atmosphere of change and insecurity.

My stepfather wasn't much of a workman. He was a blacksmith, but I guess he wasn't very good at it. He'd settle down in one place and start shoeing horses, but I guess he would hammer the shoes in too deep and cut the horse in the quick, so pretty soon he would be turning out lame horses, and he would have to leave town. In one year I can remember we lived in seven different towns, because I went to seven different schools.

Years later, after I was grown up, my stepfather got killed in an accident. He fell out of a tree. Would you believe it, he sawed off the branch he was standing on. I really laughed when I heard that.

While home was a hostile place in those years, Jack had little chance to get away from it. His stepfather demanded that he and his brother come home right after school each day and do chores around the place.

The kids in the neighborhood would come by and ask us to come out and play. We had to say we couldn't until we got the work done. At first sometimes they would help us so we would get through sooner, but they got tired of that, so after a while they didn't come by any more.

At the age of nine, Jack was sent away from home.

My stepfather told me I was eating too much. He said he was going to send me away for summer vacation with a farmer. Well, it turned out it wasn't just the summer. I stayed on that farm for four years. All of the time during the week, when I wasn't in school, I was doing farm chores. Yes, I worked by myself. There was nobody around there to work with or play with. There was just the farmer, who was a bachelor, and his sister.

At first Jack got along fairly well with the farmer, but the old man developed a habit of drinking hard cider and getting drunk. The more he drank, the more the work load fell on Jack, and the more Jack got blamed for anything that went wrong. After four years on the farm, Jack went back to his mother and stepfather, and shortly after that he had to go out to work for himself.

Up to this point, I was puzzled by what I heard. The pattern of rejection of superior authority that I have come to expect in the history of an informal leader in the factory was clearly evident. But I had also expected to hear of the formation of strong peer group ties and of an informal leadership role emerging in the childhood years. So far the story seemed to be that of a social isolate, even if the isolation was a product of circumstances beyond Jack's control.

I cast about for other areas of potential peer group and leadership experience. Thanks to my wife's accounts of her experience in a one-room schoolhouse, I was able to visualize the possibilities of this situation in Jack's case.

At that time (on the farm), I went to a one-room schoolhouse where there were children from first to eighth grades. I was there from fifth through the eighth myself.

I got a lot out of that school. The man in charge was a fellow named Adams. To look at him, you would think he was just a dirty old man. He always wore the same vest that looked like it had soup and gravy on it for 20 years. Still, he taught us a lot. And he kept order in that schoolroom without using any physical punishment on us.

He had a rule that if you finished up the assignment you were on before the day was out, you could go to the library and pick out books to read. We didn't have much of a library, but I always pushed through to get my work done in a hurry so that I could read about Tom Sawyer, Huckleberry Finn, and everything we had in the library.

We would put on plays from time to time. Generally, they would be based on stories we read in the books. Since I knew the books from the library better than anybody else, the kids would always turn to me to say how things should be done. I wasn't trying to be a leader, but they pushed it on me.

I asked him about his relations with the younger boys. He said that all of the older boys from time to time would have responsibility for three or four of the younger ones.

We would look over what they were doing and show them how to do it better. Besides that, we had responsibility for keeping order, so we had to find ways to keep the kids interested.

Outside of school, he did have time free on week ends. Since he lived far away from the other children, he would go over to play with them during most of the year, but the farm where he lived had the only swimming hole in the area, so the kids would gather there in the summer.

Jack had no opportunities to participate in organized sports. The small group had to generate its own activities every time the members got together. "Somebody would always be asking: What will we do next?" I asked if it was generally Jack who asked or was it he who got asked?

It seems like they were always asking me. I had so much time by myself on the farm that I was always thinking of things to do when I had a chance to get off from work.

Jack got his first regular job shoveling coal at the age of 14. Then he worked on a railroad section gang. When still in his teens, he started with Shawcross in an old plant that combined handwork with larger scale production methods. This was before the union was established in Shawcross.

They used to have a lineup at that time. Say about 50 men would show up each morning, and the gaffers would come out and pick maybe 20 of them to work that particular day. You never knew when you were going to be picked.

We had some real tough gaffers then. We had some fellows who would never tell you anything. They would always expect you to know what you were doing. They would raise hell if you made a mistake. Naturally, that would make you try harder, but you would get more nervous, and you would be bound to make more mistakes. You would be scared to death for your job all the time.

But there were some good gaffers, and I learned a lot from comparing the two types. The good ones to work for would explain to you what they were doing, and they would listen to you and let you talk to them.

I resolved then and there if I ever did get to be gaffer myself, I would always talk things over face to face with the men on the shop. Either I would convince the man that I was right, or he would convince me that he was right. Either way, we would talk it out right on the shop.

Jack was active in the drive that brought the union into Shawcross. In this early period, he was elected union representative for his department on two or three occasions. At this level he played a major role in working out the new pattern of union-management relations. He had no ambitions to seek higher union offices. He has not represented the Benton blowing room in the union, yet on the occasions we observed, it was Jack Carter who brought plantwide issues before the union.

Summary and analysis

We have placed the personal story of a gaffer against a context of a drastic change in the powers of the gaffer. In the pre-union days of the old Swedish craftsmen, the gaffer was king of the blowing room. He could refuse to have a man in his shop, and there was no one to oppose his will. If he wanted to get rid of a man from his shop, all management could do was place the man somewhere else or lay him off.

The gaffer held a prestige position in plant and community. His technical knowledge was unchallenged. If he did not like the way a subordinate was working, he could "go back" to that position and show the man the way it should be done.

By the time Jack Carter came on the scene, the situation had markedly changed. The union had established seniority as the main criterion for promotions. The foreman was doing the best he could to consider the gaffers' preferences, but he could not allow any gaffer an absolute veto, and he—not the gaffer—made the assignment decisions. If a gaffer wanted to get rid of a man on his shop, the foreman would try to place the man in the same job on another shop. If he found no one willing to make a swap, the foreman would simply tell the complaining gaffer that he would have to live with the situation.

The new generation of gaffers lacked the years of experience of the old Swedes. They did not have a reputation for technical expertise at all positions on the shop, and they lacked confidence in their own technical abilities. They hesitated to "go back" to demonstrate an operation for fear that they would bungle the job and look foolish.

The old gaffers' leadership was based upon high prestige for technical competence, high confidence in their own technical abilities, and unchallenged support from management for all their decisions. The new generation of gaffers lacked prestige, self-confidence, and management support.

When the old leadership role was no longer viable, most of the gaffers were confused and frustrated. Only Jack Carter worked out a successful new pattern. Recognizing his own technical limitations and the lack of management support, he developed a style of social leadership. He solved technical problems, not through the issuing of orders and instructions but through a process of consultation that brought forward technical ideas worth trying. He handled frictions within the shop by direct confrontation, thrashing things out, and assuring his men that the problems between them and him would remain in the shop. On the rare occasions when he had to involve the foreman, he took his man with him to the foreman so that no one could claim he was going behind a man's back. This pattern yielded sentiments toward the gaffer such that his men could talk about errors that had been made without any feeling of the need to defend oneself and blame someone else.

How did Jack Carter get that way? Tracing his personal history, we found an early rejection of the authority of his stepfather, the old farmer, and of some of the old gaffers under whom he worked. But Carter's relations with authority figures were not all negative. He speaks warmly of Mr. Adams, the teacher in his one-room schoolhouse. He also speaks with appreciation and approval of those gaffers who would explain to him what he was supposed to do and listen to what he had to say.

Despite the enforced isolation of much of Carter's childhood, around the one-room schoolhouse Jack did become actively involved with his peers and also with children younger than himself. It is here that we see emerging the informal leadership pattern that we observed on the floor of the blowing room.

Discussion questions

1. You are called in by management to ask whether you would recommend developing a leadership training course for gaffers so that the other gaffers can learn some of the skills displayed by Jack Carter.

a) If you would recommend such a course, indicate in general what the content would be and how it should be taught.

b) If you would recommend against such a course, indicate other approaches that should be used in helping the gaffers to solve their problems.

2. The blowing room presented unusual problems in supervision. Could management have handled these problems more effectively? If so, indicate how.

3. Review your own personal history in relation to your behavior and relationships in the work situation. To what extent do you see a fit between the past and the work situation under discussion?

4. Do the same assignment as in number 3 on the basis of interviewing another person.

5. Locate some person who has held the position of strawboss, working foreman, or group leader. Interview him to elicit information about the human relations problems involved particularly in that position.

11. Man, group, and process

THIS IS THE STORY of a crisis in the working life of Joe Sloan. We begin our story with the final scene. Then we go back to follow his individual development, his changing role in the work group, his changing relations with management, in the context of the technology and work processes in the Hi-Test Aviation Gasoline Plant.

This case will provide another opportunity to try out our theoretical framework and, in the process, to explore further certain aspects of the relations of man to job, group, and organization.

The man who walked off the job[1]

On the morning of Monday, April 12, 1943, Joe Sloan, a poly (No. 1) operator at the Hi-Test plant, walked off his job. Why did he do it?

Johnny Hudson had been on tour (shift) with Joe Sloan at the time of the incident. He explained that they had been in process of shifting over from production of isoheptene to the regular product, iso-octane, which, blended with other hydrocarbons, yields aviation gasoline. To make the shift, they had to empty the pipes of isoheptene, venting the vapors and liquids onto the floor of the control room. Hudson said that for a few minutes, until the liquid evaporated, it was all over the floor and its fumes filled the air. He went on:

It was really a hazard, but I didn't know what Joe was going to do until he just tapped me on the back and says, "Johnny, I am leaving you with it." I sure was sorry to see him go.

The foreman, Tom Lloyd, gave this account:

I was down at the catalyst plant when Sloan called me. He says, "Come on up here. I have something I want to show you." When I got there, he was purple in the face, and he shook his finger under my nose. He says, "I have

---

[1] This chapter is based on my "Engineers and Workers: A Case Study," *Human Organization*, Vol. XIV, no. 4 (1956).

told you about this time and time again. I have told you to do something about this, and you have done nothing. A man ought not to have to work in conditions like this."

Now, he was in the right about it. We should have connected those lines up outside so that the place wouldn't have been flooded. We have done that now. It was just one of those things I hadn't got around to although I had always meant to do it. But that thing had happened fifty times before, and the men had just taken it so when Sloan made such a fuss about it, I couldn't help thinking it was funny. I must have smiled, but I tried to keep a straight face. I says to him, "Now you get off me." After that he calmed down a little but he said, "I don't think a man ought to have to work under such conditions." I says, "That's right. He don't have to." Sloan walks around the pump a couple of times and then he comes back to me and says, "I don't think I will work under such conditions." Then he taps Johnny Hudson on the shoulder and says the same thing to him. After that he goes up and talks to Jess (Jess Douglas, plant manager). From what Jess said to me, I don't think Sloan had anything against me personally. He just said, "I got fed up and decided to leave."

The foreman was asked whether Sloan would be allowed to return.

Well, I don't know about that. If he had waited until we got that pump going, it would have been different. But he just left his fellow workmen on the spot. That was bad. Anyway, I don't think he wants to come back.

Lloyd went on to say that he thought Sloan had been sorry that he had turned down an aircraft factory job offered him some time before and had used this incident to force the company to give him his release so that he could take the job after all.

Plant Manager Jess Douglas made this comment:

That certainly hit me like a ton of bricks. Sloan has been a very good operator. I knew he had a hot temper. He had had one run-in before with the superintendent here before me. I never found out just what it was. I knew he was unhappy in his work. I told him there would be some possibility of getting in another line when he got his correspondence course finished. Franklin (personnel man) and I had talked with him yesterday afternoon. I wasn't really able to satisfy my curiosity about his reasons for quitting, but at least we got it settled on an amicable basis. It will go on the records that he resigned for ill health. He will get two weeks' sick pay before he is out, and then we will give him recommendations for any job that he applies for. I told him that I did not think a man of his caliber should have flown off the handle that way and he admitted it.

On April 15, Joe Sloan was interviewed as he came in for his paycheck. He began by showing a letter from his doctor saying that he was suffering from "a severe occupational neurosis probably due to a fear of explosions." He went on:

I didn't really resign, if that's what you want to know. I got out under pressure. When I came up to talk to Douglas on my way home, I didn't think

I was quitting, but when we were about half way home, he told me he didn't think I ought to come back. When he and Franklin talked with me at home yesterday, Douglas said, "If I were you, I wouldn't have the face to come back in the plant after leaving in the face of hazard." I says, "Do you mean that you wouldn't do anything about that?" And he says, "I wouldn't have the face to go back in the plant after that." I told him I had called it to the attention of Tom several times, and he had done nothing about it. This time there was gasoline on the floor and gas vapors in the air. The windows were open and the wind was blowing from the north toward the furnace. I said to him, "It looks like a man has to quit or get roasted like a pig to get any action, don't it?" And he says, "I wouldn't say that." But right after I left they did fix up that connection outside the control room.

Sloan was asked what it was about this particular incident that had made him take drastic action. (The changeover from isoheptene to iso-octane occurred about once a month.)

Well, I jumped out Tom about it and he just said, "Get off me." so I took that to mean that he wasn't going to do anything about it. I had just stood enough. That was all.

He added that he thought he had been let out because management had identified him as being active in the CIO drive to organize the plant but said he could not prove this.

He said that this was the first time in six months that he had awakened in the morning without a headache. His doctor had put him on a strict diet of milk and custards to guard against stomach ulcers.

The Sloan case aroused much comment among the workers, some of which is presented here. Said Ed Logan, a hydro-stillman (No. 2) operator and one of the most popular men in the plant:

It's too bad. Joe has always been a little hot-headed, but I've never known him to do a man an injustice. Now there are some men in here that are already talking against him. It is that selfishness that you see all over here. Now I stand to gain more out of this than anybody else. But I would be tickled to death to see him come back. I talked with him for an hour and a half at his house last night about it.

Frank Swanson, a fractionator (No. 3) operator who had worked under Sloan for many months, had this to say:

He was a smart boy, but there must have been a cog loose somewhere. A man shouldn't fly off the handle like that.

Mark Walling, a poly (No. 1) operator on another tour (shift), made this comment:

Sloan will be hard to replace. This place is losing a damn good operator. . . . They just say the man blowed up. But why does a man blow up like that? They ought to try to find that out.

Walling puts the problem of this case very well: Why did Joe Sloan blow up? And we might ask, what was Joe talking about when he said, "I had just stood enough."

To the men of Hi-Test plant, that was a real puzzle. While some of them had their theories, no one was able to explain it even to his own satisfaction—not Plant Manager Douglas, not Foreman Lloyd, and not fellow workers. Even Joe Sloan himself could not go much beyond describing the emotions he experienced and the actions he took in the crisis.

To solve the problem, it will be necessary to fill in some general background about the company and plant, examine Joe Sloan's relations with employees and management, and review some of the events of the months leading up to his walkout. The subsequent materials will be focussed on Joe Sloan as much as possible, but it will be necessary to include some data bearing upon much broader problems.

Technology and process

Let us now present the physical setting in which this drama took place.

Hi-Test consisted of three operating units which, to the layman, presented a veritable technological wonderland.

The motive power for the process was generated in the engine room where six huge engines pounded away ceaselessly. They were in the charge of an engine operator, who worked alone with the machines and the noise.

Near the engine room was the catalyst plant where an operator with a crew of ten men handled the chemical process that produced the catalyst used in making the gasoline.

The heart of the operation was the control room where the wall was lined with sensitive automatic meters to record every change in the process. Here worked the poly operator (No. 1), hydrostillman (No. 2), and fractionator operator (No. 3).

On its way from gas to iso-octane, the principal component of aviation gasoline, the liquid-gas traveled through hundreds of yards of steel tubing. The tubes carried it through a cracking furnace where it was subjected to a temperature of 1,300°F. Two cooling towers ran water over the tubes, four fractionating columns separated lighter from heavier parts, several stills distilled the substance, and so on, until it ran off at the end into storage tanks.

The catalyst plant was a chemical manufacturing unit, not connected with the steel tubing which linked the engine room with the control room. The latter two units were directly dependent upon each other in both technical process and human action.

The work duties of the control room were largely divided between the fractionator operator (No. 3) and the hydro-stillman (No. 2). When the works was opened, the poly operator (No. 1) was responsible for control room, catalyst plant and engine room, but there were charts in the control room registering the engine room operations so little human contact was necessary there. The poly operator rarely walked over to the engine room. The engine operator usually came into the control room once a day to join the others at lunch and perhaps once more during the working day. There was nothing to take the poly operator into the catalyst plant except his responsibility for checking on work activity. The catalyst operator was rarely seen in the control room.

The work of the three control room men (for each shift) is difficult to describe; except for regular hourly samples of product for testing to be drawn from various pieces of equipment, the activity depended very largely upon the condition of the process. When operations were going smoothly, the men had little to do but watch their charts. When operations were not going quite right, there were adjustments to be made almost constantly. Since any adjustment made by the fractionator operator affected operations in the area of the hydro-stillman (and vice versa), this would be a period of accelerated interaction between them and with the poly operator.

An emergency would generate greatly accelerated activity. For example, if one engine broke down, the control room men had to respond quickly in order to lighten the load on the other five. Otherwise, the other overloaded engines might all go down, and the process would come to a very costly halt.

The poly operator had a large and heavy responsibility, but few specifically assigned duties. Every hour he was required to look into the cracking furnace from both sides, to check the condition of the tubes. Grey shadows on the white-hot tubes indicated carbon deposits that might cause a blowout, pouring vapors into the furnace and setting off a fire that would play over the outside of the furnace. If these carbon deposits could be blown out, the life of the tubes would be prolonged. While the poly operator had certain other checks to make, his job consisted primarily of coordinating the activities of the other two men.

It was technically possible to operate the control room with only two men, and in fact, the plant was set up on this basis. However, the company found it necessary to set up the poly operator position to assure a proper coordination between the other two men.

Personal and organizational history

This was a young and rapidly growing company. Joe Sloan was a young man—only 29 when he walked off of the job—and he had expected to grow with it. Indeed, he had gotten off to a rapid start.

An only child, he had been forced to drop out of high school after three years by the death of his father. He was bright and eager to get ahead, and at first it seemed that the company was wide open with opportunities for him.

Sloan had been only a few years on the job when management set up a pilot plant to test out the possibilities of making aviation gasoline from natural gas. The men selected to work in the pilot plant were chosen solely in terms of management's estimate of their ability, and Sloan was among them.

When the Hi-Test plant was put into operation in 1938, management continued to consider the work there of a difficult and experimental nature. In its other operations, management had generally been following seniority in promotions, even though there was no international union in this situation with a contract emphasizing seniority. Feeling that the skills necessary to operate the new plant were not generally available in the work force, management manned Hi-Test at first entirely without regard to seniority. It was only somewhat later that men began moving into Hi-Test on the basis of their seniority.

Thus Sloan found himself in the top operating position of the new plant at the age of 24. Everything looked rosy to him at the time. He found the new job challenging and interesting. He assumed that when he had shown he could master this job, a promotion into management would not be long in coming.

But poly operator was as high as Joe was ever to get in the company. Shortly after he had attained this position, a new general manager of the natural gasoline department laid down a new policy: only college graduates were to be appointed to positions such as foreman and staff engineer. (Actually the policy was changed in 1944, under pressure of exceedingly rapid wartime expansion and manpower shortage. But that was too late to do Joe Sloan any good.)

Joe did not give up hope of advancing at once. At the time, management had not made it entirely clear whether a man who satisfactorily passed a correspondence school course in chemical engineering might be allowed to cross the barrier. Management encouraged workers to take such courses but made no commitments as to promotions. When I first met him early in 1943, Sloan was within half a year of completing his International Correspondence School (ICS) course in chemical engineering, reportedly with high grades. Nevertheless, he was pessimistic about the future. He described his feelings in this way:

I feel like I am just bumping my head against the ceiling here. There isn't much chance of getting a better job. I would like to get an engineer's rating. There are always new things to do and it is interesting work. But if I can't get that kind of job, I won't stick to this company for life. If I can't get ahead after this war, maybe I will go into business for myself. I have been thinking about getting into the cosmetics business. With what I know about chemistry, I think I might make a go of it. I thought of quitting once before, but then the army began getting close to married men. I'm only here to stay out of the army.

As Sloan remained on the same job, his sentiments toward the job itself changed. He said:

The first year I found it interesting. There was a lot to learn. But after that it got monotonous. Now it is just routine. Of course, from time to time the process is changed, and that gives you something to work on, but otherwise it is just routine and I get sick of it. . . .

While Joe Sloan remained in the same official position for a period of five years, the status of that position declined as the difficult and experimental operations became routine. Sloan describes the change in these words:

When we were chosen, we had a meeting with Bill Jones (foreman) and the superintendent. Bill told us we were supposed to be above the men, that we could not belong to the company union, we were really supervisors. At that time we were in charge of the catalyst plant. Bill told us to go down there every once in a while and see if anybody was not working and report to him. The men resented that snooping. I wouldn't snitch on the men myself, but we had one snitcher among the poly operators. I don't blame the men for the way they felt about that. One time Gasper (poly operator) and Thompson (catalyst plant operator) got into a fight and as a result of that Bill Jones told us we weren't over the catalyst plant any more.

There used to be poly operator meetings with Bill Jones. We would get together and talk over things. If we had discussed operations, it might have done some good, but Gasper would lead off with some crackpot idea. Chester and Martin would take one side and Walling and I would take the other side. We were pals then; that was before he double-crossed me.

At that time the poly operators in Texas had got a couple of raises and we had not been raised here at all. When the plant started out, we were supposed to get within $10 of what they got in Texas (per month). We got together and asked to discuss the salary with the company. I was appointed spokesman. They knew I wasn't afraid to talk, and they thought Gasper would talk too much.

I talked about the responsibilities of the job. They were expecting us to act like supervisors but still we were not getting that pay. After that, they decided to cut out some of our responsibilities. They didn't give us a raise at that time. That was when the poly operator meetings were dropped. We had been coming in on our own time like supervisors. If we were just operators like the rest, they would have had to pay us extra for those meetings.

In the first four years at Hi-Test, Sloan served under two foremen, recently graduated chemical engineers, who were highly unpopular with most of the men. This presented problems to Sloan, because while these foremen had a strong distrust of the abilities and sense of responsibility of the other operators, they did have some confidence in Sloan's ability and also in that of Mark Walling, the second-youngest poly operator. In other words, the young foremen were thought to favor the young and ambitious poly operators.

Sloan described his relations with foremen and fellow workers in this way:

> I was plenty unpopular when I came on this job at first. I was very young then, and I was an only child in my family. My wife was one of 10 children. She didn't know anything about psychology from the textbooks, but she was able to help me a lot.
>
> This was my first job handling men. I made a lot of mistakes. I was too conscientious. The trouble was I believed what Jones and Fitch (former foremen) told me. They told me that I should push the men, that I should stand behind them and keep them working. I don't think I was nasty about it, but the men didn't like it. Then I saw that Walling's crew was producing less than any of us, and he was getting all the credit, so I changed my motives. Then one man on my crew squealed on Edwards (fractionator operator) to Bill Jones. Edwards knew I got along good with Jones so he thought I had squealed, and he wouldn't talk to me for a month. That's all straightened out now. Those men know that whenever I have a complaint about them, I will take them with me to the foreman.
>
> Then I got in trouble too because I didn't smoke on the job. The men used to step outside to sneak a smoke. When the supervisors caught onto it, they thought I had squealed. I just didn't think it was right to smoke around a gasoline plant, but I never did squeal. Then when the men were taking gasoline, I didn't want to do that either and when I didn't do it, they were afraid I would squeal on them. Then I got into some trouble down at the catalyst plant. I really didn't have anything to do with it but I just got roped in on it. The fight was between Thompson (catalyst operator) and Gasper (poly operator at Hi-Test), but Thompson had been claiming that I hadn't been labelling the used catalyst right. I don't know who made the mistake there. It was such a little thing that I didn't pay any attention to it. But that got taken out on me.
>
> Being the youngest man here, I have been very careful about handling the men. Whenever a man gives me an idea, I try to tell it to the foreman in his presence. The men know that so they give me plenty of ideas. Now Johnny Hudson has had no technical education, but he has a good practical mind, and he will think of something good maybe once a week.
>
> Those poly operator meetings never did any good. The men would just get together and gripe about the operators on their tour. The poly operator would get down on some man, and he couldn't do anything right. Whenever they began tearing down a man, I would say, "Put him on my tour, and I will make it a good tour." Then the supervisor would tell me they put the new men on my tour because if they couldn't do the work, I could. That way, I have always got the newest operators. Johnny Hudson is a good man. He is a good hydro-stillman. His only trouble is that sometimes he gets excited and wants to do the wrong thing, and I have to stop him. They wanted to put Swanson on another man's tour and that man wouldn't have him, so I got him. I have never known a man who was more willing or more stupid. You tell

him how to do a thing 100 times, and he doesn't know any better the 99th time than he did the first time. (Swanson was a man in his fifties with long seniority but little experience relevant to Hi-Test.) . . . .

Bill Jones used to listen to what the men would say about other operators. He trusted me, and so some of the men suspected that I was snitching on them. That's what Charley Lester (hyro-stillman) thought when Bill got down on him, but I never did it.

For a time both Sloan and Walling seemed to enjoy a favored position with management. They were good friends. Then a change occurred to leave Sloan somewhat isolated insofar as the poly operators were concerned. He describes it in this way:

Chester and Martin had the most seniority. I was the youngest so I knew I couldn't get anything by myself. But Walling was the next youngest, and while we stuck together, that balanced things out. At that time the poly operators rotated working with different crews and getting different days off. Chester and Martin didn't want to rotate. Naturally, they had the seniority, so with this system, they could choose their days off. They talked to Walling and they finally persuaded him. So Chester picked Friday and Saturday, Martin got Sunday and Monday, Walling Wednesday and Thursday, and I got Monday and Tuesday. (By this time Gasper was doing office work and was not included.) We were off two days one week and one day the next (averaging 44 hours a week). I knew I wouldn't get anything because I didn't have the seniority, but I didn't like the way they did things. Whenever there was any change, I wouldn't be consulted, I would just get what was left. That is what I would have got anyway, but it would have been a nicer way to do it if they had consulted me first.

About a year before his walkoff, Joe Sloan's career was very nearly terminated abruptly. While Sloan was looking into the cracking furnace, examining the white-hot tubes for carbon deposits, a tube blew out outside of the furnace and burst into flames just a few feet behind them. If the accident had happened closer to him, he could have been severely and perhaps fatally burned. Sloan confessed to me that after this experience he never again looked into the cracking furnace from this particular side, though he continued to check the other side. He freely admitted that there was just as much danger on the other side, but he could not bring himself to take up again the position he was holding at the time of the accident. Several weeks after his walkoff, Sloan commented to me in this way about his accident:

I had that accident a year ago. Ever since that time I didn't feel right about that equipment. Not just the cracking furnace. I was more afraid of that 750-pound (pressure) equipment. . . . We used to have a couple of weeks of testing work around the yard every so often. I remember I always used to feel better in that two weeks. The rest of the time, for the last six months, I worked in the plant. I always used to wake up in the morning with a headache.

The union drive

Management had provided its workers in this area with a company union in 1935. A CIO union had made two previous attempts to organize Hi-Test and other plants of the company in this area. Late in 1942, a new organization drive was begun.

At about the same time, higher management, having become aware of friction between workers and local management, made some strategic replacements. Tom Lloyd came in as foreman for Hi-Test and the catalyst plant, and Jess Douglas came in as plant manager immediately above him.

At the time of my study, both men had become highly popular with the workers. Lloyd was a chemical engineer, like his predecessors, but at 36 he was a good deal older and more experienced than Jones and Fitch had been. Furthermore, having had no previous experience with Hi-Test, he had to trust the workers to handle the operations effectively. He respected them and they respected him.

Sloan describes the response of the poly operators to the unionization drive in this way:

When this latest CIO drive got started way back in the fall, the poly operators went to Douglas (plant manager) and asked him to give us a new classification. We didn't ask any more money. We just asked to be called shift foremen, and then we wouldn't have to take a stand one way or another in this union business. Douglas wouldn't even discuss the matter with us, so if we go for the CIO, they can't complain. We are all for the CIO in here except for one man. I would do more organization for the union if I didn't have to watch my step because I still have hopes of going up.

In early February of 1943, the poly operators suffered a severe symbolic blow to their status. The company was then engaged in contract discussions with its company union. The Hi-Test operators had little faith in the company union but were naturally interested in any news of the discussions.

The Hi-Test representative (a fractionator operator) had been arguing for a special increase in pay for poly operators. He was claiming that, in view of the great skill and scientific knowledge required of the poly operators, they should be paid the same as the top operators in the company's refineries.

Management was not yielding on this point, but the discussion proceeded calmly enough to the end of the formal meeting. It was after the formal meeting that Masters, chief company negotiator, speaking casually to some of the men, made the remark that hit the Hi-Test plant and the whole works area with dramatic effect. The Hi-Test representative reported it in this way:

Did you hear what Masters said about us? He told us that we were only watchmen. He said, "Down there in that plant you have got automatic controls and charts. If anything goes wrong with the meters, you just call a meter man. If anything goes wrong with the engines, you call a repairman. If anything goes wrong with operations, you call an engineer, and he tells you what to do. There is no skill in that work. You just have to watch the charts."

My data do not show how Sloan himself responded to this statement. However, the statement was resented bitterly by all of the men with whom I discussed it. Given Sloan's youth and ambition, we can safely assume that he felt strongly about it. This symbolic blow seemed to show just to what extent management had downgraded the status of the poly operator since the opening of the plant, when he was considered really a part of management.

Sloan's last six weeks

On March 1, long awaited transfers of Hi-Test men to the synthetic rubber plant in Texas were carried through. There was no worker criticism of the way the transfers were handled. The company had asked for volunteers, and the plan had been explained in a company union meeting.

At the same time, the company announced a lengthening of the work week from 44 to 48 hours, to meet the manpower shortage. Since only one Hi-Test operator elected to make the transfer, the new work schedule left the plant with a manpower surplus. One of the poly operators would have to serve as a hydro-stillman for half of his six days. The new schedule also meant that the regular three-man teams which had been together for months were now broken up.

Management elected to make the personnel changes on a strict seniority basis, so the demotion fell to Sloan. However, Plant Manager Douglas explained to him that he would retain his poly operator classification and rate of pay. With the additional four hours of overtime at time-and-a-half, his monthly income was substantially increased.

Shortly after this, Sloan took his two-week vacation. My first opportunity to interview him again on the job following his demotion came on March 23. Sloan was hydro-stillman on evening tour (3 P.M. to 11 P.M.) under Poly Operator Walling.

Sloan said that he had been offered a job as a chemist in an aircraft plant. He had gone to talk with the personnel man there and had been shown through the plant. The money would be somewhat less than he was now getting, but "it would be a clean job and the chances for advancement might be better." He did not take it, he said, because he wasn't sure what the job would look like a year from now.

I went to see Franklin (personnel man) on this to find out how I stood with the company. This was the first time I have ever gone to talk with

Franklin. It was amusing and aggravating at the same time. He spent the first half hour telling me that he had never told a lie, then he talked for about an hour telling me how important engineers were to the company. He wanted to make me feel satisfied with my job. Then when I brought out that letter that he had signed congratulating me on my ICS course, and saying that there would be a possibility of advancement if I got through with it, he had to talk himself all around those things that he had been saying. I'm sure he hadn't remembered signing that letter at all, and he didn't give me a chance to bring it in until he told me all this about the college men. He didn't want to say that he had lied in this letter or that he was giving a different picture in talking to me, so he just talked around in a circle for a while. I didn't get any satisfaction out of that.

I went and talked with Douglas (plant manager). I know I can count on him to tell me the truth. I asked him if he thought this letter Franklin had written me was a lot of ballyhoo. He said, "It kinds of looks that way, don't it?" He didn't build me up or tear me down. He just told me where I stood with the company. He told me there was no danger of me being bumped back (into a lower pay and status classification). I felt better knowing that.

Now, I am satisfied with what I am doing. I don't worry about it any more.

I asked if that last statement did not represent a change in his feelings about the job. He agreed. I asked him to explain the change. He said he couldn't, except that perhaps he felt better knowing where he stood.

Later in this same week Poly Operator Martin went to the hospital for an operation. It was expected that he would be out for two months. Sloan assumed that in this case he would be returned to full time on the poly operator job, but Tom Lloyd decided that the job should be open to bids and filled on a seniority basis. Johnny Hudson, the hydro stillman who had worked under Sloan for many months, had much more seniority than Sloan and was awarded the poly operator position. Sloan retained his poly operator classification and pay but continued to divide his week between poly operator and hydro-stillman positions.

Commenting on this change after he had left the plant, Sloan said that he had indeed felt discriminated against, but he added,

That didn't bother me. I won't say I understood the reasons for that decision, but I didn't complain about it because I thought too much of Hudson. He was my best friend in the plant.

On April 4, the representation election was held, and the CIO union lost by a narrow margin. (The watchman statement had by now receded into the background.)

The union drive will be discussed in Chapter 14. For present purposes, our only concern is its effect upon Sloan. He said that the CIO defeat was a disappointment to him, although he had had no great hopes that things would be different if the union came in.

On Tuesday, April 6, at 6:30 P.M., Tom Lloyd received a telephone call from the main office with the order to start the tri-isobutylene run as soon as possible. He had known some time in advance that a product of this nature was to be made, but it was not until this time that he was given the exact specifications (initial boiling point and dry point temperatures). Lloyd asked if he could start the run the following morning, but he was told that this was a rush order so that it was necessary to start work immediately.

Since Lloyd was not familiar with the detailed operations of the fractionating column, he telephoned Dan Benton, his staff engineer, and asked him to return to the plant to take charge of operations at once.

The fractionating column in which the product was to be made was under the direct charge of the fractionator operator, but having had a good deal of fractionating experience, the hydro-stillman was naturally interested also, and both men normally worked under the supervision of the poly operator.

To this group were added Lloyd and Benton, who ordinarily spent little time within the plant. During the run, Lloyd spent most of his time at Hi-Test, consulting with Benton and the operators. He also took samples from the fractionating column up to the laboratory in order to run distillation tests on them. When he went home to sleep, he called in Catalyst Operator Thompson to do the distillations.

Benton was in active charge from Tuesday night until Friday morning. During that period, he was in the plant almost continually, getting only ten hours of sleep. At the start, he took over the No. 3 fractionating column himself and directed the fractionator operator in all changes. Since the plant was operating in a routine manner otherwise, there was little for the poly operator and the hydro-stillman to do except watch Benton and the fractionator operator.

Benton had certain definite ideas as to how the run should be started, and it appeared that by Thursday morning he had been successful. The product at that time tested to specifications, but by the time the test results were reported, the column had become flooded and was no longer making the product. Having been unsuccessful in this effort, Benton listened to the suggestions of the operators and tried out a number of their ideas.

At the start of the daylight tour (7 A.M. to 3 P.M., Friday) fractionator operator Kendall gave his opinion to Lloyd that no further progress could be gained along the lines then being pursued, and went on to outline his ideas as to how the fractionating column should be handled. Lloyd had a high regard for Kendall and therefore decided to turn the column over to him without restrictions or supervision. By now Benton was physically and mentally exhausted, and Lloyd sent him home.

At the end of Kendall's tour, he still had no results, but he was able to convince Lloyd that he was moving in the right direction. Lloyd ordered Kendall to work another eight hours, remaining in charge of the key column. Walling was poly operator on evening tour (3 P.M. to 11 P.M.). Lloyd instructed Walling to pay close attention to the way Kendall was operating the column.

At the end of evening tour, the product was still to be made. Lloyd sent Kendall home and held Walling over for another eight hours, ordering him to take exclusive charge of the column. Early Saturday morning, 22 hours after Kendall began trying his plan, the product came over, and shortly the brief run was completed.

One operator expressed the general viewpoint of the workers when he said:

It wasn't until they left it to the operator that they got the thing lined out. Sure, it would have gone much faster if they had made it that way in the first place. The operator knows these columns better than the technical man.

During the week of the run, Sloan had worked Monday through Wednesday on graveyard tour (11 P.M. to 7 A.M.) as a hydro-stillman under Walling. Thursday through Saturday, he worked as poly operator, but when the product was finally being made, he found Walling held over to retain charge of the key column, so Sloan had nothing to do with the making of this experimental product.

Some weeks later I asked Sloan to tell me particularly about his reactions to the tri-isobutylene run. He said it had not bothered him particularly. He went on,

Now I don't have anything against Benton. I like Dan. But we hadn't been accustomed to having an engineer supervise operations like that. He was around all the time telling the fractionator man what to do. Lloyd was there most of the time too. He didn't really do anything. He would just talk to Benton and with the rest of us, figuring out what to do. Then he spent some of his time running distillations. . . .

One night when I was on tour, we had Thompson in there from the catalyst plant running distillations for Lloyd while he slept. We had never had a man from the catalyst plant work in there with us before. Thompson (a company union representative) and I got into a hot argument about the company union and the CIO. It didn't really amount to anything, but I didn't like to have Thompson around all the time. He has the type of overbearing personality that don't appeal to me. . . .

One night Tom Fitch (Lloyd's predecessor as foreman) called the plant at 2 A.M. He had something to do with the run from the main office end . . . Fitch knows the operations here a lot better than Lloyd . . . Lloyd was in the plant with us at the time. I asked him why he thought Fitch had called. "Oh," he says, "he probably just wanted to show he was interested in his job." I said to Lloyd, "Then why are you down here now? For the same reason?" He didn't have anything to say to that.

On this particular week, Sunday was Sloan's day off. He returned to work Monday on daylight tour as hydro-stillman under Johnny Hudson. This was the first time Sloan had worked under his former hydro-still-man. It was this morning that the control room was flooded in the course of the changeover from isoheptene to iso-octane, and Sloan walked off the job.

How analyze the case?

We have here a complex story that evolves over years with many small and large changes. In order to make sense out of the case, we will need to follow a time line, seeking to identify distinct periods. Within each period then we will examine interactions, activities, sentiments and transactions.

Ideally, we would like to start with personal history data that would give us a systematic picture of the personality of Joe Sloan at the time he went to work for the Blank Oil Company. In this case we have only fragments of information: Joe Sloan was an only child, who would have gone on to college, if his father had not died when he was in high school. As Joe himself acknowledges, he had rather limited peer group experience when he first went to work.

From this rather sketchy beginning, we will be able to follow Joe Sloan in much more detail through five periods of his working life.

1. Sloan's rapid rise

Sloan's first months with Blank Oil Company represented a success story: bright, young man works hard and moves rapidly ahead.

In *interactions*, in the pilot plant period and in the early period of operation of Hi-Test, Sloan enjoyed a high frequency of interaction with management personnel, being as free to initiate interaction to them as they were to him. While he presumably interacted more frequently with fellow workers than with management even in this period, his interactions with management accounted for a much higher proportion of his total interactions than at any later period.

In *activities*, Sloan found the job intensely challenging. There was always something to do, some new problem to solve. He found management people responsive to his attempted initiations of activity changes, and he was a frequent initiator of activities to subordinates.

In *sentiments*, we note Sloan's high commitment to his job. He took pride in his ability and growing knowledge and in his rapid progress. He also found the job intellectually interesting. To members of management above the foreman level, Sloan presumably had favorable sentiments—at least he never mentioned any negative evaluations to me later when discussing this period. He had rather ambivalent feelings toward his first two foremen, Jones and Fitch, but considered himself well regarded by them. He had ambivalent feelings toward fellow workers at this time and acknowledges that he was not popular with them. Apparently this lack of integration in the work group at this time did not cause him serious concern, as he expected soon to move into management.

In IRR, we find in this period that Sloan was reaping the rewards that at least equalled if they did not surpass his investment. He had high aspirations, but as he judged from his own rate of progress, his expectations were equally high. Sloan felt he owed a lot to the company, and he was determined to do everything he could to advance the company's welfare.

2.   Reactions to blocked progress

The beginning of his second period coincides with announcement of management policy that only college graduates were to be given foreman or other management positions. Along with this came the termination of the weekly poly operator meetings with the foreman, elimination of poly operator supervision over the catalyst plant, and announcement that the poly operators were now free to belong to the company union. This last item was important because it definitely placed poly operators below the line separating management from workers and at the same time offered nothing of interest to the poly operators.

We note a marked reduction in the frequency of Sloan's *interaction* with management people. Correspondingly, he spent an increased proportion of time interacting with fellow workers. We now see him taking on something of a leadership role among the workers. It seems unlikely that observation would have established Joe Sloan as *the* informal leader among the Hi-Test workers in this period, considering his youth and the previous negative sentiments toward him. Probably he was chosen as a spokesman for the group because the other workers recognized that he was highly regarded by management and also had the nerve to speak up to them. Whether informal leader or simply spokesman, this new role brought Sloan into a much more central position in the interactional network of workers.

In *activities*, we note now a marked change in job content. By now the once challenging job had become a routine set of activities, often providing long stretches when there was literally nothing that the poly operator was required to do.

In this period, Sloan's sentiments toward higher management became negative, and his resentment against the supervisory style of foremen Jones and Fitch was now not relieved by his identification of himself as a future member of management. In this period, he found himself more integrated as a member of the work group, with a mutuality of favorable sentiments.

In IRR, this was a period within which his investments in seniority, skill, and education (the ICS course) continued to increase, while there was a sharp drop in the rewards apparently available to him. He now found himself with a substantial deficit, and for the first time he began to look negatively upon his job and think of the possibility of leaving the company.

In this period, as he was losing ground, Sloan attempted to initiate a number of transactions whose success would have brought his own IRR more closely into balance. Management refused to respond to any of the transactions offered.

3.   Failure of group efforts

This period was marked by the breakdown of worker efforts, under Sloan's leadership, to gain higher status for the poly operators. In this same time period, we see Sloan losing his position among the poly operators as the older seniority men combined against him to pick their preferred days off. This served to put Sloan somewhat outside of the main stream of informal interaction among workers. His interactions came to be more concentrated within his own work team.

In *activities*, the intrinsic interest of the job remained at a low level. Sloan was no longer involved in worker-wide attempts to initiate activity changes for management.

In *sentiments*, Sloan continued to have negative feelings toward higher management, but he held favorable sentiments toward the plant manager and toward foreman, Tom Lloyd. His sentiments toward fellow workers were now mixed, as he came to feel somewhat isolated from others and fully involved only with members of his own team.

In IRR, this was a period of increasing investments in seniority and in formal education. While the job did not change in this period, with the determination of days off being made on a seniority basis, Sloan found himself suffering under a standard which had not been applied at the time of his rapid progress. The IRR deficit was now further increased.

4.   The final six weeks

In this period, begun by the transfer of workers to the rubber plant and the extention of the work week from 44 to 48 hours, Joe Sloan experienced both the break up of his established pattern of *interaction* and *activities* with the regular members of his work team and the weekly alternation in position from poly operator to hydro-stillman. This meant that he was under pressure to work out his interactional relations with those that he had not worked closely with before and to shift back and forth between those interactions appropriate to a number one position and those appropriate to a number two position. In the last week, he also experienced the highly disorganized interactions accompanying the tri-isobutylene run.

In *activities*, Sloan at last experienced some variety, but this consisted of shifting back part time to a lower level position through which he had passed earlier. Now also for three days a week he was in the familiar position of initiating activities for two subordinates, whereas for the other three days, he had to respond to the initiations of another poly operator. Finally, the tri-isobutylene run presented perhaps the most interesting technical problem faced by the plant in many months, a problem holding high intrinsic interest to Sloan, and yet he was barred from playing any important role in its solution. We see him attempting to take out his frustration in initiating to the plant manager and the personnel manager but receiving little response from them.

In *sentiments*, he remained negative toward higher management. He continued to look favorably upon the plant manager, but his sentiments toward foreman Tom Lloyd began to go sour. The tri-isobutylene run provides the first instance I have on record of Sloan speaking critically to the foreman. His sentiments toward his fellow workers continued to be mixed, and now finally he was without any work group that he could call his own.

In IRR, Sloan added slightly to his investments (in length of service). While the additional overtime increased his paycheck, it did not change his earnings in relation to others around him and thus could not be regarded as a significant reward. At the same time, he lost the position of full time poly operator not once but twice: when he was bumped back on a seniority basis at the beginning of the period and again when one other poly operator was ill and Sloan, instead of regaining his position, found his former subordinate promoted over his head. Sloan also lost the satisfactions that go with being part of a steady work group. His IRR deficit sharply increased.

Once again Sloan attempted to initiate transactions with management. No longer did he act as a representative of a group. He sought some personal reassurance regarding his future with the company. The best he could get was a statement that he would not lose his poly operator classification, and this did nothing to reduce the IRR deficit.

5. The final day

The final day placed Sloan in a new situation, both from the standpoint of *interactions* and *activities*. For the first time, he had to respond to Hughes, who had been his hydro-stillman for many months. Instead of directing the activities of Hughes and the fractionator operator, he had to follow directions.

With the venting of the lines on the control room floor, Sloan found himself temporarily in a disorganized and dangerous work situation. He initiated interaction with foreman, Tom Lloyd, and attempted to initiate activity to him. When Lloyd refused to respond, Sloan's initiatives had failed once more. In the context of his steadily increasing frustrations, this incident provoked negative sentiments toward everything and everybody associated with the job. Joe Sloan walked off the job in the face of a legitimate complaint, and yet this would have been but a minor problem except for the depressing series of changes in interactions and activities and the great IRR deficit that Sloan had experienced.

General conclusions on Sloan

What hit Joe Sloan? We have followed the accumulating problems through time. We can now identify them in a more topical framework. Joe Sloan experienced the following four kinds of losses or threats:

1. *Status loss.* This is another way of saying that Joe Sloan experienced an adverse shift in IRR. We should further note that this negative shift was proceeding at an accelerating rate.
2. Marked *reductions in opportunities to initiate activities* for others.
3. *Instabilities and fluctuations in interactions* (climaxed by the tri-isobutylene run).
4. *A threat to physical safety.*

Was Joe a peculiar fellow to "fly off the handle" in this way? I would argue that any normal individual reacts to such a combination of adverse changes by becoming upset. He is likely to try to redress this disturbance by (1) protest activity (initiating to others, promoting transactions designed to restore his equilibrium), or (2) withdrawal from the situation. On a number of previous occasions, Joe Sloan had tried the protest activity solution and found this unrewarding. This new crisis therefore propelled him toward the withdrawal solution.

The case also enables us to say something in general terms regarding IRR, level of aspiration, and upward career progress.

The Joe Sloan case also suggests a generalization regarding age, progress in the organizational hierarchy, and level of aspiration. Other things being equal, the more rapidly the individual rises in the organizational hierarchy, the more serious is his adjustment problem when further advancement is blocked. Under these circumstances, blocking can be expected to lead to strong negative sentiments and to a desire to leave the organization. (While Sloan did not intend to quit on the day of the walk-off, note his statement that he would have resigned much earlier had he had not wished to avoid conscription.)

This proposition suggests that if Joe Sloan had moved up at a slower pace, he would not have been so seriously disturbed by the blocking of his progress. Speculation as to what might have been does not, of course, provide any evidence in support of the proposition. It simply suggests a corollary for the proposition that might be tested in future research.

Technology, work process, and symbols

Let us now look beyond Joe Sloan and see if we can draw from this case some tentative conclusions regarding technological environment and symbols, interactions, activities, and sentiments.

We have already noted that the technology tends to channel within certain limits the interactions and activities of workers and supervisors. This case suggests that the technology and work process also tend to establish the symbols men use in evaluating the rank or status of the job.

Management's initial evaluation of the technical difficulty of the position led to the symbolic placement of poly operators between workers and management.

Along with this symbolic separation from workers went certain activities and interactions of poly operators, not shared in by hydro-stillmen and fractionator operators. The poly operators met as a group for discussion with their foreman. They were also charged with supervision of the catalyst plant.

Along with this pattern of symbols, interactions, and activities went a complementary set of sentiments. Management people felt a high regard for the poly operators. The poly operators felt themselves superior to other workers. This did not mean that the poly operators held favorable sentiments toward their foreman in this early period. At least, at the time of our research, the poly operators were highly critical of these previous foremen. On the other hand, much of this criticism was directed at the way the foreman would "get down on" a given hydro-stillman or fractionator operator and would try to set the poly operators apart from their two immediate subordinates. At least, Sloan and Walling felt that Foremen Jones and Fitch had confidence in them. They did not feel the brunt of the foremen's criticism.

While the technology did not change substantially in the several years following the opening of the plant, the work process came under routine control. Management now introduced verbal symbols congruent to the changed situation: the poly operators were told they were now free to belong to the company union. While this did not serve to increase the interest of the poly operators in the company union, it tended to channelize their identification toward workers instead of toward management. A broad company policy announced in this period had the same identification effects: this was the decision that only college graduates would be promoted into management.

Interaction and activity changes accompanied these symbolic changes. The poly operator meetings with foremen were abandoned, and the poly operators were relieved of their responsibilities for supervising the catalyst plant.

In the early period, when constant difficulties were encountered, the poly operator had to initiate for hydro-stillmen and fractionator operators with a high frequency to coordinate the work of the plant. As the work became routine, the intervention of the poly operator was needed much less often. The other two men simply reported to him when they made changes in operations, and he seldom had to tell them what to do. This further served to reduce the perceived status of the poly operator.

If the poly operator had been responsible for the work of 10 men, the sheer numbers involved would have made for significant interactional differences. In spreading his interactions over ten men, the poly operator would not have been able to interact with any individual with a high frequency. Thus, his position would have appeared to be separated from theirs both to himself and to his subordinates. When the poly operator had only two men with whom to interact in the test room (plus an occasional visit from the engine operator), and when he did not often interact with the foreman except in contacts shared with the other two workers, his interactions were bound to strengthen the poly operator's identification sentiments toward the workers. When you are thrown together for eight hours a day with two other men, with few other interactional opportunities, and with a technology that permits free interaction, you are bound to come to think of yourself as a member of that work group and to be so regarded by others.

The poly operators responded to this situation by changing their sentiments toward the job itself, toward other workers, and toward management. They came to recognize that the job had become more routine even as they resented this downgrading of its prestige. They came to identify themselves more with their subordinates and to look with unfavorable sentiments toward management in general, even when interpersonal relations with Foreman Tom Lloyd were harmonious.

In an effort to re-establish their lost superiority, poly operators asked for the title of "shift foreman" and then sought to equate their work with that of high status refinery operators. Having been rebuffed at these efforts of symbolic redress, the poly operators now received the heaviest symbolic blow of all: the watchman statement.

This word considerably exaggerated the loss of skill and status in the job, at least as viewed by local management. This made the symbol particularly offensive. On the other hand, it did clearly mark out the direction in which interactions, activities, and sentiments had moved since the opening of the plant.

Let us see if we can use the case to set up tentative propositions in a more general and abstract form.

Symbols tend to reflect the current pattern of interactions, activities, and sentiments in an organization. At the same time, the introduction of a new symbol may serve to signalize for participants that a change has taken place and thus to set off new interactions, activities, and sentiments in reaction to this change. More specifically, if managers apply to workers symbols implying a reduction of the status previously held by them, then these symbols can be expected to strengthen the workers negative sentiments toward management and to set off interactions and activities directed toward re-establishing the status level the workers previously enjoyed.

The case of the poly operators suggests a general proposition regarding the relations among three levels in an organizational hierarchy. Let us refer to foreman level as A, the poly operators as B, the hydro-stillmen and fractionator operators as C.

As B's interactions with A (in situations not shared by C) are sharply reduced and B's interactions with C are increased, we can expect these changes in sentiments: (1) to all parties concerned, the status of B in the organization will be seen as having declined; (2) B will now tend to identify himself more with C and less with A.

Note the sequence of analysis we follow in such a case. We begin with such concretely observable items as the technology and the work activities. We see that management *sentiments* regarding technology and the complexity of the work activities, at the beginning of our case, tend to influence (1) the number of men placed in the plant, (2) the characteristics of the men placed there, (3) the status or rank of the poly operators, and (4) the interactions and activities of the top operators with the foremen and with fellow workers (including the catalyst plant).

Unfortunately, we have no observational data for the early period to compare poly operator interactions and activities in Hi-Test with what we observed in 1942–43. When workers and supervisors alike say that the job has become more routine, we infer that comparing the later with the earlier period, interactions and activities have become much more stable and subject to far fewer sharp fluctuations. Awareness of these changes affects management sentiments on all of the points noted above except the number of men in the plant. The characteristics of the men required for the job are seen as having changed (seniority replacing ability as the primary criterion of choice). The status of the poly operators is seen as markedly lower than before. Interactions and activities involving poly operators exclusively with the foremen are terminated, and the supervisory activity of the poly operator is sharply curtailed.

Such changes may bring forth from workers (1) compensatory interactions and activities or (2) withdrawal from the situation. In this case, we have seen examples of both types of responses. Joe Sloan's walk-off was clearly a withdrawal, but earlier he and his fellows had made several compensatory efforts (the shift foreman proposal, the claimed equivalence with refinery operators). In Chapter 19, "Enter the Union," we shall be examining a more far-reaching compensatory effort.

Discussion questions

1. Select what seem to you the most important symbols in this case. For each symbol, indicate how it served to support the existing IAS pattern or how it precipitated changes in the pre-existing pattern.

2. Could members of management have acted toward Joe Sloan in ways that would have tended to keep him on the job? Indicate the points at which a member of management might have taken a different action or made a different decision in order to get more favorable responses out of Joe Sloan.

3. Review each of the changes in management behavior you have recommended on the basis of their favorable impact on Joe Sloan. To what extent would each of these changes have had negative effects on management's relations with other workers? (In other words, since management cannot afford to run the plant exclusively in the interests of one individual, you are asked to examine to what extent changes favorable to this individual would have resulted in negative effects in management's other relationships.)

Part V

VERTICAL RELATIONS

THE VERTICAL DIMENSION provides some of the main elements of the structure and functioning of organizations. While in later chapters we will be arguing that the importance of vertical relations has been overstressed to the neglect of other equally important relations, the man-boss relationship is clearly of great importance to any understanding of organizational behavior.

We begin with a description and analysis of the changing role of the first-line supervisor. In Chapter 13 we review the voluminous research literature to assess the relationships among supervisory leadership styles, morale, and productivity. Since that literature has yielded few firmly supported propositions, in Chapter 14, on "The Supervisor in the Social System," we go on to present a different scheme of analysis and apply it to a case.

12. The first-line supervisory position

WE BEGIN our examination of the management process by considering the role of the foreman. It is often said that the foreman is the key man in management from the worker's point of view, that he represents the company to the workers. We shall have occasion to question this emphasis as we go along. But the foreman, who directs the work of production or process in the plant, is at least a convenient point at which to begin.

"The" foreman does not exist

First, a caution against a very common semantic fallacy: mistaking a word for a thing. We often unconsciously assume that because we can speak of *the* foreman, such an individual and such a position actually exist. This leads people to try to discover how *the* foreman should be selected, how *the* foreman should be trained, and how *the* foreman's behavior should be evaluated. This leads further to the assumption that *the good* foreman will have the same abilities and skills, regardless of differences in first-line supervisory job situations. Nothing could be farther from the truth.

We must begin our analysis by recognizing that the technology and the nature of the tasks performed by the workers tend to shape the role and influence the behavior of the foreman. Comparisons among the cases already described will show something of the range of possibilities.

We have seen that the foreman on the assembly line has large numbers of very brief interactions with his workers individually and very rarely interacts with more than one individual at a time. By contrast, the foreman in the Benton Blowing Room has extended conversations with individuals and sometimes with groups of men. On one occasion, we noted the Benton foreman spending more than two hours with Jack Carter, observing him at work and discussing his work problems with him. Such an extended period of interaction would be completely out of the question on the assembly line.

In our study of the Blank Oil Company, we noted that the foreman of

303

the engine repair crew also related himself to his men in a way that would have been impossible on the assembly line. The men worked in small groups, and at times the foreman would be observed standing with a group of men, carrying on a lively discussion involving the diagnosis of mechanical problems, with items of small talk thrown in.

The foreman's interactions may vary markedly even within the same organizational unit. While the men in the Hi-Test control room complained bitterly about their former foremen, Jones and Fitch, and reported being under constant pressure from them, the engine operators reported that they rarely saw these foremen and were simply left alone by them.

The foreman's job may also change markedly through time. In examining the problems of Tom Walker in the barrel department (Chapter 14), we will see how the changing nature of the production in the department drastically affected his relations with other organizational units, and then with his own workers.

The Tom Walker case also underlines the importance of looking at the foreman's job in terms of a whole network of relations. We customarily think simply of the foreman's relations to his subordinates, and sometimes we consider his relations with his own immediate boss. In examining the foreman's job, we need to consider also the relations he needs to develop and maintain with other foreman in related departments and with staff and control people. In the assembly line studies, we have seen the foreman interacting more with people outside his department than with his workers. Changes in his relations with the people outside his own department often affect the foreman's relations with his workers.

While all of this distinctions need to be noted, we can make some general statements regarding the historical evolution of the first-line supervisor's position, and also, regarding the social characteristics of the men we find in that position.

The changing nature of foreman positions

It is often said that the foreman's position is weaker today than it was many years ago. What is meant by this statement?

While there were differences from company to company and even department to department, in manufacturing plants 50 years ago the foreman really ran his own department. He had the authority to hire whomever he pleased and to place workers wherever he wished in the department. He also had a free rein on disciplining workers, including firing them. His sovereignty was only beginning to be disturbed by the growth of staff specialists, and he had no union to question his decisions.

All this has changed in most plants. Industrial engineers come in to study and change job methods, and in some cases, to set incentive rates.

Design engineers move in to introduce technological changes at a rate much faster than 50 years ago. Cost accountants establish much more elaborate systems of record keeping and paper work than the old foreman faced. The union provides a channel of appeal against the foreman's decisions, and it is this force which has helped to bring the personnel man into the foreman's sphere of action. Between them, union leaders and personnel men see to it that a system of job classification and orderly progression from job to job is developed, so that the discretionary powers of the foreman are severely curtailed.

Moving up from worker to foreman

Years ago it was the universal rule to choose foremen from among the workers. This picture has been steadily changing, so that company after company is recruiting its supervisors from among college-trained men; even when promotion to the foreman level is left open to workers, we are likely to find that there is a ceiling one or two levels higher up on promotions of ex-workers.

In part this has been a natural development of advancing technology, which tends to require special training for management positions. We must explain it also in terms of the widening social cleavage between management and the workers, which makes it increasingly difficult for management to find workers who can function in the middle of a latent conflict situation.

We find in some cases that the workers who are promoted are unable to handle a foreman's job and must be dropped back to the worker level. How can we explain such failures?

We must first examine the basis of selection. In going through the personnel records of one plant, we picked out the following estimates of two workers written by the plant superintendent:

Employee has the ability but lacks courage to face criticisms of fellow employees. Was considered as supervisory material until further consideration exposed above trait.

Employee has an excellent knowledge of machine operation and could become pacesetter if he so desired, but is influenced by his group and lack of determination to force his crew.

Here two men were denied promotions because they were considered to be loyal to their work group, and it was assumed that such loyalty was not compatible with management's objectives. This is a very common management reaction. The worker who fits with the group is ruled out on those grounds. But what alternative is there for management? If the promoted worker has not been a respected member of the work group, then naturally the workers resent him intensely in his new position and resist his authority. Many foremen have been defeated by such opposition.

Nor can the problem be solved simply by promoting the leader of the gang, as is sometimes done by management. If management and workers were on the same team, pulling in the same direction, then the informal leader would obviously be the best choice. When a marked social cleavage separates workers from management, then the man who crosses the line must immediately ask himself whose side he is on. If he tries to keep close to the work group, then management looks upon him with distrust. If he conforms to management's expectations, then the workers feel he has sold them out. Some foremen we have observed try to "ride the fence," playing the workers' game when among them and conforming to management's logics when in contact with higher management. When the pressures on the foreman from above are not too severe, it seems possible to maintain this position—and we have seen it done—but the foreman always runs the risk of losing the confidence of both sides. At best, this is hardly an effective approach to the problem.

There are other factors which make for difficulty in the adjustment of the ex-worker foreman. At best, this is a difficult transition to make. In many cases a man will take 10 years or more to work up to the highest non supervisory job, so that he will have become thoroughly habituated to the work routines by the time he is faced with an entirely different sort of job. The job of handling men is quite different from that of handling machines. The new foreman must break away from hand-and-body manipulation of machines and from close concentration upon the details of a narrowly restricted job. He must see the pattern of jobs and men in relation to each other. He must learn to think in somewhat more abstract terms.

Many men fail to make this adjustment. They apparently do not feel secure unless they have their hands on a machine, and they pitch in to do jobs themselves to the extent that direction and coordination suffer.

A promotion clearly involves changes in the thought processes of the new foreman. It also involves a very important transition in human relations. It is in facilitating this transition that many managements are particularly inadequate.

Anthropologists have shown that all well-integrated societies have ceremonial ways of handling such social transitions. When, for example, the boy approaches the age of maturity, it is not left to him to become a man by himself. The society organizes an elaborate *rite of passage* to channel and support this change. While the content of the ceremonials varies widely from tribe to tribe, the form and function are much the same. First the individual is removed from the ordinary associations of his daily life—together with others making the transition at the same time—and brought into intimate and frequent contact with the adult males of the tribe. There follows a period in which the novice is ceremonially instructed in the technical and social aspects of the new role he is to play. The rite comes to a close when the novice is reintroduced to the society, and ceremonies are performed to give recognition to his new role.

Such rites are essential for the handling of social transitions. They help the individual to think, feel, and act in terms of the new role, and they help the total society to recognize the transition that has been made and to give recognition to the new role.

While ceremonials tend to be much less emphasized in our own society, we do give some attention to celebrating such transitions as marriage and school graduation. Unfortunately, with certain notable exceptions, ceremonials play a very small role in the life of the modern factory. It is perhaps at this point that management experimentation should be encouraged.

While we cannot expect a system of ceremonials to establish harmony within the factory when other important factors stimulate conflict, the transition from worker to foreman is of profound significance to the individual and to the whole factory. This suggests that more attention should be given by management to exploring the nature of the transition and to experimenting toward the development of more effective ways of bringing it about.

Perhaps some companies have been providing such ceremonials without planning it that way. Harrison Trice reports this experience with a company that had an elaborate program for the selection and training of foremen.[1] At management's invitation, he spent a summer studying both the company's testing program for potential supervisors and the two-week training program provided for those selected. Trice could find neither a relationship between the men's test scores and their subsequent performance as foremen, nor any evidence of the effectiveness of the two week training program. Trice expected that management would be discouraged by his negative report, but the personnel manager accepted it with equanimity. He said that he had thought for some time that the facts would turn out to be what Trice had reported. Nevertheless, the program's real value might lie in the effect it had in making the new foremen feel that they were really foremen and making the workers feel that it was indeed something to become a foreman. He explained that in fact management gave little attention to the test scores in making its selection of foremen, but that the candidates took the process most seriously and reported that they had really gone through an ordeal when they had finished the testing program. Similarly, whatever other effect it might have, the two-week training program did isolate the new foremen from workers and perhaps helped them to get adjusted to their new role.

The ceremonials appropriate to a primitive society could hardly be accepted in the United States. We would regard them as meaningless evidences of superstition. In a society oriented toward science and hard practical facts, it may well be that we need to develop ceremonials that will *appear* to be based upon science and practical concerns, even when they have no such demonstrated connection. In a period when the person-

---

[1] Personal communication.

ality testers are under fire for not being able to prove their claims, this approach to testing may give them a new lease on life.

The college-trained foreman

Today, while the opportunities of advancement for workers are narrowing, supervisors are being recruited in large numbers from men who are graduates of colleges and universities with degrees in engineering or chemistry, business management or nonprofessional subjects.

These "outsiders" have a difficult adjustment to make. In the first place, they are members of the middle class, and family background—or at least the educational process—has given them a social outlook far different from that of the workers. Furthermore, they generally come in to supervise experienced workers who are older than they and who feel keenly that the supervisory jobs should not be given to "outsiders." As one worker put it:

> You want to know what's the matter with this place? There's no hope! It's just like we were beating our heads against a brick wall. We're stopped where we are. If they need a foreman, they bring him in from the outside.

The college-trained foreman, therefore, is under pressure from the moment he starts work. Of course, he does not begin to supervise as soon as he sets foot inside the plant. If this is his first supervisory job, management generally provides him with a training program which involves observation of machines and processes as well as some formal instruction from management. The man may be provided with some reading matter on problems of human relations, but the emphasis is generally upon study of technology and of management procedures. Even where human problems are emphasized, we find that people cannot readily learn new ways of behaving by reading subject matter which is not closely tied to practice.

When these new men move into supervision, we frequently find conflict arising over the problem of *knowledge*. How much does the supervisor know about the jobs performed by workers? How much does he need to know?

Here we must distinguish between the college-trained engineer or chemist and the college man without this technical and scientific background.

The well-trained technical man knows a good deal about machines and processes. His problem is that he often fails to recognize the limits of his knowledge. He does not realize that the skilled and experienced operator inevitably has a more intimate, detailed knowledge of his machine or process than the foreman can or should have. Thus the foreman tries to impose tight controls over the operations, making no provision for the skill or judgment of the workers. This sort of approach is self-defeating.

We have seen this problem in the Hi-Test plant. Former Foremen Jones and Fitch had always given their operating instructions in great detail and were highly critical of the men when the operating results did not come up to what the foremen predicted on the basis of their instructions. Through their day-to-day experience, the men learned that often the detailed instructions issued by the foremen would not in fact lead to results that the foremen called for. The workers could not point this out to the foremen because the foremen, being technically trained, refused to acknowledge that the workers might know more about some aspects of operations than they did. Therefore, in order to escape criticism from the foremen, the workers took to "boiler-housing" their record of operations on the daily operating data sheet. They wrote down in full detail the operating steps the foreman had directed, but then went ahead to operate the plant so as to come out with the result that the foreman required. In many cases this meant that the actual operating steps were far different from those indicated on the data sheets. These foremen thus never knew exactly how the plant was operating. Their relations with the workers prevented them from obtaining the accurate records necessary for scientific experimentation and for technical improvements in operation.

The successor to Jones and Fitch, Tom Lloyd, recognized that efficient operations, as well as good morale, depended upon supervisory recognition of the knowledge and skill possessed by the workers. Lloyd's evaluation of the skills of his men is best shown in this comment upon the Masters "watchman statement":

Masters told the truth, but that was only part of the story. He said that the men were only watchmen, that they had to watch the charts and call in specialists for anything they needed done. It is true they have all these indicators, but they have to do more than just watch. A man has to know that if he sees one thing on a chart over here, he has to look at another chart to see how that fits in. He uses those charts to diagnose the situation. He acts like a doctor. The doctor doesn't only read your temperature and check your pulse. He uses those things to tell him what needs to be done. A man in operations needs experience to do that. The engineers can't do it for him.

The experience of the tri-isobutylene run (see Chapter 11) demonstrated the soundness of Lloyd's statement—even though at the time he failed to apply it to his problem. Somehow, when the crisis was upon him, he believed that the technical man (Dan Benton) could operate better than the workers. By having Benton supersede the operators, Lloyd upset the relations among the men and between men and management, and also failed to achieve his operating goals.

In college, the engineer is not taught how to operate fractionating column number 4 at the Hi-Test plant. He learns the basic principles of chemical engineering that will enable him to understand the fractionation process and perhaps to make basic improvements in the process. But somehow a complex piece of equipment never acts just exactly as theory dictates. The skillful operator, through long hours of experience on his job, learn things about it that no engineer with a much broader range of duties can ever possibly grasp. Even in much simpler jobs, we have found this to be the case. Therefore, the problem of efficiency as well as the problem of cooperation depends upon an effective combination of technical knowledge and worker-operating skills.

In such a situation, some workers will learn what adjustments to make without understanding why. There will be at least a few others, like Joe Sloan, who develop both the "feel" of the job and some of its scientific foundations. Even in the growing complexities of modern technical processes, these men seem qualified to move up into management. In fact, there are other companies in the same industry with the same processes which have not had a flat policy against selecting foremen out of the ranks. In one company, for example, while the management people are largely college trained, there has been a practice of teaming the college and noncollege man together out in the fields and plants. In one place, the superintendent will be a college graduate and his assistant a man up from the ranks; in another installation, it will be the other way around. In this way, the necessity for combining job knowledge with technical knowledge and with a variety of social experience has been recognized.

The college graduate in business management or other nonengineering subjects faces a similar problem, but one which is more difficult in some respects. He does not go in equipped with scientific and technical knowledge. He is chosen because he is thought to have "supervisory ability." According to this theory, if he has such ability, he will be able to pick up on the job the technical knowledge he needs. However, he runs into immediate worker resistance on this score.

One worker expressed his resentment in this way:

They put in men as foremen who don't know anything about the machines. The idea behind that is that knowledge about the work isn't necessary, that all the boss needs to know is how to supervise men. Supervise what? How can you supervise a man if you can't tell him what to do?

Another worker made this comment:

They'll send in a foreman that doesn't know a damn thing about the work. We'll show him a little about the work. Then he'll come around and give us orders. Maybe then he knows something, but he doesn't know all of it. He'll jump on you just to show his authority.

It is not easy to learn the job this way. A worker told us this story of worker resistance:

The other day we were having trouble, and finally we got the job to running right. The foreman came out and asked what we did. I told him, "Oh, just some minor changes." All we did was tighten up the screws, but if I'd told him that, the next time we had trouble, he'd come out and tell us to tighten up the screws.

And maybe the next time the trouble wouldn't be the same thing, but he'd be telling us to tighten up the screws and getting us all fouled up.

If we tell them anything, they'll be sure to be using it on us later. Either getting us fouled up doing the wrong things or trying out their God-damned experiments. The way to do is to keep things to ourselves for our own protection.

And so the workers do their best to keep the new foreman from learning the job. They answer questions either in a noncommittal manner, or else they simply feign ignorance.

We have seen foremen react to this situation in two ways. First, they may believe that the workers really do not know the answers to the questions. And yet it is clear that any man of average intelligence who has operated a machine for several years should know the answers. Therefore, it follows that the workers are stupid. This sentiment, of course, leads to a further deterioration of supervisor-worker relations.

Or the supervisor may recognize that workers know more than they are willing to tell. Then the problem becomes one of finding ways of forcing workers to divulge information. As one worker told us:

These guys think I'm supposed to teach them. That foreman said to me, "I want you to tell me what I want to know! If you won't tell me, I can make it tough for you!"

The worker who told this story spoke with intense bitterness. And all the other workers in the plant, of course, had heard the story and reacted against the foreman.

Clearly, these foremen are in an exceedingly difficult position. They lack the support of a technical background, and their training period does not provide them with anything beyond superficial knowledge of machines and processes. They are supposed to have "supervisory ability," and yet they have very inadequate knowledge of the activities they are expected to supervise. Perhaps they could pick it up in time, but they want to make a showing with management by carrying on the supervisory activity their role demands. Therefore, we often find them stepping in and giving orders based on very incomplete knowledge. This antagonizes workers and stimulates them to withhold their knowledge to make it as difficult as possible for the supervisor to learn his job.

And finally, workers do not believe that a college education creates "supervisory ability." They feel that the supervisory jobs rightfully belong to them, and they have no incentive to help the "outsider" make good as foreman.

Status symbols in the supervisory relationship

Status symbols play an important role in the supervisory relationship. The workers are quick to catch any attitude of social superiority on the part of foremen, and any such manifestations are hotly resented.

One worker said of a new foreman:

He wants us to call him *Mister* Thomas. Every time he walks past I feel like walking up to him and punching him in the jaw. One of these days I'm going to do it.

Another worker made this statement:

These bosses run around here acting as if they're better than we are. We had a foreman here that used to take a drink with some of the fellows after work. The superintendent told him that he shouldn't mix with us, that he was supposed to belong to a *different class*.

When workers describe a good foreman, they speak in these terms:

One thing about Jessup, he didn't go around in a suit and white collar. He changed his clothes, and five minutes after seven he was out on the floor with the men. . . .

He spent his time out on the floor, not in the office. He used to wear work clothes, and when anything went wrong, he wasn't afraid to step in and get dirty. . . .

I'll tell you why Taylor was a good foreman. He knew these machines, and when the boys got into trouble, he'd step right in and help them out of it. He'd lend a helping hand. I've seen him outside on a cold day, helping a couple of fellows push a truck.

These points raise some fundamental problems in supervision. The workers' comments run directly counter to well-entrenched theories held by some management people. According to these theories, the supervisor's job is to direct work activities; it is not his job to help operate the machines, except insofar as the help is offered in the form of instruction and advice. Furthermore, to maintain the respect and dignity due management, supervisors should emphasize the status distinctions setting them off from workers. Management thinking here follows the "familiarity breeds contempt" adage: If workers get to know foremen as people, they cannot give them the respect due management.

We find these theories to be unsound. We must question first the assumption that workers will respect superiors who emphasize status distinctions and who are careful not to meet them on an equal plane. All our evidence indicates that this is simply not true.

This does not mean that the foreman should participate on an intimate basis in the social activities of his workers. If he becomes too close to some men in his department, he will be suspected of playing favorites. The foreman must seek to avoid becoming closely identified with any worker clique. However, it is quite possible to establish good informal relations with workers without joining any faction.

It is well recognized by management that the foreman who can't keep his hands off the machines is not doing the supervisory job for which he was hired. The mistake is made when this sound observation is extended into a total prohibition of manual work on the part of the foreman. The foreman who lends a hand in emergencies and is not above helping out occasionally on an unpleasant job does not jeopardize his supervisory activity. On the contrary, he builds the cooperation which makes for effective supervision.

Workers recognize that the foreman's responsibilities do not allow him to be constantly at hand when they need help. They do not expect him to do the work of a worker, nor will they respect him for doing the work they feel they should be doing. The time and effort he spends in lending a hand may be very small, and yet it can serve to build the loyalties upon which effective organizations depend.

Furthermore, the foreman, in showing that he is not above getting his hands dirty, makes an important status point. He narrows the gap between himself and the workers and demonstrates in this way his regard for them and their jobs.

This does not mean that all status distinctions between workers and supervisors should be wiped out. In large organizations especially, gradations of status are important in organizing the relations of the members to each other. The clothes worn, the size, location, and furnishing of the work or office space, and many other points serve to place people in the structure. If men do not behave in accord with the status symbols attached to their positions, they are subjected to criticism from subordinates as well as superiors.

The question is not whether status distinctions should or should not exist. The foreman's desk, telephone, paper work, etc., all serve to set him apart from workers, even when he does not make a point of distinguishing himself in the clothes he wears on the job. The question is: Does the foreman accentuate or minimize these status distinctions?

There are two compelling reasons for minimizing such distinctions between foremen and workers. First, American workers like other Americans are brought up to believe that all men are created free and equal, that they are "just as good as anybody." Therefore, while they will accept status symbols that seem to be a natural part of the supervisory job, they deeply resent those which smack of social pretensions. They have no respect for the man who tries to set himself above them as if he belonged to an entirely different species.

Second, if status distinctions between any two adjoining levels of an organization are too large, effective communication between them breaks down. According to this view, the organization can function effectively with a very great spread in status symbols between worker and company president—providing the levels in between are separated step by step by far smaller graduations in status. If management insists that there shall be a sharp break in status between bottom supervision and the workers, then of course we have a social cleavage under which cooperation breaks down.

It is not easy to generalize upon the handling of status symbols. For example, we cannot make a flat rule as to the sort of clothes the foreman should wear, for clothes do not have an absolute meaning apart from the social context. They are symbols whose meaning will vary from organization to organization according to the social experience of the members. To adjust successfully to his job, the foreman must learn how people react to these status symbols and govern his own behavior accordingly.

Probably, an examination of his *functions* will serve as the best guide to his behavior on the job. He should get across the idea that he acts differently from the workers not because he belongs to a different social class, but because his job requires a different sort of activity. Since his functions call for the direction and organization of work, it is obvious that he cannot afford to spend large parts of his time at machine or work bench; on the other hand, it is perfectly reasonable for him to give the occasional help over rough spots which builds loyalty and adds to the effectiveness of his supervision. Other status questions can be answered by applying the same yardstick.

This is, of course, no automatic formula. There is always room for the exercise of judgment—as there is in most of the foreman's activities. Nevertheless, if the foreman follows this general approach, it will be possible for him to build up a close and effective working relationship with his men.

Status and positive exchange transactions

The presence or absence of positive exchange transactions between workers and foremen tends to influence worker perceptions of the status distance between these two social categories.

Ann Lindstrom and her fellow waitresses spoke favorably of earlier supervisors who "were always ready to do a favor for you." Of Ellen Geiger, who was not responsive in this way, they would say, "She is too high up for us." Jack Carter spoke warmly of the foreman who gave him the special attention that helped him to master a job on which he was failing. Joe Sloan and the men in the Hi-Test plant felt confident that they could get help from Tom Lloyd when they needed it. In the previous section, we have quoted two men who described a good foreman primarily in terms of his willingness to "step in and work" when something went wrong or to help "a couple of fellows push a truck." Implicit in all these worker comments about the good foreman was the notion that the foreman's official duties did not require him to be helpful to his subordinates: "He would *go out of his way* to do something for you."

In the chapter on "Transactions," we have distinguished between balanced and unbalanced positive exchange transactions. In the superior-subordinate relationship, the positive exchange transactions tend to be somewhat unbalanced, as the superior has more opportunities to help his subordinates than they have to reciprocate. By doing things for his subordinates, the superior can increase their responsiveness to his initiatives—providing he keeps the exchange on an implicit basis. That is, if he states that the men are obligated to do X for him because of all he has done for them, he destroys the *perceived* voluntary nature of the exchange, and reciprocity breaks down.

Even recognizing the unbalanced nature of the positive exchange transactions, our cases suggest that workers feel closer in status to a supervisor who will "do a favor for you" than to a supervisor who refuses to get involved in positive exchanges at all.

Communication, interaction, and the initiation of activities

Doing a favor is often (but not always) a response to a request by the favor receiver. Sometimes the giver acts on his own initiative: he steps in to help when he notes that his people are having difficulty with some aspect of their work. In other words, the supervisor is responding to a perceived need on the part of his subordinates.

The supervisor who responds to requests for help from his subordinates, or who volunteers help that is desired but not asked for, is described by subordinates as a person "you can talk to—he will listen to you." In terms of our schema, workers are describing a situation in which they feel free to initiate interaction with the supervisor (and in fact do so frequently), and one in which, on occasion, there are extended periods of interaction (discussions, conversations) between the worker and the supervisor.

This openness of communication between superiors and subordinates has powerful effects upon building favorable interpersonal sentiments. At the same time, we must reject the often expressed notion that "good human relations are just a matter of good communication." There are times when the worker just wants to get something off his chest, in which cases a sympathetic listener performs a useful role. But there are many cases in which the worker wants the foreman not only to listen to him but to do something about what he says: He wants to *initiate activity* for the foreman. The worker does not expect the foreman to act in response to every complaint or suggestion, but if the foreman never or hardly ever so responds to worker initiatives, then the worker loses interest in talking to that foreman, even for the purpose of simple self-expression.

The foreman's ability to take action on a worker complaint or suggestion depends not alone upon his personality and technical competence. It depends also upon how much freedom of action he has within the management hierarchy. Many foremen have lost the confidence of their workers because the actions the foremen themselves wanted to take were not within the powers delegated to them, and they were not able to persuade other members of management to act. The relations between the foreman and his subordinates must therefore be seen in the larger context of the organization structure.

The same point may be made regarding the minimizing or maximizing of the status differential between workers and the foreman. A foreman may be inclined to play down the status differentials that separate him from his men, but by so doing he can lose his chances for promotion, or even for holding his job, if higher management people feel that the effective foreman is one who accentuates status distinctions between himself and the workers.

Summary and conclusions

The points discussed in this chapter may be summarized in the following way.

1. We find few uniformities in the interactions and activities required as we compare the foreman's position in situations where there are marked differences in technology and work flow.
2. In general, foremen do not have the power of unilateral decision making that was more commonly observed among them half a century ago. Their power has been checked by the growth of unions and also by the growth of staff and control groups within management. The foreman now faces the major problem of integrating his interactions and activities with those of other management personnel.
3. The process of moving up from worker to foreman involves a difficult social adjustment. The worker who is well integrated into his work group finds it hard to initiate activities for this group which have not been customary with them. The man who has not been well integrated may find it easier to attempt such initiation but is likely to run into strong resistance.
4. As technology and applied science advance in industry, there is an increasing tendency for management to appoint college graduates even to first-line supervisory positions. These men are likely to face a serious problem of status cleavage in their relations with the workers. The conflict often arises around their failure to recognize the knowledge workers gain through experience.
5. Symbols tend to draw people together or to push them apart. In a society like ours, which tends to de-emphasize status symbols, worker responses to foremen are likely to be more readily obtained when symbolic status distinctions are minimized. However, this de-emphasis upon status distinctions cannot be carried out by the foremen alone. The inclination and ability of the foremen to de-emphasize distinctions may depend importantly upon behavior of higher management people.
6. The foreman or supervisor who is both liked and respected by his men is one who enters into positive exchange transactions with them.

7. Workers respond positively to a supervisor with whom they feel free to initiate interaction and for whom, from time to time, they are able to initiate activities.

References

Gardner, Burleigh B., and Whyte, W. F. *"The Man in the Middle: Position and Problems of the Foreman,"* *Applied Anthropology* (spec. iss.), Vol. 4 (Spring, 1945). Also available in the Bobbs-Merrill Reprint Series in the Social Sciences, No. 91. An early analysis of the foreman's role, based on research by the Committee On Human Relations in Industry at the University of Chicago.

Roethlisberger, Fritz J. "The Foreman: Master and Victim of Double Talk," *Harvard Business Review* (spring, 1945), pp. 283–98; in condensed form in Lawrence, Paul R. *et al.* (eds.). *Organizational Behavior and Administration*, rev. ed. Homewood, Ill.: Richard D. Irwin, Inc., and The Dorsey Press, 1965, pp. 434–38. A classic statement on the foreman's problems.

Walker, Charles R.; Guest, Robert, A.; and Turner, Arthur N. *The Foreman on the Assembly Line.* Cambridge, Mass.: Harvard University Press, 1956. A systematic study with quantified interaction measurements of foremen.

Discussion questions

1. You are called upon to advise an executive who is considering problems at the foreman level. He wants to know about the advisability and possibility of strengthening the foreman's position. What would you reply?

2. Select a supervisor under whom you have worked. Examine his relations with subordinates in IAS and transactional terms. To what extent does this case fit the discussion of the supervisory position in this chapter?

3. Interview another person about a supervisor under whom he has worked. Examine this case as in Question 2.

4. Reviewing Chapters 9 to 11, what similarities and differences do you find in the role of the supervisor in Chandler's Restaurant, the Benton blowing room, and the Hi-Test plant? What problems do you find posed by such a variety of work situations in attempting to generalize about the supervisor's role?

5. Read the "American Radiatronics Corporation" case in Paul R. Lawrence, John A. Seiler *et al.* (ed.), *Organizational Behavior and Administration* (rev. ed.: Homewood, Ill.: Richard D. Irwin, Inc. and The Dorsey Press, 1965), pp. 345–76. Give special attention to the role of Ralph Langley, general foreman, who was, in effect, immediate supervisor of the nuclear tube assembly room. Examine his relations with subordinates and others from an IAS and transactional point of view. How do you explain the changes in worker performance noted in the case?

13. Supervision, morale, and productivity

In the last chapter, we have examined the evolution of the role of the first-line supervisor and noted some of the major problems he faces. Our data have come largely from field interviewing of foremen and those who make up his interactional network. We shall now seek to determine what we can learn from survey research on the man-boss relationship.

Survey researchers have focused more attention on the man-boss relationship than on any other aspect of organizational behavior. Students of supervisory leadership have been concerned with two now classic questions: What is the impact of the supervisor's leadership style on productivity? What is the impact of his style of worker satisfactions? Out of these questions arises a third: What, if any, is the relationship between productivity and worker satisfaction?

Does virtue pay off?

Must virtue be its own reward? Or does virtue also pay off? These questions underlie much of the interest in studies of the relationship between productivity and worker satisfaction. Early investigators clearly hoped to find that a supervisory style in line with democratic values would not only produce more job satisfaction for subordinates but also higher productivity. In fact, some of the early studies did seem to support this point of view. The supervisor who seemed to be concerned about meeting the needs of employees (employee centered) appeared to make a better production record than the supervisor who just concentrated on getting the work out (production centered). The same general conclusion was reached when supervisory style was dichotomized between general and close supervision, the supervisor who frequently checked on performance and issued detailed orders being characterized as a close supervisor. The supervisor who provided more autonomy for his subordinates was rated a general supervisor.

This neat pattern failed to hold up in a series of subsequent studies. In a recent critical review of this literature, Robert Dubin[1] argues that no systematic relationships between worker productivity and worker satisfaction have been shown. In support of this judgment, Dubin quotes the following general conclusion from Robert L. Kahn,[2] one of the leading figures in survey research on organizational behavior:

None of the major indices of satisfaction (job, supervision, company, etc.) proved either to relate to productivity or to mediate significantly between productivity and such independent variables as role differentiation, delegation, or employee orientation.

Indices of worker satisfaction were developed by means of factor analysis, which showed four well-defined dimensions of satisfaction: satisfaction with supervision, with the job itself, with the company as a whole, and with the extrinsic rewards of money, mobility, etc. None of these indices was significantly related to productivity.

Why did the hoped for relationships disappear on further research? One problem seems to be that investigators have tended to lump all supervisory positions together. The difficulties of this procedure are well illustrated in the findings of an often quoted leadership study carried out at Ohio State University.[3] The Ohio State group was working under a somewhat different conceptual approach than that earlier followed by the Survey Research Center at the University of Michigan, with its categorization of employee-centered versus production centered supervisors. On the basis of factor analysis, the Ohio State group worked out two dimensions of supervisory behavior—*as perceived by subordinates*. These were "Consideration" and "Initiation Structure." The "Consideration" dimension seems to point to a concern for the welfare and interests of subordinates and is thus closely related to the employee centered orientation. "Initiation Structure" has to do with the giving of orders and information and generally specifying what the subordinate is to do and under what conditions he is to work. Initiation structure seems to be closely akin to production-centered supervision.

The results show that the more efficient foremen (as rated by their superiors) are inclined to show more initiation structure and less consideration than the less efficient foremen—the evaluations of initiation structure and consideration coming from the perceptions of subordinates. But when the investigators examine their findings in terms of types of jobs, a different and rather more interesting pattern emerges:[4]

[1] Robert Dubin, "Supervision and Productivity: Empirical Findings and Theoretical Considerations," in Robert Dubin, George C. Homans, Floyd Mann, and Delbert Miller, *Leadership and Productivity* (San Francisco: Chandler Publishing Co., 1965).

[2] Robert L. Kahn, "The Prediction of Productivity," *Journal of Social Issues*, Vol. 12 (1956), pp. 41–9.

[3] E. A. Fleischman, E. F. Harris, and R. D. Burtt, *Leadership and Supervision in Industry* (Columbus: Ohio State University Press, 1955).

[4] *Ibid.*, pp. 103–4.

Results indicate that there appears to be a difference between production and nonproduction departments in the requisite kinds of leadership. In the nonproduction departments, the foremen who are rated most proficient by their own supervisors apparently motivate their work groups to get the job done by creating a friendly atmosphere and by considerate behavior with a minimum of emphasis on work methods, standards, and structuring of activities. [In the case of production department foremen] considerate behavior is very good from the morale standpoint, but not so good for proficiency, as judged by the foreman's own boss.

Differences in supervisory jobs

While the investigators in this study present no behavioral observations that would help to explain the differing patterns shown by different types of jobs, one hypothetical comparison may help to explain the findings. Suppose we were to compare a foreman in charge of a machine repair crew with a foreman in charge of a mass production department. We are likely to find that a "good" maintenance foreman with the assignment described will behave quite differently from a "good" production foreman. When the maintenance foreman puts his men on a given machine repair job, we would not expect to find him pressing to get them to get to work immediately with the repair job. We may find him engaged for 15 minutes or even half an hour in apparently relaxed conversation with his men before any systematic work gets done. What is going on? The foreman recognizes that the making of a correct diagnosis is the most important element in efficiency in his type of work. He can expect that if he and his men first spend some time in working out a diagnosis to their problem, they will finish the job much sooner than would be the case if they went to work right away upon encountering the job.

The production foreman rarely encounters such a problem in diagnosis. The work of his subordinates is programmed for him and by him, and productivity depends to a much greater extent upon seeing to it that the planned operations are carried out in the planned sequences.

Dubin uses the contrast noted by the Ohio State group between production and nonproduction work to raise the question: Under what circumstances can we expect supervisory style to have a measurable effect upon productivity? Using the categorization of work situations by Joan Woodward, he argues that the supervisory style is likely to have little observable impact upon productivity in mass production or continuous process operations. In mass production situations, the work is highly programmed by technology, work flow, and engineering specifications. The foreman may indeed play an important role in keeping work activities coordinated, but the impact of technology, work flow, and engineering aspects of the jobs will be so large that the influence of the foreman will be quite elusive and almost beyond measurement. In the continuous process industry, workers do not physically produce the product, but rather monitor machines and equipment through which the chemical processes flow. When the process is going best, workers have the least work to perform. Furthermore, the chemical system is made up of highly interdependent parts so that the apparent performance of a work group under foreman B may be strongly influenced by the performance of the work group under foreman A.

Dubin argues that it is only in the cases of unit and small-batch production that supervisory style should make a measurable difference. Furthermore, he claims that where such differences have been shown, the technology has been either of the unit or small-batch type.

Another difficulty involved in many studies of the man-boss relationship is that they have involved examination of this vertical relationship entirely out of the context of other relationships that affect both foreman and worker. Charles Walker and his associates, in studies of the automotive assembly line, have found that those foremen who were more active in lateral relationships tended to be rated more effective by their subordinates.[5] Quentin Ponder,[6] in his study of "The Effective Manufacturing Foreman" comes to a similar conclusion. In distinguishing between effective and ineffective foremen (as rated by their superiors), he finds that there is no significant difference in the percentage of time spent with subordinates, the effective spending 19 percent while the ineffective spent 17 percent. On the other hand, there is a marked difference in time spent with staff and service people, the effective spending 32 percent of their time compared to 20 percent for the ineffective.

While we have no quantitative data, our studies in the restaurant industry support this same point. The dining room supervisors best liked and considered most effective by the waitresses were those who displayed skill in managing the customers, thereby relieving the pressures on the waitresses.

"General" versus "close" supervision

A further problem in this area of study has been that of conceptual clarification. What is meant by "general" or "close" supervision? We should recognize that in the questionnaire studies who is rated a close or a general supervisor depends entirely upon the perceptions of subordinates. Few students of the field have been concerned with checking subordinate's perceptions with observed behavior. A clue on the possible operationalizing of the close versus general supervision dimension is provided by the Ponder study of effective and ineffective foremen. While it was found that the two categories of foremen had almost no difference in the

[5] Charles R. Walker, Robert A. Guest, and Arthur N. Turner, *The Foreman on the Assembly Line* (Cambridge, Mass.: Harvard University Press, 1956).

[6] Quentin Ponder, "The Effective Manufacturing Foreman," *Proceedings of the Tenth Annual Meeting* (Madison: Industrial Relations Research Association, 1957).

amount of time spent with subordinates, there turned out to be a great difference in the frequencies of interaction. The effective foreman had fewer contacts, but spent more time within each contact. Apparently, the effective foreman engaged in discussion with subordinates about the nature of the work assignment and covered the topic in such a way that the worker was able to proceed for extended periods of time without intervention of the foreman. The ineffective foremen used their interactions to check what had been done and to issue instructions for a short time span of activity. This interactional difference in supervisory styles suggests the possibility of operationalizing general and close supervision. Until we have such behavioral observations to relate to subordinate perceptions and attitudes, we will be on weak ground in attempting to describe the effects of a particular supervisory style.

Forgetting for a moment the conceptual problem, does research show that general supervision works better? The evidence suggests that—in our culture—the general supervisor tends to be rated higher by subordinates than the close supervisor. (Whether this holds true in other cultures is a question we will address in the final section of this book.) We have already noted that general supervision shows no consistent pattern of relations with productivity. In order to establish relations here, apparently we must examine situational variables. Sayles and Strauss generalize in this way:[7]

> It would seem that general supervision works best (1) where the work provides intrinsic job satisfaction; (2) where the work group accepts management's objectives; (3) where worker and union-management relations are reasonably harmonious; (4) where consistency and coordination are relatively unimportant; (5) where technology permits individual discretion; (6) where subordinates desire responsibility; (7) in the long run rather than in the short run; and (8) where the pattern of supervision is consistent throughout the organization.

In effect, Sayles and Strauss are telling us that no direct correlation between general-close supervision and productivity is to be expected but that relationships are indeed to be found if we think in terms of moderating variables. That is, in situation A, general supervision yields higher productivity, whereas in situation B, general supervision yields no higher productivity or perhaps even lower productivity. Our problem then becomes one of determining the salient features that characterize situation A and distinguish it from situation B.

The programming of behavior

Much of the work on the man-boss relationship seems to be based upon the assumption that the foreman is the most important person affecting

[7] Leonard Sayles and George Strauss, *Human Behavior in Organizations* (Englewood Cliffs, N.J.: Prentice-Hall, 1966) p. 175.

the worker's job situation. We are now coming to recognize that in many situations the foreman may turn out to be a relatively insignificant figure, whose behavior is largely controlled by policies and pressures coming down upon him from above and from staff specialists. This conclusion has led a number of investigators to advocate a broader approach to supervision. Here we may distinguish between two types of approach, one which emphasizes delegation of authority and responsibility and the other which emphasizes participative processes. Let us look first at delegation, which may be considered another term for general supervision.

In a complex organization, we cannot expect that activities will be coordinated if each individual is free to make his own individual decisions on what is to be done. To a greater or lesser extent (depending upon the technology and nature of the work), work activities and interactions need to be programmed. How is management to assure that workers and lower level supervisors will behave as management intends? One method is simply that of telling people what to do. To read some of the literature, one would get the impression that this is the only way in which behavior is controlled. In fact, it is only one among a number of possibilities. Furthermore, if the organization relies entirely or predominantly upon the giving of instructions and orders for the channeling of work activities, one result is bound to be a growth of negative sentiments of workers toward their superiors and toward the company. This heavy predominance of initiation of interactions and activity from above tends to produce such negative reactions. George Strauss argues that if work behavior is channeled in other ways, subordinates generally find this more acceptable than the direct human subordination that is found in situations where the supervisor intervenes with a high frequency to direct activities. Strauss identifies not one but five means of programming work activity.[8]

1. *Giving of orders and instructions.* We list this without further discussion simply so as not to overlook the obvious.

2. *Establishment of rules* (standard operating procedures). They may be in written form or unwritten, providing their application is understood. They may be imposed unilaterally, agreed upon after consultation, or bargained between two parties. We need to distinguish between the way rules are arrived at and the functions they perform in the programming of behavior. If the subordinate has a set of rules to guide him, he can proceed with less personal direction from the superior than would otherwise be necessary. (Ways of arriving at rules will be discussed later in this chapter and elsewhere.)

3. *Setting of goals.* Here management hopes to establish the objectives toward which subordinates are to work, and management assumes that if objectives are specified and accepted by subordinates, they can then be left free to move toward those objectives in the most effective means that

[8] George Strauss, "Some Notes on Power Equalization," in Harold J. Leavitt (ed.), *The Social Science of Organizations* (Englewood Cliffs, N.J.: Prentice-Hall, 1963), pp. 71–5.

they themselves can devise. Rules specify the *means* that are to be applied in work activity, whereas goals specify the *ends* of the activities. The assumption here is that, where subordinates are committed to goals satisfactory to management, management does not need to concern itself in detail about the means used to reach these goals. This approach underlies the philosophy of "management by results"—a man is not to be judged by the means he uses but rather by the ends he achieves. At the worker level, we see this most clearly in the case of incentive rates. With all the qualifications discussed earlier, we can assume that in an incentive-rate situation workers have the objective of making money, and that therefore the foreman will not need to supervise his men so closely as would be the case in a nonincentive situation. In fact, we have the impression (unsupported by quantitative data) that in incentive-rate situations foremen initiate interaction with workers less frequently than in work situations of comparable technology and without incentives. In an incentive situation, the foreman is less likely to worry that when he is not present his workers may be "goofing off."

4. *Indoctrination.* Here also we are dealing with goals, but in a rather different sense. In number three, we refer to objectives specified by management toward which the activities of subordinates are directed. As long as organizational members orient their activities toward these objectives, management may not be concerned with level of commitment (or the intensity of sentiments) of subordinate attachments to the objectives. In the case of indoctrination, we are dealing with the *internalization* of organizational goals and standards of behavior. Through experience and often through an educational process, members come to accept the goals and the standards of behavior advocated by the organizational leaders as if they were part of the individual's personal value system. Nor is the commitment to a specific and limited objective. The individual assumes a diffuse commitment to objectives and standards of behavior. We see indoctrination most clearly in institutions such as the church and the military where a large part of the training is aimed as much toward getting a commitment to the organization's goals as it is toward providing mastery of the technical aspects of work activities. The internalization of goals and standards of behavior also occurs in the social process whereby the student becomes a professional—doctor, lawyer, scientist, etc. However, here the educational process leads toward a commitment to the norms of the profession, and those norms are not necessarily entirely compatible with those of a particular work organization. In fact, we often find cases of role conflict, in which the goals and standards of behavior that have become internalized by the individual as a professional do not lead him toward the goals that are being promoted by management.

5. *Technology and work flow.* As we have noted in earlier chapters, technology and work flow tend to channel human activities and interactions. This is not only the case with the highly mechanical programming

involved in the automotive assembly line. The impact of technology and work flow is equally apparent in service industries such as department stores and restaurants. Here it is not necessary for the supervisor to indicate when a sales girl or waitress should initiate interaction with a customer. The arrival of the customer at a certain time and place is enough to propel the worker into the appropriate activity.

If we consider that there are at least five major ways of programming human work activities, we can recognize the fallacies of dealing in a concept such as delegation solely in terms of the immediate interpersonal relationship. We can make sense out of "delegation" only if the immediate interpersonal component is examined in the context of the other means of channeling activities.

Participation management

The early work on supervisory styles indicated that the influence the individual foreman could exercise on his subordinates depended very much upon the behavior of higher management people toward the foreman. If the foreman who desired to supervise in a "democratic" manner found himself operating under higher management that directed activities in an "autocratic" manner, then the foreman would either have to conform to the style of supervision imposed upon him from above or else abandon his supervisory position. This conclusion emphasized the limitations of looking at styles of supervision simply from the standpoint of the foreman-worker relationship. Proponents of this new approach argued that management needed to take the whole system into account and to build a participative approach at each level of the organization.

But what does participation management mean? Here we face an extraordinary situation: this approach to management development has become the most popular among management educational programs in spite of the fact that its proponents have been exceedingly vague regarding the components of participation. Or perhaps the very vagueness of the ideas accounts for part of the attractiveness of the approach, since "participation" seems to be so much a part of the democratic philosophy in which we all believe.

Let us cite as an example one of the well-known studies in the field: *Changing the Structure and the Functioning of an Organization: Report of a Field Experiment,* by Stanley Seashore and David Bowers.[9] Here the experimental intervention was designed to promote more participatory management in the following respects. The cohesiveness of work groups was to be increased, and supervisors were to work more with and through these groups. Supervisors were to evidence more "supportive behavior."

[9] Stanley Seashore and David Bowers, *Changing the Structure and the Functioning of an Organization: Report of a Field Experiment* (Ann Arbor, Mich.: Survey Research Center, 1963).

They were to consult more with their subordinates and involve them more in decision-making. Note that these specifications contain a variety of elements. The cohesiveness of the work group was expected to be a resultant of the intervention, but it was not specified how managers were to behave to achieve this result. The consultation aspect gives some picture of anticipated behavior, but just what it means for supervisors to emit "supportive behavior" is not specified.

The conceptual and methodological problems of the participation approach are clearly illustrated in the following passages from the field notes of the Survey Research Center's "agent," who was both observer and change agent in the case. He wrote the following report after a conversation with the manufacturing manager of the plant:[10]

. . . Mr. Jones has undertaken an application of participation management which is of rather awesome proportions.

Mr. Jones is forming project teams to handle some of the large orders. Each team includes the men actually running the machines for each of the operations involved, and the team, as a unit, follows their particular order or project through the manufacturing process. These teams cut across the jurisdiction of the several group leaders, foremen, and area supervisors, and are supposed to work with these men as they need to. . . . Mr. Jones explicitly associates this change with our research project. . . . It is certainly a large-scale, visible, and vulnerable application of the ideas we have been trying to introduce, and a failure would be very hard on Mr. Jones and on the plant. . . . Mr. Jones has conceived and activated this effort entirely on his own.

While the description of the Jones plan is too fragmentary to give us any detailed knowledge of the changes in human relations it involves, it is clear that the plan encompassed a reorganization of interactions and activities along the horizontal dimension—following the flow of work. This is a dimension entirely left out of the specifications for participation management provided us by the authors.

The Jones intervention can only be included under "participation management" if we give participation credit for every type of management action that does not involve the autocratic exercise of authority. If we broaden the term to include so many meanings, then it has come to be really meaningless.

More recent work has indeed provided a clearer focus on the behavioral meaning of "participation management." Probably the most important case study yet made with that approach is *Management by Participation*,[11] which describes and analyzes the attempt of the Harwood Manufacturing Company, aided by researchers and consultants, to extend its own style of management to a newly acquired subsidiary. Harwood and

---

[10] *Ibid.*, p. 40.

[11] Alfred J. Marrow, David G. Bowers, and Stanley Seashore, *Management by Participation* (New York: Harper & Row, 1967).

its president, Alfred J. Marrow, are well known to behavioral scientists for the company's imaginative action-research projects on participative leadership styles.[12] Previous projects had involved small-scale studies of work groups and departments, The subject of this book is an exceedingly ambitious case of planned change presented by researchers, consultants, and the key executives who took part in the program. The case involved not only "sensitivity training," which is often associated with the participation management approach, but also such other management interventions as changes in work systems, job design, piece rates, and standards. Technical training was also provided for workers and managers.

The study presents an interesting account of the introduction of the various changes and some convincing measures of the impact of the program. The total effect seems to us both impressive and frustrating. It is impressive in its documentation of the wide variety of change efforts, but this also is a source of frustration. We start reading with the hope that here at last we are going to discover what participation management really is, but the interventions that could be called specifically participative are so interwoven with the application of standard management and technical techniques that we must abandon hope of determining to what extent the results achieved can be attributed to participative techniques.

This is not to criticize the designers of the action-research program. They quite properly concluded that the problems they faced required the application of a wide variety of interventions. Their experience indicates the complexity of our problems in organization theory. We cannot get very far if we remain at the level of trying to correlate supervisory styles with certain other variables. As we expand our focus to put the man-boss relationship in the broader context of the total organization, we find, as did the Harwood action-research team, that we must consider not simply the larger network of human relations but also the technology, the work flow, piece rates and other aspects beyond interpersonal relations. In effect, we are faced with the problem of developing effective ways of analyzing the socio-technical system.

That is the main task undertaken in this book. In later chapters, we will consider other aspects of this socio-technical system. In the final part of this book, we will then pull our thoughts together to answer the question: What have we learned so far?

Conceptual clarification

Can we clean up our conceptions of delegation and participation so as to make them more useful concepts? George Strauss has suggested a framework which may be helpful. He focuses his attention on decision-

---

[12] Lester Coch and John R. P. French, Jr., "Overcoming Resistance to Change," *Human Relations*, Vol. 1, no. 4 (1948), pp. 512–32.

making and looks simultaneously at who makes the decision and whether the decision grows out of a pair or group situation (set event). This gives him the following framework:[13]

Decision Made by	Decision Involving	
	An Individual	A Group
1. Superior	1A. Individual direction	1B. Group direction
2. Joint decision	2A. Consultation	2B. Group meetings
3. Subordinates	3A. Delegation	3B. Group decision making

We see here the essential structural difference between pair and set events. Delegation necessarily involves a pair relationship—though no interpersonal event may take place at the time the subordinate makes the decision, if his superior earlier "delegated" to him the right to make the decision. While we sometimes think of a superior consulting a group, it will probably clarify our thinking to reserve consultation for a pair event and follow Strauss in using term "group meetings" for the consultative process in set events.

In the Strauss formulation, what takes place when the superior or the subordinate make the decisions, whether in pair or set events, is reasonably clear. In situations where decisions are made "jointly," we may need to recognize further distinctions. At least, supervisors and executives argue that there is a distinction between situations where the decision evolves out of a discussion between superior and subordinate(s) and situations where the superior enters into such a discussion, but reserves the right to make the final decision himself. It remains to be seen whether this distinction will hold up in field observation. If the superior consistently makes his own decision, regardless of what subordinates have said, then we might expect subordinates to deny that they had been involved in either consultation or group meetings. Perhaps only if the superior responds to some extent to initiatives from subordinates can consultation and group meetings persist as a management pattern.

We might also make distinctions of scope in the subject matter of decision making. In the case where superior involves subordinates in decisionmaking, do they participate in decisions regarding the objectives of his department or organization, or only in decisions regarding the means whereby those objectives shall be reached? If involvement is limited to discussion of means, with the objectives being either assumed or predetermined by the superior, will the effects be the same as in the case where both objectives and means are open to subordinate influence?

---

[13] Strauss, *op. cit.*, p. 58.

Conclusions

Early writers in the field pursued the hope of finding simple relationships between two variables: supervisory style and productivity. Early studies suggested that these planners had nearly reached their goal. Looking back now, we can see that this early progress was an illusion.

The two-variable approach proved to be such an oversimplification as to make scientific progress impossible. The approach took no account of differences in technology and in the nature of work. It concentrated entirely on vertical relationships and neglected to consider the horizontal dimension, whose importance is ever more clearly demonstrated with new research findings. The approach also suffered from conceptual vagueness and confusion. While the writers talked about the behavior of supervisors, actually their data were not based upon observations of behavior, but rather upon perceptions of that behavior by subordinates. Finally, we have come to recognize that it is hopeless to try to draw firm conclusions through studying the man-boss relationship in a vacuum. We are looking at only two points in a social system of mutually dependent relationships.

Much of what has been said in this chapter must appear to readers as destructive in nature. Nevertheless, progress depends upon recognizing the sources of past errors and attempting to build a new conceptual framework and new research approaches that will not be subject to the weaknesses of past research.

This rebuilding process is now well under way. Despite the oversimplifications involved in so many earlier studies, the weight of evidence does seem to support a positive correlation between *general* (as opposed to *close*) supervision and favorable sentiments of workers toward their supervisor. While the presumed global relationship between general supervision and productivity has not withstood further examination, Dubin's hypothesis that the relationship holds under conditions of unit or small-batch production seems worth further testing. Here again we find a case where the presumed relationship holds only under certain conditions—and we find that the technology and work flow indicate some of the most important conditions to be specified before supervisory style—productivity relationships can be predicted. Through this analytical pathway, we have linked research on the man-boss relationship with the studies by Woodward and others on technology and formal organization structure.

We have also used this chapter to attempt some of the clarification of concepts that is essential to any scientific advance in this sector of our field.

References

Dubin, Robert; Homans, George C.; Mann, Floyd; and Miller, Delbert. *Leadership and Productivity*. San Francisco: Chandler Publishing Co., 1965. A very useful examination and critique of the literature on these issues.

Fleishmann, E. A.; Harris, E. F.; and Burtt, R. D. *Leadership and Supervision in Industry.* Columbus: Ohio State University Press, 1955. Representative of the best work of the Ohio State University research program.

Marrow, Alfred J.; Bowers, David G.; and Seashore, Stanley. *Management by Participation.* New York: Harper and Row, 1967. The best account of a comprehensive effort to introduce a participative approach at all levels of an organization.

Strauss, George. "Some Notes on Power Equalization," in Leavitt, Harold J. (ed.) *The Social Science of Organizations.* Englewood Cliffs, N.J.: Prentice-Hall, 1963. A very useful critique of the participation management literature.

Discussion questions

1. Assume that Dubin's hypothesis is correct: that, under conditions of unit or small-batch production, positive correlations are to be found between general supervision and productivity, general supervision and worker satisfaction, and worker satisfaction and productivity—but not under conditions of mass production or process production. Why should the relationships hold in one context but not in others?

2. Interview a person regarding the leadership style of a first-line supervisor under whom he has worked. Report his description of this supervisory style. Would you characterize the style described as close or general supervision? Participative or authoritarian supervision? What problems do you encounter in seeking to make those judgments?

3. Interview two men with management experience. Ask each of them to tell you what he means by participative management. To what extent do you get clear and similar statements from both men? If you find discrepancies, how do you account for them?

14. The supervisor in the social system

In the last chapter, we have concentrated primarily upon the deficiencies of past research upon supervisory leadership styles. Eventually, the reader should get tired of hearing about what was done wrong and ask the author the difficult question: How would you do it better?

This chapter undertakes some answers to that question. To make those answers as concrete as possible, we will present them through a description and analysis of the case of Tom Walker, foreman of the barrel department in a steel fabricating plant.

Let us begin with a word of caution. I cannot present the reader with all of the data he should expect to gather if he himself were making a field study of such a case. The case came to my attention after I had finished the *Pattern for Industrial Peace* study of union-management relations in this plant and was simply making a brief visit to the plant to pull together some loose ends of the union-management study. My curiosity was piqued by what I had heard had happened in the barrel department, and this led me to spend part of a day on Walker's problems. Still, the foreman was then peripheral to my research interests, and I did not have the wit to see that the case warranted a good deal more attention than I gave it. I must acknowledge certain gaps in the data. These would be serious for a research report. However, my purpose is not to prove the correctness of my conclusions; it is to use the case to indicate the types of data needed and the ways in which the data are analyzed.

From success to failure

In the years 1947–48, Walker's department set production record after production record. In 1945 he had taken over a department that lagged far behind the same departments in the corporation's two other fabricating plants, and by 1948, Walker's department had the best cost and production record of the three. His relations with workers and with the union were also excellent. Even in a period of intense union-management conflict that lasted into 1947, Walker had been considered a relatively good foreman by union officers. The years 1947–48 marked a sudden change to cooperative relations throughout the plant. No one credits Walker with having played a major role in bringing about the plantwide change, but higher management acknowledges that he did an especially good job in building cooperative relations in his own department. The 1937 strike that led to the organization of the union began in the barrel department, and ever since that time the barrel department has seemed to be the bellwether in union-management relations. If the union-management problems of the barrel department had not been solved, the overall cooperative relations could not have been established. All in all, Walker looked like an important man and a highly successful man in 1948.

By the spring of 1950, productivity was down and costs were up in the barrel department. There was growing friction among the workers, between the workers and the foreman, and between Walker and other members of management. The union officers turned against Walker. Finally, management transferred him to a less important department. He took a substantial cut in pay and found himself supervising 15 men instead of 70 or more.

Before we analyze this case, we must first set the stage with a description of technology and work flow and of the formal organization structure.

Technology and work flow

There were three production lines in the barrel department: the main line, the aux (auxiliary) line, and the side line. On most days both main and aux lines operated. The side line was used just for special jobs that come up less frequently.

The main and aux lines were similar and the following description holds for both of them.

These were called assembly lines because the barrel shells moved from work station to work station as the successive operations were performed. However, they differed from automotive assembly lines in that the operator himself had direct control over the speed of production. The job could be performed at different speeds at different points on the line, so that barrel shells might pile up waiting at one point and be clear at other points. Men worked in pairs on either side of the line at most points.

The line began where men known as rollers took sheets of steel and put them on a machine that shaped them in circular form. The shells then rolled to the welders who welded the two sides together. Then the testers checked the welding for leaks. Next came the beader men, who put the shells on a machine that put the beads (protruding ribs) into them. The shells then rolled into a spray booth, where their insides were sprayed with paint or lacquer. The double-seamer operators attached both ends of the barrel. The barrel might then go on to another spray booth where an outside coat of paint or lacquer would be applied. Some orders called for a baked enamel finish, and the barrels were carried through bake ovens on conveyors for that purpose. Conveyors carried the completed barrels directly into the shipping department. There were numerous variations of this procedure, depending upon the specifications of the order, but those were the basic steps.

Vertical and nonvertical relations

The foreman of the barrel department had an assistant working with him. The foreman reported to an assistant production supervisor and a production supervisor. There were two additional levels of line authority: the vice president in charge of production, and the president of the subsidiary.

The foreman received his orders as to what sort and number of barrels were to be produced from the production control department. These orders covered a period up to two weeks, within which time he could make adjustments in his own schedule. On the basis of these orders, he requisitioned the sheets of steel he would need from the steel storage department and the number and types of covers for barrels from the punch press department. At the other end of the line, he notified the foreman of the shipping department as to the number and types of barrels to be produced, and the destination of the orders.

Foreman Walker also dealt with the accounting, maintenance, and inspection departments. The accounting people handled timekeeping and rate-setting for the barrel department. While no new rates were set in the 1948–50 period, the timekeeping job was a daily function. One maintenance man was regularly assigned to the barrel department, but much maintenance work required the assignment of extra men. The inspector carried out the customary job of enforcing quality standards.

Since the plant was unionized, Walker also dealt with the steward and other union officers.

1947–48: The pattern of success

Tom Walker had arrived at his foremanship position in 1945 after spending a number of years working up from worker to group leader. A white man in a department which by this time was more than half Negro, Walker had never had any problems in intergroup relations and in fact he got along very well with Ed Hodges, a Negro, who was union president (1940–48) and who, like Walker, had spent all his working time at the plant in the barrel department.

In his *interactions*, in this period, Walker appears to have had more frequent contact with workers than with any other category of plant personnel. He spent much of his time around the production lines and enjoyed an easy informal relationship with his men, with initiations of interactions going in both directions.

Walker had infrequent contacts with production control people because until well into 1948 the plant was operating in a seller's market for steel barrels. This meant that production was limited to long runs on a small number of types of barrels. Walker had little problem in adjusting his own plans to the simple schedules passed down to him by production control, and there was no need for extended contacts with production control.

For maintenance, Walker had a maintenance man assigned permanently to his department and under his orders. He only had to call on the maintenance foreman for problems beyond the capacity of a single repair man. When machines operate for long runs with infrequent adjustments, they tend to break down much less often than under short runs and frequent adjustment conditions. Thus, until well into 1948, Walker seldom had occasion to call on the maintenance foreman.

In the flow of work, Walker had to initiate interaction (and activities) for fellow foremen in steel storage, punch press, and shipping. Under conditions of long runs on a small number of types of barrels, these contacts, too, were infrequent. If he was running a certain type of barrel for a whole week, Walker needed only to make a single order for steel sheets and for covers (with daily requirements specified in each case). Similarly, he needed to provide the shipping foreman only with the number of barrels to be shipped to one or two buyers.

There was a timekeeper who was responsible for keeping records on hours worked in this and several other departments. In the time now under discussion, Walker nearly always worked with a stable crew, so that the timekeeping task was routine and provided no particular cause for interaction between foreman and timekeeper. Walker always had a quality inspector in his department, but in the 1947–48 period, there was little interaction between foreman and inspector. In a seller's market, the plant was shipping out all barrels that were not obviously defective. The defects spotted by the inspector, therefore, were likely to be so obvious as to give no cause for controversy between inspector and foreman.

Tom Walker interacted frequently with Production Supervisor Short, two levels above him. Interaction was initiated freely in both directions. On Walker's interactions with the assistant production supervisor and with Walker's own assistant foreman, we unfortunately have only fragmentary data.

To assess *activities*, let us first look at the content of the foremen's job. Here again our data are inadequate, but at least we can make a distinction among three aspects of the job: paper work, technical, and interpersonal. On the record-keeping and planning aspects of his job, which revolved around the paper work, Walker was known by superiors as well as by subordinates to be rather inefficient, and he made no secret of his distaste for this sort of work. On the other hand, this deficiency was no great handicap in the period under discussion, for long production runs and a stable work crew required a minimum amount of paper work. On the technical side, Walker had a knowledge of the machines which was entirely adequate for this period.

Let us examine the interpersonal relations in terms of the initiation of activities. He was responsive to criticisms and suggestions from subordinates, and they, too, were inclined to "put out" for Walker. Union President Hodges came to him first on worker problems in the department, and Walker went to Hodges first when he had problems with workers. Each man was able to initiate activity changes for the other. With Al Short, there was similar reciprocity. Furthermore, Walker had found that when he got in disputes with other members of management and took them to Short, the production supervisor generally ruled in Walker's favor.

The area of interpersonal difficulty in this period was that between Walker and other foremen and members of plant staff. There was one-sided initiation of activity by Walker to certain other members of management. While this was distinctly unrewarding to the others, it got Walker what he wanted. The others learned that they had to contend with sanctions from Short if the problems of the barrel department did not receive the attention demanded by Walker.

The activities carried on by Walker in this period added up to success, both in terms of productivity and in terms of worker-management relations.

For *sentiments* and *symbols,* let us look first at the job itself. While Walker freely acknowledged that he did not enjoy paper work, he had to spend little time on it. He did enjoy his technical and interpersonal activities, and he enjoyed the reputation for success that he had attained with higher management, as well as with his own workers.

Walker had favorable sentiments toward his workers. He was inclined to describe them as "a good bunch of fellows." The workers generally reciprocated these favorable sentiments. They considered Walker a very good foreman, although they were not blind to certain faults. They knew that Walker was sloppy in his paper work and sometimes mixed up his assignments in such a way that workers themselves had to provide him with the correct information. They thought he was inclined to be somewhat excitable and given to frequent use of profanity. At this time, the profanity was rarely resented. Workers seemed to look upon Walker as a rather colorful character and would explain, "That's just the way Tom is."

Walker and Union President Hodges liked and trusted each other. Walker had come to consider the union president as almost a partner in the running of the barrel department.

With Production Supervisor Short, Walker had a lot in common: they both loved barrels. Before coming to this plant to his production supervisor's job, Short had been foreman of a barrel department in another plant of the corporation. Short continued to think of the barrel department as the heart of the plant, and he was always inclined to look out first for the interests of the barrel department.

With other foremen and staff people, we find a reciprocal pattern of negative sentiments. Walker did not like them and they did not like him. When I attended a monthly meeting of the Foreman's Club in the plant in 1948, I noticed that in the social period before and after the formal program, Walker spent nearly all of the time by himself. Clearly, he was no part of any informal group in management.

This period produced several symbols that were important in representing the success of Tom Walker. As his barrel department approached and then passed the performance of other barrel departments in the corporation, there were increasingly frequent occasions of recognition of new production records. Management kept a record of the top production for an eight-hour day on each type of barrel made within the corporation. Every time Walker's department hit a new record on any type of barrel, he got a telegram from the plant manager to post on the bulletin board. The plant manager also had a plaque made and hung in the department, with the record number produced for the type, the date, and the names of all the men working on the crew at the time.

In addition to this higher management recognition, Al Short personally rewarded the barrel department foreman and assistant foreman with bottles of whiskey and bought cigarettes and cokes for all of the men in the crew. When new records were made—as they were—in other departments, the other foremen got the higher management telegram and the plaque, but they got no tangible recognition from Al Short. This differential treatment served to symbolize the superior position enjoyed by the barrel department and Tom Walker.

The victories Walker won in arguments with other foremen and staff members also came to be symbolic of his important position in the plant.

In *transactional* terms, Tom Walker was engaged in positive exchanges and joint payoffs with the workers. He was responsive to requests for assistance from his men, and he depended upon them to tell him when his instructions were incomplete or erroneous, thus saving him from some costly mistakes. Walker and the workers shared the recognition on the production records.

With Union President Ed Hodges, Walker engaged in positive exchange, trading, and joint payoff transactions. Each man relied upon the other to help him out, and this at times became explicit as they worked out the terms of an informal agreement together. The two men shared the credit both for the change from union-management conflict to cooperation and for the spectacular increases in production.

With Production Supervisor Al Short, Walker found himself in a positive exchange and joint payoff situation. He could always count on

Short's support, and the men shared credit for the barrel department improvements.

With other members of lower management, Walker was in a mutual-minus situation. However, in transactional terms, the relationships were not balanced. Walker could impose his minus on others, and his firm alliance with Short prevented the others from getting back at him openly.

What changed?

When I have asked students to guess what changes might have accounted for the downfall of Tom Walker, the first thought to come to mind is some sort of technological change. This is a reasonable guess, for technological changes often do give rise to disturbances such as we are describing. But the guess misses its mark in this case, for no significant changes in the machines took place between 1948 and 1950. On the other hand, there were important changes that affected the way these machines operated and produced.

During the year of 1948, the seller's market came to an end, and the plant found itself in a buyer's market. In the seller's market, having more potential orders than could be filled, management was able to concentrate its production on a limited number of models and turned down orders that presented any unusual production problems. Now salesmen were urged to go out and sell more aggressively, which meant also that they were encouraged to be more accommodating to customers and accept orders for smaller lots and wider varieties than they had booked before.

There also occurred in 1948 two personnel changes of major significance to Walker. Al Short left the company, to be succeeded by Jess Wiley, who had been in charge of production in one of the company's smaller plants. Union President Ed Hodges left to become international representative. The steward in the barrel department, Lou Halsey, remained in that position, but in the past the union president had in effect represented the barrel department. Walker thus had to work out a relationship with a new person on the union side.

1949–50: The pattern of failure

In *interaction* terms, these changes meant greatly increased interaction and also increased initiation of interaction from Walker to the feeder departments and to shipping, since the new production mix involved a wider variety of orders. As the much more frequent changeovers of machines led to increased incidence of breakdowns, Walker found himself calling on the maintenance foreman much more frequently. Since there had been no introduction of new machines throughout this period, somewhat more frequent breakdowns could have been expected even under the former production conditions.

The production changes brought about increased initiation to Walker on the part of the inspector and the timekeeper. As management felt called upon to raise quality standards, the inspector suddenly became a much more important figure than he had previously been. In effect, he was intervening much more frequently to inform Walker regarding quality failures—and in many cases these represented conditions that Walker had "got by with" in the seller's market.

The changes also increased the involvement of the timekeeper in the barrel department, since the new production situation required much more shifting about of workers from line to line and in and out of the department.

With Wiley, the new man in the position of general production supervisor, Walker felt less free to initiate interactions than he had with Short, and he found Wiley initiating more frequently to him. Walker reported spending more time with Steward Halsey than he had with Union President Ed Hodges, but it is unclear what the distribution of initiation of interactions was.

There was a major shift in the composition and stability of the work force. For many months, Walker had been running with a regular complement of 58 men. With more complex models now in production, the regular number increased to 71, and approximately twice a week 10 to 12 additional men were brought in from other departments. Walker thus found himself interacting with more men and with some men with whom he had no previously established relationship. Reports indicate that Walker also increased his initiations to workers and that they reduced theirs to him.

In *activities*, we note a great increase in the complexity of the foreman's job. The shorter runs and the greatly increased variety of models produced all added up to more paper work and increased importance of planning. Walker's average production declined. He no longer found it possible to make any production records.

Walker felt that Wiley, the new general production supervisor, exercised more control over him than had Short. Walker had been free to answer union grievances according to his own judgment and was required to consult his superiors only when in doubt. Higher management felt that this practice allowed some departments to get "out of line" with others. All the foremen were thereupon required to check the answer to each grievance with the general production supervisor, Wiley, even though the foreman might be certain he knew the right answer. While this change affected all the foremen, it probably had a greater impact upon Walker than others since in the past Walker had been more inclined than others to work out union-management problems on the spot.

Walker stopped appealing for help to Wiley, for he found that the general production supervisor was not inclined to serve as arbitrator in intramanagement disputes and, when forced to do so, was likely to rule against Walker. Wiley reported that as soon as he had learned his way around the plant, he discovered that Walker was involved in serious friction with inspectors and time keepers, and with the foremen of the machine shop, punch press, steel storage and shipping departments. Wiley reported that he handled such arguments in this way: he would rebuke the two parties for getting excited over the issue and tell them they were being childish. He would then advise them to settle such problems among themselves.

Wiley gave this illustration. He found Walker engaged in a furious argument with the timekeeper—over six cents. Wiley listened to the stories of the two men and decided in favor of the timekeeper. Walker then protested that he could not make any record for himself when his boss acted that way. Wiley countered by saying that six cents did not mean anything; Walker should be thinking of more important matters.

Other people in management were no longer as responsive as before. Walker would demand action and the recipient of the demand, now that he was under no pressure from the superior to take care of the barrel department first, would make sure that he responded to Walker only after he had taken care of other people.

The new period brought important activity changes to the workers, and these were not limited to those arising directly out of the new production mix. Either just before or just after Ed Hodges left the plant —the record is not clear—Walker worked out with the union a new procedure on the handling of situations where a job would run out for a particular worker during the working day and there would be nothing available for him to do the rest of that day. Under the previous system, the man who found himself without work would be sent home for the rest of the day, whereas those who were on continuing jobs remained at work. According to the new system, when work ran out for a man at his station, he could look around to see whether there was still work for any other men in his classification in the department. If he had more seniority than any of these men, he could "bump" one of them, thus sending somebody else home, while he remained at work.

Such a change would have had little significance up to 1948. With the long runs and similar work requirements from model to model, it was a rare occasion when a man would find his work running out with nothing else to do. Furthermore, these occasions could easily be foreseen, giving the foreman the opportunity of placing the affected worker somewhere else in the plant. Now, with much more rapid changeovers from model to model and with a greater variety of work requirements, the surplus manpower situation came up with greatly increased frequency. Under the previous arrangement, the worker whose work ran out could regard it simply as a matter of bad luck—a loss suffered at the hands of impersonal forces. Now lower seniority men found themselves losing out at the hands of higher seniority workers, and the losses could be attributed directly to the union steward and the foreman.

Up to this time, the barrel department had appeared to have a highly cohesive work group, but now the evidences of friction and conflict increased. There was a marked cleavage between high- and low-seniority men, with the low-seniority people putting on so much pressure through the local union and with the international representative that they were able to bring about the resignation of the steward.

Friction within the worker ranks also showed itself in the rhythm of work on the assembly lines. In the earlier period, those who found they could do their operations faster were inclined to slow down so as not to pile up barrel shells at the succeeding work station, thus obviously drawing to management's attention where the bottleneck was. Now these restraints were less often observed, and pile-ups on the line were more frequently evident.

In this period, the workers also found their IRR becoming less favorable. While they claimed they had to work just as hard as before and perhaps even harder, their incentive earnings went down. Theoretically, a piece-rate system is supposed to operate so that more complex and slower jobs will have higher rates and therefore workers will not lose money as they shift from the simple to the more complex tasks. Experience shows that actual earnings rarely work out this way. The problem is further compounded by the difference between long and short runs. Workers almost always find that they can make more money on long runs than on short runs. Thus, workers found that they had impersonal as well as personal complaints.

In *sentiments*, Walker found himself in a highly negative situation. While he argued that the problems were not his fault, he recognized that he had lost the reputation for success.

Walker was now showing increasing signs of tension. Vice President Northrup gave this illustration. He had been in the office of Lou Fisher, assistant to General Production Supervisor Wiley. The phone rang and Fisher picked it up. Northrup said that he could not understand what was being said, but noticed that the voice was so loud it drove Fisher away from the receiver. Northrup picked up the other phone in the office to listen in. He reported that he had never heard anyone so explosively raked over the coals as Walker was then raking Fisher, a man who was his immediate superior. Finally, Northrup broke in and told Walker to come up to his office. Walker came up somewhat chastened, and Northrup told him that it was outrageous for a man to talk that way to anybody, let alone his boss. They talked at some length and Walker agreed that he had been "out of line." But Northrup did not notice any change in Walker's behavior after this talk.

The new workers had never liked Walker, and now the old-timers were turning against him. The new workers had never been able to excuse profanity, apparently directed at them, as just an interesting feature of the colorful character who was their foreman. By now the old-timers also began to feel irritated by the profanity. The men also recognized that their jobs were no longer as attractive as they once had been, as the work itself became less smoothly organized and their earnings went down.

We also note major changes in symbols. No longer was Walker's success symbolized by plaques for production records and bottles of whiskey. No longer was his high standing certified by his victories over other management people. Here, the six-cent case with the timekeeper serves to measure the extent of Walker's fall. Whereas before he had won arguments with all sorts of people on his level if not above him, now he lost an argument to a lowly timekeeper. In this light, we can see that the six cents was not nearly so trivial to Walker as it appeared to Wiley.

Views of steward and foreman

The beginning stages of my interview with Jim Carter, the new steward in the barrel department gave me no keys to the puzzle. As a last resort, I shifted from treating him as a passive respondent and asked for his own explanation of what had taken place. I told him that either I had been mistaken in my assumption that Walker was a highly successful and popular foreman up to 1948, or, if I had not been mistaken, then I still did not understand how things could have changed so drastically in such a short time. When I asked thus for his help, Carter opened up and gave me the best account of Walker's growing difficulties than I had received from anyone. He began by saying that personally he had always liked Walker.

In the first place, it made a lot of difference when Hodges left that department. When you have a president in the department, he carries a lot more weight than just a steward. People listen to him, the foreman really listens to him. When Hodges left, that made a lot of difference. The steward in that department never had done very much. He didn't do very much after Hodges left. I don't think Walker listened to him.

You know Walker had been in that department for many years. He worked himself right up and at first the men were pleased when he got the job. Besides that, after that long strike (1946) they really wanted to work and make some money, so he was in a position to make a good record. And those production records he began making in that department made trouble for him in the long run. The men thought that those records were all right, but not as an everyday proposition. They didn't like it when he expected them to do every day what they had done once as a special thing. It was all right after that six-months' strike, but it went on and on, and the men were getting tired.

Walker would go after the men who slowed down. You know, in the production line there are some men who have easy jobs and some men who have hard jobs. The fellows with easy jobs can go a lot faster, and they pile up the production where they are and roll the barrels down the line to the next fellow after them.

Carter explained that there had been no problem of one man urging another man to speed it up, but people who worked faster passed their production along to the next point and the foreman could easily tell where the bottleneck was. Then he would come around and say, "What's the matter?" The worker would reply, "I'm going as fast as I can." Then Walker would tell him that he knew that wasn't true because the man had done more before and he would cite the production record. He would say, "What's the matter, are you sick? If you are sick, you ought to go home. If you can't get out production, I'll have to take you off here and put somebody in who can." Carter said that the man might speed up for the moment, but he would resent Walker for it and he would also resent the other men on the line who had made him look bad.

Another thing, Walker used pretty rough language. People would come to me and complain that he was cursing them out. Now you might listen to him and you could tell that the cursing wasn't really addressed at the men. Mr. Walker was just cursing, but still people took offense. You know, he used to talk that way all the time and nobody paid any attention. They would say, "That's just the way Tom is. It don't mean nothing."

Now when the men wouldn't get the production up and things were going bad, Mr. Walker would get excited. He would lose his temper before the men would. And that's bad. He would become more and more excited when he couldn't get the production up.

It got so that people were only doing what they had to do. You know, on a line like that, all the jobs fit together and you need to work along with the other fellow in order to do a good job. But it got so that it was just every man for himself. Every man was doing just what he had to do and nothing more and the whole line suffered. Another thing, in the old days when Mr. Walker would give an order and a worker would know that there was a mistake in it, he would bring it up to Mr. Walker so that they could make a correction and the mistake wouldn't go through. But when Mr. Walker got so excited pushing for that production, it seemed like he wasn't interested any more in what the men thought. He was just telling them what to do and it got so that they would go ahead and do it even when they knew it was wrong, and they'd be glad it was wrong so they could show him up.

A couple of times Mr. Walker called me in and told me that a certain individual wasn't doing the job he should do. I went over and watched the man. If a man is really laying down on the job or sabotaging or something like that, I'm supposed to talk to him. But the man would be just doing what he had to do and nothing more, but nothing less either. In a situation like that I couldn't help the foreman. If he wants the men to do a little more, he's got to win their cooperation. There is nothing I can do for him.

I look forward eagerly to getting Walker's own version of the case. I found this was impossible.

In the 1948 period, when I was carrying on an intensive study of union-management relations, Walker talked with me frankly and freely. When I returned to the plant for a brief visit shortly after his demotion, he greeted my opening interview question with a broad grin and this statement: "Well, you know how it is, Doc. There are a lot of things I could tell you, but you know you talked to a lot of people when you were here last time, and some of them aren't here any more."

He was referring particularly to Al Short, his former general production supervisor, who had been fired shortly after I left the plant in 1948. The firing grew out of conflict between Short and the union, in which top management became convinced that Short had deliberately failed to live up to certain agreements negotiated with the union. I was not even aware of any such difficulties until I was informed that Short had been discharged, but the coincidence between the termination of my study and the discharge gave rise to suspicions in the mind of the demoted foreman that I was unable to overcome. He simply laid all of his difficulties to mechanical problems and said that no one could have done a better job keeping those machines running.

Walker's transactional deficit

In the earlier period, in nearly all relationships Walker came out on the plus side. The exceptions were in his relations with other members of lower management. Even here, because he had the support of Al Short, he was able to impose penalties on others without suffering negative consequences.

With steward Halsey, Walker was unable to establish the transactional pluses that had prevailed in his relations with Union President Ed Hodges. With the new general production supervisor, Wiley, Walker missed the positive exchanges and joint payoffs he had enjoyed with Al Short. The personnel change also had an important indirect effect: Wiley declined to support Walker in his conflict with other management people, so they in turn were free to take out on Walker the reprisals they had refrained from taking before.

With the passing of the era of production records, Walker also lost the possibility of sharing in joint payoffs with the workers, the union president, and the general production supervisor. It was now more of a question of determining who was to blame for inferior performance.

Note how the steward describes the appearance of negative exchanges and the disappearance of positive exchanges between Walker and his workers. Walker got after workers for failing to produce, and the workers got back at him as best they could. Given Walker's sloppiness in paper work, failure to inform the foreman when the worker noticed a mistake proved to be a potent reprisal.

Note also the changes in transactional frequencies in particular sets of relationships. When there was a low level of interaction and initiation of activities between Walker and other foremen and lower management people, the negative transactional elements were of little importance.

Now the changes in production schedules multiplied the interactions between Walker and these others and added greatly to the deficit in Walker's balance of transactional values.

General conclusions

If a social system is characterized by the mutual dependence among its parts, the nature of this mutual dependence can only be assessed through examining how the parts change through time.

To apply our approach, we need to assess *interactions* (I), *activities* (A), *sentiments* (S), and *transactions* at time one and then note the changes in each element by time two, three, four, and so on. Of course, our concepts are not variables within themselves. For I, A, and S, we need to specify variables which are subject to measurement. Methods are now available to provide measures of a number of the variables.

In this illustrative case, it may seem that we did no measuring at all, that we are simply presenting a "qualitative" interpretation. While it would have been highly desirable to do much more than was done in specifying and measuring variables in this case, I would argue that even the rough data we have provide the basis of measurement. For example, we do not know how frequently Walker interacted with the foremen in the steel storage, punch press, and shipping departments in the 1947–48 period, but we do know that the frequency of his interaction with them was greatly increased in the 1949–50 period. If we can determine that the interactional frequency in 1949–50 was greater than in the period 1947–48, the statement of "greater than" is a quantitative conclusion.

This is not a defense of crude quantification, except insofar as I would argue that if we can go this far with crude quantities, we should be able to go much farther with more refined and precise measurements. We have been able to go as far as we have with Tom Walker's case because the changes involved were so large that we have not needed precise measurements in order to appreciate their importance. More systematic efforts at quantification will enable us to deal meaningfully with much smaller differences.

What light does Tom Walker's case throw upon studies of supervisory leadership? Suppose we ask: Was Tom Walker a good foreman? The only answer we can give is: He was a good foreman in the situation prevailing up to 1948, and he was a poor foreman in the situation prevailing in 1949–50.

Suppose we use Tom Walker to have another look at the perplexing problem of the relationship of supervisory performance to the dimensions of employee-centered versus production-centered leadership or general versus close supervision. Even in studies where statistical correlations have been shown—which, as we have seen, is not always the case—the investigator is left with the troublesome question: Which is the dependent variable? In other words, did the foreman's work group perform well because the foreman was employee-centered or was the foreman able to be employee-centered because his group was performing well? The same question can be asked regarding general versus close supervision.

While we have no survey data in this case, the evidence we do have suggests that the workers would have rated Walker an employee-centered supervisor in 1948 and a production-centered supervisor in 1950, a general supervisor in 1948 and a close supervisor in 1950. As Walker got into trouble, he pushed for production, increasing his initiations of interaction and attempted initiations of activity to the men.

We see from this case that causation can run in either direction. There is no theoretical or practical profit in trying to determine which is the hen and which the egg. If we are to make scientific progress in studies of supervisory effectiveness, we need to get out of the little box of the man-boss relationship and look upon this relationship simply as one part of a broader social system.

Discussion questions

1. Management did not anticipate in 1948 the problems that Tom Walker was going to face in 1949 and 1950. If members of higher management had been equipped with the conceptual framework used in this chapter, to what extent should it have been possible for them to anticipate these difficulties? (Do not assume that management had a research man available to study the problem. Consider what items of information were necessary to make accurate predictions in this case. Did members of higher management probably have this information? To the extent that they lacked some of the necessary information, how difficult would it have been to gather this information through ordinary channels—if they had known what they were looking for?)

2. Assume that in 1948 members of higher management had been able to anticipate the main outlines of the difficulties Tom Walker was to encounter in 1949 and 1950. What steps might have been taken to deal more effectively with these problems? Do you find missing some information that you consider important for your answer to this question? If so, what information is missing? Why do you need it? In what ways would the missing information help you to develop your answer?

Part VI

LATERAL AND DIAGONAL RELATIONS

IN CHAPTER 14 we have seen that we cannot understand the relations between supervisor and subordinate without placing the supervisor in his network of lateral and diagonal relationships.

In Part VI we devote three chapters to case studies of the relations with operating units of maintenance, cost control, and personnel departments. These chapters illustrate a wide variety of types of problems that tend to arise in lateral and diagonal relationships. In Chapter 18 we try to systematize these and some other materials in order to discover the "Patterns of Lateral and Diagonal Relationships."

15. Maintenance and operating organizations

MAINTENANCE organizations must be examined in the context of inter-group relations. The effectiveness of a maintenance organization is judged in terms of the way it serves the operating division and departments. In this respect, maintenance organizations have problems distinctively different from those of most production organizations.

In maintenance, it is exceedingly difficult to plan a steady flow of work. If the operation is large enough, management can make estimates of the load of repair work to be expected from month to month, so as to make possible some routinization of activities. Preventive maintenance can be scheduled even more precisely. Nevertheless, even in the largest maintenance organizations there will be unavoidable and sudden changes in the work load, which make for difficult administrative and human problems. Even when the work from one unit to the next appears to be the same, there may be wide differences in the amount of labor and cost of materials required. Two specimens of the same machine seldom break down in an identical manner. Furthermore, the efficiency of repair work depends in large measure upon skill of diagnosis. A mechanic may spend hours making repairs indicated in his initial diagnosis, only to find that the "repaired" machine still does not run properly and that a different approach is required. This is one of the reasons why cost estimates of repair work are notoriously unreliable.

Given these difficulties, how shall management organize its maintenance activities? There seem to be two main approaches to this problem, with many variations in between.

1. *Decentralization.* Here a small maintenance group is attached to each operating unit. This has the advantage of making maintenance assistance readily available so that a minimum of operating time is lost. But how large should this maintenance group be? If it is large enough to take care of most of the problems that can be expected to arise in the department, then there are bound to be many times when there are idle maintenance men in the department, just waiting around between machine breakdowns. If the maintenance force is reduced to the point where

the men can be kept busy most of the time, then there are bound to be peak load periods when they cannot handle the problems without causing serious delays in the operations.

Any company which decentralizes its maintenance can be expected nevertheless to retain some central maintenance unit to cope with the problems that cannot be handled within the departments. The problem then becomes one of balance: How much should be done by departmental forces? How much should be done by a central force? Some companies fluctuate back and forth between centralization and decentralization.

2. *Centralization.* There will be few cases of complete centralization. Wherever interruptions of operations are costly, it is the usual practice to keep at least one maintenance man in the department, so that minor repairs can be made quickly.

Within a pattern of centralization, there are two general types of controls exercised on the scheduling of maintenance. According to one system, maintenance work is scheduled by the maintenance supervisors themselves; thus the head of the machine shop schedules the work for his shop, the head of the heavy equipment repair shop makes work schedules for his group, and so on. No doubt, there is something to be said for combining, all together, the complementary activities of directing work, requisitioning men and materials, and scheduling work. At the same time, this puts the maintenance supervision in the middle of a difficult area of interdepartmental problems.

The machine shop or the heavy equipment shop work not for one department but for a number of them. This raises the question of priorities in getting the work out. Should the work be done strictly in the order that the jobs come into the shop? This seems like the fairest system, and yet it fails to allow for differences in degrees of urgency. Suppose a routine job for department A is next in line, but then an urgent job comes in from department B—with the supervisor from department B claiming that his production is crippled until he can get the job done. Then it would seem that the department B job should be done first. But how are differing degrees of urgency to be weighed? The maintenance man who has discretionary powers in these matters is bound to be the focal point for pressures from operating people.

To avoid these pressures and the inequities that may arise in servicing different departments, management may establish a department charged with centralizing the scheduling of maintenance work. All orders for maintenance must then come into this department, and the departmental personnel would then go out to the appropriate shops to tie in each new order with the existing schedule for each shop. To do this efficiently requires much more than simply marking down a sequence in the order of jobs. The schedule cannot be a realistic guide unless the person making out the schedule estimates the number of men required on the job, the number of hours of labor required, the parts and equipment needed, the expected speed of their availability, and so on. This may also necessitate establishing cost estimates on each job, and even determining the exact number of men who are to work on the job. In other words, this involves a division of managerial functions—which traditionally rest with the foreman—between the man making up the schedule and foreman. Some friction is to be expected from this division, as we shall see.

The management of maintenance activities also raises some interesting questions involving the relations of craftsmen and engineers. In mainte-nance organizations, craftsmen without college training are likely to rise to higher levels than in many operating units. These status differences may give rise to frictions, and we also find that engineers and craftsmen tend to have far different views of machines and mechanical problems, which again can be a source of friction.

Some of these problems will be illustrated in the cases described below.

The standardization program

First let us consider the problem of standardization in purchasing. As a rule, we find that when decisions are made by people who are to be directly involved in carrying out the decisions, those individuals respond with higher morale than is the case when the decisions are made above their level. Other things being equal, decentralization in decision-making seems to contribute to high morale. But decentralization can also lead to problems.

In the case of the Overseas Corporation, the general foremen had been given the responsibility of making decisions regarding the tools and equipment they needed in their units. Depending upon the amount of money involved in the given purchase, some of these purchase orders had to be approved at higher levels, but no standards had been imposed on a companywide basis.

Since different general foremen had different ideas about the best machines and tools for particular jobs, management found itself with a wide variety of machines and tools spread throughout its operations, even when the same type of job was involved.

This approach presented management with a financial and a warehous-ing problem. Having available replacement machines and parts for all the machines then in use led to a very high inventory. This was aggravated by the distance of the company from the United States, whence came most of the machines. Since freight shipments would be several weeks enroute, and since air freight would be prohibitively expensive if not impossible, Overseas Corporation had to maintain many more spare units on hand than would have been necessary at a United States location.

This also involved a serious problem of obsolescence. There was a good deal of movement of personnel from job to job and from area to area within the company's operations. Thus, General Foreman Smith might be convinced that the ABC machine was the best possible one for his needs and would therefore insist that spare units and parts be locally warehoused. Then his place would be taken by General Foreman Jones, who firmly believed that the XYZ machine was more adequate, and therefore insisted that extra units should be provided for this machine. This meant that the spare units for ABC would simply remain in dead storage. By the time that a new general foreman succeeded Jones and reconsidered the use of the ABC machine, that machine was likely to have become obsolescent through technical progress within the ABC or other companies.

This type of system led the company into an inventory of many millions of dollars. When higher management began looking into the problem, it was apparent that a large proportion of this inventory would never be used.

Recognition of this problem led to a standardization program. Standardization committees were established in the main office and in each division. The aim was to establish a standard approved list of machines and tools that would cover all the major parts of the company's operations. Once this list was put into force, a general foreman could order something which was not on the list only if he received approval from the divisional standardization committee or from a member of that committee who was delegated the responsibility of judging such requests. There was also a provision for carrying some of these requests as high as the main office standardization committee, but what distinguished the requests that went all the way to the top from those that were handled in the division office is not clear from our records.

From the standpoint of higher management, the new system was exceedingly effective. Some months after its installation, the inventory of machines and parts was down to less than half the figure that had been reached before standardization. Results could be shown in dollars and cents. On the other hand, the new system carried with it certain costs in friction and increased demand on supervisory time and effort—though these were never directly measured.

Let us see how the new system worked, from the point of view of the general foreman. While he might agree that standardization was a good thing as a general principle, he often complained against the judgment of those who made the standardization decisions, and often felt that he badly needed some item that was not on the approved list. In such a case, his first step was to check with the warehouse to see if by chance the type of item he wanted was still in stock. If he did not find it—and usually it was not there—he then had to draw up a written request and justification for the purchase. Before and after taking the step, he generally spent a good deal of time consulting with local management people about his proposal, marshalling his own arguments and trying to persuade those who might be consulted by the divisional standardization committee.

Ordinarily it took some weeks for the written request to go from a general foreman to the stage of final action at divisional headquarters. In the meantime, the general foreman had to wait and possibly substitute some makeshift arrangement while he was waiting. This sometimes led him to place an order with the machine shop to have the item in question manufactured. This was, of course, a costly procedure, for the machine shop was not set up to manufacture such items in quantity.

As often as not, the general foreman's request would be turned down by the divisional committee. In fact, the standardization program cannot be expected to work unless most requests for substitute items are turned down. But what does a general foreman do when his request is vetoed? Let us consider "The Case of the Tool Kits" for illustrative purposes.

Our story begins on a November 8, when a general foreman submitted a requisition for the purchase of four tool kits to be used in the servicing of a unit of a certain type of machine. The cost involved was approximately $50.

On January 6, the requisition was approved by local management. (Why it took almost two months for the requisition to get out of the local organization we have no idea.)

On January 12, the requisition was received in the division office. On February 8, the standardization committee raised a question as to whether the use of the kits would affect the manufacturer's warranty on the machines. It was requested that the requisition be held up for the decision of the engineer, who was then out of the city. When he was able to give his attention to this matter, the engineer recommended against accepting the local requisition. His decision was upheld by a representative of division management. The cancelled requisition was returned to the local unit on April 4.

Almost six months had passed since the original request, but our story is not over yet. On May 27, the general foreman resubmitted the requisition, together with a more elaborate statement justifying the order.

By August, when I left the local scene, a final disposition of the tool kit case had not been made, so I cannot tell the end of the story. However, I can provide this information regarding the bases of decision-making, both in the divisional office and in the local situation.

I learned that the division turned down the requisition not only on the question of the manufacturer's warranty. The action was also taken in line with general company policy to have repair and servicing of machines done outside of the company whenever adequate facilities were available and there seemed a good chance of saving money. This seemed like a case in point because there was a service agency in the division office city for the machines in question.

At the local level, the situation looked entirely different. The manufacturer's warranty was brushed aside on these points:

1. Most of the machines in question were so old that they did not come within the warranty period.
2. Anyway, a warranty can apply only if the machine is sent back to the

manufacturer (in the United States), and then only if he is convinced that the difficulty is due to faulty materials or workmanship. This is a costly and long, drawn out procedure at best.

Regarding the possibility of having the servicing done in the division office city, the craft people made this point. With the tool kit, the unit could easily be serviced without being removed from the machine. The job took no more than half an hour. If the unit were sent out, it had to be removed from the machine, which took at least two hours time. In other words, having the work done outside would cost the company more before the unit even got out of the local shop.

Obviously, this is an extreme case. It does not represent the average situation. Rather, it represents the situation as viewed by some of the general foremen. As one foreman sought to explain his point of view to me, he brought up this case to symbolize everything that was objectionable about the system. Thus the case is highly significant—even though it is not typical—in that it exemplifies the point of view of the general foremen.

The hostile sentiments of the general foremen toward the system were directed particularly against the engineers, whom they saw as being in control of the standardization committees and procedures. The prevailing sentiments of many of them can be summed up in these terms (paraphrased from my interviews):

The engineers don't really understand our problems. Furthermore, they aren't interested in our problems. If the engineer who is making the decision doesn't accept my reasoning, why doesn't he call me up and try out his answer on me or ask me to explain it further? The trouble is, engineers think they know it all. They think we are stupid. Now they have set up all this complicated system so that the general foremen are pinned down in useless paper work more than they ever were before.

The engineers in division headquarters had a different view of standardization problems and a matching set of sentiments toward the general foreman. They regarded the average craft supervisor as an illogical individual, who was inclined to develop strong personal attachments to particular machines. He was also thought to be a stubborn individual, inclined to resist change even when it was obviously indicated.

It is not my intention to finish this case with a balance of profits and losses under the new system. There was no such balance available. The gains achieved under the new system were to a large extent measurable—and measured—in the reduction of the inventory. The costs of the new system were not measured, but some of them were potentially measurable. If management were concerned with striking a more realistic balance, other sets of figures could be gathered. For example, it could be found how much time each member of a standardization committee was spending on this task and this could be charged as a fraction of his salary. Field studies could at least bring forth some useful estimates of the time being spent by general foremen on the new procedures. (Ideally, we should be able to compare this with the time they were spending in acquiring tools and equipment under the earlier system.) No direct dollar value can be put on the increasing frictions between craft supervisors and engineers or on the increasing frustrations felt by craft supervisors, but these two costs are obviously incurred in achieving the gains of the new system. Quite apart from dollar values, management had no way of registering these changes in interpersonal sentiments and thus considering them in management decision making. This matter of factors measured and factors unmeasured presents a problem in management to which we shall return later.

The area coordination system

The Overseas Corporation provides us with another problem in organizational structure and relations as we examine the operation of the area coordination system.

The maintenance and construction organization of the corporation was a new structure designed to achieve better coordination of maintenance and construction activities. It must be viewed against the background of the type of organization which preceded it. In the old days the craft organizations were supreme. Each craft was headed by a general foreman. The general foreman reported to a master mechanic or craft coordinator.

Under this type of organization, craft supervisors received work orders from the "owners" of equipment and the supervisors themselves had considerable freedom of action in scheduling the work in their shops. This led to an emphasis upon the relationship between a man and his boss from the bottom to the top of the line of authority. Such an organization may be well adapted to putting out high quality work in each craft.

However, the basic problems of maintenance and construction cannot be solved in terms of a man-boss relationship. Nearly every job that comes in to maintenance and construction requires the work of more than one craft, and some jobs may call for the work of half a dozen. Under these circumstances, the efficiency of the work depends at least as much upon intergroup relations as it does upon the relations within each craft group.

Furthermore, as we have already noted, it is characteristic of work in maintenance and construction that the flow of production is not even and steady. There will be shortages of men in some shops, while others find themselves with surpluses, and sometimes these shortages and surpluses occur simultaneously within the same craft but in different installations operated by this craft. Efficiency obviously depends upon a full utilization of manpower, and in maintenance and construction this seems to require the ability to move men from shop to shop to meet the fluctuating needs.

The new maintenance and construction organization, then, was designed to increase efficiency through the coordination of intergroup relations and through a more flexible assignment of workers.

The maintenance and construction organization established what were, in effect, two parallel lines of authority. Under the chief of the maintenance and construction organization was the area coordination organization, and under the craft coordinator, a number of craft groups. The area coordinator and his assistants were responsible for receiving orders for work from the "owners" of equipment and for preparing a production schedule. This schedule was supposed to determine on what day a given craft should start work on job X, how many men would be assigned to the job, and how long the job should take. The assignment of men also involved the power to shift workers from place to place to meet work requirements.

The area foremen and the supervisors below them were responsible for determining the best methods of doing the work, for training their men, for directly supervising the work, and for evaluating workers and determining job classifications and pay increases. Since they did not have control over the number assigned to them from week to week or the freedom to decide when a particular job should be done or how many men should be assigned to it, they had given up certain important functions they previously performed.

The job description stated that area coordination and craft supervision groups were to work together as a team. However, the description also clearly stated that the area coordinator was the captain of the area team.

We found a good deal of friction between the area coordination and craft supervision groups, with the craft supervisors feeling that they were the underdogs in that situation. Although the assistant area coordinators and the area foremen appeared on the same level on the organization chart, many craft people felt that the assistant area coordinator had the higher status with management as well as more power.

It was quite natural for craft people to have these sentiments regarding status and power, because the craft people no longer had the full control over the work that was once theirs. Furthermore, in planning the work schedule, the assistant area coordinator was frequently in the position of telling the foreman what to do, while the official distribution of functions and responsibilities provided the foreman with no opportunity to tell the assistant area coordinator what to do.

Craft supervisors also complained that the area coordination people were so preoccupied with the equipment and paper work that they neglected the "human element." What did this mean? This question is best answered by a story that was told us by a craft supervisor:

I think this problem we had about Holy Week really shows you the point of view of those people. Thursday and Friday of that week are religious holidays. Instead of that, area coordination told us that we were going to have to work those days—to get an emergency job done. Besides, we weren't going to work just one shift; we were going to have to work three shifts right around the clock. Spread as thin as we are, that would have meant that all of the expatriates and all the national foremen would have had extra hours to cover the job. Besides, we couldn't have required the men to work on those holidays. We would have had to ask for volunteers, and we knew damned well that we couldn't get enough men to come out and work on those days and those hours to be worth the effort.

I argued with area coordination. I told them just what I thought of their point of view. I told them there were other ways of getting that job done. But I might just as well have been talking to a stone wall. Their attitude was that they were running things around here, and we just had to do whatever they told us. They couldn't think of anything but the jobs to be done and their pieces of paper. The human element didn't enter into their calculations at all. The area coordinator even said to me that he didn't have to worry about personnel. That was my problem.

Well, I argued with them until I saw it was just going to do no good. Then I went to my general foreman and told him what I thought about it. He took it on upstairs and now we hear that the plan has been called off. But the fact that they told us they were going to carry on such a work schedule gives you an idea of their point of view.

Another craft supervisor made this comment:

Some of these people in area coordination don't consider the individual at all. Lately here they came through with a schedule that would have required Sunday work out of us every Sunday for a period of two months. Now, of course, I am supposed to be on call 24 hours a day, seven days a week, but outside of my six regular days, I am only supposed to be called in if it is an emergency. How can it be an emergency if you can schedule the work two months ahead?

While something like the Holy Week work schedule problem or the Sunday work problem only come up occasionally, such incidents made craft supervisors feel that they were at the mercy of the area people. To be sure, if the area man pushed you too far, you could appeal to your general foreman, and he could go upstairs and perhaps get the decision changed. However, this possibility seemed open only on a large and dramatic issue. In the normal routine, the craft supervisor might feel subjected to many unnecessary inconveniences in the personnel field without being able to do anything about it.

Was this area-craft friction inevitable? Apparently not, for we found several cases where the assistant area coordinator and the craft supervisor were getting along well.

We looked into one such relationship and discovered two possible explanations for the harmony we observed. In the first place, the men had worked closely together before the maintenance and construction organization was set up and they had always been good friends. In the second place, the actual procedures that the assistant area coordinator used were different from those that were customary.

We heard many complaints from craft supervisors that the area people would give them a work schedule already completed without consulting them at any point. They often felt that the area people were young upstarts who did not really understand the craft problems. The found that the work schedules were often impractical, but to institute a change when a schedule was already made out involved an argument with the assistant area coordinator and possibly even an appeal to a general foreman.

In the case of the area foreman and the assistant area coordinator who got along so well, the work schedule really could be called a joint product. Before he took his first steps in making up the schedule, the assistant area coordinator would go to the foreman to discuss the work in prospect for the coming week, the technical problems that might be involved, the number of men that would be required, and so on. Whenever possible, they would go out to look over the jobs together—and on these occasions the United States foreman generally took his national foreman with him, so that all supervision was involved in this planning process.

Next, the assistant area coordinator would prepare a tentative work schedule for the week and bring this in to the area foreman for discussion. At times the area foreman would disagree with the assistant area coordinator as to the number of men required for a particular job. In such cases, he told us, sometimes the assistant area coordinator would accept the foreman's estimate, sometimes they would agree on a compromise, and sometimes the foreman would agree to go along with the scheduled number of men. Since he felt he played an important part in making up this work schedule, the area foreman never found it difficult to come to an agreement regarding the various aspects of scheduling.

As the last step, the assistant area coordinator presented the completed and official work schedule to the area foreman. Since this only put in final form what the two men had already thoroughly discussed and agreed upon, there was never any problem at this point.

When two men work together well in a situation where friction might be expected, it is often said that the harmony is due to their particular personalities. In this case, while their past association certainly helped the two men to learn how to get along with each other, we should emphasize that the procedures they followed and the ways in which they organized their relationship were objectively different from what we observed in cases of friction.

The harmonious relationship did not arise simply by accident, because the two men happened to like each other. At the same time, we should note that the procedures they worked out were not based upon management directives.

The struggle at Milo

Men Who Manage, by Melville Dalton, provides us with the most intensive study available of relations within management, of the exchange of favors and penalties, of factional maneuvering and power struggles.[1] One of Dalton's cases, taken from Milo, a very large manufacturing plant, involved the relations between maintenance and operations.

Dalton sets the stage for us in this way:

For a decade the records of all repair work were prepared by the maintenance shops in which the work was done. This record included time and materials for doing the work. The shops sent a copy to the auditing department, which charged the cost to the given head. Over a period of several years friction developed between operation and maintenance groups. Some heads of operation complained about the backlog of over 1,500 uncompleted orders in the various shops, while foremen of maintenance protested about being "pushed around" by operation executives.

Hardy (assistant plant manager) and the assistants to Stevens (plant manager) investigated and found that some heads had hundreds of unfinished orders while others had none. The condition was hushed up to prevent invidious ascription of good or poor leadership, when obviously there could be no poor leaders.

The backlog belonged almost entirely to the less aggressive and less astute heads. Once their orders and worn equipment were delivered to the shops, they assumed that the work would be done as soon as possible, and attended to more urgent matters. Or if they did inquire at the shops, they put no pressure on maintenance foremen. On the other hand, the chiefs abreast of their repair work were there because they checked constantly on the progress of their orders. They expedited the work by use of friendships, by bullying, and by implied threats. As all the heads had the same formal rank, one could say that an inverse relation existed between a given officer's personal influence and his volume of uncompleted repairs.

For example, a dominant chief would appear in person and tell the maintenance foreman that certain jobs were "hot" and were holding up production. Some operation chiefs threatened to block their flow of informal favors to maintenance officers. These favors included (1) cooperation to "cover up" errors made by maintenance machinists, or at least to share responsibility for them; (2) defense for the need of new maintenance personnel; (3) support in meetings against changes recommended by staff groups that maintenance forces opposed; (4) consideration, and justification to top management, of material needed by maintenance for its success and survival in meeting the demands of operation.

---

[1] Melville Dalton, *Men Who Manage* (New York: John Wiley & Sons, 1959).

Confronted by an aggressive executive demanding special service, the foreman would look about his shop for machines with jobs that could be removed with least danger of offending other executives concerned. He would "pull" the partially repaired job of some less bellicose supervisor and replace it with that of the demanding head.[2]

This problem led to a good deal of discussion within local management ranks and between the top local management people and men from the central office.

Working with the main office, top local management developed a two-point plan to deal with the problem. One part of the plan was the installation of a piecework incentive system for maintenance workers— which will not be discussed here. The part that will receive our attention was a new organization structure and control system.

The field work department (FWD) was designed to take over the estimating and scheduling of all maintenance work. The staff of FWD, nearly 100 strong, was drawn from a pool of experienced operations and maintenance men. In addition to having a general familiarity with Milo technology and production processes, each FWD man was a specialist in some aspect of maintenance work, such as boiler repair, motor repair, carpentry, and so on. The large staff was placed under a superintendent of maintenance who had earlier been in operations himself. The FWD was housed in a new building, which was isolated from other structures, so that the planners would be removed from the immediate pressures of operations or maintenance men.

The new system gave each operations department a specific annual series of numbers for use in writing maintenance orders. If one department had a series from 5,000 to 10,000, an order number anywhere within that range would identify the order as to the department of origin and place it in a time sequence, so that job number 5070 would be begun before job number 5071. Each order was punched on a time clock as it entered FWD, so that an order from one department would take its chronological place in line ahead of an order from another department that came in later. In other words, the scheme was designed to function completely on an impersonal basis, with order numbers and time clock numbers being substituted for personal relations.

For each job, FWD specialists in materials, routing, and machines, would estimate the cost of materials and labor and indicate the shops and routes among machines and operations that the job should follow. Before the maintenance work was actually begun, the cost estimate was submitted to the executive who had issued the maintenance order, for his signature. The order was then placed in a pouch with blueprints and instructions and sent to the shop assigned to the job or to the first point of

---

[2] *Ibid.*, p. 34.

the job. The actual cost of the job was later computed on the basis of records of materials used and labor supplied at each phase of the work.

The FWD system was remarkably successful in breaking the log jam of maintenance orders. However, the new system produced results which had not been anticipated by the plant manager and assistant plant manager.

In effect, the new system reversed the performance scores of competing groups of superintendents. In group A were those superintendents who had been most aggressive towards maintenance in the past and most successful in getting work out of maintenance ahead of their less aggressive competitors (who were also more inclined to follow the rules). Group A men now found that their actual costs were running well above estimated costs, and these discrepancies were a source of considerable embarrassment.

The superintendents in what Dalton calls group B enjoyed a sharply contrasting experience. These were the individuals who had previously exerted no pressures on maintenance and had dropped far behind in their maintenance work. According to Dalton's evidence, they seemed to be outsiders as far as the informal power system was involved. But now, thanks to the operation of the FWD system, they were not only getting their work done much more rapidly, but their actual costs were running well below estimated costs.

The group A men now began to express resentment against FWD. This began with sarcastic remarks regarding "pencil pushing," "red tape," and so on.

The group B superintendents were not as strong partisans of the new system as might have been expected, according to Dalton, because their actual job costs in some cases were so far below estimates that they too feared embarrassing questions from higher management.

What is the explanation for the discrepancies between estimated and actual costs? As I have already noted, the estimation of maintenance costs is extremely difficult, so that discrepancies will certainly be expected—but to find one group of superintendents consistently overestimating costs and the other group consistently underestimating them is unexpected.

Dalton found the explanation in the behavior of maintenance foremen. Apparently in the period before FWD, these foremen had been exceedingly resentful of the pressures that the group A operations superintendents placed upon them. They received exceedingly few favors and many threats and penalties from these superintendents. Apparently, it was only at the higher level of maintenance department management that there existed any exchange of favors with the department A superintendents. Since the group A superintendents had the most powerful positions in the informal organization of the works, maintenance department management could gain increased appropriations and other favors through cooperating with these superintendents.

Protected by FWD from the direct pressures of group A superintendents, the foremen were now in the position to pay off on some old scores. This they could do by charging to group A jobs the working time which their men actually spent on group B jobs.

As the pattern of excess costs for group A superintendents developed, those individuals naturally became suspicious and began to investigate. While they were not able to prove the existence of a general pattern, they did discover several cases of improper charges and used these with top local management to discredit the system. Apart from these few cases of proven violations, the group A superintendents were no doubt able to gain additional support for their point by view by pointing out that the very inaccuracy of cost estimates by FWD was evidence of inefficiency. The FWD organization was set up to provide better cost estimates as well as to provide for better scheduling, so that the gross inaccuracy of the FWD cost estimates became a source of embarrassment to the proponents of this system.

The fight over FWD also became involved in a problem of maintenance piece rate incentives. These had been introduced, at the same time as FWD, as another means of speeding up the work. The speed with which the incentives were introduced resulted in an unusually large number of "loose" rates being established. Group A superintendents attributed some of their cost problems to this source also. They were unable to get the incentive program thrown out, but the FWD did fall before their attack.

For some time several of the departments had had their own small maintenance crews to handle simple repairs that needed to be done quickly. Now top local management decided to place large crews within the departments to handle all maintenance problems. FWD was reduced to a "skeleton crew" of less than a dozen men, and its personnel was absorbed elsewhere in the plant. Relatively large maintenance groups were then attached to each of the major operating departments and placed under the direct control of the departmental management.

Friction between maintenance and operations now shifted to within the operating departments. Dalton reports this complaint by an operations foreman:

It was bad enough when we had to put up with central maintenance. We at least felt free to run our production the way we wanted to. Now it's worse than ever. Higgins comes around and sticks his nose in to tell you your men aren't taking care of the equipment. He thinks they should work with one hand and hold an oil can in the other. He tried to tell me last week when we had a breakdown, that it was my fault—that I hadn't let the line stay down long enough the last time to let him do a good job! What the hell does he expect? That line is supposed to be moving, not standing idle. He comes nosin' around and tries to pass the buck. Jesus Christ! I know my equipment. We never had any trouble in here till they sent him over from the shop.

The following day Dalton encountered the maintenance foreman and opened the conversation by saying that he had heard that the two men had had an argument the day before and wondered whether the production foreman had landed any punches "below the belt." The maintenance foreman replied in this way:

You're damned right he did! That's the only way he knows how to fight. He skips on his maintenance costs to get a little extra production. Hell, he could get a damn sight more production if he'd keep his line lubricated. Go over and look at his cranes—the wheels and gears shine like the sun!

In the long run he's going to get less production and more costs. But you can't tell him a damn thing. He knows it all. I came out a while last night to see that everything was all right. And it's a damn good thing I did. I saved him a thousand dollars in maintenance costs by spotting the leaky line and defective gauge on his_____tank. He might have had a blowup with lost time cases. And if he hadn't, he'd at least have damaged enough material so that the reprocessing would have cost over a thousand dollars and would have cut hell out of his production. And that's not all. He's in the hole on his costs now—I saved him from an ass-eating. But hell, he never has a kind word for maintenance, and least of all for me. It's always "gimme, gimme," with nothing ever coming back.

When these frictions came to the attention of management at higher levels, the assistant plant manager suggested that in the future responsibility for maintenance costs would rest with the maintenance foreman. This encouraged operations people to give even less thought to maintenance and to concentrate on production regardless of cost.

We have now followed maintenance foremen through a complete cycle. Our story began before FWD, when they were the harrassed victims of the aggressive operations superintendents. FWD gave the maintenance foremen protection from these aggressions and put them in a real power position so that they could markedly affect the performance records of the various operating departments. Having used their power with more freedom than discretion, they found themselves at last shorn of the protection of FWD and placed under the direct control of operational management.

While this is the end of our present story, there is no reason to believe that this cyclical rise and fall of maintenance in relation to operations may not have continued in this organization and is not to be found in many another. Our data suggest that the relations between operations and maintenance are often fraught with friction and instability.

Conclusions

Let us see now what general conclusions we can draw from these cases, focusing particularly on the relations between maintenance and operating organizations.

We see first a problem in the evaluation of the two activities.

Although maintenance is essential in most companies, it is usually thought to be of less importance, and therefore of lesser status, than operations.

There are other differences in the evaluation of activities not directly related to status. As Dalton points out, the maintenance men tend to view their work from a craft point of view, which means that they place particular weight upon the way work is done. Operations people tend to emphasize the end product and to be impatient with the maintenance man's concern for the proper care of equipment and the proper operating methods.

We see status problems also in the characteristics people bring to their jobs. In general, the maintenance people tend to have somewhat lower educational backgrounds and community status than men at the same level in operations. This makes it easier for outsiders to establish control over what would seem to be maintenance functions, and more difficult for maintenance supervisors to initiate activity toward these outsiders. This we have seen in the standardization case of the Overseas Corporation, where the important functions of choosing materials and equipment for maintenance work were strictly limited by controls established outside of the maintenance organization. We encountered consistent and bitter complaints from maintenance people regarding their inability to initiate for these outsideres.

While we encounter problems of low organizational status in maintenance in all of these cases, we see one significant difference between the Overseas Corporation and the Milo Corporation in this respect. In Milo the maintenance shops constituted just a small part of a large complex of plants, with most of the activities being concentrated in production. This may help to explain why the FWD collapsed at Milo, whereas the area coordination system survived at Overseas. We have noted the resentments the maintenance supervisors expressed toward the area coordination system and their sentiments favoring continuation of the system. Presumably the supervisors within maintenance at Milo also favored the continuation of FWD. The difference was that at Milo the production superintendents were in a sufficiently powerful position to undermine FWD, whereas only one third of the personnel of Overseas Corporation in this area was devoted to operations, which gave the top operating people less opportunity to exercise influence upon the high level managerial decisions that would have been necessary to change the organization structure.

Also, the nature of maintenance activities generally tends to place operations in the position of initiating activity for maintenance. This also tends to fix the status of maintenance below operations. When group A consistently initiates for group B and group B has little opportunity to initiate in return, we find people evaluating group A as having higher status than group B.

If we were dealing with only one operating department and one maintenance shop, this pattern of one-way initiation might be expected to stir negative sentiments of maintenance people toward operating people, but it would not give rise to the serious problems of coordination we have seen. When several operating groups are trying simultaneously to initiate activities for maintenance, serious problems of coordination do arise. Given the pattern of rare initiation of activity, together with the low status accorded to maintenance, a situation results in which it is difficult for maintenance people to resist the pressures placed upon them and to establish their own independent system of priorities.

The establishment of the area coordination system and of FWD both had the same effect in one respect: they blocked off direct initiations from operations to maintenance. The new approach still provided for one-way initiation of activities, but this time from the planning group to maintenance.

These cases illustrate for us the importance of symbols, particularly cost symbols. Management in the Overseas Corporation had elaborate figures on the volume of inventory before and after standardization. The difference of some millions of dollars seemed to make it obvious that the standardization program was a great success. But we have noted that management made no effort to produce the symbols representing the costs of the change. Some of these costs would have been easy to calculate, according to standard accounting methods, and some would have been exceedingly difficult. Let us examine further what would have been involved.

Determination of the number of man-days spent by members of the standardization committee and their staff on investigation, deliberation, and decision making on purchase orders could readily have been converted into salary costs at this level. Estimates of the time spent by foremen, general foremen, and their clerical personnel in preparing the more elaborate purchase orders and justifications and in deciding upon strategies to pursue to win favorable decisions from the standardization committee could similarly have been converted into salary costs. The costs in production delays and inefficiencies to be attributed to the increasing time span between placing a purchase order and receiving the item presents a much more complex problem, but investigation of a sample of cases might have provided a formula for estimating these costs.

Increasing negative sentiments of foremen and general foremen toward the engineers and higher management and lowered job satisfaction of the foremen and general foremen present a different type of measurement problem. Such changes can be measured through survey techniques, but the differences found cannot be converted directly into dollars.

We are often told that you cannot add together unlike elements. That is, we can only compare the value of 12 oranges and 25 potatoes if we use the same set of symbols (money) to represent the value of the orange and of the potato. While the time of people who are paid for their time is readily convertible into money, that is not the case with sentiments.

Does this mean that elements which cannot be converted readily into money should not be measured? To pursue the analogy, let us assume that management has precise measures of its potato yield and no measures at all for its orange yield—and no recognition of any possible interconnection between the two. In that case, naturally management will bend all efforts simply to increase the potato yield. On the other hand, if management also measures oranges and recognizes the possible interconnection between potatoes and oranges, management is then able to consider how many oranges it is prepared to lose in order to increase the potato yield by X amount. Or management can consider several alternative ways of increasing the potato yield to determine which method will best minimize the loss in oranges.

To return to time, money, and sentiments, the inventory savings were so large in the standardization program that it seems unlikely management would have abandoned it, even facing the figures on the several categories of losses involved. However, if management had had available sets of figures on the various offsetting costs, including negative supervisory sentiments and lowered job satisfaction, then management might well have sought to modify the standardization program so as to reduce or avoid some of the costs observed. In other words, while management still could not put a dollar loss value on the generation of negative sentiments, if management had recognized that measurable costs in sentiments were involved in the new program, then management would have been more likely to consider possibilities of reducing these costs. In competition for executive attention, the unmeasured items are likely to lose out to the measured items.

In the Milo case, maintenance costs were important symbols of success or failure. Before FWD the group A superintendents utilized their relations with the maintenance superintendent in such a way that the figures exaggerated the quality of their performance. Under FWD the cost symbols shifted sharply against the group A superintendents. This naturally led them to bend every effort toward eliminating the system which produced the symbols that reflected adversely on their performance.

Maintenance-operations relations tend to channel the types of transactions that occur. Operating people are generally in the position of initiating activity for maintenance people, and there are few opportunities to initiate in the other direction.

In other words, operating people often ask maintenance to do things for them, and maintenance seldom asks for help in return. Few positive exchange transactions are likely to occur at these junction points.

That general conclusion needs to be modified in terms of relationships at different points in the two structures. The foremen and general foremen of maintenance were constantly on the minus end of transactions with operating people, whereas the superintendent of maintenance could engage in positive exchanges and trading with the production superintendents. That is, he could give special help to influential production superintendents and get in return support for an expanded maintenance budget and other payoffs valuable to him. The maintenance foremen and general foremen, not sharing in these payoffs, were naturally hostile to the aggressive superintendents and ready to "get even" whenever the opportunities arose.

References

Dalton, Melville. *Men Who Manage*. New York: John Wiley & Sons, 1959. An "inside story" of maneuvering within management and between management and union written by a sociologist with several years of experience as participant observer.

Sayles, Leonard, and Strauss, George. *Human Behavior in Management*. Englewood Cliffs, N.J.: Prentice-Hall, 1966. See Chapter 16, "Specialization," pp. 393–422. Deals with various types of lateral relations.

Gardner, Burleigh B., and Moore, David G. *Human Relations in Industry*. Homewood, Ill.: Richard D. Irwin, Inc., 1964. See Chapter 7, "The Factory Organization and Division of Labor," especially pp. 201–5 on "Service Organizations." A good, brief introduction.

Discussion Questions

1. You are a consultant to an executive. He wants to know whether, in a large new plant the company is building, the maintenance activities should be centralized or decentralized. What would you need to know in order to develop your recommendations? With each item of information you specify, indicate its implications in terms of organizational behavior.

2. Assume that the decision in the above situation is to set up a centralized service. What difficulties could be anticipated?

3. Assume that the decision is to establish a decentralized service. What difficulties could be anticipated?

4. You are the plant manager. The maintenance superintendent proposes establishment of a program of preventive maintenance. What factors are likely to have led him to this recommendation? If you accept his recommendation, what changes in behavior and sentiments on the part of what people should you anticipate?

16. Cost control, production, and people

Budgets and the budgeting process are central features of our highly industrialized society. To produce a product at a profit, management needs more than machines and technical processes. Management also needs a means of keeping score—calculating the score for the total organization at appropriate time intervals and also calculating the score for each unit making up that total, so that the contributions of the units can be evaluated.

Budgets are generally prepared annually, and they are often broken down into monthly and weekly totals. Each budget can be looked upon as a goal for the organization, as determined by top management. The goal is based in part upon past experience but also represents a projection of a future desired state of affairs. The budget may specify goals for production, labor costs, maintenance costs, materials costs, amount of waste or scrap, and so on.

In terms of our scheme of analysis, what are budgets? They are symbols designed to represent a planned state of organizational performance. The symbols have effects upon the sentiments of people and in turn affect their activities and interactions. In this way, the impact of budgets is felt throughout the social system even by those who give little direct attention to budgets. The purpose of this chapter is to explore some of the ways in which budgets affect sentiments, interactions, and activities in the social system.

Most of the material in the present chapter is drawn from *The Impact of Budgets on People.*[1]

What do budget symbols mean to people?

In a study of four plants, Argyris and Miller asked each factory supervisor to name the department which affected him most and then the

---

[1] Prepared by Chris Argyris for Controllership Foundation, Inc., under the direction of Schuyler Dean Hoslett, with the assistance of Frank B. Miller, Jr. (Ithaca, N.Y.: Cornell University School of Business and Public Administration, 1952).

second most important department. A total of 56 percent considered production control as most important and 44 percent named the budget department; *all but one* supervisor who named production control first chose the budget department as the second most important department.

These sentiments should be interpreted in terms of the flow of interactions and activities within the plants. If we just looked at the efficient functioning of production departments, we might assume that their supervisors would consider the maintenance department as the most important one for them. One could argue that without efficient maintenance, production would break down. However, as a general rule the production departments initiate interactions and activity changes for the maintenance department, whereas production control and cost control constantly initiate interactions and activity changes for the production departments. The budget people also have control of one of the key sets of symbols in the organization and thereby indirectly bring rewards and penalties to the production supervisors.

How do the budget people see their own role? One man says, "If I see an inconsistency, I'll go to top management and report it. No, I never go to the supervisor in charge. It is our job to report any inconsistencies to the top management."

Another man gives this picture:

As soon as we examine the budget results and see a fellow is slipping, we immediately call the factory manager and point out, "Look, Joe, you're behind on the budget. What do you expect to do about it?"

True, he may be batting his brains out already on the problem, but our phone call adds a little more pressure—er—well, you know, we let them know we're interested.

The important thing for us to do is follow up. The supervisor's interest lags unless someone is constantly checking up on him. A little pressure. If you don't, the tendency is to lag. You can't blame supervisors. They are interested in the machines.

I think there is a need for more pressure. People need to be needled a bit. I think man is inherently lazy and if we could only increase the pressure . . . I think budgets would be more effective.

The factory managers, superintendents, and higher level supervisors see budgets in much the same light. Consider these two comments:

The job of budgets is to see to it that we *never forget* we've got a job to do. Sure, we apply pressure with budgets. I guess budgets aren't worth much unless they have a kick in them.

I go to the office and check that budget every day. I can then see how we're meeting the budget. If it's O.K., I don't say anything. But if it's no good, then I come back here (*smiles*) and give the boys a little . . . Well, you know. I needle them a bit. I give them the old . . . hm . . . well . . . you know what . . . the old needle.

The factory foremen take quite a different view of budgets. Budgets represent pressures on them—that they cannot pass down to the workers. These two comments are illustrative:

You can't use budgets with the people. Just can't do anything like that. People have to be handled carefully and in our plant, carefully doesn't mean budgets. Besides, I don't think *my* people are lazy.

No sir, I can't use budgets to increase production. I don't dare go up and say to a man, "My budget is *up* $5,000 this year, John." He'd look at me in scorn. No sir, anything like that is using a *whip*. And the men *don't like it.*

How do the workers see budgets? They often recognize that management people are worried about costs, but with the foremen afraid to put the cost situation to them, they remain uninvolved in the struggle.

Problems with budgets

This discussion suggests several important problems involved in the application of this set of symbols.

1. *Pressure.* The budgets are seen as sources of severe psychological pressure on the part of management people. This problem may be perhaps most acute at the foreman level, because the foreman receives the pressure and has no one to whom he can pass it on without fear of damaging reactions.

2. *Budget results indicate the score but do not reveal the plays that went into making up the score.* As one factory supervisor said:

Let's say the budget tells me I was off. I didn't make it. That's of interest. But it doesn't tell me the important thing of why I didn't make it, or how I am going to make it the next time. Oh sure, they might say all I need to do is increase production and cut out waste. Well, I know that. The question is how to do it.

3. *The goal is always rising.* As one man commented:

If I meet this budget, those guys up there will only raise it. Oh, you can't let them know that you made the budget without too much trouble. If you do they'll up it as sure as hell.

4. *It is often charged that the goal is too high.* One factory supervisor made this comment:

Budgets should be realistic. They should reflect the true picture. Take the error budget for example. There is something. The error figure is way too low. I know it. The people know it and so do the financial people know it.

So I suggested to the financial people that they should increase it. They refused. They feel that if they increase the budget to a realistic level and the people meet it, they'll have no reason to cut down errors.

We, on the other hand, feel differently. Our people see the figure and they know it is ridiculously low. So they say, "Oh, those financial guys do that so they can have the opportunity to wave the flag."

5. *In many situations, production management people do not partici-pate in the goal-setting process.* At least this is true at the level of factory superintendent and below.

Most of the controllers interviewed spoke about encouraging the par-ticipation of the line people in the budget-making process, but they seemed to view the budget people as the active agents and the supervisory people as the passive accepters in this so-called participation process. Argyris paraphrases the comments of a number of controllers in this way:

We bring them in, we *tell* them that we want their frank opinion, but most of them just sit there and nod their heads. We know they're not coming out with exactly how they feel. I guess budgets scare them. . . . Some of them don't have too much education. . . .

Similarly, the controllers refer to another phase of the participation process as they outline what happens when they present the budget to the supervisor:

Then we request the line supervisor to sign the new budget. Then he can't tell us he didn't accept it. We found the signature helps an awful lot. If anything goes wrong, they can't come to us, as they often do, and complain. We just show them their signature and remind them they were shown exactly what the budget was made up of. . . .

Needless to say, the supervisor who is asked to sign on the dotted line —and knows he has no alternative—can hardly feel that he is participating in the budget-setting process.

The impact of people

What impact do these budget-making and enforcing procedures have on the sentiments, activities, and interactions of people?

1. *The budget man achieves his successes by pointing out the failures of departmental managements.* The procedures described put budget people and supervisors in a competitive transaction situation. Further-more, the transactions tend to be "rigged" so that the supervisors cannot win. If they meet the budgets established for their departments, they escape penalties, but they do not win. Only by exceeding the budget standards can the supervisors win. Since the budgeteers control the sym-bols of success and failure, they are inclined to set the standards so high that surpassing them is highly unlikely.

There is no doubt that this system stimulates the supervisors to take budget and costs very seriously. At the same time, it leads to strongly negative sentiments toward budget people on the part of factory supervi-sors. Is this a necessary price that must be paid for developing an efficient and cost-conscious organization?

2. *Budget and cost control procedures, as often used, tend to put and keep supervisors in a failure situation.* In fact, some controllers and other

executives seem to feel that the only way to get supervisors highly motivated regarding costs is to have the budgets so tight that supervisors are nearly always falling at least somewhat short of meeting the budgets. The assumption seems to be that men are naturally lazy and will relax as soon as they have reached a goal set before them. If this assumption were true, it would then follow that great care must be taken to set goals that are rarely reached.

On the other hand, if we assume that most people in industry are concerned with doing a conscientious job and would get especially strong satisfaction in meeting or exceeding the goal set before them, then it is obviously a mistake to set goals that can rarely be met.

Research suggests that constant failure to meet goals has a depressing effect upon both the morale and productivity of the individuals involved. This does not, however, suggest that the lower the goal, the better the morale and performance. People seem to perform best and to achieve the greatest satisfactions when they are called upon to put forth special efforts to meet the goal, but then do find it within their reach.

3. *As often administered, budgets promote interdepartmental friction and an orientation toward the past.*   That is, budgets provide supervisors with an incentive to discover faults in other departments so that they and their departments may escape blame. Wherever the blame is finally placed, the effort to pin down responsibility involves a canvassing of past events and may divert considerable time from current activities and planning for the future.

An illustration of this effect is provided by a case presented by Argyris in these words as he describes a management meeting and the events that followed:

Present at the meeting were the supervisors of the two departments, two budget people, the supervisor of the department that supplies the material, and the top executive whom we shall call the leader.

LEADER: I've called you fellows down to get some ideas about this waste. I can't see why we're having so much waste. I just can't see it. Now (*turns to one of the supervisors*), I've called in these two budget men to get some ideas about this waste. Maybe they can give us an idea of how much some of the arguments you're going to give are worth.

COST MAN 1 TO LEADER (*Slightly red*—seems to realize he is putting the supervisors "on the spot."): Well, er—we might be wrong, but I can't see how. There's an entire 1 percent difference and that's a lot.

SUPERVISOR A TO SUPERVISOR B (*Trying to see if he could place the blame on Supervisor B.*): Well, maybe—maybe—some of your boys are throwing away the extra material I sent back to your department.

SUPERVISOR B (*Becomes red, answers quickly and curtly.*): No, no, we're reworking the extra material and getting it ready to use over again.

SUPERVISOR A (*Realizing that the argument wasn't going to hold much water.*): Well—you know—I've been thinking, maybe it's those new trainees we have in the plant. Maybe they're the cause for all the waste.

LEADER: I can't understand that. Look here—look at their budget, their [trainees'] waste is low.

The meeting continued for another 20 minutes. It was primarily concerned with the efforts of Supervisors A and B to fix the blame on someone except themselves. The leader terminated the meeting as follows:

LEADER: All right, look here, let's get busy on this—all of you—all of us, let's do something about it.

Supervisor B left the meeting, flushed, tense, and obviously unhappy. As he passed through the door, he muttered to himself, "Those g—— d—— budgets!" (Note that the budgets are immediately blamed for the unhappiness.)

Supervisor B hurried down to his area of the plant. He rushed in the office and called his subordinates abruptly. "Joe—get over here—I want to speak to you—something's up."

The subordinates came in, all wondering what had occurred. As soon as they had all assembled, the supervisor started:

SUPERVISOR B: Look, we've just got to get at this waste. It makes me look like ——. Now let's put our heads together and get on the ball.

The supervisors set to work to locate the causes for the waste. Their methods were interesting. Each one of them first checked to see, as one of them put it, "that the other guys (departments) aren't cheating us." A confidential statement finally arrived in Supervisor B's hands from one of the subordinates to the effect that he had located the cause for waste in another department.

Supervisor B became elated, but at the same time was angry at the fact that he had been made to look "sick" at the meeting with the leader.

SUPERVISOR B: . . . I'm going to find out why they are making the waste. I don't mind taking a little——, as long as it's me that's doing the trouble.

Supervisor B roared out of his office and headed straight for the office of Supervisor A, where the confidential sources had reported the waste. Supervisor A saw him coming, and braced himself for the onslaught.

SUPERVISOR B:——, I found out that it's your boys causing the waste.——, I want to know why——. . . .

SUPERVISOR A (*Cuts off Supervisor B . . . spits out some tobacco and says*): Now, just hold on to your water. Don't get your blood up. I'll tell you. . . .

Briefly, we have tried to show, by a running account of one small problem, the effects budgets can have upon people. In this cost-conscious plant, five or six people on the supervisory level spent many man-hours trying to place the blame on someone else.

4. *As usually administered, the budget process does not involve workers.* As the foremen point out, it is probably fortunate for management that the process does not reach workers—as it is ordinarily carried out. If the foremen did indeed transmit to workers the cost pressures they themselves feel, the losses incurred by management would certainly outweigh any gains that could be made. On the other hand, the behavior of workers is certainly of great importance in creating the figures that the budget process reports. Therefore, it does seem ironic that workers are

left out of the process altogether. We may ask whether there might not be some way of involving workers in the process without incurring the losses that would normally be expected.

The budget-making process

The process by which the budget is made up has important consequences for the reactions of operating people to that budget. Let us consider two contrasting cases.

The first is taken from the company in the Argyris-Miller study, where production supervisors reported feeling under the most extreme budget pressures. Here we found a common belief that accountants were running the company. In fact we found that a very high proportion of the men in top management were accountants by educational background.

Let me digress to point out the general significance of this phenomenon. While most large companies recruit men of a variety of educational backgrounds and promote to higher management levels men from the several functional specialties, we often do find that one particular category of men has much more than its proportionate share in the higher positions. Thus we find members reporting that company A is run by engineers, company B by salesmen, company C by accountants, and so on.

The effects of such a promotional emphasis may go far beyond the careers of individual members. Men of a given category are likely to see the organization and its problems in similar ways, and when they hold the dominant positions, they are able to impose their own views upon the structure and procedures of the organization.

In the accountant-dominated company, the controller in the main office was naturally a powerful figure. Furthermore, his power extended into every plant. Reporting directly to the controller, and independent of the plant manager, the plant controller was responsible for the direction of the plant office and also for the budgets for office and plant. The controller would hand down to each plant controller the targets they should seek to establish so that the figures for each plant would fit into the overall company budget the controller was to recommend to the president and board of directors. The plant controller would then work out the figures for departments and the plant as a whole.

In this process, the plant controller was not required to seek out the collaboration of operating management. Collaboration did not generally take place, and sharp conflicts between plant manager and plant controller were commonly observed. In the one case where we found collaboration, it seemed something more than a coincidence that the plant manager himself was an accountant. While this may have helped to smooth relations between the two men, it did nothing to relieve budget pressures perceived at lower operating levels. In fact, we see the plant manager calling cost men into meetings with superintendents to help him apply the pressure to them.

In the second case, while we have much less systematic information, the process seemed to be quite different. In this company, the vice-president and controller was considered to be a staff man responsible for establishing the cost control and accounting procedures for the company as a whole. He was also looked upon as a technical consultant to the cost control people in the plant. However, each plant manager had a plant controller reporting directly to him. It was the plant manager who presented the preliminary budget for his plant to the general manager and the president of the company. At least in some cases, this preliminary budget grew out of considerable discussion that the plant manager held with his superintendents and with his controller.

The president then reviewed with his general manager the preliminary budgets submitted from the plants. He reported that he sometimes acted to tighten up a plant budget but at least as often decided that the goals set were unrealistically high and should be somewhat reduced. It was his aim to establish budgets that *could be met*. The involvement of the supervisors in the budget-making process and the establishment of goals that seemed reasonable to them combined to make them feel under less budget pressures than the supervisors in the first case reported.

Summary and conclusions

Budgets provide the primary set of symbols by which the performance of managers and supervisors is judged. The budget-making and implementation process is therefore highly *salient* not only to the budget makers but especially to the people whose performance is so judged. Supervisors are not likely to be indifferent toward the budget and cost control people.

If budgets are established without any participation in the process by departmental supervisors, we can expect the supervisors to hold strongly negative sentiments toward the budgeteers. The budget makers are likely to have a negative view of human nature and feel that men will be too lazy to perform well unless they have exacting standards imposed upon them. Supervisors who work under such tight standards that they find themselves constantly experiencing failure tend to become demoralized.

As often administered, budgets tend to focus supervisory attention on the past rather than on present or future. If higher management relies heavily upon budgets to control subordinates, the supervisors find themselves so often called upon to justify past failures to meet the standards that they find it difficult to think of the present and plan for the future.

Pressure from budgets tends to promote interdepartmental friction. If the departmental supervisor is called to account by superiors for falling short of his budget, he may consider three possible strategies of response:

1. Undertake to do better in the future.
2. Claim that the budgetary standards are unfair.
3. Claim that sub-par performance was due to problems created for one's own department by some other department.

The first strategy provides no immediate solution. It will take some time to demonstrate this improved performance, whereas the superior is applying "the needle" to past performance. Furthermore, the supervisor assumes that if he really does better in the future, the standards will be raised further so that he will again be in a failure situation. The second strategy is no more promising. The manager who is trying to apply pressure with the budget is not likely to respond favorably to a strategy that would tend to disarm him. Thus the third strategy may appear to the supervisor as his only possible escape. He therefore tries to blame other supervisors for his apparent failure—and at the same time to be on guard against others who, in the same situation, would like to pin the blame on him.

Can these negative effects of budgets and cost control be avoided—without the loss of performance? Suppose we ask each supervisor to make up his own budget. To relieve him further from pressure from above, suppose we even leave it to him to report to superiors at the end of each period how he did in relation to his own standards.

We can imagine this strategy working well in a small organization and as part of a general program to involve supervisors in decision making. We cannot imagine the strategy working in a large organization, no matter what the leadership philosophy of top management. Budgets are not used simply to put pressure on supervisors. They are used by higher management in relation to current performance figures to assess the relationship between past plans and current performance, to plan future production and financial requirements.

We assume that higher management must continue to be involved in budget setting, but we do not have to assume that the process will be carried out without any participation of the supervisors whose perform-ance is being judged. Supervisors will respond less negatively to budgets and budgeting specialists if they themselves play a more prominent role in the process than is generally the case.

We also suspect that few managements are exploiting budgets in terms of their teaching and learning potential for budget specialists and supervi-sors alike. One supervisor gave us this clue in these words:

So they tell me that I didn't make my budget. Well, that is of interest, but the real question is: Why didn't I make the budget? They don't give me any help in answering that question.

In many plants, the cost control specialists present their findings on departmental performance not to the supervisor but to his superior. The cost control man may interact with the supervisor only when he is called in by a manager to help prove to the supervisor how badly he performed. In this highly negative situation, the supervisor is not likely to admit that he does not fully understand the budget or ask the cost control man to help him to interpret it and to use it more effectively in his department.

This suggests an approach along different lines: In this approach, the supervisor and the budget specialist work together in preparing the departmental budget. Each month they again get together to review performance figures against the budget. The budget specialist uses the budget not as a club but, in relation to performance figures, as a diagnostic instrument. He tries to help the supervisor to understand the budget so that he can even arrive at his own diagnosis. In the process, the budget specialist gains from the supervisor a far more realistic picture of departmental operations and problems than he would otherwise have. Thus, even if he alone prepares the first draft of the departmental budget, it is more likely that the supervisor will find it realistic and reasonable. The process also should influence the budget specialist's sentiments toward the supervisor. With this approach, he is less likely to consider the supervisor a lazy man who needs to be "needled" and more likely to consider him a responsible individual who is eager to improve his performance.

Since we do not have research data to back up this proposed approach, the argument must remain speculative. Nevertheless, note how we have gone about changing the sentiments of supervisors toward budget specialists (and vice versa) and the sentiments supervisors have toward themselves and their jobs. We have proposed a reorganization of the interactions and activities of budget specialists and supervisors. We proceed on the assumption that if changes are introduced in I and A, changes in S will necessarily follow. If this fundamental assumption is correct, then our framework can at least guide us to changes that are worth trying out.

References

Argyris, Chris, under the direction of Schuyler Dean Hoslett, with the assistance of Frank B. Miller, Jr. *The Impact of Budgets on People.* Ithaca, N.Y.: Cornell University School of Business and Public Administration, 1952. The first organizational behavior study of the human impact of cost control and budgeting procedures and still the best thing of its kind.

Gardner, Burleigh B., and Moore, David G. *Human Relations in Industry,* rev. ed. Homewood, Ill.: Richard D. Irwin, Inc., 1964. See Chapter 7, "The Factory Organization and the Division of Labor," especially section on "Control Organizations," pp. 205–14. A good, brief introduction.

Discussion questions

1. Select an organization with which you are familiar. How are the symbols of success/failure established? Who participates in the goal and standard-setting process? With what consequences?

2. Interview a person with some experience in a work organization where he has been involved either in setting up the symbols of success/failure or in having them applied to him. Answer the same questions as above.

17. The role of the personnel man

Who is the personnel man? What does he do? Where does he fit into the organization?

In this Chapter, I am not trying to provide technical answers to those questions. The student must turn to text books in personnel administration to find the detailed specifications of the personnel man's job and the directions as to how he goes about developing programs of wage and salary administration, merit rating, and so on. I shall seek rather to provide a social answer to those questions: to examine the role of the personnel man and the way he plays that role in the organization.

The evolution of the personnel department

Personnel departments, as we find them today, should be seen against the background of their evolution. They have arisen primarily in response to certain pressures upon the management organization. In large measure, these pressures have been generated by unions.[1]

The industrial relations department is one of the union's chief contributions to the management organization. Even some of these departments in nonunion companies must be considered in large measure a response to the push of unionization. There were specialized industrial relations functionaries in the mass production industries before the advent of unions, but in most cases their activities in the twenties and early thirties were confined to the process of initial employment.

By the 1940's, industrial relations activities had expanded greatly, and the top man now generally carried the title of manager of industrial relations or of employee relations or personnel. He was still outranked by the vice presidents of sales, engineering, manufacturing, and so on.

The records show that the personnel man has now arrived, at least insofar as formal management recognition of his importance is concerned.

---

[1] Most of this section is from my chapter on "The Impact of the Union on the Management Organization," in Conrad M. Arensberg *et al.* (eds.), *Research in Industrial Human Relations* (New York: Harper & Bros., 1957), pp. 171–4.

Dalton E. McFarland[2] has made a survey with responses from line executives and personnel executives, the sample being divided equally in three parts, companies with 500 to 999 employees, those with 1,000 to 4,999 and those with over 5,000.

Based on the responses of 245 top personnel men, he finds 6.6 percent reporting to the chairman of the board, 51.1 percent reporting to the president, and 18.9 percent reporting to the executive vice president or to a group of vice presidents. The remainder report to such officials as treasurer, secretary, controller, line vice president, staff vice president, manager, or superintendent. This distribution suggests that probably over two thirds of the top personnel men have attained the rank of vice president.

The union created an obvious need for the development of negotiators within the industrial relations department. In some companies with many plants and many different contracts, a group of men can spend all of their time throughout the year in preparing for negotiations and in negotiating contracts. But this is not all. Unions create other needs involved in the day-to-day administration of the work force.

Unions have weakened the workers' dependent relationship upon management. Years ago, many management people prided themselves upon taking personal interest in the welfare of their workers. This meant that they might grant special consideration to workers beset with personal difficulties or unable by reason of health or age to carry on their regular jobs. But these favors were generally based as much upon attitude toward management as upon need. The "loyal" employee might expect to be "taken care of," whereas there would be no favors for the "troublemaker."

Union pressure has generally put an end to this sort of situation. Unions insist that what a man receives in pay, in hospitalization benefits, in his retirement plan, and so on, shall not be subject to the discretion of management, but shall be determined by policies established to some degree through contract negotiations.

On all fronts, the union has demanded standardization, and management has had to hire specialists and develop special activities in order to meet these demands.

To justify its wage and promotion system, management has had to develop procedures for job descriptions and job evaluations. Taylor's scientific management movement began such activity before large-scale unionization, but it was immensely stimulated by union pressure.

Unions have exercised heavy pressure through the grievance procedure on matters of discipline and promotion. This has led not only to the creation of a set of functionaries to deal with the union on grievance

---

[2] Dalton E. McFarland, *Company Officers Assess the Personnel Function* (AMA Research Study 79, New York: American Management Association, 1967).

procedures, but also to efforts to standardize management's policies and to build up the necessary paper records for dealing with the union.

In the past, management has claimed the right to promote the ablest individual, regardless of seniority. But how is ability to be determined? Before unionization, in some cases promotions simply went to the workers who were able to ingratiate themselves with the foremen. Such favoritism accounts for much of the union pressure to establish seniority as a basis for promotion. Even before unionization, many managements followed seniority in promotion in most cases, and today most managements seem willing to promote by seniority in relatively unskilled jobs. However, most managements seek to retain the right to consider ability on skilled jobs. In some cases, unions are willing to agree on this in principle, but they demand proof of relative qualifications. This has forced management to examine its jobs carefully and to keep more adequate records upon the performance of individual workers.

Unionization frequently released a flood of grievances and complaints against foremen. Often this led higher management people to see the foreman as a scapegoat for all the ills of worker-management relations. If this were true, then something had to be done to train the foreman to establish better human relations with his workers. This interest led to the widespread development of training programs in American industry. The union influence did not stop at this point, for as the more sophisticated management people began to recognize that some of the problems had their roots above the foreman level, the emphasis in training shifted toward higher levels in the organization.

Union pressure for fringe benefits created a need for a new type of specialist within the industrial relations organization: a man who knew something about principles of insurance and actuarial problems.

These new activities have led to a professionalization of the personnel field. In making its first response to the union, management often looked toward some individual whose sole or main qualification was that he got along well with people. Such an individual may find favor with workers and union officials at the outset, but management soon finds that just "knowing how to get along with people" is not enough. Including as it does contract negotiation, wage and salary administration, selection and employment, safety, merit rating, job description, job evaluation, grievance handling, training, benefit programs, and so on, the field of industrial relations has become highly technical. The industrial relations administrator does not need to know the technical details in all of these areas, but he must have a general familiarity with them sufficient to know whether his subordinates are talking sense or nonsense. Furthermore, the stakes in industrial relations have become so high that management cannot tolerate the well-meaning bungler who merely happens to "like people."

We now have college and graduate school programs designed to train men in industrial relations, and industrial relations men in industry are seeking to enhance the standing of their field through clothing it with professional regalia. While this urge toward professionalization may have some roots in a desire to add to the prestige of the field, nevertheless the job functions have become sufficiently technical and specialized to lead naturally in the direction of professionalization.

While noting the influence of unions, we should not think in terms of a simple cause–effect relationship. Before the advent of unions, there were people in management who would have liked to develop an improved human relations program but found themselves blocked by management's preoccupation with the "practical" matters of costs, technology, etc. Possible slowdowns and strikes being matters of obvious practical concern, unions have greatly strengthened the hand of many people who were privately (but ineffectually) committed to a broader social viewpoint.

How to organize the personnel department

An earlier study by McFarland[3] shows four general patterns for the organization of the personnel department.

1. *The integrated department*, found in 69.6 percent of the cases studied, was by far the most common pattern, with labor relations and personnel activities combined under a single personnel executive, who reported directly to a high-level line official.
2. *The extended department* is an integrated department, as above, but with the addition of other functions such as a community or public relations. This was found in 16.7 percent of the cases.
3. *The split function organization* involves the separation of personnel from labor relations, with the executive of each function reporting to some higher company officer. This was found in 8.8 percent of the cases.
4. *The staff-coordinated department* involves either an integrated or extended staff unit but one which reports to a central staff executive rather than to a high line official. This was found in 4.9 percent of the cases.

McFarland notes that personnel men in industry generally have very little influence in the design of formal organization. They rarely have much to say even about how their own department should be structured. In fact, he notes a fairly widespread use of what he calls the "trash can" approach to assignment of functions in the personnel department. Higher officials have a tendency to assign to personnel functions that do not seem to fit very well anywhere else—whether or not they fit well in personnel.

---

[3] Dalton E. McFarland, *Cooperation and Conflict in Personnel Administration* (New York: American Foundation for Management Research, 1962), p. 24.

While we have seen that top personnel men generally have been quite successful in achieving high organizational rank, their lack of influence on organization structure suggests that their power in the organization has not risen as rapidly as has their status.

The nature of personnel functions

The personnel department has a broad, general responsibility for employee relations: for the adjustment of workers to the job situation and for the handling of worker problems that arise in this situation. In many companies, this same general responsibility is extended to supervisory levels. Sometimes we find such responsibilities even for higher level personnel, with executive development and placement programs being found in personnel departments, but perhaps more often these functions are kept outside of personnel.

While this broad area of responsibility is well recognized, it is often assumed that the personnel man does not have any authority for the carrying out of these responsibilities. According to traditional organization theory, he is a staff specialist. It is his job to provide management with special personnel services and also with advice regarding personnel problems.

Is is true that the personnel man does not exercise authority? Consider the comments of three personnel executives:[4]

Well, its staff with a lot of things, but with the basic policies it's my job to put them down, tell everybody what they are, and see that they are enforced. Now, it's all in the way you do this. We are supposed to do it in certain ways and not in other ways. We are prevented from doing it by force or by the use of authority, but nevertheless we must take vigorous action in order to get that job done and get it done right.

The line management knows that we will be in hot water in a hell of a hurry if personnel recommends something and they don't do it. When we tell them something should be done in a certain way they usually follow it, because if they are wrong, it will be their neck.

This job is supposed to be sort of a staff job, but I got more authority around here than anybody who is really supposed to have authority. People around here know that when I say something they might just as well assume it is an order and follow it, because if they don't, they will hear from the top man. They come to me with an awful lot of things to decide, and usually they find out they are better off if they let me decide them than if they try to decide them for themselves.

Are these statements extreme? Perhaps, but they point to the general problem of distinguishing between traditional theory and actual practice. If, by authority, we mean the ability of an individual to tell another individual what to do *and directly* to apply sanctions on him for failure

---

[4] *Ibid.*, pp. 94–6.

to comply, then generally personnel men do not have authority outside of their own departments. However, as other executives find out, the personnel man may be in a position to bring in heavy sanctions through his organizational superior, and thus he is able to tell people what to do and get it done just as readily as if he himself could apply sanctions.

Personnel men often have the direct power of veto in certain activities. For example, let us say that the company has a policy regarding merit increases for employees. The policy will spell out the frequency with which individuals can be considered for increases, the grounds for increases, the proportion of workers in a given department that can be given such increases at any time period, and the procedures to be utilized by supervisors in proposing men for merit increases. Generally such procedures require approval by the personnel department. Thus the personnel man has a direct veto and can only be overruled by appeal to a superior officer. Since the supervisor will have lower status than the personnel man, and therefore needs the backing of his line superior to challenge the ruling of the personnel department, we can expect such appeals to be rare. The supervisor is much more likely to wind up the case by telling the worker in question, "I put in for an increase for you, but the personnel department turned it down."

When the personnel executive speaks of "enforcing policy," he is telling us that he also has an inspection function. To get policy enforced, he has to develop information on violations, so he and his associates in personnel have to be able to go over records and look around to determine who is doing what wrong. Later in this chapter we will consider the implications of these inspection, enforcement, and vetoing activities for the development of the consulting role of the personnel man.

What functions can the personnel man carry out to contribute to the work satisfaction of organizational members and to the efficiency of their performance? We now recognize that satisfaction and efficiency are both strongly influenced by the formal structure of the organization, by technology and work flow, and by the way changes are being introduced into the formal structure and into the technology and work flow. Generally speaking, personnel men claim neither power nor expertise in these areas, and line managers rarely look to them for advice when contemplating such changes. For example, in a division of a large company I once studied, the divisional personnel manager was very highly regarded by the division superintendent, to whom he reported, and the two were often seen together. Nevertheless, a drastic change in organization structure in this division was carried out with only minimal involvement on the part of the personnel man. He knew nothing about the plans until he sat in on the management meeting at which all the changes were announced. He played no part in this meeting except to suggest that the experts who had worked out the reorganization plan should take pains to explain it carefully at lower levels of the organization. (It is always a safe thing for the personnel man to suggest that communication is important and more attention should be paid to it. Such a statement will always elicit agreement—whether or not any further action results.)

The personnel man, in describing this meeting to me, did not seem to be expressing any dissatisfaction with his own role and that of his department. In this particular company there was another department which handled problems of organization structure. The personnel department kept itself busy with personnel programs: wage and salary administration, safety, fringe benefits, and so on.

If the personnel man is generally ruled out of areas having such a critical impact upon satisfaction and efficiency, what can he do to discharge the responsibilities so generally accorded him? There are three types of activities that have been utilized, with varying emphases and degrees of success: personnel counseling, training, and consulting.

Personnel counseling

Personnel counseling in industry has been of two general types which we may describe as social work assistance or psychotherapy. While we will here be primarily concerned with the psychotherapeutic approach to counseling, let us not overlook the possible continuing utility of the social work assistance approach.

Suppose an employee comes to consult a personnel man about the health problems of a child. The employee is not likely to be satisfied with a nondirective answer: "You are worried about your child's health?" Many employees simply lack information about the available facilities and institutions in their city designed to provide the type of assistance they may need. If the personnel man is equipped with the relevant information, he can provide a welcome service to the employee without any negative consequences.

On the other hand, we must recognize that many problems workers face are not to be solved simply through the provision of information. Does the worker need advice? The early history of personnel activities in the United States provides examples of many programs designed to advise workers on how to solve life's problems according to accepted social work standards. The weight of expert opinion is now running against this advice-giving approach. The assumption now is that the problems of the individual cannot be solved for him by someone else. He must work his own way through to the solution of his problems, but a skilled counselor can help him to find his path.

The counseling approaches of Carl Rogers[5] and of the Western Electric program developed independently but along the same lines in the

---

[5] Carl Rogers, *Counseling and Psychotherapy* (Boston, Mass.: Houghton Mifflin Co., 1942).

mid-1930's. Both were based upon the assumption that a person may need help in talking his problems out more than he needs advice, and counselors were trained to take a nondirective approach. Since we now have an important book reviewing the development and history of the counseling program at Western Electric Company and since this has been the best known counseling program in industry, we will review it in some detail here.[6]

A special counseling organization was set up in the Hawthorne plant of Western Electric Company within the personnel department in 1936. Personnel counselors were assigned to various areas in the plant. They were free to spend much of their time in the workplace, observing and engaging in informal interaction with workers and supervisors. Each counselor also had his own office separate from the factory workplace, and he was free to make appointments with workers (and with supervisors) for interviews in this office. Workers received their regular hourly pay while in the counselor's office.

Dickson and Roethlisberger described the role of the counselor in this way:[7]

But the role of the counselor was not just that of a disinterested observer; he was also trying to improve his skill in the direction of opening up avenues of communication between persons and helping persons to help themselves. He was not just a researcher seeking knowledge; he was also a practitioner trying to improve his understanding, skills, and sensitivities about others and himself and by this improved practice trying to make helpful interventions. He was trying to clarify situations for others as well as for himself. The role prescriptions for this orientation were:

1. *Listen—don't talk.*
2. *Never argue; never give advice.*
3. *Listen to*
   a) *What the person wants to say.*
   b) *What he does not want to say.*
   c) *What he cannot say without help.*
4. *Become sensitive to the expression of feelings.* Learn to recognize and reflect them.
5. *Help the person to clarify and accept his own feelings.* Do this by summarizing from time to time what has been said (e.g., "Is this the way you are feeling?"). Always do this with great caution, that is, clarify but do not add or twist.
6. *Help the person to make his own decisions; do not make them for him.*
7. *Try to understand the person from his point of view; do not put yourself in his shoes.* Put him in his own shoes.

---

[6] W. J. Dickson and F. J. Roethlisberger, *Counseling in an Organization: A Sequel to the Hawthorne Researches* (Boston, Mass.: Harvard University Graduate School of Business Administration, 1960).

[7] *Ibid.*, p. 42.

8. *Never forget that you are involved in the situations you are observing.* Learn to recognize and accept your own feelings. Don't try to escape from them—learn to accept them and deal with them through skill and understanding.

   a) Take it easy.

   b) Stay loose.

   c) Be flexible.

   d) Internalize these role prescriptions so that they become congruent with yourself. Don't be a copycat. Be true to yourself.

   e) Be natural.

It is sometimes claimed that the counseling program in Western Electric was based on the assumption that the problems troubling workers primarily had their origin outside of the plant situation and that the program was designed to encourage the workers to think that this was the case. An analysis of the "topics of concern expressed by 736 employees who requested interviews with counselors, September, 1953–December, 1954" leads to the following general statement:[8]

. . . We can see that far more (63 percent) of these employees were concerned about work-related problems than about personal problems, and that men outnumbered women in this respect—66 percent contrasted with 60 percent. More women than men were concerned about personal problems and interpersonal relations at work, and more men than women were concerned about other job factors. These findings support what are generally held beliefs about these matters. The dominance of work-related concerns among both men and women, however, should serve to dispel any assumption that employee concerns were primarily about matters unrelated to their work situations.

From its outset, the personnel counseling program was plagued by a number of dilemmas which were never satisfactorily resolved. Let us review them here.

1. *The relations between counseling and research.* At the outset, it was assumed that the data gathered in the counseling program would somehow be utilized for research purposes, though how this was to be done was not classified in advance. The program did from time to time issue general reports about the state of morale in the plant, about reactions to the introduction of technological changes, and so on, but these were simply based upon interpretation of bodies of interview material collected for therapeutic purposes. The role definitions for the counselors apparently precluded the systematic work on particular problems that would be necessary for research purposes. As time went on, apparently even general interpretive reports became less frequent.

---

[8] *Ibid.,* pp. 70–72.

2. *Relations with supervision.* Suppose a given supervisor was having difficulties with his subordinates and suppose the counselor had gathered a good deal of information that would tend to explain the sources of the difficulties. Could the counselor then go to the supervisor and offer to feed back the data gathered, in general terms, so as to help the supervisor understand his situation? Apparently some supervisors expected or hoped that this would be done. It naturally stirred their anxieties, when they were involved in friction with subordinates, to see the counselor carrying on interviews in which the subordinate's picture of his supervisor must have played a prominent part. But, according to the rules of the counseling program, the counselor could not provide the supervisor with such feedback, since this was considered a violation of confidences, even when the interpretation was provided without naming names of informants. The best that the counselor could do was interview the supervisor himself, hoping that it would help the supervisor somewhat to talk his problems out.

3. *Service to management?* In the very nature of the program, it was exceedingly difficult to provide any concrete evidence that personnel counseling was performing a useful service to management. From time to time, the counseling organization did use the interview data to provide materials for supervisory training programs. While this was appreciated, the contribution seemed relatively small in relation to the large amounts of money being invested in the program. Many management people were naturally concerned with such questions as "What are they doing?" and "Is it doing us any good?" The best defense for counseling was found in testimonials that came from individual supervisors and managers, who claimed that they had found the program helpful, but even these endorsements were phrased in such general terms as to be hardly convincing to the skeptical.

4. *Individual or organizational therapy?* The designers of the personnel counseling program hoped that counseling would not only aid individuals to solve their personal problems but would also somehow contribute to the solution of organizational problems. As time went on, it became increasingly evident that while the program was helpful to some proportion of the individuals interviewed, it had little if any impact upon organizational problems.

5. *Frustration of counselors.* Many of the counselors gained a high degree of skill in interviewing so that they were able to develop a penetrating picture of organizational problems as well as the individual adjustment problems of the interviewees. This naturally led them to develop ideas as to what might be done to solve one or another organizational problem. As they found no way of bringing those ideas to bear on the organization, they naturally came to doubt the value of their work and became increasingly restive with the role they were playing.

Dickson and Roethlisberger close their analysis with this remarkably frank evaluation:[9]

> So, viewed as an experiment, the counseling program had demonstrated well not only the utility of counseling for certain persons but also its limited utility for securing the organizational changes that were required to achieve its goals. It had pressed a certain set of ideas to its limits and, by so doing, learned something, as is said, the hard way.

Personnel counseling at Western Electric lasted for 20 years, being finally terminated in 1956. Now that this most ambitious effort has come to an end at Western Electric, it seems unlikely that any other company will try anything like it. This is not to say that the program did no good. It is to say that there must be other approaches to the solution of human problems in the work situation that would produce more generally satisfactory results with the same investment of money and talent.

Training

At the outset we must distinguish between training in job skills and human relations training. While there are certainly better and worse ways of training a worker to become a lathe operator or a mechanic, in general there seems to be little doubt regarding the payoff of effort and money put into such training activities. At least for our purposes, we can assume that such training does enable workers to learn their jobs better and faster.

Our concern is with human relations training: with programs designed to make supervisors and managers more effective in handling their interpersonal relations on the job. Do such training programs in fact help the trainees to do better? Is it possible even through such training programs to effect changes in the way the whole organization functions? The best we can say in answer to both questions is that it is not yet possible to give a positive answer with any assurance. The early research in training evaluation has hardly been encouraging.

Edwin A. Fleishman, Edwin F. Harris, and Harold E. Burtt, at Ohio State, found that the International Harvester Company program had effected no gain in these supervisor-worker relationships—and perhaps it had even resulted in a slight loss.[10] The University of Michigan Survey Research Center's study of a training program in two divisions of the Detroit Edison Company showed a small overall gain.[11] However, it was

---

[9] *Ibid.*, pp. 447–48.

[10] Edwin A. Fleishman, Edwin F. Harris and Harold E. Burtt, *Leadership and Supervision in industry: An Evaluation of a Supervisory Training Program* (Monograph No. 33, Bureau of Educational Research [Columbus: Ohio State University Press, 1955]).

[11] Norman A. Maier, *Principles of Human Relations* (New York: John Wiley & Sons, 1952), pp. 184–92.

found that there had been a loss of ground in one division, which was more than compensated for by gain in the other.

How can we account for these results? Were the programs in themselves no good? No doubt better training can be given, but probably these courses were a good deal better than the average in industry today.

We find the best explanation by looking at the two divisions in the Detroit Edison study. The researchers found that in the division where progress had been made, the foremen were led by a higher management that supervised them very much in line with the principles developed in the course. On the other hand, in the division that lost ground, the foremen were under superiors who directed them in a manner that was entirely out of harmony with the program.

These findings suggest that the effectiveness of a training program for lower level supervisors depends in a very large measure on the way that program is supported at higher levels in the organization. Nor can that support be simply verbal. Real success depends on the actions of top management in its day-to-day behavior.

The lack of positive results from training directed at the first-line supervisory level only has led trainers to seek to develop programs aimed at higher levels of management. There have also been efforts to develop new types of training. While it is generally felt that a case-discussion approach is better than simply giving supervisors lectures on good methods of supervision, it has become apparent that case discussion hardly presents a satisfactory answer. It seems quite possible for many people to analyze someone else's problems in a very effective fashion and yet be unable to apply the same analytical skills to problems in which they are personally involved. Human relations trainers have therefore sought to develop training methods that would more directly and more personally involve the trainees.

The most common name of such training approaches is "sensitivity training." Here the trainer seeks to get his group to focus directly upon the interpersonal and organizational problems they face in the work situation and upon the problems they have in relating to each other in the discussion group. There seems no doubt that trainees participating in such sessions do become much more personally and emotionally involved than is generally the case with discussions of cases outside of their own experience.

There is also a simulation approach that has been developed by Herbert Shephard and others. Here the aim is to develop in a training laboratory situations that will be analogous to problems commonly faced on the job. In Chapter 8 we have described at some length training exercises designed to help trainees understand and cope with intergroup rivalry and competition problems. Here again there is no doubt that participants in such simulated problems become very much personally involved, so that the trainer, in the subsequent discussion, can deal with both the intellectual and emotional problems encountered in the situations under study.

Let us consider the training approach of one of the ablest practitioners in the field: Chris Argyris.[12]

What is Argyris trying to do? In recent years he has been focusing primarily upon problems of communication and interpersonal relations at high levels in organizations. The concentration on high levels is explained by Argyris's belief that only the top officials have the leverage upon the organization to bring about the kind of far-reaching changes that he has in mind.

Argyris argues that most hierarchical organizations operate so as to limit communication among members of management to technical, rational considerations. The expression of emotion in committee or other business meetings is discouraged. When the formal leader of the discussion finds an individual becoming emotional, it is thought that he should change the subject or take other actions which would prevent the open examination of feelings in the group situation. When this kind of communication norm prevails, the subordinate may find himself seriously upset by proposals for action from his organizational superior to which he feels he is prevented from making any effective reply. Since to express how he feels would seem to reveal him as a person incapable of controlling himself adequately, he can only try to phrase objections in technical, rational terms which may have no relationship to the real problem as he sees it. When communication proceeds in this fashion, according to Argyris, superiors universally receive assent from subordinates for actions they propose, only to find out later that the actions have not been carried out as they had hoped. This leads them to "sell" their own point of view even harder next time, thus still further stifling the possibility of feedback which would reveal to them more of the nature of the interpersonal problems with which they are dealing.

The Argyris prescription for this condition is not a substitution of emotionalism for technical, rational discussion. He advocates what he calls "openness" or "authenticity," which is his particular combination of rational *and* emotional communication. Openness does not mean that each individual should express whatever is on his mind regardless of any concern for the feelings of others. The aim is to create a situation in which the members of an organization who are working closely together can each express how they feel about problems in their relationships in such a manner as to help those with whom they are communicating to express themselves in a similar open manner. The theory is that the emotional problems within the group do not simply disappear when they are not faced by members of the group; rather they tend to obstruct the carrying out of the rational plans of the members. The theory holds further that the technical problems can be more effectively resolved if emotional problems are not suppressed but are dealt with along with a development of rational plans.

Argyris believes that the barriers to his desired authenticity stem in part from such environmental forces as the organization structure, the budget and

---

[12] The discussion of the Argyris approach is taken from W. F. Whyte and E. L. Hamilton, *Action Research for Management* (Homewood, Ill.: Richard D. Irwin Inc., and The Dorsey Press, 1964). For Argyris' own reports on his approach, see particularly, *Interpersonal Competence and Organizational Effectiveness*, and *Organization and Innovation* (Homewood, Ill.: Richard D. Irwin, Inc. and The Dorsey Press, 1962 and 1965, respectively).

other control systems, the technology, and so on. He therefore does not see a change in interpersonal relations and perceptions at the top level as a solution to the basic human problems of organizations. He rather looks to these interpersonal changes as providing the necessary first step toward the facing of the structural changes that need to be carried through.

The change agent cannot do everything at once. Should he seek to change organizational behavior through working on the quality of interpersonal communication or through restructuring activities and interactions?

Argyris has demonstrated that his strategy may result in significant changes in the behavior of those going through the training experience. He acknowledges that these changes do not readily filter down through the organization, so that further research-training efforts may be needed at successively lower levels. He also recognizes that the favorable changes in interpersonal relations can be neither maintained nor extended unless they are supported by the sort of environmental changes we have been emphasizing.

Argyris has not yet demonstrated that executives who go through a training experience that reshapes their own interpersonal relations will necessarily go on to change the social, economic, and physical environment of the organization so as to support the kinds of changes in interpersonal relations he has introduced. For this reason I question the emphasis he places upon T-group and related types of training. If we indeed do agree upon the importance of the environment of work, then it seems to me more promising to design interventions that will have a direct impact upon the work environment, rather than seeking to get at that environment through human relations training. By following this environmental route, we will indeed need to do some training as we go along and we may find the Argyris approach to training particularly effective at the top levels of the organization. This is not an either-or argument. We do not yet have a study which effectively integrates our environmental emphasis with the interpersonal sensitivity emphasis of Argyris. A project which attempted such integration would offer much to both approaches.

The Argyris effort leaves still unresolved the problem of moving from laboratory training into the plant situation itself. There seems general agreement that it is a good idea to give supervisors or managers their first exposure to sensitivity training in a laboratory situation, where they will be less inhibited in discussion than they would be back at the plant. But can his kind of training then be carried directly into the plant? One exponent of this point of view writes in this way about the experience in his own company, TRW Systems.[13]

I think one important theme of the nearly four-year organizational change effort at TRW Systems is that of using laboratory training (sensitivity training, T-grouping,) clearly as a means to an end—that of putting most of our energy into on-the-job situations, real-life intergroup problems, real-life, job-family situations, and dealing with them in the here-and-now. This effort

[13] Sheldon A. Davis, "An Organic Problem-Solving Method of Organizational Change," *The Journal of Applied Behavioral Science*, Vol. 3, no. 1, 1967.

has reached a point where sensitivity training, per se, represents only 10 to 15 percent of the effort in our own program. The rest of the effort, 85 to 90 percent, is in on-the-job situations, working on real problems with the people who are involved in them.

If we can judge from other research on learning, we would assume indeed that the closer the training experience can be brought to real life problems, the greater the possibility that what is learned in training will be carried over into the life situation. On the other hand, it remains an open question to what extent the particular characteristics of the TRW Systems Company make this extension of sensitivity training more applicable than might be found in other types of companies. TRW Systems is moderately large, employing about 13,300 persons, and is highly oriented toward technical innovation. About one third of the personnel are professional engineers and half of these even have advanced degrees. While the writer does not give figures for other types of personnel, we would assume that if we added to the professional engineers, other professionals, technical people, and white collar workers, the total would come to far more than half of the 13,300. This is not said in order to discredit what is being done at TRW Systems but to point out that we need to consider not only whether sensitivity training can bring about the constructive changes in any organization, but also whether the approach is much more adapted to some types of organizations than others.

Our general conclusion is that while the sensitivity training efforts are currently far outrunning the research that provides data on constructive results, this general approach does hold more promise than either the very old-fashioned lecture method or the only somewhat less old-fashioned case-discussion method. While the future does look promising with this approach, we must raise some cautions about what this promises for the personnel man. In the first place, we must recognize that a good deal more skill is required for training with this approach than in the lecture or case-discussion approach. Unless the personnel man is prepared to take some time out to get this training, he is well advised to keep out of this area. In fact, most such training has been provided by specialists brought in from outside the company. On the other hand, there is an increasing trend for men in the employ of the personnel department to collaborate with outside specialists and eventually to take over more of the training load.

The personnel man as human relations consultant

The personnel man is expected to be a consultant to line management on human relations problems. If he plays the role effectively, he can indeed meet some of his responsibilities for the morale of the organization.

This is true enough, but how often does the personnel man really play this role? And how effectively does he play it? My experience suggests that there is far more talk about staff advising, in this field, than there is of actual advisory behavior. What are some of the main obstacles against the utilization of this advisory role?

1. *The need for justification.* Personnel men seem still to need ammunition to justify the value of their contribution to the organization. The production man can point to the volume of production, to costs, and so on. The engineer can point to new machines and processes developed and installed. All this is very concrete. The effective consultant performs in a manner which makes it very difficult to measure his contribution. He stimulates other people so that they may come to look upon some of his contributions as their own ideas—and then how does the personnel man get credit for his contribution? Furthermore, it is hard to imagine how the personnel department, in its annual report, could make a case for the value of its advice. We are inclined to expect the receiver of advice to report how helpful it was (which he often fails to do). When the man who gives advice publicly places a value on that advice, this seems boastful and is resented by those receiving the advice.

There is therefore a sense of security in personnel programs. The personnel man can report the number of training programs given, the number of supervisors involved in them, the accident record, the new wage and salary classification system, and so on. There is a natural tendency to concentrate on those aspects of the job that can concretely be reported to higher management. For the personnel man, they become the symbols of organizational performance.

2. *The confidentiality problem.* For the personnel man to function effectively as a consultant, people must be willing to talk with him freely and frankly. Their willingness to do this will be determined in part by their estimate of what he will do with the information they give him. Will the information be treated confidentially? Just what does confidentiality mean?

This problem is illustrated by comments I received in one study from a superintendent of field operations. He explained his failure to call upon personnel men for help in this way:

They tell me that they are just a staff organization. They are here to help you, and you are supposed to bring any problem you want to them. Several times I had a problem somewhere in my group and wanted to consult somebody, so I went up to personnel and told one of them my story. The answer I would get would be, "Let me think about that one. I'll get in touch with you on it."

The next thing I would know, the big boss would call me on the phone, and he would want to know what I was doing about such-and-such. Well, I would tell him I was working on the problem and thought I had it under control. Now the first time that happened, it might have been just a coincidence. But the second time was just once too often. When things like that happen, you feel that you just can't trust them. Now, I feel the less they know about my problems, the better off I am.

When I reported this incident to the personnel people in the central office (without identifying either informant or the man he complained against), the story was greeted with a great sense of outrage. Such a violation of confidences was considered reprehensible, but also extremely rare.

I wonder how rare it actually is. In this case, the man complained against was considered one of the leading district personnel men in the company and shortly went on to a higher position. His close relations with the district manager, to whom he apparently gave the information, might help to explain his advancement. I do not intend to give the impression that this passing of confidential information was a calculated move to win the favor of higher management. The field superintendent worked in a building some distance removed from the district manager and his chief personnel man. The personnel man had an office almost adjoining that of the district manager, and the two were frequently together. The district manager felt rather isolated from the field situation and looked upon his chief personnel man as an individual who really had his finger on the pulse of the organization. Given the fact that the personnel man spent much time with the district manager and little time with the field superintendent, it is easy to understand how the personnel man could let slip comments regarding the field superintendent's problems without even stopping to think of the possible effects on the field superintendent or of the problem of confidentiality.

I suspect, further, that confidences will not be respected within an organization unless certain standards regarding what is and is not confidential have been made explicit. Along with this must go a rationale for the protection of certain information. If confidentiality just depends on the personal ethics of an individual, then there are bound to be varying interpretations of what confidentiality means.

3. *Inspector versus consultant.* Who enforces personnel policy?

In one case I studied, top management became aware of certain difficulties out in the districts that seemed to stem from failures of local management to act in accordance with the contract and company personnel policies. After several problems had arisen over a period of several months in various districts, the president of the company expressed his concern to a personnel man and told him that his department should conduct an "audit" regarding the application of the company's employee relations policy in each plant.

Since the event took place in the elevator of the main office building and since the personnel man was not in charge of his department, he hoped he was safe in forgetting about it. In fact, the president took no further action to require an "audit." However, the fact that the personnel people were so concerned about the possibility of this undertaking suggests that they recognized a problem of role conflict.

It is clearly impossible to be an inspector and a consultant at one and the same time. If the functions are divided within the department so that some men are inspectors and others are consultants, will the consultants be accepted by the operating organization? Or will their identification with the inspecting department render them impotent as consultants? I do not know the answer to these questions, but any management that wishes to develop the role of *consultant* for the personnel man must also be concerned about what, if any, responsibilities he has as *inspector*.

4. *Training for the consultant.* What training does the personnel man have to serve as a consultant in human relations? He may know much of the technical aspects of personnel, but in all too many cases we find he is just a nice chap who likes people, remembers the Golden Rule, and is in favor of "good communication." If those items represent the sum of his human relations equipment, then it is fortunate that he has little opportunity to give advice. An advisor needs some tools to analyze the situations on which he is giving advice.

5. *The advisor without data.* The accountant, the engineer, and other specialists have data that they use to back up their recommendations to management. Unfortunately, everyone in management considers himself a natural hand at human relations. Furthermore, much of the data that the personnel man has is also common knowledge to the rest of the organization, whereas the accountant and the engineer have command of data which is not known to other people until they themselves present it. How is the personnel man going to serve as an advisor to management on human relations when he has no data of his own on which to base his advice?

Summary and conclusions

Over the past three or four decades, the personnel man has risen markedly in status in the industrial hierarchy. Union pressures have been a major force in bringing about this ascent, since unions have pressured top management to give attention to human problems that might otherwise be overlooked.

Does the personnel man have authority? We have seen that this is an unrealistic question. The organization chart indicates that he is not expected to exercise authority, yet we often find him telling people what to do or vetoing proposed actions.

The authority question should be seen in transactional terms. The individual who has subordinates directly reporting to him may be able to develop positive exchange, trading, and even sometimes joint payoff transactions with them. This is less likely to develop between the personnel man and the line management. Their interactions are likely to be much less frequent, which in itself inhibits the development of plus-valued transactions. If the personnel man has the power of approval or disapproval of salary or other personnel proposals of the manager, he gets little if any credit for approval and produces negative values with disapproval. Can the personnel man contribute plus values to line managers? It is assumed that the advice he is asked to give them provides these plus values, but we have found important limitations on the production of such values.

It is an axiom in the counseling field that unsolicited advice is seldom positively valued. If the personnel man is to build up credits in this activity, others must come to ask for his advice. We have noted common situations in which the personnel man produces negative values for the line manager, and this naturally reduces the probability of the line manager coming to him for plus values.

The human problems we have been studying tend to be intimately related to formal organization structure, technology, and the flow of work. In most organizations, these topics are the property of other specialists, and a few people would be likely to call on the personnel man for guidance in these areas. If he were called upon, it is unlikely that he would have anything useful to offer, because the education and experience of the typical personnel man has led him to place "human relations" in a separate compartment from organization structure, technology and work flow.

Consultation also suffers from the liability that it is difficult to symbolize in ways that would make the personnel man's contribution apparent to his superiors. This encourages personnel men to concentrate their time on "programs." While the results of such programs are never measured, at least the number of training courses given, the number of departmental wage and salary studies completed, and so on, can be reported and made to sound very concrete.

Among the many programs to be found in this field, we have singled out for special attention personnel counseling and human relations training. We have found the Hawthorne-style counseling program an ambitious and extremely costly enterprise which did not seem to yield results that would recommend it to other firms. In human relations training, the results have been similarly meager so far. Sensitivity training seems to be an approach that produces a high level of emotional involvement on the part of participants, but how this involvement under laboratory conditions is to be carried over into new behavior in the work situation is not at all clear from the research literature so far available. Even the strongest proponents of such types of training acknowledge the fundamental importance of organization structure, technology, and work flow. This suggests that the most promising direction for future human relations training efforts would be one which sought to integrate changes in interpersonal relations with changes in the structural aspects of the work environment.

References

Argyris, Chris. *Interpersonal Competence and Organizational Effectiveness.* Also *Organization and Innovation.* Homewood, Ill.: Richard D. Irwin, Inc. and the Dorsey Press, 1962 and 1965, respectively. Detailed case reports presenting the Argyris strategy of organizational intervention.

Dickson, W. J., and Roethlisberger, F. J. *Counseling in an Organization:* A *Sequel to the Hawthorne Researches.* Boston: Harvard University Graduate School of Business Administration, 1966. A history of the rise and fall of the famed Hawthorne counseling program.

Fleishman, Edwin A.; Harris, E. F.; and Burtt, Harold E. *Leadership and Supervision in Industry: An Evaluation of a Supervisory Training Program,* Monograph No. 33, Bureau of Educational Research. Columbus: Ohio State University Press, 1955. A classic study of the impact of a supervisory training program.

Gross, Neal; Mason, Ward S.; and McEachern, A. W. *Explorations in Role Analysis.* New York: John Wiley & Sons, 1958. Presents a framework and cases relevant to examination of problems of role conflict, such as those experienced by the personnel man.

McFarland, Dalton E. *Cooperation and Conflict in Personnel Administration.* New York: American Foundation for Management Research, 1962. Also *Company Officers Assess the Personnel Function.* New York: American Management Association, 1967. Two wide-ranging studies on the role of personnel men and how they are perceived by their organizational superiors.

Whyte, W. F., and Hamilton, E. L. *Action Research for Management.* Homewood, Ill.: Richard D. Irwin, Inc. and the Dorsey Press, 1964. A case study of an action-research project designed to change the role of the personnel man.

Discussion questions

1. Find yourself a personnel man or someone who has some experience with personnel men. Interview him to determine:

a) The nature and extent of the personnel man's activities.

b) The personnel man's conception of what he does and of what he thinks others expect of him.

c) The extent of the discrepancies between his conception of his role and the expectations others have of him.

2. To what extent does the concept of "role conflict" provide a useful tool for analysis of the problems of the personnel man? For this purpose, consult particularly pp. 281–318 in Gross, Mason and McEachern (see references). Examine also the two studies of McFarland (see references).

3. Read *Action Research for Management* (see references). To what extent do you think the restructuring of the role of the personnel man described in this book would be applicable to other situations?

18. Patterns of lateral and diagonal relations

Up to this point in Part VI, we have been examining lateral and diagonal relations in terms of case studies of the relations to production departments of maintenance, cost control, and personnel. For want of research data, we have not had a special chapter on one very important department: production control. However, in our chapter on maintenance-production relations, we have in effect given substantial attention to the kinds of problems that arise in production control departments. Whenever maintenance activities grow beyond small-scale mechanical tinkering and get into major repairs and even the fabrication of parts, the scheduling of work presents the same problems as are found in regular production shops. In fact, work-scheduling problems in maintenance are likely to be a good deal more complex because the tasks are much less standardized.

We are omitting one important department or set of departments—engineering. Engineering activities are of such importance that they deserve special treatment. We will consider the impact of engineering in several chapters in Part VIII, which deals with the introduction of change.

The purpose of this chapter is to go beyond the case discussions and to build a systematic framework that would apply to those cases and others. We will set up a typology based on the way interactions and activities are structured. With that approach, we will see that one department may be involved in more than one type of interaction-activity structuring. The framework for this chapter is taken from Leonard Sayles,[1] with minor modifications. I add one category not specifically discussed by him (scheduling relationships), introduce a minor modification into the treatment of auditing relationships, and postpone the treatment of innovating relationships to our discussion of the introduction of changes in Part VIII.

1. Work flow

As organizations grow and diversify in number of activities, with the

---

[1] Leonard Sayles, *Managerial Behavior*. (New York: McGraw-Hill Book Co., 1964).

consequent division of labor, work flow problems become an important focus of management attention. In a company with stable technology and a stable product mix, relations among work units and departments could be routinized. That is, the sequence of activities and interactions could be specified at least in general terms in advance, and most uncertainties could be eliminated. When conditions are changing (as they are in most U.S. companies most of the time), change in any part of the work flow involves changes in other parts. That is, the industrial engineers cannot be content simply with specifying materials to be used and work methods to be applied in the production department. Changes in production methods and materials will almost certainly involve changes imposed upon assembly departments and also upon packaging and shipping.

We can conceive of work flow in the factory in terms of the downstream-upstream dimension. As we move downstream, we are following the sequence of activities through which the materials flow: for example, production, assembly, packaging, and shipping. Upstream movement is in the opposite direction.

If the plant is set up without any conscious attention to these matters, we generally find that the initiation of interaction and of activities between work units tends to follow the downstream direction. That is, the work units that are located farther upstream tend to make their plans first and then communicate them to the downstream units and expect those units to make the appropriate adjustments. Downstream supervisors find that this procedure often places them in difficult situations where the plans made by upstream units impose considerable difficulties on the units father downstream. Downstream supervisors often argue that if they were consulted in the planning process, they would be in the position to suggest modifications in upstream plans that would make the work of their own departments much more efficient. There is thus a natural tendency for downstream supervisors to try to plug themselves into the interactions and activities in the earlier stages. We will consider later in this chapter problems of introducing change into the interaction-activity structure in the work flow. In Chapter 27 on "The Development Process," we will take a more detailed view of a case example, the relations among engineering units and production in the design of a new TV set.

Walton, Dutton, and Fitch[2] have examined the concomitants of conflict-cooperation in the relations between sales and production department and production planning and sales service departments in a multiplant company. They are here looking at an important set of relationships which is often fraught with conflict. The success of sales people may

---

[2] R. E. Walton, J. M. Dutton, and H. G. Fitch, "A Study of Conflict in the Process, Structure, and Attitudes of Lateral Relationships," in A. H. Rubenstein and C. J. Haberstroh (eds.), *Some Theories of Organization* (Rev. Ed.; Homewood, Ill.: Richard D. Irwin, Inc., and The Dorsey Press, 1966), pp. 444–65.

depend upon giving their customers special services in modifications of standard products and in delivery dates which can make for serious problems in manufacturing. Sales people would like to have maximum flexibility in the variety of designs they can offer and maximum speed in delivery dates. Manufacturing people naturally would like to standardize on a few production items and have lead times long enough to allow for any manufacturing difficulties that may arise. While these problems are built into the sales-production relationship, we find cases where relations are full of conflict but also cases where relations seem to be quite harmonious. What makes the difference?

Walton and his associates studied six plants of a company engaged in the production of metal doors and window products. They made their selection on the basis of the reputations these plants had with knowledgeable higher management people: some were reported to be marked by continuing and serious friction while others were reported to have exceptionally smooth relationships.

The sales and production departments were in different lines of authority, reaching a common superior to the district sales manager or the production superintendent only three levels above those positions. Thus it would not have been feasible to try to handle the disagreements on the basis of arbitrating them before a common superior.

The researchers were not content with higher management's evaluation of the quality of relations between the units in these six plants. They worked out their own rating on the basis of intensive interviews with 15 to 20 of the key personnel involved in the relationships: sales manager, production manager, field sales manager, plant superintendent, field salesman, foremen, shipping manager, sales service manager, production control manager, and office clerks. In each case, interviewers sought data not only on the evaluation of the quality of the relationships (the sentiments), but also on the interaction and activity patterns involved.

If we translate their findings into our own framework, we find that the relations that were evaluated as more harmonious involved more frequent positive exchange, trading, and joint payoff transactions and fewer negative exchange and competitive transactions than those relationships rated as less harmonious. The more harmonious relationships were also characterized by distinctive interaction-activity patterns, when compared with the less harmonious. Putting together the sentiment and transactional data, we find that, when compared with the more harmonious relationships, those showing *more negative inter-unit sentiments* and *more frequent negatively valued transactions* showed the following conditions:

1. *Fewer persons were involved in the inter-unit interactions.* Why should this be the case? Under conditions of negative inter-unit sentiments and negatively valued transactions, the head of each unit is afraid

that if he does not keep control of relations with the other unit, his subordinates may make commitments that will damage the position of his unit. The safest procedure, under this assumption, is to centralize interactions between the two units as much as possible, channeling those interactions between the heads of the two units.

2. *There are more formal rules and they are more strictly enforced.* To hold or improve the position of his unit, each head tries to specify the rules to be followed by his subordinates and to get from higher management the promulgation of rules that will control the behavior of the opposing unit.

3. *There is a greater resort to outside pressures to influence the other party.* Under the specified conditions of sentiments and transactions, leaders of the two units have limited faith in their ability to influence the other party directly and thus are inclined to look for allies in their local situation or in higher management.

4. *There is less experimentation on procedures.* Managers of each unit hesitate to try out a new procedure. Suppose it works out to the disadvantage of their own unit, but the other unit is happy with the new procedure. In this case, the managers fear that their unit will be stuck with the change.

Note here how an item of easily available interaction-activity information can be used to predict sentiments, transactions, utilization of rules, resort to outside pressures, and experimentation on new procedures. The research men or company executive needs only to inquire how many people are involved in inter-unit interaction in order to be able to make predictions on these other points. Of course, certain cautions need to be introduced in applying this framework. Predictions are likely to be more accurate at the extremes. If we find that inter-unit interactions are so highly centralized that they are all or nearly all channeled through the two unit heads, we can be very confident in predicting that we will find a conflict situation with all the described concomitants. On the other hand, if we find that anyone in either unit is free to contact anyone in the other unit, we can be confident that we will find a harmonious pattern. It is when interactions are not left entirely free between units, yet are not limited to the two unit heads either, that prediction becomes more problematical.

Furthermore, while Walton and his associates found their various hypotheses all substantiated and some at a high level of statistical significance, they found only one perfect (1.00) correlation—the more negative the sentiments, the more frequent the use of extra-plant relationships to influence the other party. Thus we can not expect here—or in any other organizational behavior case—to make a prediction with 100 percent probability of success. The Walton group study indicates that with a minimum amount of readily accessible information, we can improve our predictions substantially beyond a chance basis.

2. Buy-sell relationships

Sayles speaks of these as trading relationships, but I prefer to call the relationship itself "buy-sell" to keep the terminology straight, since I want to use "trading" as a specific type of transaction that occurs in many relationships other than those of buy-sell.

Buy-sell relationships link the firm to the outside world, but there are also many such relationships that occur within large companies. In fact, some firms (General Motors, for example) have a policy of encouraging managers engaged in buying components for their units to get competitive bids from outside as well as available inside sources. If the inside unit loses the sale, as sometimes happens, managers of that unit are naturally unhappy, but top management people feel that the inside-outside competition may help to increase the efficiency of the inside units.

Even when buy-sell relationships are built into the organization, that is, when unit A regularly produces for unit B, C, D, and so on, there may still be room for trading transactions. Sayles puts it in this way:[3]

In effect, there is a wide variety of "terms of trade" to negotiate: what, when, how, and for how much the work will be performed. Often there are efforts by "buyers" to improve the terms once they are negotiated, e.g., by asking for a few "extras" or an earlier completion date. The buyer not only supplies a budget or an approved activity (which will justify the existence of the seller), but he may also be called upon to supply waiting time, special manpower, tools, space, even good contacts with supply sources of one kind or another, or special informal favors in the area of organization politics. All are analogous to a market price.

In the buy-sell relationship, each side tries to improve its own position within the larger organization. The manager of the selling unit recognizes that he raises the value of his unit to the company by being able to sell more, and that furthermore he can improve performance of his unit by selling especially those items that the unit can produce especially well and at low cost. To the extent that he makes such gains, he stands to increase the satisfactions of members of his own unit.

The buyer also has an interest in negotiating the terms of trade. To the extent that he can get the needed item at lower cost, receive faster delivery, and get better quality, he can improve the performance of his own unit, improve the position of his unit in the company, and increase the satisfactions of unit members.

While both buyer and seller have something to gain from working

---

[3] Sayles, *op. cit.*, p. 61.

together, according to the terms of trade agreed upon, the advantages
might be predominantly on one side or the other, and the problem for the
negotiators is to arrive at an agreement which will provide a reasonable
balance of advantages and disadvantages to both parties.

While the actual trading transactions are of the first importance, we
find that men who are skillful in developing these buy-sell relationships
make a large investment of their time and interactions in preparing the
way for the trading transactions they wish to initiate. The manager needs
to get around to gather information on potential buyers and sellers and
what they need or have to offer. He needs also to use this social circulation process as a means of providing interpretation and information about
the capabilities and needs of his own unit. Sayles provides these two
illustrative statements from individuals successful in the buy-sell relationship:[4]

(A potential "seller"): I never miss a chance to go out to lunch with a
department head who may be able to use our services. You've got to keep
telling people what you can do for them if you expect to build up the
reputation of your department and its activities.

(A potential "buyer"): You can't rely on written memos or reports to
keep up with what's going on in the company. Many times some group is
working on something which could be very useful to you, if you knew about
it. So whenever I have some free time, I wander around to keep current. Then
when we have to farm out something or have some difficult problem, I know
where to go and, just as important, *who* to go to, who can help us.

3.   Service relationships

Service units are typically on the receiving end of initiations of
interactions and activities from units that need their services. If the service
unit responds to only one other unit, service personnel may chafe under
pressures, but they do not have conflicting pressures to contend with. If
the service unit is on the receiving end of demands from two or more
organizational units (as is typically the case with maintenance departments), then work schedulers and supervisors in the service unit must try
to cope with competing pressures and with the escalation of demands as
each unit tries to make its claims sound more urgent than those of other
units.

Considering the predominant flow of initiation into maintenance, we
might assume that the most successful maintenance supervisor would be
one who could tolerate high frequency of incoming initiations. This may
indeed be a limiting condition for success in this position, but it does not
appear to be a sufficient condition, even if we confine ourselves to the
interactional aspects of personality. That is, we can predict that any
individual who cannot respond to a high frequency of initiations of inter-

[4] *Ibid.*, pp. 65–66.

actions and activities to him from a wide circle of people will not be able to function effectively in that particular supervisory position. But this limiting condition suggests a door mat type of personality which hardly conforms to the picture we have of a successful supervisor, based on other research. While we have no measures of success or failure in these terms, Sayles suggests that the more successful service managers develop a pattern of initiating interaction and activities toward the units that initiate work orders for them. Instead of simply responding to work orders as they come, the service manager takes the initiative to urge upon other department managers and supervisors changes in their work plans which will facilitate the work and improve the performance of his department. He also seeks to get them to change the procedures of scheduling the work in ways that will ease the burdens he feels.

There may be a more comprehensive approach that some service managers are able to take. In the question of maintenance, the department manager may get management acceptance of a program of preventive maintenance. While he argues that a regular program of servicing the machines will in the long run make for fewer breakdowns and less lost time, the proposed program introduces significant changes in the structuring of interactions and activities. The introduction of a preventive maintenance program gives the department manager greater control over the activities of his own department. It also enables him to initiate changes in the activities of other department managers and supervisors.

While the facts and figures the maintenance manager presents to support his proposal will carry some weight with his peers and his superiors, acceptance or rejection of a proposal that provides for increased initiatives from the service department is likely to depend more upon the distribution of power and influence among production and service departments. While no a priori determination can be made on this, we assume that the power and influence of maintenance managers will depend to some extent upon the distribution of personnel and investment of resources from department to department. In a company where the maintenance department is small in relation to the production units, the chances of the maintenance manager putting over such a scheme would seem to be much less than would be the case in a company where the proportion of personnel and of investment by the company are much more heavily concentrated on the maintenance side. In any case, this was the hypothesis we called upon to explain the elimination of the FWD System at the Milo plant and the survival of the area coordination program in the Overseas Corporation (Chapter 15).

4. Scheduling

In a small plant, the scheduling of service activities may be simple enough so that it is not necessary to use specialized personnel on work scheduling. The work orders then simply come into the unit manager, who plans the work schedule for his department and also handles the relations with other departments, seeking thus to decrease the pressure in his own department. In a large and complex organization, with many units initiating for the service unit, work scheduling becomes such a complex and crucially important problem that management is likely to establish a special work scheduling unit.

In Chapter 15 on maintenance, we have examined two systems for dealing with other departments in terms of work scheduling. While both of these systems generated some new problems for management, we must recognize that when the maintenance operations attain a magnitude such as found in these two cases, it becomes impractical for management to expect that the work scheduling will be handled entirely by the maintenance supervisors.

In production departments, when scheduling problems become complex, management usually finds it advisable to set up a separate production control or production planning department. This is obviously a vitally important unit in many large production organizations, but unfortunately we know of no behavioral science studies of this relationship in production organizations. The best we can do is extrapolate from our cases in maintenance scheduling.

There we found scheduling personnel in a powerful position, constantly initiating activities for work supervisors. In those situations where the relationship appeared most harmonious, we noted a marked change in the interaction-activity pattern of scheduler and work supervisor: the scheduler would engage in considerable consultation with the supervisor before drawing up the schedule.

5.   Auditing and standard setting

While Sayles sets up auditing as a type of relationship, I prefer to consider auditing and standard setting together, for I assume that frequently (though not always) the same unit is involved in both activities.

By auditing we mean the systematic checking up on the performance of individuals and groups outside of one's own organizational unit. This is the type of activity carried on by an inspection department. Sometimes the personnel department is called upon to check on the compliance with company personnel policies. Industrial engineers are involved not only in setting standards for work performance but also in checking on the functioning of the system. Our Chapter 16 on cost control and budgets gave special attention to the types of pressures in production departments that come out of this kind of auditing activity.

Here again we are faced with a built-in situation of potential conflict. We cannot expect the performers to feel kindly toward those who are checking on their performance. However, experience and research suggests certain possibilities of reducing the level of friction. In dealing with budgets and cost control, to the extent that production supervisors and managers play a part in establishing the standards against which they are judged, to that extent will they have more favorable sentiments toward those standards and also toward those responsible for standard setting and for the auditing of performance.

6.   Stabilization

In a large, complex organization, there are endless opportunities for one unit to make decisions that put it "out of line" with other units or that may establish precedents that appear to commit other units to accepting decisions that have been considered neither by them nor by top management. One way of preventing "out of line" conditions from arising is through establishing what Sayles calls stabilization relationships.

Higher management rules that certain types of decisions that may tend to produce these "out of line" conditions must have the approval of an individual or group charged with these special stabilization responsibilities. The stabilization personnel in such cases do not initiate activities, but must have proposals referred to them, and they may then either approve or veto the given proposal. Usually, the proposer has the right of appeal to higher authorities in case of a veto. Since he recognizes that higher management has established the stabilization relationship for the specific purpose of effecting a veto on some lower management decisions, he is naturally reluctant to push the appeal unless he feels he has a very strong case.

Personnel men often find themselves in the stabilization position regarding personnel policies. For example, the policy may state that individuals are to be considered for merit pay increases only once a year and that any exception that a supervisor wishes to make must be referred to personnel for approval. Similarly, the policy may call for pay increases automatically every six months until the worker reaches the mid-point of the rate range for his position, but require that beyond that point standards of merit shall apply and only a certain proportion of the men who have reached the mid-point in the range in any given year may be considered for increases. The supervisor then has to submit his proposals for pay increases to personnel to show that he is following policy or to make a special case for departing from policy.

In our chapter on maintenance and operating organizations, we have examined in some detail a stabilization example: inventory control. In an organization large enough to have a number of units using the same or similar machines and materials, if individual supervisors are free to order whatever in their judgment is best for their purposes, management is likely to be confronted with an inventory situation that has got out of control. General Foreman Jones has great faith in machine X and wants to be sure that he has replacement units of X readily available. When General Foreman Smith succeeds Jones, he announces that he has no faith in machine X and must be well-supplied with replacement units of machine Y. If his orders are complied with, the warehouse will have several units of machine X sitting in dead storage until the time when any supervisor would agree they had become obsolescent.

To avoid such pileups of unused and unusable equipment, management sets up a standardization committee to study the machine and material requirements of the plant or plants in question. The committee then develops an approved list of standard items. Now any supervisor who has been given the power to requisition from the warehouse or to write out a purchase order may take direct action in regard to any of the items on the approved standard list. If the supervisor wants an item not in this standard list, he has to write out a special requisition which includes a statement of why he needs this particular item and why an item on the standard list will not serve his purposes. As we have seen in the Overseas Corporation case, this can be a cumbersome and frustrating procedure for supervisors.

Given the structure of relationships involved in stabilization activities, we cannot expect the stabilizers to be viewed with positive sentiments by those men whose proposals they must approve or veto. The stabilizer is likely to get no credit for his approval. He is only allowing the supervisor to do what that supervisor would have done anyway if the stabilizer had not got in the way. The stabilizer naturally provokes negative sentiments when he vetoes a proposal by a supervisor.

If stabilizers are to do the jobs allocated to them, probably there is no way of eliminating such negative sentiments completely. Research in other situations suggests that the intensity of the negative sentiments may be reduced if the stabilizers encourage those whose decisions they must review to discuss with them the policies and procedures that are being applied. If the stabilizers seem to be responsive to proposals for changes in policies and procedures, they may reduce to some extent the animosity directed toward them.

7.   Advisory relationships

We have already reviewed the problems of the personnel man in his advisory role. Any other specialist may also become involved in an advisory or consulting role, but field observations suggest that advice rarely flows as freely as the apparent needs would seem to demand. Why should this be the case?

It is a well-recognized principal in the field of counseling that advice is not likely to be valued unless it is requested. Taking the initiative to offer unsolicited advice to another person is not likely to lead either to the use of that advice or to an improvement of the relations between advice-giver and advice-receiver. Therefore, the potential adviser must avoid taking too much initiative in the offering of his advice. But suppose the adviser sits back and waits to be called on and the potential recipient of advice never makes the call.

Blau has pointed out that the act of seeking advice from another person may be interpreted by both parties as implying a status subordination of the receiver to the giver. This presents a naturally inhibiting influence.

How do mutually valued consulting relationships develop? Cases that I have observed indicate that success in this relationship depends upon establishing a more balanced pattern of interaction and activity initiation than we customarily think of being involved in advice giving. We might consider it in terms of the five points below:

1. The specialist builds up a certain frequency and regularity of interaction with the operating man before seeking to bring about any innovations.
2. This means, in effect, that the specialist does not simply cook up his innovation in his own mind and then move right in and try to bring it about. Instead, he deliberately withholds his innovating efforts until he has established a personal relationship which will make them more acceptable.
3. Before he seeks to innovate, the specialist concentrates on familiarizing himself with the operating man's situation and problems. Some of this is done through observation, but a good deal of it is done through interviewing. This means, in effect, that the specialist gets the operating man to explain his situation as he views it himself, and to take the initiative in their relationship.
4. The specialist tries to build his innovations into a pattern of reciprocal initiations and exchange of valued activities. That is, he is not exclusively asking the operating man to change his behavior. He is also providing opportunities for the operating man to call for help from the specialist.
5. The specialist helps the operating man with activities for which the operating man receives rewards.

Combinations, natural and unnatural

In these seven relationships discussed before, we have made no assumptions regarding the extent to which a single individual or a single unit could or should be involved in two or more of these relationships. In our chapter on the personnel man, we have already noted that such specialists may be involved in service, auditing, stabilization, and advisory relationships. What happens when some relationships are combined?

I make the assumption that certain of these relationships are mutually compatible and others are not. By compatible, I mean that in some sets of relationships the role requirements of the actor fit together, whereas in other relationships, what he is expected to do in one role conflicts with what is expected of him in another.

There has been little research on this question yet in industry, but let us consider the examples pointed out in our discussion of the personnel man. There I argued that the advisory relationship was not compatible with auditing and stabilization relationships. Auditing and stabilization seem to me mutually compatible.

Lateral or diagonal relations?

In this chapter we have been discussing relationships that are distinguished by not involving the direct exercise of authority. Does it make a difference whether we are dealing with lateral or with diagonal relationships—that is, whether the interacting individuals are at the same status level or whether one is superior to the other?

Consider the case of Harry Holmes, vice president for industrial relations, who prided himself that, although frequently called upon for advice, he never gave orders to an operating official. Harry was a man in his sixties who had come up through the ranks in the company and acquired a tremendous respect on the part of workers and managers alike. The plant manager was consulting Harry on an action he wanted to take. Harry advised him against it. The plant manager persisted, rephrased all his arguments, and said he was determined to proceed. Harry shook his head once again and said: "If that's the way you feel about it, go ahead. It's your decision to make. But that sure is going to get you into a lot of trouble." The plant manager thought it over some more and decided not to do it after all.

Harry Holmes told us the story to show that he only served in an advisory capacity to the line. The plant manager was free to accept or reject his advice. Now, I don't know how this exchange looked to the plant manager, but I know that situation well enough to imagine the plant manager's reaction. If he went ahead, he knew very well that Harry Holmes would take no action to stop him, because Harry was very conscientious about avoiding the exercise of authority. If the plan worked all right, then there was nothing to worry about. On the other hand, if he went ahead and the labor relations difficulties anticipated by Harry Holmes did materialize, what then? The general manager would ask him why he hadn't consulted Harry Holmes, and he would have to admit that he had consulted Holmes but had refused to take his advice. Or the general manager would ask old Harry why he hadn't advised the plant manager. Harry wouldn't want to hurt the plant manager, but he was an honest man, and he would have to say, "Well, I told Joe that that would lead to trouble, but he was determined to go ahead anyway," or words to that effect.

In this example, merely saying that Harry Holmes served in an advisory capacity does not explain the situation. On the other hand, it is equally misleading to say that Harry Holmes exercised authority.

If we define authority in terms of the direct exercise of sanctions, then Harry Holmes was not exercising authority. However, he was in the position where, whether he wanted to or not, he brought sanctions to bear upon the situation indirectly. Harry Holmes' sanctioning power was derived only in part from the formal position he held. At least as important was the set of relations he had developed with the top management people and union leaders over the years.

Suppose the very same advice had been given the plant manager by his plant personnel manager—a man diagonally below him. In that case, we can assume that the plant manager would have been much more likely to perceive the personnel manager's statement as advice which he was perfectly free to accept or reject.

Consider the following example given to Leonard Sayles by a manager of a service department.[5]

Our department has the job of shifting office furniture. I found the man I had in charge of the operation couldn't take it any longer. Each department that wanted work done brought in the big brass, so on any particular day he might have three or four division heads claiming that their people had to be taken care of first. Now I make them come through me, and I make up a schedule of priorities for the immediate manager.

In this case the service department manager is recognizing that pressures coming into his department diagonally downward can be too severe for the recipients. To protect his subordinates, he eliminates the downward-diagonal initiative and channels all of the initiatives from outside along the lateral dimension, through himself. Having higher status than his subordinates, he has more resources to bring to bear in coping with outside pressures.

Changing work flow and status relations

The flow of work from upstream to downstream has important implications for the status of departmental supervisors and for the degree of control each has over the activities of his department. Other things being equal, the farther downstream you go, the more programmed your activities tend to be, the less freedom of action you are likely to have, and the more the activities of your department tend to be predetermined by activities of preceding units. While they do not conceptualize the problem in just these terms, skilful downstream supervisors are well aware of the problems posed by their position in the work flow and often engage in maneuvers designed to modify that position.

We are indebted to George Strauss for a classic case of this nature: that

---

[5] *Ibid.*, p. 81.

of the purchasing agent. While the purchasing agent initiates for salesmen outside of the company, he generally finds himself at the end of one or more work flow lines within the company. Various specialties of engineering, as well as production supervisors pass their orders down to the purchasing agent. Furthermore, in many situations he finds he is viewed as nothing but an order clerk. The man who writes the order specifies exactly what he wants, leaving the purchasing agent nothing to do beyond filling out the necessary forms. The purchasing agent complains particularly of the habit of some engineers of specifying what they want in terms of brand names. Since the alternative to specifying by a brand name is to draw up a detailed set of specifications concerning all the relevant properties of the item to be purchased, engineers naturally find that they can save considerable time by simply writing down the name of a brand that they feel will do the job quite adequately.

If the purchasing agent receives a set of specifications, he can draw upon his knowledge of the market and use his ingenuity to find two or more alternative items, analyze data on prices and quality, and make a recommendation back to the engineer. He may even feel that one particular aspect of the engineer's specifications is not really necessary and that, if this aspect can be modified, he can give the engineer much better value for the money. He then goes back to try to persuade the engineer to accept the modification. If he simply receives an order for a brand name, he can do nothing beyond what is well within the powers of an ordinary clerk.

Assuming that the purchasing agent is ambitious and would like to demonstrate his value to the company, he seeks to build up the complexity and importance of the content of his job.

Strauss gives this analysis of the way the ambitious agent views his job:[6]

The ambitious agent feels that placing orders and expediting deliveries are but the bare bones of his responsibilities. He looks upon his most important function as that of keeping management posted about market developments: new materials, new sources of supply, price trends, and so forth. And to make this information more useful, he seeks to be consulted before the requisition is drawn up, while the product is still in the planning stage. He feels that his technical knowledge of the market should be accorded recognition equal to the technical knowledge of the engineer and accountant.

Specifically, the ambitious agent would like to suggest (1) alternative materials or parts to use, (2) changes in specifications or redesign of components which will save money or result in higher quality or quicker delivery, and (3) more economical lot sizes, and to influence (4) "make or buy" decisions. The agent calls these functions "value analysis."

One way of looking at the agent's desire to expand his influence is in terms of interaction. Normally orders flow in one direction only, from

---

[6] George Strauss, "Tactics of Lateral Relationship: The Purchasing Agent," *Administrative Science Quarterly*, Vol. 7, no. 2 (September, 1962), pp. 163–64.

engineering through scheduling to purchasing. But the agent is dissatisfied with being at the end of the line and seeks to reverse the flow. Value analysis permits him to initiate for others. Such behavior may, however, result in ill feeling on the part of other departments, particularly engineering and production scheduling.

The purchasing agent can only bring his "value analysis" to bear if he gets himself in on early discussions of engineering and production plans. He comes to recognize that, if he is not informed about the purchases required until the papers arrive in his office, he faces what Sayles and Strauss call "the completion barrier." By the time the purchase orders reach the purchasing agent, the engineers feel they have completed one project and already started on another. The purchasing agent recognizes that this makes it extremely difficult to get the engineers to consider alternatives to what they have ordered. Almost any change might involve considerable additional work on the part of engineering. Purchasing agents argue that if they can get in on the planning discussions, they can feed in information regarding available machines and equipment, delivery times, and, in general, alternative purchasing strategies. If the purchasing agents are successful in establishing this claim, they will have brought about a marked reorganization of the flow of work and of the interactions and activities associated with this flow.

Power and performance

This description of problems arising along horizontal and diagonal relations may give the impression that life in management is nothing more than a constant struggle for power and status. Indeed, these elements are necessarily involved, but they are not the whole story. Furthermore, the struggle for power and status should not be interpreted simply in terms of personal desires for self aggrandizement. Most people in management have strong urges to "get the job done." They recognize that those who gain more power in the organization also gain more control over the elements necessary to get the job done in their own departments. Each manager is therefore likely to pursue strategies that he hopes will expand his influence over the elements necessary to get the job done in his department and reduce his dependence on other departments, or at least build up such relationships with other departments as to facilitate getting the job done. The manager necessarily finds himself maneuvering to increase his own influence among others who are doing the same thing. If the manager is completely oblivious to power considerations and just tries to pay attention to getting the job done in his department, he is likely to lose control and influence over external matters affecting his department and find that the production job is suffering because he has not been enterprising enough to structure the relations of his department effectively into the larger network.

The manager will not be able to increase his influence just because he wants to do it—since he is competing with many others who have the same objective. While we certainly need to recognize that there are other factors than performance that affect the influence an individual holds in an organization, let us not neglect performance. To a substantial extent, in most organizations, the individual's ability to increase his influence will depend upon his performance. The purchasing agent who demonstrates that he can save money, speed deliveries, and bring superior products to the attention of others *if* he gets in on the process early—will get in early. If he cannot substantiate such claims, he must be content with the status of order taker.

Summary and general conclusions

Following Sayles, we have found eight types of lateral relationships:

1. Work flow
2. Buy-sell
3. Service
4. Scheduling
5. Auditing and standard setting
6. Stabilization
7. Advisory
8. Innovation (To be dealt with in Part VIII.)

Each of these relationships involves a particular structuring of interactions and activities, but we have noted that this structuring is not predetermined in detail. The skillful manager can note the structuring that is likely to arise in his position and assess the likely impact of this structuring on the sentiments of others toward him and upon his status and influence in the organization. If he does not like the conditions he sees "naturally" arising, he may take certain steps to modify the pattern and thus change the sentiments of others and his own status and influence.

In general, those groups upstream in the work flow will exercise more influence downstream than is exerted on them from downstream. Downstream managers often seek to increase their influence over their own work and the work of others through getting themselves into interactions and activities farther upstream.

These relationships are not distributed on a one-relationship-per-department basis. Members of a single department often find themselves engaged in two or more of these relationships. Some of these are compatible, some are not. We have particularly noted the difficulties posed for the advisory relationships when a manager also finds himself engaged in auditing and standard setting or in stabilization relationships.

Whether the relationships are lateral or diagonal affects perceptions of the advice that is given or received. A given statement offered diagonally upward or laterally is likely to be seen as advice, whereas the same statement sent diagonally downward is likely to be seen as having the force of an order.

Whether the relationship is lateral or diagonal also affects the "pressures" felt by the man on the receiving end of initiations of activity. We would expect the pressures to be felt least when the receiver is on the upward end of the diagonal and most when he is on the downward end, with the lateral relationship falling in between. Thus, if a manager finds that one of his subordinates is feeling excessive pressure diagonally downward, he can relieve this pressure by insisting that these initiations from other units be directed laterally through himself.

References

Sayles, Leonard. *Managerial Behavior.* New York: McGraw-Hill Book Co., 1964. Presents the framework largely followed in this chapter.

Discussion questions

1. Examine the roles and problems of engineers from the standpoint of the relationships framework of this chapter, using Chapter 13 of Leonard Sayles' *Managerial Behavior* for case material. How many of the relationships in our *Organizational Behavior* chapter does the engineer get involved in? To what extent are these relationships mutually compatible?

2. Locate a man whose principle responsibilities have required him to handle lateral and/or diagonal relationships. Interview him to determine to what extent his job requires him to act in each of the relationships examined in this chapter. To what extent are the dilemmas and problems he faces due to incompatibility among these relationships?

Part VII

UNION-MANAGEMENT RELATIONS

WHERE UNIONS ARISE, we must recast our structural analysis of organizations to include the dimensions of union-management relationships.

In Chapter 19 we examine two union organizing campaigns in order to assess the forces that lead workers to accept or reject the appeals of unionization. In Chapter 20 we follow the changes that tend to take place as the union-management relationship evolves from the initial stage of official recognition toward the institutionalization of the relationships— that is, toward a regular pattern of interactions, activities, and sentiments among representatives of the two parties.

While we can make some generalizations regarding union-management relations for a plant or a set of plants in the same area, taken as a whole, as we move from plant down to departments and other work units, we find a wide variety of situations. Factors accounting for some of this variety are analyzed in Chapter 21 on "Work Unit Cohesion and Militancy."

In Chapter 22 we return to a consideration of the broad "Patterns of Union-Management Relations" as they manifest themselves at several organizational levels within the plant.

How do you move a given union-management relationship from conflict toward cooperation, or vice versa? To some extent such changes may come about gradually through changes in interactions and activities that take place during the year. "The Collective Bargaining Process" is not only the most dramatic aspect of a union-management relationship; it is also the aspect most likely to generate changes in the pattern of union-management relations. In Chapter 23 we examine the bargaining process in order to learn how such changes are generated.

19. Enter the union

WE HAVE ALREADY MET with unions in this book, for it has been impossible to discuss the response of workers to their environment without getting into some discussion of union activities. Up to now, unions have been in the background of our discussion; we have taken them as given (not to be explained) as we have focussed on other aspects of organizational behavior. In Part VII, unions and union-management relations will be our main focus of attention.

Why do workers join unions? The differences in personality and organizational experience that incline some men to join and others to reject unions have been analyzed in Chapter 4. In the present chapter, we will be concerned with the impact of organizational changes upon worker voting intentions and with some of the forces influencing managerial response to unions.

To examine worker responses to unionism, we will observe the impact of the CIO drive upon the Hi-Test plant and its related facilities. We will then turn to the case of S. Buchsbaum and Company to analyze managerial reactions to a strike for union recognition.

1. The union organization drive at Hi-Test

In my first study in industry in 1942–43, I had the good fortune to spend five months, two to three days a week, with workers and management people of Blank Oil Company at a time when the Oil Workers International Union (CIO) was seeking to organize the workers of Hi-Test plant and other surrounding installations in the city. I make no claim that this is a typical case, but we shall see that it involved many of the forces that actually do come to bear in such situations.

We have already met Hi-Test and Blank Oil Company in Oil City through our story of Joe Sloan. Joe will be one of the characters in this story, but a minor one, as we concentrate upon groups in conflict instead of upon the conflicts faced by any one particular individual.

This was the third attempt of the CIO union to organize the workers in this area. The two earlier attempts had won some supporters but had fallen far short of success. This third attempt culminated in a representation election in April, 1943, which the CIO union narrowly lost. Both workers and management people agreed that the union would have won if the election had been held just a few weeks earlier. With the decision thus hanging in the balance during the time of my field study, I had the opportunity to observe the forces that moved men for or against the union.

Why did the CIO union come so close to winning in 1943 when earlier drives had failed to provide any serious challenge to management's control? To answer this question, we need to look back upon the state of human relations in the organization in an earlier era.

In the "good old days"

In the early days of the company, problems of supervision were relatively simple. Even in the manufacture of natural gasoline, where scientific knowledge was constantly applied to the processes, operations were of a rather routine nature. Men who had worked in the old type gasoline plants told me that an experienced worker in such an establishment required very little supervision. The operations of one day were just like those of the preceding day. Frequently the men would not see their immediate supervisor inside the plant from one day to the next. This, of course, minimized the opportunities for conflict over supervision.

In this stage of the company's development, both supervisors and men had the same social backgrounds. The supervisors were men who had worked their way up through the ranks, demonstrating their capacities on the job. The workers knew that a man who showed talent in handling men and equipment could look forward to graduating into supervision. No technical education was required. There was no sharp social line drawn between the men and their supervisors, and there were many social activities, such as picnics and stag parties, in which they all participated, looking upon themselves simply as fellow employees of Blank Oil Company.

Even for those who did not graduate into supervision, there was a road to distinction gained through long and loyal service to the company. The man who had been with the organization from its start—or shortly thereafter—enjoyed a special prestige and came to look upon it as his company. The executives cultivated this feeling of loyalty through awarding service badges of increasing distinction for each five years in the company's service. The long-time employee enjoyed a job security which was almost absolute. He could not be discharged by his foreman or plant superintendent, and the executives were careful to protect his interests in cases involving discrimination by those in immediate authority.

The great strength of the company's personnel work in this era was its informality. There was no special personnel department. The executives in the main office took pride in remaining in personal touch with their employees in the field. Long after the organization had become too large for its founder to keep up the personal contacts, the natural gasoline department maintained those ties through General Superintendent of Field Operations Fred Fitzgerald.

As one worker put it:

All the men loved Fred. Any man that would work for the company a year, Fred knew him by his first name, and he knew something about him. When he came through the plant, he would stop and talk to the men. Then we used to have big picnics every summer. He would come down carrying some old clothes in a suit case. He would go off behind a tree and get into those old clothes and play ball with the boys. . . . You never heard anything about unions around here when Fred was alive.

Another man had this to say:

Fred Fitzgerald used to come around to these plants often. Yes, several times a year until a little while before his death, when the company was getting so big that he couldn't get around so much. He knew most of the men. He had grown up from ditch digger with the company. He would come around and ask you how your wife and kids were. He would know how many children you had, and if they had been sick, he would know about it. If you ever wanted to go see him, you could go up to his office and you could talk to him for an hour or two hours. He would never hurry you. If your story was right, you could depend on him to do something for you. If it wasn't right, he found out about it.

I will never forget one meeting where Fitzgerald spoke to us. There was some trouble in that field and the men were getting organized into a union. He called a meeting and he talked to us like this: "God damn it," he says, "What the hell do you guys want a union for? If you have some grievance, tell me and we'll fix it." After that the men got right up and cussed back at him. That's what he wanted. He wanted them to talk and they knew it. When a man would make some complaint, Fred would turn to the superintendent and say, "Why hasn't this been taken care of? Let's get some action on it."

From the standpoint of his living memory among the men, Fred Fitzgerald died just at the right time. In the last few years of his life, the company was expanding so rapidly that Fred was seen in Oil City less and less. In this era, he personally was the connecting link between the main office and the Oil City workers. A few years more of organizational growth might have strained this personal link to the breaking point.

So the era came to an end in 1939 with the funeral of Fred Fitzgerald in the main office city. At the time of the funeral, it was only with the greatest difficulty that local supervisors were able to persuade enough men to remain on their jobs to keep the operations going. From Oil City and in fact from all over the holdings of Blank Oil Company in the natural gasoline department, the workers travelled at their own expense to the main office city to participate in the largest and most impressive funeral the town had ever known. Their grief at the loss was genuine and deep.

What would take the place of this communication channel between workers and higher management?

The company union

Several years before Fitzgerald's death and in response to an earlier CIO organization drive, management had given birth to a company union. How did the company union look to the men? The following picture was given to me by a man who was a representative of the company union in its early period:

> The company called a big meeting of all of the men. The superintendents were there. They told us the organization was all ours. We could do with it whatever we wanted to. It was all their idea. The men hadn't any idea of starting an organization. For about a year and a half we held monthly meetings in the club house. The company would put up refreshments, and they furnished entertainment. We had some nice programs. We would get 100 or 150 out to each meeting. We set up a lot of committees and we were working on them. We did not have any grievances at that time. We were well-satisfied, but we were just trying to work things out for the betterment of the men and for the company too. The superintendents did not hear nothing of it for a while and I guess they got suspicious so in one of our meetings all the superintendents and the division superintendent too came up. They held the floor for the whole meeting. There wasn't much that the men could say. They just told us that we should take more of an interest in the company. We had been taking an interest in the company. But they did not know what we were doing so they were suspicious. They told us that after that meeting the superintendents would have to come to every meeting. That really broke it up. I don't remember; we may have had a meeting or two after that, but we never got any real attendance. It was the company's fault. The company killed that company union.

The Hi-Test company union representative made these comments:

> That company union is all right in a way. You can really get things with it when the (CIO) union puts on the pressure. It can't get anything when the company is not afraid of the CIO.
>
> There was one man here that used to be a representative in the company union, and one time the superintendent called him into his office and told him, "You are spending too much time on that company union. I think you would be better off if you spent your nights home with your family." (He was referring to the man previously quoted.)

Our first informant tells us that management killed the company union in its early stages. Insofar as widespread membership participation and interest was concerned, this seems to be true, but as a paper organization —with occasional bursts of activity by some of its officers—the company union lived on and was to play an important role in the representation election of 1943.

The Masters' crack-down

Ed Masters took over the position of general superintendent of field operations upon the death of Fred Fitzgerald in 1939.

It would have been difficult for any man to step into the shoes of Fitzgerald, especially during this period of rapid expansion. The task was made doubly difficult by the nature of the situation which had developed in Oil City.

The company's operations there were marked by an exceptional laxity of supervision. The superintendent in charge was a competent gasoline man but an inveterate gambler. For months he had been organizing crap games in tool sheds, warehouses, and other secluded spots. With the encouragement of the superintendent, gambling activities grew completely out of control, and large numbers of men were neglecting their jobs to roll the dice.

The stealing of gasoline was also a problem. It had become a time-honored custom for men throughout the industry to help themselves to the gasoline they needed to run their cars. There was, of course, a rule against this practice, but the supervisors made no attempt to enforce the rule, and the employees, like human beings everywhere, judge rules more by the behavior they experience and observe than by official notices. There had been two cases of men being fired on this charge, but when the cases had been appealed, Fred Fitzgerald, in consideration for the long years of service of the culprits, had simply given them a warning and transferred them to another area.

The new general superintendent of field operations was sent in to clean up this situation. Since he had been working in another area, he had no personal ties to link him with the men in Oil City. He was entirely an unknown quantity to them.

The general superintendent's first move was to warn his immediate subordinate that the gasoline stealing practice was to be stopped. The response to this was the posting of warning notices in the plants. Some of the men took the notices seriously and stopped taking gasoline. One of them told me, "I figured that this time the company meant business." Others did not take this notice any more seriously than earlier ones which had made the same announcement.

Suddenly the blow fell. Seven men were caught stealing gasoline and were fired. The superintendent and the district superintendent were fired, and the top man in Oil City, the division (state) superintendent, was transferred. Men who were completely unknown to the workers were brought in as plant superintendent and district and division superintendents.

The disruptive effects of this blow were impressive and far-reaching. Rumors of continued crack-down ran wild through the working force. There was endless speculation as to the character and policies of the new management people. The reorganization was so sudden and complete that for some days there were a number of employees who did not know to whom they were responsible and what they were supposed to do. There was a general feeling that the firings marked the end of an era of easy-going, friendly control in favor of harsh, impersonal action.

The workers took up a collection to pay for sending their company union representatives to the main office to plead with General Superintendent Masters that the seven workers be put back on their jobs. As one member of the delegation reported to me:

> We talked it over for a day and a half and finally he (Masters) agreed to put four of those men back to work. They did not go back on the same classifications so they really lost some, and those other men didn't go back at all. When we came home, we thought we had accomplished something, but when we talked to the men, we began to think we didn't do so much. They thought we had sold out. All those men should have been put back to work.

It must have seemed to the general superintendent that in view of the serious nature of the charges, he was leaning over backward to be lenient with the men; therefore, they should be satisfied. This view, however, overlooks the unsettling effects of the crack-down upon the organization of human relations in Oil City. The men had become accustomed to getting along with their superintendent, and they had built up ties of work cooperation and friendship with the employees who were fired. It took some time to become accustomed to the new supervisors and to the absence of old employees. The social situation was so disturbed that it is difficult to conceive of any settlement the company union representatives might have obtained that would have satisfied the men. One of the results of the trip, therefore, was to weaken the company union by making many of the men feel that they could not serve as representatives without being suspected of selling out the workers' interests.

Masters' first personal appearance in his new position in Oil City did nothing to reassure the men. He called a meeting of the local superintendents. At this meeting, one of the superintendents ventured to say something about cooperation with the men. According to both worker and local management informants, Masters stood up, shook the back of his chair angrily and said:

> To hell with cooperation! I don't want cooperation from the men. All I want is a good solid eight hours' work—on their feet.

The last phrase referred to the men's practice of sitting on packing boxes or benches at times during the course of their work. Since the work at Hi-Test, for example, mainly involved watching charts on the wall, the men felt that they could perform this part of the job just as well sitting down as standing up. Apparently Masters believed that sitting down did not constitute working, and the packing boxes and benches were thrown out immediately after this statement. During my five months at Hi-Test, I never once observed one of the workers sitting down except during the 30-minute lunch period, and even then the men told me that this was probably contrary to Masters' orders, and if he ever visited the plant during the lunch period they would have to see to it that he found them eating lunch on their feet.

While four years had passed since the Oil City shakeup, it still loomed as a major landmark in the history of employee relations in this area. Nearly every man who discussed the causes of discontent with me would, without any prompting, carry his story back to that unsettled time. The shakeup did not leave scars only upon those who had been engaged in gambling and gasoline stealing. Joe Sloan said, "It changed me from a Republican to a Democrat, from anti-union to pro-union—overnight!"

The situation at Hi-Test

For this representation election, the bargaining unit involved over 200 men. Besides the Hi-Test plant, there was in the same plant yard the closely related catalyst plant and an older plant manufacturing natural gasoline. A few miles away there was another gasoline plant, and the company's labor gang was also included in the unit.

There were only seventeen men attached to Hi-Test, so we certainly cannot undertake to explain the whole campaign in terms of Hi-Test. Nevertheless, these men held the highest status jobs in the area and were in a strategic position throughout the struggle so that their experiences and reactions cast light upon the whole process. A further reason for dealing primarily with Hi-Test is that it is from this plant that I have solid research data, whereas my study touched only lightly on other units.

In telling the story of Joe Sloan, we have already covered some of the important factors involved in the struggle over the union at Hi-Test. We need only review them here.

This was a new plant producing by a relatively new process. The workers were not serving under the old-time, up-from-the-ranks foremen, but under technically trained college graduates. The workers who had moved into the plant first were young and ambitious and had fully expected to move up to higher levels.

We have seen how the status of the jobs at Hi-Test declined, and we have seen the ceiling close in against promotion into supervision of noncollege men. Given this background, there should be nothing mysterious about the fact that some of the most dissatisfied men employed by the company in Oil City were also the most highly paid men.

While the plant was first staffed entirely without regard to seniority, a few months later half of the original working force was transferred to a new plant of the same type in another area. Positions thus opened up at Hi-Test were then filled according to the regular procedure, primarily upon a basis of seniority. The result was that of the original crew, only the poly operators and two hydro-stillmen remained.

This history accounts for the unusual distribution of seniority and age among the men. Though the average seniority varied insignificantly between poly operators and their subordinates, there were striking differences in the ages of the men at the time of my study. The poly operators averaged 32½ years, the hydro-stillman 35½ years, and the fractionator operators almost 45 years.

This situation meant that the young poly operators had no place to go with supervision being closed to them, and the men at lower levels were discouraged because younger men were ahead of them.

For most of the time up to the entrance of Tom Lloyd in 1942, the Hi-Test plant had been under the supervision of Bill Jones and later, Tom Fitch, both of whom were chemical engineers. While Jones was finishing his college career, he put in some time as a worker in Hi-Test, and the change from worker to foreman made difficulties for him later. Perhaps the most understanding discussion of Jones' problems was furnished me by one operator in these words:

When Jones was on operations, he was no better than the rest of us. We used to have a bench in here and he would spend plenty of time on that bench. Then when we were supposed to clean up, he would just take a mop and push it around the pump and that was all. After he was foreman, one of the first things he had to do was throw that bench out. Now I happen to know that it was orders from the superintendent but the men don't consider that. They just said, "He used to spend more time on that bench than anybody and just as soon as he gets up there he takes it away."

One day I heard the division superintendent criticize the clean-up work. Then the next day Jones was on us for the cleaning up. The men were griping again. They would say, "Of all the lousy clean-up men he was the worst and now that he is up, he is getting after us."

They never should put a man above a group that he has been working with because those men don't like to think of him as a supervisor. It is all right if you send a man away for a couple of years and then bring him back. By that time they can get used to the idea.

I think the university and the company ruined Bill Jones. The university taught him the technical side but it did not teach him anything about handling people. The company put him in charge of operations because he was a smart man. He never could handle the men.

Another worker added, "We teach them (the technical engineers) all they know about operations, and then they turn around and boss us."

Both Bill Jones and Tom Fitch delivered their orders down to the last detail. In many cases the men were not told the general objective of their work; they were simply ordered to make certain specified adjustments. Whatever the reasons for this procedure, it tended to reduce the work of the operators to mere mechanical manipulation and discouraged study and initiative.

The foremen went still further to discourage initiative. As one of the men reported:

Suppose you had a suggestion to improve operations. You might take it up with Tom Fitch. Before you got hardly started telling about it, he would begin shaking his head and tell you it was no good.

The men said that they sometimes found that the ideas they had suggested to Jones or Fitch were later put into effect—but they were given no credit for their suggestions. After several experiences of this kind, they stopped making suggestions.

Favoritism was the charge most frequently leveled against Jones and Fitch by the men. As one operator expressed it:

There was one poly operator that could never do anything wrong. That's the way Bill Jones looked at it. He would hold that man up to us as a model. Whenever he had anything new to try out, he would start it on that man's tour. He never gave the rest of us a chance. Now we didn't think that man was any better than we were, so naturally we resented it.

It was well known among the men that Jones and Fitch had confidence in some of them and placed no reliance on others. While he was holding monthly poly operator meetings, Jones used them as a forum to air his views about the men. At one time he gave the names of three men that he was "down on" and asked one of the poly operators to tell them of their precarious position. The poly operator countered by saying that if Jones had criticisms of his men he should make them to their faces. The men thoroughly resented talk behind their backs.

One of the men discussed the problem in this way:

Jones and Fitch used to get down on a man and then they would blame everything on him. There was one man here that they really ran off the place because he couldn't take it. Then at one time Bill Jones was down on X and X couldn't do anything right. Later Fitch was down on Y. It got so bad once Y almost hit him with a hammer.

Another man confessed that he had had difficulty restraining himself from using his fists on Fitch when the foreman was "down" on him.

The men felt that these personal criticisms were unfair. They said that they were all skilled men, and while they all made mistakes, there were no operators so inferior to the others that they deserved to be especially singled out. Furthermore, they felt that the foreman could be mistaken in fixing personal responsibility because a man's difficulties might arise from conditions left to him by the operator on the preceding tour. It was the men's opinion that the foremen simply felt the need of having scapegoats upon whom they could vent their feelings of irritation over any operational difficulty.

This situation directly affected the technical side of operations. Tom Fitch frequently gave detailed orders designed to meet certain operational specifications. The operators, judging from their long experience with the equipment, sometimes felt that the stipulated adjustments would not yield the desired results. Knowing that they would be blamed if the objective were not attained, the men simply operated the equipment so as to reach that objective and "boiler-housed" the chart readings. That is, they put down the readings that Fitch would think correct instead of those actually obtained. This practice was exceedingly widespread. The men looked upon it simply as a way of protecting themselves from unfair criticism. As a consequence, while Fitch may have suspected that the men were "boiler-housing" their readings, he never knew exactly how the plant was operating. His behavior prevented him from obtaining the accurate records necessary for scientific experimentation and for technical improvements in operations.

The men said that the records were falsified for another reason also. There were certain men who, in order to escape criticism or win the favor of the foreman, would cover up their own mistakes by recording fictitious readings but would leave conditions such that their relief operators were bound to get into difficulties.

Similarly, there were some who, when they got into difficulties, complained to the foreman that the men they relieved had left conditions in a mess. The men all say that Jones and Fitch encouraged them to make complaints about their fellow workers. This was one way of gaining favor with the supervisor. It created a problem even for those who did not "squeal" on their fellows, as Joe Sloan commented:

> Tom Fitch used to listen to what the men would say about other operators. He trusted me and so some of the men suspected that I was snitching on them. That is what X thought when Tom got down on him. When I found that out, I got Fitch to tell X the truth, that it wasn't me that squealed. Things like that gave me a lot of trouble.

In this period, Jones and Fitch were also in charge of the catalyst plant. We do not know in detail their effect upon that plant, but one event stands out in the memories of the men there. As a catalyst operator commented:

> When Bill Jones was down here he used to stay until 11 o'clock when we had lunch. Then he would go out. At 11:30 sharp, he would come down here on his bike. He would be off it and come a-running into the plant, before it stopped. He was such a lazy bastard himself, he couldn't believe that other men were not as lazy as he was. One time he called us a bunch of WPA

workers. We had a meeting and were trying to get a better classification and get a road out of here. Masters was there too.

Tom Lloyd, who succeeded Fitch as foreman, made this comment:

You can imagine how that hit the men. That was two years ago, and still sometimes when I try to get a man down here to do a better job, he tells me "What do you expect? I am nothing better than a WPA worker."

New supervision at Hi-Test

Had Jones or Fitch been in charge at Hi-Test and in the catalyst plant at the time of the representation election, a CIO victory would have been assured. Recognizing finally the difficulties arising between the men and supervision, management made some strategic replacements in 1942. Tom Lloyd came in as foreman, and Jess Douglas took over as plant manager over Loyd and over the superintendent at the neighboring gasoline plant. By the time of my study, both Lloyd and Douglas had become popular and respected among the workers.

Tom Lloyd handled his men in a manner entirely different from that used by Jones and Fitch. He began with certain advantages. He was 36 years old. Some of his subordinates were older, but half of them were younger. He had not served alongside his men in operations. He gained his experience elsewhere, came in to win a good reputation supervising the catalyst plant, and made the transition to take over the Hi-Test plant without difficulty. He could not be looked upon as an inexperienced youth who had been taught his job by the men he was then called upon to boss.

Lloyd built skillfully upon this foundation. His relations with his men were carried on in an informal, friendly manner. While his predecessors were noted for "throwing their voices," I never heard him talk to his men in anything above a conversational tone.

Lloyd respected the ability of his men and had confidence in their judgment. One operator expressed it this way:

Tom Lloyd is entirely different from Jones. Bill Jones would come down here and tell us what changes we had to make and that was all. If we could figure out from that what we were making, all right, but he never told us. Tom comes down here and tells us that we have to make a certain product and asks us how we think we ought to go about it. He will say to us, "You fellows know more about this than I do, what do you think?" Of course, he really knows a lot more than we do, but that flatters our egos, and we will figure out with him the way we ought to do it.

This did not mean that the foreman simply let the men run the plant as they saw fit. He set the objective and worked out the plans with them. He carefully checked the operating records of each day, as recorded by the men hour by hour on the daily operating data sheet. Since the records were no longer "boiler-housed," they furnished him with an accurate picture of operations.

The new foreman did not devote as much time to the details of operations as did Jones or Fitch. Lacking their experience of working on tour in this plant, he was not in a position to provide this detailed supervision. In general, he appeared in the plant only once or twice a day and sometimes not at all. Compared with the great frequency of supervisory activity by Jones and Fitch, this restraint of Lloyd's activity seems to have helped to re-establish the equilibrium of the working group.

The details of operation were not overlooked by the supervisor. They were entrusted to his assistant, Engineer Dan Benton. Since Benton had run tour in Hi-Test, he knew the equipment well. He was able to handle certain problems which could not be dealt with by the operators. For example, at one time one of the fractionating columns was giving a good deal of trouble. To solve the problem, it was necessary to give that column more concentrated attention than the fractionator operator could spare from his other duties. Besides, each operator might have had his special ideas as to what should be done, whereas the problem really required the experimental application of a uniform policy for more than the eight hours spent by any one operator on tour; Benton provided the uniform policy and the careful attention. Nevertheless, he did not simply take the column away from the operator. The problems were freely discussed and on occasion Benton tried out ideas suggested by the operators. When differences of opinion arose between Benton and the operators, I observed points being conceded on both sides. Benton recognized that the men had an intimate familiarity with operations which could not be gained by a technical engineer in a few months of running tour. The men recognized that Benton's technical background enabled him to gain an important perspective on operations which they necessarily lacked. Bringing these two types of knowledge together on an informal, give-and-take basis was an immense aid toward building harmonious employee relations.

Lloyd checked up on his men in a manner quite different from that used by Jones and Fitch. In discussing with me his use of the daily operating data sheet, he said:

That sheet is not there primarily for my checking. The purpose of it is to enable the men to know what they are doing. By just looking over that sheet, I can tell how things are going. If something is wrong, I just ask the men to explain it to me. I never try to fix responsibility or say who is to blame. If a man's explanation is weak, he knows it as well as I do. I don't have to tell him. In telling me, he tells himself. That is all that is necessary. These men are very sensitive; they have thin skins, and they take great pride in their work.

Lloyd expected his men to do good work and they wanted to do their best for him. One of them expressed the feelings of the group when he said, "I never wanted to do anything for Bill Jones that I didn't have to do. I'll do anything I can to help Tom Lloyd."

The new management team had smoothed over relations at Hi-Test to a considerable extent. Without question, this served to weaken the interest of the men in the CIO union, but it did not kill their interest altogether. As Joe Sloan and others argued to me, Masters was still in power in the main office. Management's policy was to be good to the men while the CIO threat lasted. If the CIO lost the election, how long would Lloyd and Douglas last in their positions? What was to prevent Masters from sending in other men like Jones and Fitch?

The men's relation to the foreman is important but that does not blot out all concern with higher management.

The campaign

Since my research was carried on within the plant, I can only give a sketchy picture of union organizational activities outside of the plant. I shall report primarily the impact of the campaign upon men on the job.

The two union organizers held monthly meetings and did a good deal of visiting of the men in their homes. Several company employees became informal organizers for the union, talking it up on the job. However, they distributed no literature inside the plant gates, so far as I could tell. One man just let his friends know that he had literature in his car outside the gate.

The literature passed out by the union emphasized that collective bargaining was a democratic process and pointed to the great gains that had been brought to workers through the labor movement. It also promised higher wages, increased job security, and stricter adherence to seniority in promotions.

These promised benefits did not seem to stir any great enthusiasm among the workers in the Hi-Test plant. Since some of these men had moved up very rapidly in classification and pay, wages were the last thing they complained about. In fact, while we can assume that these workers, like any others, would have been glad to have more pay, I found that wages were referred to very seldom in all of the discussions of unions that I heard. In a rapidly growing company, the men were more concerned about new jobs opening up than about losing their jobs. There was, however, a good deal of talk about the Masters crack-down, which involved the discharge of several men.

The seniority issue really cut both ways. Probably a majority of the men were in favor of having promotions follow seniority, but this had been the policy more and more adhered to by the company in recent months. Furthermore, there were a number of men who had risen rapidly because management had disregarded seniority earlier, and these men could hardly be enthusiastic for strict seniority.

The CIO drive seemed to have stalled well short of an assured majority when, at the beginning of February, Masters made his watchman statement, quoted in the chapter on Joe Sloan. Let us now provide the union-management setting into which that statement fitted.

It came at a time when management was negotiating with the company union on wages and several other matters. Lester Harper, company union president, described for me the past history of company union-management negotiations, leading up to the current activities:

In 1941 the men began to think that we had a general increase coming to us. The company union got out petitions and was beginning to circulate them around. Before we got the petitions to the company, we read in the newspapers that we were going to get an increase. Later on in the year, the men thought we had another increase coming and we got out the petitions again. The same thing happened. Before we could get the petitions to the company, we read in the papers that we were getting a second increase. . . . Yes, it would have strengthened the company union if the company had gone through us on that.

Last February (1942) I wrote a letter to J. L. Weber (vice president of the company) saying that the men thought we had another increase coming to us. He wrote back to tell us that he could meet with us to discuss it, but he was very much tied up on priorities and other questions and he would appreciate it if we did not insist on that meeting. He told us we could not get the increase anyway. . . . It seems like when the men go up to Weber and he says no, they just back off and don't do nothing more. We just let it ride until August. By that time the cost of living had gone up some more and I wrote him a strong letter saying unless he met with us our representation plan would break down altogether. That was the beginning of these negotiations.

The possibility of the breakup of the company union apparently was not lost on Mr. Weber. Management met sporadically with the company union representatives through the late fall and winter.

The Hi-Test representative in these negotiations was Andy Taylor, a fractionator operator. Poly Operator Mark Walling described to me the circumstances of Taylor's election to represent the men:

Do you know how Andy got elected? They put a ballot box down here and it stayed here for three days without anybody putting any slips in it. Before that when we had to sign up whether we wanted the company union or not only two men out of 15 voted for the company union and they crossed their names off when they learned they were the only ones. Well after that box had been there for three days, Ed Lester (hydro-stillman) and I got an idea. We took some slips of paper and wrote the name of Andy Taylor on them all, and we signed the different names of the men on all of them and that is how Andy was elected. We never thought he would take it seriously, but he did. Don't ever tell him because I think he doesn't know. Actually, he doesn't represent anybody but himself.

Whomever Taylor represented, by virtue of his election he was included in the negotiating meetings, and thus he became a channel of communication from the Hi-Test plant to the management negotiators and back again.

While the men at Hi-Test had little respect for the intelligence, dependability, or working skill of Taylor, they were naturally interested in whatever he had to report of the negotiations, and presumably some of them gave him suggestions as to things to bring up in the meeting. In fact, it was Andy Taylor who was making the argument for a higher classification for the poly operators when Masters broke up the meeting by calling them a bunch of watchmen (see Chapter 11).

The "watchman" statement had an immediately disturbing effect within Hi-Test. The day after it was made, the chief engineer of the division happened to drop in at the control room to ask the fractionator operator what was the trouble with the number four fractionating column. The operator replied curtly, "You're the engineer. You're supposed to tell us."

This embarrassed the chief engineer, because he had not the slightest idea what was wrong with the column, and only men who had worked closely with it could have been expected to know. The statement also upset relations of Dan Benton, the plant engineer, with the men. As he had been working primarily on the fractionating columns, sometimes, without thinking of the proper organizational channels, he had been directing the fractionator operator to make certain changes. No protest had come out of this until immediately after the watchman statement, when a poly operator complained to Foreman Tom Lloyd that his engineer was bypassing the poly operator.

For several days after the statement, Hi-Test men signed the daily operator data sheet as "the watchman," and there were a number of phone calls from other parts of the company's operations, asking to speak to the "chief watchman."

Several weeks later, a worker who had been very active for the CIO union made this comment upon the impact of the statement on the union drive:

After Masters made that statement about us all being watchmen, the CIO signed up 50 percent of the men that it had. I signed up quite a few names myself. I signed up men that had been strong against it before. There was one man with the company 20 years. He was proud of his position as an operator, and he thought the company appreciated his work. He thought he could take care of himself. When Masters made that statement, this fellow got mad and signed a pledge card. He figured that if that was what the company really thought of him, he needed the protection of a union.

Had the election been held shortly after the watchman statement, it probably would have been a landslide for the CIO. In fact, the CIO organizers were reported to be jubilant at the time. For the first time they had an issue really capable of exciting the men—and presented to them by management. The union literature now reminded the workers of the watchman statement and played up General Superintendent of Field Operations Masters as the villain whose evil doings could be checked only by a strong union.

Local management's counteroffensive

Local management people were disheartened and almost ready to concede the election to the CIO. Not so with Division Superintendent Al Wenzel, the immediate subordinate of Masters and the immediate superior of Plant Manager Douglas. The date for the representation election had not finally been set, and he hoped that, given a little time, the watchman statement would recede into the background and effective counteraction could be undertaken.

First Wenzel had to take steps to make sure that matters did not take still another turn for the worst. Reports coming back from the main office city indicated that Masters was angry at the reaction to his watchman statement. He was arguing that management was wasting its time negotiating with the company union. The workers really needed to be shown who was boss in this situation. Therefore he ordered that the surplus manpower in the Hi-Test plant and surrounding plant yard be bumped back immediately to lower classifications.

Some months earlier, when working hours had been lengthened from 40 to 44 per week, local management found itself with several more men than were actually needed to man the operations. The local management argued that there was no need to bump these men back immediately. The company was expanding rapidly. In the spring of 1943, a new large synthetic rubber plant was to be opened, and men from Oil City would be vitally needed to help man the new operations. Wenzel's plan was to hold the men in their current positions until the new jobs opened in the synthetic rubber plant. At that time, Oil City working hours would be further lengthened to 48 a week, and he hoped that this lengthening of hours, timed to coincide with the transfers to the rubber plant, would enable him to make personnel changes with a minimum of bumping back. In fact, if enough men volunteered to move to the new operation, there might not have to be any bumpings at all. But now Wenzel received the order to cut the men back immediately.

Foreman Tom Lloyd described the new "get tough" policy in this way. He laid the change in part to a decision of the National Labor Relations Board. The contract between the company and the company union had a provision regarding arbitration of matters on which the parties did not agree. Management claimed that this clause did not apply to wage rates. The company union representatives argued that it did, and the government had upheld this view:

It looks like Masters has got some backing from higher up. The old appeasement policy is out. From now on the company wants us to get tough.

It seems that they did not think they had to abide by the contract with the company union and the company union did. Now they have found that they have to abide by that contract so they say, "If the men are going to cut all the corners they can on the contract, we are doing the same thing. We will show them who is running the company."

I guess they have given up on the company union. Franklin (Oil City personnel man) told us about the new policy. He and Wenzel had been up to the main office over the weekend, and when he came back he called local management together and he told us that we would have to get tough. From now on we are not supposed to make any concessions to the men. . . . Now they are telling us that four men have to be bumped back. One out of Hi-Test and two out of the catalyst plant. If the men protest, we are supposed to can them. In the past I have never had the power of firing a man. I can only recommend it to my superiors. Now I can fire anybody I want to.

Of course, the local administration hates this like hell and Franklin doesn't like it either. He told us, "I'm afraid the men will think that I am the son-of-a-bitch that brought up this policy. But they told me, if I didn't like it, they would put men down here that did."

This is really something new. In the past we have had the one big happy family policy. It never got this tough before.

Wenzel's first response to the cut-back order was to stall. He pretended not to understand it. After waiting a day so that he knew Masters would be out of the main office city, he called a personnel man in the main office to ask for clarification as to whether the bumpings had to be done at once. This gave him an opportunity to suggest the disruptive consequences of such a move. The personnel man said he would take the matter up with Vice President Weber. Shortly the word came back from Weber that the bumpings could be postponed.

Now Wenzel could proceed to reactivate the company union, which had become dormant after the watchman statement. Wenzel explained to me that it was really his own fault that the CIO drive had gone so far. The great mistake he had made was in not keeping the company union alive. He said he knew that earlier superintendents had just not wanted to be bothered dealing with the company union and he had allowed them to discourage the men. He had had other things to do so he had not called regular meetings with the company union. But now he was going to stir things up again, if it was not too late. He called Franklin, the personnel man, and told him to get in touch with Les Harper, company union president, so that Les could "demand" another negotiating meeting with the company on the following Saturday.

Meanwhile Division Superintendent Wenzel and personnel man Franklin were keeping themselves informed about union developments. Did they have spies? One management man told me that on the morning following the last CIO meeting, Wenzel had a complete list of all the company employees who had attended. Wenzel denied this. He said, "We

only had four of the names. We are not interested in all those names."
Franklin added:

We just felt that we ought to know what was going on there. How
are we going to know if the CIO is a good thing for us or not unless we know
about those things? Maybe we want to go in with the CIO. The man that
brings us that information does it entirely voluntarily. He feels very strongly
about this, and he thinks that it is in his own interest as well as for the company to find these things out.

In early March it was time for the annual election of representatives to
the company union. In Hi-Test the first ballot showed two votes for Joe
Sloan; two for Frank Kendall, a popular fractionator operator; one vote
each for two other men; and the rest of the votes for "CIO," "Jesus
Christ," and various obscenities.

The next day, when the run-off election between Kendall and Sloan
was scheduled, Foreman Tom Lloyd urged the men to take it seriously.
He argued that they had nothing to lose in doing so. If the CIO union
won the representation election, the company union would be out, but if
the company union did win, the men would at least have a representative
in on the making of a new contract. The men did take the run-off more
seriously, and they elected Frank Kendall.

While the campaign between the CIO and the company union was
fought out on a day-to-day basis, the sentiments of the men corresponded
to their acticipations of future situations. Suppose the CIO won, how
would things be different? Suppose the CIO lost, how would the men fare
without a CIO union? And if a man favored the CIO or the company
union, how would this affect his future with the company? To some
extent these considerations were inevitable among the men, but to some
extent they were stimulated by contacts between the men and Division
Superintendent Wenzel and personnel man Franklin.

To some of the men, the entrance of the CIO would mean a clarification of the relations between the men and management and an elimination
of favoritism. As a Hi-Test hydro-stillman put it:

If we had a union come in here, we could take care of things like that
(promotions outside of seniority). The men wouldn't be so uncertain any
more. The company would have a line to walk, and the union would have a
line to walk. The union could keep the company from getting out of line, and
the company could keep the union from getting out of line.

But did the men really want an impersonal system? Would some of
them rather prefer to take their chances with what management might
offer them individually? In early March I had this report from Poly
Operator Mark Walling:

Did you hear what Wenzel said to Jess Kemmerer? (poly operator). . . .
Well this is what Wenzel said, and he probably meant for Jess to pass it on to
us. He said, "Any one of those poly operators could have had the job that

Tom Lloyd has now if they had just kept their noses clean." I went down to see what he meant about that. He told me the same thing, and when I asked him to explain, he just said, "Well, you know how conditions have been down there." It was obvious what he wanted to do. He wanted to make the poly operators ease off the CIO. Al is a good fellow, but he is a big bull artist. I happen to know because Tom Lloyd told me that he was promised his job almost six months before he finally got it. They had to wait all that time to make a job for Fitch somewhere else. If he was in line for that job, how would we have a chance at it?

Wenzel gave me his own version of the conversation:

I knew he would tell out there what I told him, but maybe I talked too much. I told him that he could get ahead himself if he just kept his nose clean and did his work. By that phrase, keep his nose clean, I just meant that he should keep out of trouble with the supervisor, and he felt guilty about the CIO, and he felt that I was referring to union activity. The outcome of that is just the man's personal business and I wouldn't interfere with that.

Is that all Wenzel meant? If so, why did he refuse to clarify the remark when Walling asked for an explanation? When the men were preoccupied with the CIO drive, it was inevitable that any such remark of Wenzel would be interpreted just as it was interpreted, and the division superintendent could hardly have been unaware of this.

Could such remarks discourage the men from supporting the CIO? I put this to Mark Walling.

Not a bit. We all know that Al is a big bull artist. We know that they wouldn't put a man in that position without a college education anyway.

But were the men actually that certain? The men knew the current company policy against promotion into management for noncollege men, and yet several of these Hi-Test operators had told me that they had not entirely given up hope of somehow getting into supervision. Was it entirely an unrealistic hope? It certainly seemed so at the time, but before the war was over, management was finding such difficulty in getting enough college men to take foremen's jobs in its rapidly expanding operations that the policy against promotion of noncollege men was rescinded. Whatever the facts of the case, the men listened avidly for reports from Wenzel about their promotion prospects even as they damned the division superintendent as a "bull artist."

A week later, Walling brought back another report on management's point of view, this time from a conversation with personnel man Franklin. He had asked Franklin what the company would do if the men went CIO.

He said he thought it would be pretty rough. All the human side would go out of it. The company would just cut all the corners that it could. I wish I knew what was the best thing for us to do. Do you think the company will get rough?

I asked him if he had ever considered that possibility before.

No, not until I talked with Franklin. I wonder what they might do? Maybe they will cut the poly operators out of here and just leave two men to run the plant. What do you think they could do?

I answered that different companies react in different ways and asked him what he thought he himself would do.

I don't know. Just figuring out for myself, I think the union would be the best thing, but I wish I knew how it would affect the men.

I asked him if he thought his known connection with the union might handicap him personally with the company.

Yes, I think it has.

It is extraordinary that a poly operator such as Walling would consider the possibility of the company eliminating the poly operator position. The plant had originally been run with only two operators, but management had found it necessary to place a third man in charge in order to coordinate the work of the two. The poly operator position had not been created to please the men, and it is hard to imagine that it would be eliminated in order to punish them. But such were the tensions and anxieties in this situation that Walling was able to imagine the elimination of his own job.

Division Superintendent Wenzel had been able to stall off the Masters get-tough policy, so that no men were bumped back before the transfers to the rubber plant. Now he took the initiative to bid for full local control of the campaign in a meeting at the main office. He and Franklin had been called to the main office to discuss management strategy and tactics against the CIO in a meeting with Vice President Weber and General Superintendent of Field Operations Masters. Wenzel reported to me that Masters did most of the talking at this meeting and seemed to be assuming that in the final weeks before the election, his assistant would be in Oil City taking command of the situation. Wenzel assumed—and probably correctly—that the mere presence of anyone identified with Masters in Oil City could be worth a number of additional CIO votes in the election. He therefore urged Vice President Weber to leave the whole campaign to Franklin and himself. This was a local problem, he argued, and he knew how to handle it. Weber agreed. No one from the main office was seen in Oil City until after the election.

Having secured control over management action in the crisis, Wenzel now found events playing into his hands. It had come time to arrange the transfers to the rubber plant. If these had been handled autocratically or in a discriminatory manner, the transfers would have provided fuel to warm up CIO sentiment. As it was, several of the strongest CIO supporters among the men commented to me that management's handling of the situation had been perfectly fair and reasonable.

A company representative from the rubber plant had met with local management and with the company union representatives to describe the opportunities at the rubber plant, the nature of the community situation, and so on, and to respond to any questions. The men were then free to schedule individual appointments with him to explore the prospects the rubber plant might offer them. No one was required to transfer, and men were given time to make up their minds. On its side, management was not required to accept for the rubber plant everyone who was ready to transfer. However, I heard no criticism regarding individuals who wanted the rubber plant job and were refused the opportunity. Apparently, there turned out to be a pretty even balance between those wanting to make the transfer and those acceptable to the rubber plant representative. In Hi-Test, as one hydro-stillman transferred, it was only Joe Sloan whose job was affected.

The transfer activities had a striking affect on interest in the representation election. A sudden shift in topics of conversation among the men was reported to me by several informants. While before the transfer activities the progress of the union organization drive, and the various statements of the division superintendent bearing on that drive, had been a central focus of conversational interest, now the men were all talking about the rubber plant transfers. Each man had to ask himself whether he would be better off to stay or go. Not only did the men talk it over at home but they talked it over on the job. The men who decided to go found themselves suddenly in a situation where what happened locally no longer meant very much to them—even though they might still be around to vote in the representation election. The men who decided against leaving could not help but wonder whether they had made the right decision, and they were at least interested in hearing arguments that would provide reassurance on this score.

The farewell party

A final distraction was provided by Poly Operator Mark Walling himself—although he certainly did not plan it that way. It occurred to him that it was not right for the men to let several of their fellow workers leave for a new plant without having some kind of party in their honor. He telephoned Franklin and Wenzel regarding company support for such a party and found them uncooperative at first. Walling persisted and finally Wenzel agreed that management would furnish beer and pretzels for a party in the clubhouse. Walling then organized a collection among fellow workers to provide parting gifts for the men.

When I arrived at 8:15 at the clubhouse, the party was already well under way, and the beer was beginning to flow. There was a crap game going on in one corner of the room and two poker games were starting, one for small stakes and the other for much higher stakes.

At one table, Mark Walling was playing checkers against an engineer, whom he beat four straight games. Throughout the room, there was a lively mixing of management and workers.

When Al Wenzel entered, he joined in the crap game and immediately became the center of attention, talking loudly with the men and joking about his prowess with the dice. Wenzel moved into one of the poker games later. Through the evening, he was circulating around the hall, radiating good fellowship. When he did stop to talk for any length of time, I noted him talking with Walling more than with anyone else.

For the speech-making, a popular worker served as master of ceremonies. All of the local management people were called on for remarks. Les Harper, company union president, Mark Walling, and the men going to the rubber plant all spoke briefly.

The speeches all followed very much the same pattern; the management people, Harper, and Walling told the men what good fellows they had been to work with and stressed the advantages they would have in the rubber plant. Wenzel provoked laughter with his heckling of some of the management speakers.

After the presentation of gifts from the men by one of the superintendents, Al Wenzel had the last word. Following the customary remarks about the men who were leaving, he went on to say:

We wouldn't be here tonight if it had not been for that goddamn Walling. He has the most persuasive telephone voice I ever heard. We had decided, because of being afraid of being accused of this and that, that we couldn't come to this party tonight, but that goddamn Walling wouldn't take no for an answer, and so we are here. I am glad to say that I haven't heard a word from anybody tonight about coming events, and the first man that mentions coming events will be thrown out.

The CIO organizational drive symbolized a division between the men and management. The men were on one side, management on the other. Did the men need a union to protect them against management? Some management people considered the organization as "one big happy family." In fact, the president of the company, in one of his rare visits to Oil City some weeks before the election, had said plaintively to local management people:

I want you to know this is the same organization that it has always been. We are the same men that we always were.

He recalled the days when he used to sign the payroll checks for all the company employees and when he used to visit the families of the men when somebody was sick. But, he went on:

We have grown so big I have to think of Washington all the time. They are doing so many things that I can't see the men as I used to. But my door is still always open to anybody that wants to talk to me.

The farewell party dramatized for the men as nothing else could have the conception of the company as one big happy family—with management in the parental role. Workers and management people met on the same social level. Good old Al Wenzel was there in vest and suspenders, making wisecracks at the men and encouraging them to joke back at him. The speeches all sounded a note of fellowship among all of these men working together. And interestingly enough, although the party had been organized by Mark Walling, one of the superintendents made the presentation of gifts, all of the management men were called upon to speak, and the final talk was reserved for the division superintendent himself. In spite of everything that had happened, the management people were acting out the one big happy family concept, and the men were enjoying it.

Did the farewell party affect votes in the representation election which took place less than two weeks later? That is a difficult question to answer. A man who expressed himself for the CIO before the party could hardly admit that such an apparently extraneous event as a farewell party had changed his mind. I am certain that it did not affect the votes of those who had previously stated to me strong CIO convictions. It may very well have affected a number of men who were on the fence, but some of these men had been wavering back and forth for a number of weeks, and it would be hard to weigh the significance of even so dramatic an event as this in the wavering process.

I assume that Mark Walling himself was the man most likely to have been influenced by the farewell party. When I saw him briefly a day or two later and asked him how he was voting, he said he was on the fence. In contrast to earlier discussions, he avoided further explanations. A week after the election he commented, "There are lots of crooked things about unions."

I asked if he knew anything crooked about the Oil Workers International Union. "No, but you read a lot of things in the newspaper about that sort of thing."

Why had the corruption issue suddenly come to Walling's attention? He was probably referring to the columns of Westbrook Pegler, which were syndicated in the Oil City's daily newspaper, but this was hardly a new theme for Mr. Pegler. Why had the Pegler remarks failed to impress Walling earlier? We must conclude that something had happened to Walling to increase his receptivity to this kind of argument. His involvement as a central figure in the farewell party may well have been such an influence. On the other hand, it might be argued that since the CIO had just lost the election, Walling was in the process of adjusting himself to the inevitable. However, the CIO had already entered a protest on the election, so a man did not have to accept its results as final unless he so desired.

Negotiating for the company union

As the April 6 representation election date approached, management and the company union negotiators were meeting day after day to work out a new contract. It was management's idea to have at least a tentative draft of the contract finished before the representation election, so that word of its promised benefits could be spread before voting time. The final contract could then be worked out after the representation election —assuming that the company union won. A little more than a week before the representation election, the tentative contract was agreed upon and the negotiating meetings were terminated.

How this promise of a new company union contract affected the men I cannot document, but my record is clear as to the effect of the negotiating process upon Frank Kendall, who was the reluctant representative for Hi-Test plant. His remarks clearly show a change in sentiments accompanying the change in interactions and activities he had experienced during the negotiation period. It was noteworthy that in discussing the change of sentiments with me, he made no reference to any specific contract provisions. Here speaks a man whom I had identified earlier as one of the staunchest supporters of the CIO:

I used to think that the company was just out to get whatever it could from us. Now, I have been meeting with those men, and I have been studying them. I have come to the conclusion that they are really sincere. You can't be with a group of men for days like I was if they are hypocrites without you seeing that. I think they mean to be good to the men right now. If the company union wins this election I think they will do their level best to make things nice for the men—for a while. I think we would be better off in the company union right now, but the thing is, is it always going to be that way? I wish I knew.

After he had repeated himself several times on this theme, I asked him how he was going to vote.

I don't know. I am still on the fence. It wouldn't do for me to come back to these men and try to convert them to the company union. They would think that I was bought off. That's what they are looking for. I just don't know what I am going to do.

He told me that he had already been made the butt of jokes about the chicken barbecue dinners the management was buying for the company union negotiators. He assured me that although the men and management had eaten together, the worker representatives had bought their own lunches. He added that he had not got any enjoyment out of the experience of negotiating the contract. "It bores on me." He went on in this way:

You know, I have changed my opinion of Masters a good deal since I have been seeing him. He talks right out and tells you what he thinks. He is a little blunt about it, but you know where he stands. Walter Gruber (employee relations director) is always trying to smooth things over. I don't like that so much.

Tom Lloyd was talking to me yesterday. I didn't have the heart to tell him that I would vote for the CIO. No, it wasn't that I would be afraid to tell him.

It just don't seem right to say that. It seems like we are letting the men down. Right now we have better bosses than we ever had before. The men are just beginning to appreciate them. That means a lot.

Management's eleventh-hour effort

Management did not wait out passively the last few days until the election. Tom Lloyd described to me the last moves that were contemplated:

There will be plenty of dirty work. There will be no holds barred. The company wants to win this election at all costs. There are certain things we can do. These men that are supposed to go to the synthetic rubber plant on April 1—now we have just discovered that there are certain jobs that those men are to be kept here for until after the election. We know those men, and we know how they are going to vote. I don't think the union can protest that because these men were on the rolls March 1 when the union had a chance to go over the payroll. Then there is the district labor gang. Those men work all over the state, but it is just going to happen that on the day of the election they are all going to be working in Oil City. We don't think the CIO has been able to do much there. We are going to see to it that every man votes. I will go down on the job on Saturday and check up on all of my men. If a man has not voted, I will arrange to let him go off the job to get to the polls. If he does not want to go, I can say to him, "After all, this is a secret ballot and nobody is going to know how you vote, but it will be known whether you voted or not. And then whoever wins they can think that you were on their side. That sounds pretty logical, don't it?" Besides that we will work through certain men we can trust.

Local management people had met earlier, with each man going over the list of men under his supervision and indicating how he expected each man to vote. The summation of these estimates indicated a landslide for the company union. This suggests that we must not overestimate the accuracy of management information in such a situation. For example, I asked Lloyd to predict the votes of the Hi-Test men. He predicted nine votes for the company union, with five being on the fence and only three being definitely for the CIO. Among his nine for the company union were two men that I would have placed on the fence and two (Joe Sloan and Johnny Hudson) that I was certain were going to vote for the CIO. When I asked Lloyd on what basis he predicted Sloan for the company union, he said:

I talked with him this morning and asked him how he thought it was going to go. He said he thought the company union might win it. I didn't ask him how he would vote himself, but from the way he talked, I think he is leaning that way.

Later that same day, Sloan told me flatly that he still intended to vote for the union—but he had told Lloyd that the company union might win, as indeed he thought it might.

The final blow for the company was wielded in the labor gang by Elmer Martin, welder and company union representative. Except for several welders, the labor gang was made up of men who had very little experience with the company. Furthermore, as Lloyd noted, the gang moved around to different locations in the state and thus was cut off from very much communication with the operating units in the Oil City area. The welders were not only the most experienced men in the labor gang, but also the only skilled ones. It was natural under the circumstances that they should have high status in the labor gang and that one of them should be elected company union representative.

During the week before election, Elmer Martin took it upon himself to explain the proposed company union contract to the labor gang. The meeting was held outside of the plant yard—but on company time. Martin claims that this was his own idea, but he had to have his superintendent's permission in order to make the time available to the men for this purpose.

I had no contacts with the labor gang and so no direct way of estimating the impact of Martin's meeting. However, given the prestige of the welder and the lack of experience of the labor gang members, it seems likely that this was indeed an influential move. And 45 men in an electorate of 200-odd were involved.

For the April 6 election, the workers had three choices; the CIO union, the company union, or no union. However, management had sent out word that the men who were against the CIO union should not divide their votes; they should vote for the company union, whatever their opinion of that organization. In reality, the election represented simply a vote for or against the CIO. The activities preceding the election had not convinced anyone that the company union was an effective organization. Thus in voting the men were expressing either their desire to put their faith exclusively in management, or to turn to representation which was not under management control.

The count in the April 6 vote showed 106 for the company union and 92 for the Oil Workers International Union. The CIO immediately challenged the election on a number of grounds, the two most important being Elmer Martin's meeting with the labor gang and personnel man Franklin's presence in an automobile near the polls throughout most of election day. (A CIO organizer had asked Franklin which side he was supporting, and the personnel man had refused to answer.)

While another election was scheduled for a later time, this was the end of my research, and I left Oil City a month later.

Analysis

Let us now see if we can put the case in a more general framework. The story told suggests that the progress of unionization can be considered as both a long-run and a short-run phenomenon. That is, we found that certain basic changes had taken place within the company and in the relations between company and environment to make unionization possible. We also saw how changes taking place day to day and week by week in the months leading up to the representation election served to increase or diminish the chances of the union.

Let us approach the unionization problem from a standpoint of the way the workers visualize the organization. In terms of the present question, there are two mutually incompatible ways of visualizing the organization: vertical versus horizontal integration. When management people speak of "one big happy family" they are presenting the vertical integration image. People at all different levels in the organization are alike in that they share a common membership.

The union organizer sees the situation in terms of horizontal integration: There are two classes of people in the organization, management and workers, with a sharp dividing line separating them horizontally.

I do not mean to suggest that there are workers who see the organization purely in terms of vertical integration or those who see it purely in terms of horizontal integration. We can expect nearly any worker to see the organization in terms of both concepts, but worker A may find vertical integration the predominant concept, worker B may find horizontal integration the predominant concept, while worker C may fluctuate between the two polls in response to events taking place in the course of the campaign.

Let us now examine the forces that lead to the strengthening of one or the other concept, thus resulting in a vote for or against the union.

Long-run changes

If we consider the 10-year period leading up to the representation election of 1943, there were clearly important changes in the relation of the company to the environment of the country. At the beginning of the period, industrial unions were practically unknown. By 1943, they were an accepted part of the industrial scene, with legal protection and a federal governmental policy favoring collective bargaining. However, much the same could have been said about two earlier organizing attempts in the late 1930's, which failed to gain much headway. In other words, this environmental change does not seem to account for the 1942–43 drive coming so much nearer to success than the earlier ones.

It might be argued that the condition of the labor market provides part of our answer. In a period of wartime labor shortage, a worker need not have fears of prolonged unemployment if he is discharged for union activities. However, workers in this situation had strong claims for draft deferment, since they were considered to be working in an essential industry. As Joe Sloan himself commented, a man who quit his job or was discharged might be drafted. Therefore, while the labor market situation may be an important influence in some cases, it does not seem to be so here.

The major long-run influences seem to be two: career blocking and changes in worker-higher management relations.

The management policy of placing in supervision only college graduates served to divide the organization into two parts, with a sharp line drawn between them. The workers, thus cut off from advancement, were now less inclined to identify themselves with management and more inclined to feel, think, and act in terms of horizontal integration.

The change from Fitzgerald to Masters destroyed the connecting link between workers and the home office. Even while Fitzgerald still lived, there was from year to year a decrease in frequently of his interactions with workers, but there remained a feeling that you could go to Fred when you needed help, and he would help you. While Fitzgerald was alive, there also existed a system of reciprocity, which was well understood by the men. The positive exchange was of this nature: The workers refrained from involvement with unions, and Fitzgerald acted on the problems they had with local management people. No such reciprocity was offered by Masters.

The change from Fitzgerald to Masters also involved drastic changes on the local management scene. Before the Masters' crack-down, what Alvin Gouldner has described as the "indulgency pattern" prevailed in the Oil City operations.[1] Discipline was lax and the men enjoyed certain benefits (free gasoline, time off for gambling, etc.) which were contrary to the official policy of the company. In return, they were expected to be loyal to the particular management people who provided the benefits. Now, I am not saying that all or most of the workers were happy with the particular set of personal relations involved in this indulgency pattern. I later heard many complaints about favoritism, but this simply pointed to a situation in which a certain number of workers might look to get advantages through developing special relations with certain management people. While these channels were open, there was less likelihood of workers joining together on a basis that would establish uniform policies governing the position of individuals in the social system. When Masters stepped in, he destroyed the indulgency pattern with one blow.

The changes in potency of the company union also had a long-run impact. As worker interactions with higher management and sentiment ties to it became more attenuated, one might have expected the company union to step in and reestablish the relationship. In fact, this is apparently what higher management had in mind, and it is instructive to see how management's expectations were frustrated. As an organization with member support, the company union was destroyed at two levels. Local

---

[1] Alvin Gouldner, *Patterns of Industrial Bureaucracy* (Glencoe, Ill.: The Free Press, 1954).

management found it inconvenient to have workers raising questions about its decisions before higher management people in the company, and so stepped in to discourage worker leadership activity and to take over the union meetings. Division Superintendent Wenzel recognized that he could have prolonged the life of the company union by encouraging regular meetings and taking action to assure workers that they would get responses to their complaints, even when those complaints embarrassed local management. But a dormant company union provided less immediate bother to Wenzel than did a live one, and he took no trouble to revive it until a greater threat appeared on the horizon.

Two types of action from the main office also served in the destruction process. The company union president noted higher management's tendency to anticipate company union demands and raise wages before negotiations had even been undertaken. He also cited a statement by the vice president of the company who said, in effect: Don't bother me now; I have more important things to do in Washington, and you won't get anything anyway.

The company union therefore did not provide an institution through which workers were enabled to initiate activities for management on a regular and continuing basis. While this destroyed the company union as a real membership organization, the form persisted, as we have seen, and provided a vehicle through which management was later able to institute certain interactional changes that did have effects upon worker sentiments.

Changes in interpersonal relations

Foremen-worker relations: We can expect foremen-worker relations to affect worker sentiments toward the union to some extent. The experience of the Hi-Test workers under Jones and Fitch seemed to stimulate them in a pro-union direction. Their experiences under Lloyd seemed to modify this orientation. Some men expressed the sentiment that voting for the union seemed equivalent to letting the present good bosses down, and this was apparently a consideration even among those who continued to favor the union.

The two types of foreman-worker relations show marked contrasts in the frequency and direction of initiation of activity and in the presence or absence of positive exchange transactions. For case one (Jones and Fitch), the following characteristics of the relationship promoted pro-union sentiments:

1. High rate of initiation of activity from foreman to workers.
2. Low rate of initiation from workers to foreman.
3. Absence of positive exchange transactions.
4. Prevalence of negative exchange transactions, with the foreman penal-

izing to enforce standards and workers evading standards to escape punishment and get back at the foreman.

In case two (Lloyd), the workers were encouraged to identify with the company through the following changes:

1. Decrease in the frequency of initiation of activity from foreman to workers.
2. Increase in the frequency of initiation of activity from workers to foreman.
3. Development of positive exchange transactions between foreman and workers.
4. Elimination of negative exchange transactions between foreman and workers.

The foreman-worker relationship may influence but does not fully determine worker sentiments regarding the union. As they talked about the union, Hi-Test workers talked a great deal about Masters and the home office. Some of them saw the decision of management to place Lloyd in this position as a temporary expedient to head off the CIO and argued that management might just as readily remove the "good" foreman at any time. Nevertheless, there did seem to be some influence along the lines I have indicated.

Significant symbols: In this case, we have a number of examples in which certain verbal symbols played a prominent role in affecting sentiments and interactions.

The use by management people of verbal symbols implying low status for workers tends to promote among workers the concept of horizontal integration, and thus encourages pro-union sentiments.

In this case we have two striking examples. One of the earlier foremen once referred to men in the catalyst plant as "WPA workers" (men on work relief projects). We have Tom Lloyd's testimony that this stirred up such strong resentments that the men still talked about it years later. This obviously stirred resentment toward the management man who uttered the words and presumably toward management in general. We might also assume that it strengthened the horizontal integration concept and therefore promoted union sentiment, although we have no direct evidence on this point.

The "watchman" statement presents us with a more clear-cut case. This reawakened and fortified all the old sentiments of hostility toward Masters and the main office. Workers and local management people alike reported that the incident had a sudden and far-reaching effect on pro-union sentiments.

Worker-management off-the-job relations: The case suggests that the following conditions will tend to strengthen the vertical integration concept and thus weaken pro-union sentiments:

1. Increase of interactions outside of the line of authority between workers and management, providing this is accompanied by
2. Increased opportunities for workers to initiate activities for management and
3. Management use of verbal symbols appropriate to the vertical integration concept.

In this case, we should note particularly two areas of worker-management off-the-job interaction. The company union negotiations with management provide the first example. We saw first that these increased interactions did not promote the vertical integration concept when a management man used a verbal symbol in striking contradiction of that concept. In effect, the watchman statement broke up the meetings. When they were resumed, we cannot testify that management did in fact use symbols implying vertical integration, for such evidence can only have been gained from observation of the meetings. However, we can say that management did not again introduce any verbal symbols which were sharply at variance with this concept of vertical integration.

In the case of the farewell party, I had an opportunity to observe the verbal symbols as well as the interaction. In the first place, we should note that the party itself arose out of worker initiative. It involved workers and management people interacting together, regardless of their sentiments toward the union. Managers and workers alike, in their speeches, used symbols implying vertical integration, referring to years of experience with each other within the same organization and remarking upon what a fine thing it was that all of the members could get together in such a good spirit.

One word of caution should be stressed. The reader should not assume that management people need only to speak in terms of "one big happy family" in order to stimulate workers to see the organization in vertical integration terms. When the appropriate interaction and activity patterns are lacking, such symbols will seem incongruous and be ineffective. In this case, the symbols were appropriate at least to the immediate interaction and activity situation. This combination of symbols with interaction and activities seemed to promote the concept of vertical integration at that time. Had the representation election come several months later, this momentary reorganization of interactions, activities, and symbols could not have been expected to have any effect upon votes. As it was, the farewell party took place within a few days of the election, and there is reason to believe that it had some influence in the vote.

So far we have been discussing worker visualizations of the organization in terms of two conflicting concepts: vertical and horizontal integration. This seems appropriate to the situation where a union organization drive is in progress. Where the union has become established, we shall see that the two concepts do not appear to be so conflicting to the workers as they do during the organizing period.

2.   Symbolism for changing management sentiments

In the Hi-Test case, we have taken management sentiments toward unions as given and have sought to explain worker sentiments in the course of an organization drive. In the case to follow, we shall reverse the procedure, taking worker sentiments as given and seeking to explain a change in management sentiments.

The sentiments that counted for management in this case were those of Herbert J. Buchsbaum, president of S. Buchsbaum and Company, a firm manufacturing jewelry and plastic items. Using a labor spy, Buchsbaum had broken a strike in 1935 and destroyed the union. In 1941, Buchsbaum not only settled a brief strike by signing a union contract but went on to establish an extraordinarily harmonious union-management relationship. What happened to change the orientation of Herbert J. Buchsbaum?

In the following passages, Buchsbaum describes his pre-1941 sentiments regarding his company, his workers, unions, and union leaders. He also describes some of the important events of his labor relations experience.[2]

Nothing happened between 1935 and 1940 to change the way I felt about unions. I had a few friends who could see some good in unions, but I was arguing with them just as strongly in 1940 as I had in 1935. I thought they were crazy.

My mother has always been on the side of the workers. She used to say, "The poor people. They work so hard, and what do they get to show for it?" In the middle of the 1935 strike, she came into my office and pleaded with me to settle and take the people back. I certainly didn't want to listen to her then, because I knew that I was breaking the strike. I just said to her, "Mama, you've got the wrong idea. This whole thing was stirred up by a few trouble makers—just a bunch of reds. When we get rid of them, everything will be all right." That didn't satisfy her, but still she wasn't able to make me change —then or later.

But while I stayed the same, the world around me changed. By the time of the strike in January, 1941, the Wagner Act had been declared constitutional by the Supreme Court, and we were getting used to the idea. I didn't want to violate the law, and it wasn't just because of the penalty involved. Capital must believe in law and order because if you don't have law and order what protection is there for your capital?

The first break for the union came late in 1940 when they appealed to the government on some discrimination cases, and the National Labor Relations

[2] Andrew H. Whiteford, William Foote Whyte, and Burleigh B. Gardner, "From Conflict to Cooperation: A Study in Union-Management Relations," *Applied Anthropology* (Special Issue), Vol. 5, no. 4 (Fall, 1946).

Board ruled that I had to post a notice in the plant announcing that the employees were free to join a union for collective bargaining purposes. Posting that notice was the last thing I wanted to do, but I had no choice.

When organization started in the plant, I did everything in my power to forestall it. I gave a nickel raise and promised more. I thought that would take care of everything. If the people became discontented, all I had to do was offer them a raise in wages, and that would take care of it. But it didn't in this case. Apparently that wasn't what they wanted at all. They just wanted to be organized.

With the union trying to organize, naturally I was worried, but still I didn't think they would be successful. I thought I had everything under control, that most of the people were loyal to me and to the company.

I met with Sam Laderman before the strike, and he tried to convince me that he represented a majority of the workers, but I wouldn't believe him, and I challenged him to prove it to me. At the same time, I was on the watch for union tendencies in the plant. That was one thing I didn't hesitate about. If I found anyone who had any interest in the union or even if he was the son of a union member, I would have fired him as quick as look at him, no matter what he was doing in the plant.

When I came down to the plant that morning in January and saw that picket line, it was a great shock to me. I felt that those men had turned against me personally, that they were traitors and double-crossers. I was determined to get rid of them all, bring in a new bunch of people, and break the strike, just as I had in 1935.

I didn't see anything that could stop me. The strike could not have come at a better time, so far as we were concerned. Before the war, January was always a slack time in our business. The Christmas rush was just finished up and the first of the year inventory was being held. Few orders were coming in, and the receipts from our Christmas sales were moving into the office. The company was in a very strong financial position. In January we usually have to let out some of our people temporarily, so it wouldn't have hurt us at all to close down for a couple of weeks.

The union tried to block us from getting goods in and out of the plant, and they were pretty effective, but we were managing to move some things at night, and I was confident that in a couple of weeks the other unions cooperating with them would lose interest and we would be able to handle all our shipping and receiving.

While I made my plans to break the strike, I couldn't help noticing that it was different from our 1935 struggle. There were nearly all our own people on the picket line. I thought I knew them pretty well, even though they had turned against me. It was zero weather, and it was pretty cold out on that picket line. I stopped and talked to the boys, and I told them to come in the vestibule and picket. That's the kind of strike it was.

There was quite a bit of violence and sabotage in our 1935 strike. Expensive equipment was smashed, sand was thrown in bearings, materials were destroyed, and there were some bricks thrown through the windows.

The 1941 strike was quite different. A few people got beaten up, but the company suffered no property damage. The union had good discipline on that point. There was one time when some of our people were trying to get through the picket line into the plant. They drove up in a car onto the sidewalk and right in front of the plant entrance to get the people in. That car endangered the lives of some of the picketers, and they rushed up and wanted to turn it over. Garfield (union leader) stepped in then and wouldn't let them do anything to the car. That made an impression on me when I was told about it. I felt that these were responsible people. I didn't agree with them, but I could see that they were going out of their way not to harm the company.

Did the union leaders know what they were doing as they acted out the drama of the picket line? Here is Sidney Garfield's account of the encounter with the strike-breaker's car:[3]

I think something that made him (Mr. Buchsbaum) trust me was rather interesting. During the strike, things were pretty rough for a while and we had a number of clashes when people tried to get into the plant. One time one of the men came flying down the street about 60 miles an hour in a car and ran right up on the sidewalk to the doors of the plant and tried to let people in that way. He might easily have run over some of our boys standing around, but they got between him and the door of the plant and had him trapped there. The strikers were all for taking care of him quickly right then and there and turning the car over in the street, but I knew enough to realize that that would be a bad move because of *the great American tradition of respect for property*, so I made them leave the car alone. I don't mean that I was easy. There was one fellow who was trying to sneak in, and I pulled him out of his car and just kicked him down the street.

When this incident came up, the chief company detective was standing right inside the door with a gun in his hand, but he was afraid to use it, and I found out later that he was impressed by what had happened and had gone up and told Herb Buchsbaum about my respect for property, which apparently made some impression on Herb, too. It's the little things which make the difference.

Now Herbert Buchsbaum resumes his story:[4]

As soon as the strike started, Sam Laderman (union leader) asked me to meet with him and a committee of the strikers. I didn't want to do it, and I called my lawyer three times to try to find some way out of it. Each time he told me I had to accept the invitation because it would have been a violation of the law not to meet with them.

On the second day of the strike I had lunch with Laderman and with a business acquaintance of mine who had a contract with his union. Up to that time I thought all union people were a bunch of racketeers. My friend reassured me on this point. He said that you could count on Sam Laderman keeping his word. He told me that Sam was a real human being. He liked opera. He disliked fights. There would be nothing he would like better than being friends with the employer if it were possible. He assured me that the union was always willing to discuss things from a reasonable point of view. And Laderman assured me that our contract would contain the standard

[3] *Ibid.*

[4] *Ibid.*

clause that it would be no less advantageous to the employer than contracts the same union made with any other firm.

That made an impression on me. I still had no idea of settling the strike but I agreed to meet with Laderman and a committee of the employees on the third day.

Well, we sat around the table and began talking. I knew all the men there. We were just a small firm at the time.

The first question one of the men asked me was this: "Mr. Buchsbaum, why are you against unions?" Now that was a good question and I welcomed it. I thought that gave me a chance to win them over to my line of reasoning. I stated: "I'm against unions because they limit production. They put production down to the level of the slowest employee and at the same time force impossible wage increases, driving the company out of business."

They started talking all at once. They didn't want to limit production, but increase it. They wanted to see the company go ahead.

I asked: "How can you increase production?"

I got answers fast. Each one had a sound suggestion for his department. First spoke one of the polishers. He told of the large door behind the polishing department used for in and out shipments—how in zero weather this door was opened many times daily, obliging the perspiring men to leave their wheels and go to the washroom to save themselves from catching cold. How a simple protecting partition would save about an hour and a half per man per day. Other suggestions equally good came from everyone in the circle. I took notes that I could see would save the company thousands of dollars annually.

In that first meeting they really sold me a bill of goods. There was one thing that convinced me. When the workers began talking I saw that they had my interests at heart—as well as their own. I realized I had done them a great injustice in thinking that they had turned traitor to the company.

I came to a decision—"All right boys. I have a different slant on this now. Go out and tell all the men to come back to work. We'll sign a union contract as soon as we can write it up. Only one condition—no hard feelings or discrimination against the workers who did not join the strike. Let's say they didn't understand your point of view. I didn't myself."

Right there we agreed in principle on the terms of the contract and signed a memorandum. That ended the strike. The men went right back to work.

When we have the task of explaining a change in a man's sentiments, generally we look first for changes in the interactions and activities he is experiencing. But if the company president refuses to interact with union leaders and to get involved in any activities with them, then clearly we must look for another route for the introduction of sentiment changes.

Let us re-examine the symbols perceived by Herbert Buchsbaum in the light of the theory of cognitive dissonance.[5] Before the strike, the president had a clear and integrated set of sentiments regarding unions, union leaders, private property, law and order, and his company. He regarded union leaders as racketeers and/or Communists. They and their unions

---

[5] L. Festinger, *A Theory of Cognitive Dissonance* (Evanston, Ill.: Row, Peterson and Co., 1957).

had no respect for private property and the welfare of his business. He felt he had a legal right to protect his business from "outside agitators."

Note how the key events during the short strike produced symbols that ran counter to Buchsbaum's sentiments in every important respect. He saw Garfield in the act of protecting private property—of individuals and of the company. He heard from a trusted friend that Sam Laderman was "a real human being" and a lover of opera. It is important to note that the opera-lover symbolism did not owe its effectiveness to a common interest on the part of Buchsbaum. He confessed to me that opera bored him and that he only went when dragged by his wife. The point is that the symbolism of "a real human being" and an opera lover was sharply at variance with Buchsbaum's conception of the subhuman racketeer/Communist. The changes in labor relations in the national scene had shaken Buchsbaum's picture of his own moral position. Until recently he and his friends had been telling themselves that the Wagner Act was unconstitutional and would be thrown out by the Supreme Court. When the Court upheld the Act, this disrupted the integration of Buchsbaum's sentiment pattern. If he acted in terms of his strong anti-union sentiments, he would be acting in violation of his sentiments on respect for the law.

Finally, when Buchsbaum did meet with the union officers and the local workers' committee, he was confronted with a reversal of the symbolism of anticipated transactions. He told the committee that union-management relations necessarily involved negative exchange and open-conflict transactions. They countered by showing the possibilities of positive exchanges, trading, and joint payoff transactions.

It was probably important that the workers did not speak simply in general terms of their regard for the company and of their desire to be helpful. They cited specific conditions that could be changed, and Buchsbaum could readily translate these suggestions into the symbolism of cost savings or productivity increases. As he agreed to sign the contract, he moved immediately to set up the pattern of transactions that had been symbolized for him by the suggestions of his workers.

It might be argued that without any of the other symbols described Buchsbaum would have been forced by the law to meet with the union leaders. That is probably true, but many executives have met with union leaders under duress, have gone through the required motions, and yet have avoided coming to any real accommodation with the union. The force of the law might indeed have brought about a meeting between Buchsbaum and the union leaders, but it seems hardly likely that this compulsion alone would have brought about the sudden and drastic change in the sentiments of the company president.

Summary and conclusions

In this chapter, we have traced two union organizing campaigns, one almost successful, the other successful, one viewed in terms of worker

reactions, the other viewed from the standpoint of the company president.

In each case we have sought to examine the campaign in terms of
symbolism and of the relations of symbols to interactions, activities, and
sentiments.

In the Hi-Test case we posited two opposing symbolic representations
of the company: vertical integration versus horizontal integration. Those
who saw the company in vertical integration terms rejected the union,
whereas those who thought in terms of horizontal integration identified
with the union. We examined events leading up to the campaign and
during the campaign as they tended to promote a vertical or horizontal
orientation among the workers.

We noted that the worker ties with Fred Fitzgerald tended to make
them think in vertical terms of integration with the company. The shift
to Masters blocked workers off from any access to higher management
and was a basic influence toward horizontal integration. The early supervisors, Jones and Fitch, were so unresponsive to the workers as to stimulate pro-union sentiments. Tom Lloyd was so responsive as to give some
of the men serious doubts as to whether it was right to vote union.
Finally, we have noted that the farewell party was a large-scale and
dramatic representation of the "one big happy family" (vertical integration) symbolism.

In transactional terms, when workers find themselves engaged in positive exchanges, trading, or joint payoff transactions with members of
management, they tend to embrace the vertical integration concept and
reject the union. When few such positive transactions with managers are
available to them, they tend to explore the transactional possibilities of a
horizontally based organization.

We have examined the case of Herbert J. Buchsbaum in terms of
cognitive dissonance: the confrontation of the actor with symbols that
are at variance with his sentiments. The same reasoning can be applied to
the Hi-Test case. As the horizontally oriented individual confronts events
that seem to symbolize vertical integration (the farewell party, for example), the dissonance serves to make him more uncertain of his sentiments.
And so it is also with the vertically oriented individual when he confronts
events that seem to symbolize horizontal integration (the watchman
statement, for example).

Earlier in this book (see Chapter 4), we have examined the pro- or
anti-union sentiments of workers in terms of their previous IAS experience. In this chapter, we are applying the same type of analysis at the
group and organizational level as well.

References

Gouldner, Alvin. *Wildcat Strike.* Yellow Springs, Ohio: Antioch College
Press, 1954. A case study of a strike.

Karsh, Bernard. *Diary of a Strike*. Urbana: University of Illinois Press, 1958. Case study with particular emphasis on varying reactions of workers.

Discussion questions

1. Select an organization in which you have worked. Describe the events and accompaning symbols that inclined you toward vertical or horizontal integration.

2. Interview someone with experience in working in organizations. Get him to describe the events and accompanying symbols that inclined him toward vertical or horizontal integration.

3. Review the Hi-Test organization drive. Think first in terms of top management's objective to defeat the CIO union. What moves were correct in terms of this objective? What mistakes were made? Now think in terms of the union's objective to win representation at Hi-Test and related facilities. What moves were correct in terms of this objective? What mistakes were made? (Recognize that you have a much fuller report on management strategy and tactics than that available for the union.)

4. Review the discussion in Chapter 4 regarding personality and individual experience factors that tended to incline some Blank Oil Company workers toward the union and others away from it. To what extent could a union organizer or a management executive utilize the information and framework of analysis on these individual cases to increase or decrease the prospects of the success of an organization drive?

5. Select for analysis either the Gouldner or Karsh case studies (see references to this chapter). Apply the theoretical framework of *Organizational Behavior* to the case selected. Note especially where (*a*) the case does not provide information you need to use the framework effectively, and (*b*) the framework fails to take into account what seem to you important elements of the case.

20. The evolution of union-management relations

THE UNION ORGANIZATION DRIVE necessarily represents an attack upon management control. The aim is to persuade workers that it is unwise for them to place their faith completely in the hands of management. Management is attacked. If it is to be effective, the nature of the attack must be adjusted to the existing state of worker-management relations. The first organizers at Blank Oil Company attacked the company so vigorously that they stirred up an adverse reaction among many of the men. It was only when Masters' watchman statement came out that they learned how to attack management without attacking worker loyalty to the company.

However much bitterness enters into the struggle, union organizers seek to cast the union in the role that Leonard Sayles has called "lawyer for the defense."[1] That is, they seek to give the impression that, whatever the individual's problem, he is to look to the union for its solution. The union will fight management to get for him what he needs and deserves.

At this point, the competing and conflicting interests among workers tend to be submerged. As the workers discuss various possible rules and regulations, they may be aware that a decision which will give advantage to one individual or group will also deny it to others, but until the union is in being, no one knows which people are to get which particular advantages, and stress can be placed upon general benefits such as wage increases.

As the union receives its first official recognition, its struggle is by no means finished. For the union to function effectively, management people must change their behavior and relations substantially. This is not easily done. In fact, the changes are often accompanied by sharp attacks on individual members of management and on management in general by the union leaders. As management people gradually adjust to this new relationship, the sentiments and interactions on both sides change, and this

---

[1] Except for other references noted, this chapter is based largely on Leonard Sayles and George Strauss, *The Local Union: Its Place in the Industrial Plant* (rev. ed.; New York: Harcourt, Brace & World, 1967).

change is often accompanied by the emergence of a different type of local union leader. The first stage of fighting for recognition tends to bring to the fore what Max Weber calls the "charismatic" leader, the colorful individual who has a gift for expressing the sentiments of his people and for dramatizing the conflict situation. As relations between the parties settle down, the new situation tends to bring to the fore the bureaucratic leader, the individual who is skilled at negotiation and who prefers to work quietly rather than with great fanfare. Sometimes the same individual can change his own behavior sufficiently to serve as leader from one period into the next, but often the change in the relations among the parties leads also to a change in leadership personnel.

This sort of leadership change has been widely noted. Let us turn to a case to show how the process of changing relations brings with it a change in union leadership. Lois Dean has provided us with case studies of two union locals which she studied intensively.[2] Both of them showed the same shift from the charismatic to the bureaucratic leader. In one case, the charismatic leader was in the process of dying of cancer at the time when his control was challenged, so that we cannot attribute his downfall entirely to the changing social situation even though we can show that his successor behaved far differently from him. Let us look at the second case in which the downfall of the charismatic leader was not influenced by such a health problem.

The rise and fall of Frank Vitucci

The setting is a manufacturing plant that had been family owned, but shortly before World War II, it was taken over by the Truax Corporation. Employment rose to between 6,000 and 8,000 workers. In 1944 a union carried through a successful organizing drive. Top management also recognized the union in three other plants at much the same time. Elsewhere the adjustment to the union took place with little conflict, but in our Truax plant there were two years of struggle before the change took place.

The chief target for the union in this period was Industrial Relations Director O'Leary, a man who had been accustomed to running his own show and did not respond readily to suggestions or demands from the union.

The role opposite O'Leary was played by Frank Vitucci, a young man who had played a leading role in organizing the local. He had grown up in a poor Italian-American section of the city and had learned early in his life to settle arguments with his fists. As a teenager, he had had some success as an amateur boxer. In the union situation, he made little use of

---

[2] Lois Dean, "Front Office Leadership: The Decline of Militancy in Two Union Locals," (Ph.D. thesis, Cornell University, 1953).

his fists, but he seemed to find the same sort of satisfaction in fighting management in other ways.

One of Vitucci's admirers described him in this way several years later:

Frank wasn't the most intelligent man in the world, but he was militant. He was willing to *fight* for his rights and what he stood for. He was a low seniority man. He only had two years when he got active in the union. Ordinarily a person with so little seniority wouldn't want to stick his neck out. But Frank never cared for his own job. He liked to help the people. I can't help admiring a man like that.

A union committeeman of the later period described the two antagonists in this way:

O'Leary was a rough-and-tumble sort of man, always shouting and pounding the table, and making threats. You couldn't argue with him. Frank couldn't argue either, you see. All he knew was to shout and threaten strike. So he'd go to O'Leary, and they'd yell and shout at each other, and finally reach a settlement that way.

The quotation certainly does not make clear how the men actually reached an agreement on anything, but we have a clue from Vitucci's own comment at the time when O'Leary lost his job several months later. Vitucci was the only one who expressed regrets. He said:

O'Leary was a good Joe. He was too soft. You could badger him into anything. We won all our big grievances.

Apparently O'Leary, for all his tough talk, often found himself in an untenable position and had to give way—if the union put on enough pressure. Vitucci was the man to apply the pressure.

The gains the union made against O'Leary were piecemeal. From the time of organization in 1944 through 1945 and early 1946, they were unable to reach agreement on a general contract. Instead, the parties worked together by means of agreements exacted on specific issues. In late 1945, the union was able to persuade top management to send in another negotiator to work with O'Leary, and at last the parties reached a temporary agreement.

During the early post-war months, the union was in a precarious situation. The union fought for its life primarily through finding and processing grievances. In this period, union officers did not wait for workers to come to them. They canvassed for grievances. Contrasting his own leadership with that of his successor, Abe Carter, Vitucci says:

Every grievance Carter's bunch has now, we had 50. . . . Why I won grievances under O'Leary that I wouldn't even *call* a grievance now.

Harassment of the foremen was an important part of the union drive. One former union officer describes in this way the campaign to get old Dan McDougall:

There were a lot of those old birds around, and they caused the union a lot of trouble for a while. We had to act tough and we had to do a lot of bluffing to get around them and get grievances settled so the people would be satisfied. We had to keep creating interest in the union, you see. I'll never forget one time—it was the first time I ever saw Bob Stevens (former Truax main office industrial relations director). What happened was, we had a grievance in the drives, and one of these old-time foremen, Dan McDougall, had that department. He was a hard-boiled son of a gun, and he bucked the condition up there in the drives. The girls on the line did this operation where they had a little stick of carbon and burred off the spring. That created a lot of sparks shooting all over, and some of them were pretty big sparks. Their hands were always getting burned, and the sparks burned holes in their aprons. One girl had a spark drop in her lap, and went right through her apron, through her dress, and she had one of those rubberized girdles on, and it went right through that, and it wasn't until it actually burned her skin that she knew it was there.

It was horrible that such conditions existed. You see, they had improper ventilation. There were open windows, but no cross-ventilation, so the wind just blew the sparks back in their faces. And the odor was terrible, because there was no ventilation. Well, when that one girl got burned, that's when the grievance came up. I was a committeeman and I went up there, mad as hops. I'm storming down the aisle looking for Dan McDougall, and along comes John Perkins (assistant industrial relations director) and Bob Stevens from the other direction. I didn't know Stevens, never seen him before. Perkins was showing him through the plant that day, and he was about to take over as industrial relations director. So I just went barging up to Perkins—we had to do a lot of buffing in those days. I shook my finger at him, and I said, "What's the matter that such conditions as these are allowed to exist! If you don't get some decent ventilation in here, I'll take the whole damned department out on strike."

Well, what happened was, the company finally began to get rid of these old foremen, and although they didn't say so, I know it was because these old guys couldn't get along with the union, and the company realized the union was here to stay. They'd tell these foremen they had to play ball with the union, and if they still didn't, the company got rid of them. That's what happened to Dan McDougall. After the company told him to play ball with the union, he'd talk fine to the union officers—he and I got along swell. But as soon as we left, he'd go back to driving those people that were working for him. Well, finally, he was just having too many grievances. And we really needled him.

One time, there was a grievance on one of the lines up there, and instead of having just one of the girls write the grievance, we decided to have all 60 of them write the grievance. You see, the grievance procedure provides that when there's a certain grievance that applies to more than one person, one can write it out and you can turn in just one, but the settlement will apply to all the people that are affected. But in McDougall's case, we decided we'd have each person on the line write a separate grievance. Naturally, that would stop the line because it couldn't run unless everybody was working, and there'd always be somebody writing out a grievance.

Well, we did it that way, and by the time five or six had written,

McDougall gets in touch with personnel, all excited, and says his line is down because everybody is writing a grievance. They then start hunting for me, but naturally I've made myself scarce. They're calling for me here and there, and meanwhile I'm hiding in an oil shed between the two plants. I had a spy out and when about 57 of the grievances had been written, I decided it was time to come out of hiding. So I went up to McDougall's department and he was all upset and said, "Look what's happening here, everybody is writing grievances!" All the time, I'm looking out of the corner of my eye to see how they're doing with the grievances. When I see there are only two to go, I say innocently, "Is that so? I wonder what could be the trouble. But they're nearly through, it looks like, might as well let them finish up, and then we'll go straighten it out." So we got all 60 of them. It wasn't long after that they had to let McDougall go.

It took longer to get O'Leary, but that time came too. The grievances at the foreman level, of course, piled up to the industrial relations director. There were also plantwide issues, the most important of which came to a head in 1945. The workers had been eating their lunches on company time. The company proposed to eliminate the paid lunch period, thus lengthening by half an hour the time the workers were to be in the plant. When O'Leary did not readily back down on this issue, Vitucci and his bargaining committee decided the time had come for a show of strength. As a committee member describes the situation:

It had to come. We had to show O'Leary we meant business, and we had to show him we had the people behind us. O'Leary never believed that. He figured if it ever came to a strike, why, the people wouldn't go for it, and that would be the end of the union. Well, he got the surprise of his life.

One night as the second shift workers approached the plant, they were greeted by Frank Vitucci and several committeemen, who said simply: "We're hitting the bricks." When the day shift arrived, a picket line had already been established and the plant was closed down tight. After giving the strike order, Vitucci and his fellow workers had disappeared, so the walkout appeared to be a spontaneous wildcat.

The strike lasted a week, being brought to an end by the intervention of a representative of the international union and one from top management. The strike was settled on Vitucci's terms, and the victory strengthened his hold on the membership. In the 1946 election he won an easy victory as president against a popular worker by the name of Ed Lynch.

The 1946 negotiations proceeded in two stages. First a master contract was negotiated for the four plants including our Truax local. The understanding then was that local wage structures were to be further negotiated on a local basis. O'Leary insisted that there was nothing further to negotiate. Vitucci was equally adamant in saying that the union would strike unless an appropriate agreement was reached locally. In an effort to avert the strike, top management at last replaced O'Leary with Don

Paxton, who had dealt successfully with unions elsewhere. (O'Leary said in parting, "The union cost me my job," and no doubt he was right.)

If Paxton had entered the scene some months earlier, perhaps the strike could have been avoided. A man who is unfamiliar with local practices naturally is hesitant about making important commitments rapidly. Vitucci was not the sort of man who could wait patiently. He led the local out on strike, thinking of this as just another demonstration of strength which would be over in a few days. The strike dragged on for five and a half weeks. Out of it came a three-point agreement:

1. The union and management would work together to establish a joint system of job classifications.
2. Management would set aside an inequity equalization fund from which workers in the plant would ultimately get from one to ten cents an hour, depending upon decisions on the adjustments that were due them.
3. The union would have the authority to distribute the inequity fund.

A Vitucci committeeman described what happened in this way:

We worked awfully hard on that wage structure. We worked on it for months. . . . Everybody was pretty short-tempered. We had an awful time getting that thing set up to everybody's satisfaction. And then when we finally did, and put it into effect, there wasn't half the people in the shop satisfied. Some of 'em were ready to cut our throats because they didn't get anything out of the adjustments.

Everyone in the plant got one cent an hour beyond the increase agreed upon in the master contract, but some of the workers, where the inequities were assumed to have been the greatest, received as much as ten cents. Most of the workers received little more than the one cent minimum. To many of these people, the wage structure was technical and confusing. All they knew was that they had struck for five and a half weeks for nearly nothing. As Vitucci put it:

We should have had the company allocate the money. This way, the union took the blame. The people that got the 10 cents were satisfied. The beefs came from the guys that got the cent.

This settlement was the beginning of the end for Frank Vitucci's control over the local union. It is interesting to note that his downfall was not directly due to a failure to make gains from management. He did indeed make gains but at a cost that seemed too high to a large segment of the working force. Furthermore, his whole leadership approach was based upon attacks upon management. He was not skilled for the negotiating and political maneuvering involved in balancing various issues among segments of the membership. He was equipped to represent the union in the "lawyer for the defense" era. When the problems increasingly became ones of balancing the interests of segments of the work group—in other words, intergroup relations problems—Vitucci lost his hold.

Vitucci's successor, Abe Carter, was a man of very different personality. He had taken no part in the organizing campaign. First as a steward and later as recording secretary, he worked quietly, conscientiously and inconspicuously for the union. After becoming recording secretary with the backing of Vitucci, he began to speak up in union meetings. He spoke in a measured and thoughtful manner, with an excellent command of the language. People began listening to him with respect.

Ed Lynch, who had lost out to Vitucci in the 1946 election, began to cultivate Carter, and persuaded him to run for president in 1947. Carter centered his attack on Vitucci, charging him with leading the union into an unnecessary strike. Vitucci's campaign consisted largely of defending himself and pointing to the gains the union had made. Carter won a decisive victory.

The shift from Vitucci to Carter brought about a marked change in the atmosphere of union-management discussions. There was no more pounding on the table and shouting. Carter organized his information carefully and systematically and presented it calmly and cogently. Don Paxton, successor to the table-pounding O'Leary, replied in the same vein. The excitement gradually faded out of labor relations at the Truax local.

Along with this change in union-management relations went a growing centralization of control within the local union.

There was a marked decline in the importance of the shop steward. A man who had served as steward in the Vitucci period made this comment:

The stewards don't amount to anything in the shop nowadays. They're just not important. About the only thing they do is to write the grievance out. After that, their job is done, and the committee handles the grievance from then on. In fact, the committeeman is usually in it from the beginning, anyway. The stewards *used* to be important, though. We handled more grievances right on the floor of the shop, instead of saving them up and meeting with the company once a week, the way they do now. As a matter of fact, they haven't *got* any grievances anymore. They'll go in and meet with the company every Friday morning, and maybe they've got one grievance. In our day, we *dug up* grievances. We went out and looked for them. One time, I remember, there was a fellow named Rockwell who'd been laid off unfairly and should've been reinstated with back pay. He was working some place else, but we went out and dug him up and brought a grievance. We won it, too, and got him his job back. Maybe that wasn't necessary, but you see, we had to show the union's strength.

The decline of the steward[3]

This seemed to be a common developmental trend. Furthermore, it came not simply from the decline in frequency of grievances but from at least four other factors.

---

[3] This section, in revised form, is taken from my remarks on "The Grievance Process," *Proceedings of a Conference at the Labor and Industrial Relations Center,* Michigan State University, March 23–24, 1956.

First of all, there was *a change in the role of the foreman*. In the old days, the foreman really ruled the roost in his department. One of the first union attacks was on the foreman, as we have seen in the case of Dan McDougall. And so management generally was inclined to limit the foreman's freedom of action, to make him check with superiors before he gave an answer to a grievance. Management was afraid that if it let the foreman in department A make a settlement, this would result in a similar move by department X, and so a more uniform approach seemed necessary.

Since the steward was the man who handled the grievances with the foreman, the change in the role of the foreman had the effect of pulling the rug out from under the steward.

Second there was the *natural tendency of workers to appeal to the biggest shot that could be reached*. The steward was a fellow you knew too well. Somehow you felt that if you could contact the chairman of the grievance committee, the president of the local, or even the international representative, that would be much better. Just as in politics we think that if we can get to the United States senator rather than some local politician, we will do better, so it is in the plant. We see this not only inside the plants. When the local president, grievance man, or head of the grievance committee is out socially in the community, he may have a grievance put to him at any time. It doesn't matter what the occasion is or what the hour is. It is a 24-hour job. When this happens, as union president or chairman of the grievance committee, you are supposed to tell the man gently but firmly, "Go to the steward first." In an organization that depends upon workers' votes, it is hard to do that. Many union presidents and other high local officials fear that workers will say about them as indeed they do say, "Well, Joe used to be a regular guy, but now he's too big for us."

Third, the *technical nature of many grievances became a problem*. Ten cents across the board is very simple, but grievances involving incentive rates, for example, are very technical indeed. There may be only one or two men in the local union who are qualified to argue and settle such grievances with management. Even they may need help from the international representative or some technically trained man in the international union.

And fourth, *many grievances are in fact intergroup problems*. For example, take the hypothetical case of a department made up of polishers and grinders. A new job comes into the plant. It is a better than average job. Should a polisher get it or should it go to a grinder? Is the steward a polisher or a grinder? In either case, the steward's position is untenable. If he is a polisher and expresses the grinder's point of view, the polishers will accuse him of treason—if not lunacy. If he speaks for the polishers, the grinders will say he's looking after his own bread and butter. So the grievance by its very nature, has to be resolved by someone outside of the department. (Note that such a grievance has nothing to do with the time-honored argument of seniority versus ability. It is a question of which group gets the job.)

The union meeting

This centralization of control reflected itself also in the local union meeting under Carter's regime. While no specific figures are available, all observers report that the turnout at the meetings under Vitucci was much larger than it was after Carter had become firmly established. In part, this was no doubt due to the atmosphere of excitement in the period in which the union was struggling for its life. In part it seems also to have been due to differences in the manner of conducting the meetings. If Vitucci had ever heard of *Robert's Rules of Order*, his meetings did not reflect the book. Anyone could get up and have his say. Grievances were freely brought up and argued on the floor of the union meeting. This sometimes made for long meetings. One wonders how interest could have been maintained when meetings lasted far into the night, and maybe some people were lost to the meetings because they took too much time. At the same time, people seemed to have a lively sense of participation. There was excitement in the union-management relationship then, and the worker could also look forward to excitement at the local union meeting.

The Abe Carter meeting was far different. He knew his *Robert's Rules of Order* by heart, and he enforced them. He had his agenda carefully prepared for each meeting, and he followed it. A member who tried to raise other topics might find himself called out of order. Carter insisted particularly that all discussion of grievances was out of order, since these were matters that should be referred to the grievance committee. In time it got so that only those close to the union officers turned out for meetings. The meetings that had drawn 100 or more men regularly, and frequently much larger numbers, declined to 30 to 35 members per meeting.

There was some griping from the members about the way Abe Carter dominated the union, but there was no organized protest. Abe Carter ran the union, to be sure, but he worked diligently and he continued in his quiet and efficient way to make gains for the members.

How much centralization?

We have followed the process of centralization at the level of the local union. Does centralization go beyond this? Do we find that the top international officers have all the power in their own hands and that the local officers are little more than figureheads?

If we look at the determination of wages and fringe benefits, certainly it does appear that power is centralized at the top of the international union. In a large company, these matters are no longer negotiated at the local level. However, we must not exaggerate the degree of control that actually can be exercised from the top. Perhaps in an industry where there is very little technological change, so that work methods and procedures remain stable year after year, it would be possible to prescribe the rules and regulations from the top. In other situations, changes are constantly confronting local management and union people. Thus, they necessarily work out ways of getting together and resolving the immediate problems. If the solution that seems mutually advantageous to the local union and management people is not in accord with the written contract, this does not necessarily rule out the solution. The parties simply agree informally and take care that the agreement is not written down. In his discussion of "unofficial union-management relations," Melville Dalton makes these comments:[4]

> In one of the plants a departmental superintendent declared;
> "(The plant manager and his assistant) have both said they don't give a damn what kind of arrangements are made with the union as long as things run smoothly and it's kept out of writing."
> Grievance committeemen made similar statements. Two of those whom I knew intimately were quite specific. One stated:
> "The top people (policy makers) lay down too many hard and fast rules to follow. But we get around the contract by doing a lot of things that we can work out and keep off the record."
> The other said:
> "Top union and management are always bothering the local plant. We can work out our own arrangements if they'll leave us alone. (The plant manager and assistant) told us they don't care what arrangements we make but if we get in trouble the contract will have to be followed to the letter right down the line."

This was the only case in which a union officer admitted direct informal communication from management approving evasion of the contract, but actual behavior was similar in all the plants and had a character that could hardly have existed if local managerial and union officers had been opposed to evasion.

We see that in this way local union and management people retain a considerable amount of autonomy. At times each party has an interest in keeping the central office out of the local scene.

The meaning of grievances

Years ago it was thought that a study of written grievances would cast light upon the state of union-management relations. Students even wrote theses on such data. Happily, this is seldom done any more. We have come to recognize that written grievances do not *clearly* tell us anything,

---

[4] Melville Dalton, "Unofficial Union-Management Relations," Robert Dubin, *Human Relations in Administration* (New York: Prentice-Hall, 1951), pp. 68–78.

though they can provide valuable data when combined with other types of data.

Does a large number of written grievances indicate widespread worker dissatisfaction? In general, this seems to be the case, yet we must not assume that every grievance represents a specific problem felt by a particular worker. As we have seen in the case of Foreman Dan McDougall, the submission of 60 grievances instead of one stemmed from a decision of a union officer. This was a way of putting pressure on management. A large number of grievances, therefore, may point to problems affecting union officers particularly and not just to problems experienced by rank and file members. This is not to say that the sentiments of the union officers are of no consequence. They are of obvious importance. I am simply saying that a large volume of grievances does not point automatically to the source or sources of the problems.

Suppose the rate of grievances is very low. Does this mean that the workers are completely satisfied? No such simple conclusion can be drawn, since a low rate can grow out of a variety of influences.

First, there may be a reluctance on the part of workers to express their problems in terms of grievances. Why should this be so?

There are two factors to account for this. One is the old American tradition of individualism and self-reliance, the belief that many of us grow up with and which is reinforced in the schools, that one should be able to take care of one's individual problems. We find workers talking about this and saying in effect: "Somehow I ought to be able to handle this matter myself, and I feel a little uneasy about going to anyone else about it." It may not mean that they don't trust the union or that they don't believe in the union. Many people, apparently even in well-established unions, view this turning to the union as an admission of the helplessness of the individual.

There is another aspect: the workers' concern for management's reaction to the grievance. Workers don't like to be considered "troublemakers." Usually the worker does not fear a specific reprisal. However, he has an uneasy feeling that if he puts in a grievance, management will not forget it, and maybe somewhere along the line he will not get the breaks to which he is entitled.

This presents a problem to union stewards and officers. We have run into situations where union officers have been quite embarrassed to find themselves in the middle of processing a grievance only to find that the worker says, "Oh no. Let's forget about that. I didn't really mean it." This gives management the impression that the officer is stirring up trouble. The good worker just got talked into his grievance. Generally we found it was the good worker who began to get a little leery about this process when it came to a showdown, and decided that he would rather back out. This eventually led union officers to require that the worker sign his name to the grievance before submitting it for action.

A low rate of written grievances can also be a product of situational influences—but it can grow out of quite different situations, as the following three cases will indicate.

Donald Roy has reported on a department in which he was a machine operator.[5] The workers there had an intense distrust of management and yet hardly ever put in a written grievance. They also thoroughly distrusted the union and were convinced that it would do no good to process grievances. Why this was so, Roy did not have the data to explain, but the important point for our purposes is that a distrust of the union can balance the pressures created by distrust of management, so that workers do not see the grievance procedure as a solution to their problems. This does not mean that they do nothing. In the Roy case, the men were very active in restriction of output.

In the case reported by Dalton earlier in this chapter, the distrust of management did not seem so intense—though we have no measures of this. There was enough confidence in the union to bring worker problems to the attention of union officers. However, the union officers and management people both felt that they had more freedom for maneuvering and striking bargains when nothing was put in writing. Thus many problems that were in effect grievances were handled informally without any written record.

In my study of the Chicago Inland Steel Container Company plant, I found a sharp change from many grievances to practically none at all.[6] The later situation was one of extraordinary harmony between union and management, and yet the absence of grievances did not mean that there were no worker problems being felt or handled. I found in fact that many worker problems were being taken up and resolved, but here again there was an avoidance of written records. In this case, the motivation was somewhat different from that reported in the Dalton case. The parties at Inland had come to take great pride in their harmonious relationship. They had come to think of grievances as symbolizing poor relations. For this reason, they simply avoided writing grievances on many problems that could have been written on grievance forms. The problems were resolved informally through discussion at whatever level seemed appropriate.

This suggests that the number of grievances raised—as well as the type of problems presented in grievance form—must always be considered in the social context of a particular union-management relationship.

The evolution of rules

The establishment of a union-management relationship involves also the development of a set of explicit rules for the governing of the

---

[5] In William F. Whyte, *Money and Motivation* (New York: Harper & Bros., 1955), chaps. iv, v, and vii.

[6] William F. Whyte, *Pattern for Industrial Peace* (New York: Harper & Bros., 1951).

industrial community. These rules limit the exercise of managerial judgment. For workers, they introduce important elements of predictability into a world that is largely beyond their own control. The effects are not entirely one-sided. While the rules limit managerial judgment, they can also ease the burden of decision-making through limiting the choice of alternatives.

Our whole book could be devoted to the evolution of rules in the union-management relationship. Here we will confine ourselves to one example: the seniority system.

While workers are by no means unanimous on this point, their preferences in general are for seniority clauses which give substantial weight to length of service in decisions regarding promotions, transfers, and layoffs. Why should this be so? While workers do not put it exactly in these terms, interviews suggest that they see themselves as investing their time in the service of the organization. The investment the worker makes should entitle him to some reward. More specifically, if Jones has invested more time than Smith, then Jones should have preference over Smith in promotions or in holding onto his job in layoffs. In general, management people share the same sentiments: that other things being equal, the preference should go to the man with greater length of service.

Differences arise regarding the relative weights to be given to length of service as opposed to ability, with management people, of course, emphasizing ability. The workers, too, recognize ability differences. Their desire to reduce the weight of ability in these judgments is due partly to their distrust of managerial standards of judgment. How is superior ability to be distinguished from mere favoritism in managerial judgment?

For example, consider the case of Walt Marshall in the catalyst plant of the Blank Oil Company. A catalyst plant worker told this story about Walt, and several others vouched for its accuracy:

When Al Manton (plant superintendent) was here, there was a job opening up as reclamation operator. It was a daylight job so everybody was interested in it. I had the most seniority so I thought I should get it, but when Al comes down here to post that job, he tells us, "There is no use anybody else bidding on that job. I am going to give it to Walt Marshall." Walt used to give him chickens, and he would sell the old man eggs. I have been down here when Al came down about those eggs. He would say, "Walt, how much do I owe you for those eggs?" And Walt would say, "Oh, anything you want to pay, Al, that's all right," so Al would pay him 35 or 40 cents a dozen. Walt was open about it. He used to boast about the way he gave Al the chickens.

Of course, higher management did not approve of its foremen and superintendents becoming thus personally obligated to workers, but this kind of thing often does not come to the attention of higher management.

Anyone who has interviewed workers about the plant situation before the union came in has picked up similar stories of the establishment of personal obligations which the supervisor has then sought to discharge by giving a worker preferential treatment.

When Tom Lloyd had become foreman of the Hi-Test plant, he described to me this experience from his period of supervising the catalyst plant:

> I got into the most awful mess there I ever did in my life. After I had been there for a while, it was a matter of routine. I went to Al Wenzel (the division superintendent) to tell him I wanted to quit and join the Navy. I told him that there was no use having an engineer in that plant. One of the men could handle it. He said, "All right, can you recommend a man?" I picked out the man I thought was the best worker, and began to train him into the job. As soon as the other men found out what was going on, they began to pick on Walt. They were just like a bunch of white roosters picking on a black one. They made things hard for him, and they complained over his head. So finally we couldn't give the job to Walt. . . . Of course, it was only my opinion that Walt Marshall was the best man, but then I was in the best position to judge.

Tom Lloyd had received neither chickens nor eggs from Walt Marshall. Granting his own fallibility, he was doing his best to select the most competent man for the job. Considering Marshall's past behavior, there was no possible way in which Lloyd could have convinced the men that the decision had been made on the basis of ability alone.

Many experienced management people have come to accept Tom Lloyd's view of seniority: that it is a good rule to follow in general but that there should be exceptions to it for jobs requiring special abilities. We must recognize that for many jobs in American industry, individual differences in skill have little meaning. For example, consider the men on the assembly line. Since the jobs require such a minimum of skill in the first place, it would be absurd to try to develop a promotional system based on estimates of the comparative abilities of the workers. The more abilities a job does require, the more inclined are the workers themselves to give some weight to ability in filling the job. However, they still demand some standards of evaluation in which they themselves can believe. This puts the responsibility on management to develop standards that will seem reasonably objective. In some cases the problem has been approached through a joint union-management administration of the standards. For example, we found in a study carried on in 1946 that union-management relations in the Tennessee Valley Authority were extraordinarily harmonious.[7] No one factor could be credited with this result, but it was interesting to note that unions and management had

---

[7] William F. Whyte, "Patterns of Interaction in Union-Management Relations," *Human Organization*, Vol. VIII, no. 4 (1949).

agreed upon a set of qualifications *and testing procedures,* jointly administered, to determine the qualifications of workers applying for positions demanding real skill. Management experience in this case showed that the union members of the promotion boards were even more exacting in their insistence that workers meet high standards in the tests before being promoted than the management people were inclined to be. This suggests that when workers and union leaders have some involvement in the establishment of promotional procedures and standards, so that possibilities of favoritism are reduced, it is possible to gain from workers some acceptance of ability as a criterion for promotion.

Seniority has been traditionally considered as an issue between unions and management. More recently we have come to recognize its broad significance as a system of rules placing individuals in the social system. Even where the placement of the individuals is to be determined by seniority alone, it remains to be decided in terms of what organizational units seniority shall be figured. For example, consider the cases of Jack Carter and several other Benton glassworkers who rose so rapidly to the top in the blowing room. If seniority at Benton had been calculated in terms of the plant or department, Jack Carter would never have been able to move over from another plant in the first place. It was only because seniority at Shawcross was figured in terms of service in all of the plants in that city that Carter was able to bring his seniority with him to Benton. The life we observed in Benton was strongly influenced by the seniority system which determined in part the characteristics of workers serving there.

While a seniority system provides workers with some security against arbitrary decisions of management, it should also be viewed as an influence on and a product of intergroup relations among the workers. Seniority involves not only the individual's current position in the department but also the structure of the promotion ladder: what job or jobs the individual can promote into, what job or jobs he can be bumped down to, in case of a reduction of the force. When forces are reduced, it is to the advantage of the individual to have as many jobs under him and as few over him as possible. This limits the number of people who can bump him to lower positions and provides ample bumping opportunities for him. To some extent, the nature of the promotional ladder will be determined by the technology and skills required, but where there are many jobs of approximately equal skill, there is considerable flexibility in setting up the promotional ladder. Furthermore, as technological changes take place so that new jobs are created and old jobs eliminated or modified, questions frequently arise as to possible rearrangements of the jobs and as to changes in the promotion ladder. We often see groups of workers struggling with each other over where a new job will fit.

As the union enters and establishes itself, inevitably it limits the free exercise of managerial prerogatives. As time goes on, the union may come to share in the discharge of a number of responsibilities. In some cases, the union may succeed in taking over control. This may seem like an important victory for the union, but let us note intergroup problems that may arise when the union does in fact assume control. In this chapter, we have noted how Frank Vitucci's victory in taking over, for the union, the distribution of the inequity equalization fund led to his downfall. In another plant we studied, the union had won a victory that gave it the power to determine seniority units and lines of promotion within the plant, subject only to the proviso that management be assured that individuals would be required to accept promotions offered. At the time of our study, we found the grievance committee of the local union more occupied with seniority disputes among its own members than with any other matter. In effect, the union had taken over this area of intergroup problems. When workers did not like a given decision, they could not blame management for it. It was their own union that had done it. This led to serious frustrations on the part of local union officers. They had to wrestle with very complicated matters through long hours of discussion, only to find that whatever they decided would be rejected by many of the workers.

Loyalty: dual or divided

Many management people have been inclined to view the union-management relationship in terms of a competition for the loyalties of workers. The assumption seems to be that if the man is loyal to management, he cannot be loyal to the union, and vice versa. This may sound logical on the face of it, but is it in accord with reality?

It is at the time of organizing the union that the competition for loyalties appears to be most pronounced. In analyzing the campaign at Hi-Test, we talked in terms of vertical integration versus horizontal integration as alternative ways in which workers may conceptualize an organization. But even here, we drew attention to the case of a strongly pro-union worker who said, "This has always been a good company to work for," and went on to speak of the company in highly favorable terms. While in the organizing stage, sentiments tend to polarize, apparently even at this time some measure of dual loyalty is possible.

As the collective bargaining relationship becomes established, it is more likely to be accompanied by dual than by divided loyalty. This is perhaps the most thoroughly demonstrated proposition that we have in human relations in industry. The evidence comes from questionnaire survey studies of at least 12 union-management relationships. While the specific wording of the questions may have varied from study to study, the studies all had this in common: Workers were asked to express their sentiments toward the union and toward the company.

If loyalty toward one party necessarily involved alienation from the other, then we would expect workers who expressed favorable sentiments toward the company and management to express unfavorable sentiments toward the union and union leaders. By the same token, we would expect those who expressed favorable sentiments toward the union and union leaders to express negative sentiments toward the company and management.

So far this condition has never been reported. In one case, George W. England reports a complete absence of correlation—but *not* a negative correlation.[8] The Illini City study of five plants reports *positive* correlations in sentiments toward company and union running from .10 to .46.[9] While the two lowest correlations are not statistically significant, it is worth noting that all correlations are in the same direction. Furthermore, the combined rank-and-file correlation of .32 for the five cases is significant at the 1 percent level.

Willard A. Kerr, studying the Buchsbaum case so noted for harmonious relationships, reports "a positive Pearsonian coefficient of correlation between the total scores on the management-oriented ballot and the union-oriented ballot of .73."[10] That exceedingly high correlation suggests that dual loyalty will be most pronounced in situations marked by cooperation among the leaders of both parties. On the other hand, Father T. V. Purcell, in a study of the Swift local of the United Packinghouse Workers of America, reports 73 percent of the workers being favorable to both organizations, with only 26 percent being favorable to one and unfavorable or neutral to the other.[11] The Swift situation was not noted for union-management cooperation, and in fact, a strike had taken place before the study. On the other hand, Father Purcell reports that the workers were opposed to the strike and only went along as required by the top officers of the international.

In a study of three local unions ranging from peaceable to contentious relations with management, Lois R. Dean also finds dual loyalty expressed by the workers as a whole in each situation.[12] When she then goes on to

---

[8] "Dual Allegiance to Company and Union," *Personnel Administration*, Vol. XXIII, no. 2 (March–April, 1960).

[9] Ross Stagner, "Dual Allegiance as a Problem in Modern Society," *Personnel Psychology*, Vol. VII, no. 1 (March, 1954).

[10] William A. Kerr, "Dual Allegiance and Emotional Acceptance-Rejection in Industry," *Personnel Psychology*, Vol. VII, no. 1 (March, 1954).

[11] T. V. Purcell, "Dual Allegiance to Company and Union-Packinghouse Workers. A Swift-UPWA Study in a Crisis Situation, 1949–52," *Personnel Psychology*, Vol. VII, no. 1 (March, 1954), pp. 48–58. For a full report, see his book, *The Worker Speaks His Mind on Company and Union* (Cambridge, Mass.: Harvard University Press, 1954).

[12] Lois R. Dean, "Union Activity and Dual Loyalty," *Industrial and Labor Relations Review*, Vol. VII, no. 4 (July, 1954), pp. 526–36. Dean also reports similar findings from Daniel Katz' University of Michigan Survey Research Center study of a large automobile factory, and from Arnold Rose's study of a teamsters' local. See his *Union Solidarity* (Minneapolis: University of Minnesota Press, 1952).

check the relations among sentiments, interactions, and activities in each case, she does find interesting differences. In the conflict case, the pro-union, anti-management workers report themselves as attending union meetings in far greater numbers than the dual loyalty or other categories of respondents. A slight tendency in this direction was observed in the in-between case, whereas the peaceable situation did not show the pro-union, anti-management workers attending meetings in disproportionate numbers at all.

The author gives this interpretation of her findings:

> Where management and the union are in continuous overt conflict, dual loyalty may still exist in the plant as a whole. The union meeting appears to attract, however, an entirely different sort of person; that is, the worker who does not see union and management as having compatible goals. This worker obtains further justification for this perception from what he learns at union meetings. For if relations between union and management are strained, the union leaders are likely to emphasize the conflict and insist that any benefits the rank and file enjoy are due to the union's unremitting struggle against an obdurate management. Under these circumstances, dual loyalty breaks down, and the anti-management, pro-union worker predominates at the union meeting.
>
> The union meeting, then, has a selection and reinforcement function. The workers it selects and the attitudes it reinforces depend, at least in part, on the degree of conflict in the union-management relationship. Apparently, management need not fear that the presence of a union in their plant will necessarily cause workers to become disloyal to the company; but if union-management conflict prevails, the most active unionists are likely to be the conflict-oriented workers with strongly one-sided loyalty. If the union-management relationship improves, our data suggest that control of the union may very well shift accordingly; so that, as at Amco, the active unionists will be those who look with favor on both management and the union.[13]

How do we explain this phenomenon of dual loyalty? It might be explained in personality terms. Perhaps the world is divided between "positive thinkers" and "negative thinkers." The positive thinkers tend to view things in a rosy light, whereas the negative thinkers see the world in more somber hues. While this is a possibility, it implies that the rosy responses of the positive thinker would not be limited to the union and management but would be seen in all of the questions, with an opposite tendency for the negative thinkers. Actually, the questionnaires do not seem to show this much uniformity.

Perhaps a more plausible explanation is provided by the integration of the union-management system itself. As the union-management relationship develops, the parties are no longer sharply separated in their spheres

---

[13] *Ibid.*, p. 536.

of activity. In effect, it is union and management together who administer the social system of the plant, even in cases where there is a good deal of friction between them. Furthermore, the workers come to realize that many of the problems they face are not problems separating union from management but rather problems in which union and management agree that one group and not another will receive a given benefit.

After the excitement of the organizing period has passed, we find that rank and file workers do not generally continue to speak of "we" in referring to the union. The union, like the management, is "they" to the workers. If a worker thinks that "they" are administering the system well, he checks favorable sentiments to both parties in the questionnaire. If he thinks "they" are doing poorly, he marks off the opposite conclusion, also for both parties.

So far little attention has been given to the possibility of the existence of dual loyalty among management people. Father Purcell reports 57 percent of the Swift foremen manifesting this combination of sentiments (compared to 88 percent of the stewards), but as yet we have no figures for higher management people.[14] If the logic of our analysis of dual loyalty among workers is correct, we should find the same phenomenon among management people—although perhaps in weaker form and less widely distributed. Indeed, as we talk with management people in a situation where the union is well established, we do find such evidences of dual loyalty. These men tend to accept the union organization as part of the whole institutional system and recognize an obligation to union leaders in their positions as leaders, in much the same way that they feel obligation toward fellow members of management.

Conclusion

In this chapter, we have been following the evolution of a new institution, the union, and a new set of relations, those between management and union. We have noted the interdependence of the two institutions, as we have seen changes taking place within management affecting the union and vice versa.

As relations have evolved between union and management, we have noted three interrelated developments:

1. The issues between them become more complex.
2. Union officers become increasingly occupied with intergroup relations within the local.
3. A legal framework arises to regulate the relations between the parties. This consists of both the written law of contract clauses and the common law of past practices and understandings as to how things should be done.

---

[14] Purcell, *op. cit.*, p. 53.

These developments lead to the following two results:

1. A shift among industrial relations leaders from fighters to negotiators; from charismatic leaders to administrative leaders.
2. Centralization of decision-making activity toward the top level of local union and local management.

Let us put this analysis of the Vitucci and Carter leadership styles in interactional and transactional terms.

Vitucci built up and maintained a high rate of interaction with rank-and-file members and was particularly active in large group or mass situations. With his followers, Vitucci provided positive exchanges in pair situations and projected the image of joint payoffs—that all members would gain together.

Vitucci's relations with Industrial Relations Director O'Leary were marked by negative exchanges and open conflict, but the union leader was able to manipulate the situation so as to gain rewards for the members and to protect them from management reprisals.

Vitucci was little inclined toward the development of trading transactions. When he wanted something from management, he tended to stress the negative consequences for management in not giving him what he demanded.

Bargaining involves a complex series of transactions, with a high emphasis upon trading. This proved to be Vitucci's downfall. The settlement that gave the union leaders the right to allocate the inequity payments among the workers in effect placed workers in a competitive situation with each other. Those who lost (getting only one cent or so) naturally blamed the local leaders.

Carter followed quite a different interaction and transactional pattern. He minimized interactions with workers in large crowd situations. Had the role of president required the handling of large meetings of excited workers, Carter probably would have been unequal to the situation, but under calmer conditions he found himself well adapted to pair and small-group interactions. He excelled in developing positive exchange transactions: doing something for an individual member, getting the member's support for his plans in return.

With management, Carter fitted readily into a pattern of trading transactions. The development of this pattern was, of course, made possible by the substitution of a new industrial relations man for O'Leary, who had neither skills nor inclinations for trading.

We have noted the tendency of centralization of decision making that accompanies the shift from conflict to a union-management accommodation. Many of the problems that previously were settled locally are now being settled on a companywide or even industrywide basis. However, our preoccupation with the drama of top level power struggles should not blind us to the fact that local union and management leaders may yet retain a good deal of *unofficial* autonomy in adjusting their relations to each other.

Finally, we have noted the evolution of a semi-integrated union-management institutional system. What may have appeared to the workers in the period of the struggle for recognition as two entirely separate and conflicting organizations, now seems to be an interlocking system, administered by management and union leaders together.

But a word of caution should be added to this interpretation. I do not mean to suggest that workers come to see union and management living together in perfect harmony. The fact that the parties are dependent upon each other and necessarily work together to at least a limited extent does not mean that they never fight. It only means that, after fighting, the parties come together again to continue their joint administration of the industrial relations system. In later chapters we shall examine the influences determining the degree of conflict or harmony we actually find within that industrial relations system.

References

Dalton, Melville. *Men Who Manage.* New York: John Wiley & Sons, 1959. See especially discussion of unofficial union-management relations, Chapter 5.

Sayles, Leonard, and Strauss, George. *The Local Union: Its Place in the Industrial Plant,* rev. ed. New York: Harcourt, Brace & World, 1967. The best study of relationships and problems within the local union.

Whyte, William F. *Pattern for Industrial Peace.* New York: Harper & Bros., 1951. A case study of a change from conflict to cooperation in union-management relations.

Discussion questions

1. A union leader calls upon you for advice. He says, "We are having trouble getting good stewards. We want to know how to get better stewards." If you looked into his problem, what would you be likely to find?

2. If union members are allowed to bring up anything on the floor of the union meeting, the meetings go on so long that many members lose interest and stop coming. If the meetings are conducted in terms of strict parliamentary procedure, many members complain that the president is being a dictator, and they stop coming. Do you see any way out of this dilemma?

3. It is often said that "management gets the kind of union leaders it deserves." This is a moral judgment that is not testable. However, consider the underlying idea: that management's actions determine the kind of union leadership that emerges. To what extent is this a valid conclusion?

4. Interview a man who has been an officer of a local union. Focus particularly upon the ways in which changes in union-management relationships may have affected the problems he faced and the ways in which he played his role.

21. Work unit cohesion and militancy

On the problem of work group cohesion, there have been two major studies: those of Stanley Seashore[1] and Leonard Sayles.[2] The two men approached the problem with quite different methods.

Seashore measured cohesion entirely in terms of the responses of members of work groups and then related his findings to the productivity records for these groups. Relating attitudes to productivity enabled Seashore to make certain inferences about behavior. He found that average productivity of group members was unrelated to cohesion, as measured by the respondents' evaluation of their groups, their willingness or reluctance to leave their group, their opinions as to how well their groups "stick together," and similar items. In other words, Seashore found highly cohesive, high-production groups and, about as often, highly cohesive, low-production groups. *But* when Seashore compared the production records of individuals with others within the same group, he found a significant uniformity. In low cohesive groups, individual production records showed a wide range of variation. In highly cohesive groups, the variation was sharply reduced: the members tended to produce at approximately the same level.

According to Seashore's interpretation, the low cohesive group was one in which *norms* of behavior did not develop or were not enforced. The highly cohesive group developed *norms* regarding elements of behavior important to the members, and the amount of work put out would certainly be one such element. Thus the members would arrive at a consensus as to what amount was appropriate, and they would conform to that *norm*. Whether the norm was set high or low was then not determined by cohesiveness but rather by the relationship between the work group and management. If relations were fraught with conflict, produc-

---

[1] Stanley Seashore, *Group Cohesiveness in the Industrial Work Group* (Ann Arbor, Mich.: Institute for Social Research, 1954).

[2] Leonard Sayles, *Behavior of Industrial Work Groups* (New York: John Wiley & Sons, 1958).

tivity would be low. If relations were harmonious, productivity would tend to be on the high side.

Sayles focused his attention directly on behavior. In his studies of local unions, he had observed that militancy was never uniformly distributed throughout the plant. There would be departments where the members "stuck together" and put sustained pressure on management toward goals of interest to all of them. There were other departments which appeared to be apathetic; the members hardly ever made their views known in any concerted fashion. And there were still other departments which seemed to be highly erratic—quiescent most of the time, but given to unpredictable and explosive bursts of concerted activity. These types did not seem related to worker sentiments toward management. Sayles found departments where the general level of dissatisfaction was high and yet where the members were so sharply divided among themselves that they were unable to put any pressure on management.

The research method used by Sayles in establishing his typology has been described in Chapter 2. Here we should note that Sayles and Seashore were examining related yet different phenomena. Seashore was interested in cohesion, as measured by attitudinal items, and as related to productivity. Sayles did not measure cohesion but instead focused on behavioral phenomena that are presumably related to cohesion. He was not concerned with how members *felt* about their work groups, but rather with the extent and forms and frequencies (roughly estimated) with which they engaged in concerted activities that put pressure on management.

A further distinction should be noted. Seashore was concerned with relatively small groups. Sayles focused his attention upon departmental units, which were equivalent to small groups in some cases, but in other cases might encompass as many as 100 men—in which case it is rather misleading to speak of them as "work groups."

Since productivity is a measure of one aspect of worker behavior, it provides us with a possible link between the Seashore and Sayles approaches. We can infer that the groups that were more cohesive in Seashore's measures, and produced greater uniformity in members' output records, probably also "stuck together" more in dealing with management. But this conclusion is only speculative. We shall not be able to fit the Seashore and Sayles findings together until someone executes a project utilizing a survey and productivity measures together with the behavioral data of the type gathered by Sayles. In the meantime, those interested in further examination of research on cohesion must follow one route or the other but not both simultaneously.

For purposes of my own further exploration and exposition, I shall follow the Sayles framework. My concern in this chapter is with militancy as well as with cohesion. I shall deal with departmental units rather than with small groups.

What makes the difference between the levels of militancy that we observe as we compare one department with another? As we get below the level of the local union and examine the technology and nature of the jobs, we find some of our answers. This chapter examines cases from three local unions.

The first case involves a comparison between two divisions within a large local: one noted for the high level of activity and militancy and the other for comparative quiet in labor relations. We shall also explore certain changes which occurred within the militant division over the course of years.

The second case involves a small department which once was heavily involved in militant union activity but later became so disorganized that no concerted effort could be successful. Here again we shall examine the impact of changes through time upon the level of cohesion and militancy within the department.

The third case involves a department where, in general, the level of cohesion and militancy was very low but where on several occasions the workers managed to "stick together" and put pressure on management. We shall undertake to explain both the prevailing low level of cohesion and militancy and the occasional instances of effective collective action.

1. Smelting versus chemical division[3]

The study to be reported here involved a local union of over 6,000 members encompassing a number of plants in the same city, all of them under the control of the works manager. The city was in French Canada, which meant that the higher management people were generally English Canadians. Workers, foremen, general foremen, and union leaders were almost exclusively French Canadians.

While our project was focused upon problems of relations within management, we were naturally interested in the forces involved in a four-month strike which was in progress during the course of our research. While the workers were out in all of the divisions and plants, it was evident that union militancy was not uniformly distributed. All the evidence indicated that the heart of union militancy was in the Smelting Division. This division had provided most of the labor relations crises leading up to the strike. However, the problems were not uniformly distributed through that division. It was on the vat lines, where most of the workers were concentrated, that the major labor relations problems arose. Furthermore, the man who was union president at that time had previously been a vat line worker, and the vice president of the union for the division (who worked on the vat lines) was known locally as the most militant of the divisional representatives.

---

[3] This section is based primarily on field studies carried out under my general direction by Laurent Picard and André Bisson.

We will first compare the vat lines with the chemical division, where labor relations were markedly peaceable. Then, looking more closely within the smelting division, we will compare the vat lines with the caustic plant, where worker-management relations were quite harmonious. In each case, we shall ask what it is in the work situation that promotes or minimizes work group cohesion and militancy.

Let us compare the vat lines with the chemical division in terms of technology and the nature of the jobs.

1. *Working conditions.*   Work on the vat lines was considered hot and heavy. The men had to work in close proximity to vats of molten metal, the extreme heat presenting a problem even in winter and making conditions exceedingly oppressive in the summer. In recognition of these difficult conditions, management provided air conditioned rest rooms in which workers spent up to half of the working day. Nevertheless, the working conditions generally were thought to be undesirable. Furthermore, most of the workers had to work close to the vats, so that this sort of experience was widely distributed.

In the chemical division, there was less of a problem involving excessive heat or heavy work. Certain working areas were rather dirty, but there was a wide variation in conditions from location to location throughout the division. Working conditions were not uniform.

2. *Homogeneity versus heterogeneity.*   We found a contrast between the divisions in the nature of the jobs, and to some extent, this could be described in terms of homogeneity versus heterogeneity.

On the vat lines, there was a day crew for each section. For operations each section was divided into four parts, with crews working shifts in each part. A general foreman was responsible for each section on a 24-hour basis. The jobs were closely similar in their skill requirements, and the spread between the lowest and the highest pay was only about 13 percent. As we have noted, all of these men worked close to the vats, and this similarity in their jobs was of great importance to the men.

Finally, for the vat lines, it could be said that the pattern repeated itself over and over again from one end of the division to the other. With very minor variations, one vat line was just like any other, with the same complement of skills, positions, and working conditions.

The men here not only had the lowest average level of school grades completed of any major section of the works, but they were also highly homogeneous in general social backgrounds.

The situation in the chemical division was much more heterogeneous. There was a much wider variety of jobs and job classifications, and also a greater range in pay (27 percent) between the lowest and the highest jobs. Since the top jobs were considered highly skilled, there was also a much greater range in educational background within the division—from very little schooling for some of the laborers to a high school education for some of the top operators.

3. *Management flexibility*. The very heterogeneity of the situation in the chemical division allowed for more management flexibility and a greater degree of decentralization in the handling of labor relations problems. What was done on one vat line naturally set a precedent for the other lines, which tended to push labor problems up to high levels for solution.

4. *Interactional opportunities*. While on the job, the men on the vat lines worked together in teams. For roughly half of the working day, the men were free to interact together without restraints in the rest room. Furthermore, the men could leave their jobs for a period up to three hours without causing a serious breakdown in operations. Beyond the three-hour point, the consequences of neglect would become exceedingly costly to management, but up to this point, management would simply experience a drop in operating efficiencies. Thus it was easy for one man to check with his fellows regarding his complaints, for groups to meet with one another, and for demonstrations to build up involving large areas or even the whole division. In other words, this was what Leonard Sayles has called a high resonance situation, in which one individual facing a particular problem could readily find many others facing the same problem. Such a situation is conducive to concerted group action. Far from inhibiting interactions among workers, the technology made it easy for such interactions to take place and for pair interactions to develop into group interactions and activities.

By contrast, most workers in the chemical division were widely separated in space, and they could not leave their work areas for any extended period of time without risking serious operational consequences. Furthermore, the worker in the chemical division who faced a given problem, even if he did seek out a fellow worker, might find that the other man did not share the same problem at all. In Sayles' terms, this was a low resonance situation.

5. *Strategic importance to the management*. While we could not argue that the chemical division was unimportant to management, it should be noted that the smelting division provided almost 40 percent of the work force, whereas the chemical division provided less than half of that figure. Furthermore, management tended to think of the production of the works primarily in terms of the performance of the vat lines. It was said that most of the men in higher management had risen through the smelting division. Workers and union leaders seemed to recognize this sense of crucial importance in their division. Such a condition can be expected to encourage the workers to believe that concerted action on their part will bring concessions from management. The efforts of work group organization are likely to be rewarded.

6. *Job security*. Within this works, any reduction of the level of operations strikes the vat lines much more heavily than it does other divisions, including the chemical division. When the demand for the

product drops off, vat lines are shut down and the men on those lines are transferred to other divisions or laid off. Having no transferable skills, the men in the vat lines are unable to make any special claim as to their value with management. They are thus inclined to look to the union for job protection.

Employment in the chemical division is generally much more stable. Even a reduction in the volume of liquids processed is not likely to reduce greatly the work force deployed through the plants. There is thus less need for the men in the chemical division to look to the union for job protection.

7. *The wage inequity issue.* Management had offered a production bonus during World War II to attract men during the existing labor shortage. This production bonus made the total pay of the men on the vat lines higher than their skill justified. When the wartime labor shortage passed and management no longer needed a production bonus to attract new workers for the vat lines, management sought to reduce the size of the bonus during each contract negotiation. Thus the vat line workers found themselves sharing in each general increase, but losing a little of their bonus each time. Furthermore, the losses the vat line workers sustained were felt equally by all of them, and the threat of future losses affected all of them alike. An issue having a uniform effect on a group of workers is likely to stimulate a uniform response on their part.

The case of the caustic plant

The technological base for the differences in labor relations between the smelting and the chemical division is further substantiated if we compare two parts within the smelting division: the large vat lines versus the small caustic plant. (The vat lines employed about 60 percent of the workers of the division, whereas the caustic plant employed only a tiny fraction of this amount.)

While the caustic plant was formally within the smelting division, its technological and other characteristics were much closer to chemical operations than they were to the vat lines. The caustic plant offered a wide variety of working conditions and a high degree of heterogeneity in the job situation. The plant offered a pay range even somewhat greater than that found in the chemical division: the top job paid 32 percent more than the bottom job (compared to 13 percent on the vat lines). Since the plant was small and unique, most proposals for change initiated by workers or union officials could be carried through at low managerial levels. The caustic plant had smaller strategic importance to management than the vat lines, since it could be shut down for short periods without crippling company operations. This lessened the leverage the union and workers had in this unit. The interactional opportunities of workers in the caustic plant were also quite limited in comparison to those on the vat lines. Workers could not leave their jobs for more than a few minutes without incurring danger of explosions. No rest room facilities were provided for them. Since the caustic plant jobs were highly skilled at the top levels, and since the plant could operate economically even when other operations were reduced, the workers faced little problem of job insecurity. Finally, they were unaffected by the incentive rate inequity issue that was being fought out between management and vat line workers.

In all these respects, caustic plant workers resembled chemical plant workers much more than they did the men on the vat lines. Therefore, it is not surprising that management reported no labor relations problems with the caustic plant.

Post-war adjustments

While we have reviewed some of the influences leading toward cohesion among vat line workers in contrast to the situation prevailing in the chemical division, this cohesion and militancy was not uniformly displayed. As we review developments through the first 12 post-war years, we will see how management sought to meet its vat line problems and how these management efforts led to counteractions on the part of the union in the vat lines.

Throughout this post-war period, there was no change in structure at the top levels. The division was divided into two departments, A and B, with a superintendent for each department. Above the superintendents was a general superintendent for the division, who reported to the works manager. Changes in lower levels of the structure will be described presently.

During the period up to 1945, it appears that foremen and general foremen had had considerable authority in dealing with workers. The period 1945–52 was marked by a centralization of control. A general foreman describes the situation in this way:

Around 1945 and 1946, after the war, they took away completely the authority of the foremen. . . . Some time later, the union took account of the situation which was that the foreman was being neglected and had very little authority, and the union began to create problems that the foreman could no longer handle. They went to try to handle these problems at a higher level, and even at the level of Mr. S (works manager). At that time, the management did not permit the foremen to decide such matters. Even if the union did not understand this situation at the start, it is clear that after a certain time they saw what was going on, and it is also clear that they took advantage of it. For example, an employee might ask for a day off. The foreman would say no, and the grievance agent would then telephone directly to the superintendent without talking to the foreman, and would ask for the day off for the man. The superintendent would then telephone the foreman and tell him to give the man the day off. This sort of thing was happening right up to 1952.

This pattern of saying no at lower levels and saying yes at higher levels seems to have been maintained right up to the top.

The personnel manager at the time was the man who would say no for the works manager, but if the works manager himself could be reached and put under sufficient pressure, he would say yes. At a lower level, the foremen seemed to be in the same situation as the personnel manager. They had no latitude for saying yes. They could only say no and be reversed at a higher level.

This situation presented an open invitation to the union to put pressure on management and go on to the top for action.

This period also saw the establishment of the position of supervisor in the line of authority between general foreman and superintendent. A management man describes the situation in this way:

> Four or five years ago, the organization chart was different. The foreman did not have any authority. It was the supervisor who decided everything. The general foremen were primarily messenger boys who took questions asked by their subordinates to the supervisor for answers, decisions, or favors. On the one hand, the general foremen did not have any authority, and on the other hand, the engineers (supervisors) were practically without experience. Up to this time, the engineers remained for a very short time in the same position. The situation was that the general foreman had to ask permission of an inexperienced engineer before making any change in the process.

The general foremen at this time had gone about as far as they could expect to go in the company, and were naturally concerned about maintaining their relations with subordinates. The supervisors, by contrast, were at the beginning of their careers and looked primarily upward toward establishing the relations that would enable them to advance. Furthermore, the supervisors changed positions so often that it was impossible to develop any continuity of operations in a given sector of the vat lines. Finally, most of the supervisors had little knowledge of the workers' language, so that language was a further block to good communication. Thus, there arose a serious cleavage between general foremen and supervisors. In this situation, the general foremen felt that they had little understanding or protection from above. They saw adjusting to the men and to the union as the only possible solution in such a situation. This led to setting up, each man for himself, a principality in which he developed his relations in whatever way would enable him to survive in this difficult environment. Each principality had its own norms of behavior. The supervisors, having very little communication with the general foremen, were unaware of these differences in operating practices, and had no way of effectively controlling the situation.

1948 marked the founding of a foreman's club in response to the unprotected and unintegrated situation in which the foremen and general foremen found themselves. Some of the men would have preferred to form a union of foremen, and the new club did, in fact, serve to present grievances to management.

The foreman's club raised two general grievances with management. Club representatives claimed that many foremen were receiving a smaller annual income than the workers whom they supervised. They also complained against the supervisors and urged that they be removed from the line of authority.

In 1952 and 1953, this structural change was made. With this change and the assumption of the position of works manager by John Black, we enter into a new period.

Before leaving the earlier period however, we should note that the 1942–52 decade was marked by an almost 50 percent reduction in the labor force, accompanied by major construction programs and technological changes. Such changes no doubt complicated for management the handling of labor relations problems.

The new management approach: 1953–57

The new management approach was based upon a recognition that the foremen and general foremen were not really integrated into the management organization, and furthermore, that higher management had been exercising little control of the activities of the workers in the vat lines.

The structural change, involving the moving of supervisors out of the line and into staff positions, was the basic change which made possible the new management program.

Following the structural change, there arose these new developments:

1. The superintendent instituted weekly meetings with his staff and the general foremen to discuss policies and operations.
2. The general foremen were encouraged by the superintendent and his staff to visit lines other than their own in order to compare notes with other general foremen and have an exchange of ideas about operating practices. Up to this point, no such visits had taken place. It was only gradually, and with some difficulty, that this kind of visiting began to occur.
3. The general foremen were provided opportunities to visit another plant to observe the operation of the vat lines there and to see what ideas they could bring back. These visits seemed to provide an impetus to efforts toward improving efficiency throughout the division.
4. The superintendent set up promotion committees whose members, on a rotating basis, consisted of general foremen and staff. Previously, promotions had been made entirely from within a single vat line. Now, in the case of any vacancy, men were considered from all parts of a department. In the case of promotions from foreman to general foreman, the selection was no longer made simply in terms of men who had

been moved up to serve as vacation relief for their particular general foreman. Three or four foremen were selected from various parts of a department to serve as vacation relief general foreman during a three- to four-month period, so that management could observe their abilities at length.

5. In an effort to clear up particular trouble spots, the superintendent arranged to transfer those general foremen who were thought to be particularly strong to take over the lines of general foremen who were not thought to be doing effective jobs.

I have commented on the tendency of the general foreman, in earlier years, to develop his own semi-autonomous principality as he sought to work out ways to live with the workers and the union. Management efforts to develop and improve uniform operating practices and to shift general foremen and foremen about in order to strengthen "weak spots" naturally had the effect of knocking down the walls separating the principalities and of disturbing the equilibrium of union-management relations.

This meant that problems between workers and management which had previously been settled at the principality level now became subject to much more effective control from higher management. To meet this control at higher levels, the union leaders naturally tended to seek to mobilize resistance at the work level and exert pressure on management at levels above the general foreman.

Conflict cases

The impact of these changes in the management approach can best be illustrated by description of two cases which precipitated worker-management and union-management conflict.

The first case grew out of the new practice of transferring foremen and general foremen from line to line. A general foreman, who was considered by his superintendent to have a very strong record, was transferred to take over the line of a general foreman thought to be weak and ineffectual. Along with the strong general foreman went a shift foreman by the name of Girard. Higher management knew Girard to be a very intelligent and conscientious individual, but one who had tended to be autocratic toward the workers and who had antagonized other foremen by his pretensions regarding his greater knowledge of operations. While they had cautioned him on these matters, his behavior had not seemed to change. Nevertheless, when he was among the men with whom he had worked for several years, he had no serious problems.

At the beginning of his new assignment Girard had no difficulties requiring the attention of higher management. Then he was away for several months, on loan to another plant. He came back to the line just at the time of heightened union-management tension. He ran into his first problem one Sunday morning when the union grievance man approached him and said: "You won't empty the vats on Sunday."

Girard replied: "The vats aren't emptied when we wish but when they are ready." The grievance man remained adamant on this point. Girard then called his department superintendent to ask whether he should force the issue. The superintendent replied that relations between union and management were then at a very delicate stage and that it would be well to hold off the pouring until the next day. (Actually, some of the vats were poured off on the following shift, still on a Sunday, without any difficulty.)

Somewhat later, management added new vats to the line, and this involved a redistribution of responsibilities. At the time of instituting a new schedule for cleaning up around the vats, higher management discovered that the cleaning-up duties on most of the lines had been abandoned from six months to two years earlier. The foremen were ordered to reinstitute the cleaning-up duties.

Girard, at this point, ordered one of the men to do some cleaning up. The grievance man told him that he could not issue such an order. Girard persisted. He told the man: "If you don't want to do the work, go on home." To this the man is reported to have replied: "I will not leave. The only one who can make me leave is the plant policeman."

Perhaps Girard thought the worker was just bluffing. When he still refused to follow orders, the foreman called the plant police and had the man ejected.

This action caused a stir throughout the division. The plant police were unpopular with the men, and Girard's action was bitterly resented. On this point, he did not even have the support of fellow foremen, who openly criticized him for not being able to handle disciplinary problems without bringing in such an outside force. Then several days later, Girard got into another argument with his men. Heated words finally led to drastic action; some of the men ejected the foreman from the plant.

This was regarded by management as an intolerable challenge to its prerogatives. Those considered to be ring leaders in the expulsion of Girard were discharged, and lesser disciplinary action was taken against several others. While the union leaders sought to defend the men, at least to the extent of decreasing the penalties, they were unable to provide an effective defense. The contract did not provide the workers with the right to eject the foreman.

The second case involved a change in working methods on a broader scale.

General foreman Daniel returned from a visit to another plant full of enthusiasm for the work methods he had seen there. Calling a meeting of his shift foremen, he convinced them that adoption of these new operating methods would result in improved efficiencies and also in less work for the men. Having convinced the shift foremen, Daniel then called a meeting with the workers on each shift to explain and endorse this new organization of work. The men evidenced at least a willingness to try out the plan.

As the new working methods were put into practice, Daniel's lines became a focal point of interest throughout the division. The department superintendent and the general superintendent visited the lines to observe progress. The general foreman felt the men were responding with pride to these evidences of attention and interest from higher management.

The new methods on Daniel's lines were also the subject for lively discussion among workers and union representatives in other parts of the division.

The union vice president, Martin, now sought to intervene. He first tried to persuade the men and the grievance man on Daniel's lines to refuse to follow the new methods, but here he was unsuccessful. The men reported that they were satisfied that the methods were better for them as well as better for management. This resistance led to a period of ostracism for the men on Daniel's lines. For a short time other workers kept them out of the rest room or the lunchrooms. When this pressure failed to push the men back to the old working methods, this tactic was abandoned and the men were readmitted as before.

When the superintendent considered the methods to be firmly established on Girard's line, he took the first steps to introduce them elsewhere. Selecting another line for the change, he called a meeting of the workers on that line to explain to them what was to be done. According to the superintendent, one of the men got up and made the following statement:

> After all, we would like to cooperate, but management should understand that the men have to take orders from the union. To have a strong union we must stick together. If there are to be changes made, the best thing probably would be to contact the union heads and then the union heads would give orders to the men.

The superintendent replied: "If there are changes to be made, it is written in the contract that management has the right to make them, and not the union."

The man replied in this way:

> Well, we don't know anything about that. You are an educated man and you can show us anything you wish and make us think you are right. If you have something to discuss, discuss it with the heads of the union.

According to the superintendent, the man acknowledged later that the union in the department had had a caucus on this matter and that he had been instructed by the union vice president, Martin, to take this stand.

A short time later, the superintendent encountered Martin, who heatedly accused him of trying to break the union. The superintendent denied any desire to destroy the union and said that it was important to work together. After some further conversation, the superintendent asked for the cooperation of the union vice president, who is reported to have replied in this manner:

If you want to introduce your new system, there is only one way. Ask us and we will help you. Call a meeting with all the employees and explain it to them and we will help you.

The superintendent stated that he would be glad to do this.

Martin did not attend the meeting which the superintendent then called. Hardly had the superintendent begun his exposition when he was hooted and heckled by the men. Some of them got up and began pushing their chairs around on the floor, making such a noise that discussion was impossible.

That same evening the superintendent received a telephone call at his home from Martin, who apologized for the behavior of the men and promised cooperation in the future.

In consultation with his superiors, the superintendent had already decided to go ahead with further meetings with a change in approach. Now, instead of simply explaining the new methods to the men, he tried to elicit their suggestions for improvements in work methods which would get the new system under way. The second, third, and fourth meetings which the superintendent conducted went along without any disturbance and with a worker participation and discussion that was most encouraging to him.

When the superintendent next saw the union vice president, he was told that if he intended to have any more meetings with the men, Martin was going to tell them to refuse to attend. The superintendent expressed surprise, saying that he had understood the vice president was trying to help with the program. Martin said that he had wanted to help, but the program was dividing the union.

Blocked on the meetings, the superintendent decided to go ahead with the new program without further delay. He planned to introduce the new methods at first on those lines where he thought the general foremen had especially good relations with their men. He gave orders for the program to begin on one such line—and suddenly the other lines followed suit without waiting for similar instructions. The dam of resistance had broken, and in a short time the new methods were in use throughout the department. The superintendent reports that at this point he received a visit to his office from Vice President Martin, who was extremely angry. According to the superintendent, Martin said to him:

You have succeeded because you have control, but we will have our turn. We will stop this. The program is going because you have us by the throat.

Several months later, the whole works was shut down by a strike that lasted four months. Was there any connection between the union-management struggle in the vat lines and the outbreak of the strike? Since the strike grew out of the breakdown of negotiations on issues far transcending the vat lines, it is impossible to weigh the influence of relations within this division in the breakdown of negotiations. However, in the long series of negotiation meetings up to the strike, management people were convinced that Vice President Martin was the most militant of the whole union negotiating group. The management negotiators were convinced that while some of the men on the union negotiating team were trying to avoid a strike, Martin actually seemed to welcome the prospect.

Analysis

These cases indicate the importance of the technology and nature of the job in channeling relations among workers and in stimulating high and low cohesion. The importance of a wage issue upon group activities is evident; however, we are not simply pointing out that money is important to workers. Note that the money issue affected all vat line workers alike, and therefore, inclined them to meet it in a like fashion.

The cases also illustrate ways in which management structures and policies may affect relations within a department or division and the ways those relations within a given unit may affect the union-management relationship as a whole. Let us explore these aspects of the program further through reviewing the management approach to the vat lines under the new works manager.

The works manager believed in decentralization. As far as the vat lines were concerned, should we describe the situation in terms of centralization or decentralization? Our case illustrates the difficulties we get into as we talk in a very general way about centralization or decentralization.

The case suggests that in the period 1953–57, control of operations became more centralized within the vat lines. At the same time, control of industrial relations became more decentralized. Management's efforts to move simultaneously in opposite directions may account for some of the difficulties management eventually faced. Let us explore further these conflicting movements.

Earlier we described the growth of the semi-autonomous principalities, with each general foreman and his foremen making explicit or implicit agreements with workers and union leaders regarding the way the lines would be administered. Management's program to increase efficiency led indirectly to the destruction of these principalities and to the increase of control in the hands of the superintendents and the general superintendent. This led, in effect, to more homogeneous conditions throughout the division. No longer could problems be resolved within the principality where they arose. A problem in one area of the division tended to become a general problem throughout the division. Thus, with increasing frequency, mass demonstrations and other concerted pressure efforts on the part of the union occurred in the division.

Decentralization in labor relations began with the works manager, who refused to respond to union grievances brought directly to him from lower levels in the vat lines. He believed that these problems should be resolved as close as possible to their point of origin. At first glance, this seemed to be a good human relations doctrine. But although it worked out very well in the chemical division, it did not work in the vat lines, where the impact of many of the problems touched the entire division. Furthermore, management efforts to centralize control of operations tended to transform principality problems into divisionwide problems.

The role played by Martin, the union vice president, must be viewed in the light of these conflicting trends. Management people explained his behavior in terms of adverse reflections upon his character and personality. While the situation did not provide opportunities for us to study Mr. Martin himself, even the management account of events and problems provides us with a possible line of explanation independent of any assessment of the personal qualities of the vice president.

Under the principality form of organization, union leaders had been actively involved in the resolution of all sorts of problems. In developing the new efficiency program, the general superintendent and the superintendents were taking unilateral action. It was only when they encountered worker and union opposition, and when Vice President Martin suggested more union involvement in the discussions, that management sought to include the union in the program. But then Martin did not attend the meeting at which he was expected, and he reasserted his opposition later.

This behavior seemed inconsistent, and therefore untrustworthy, to management people, but note that management was not really offering the union leader an active role in developing the new program. The superintendents had decided what they were going to do, and they were only asking Martin to come in to give his endorsement to their program. This represented such a radical change in union-management relations in the division and in the relations between Martin and the management people that one could hardly expect the union vice president to accept it passively.

We should also note one important respect in which the decentralization program in labor relations was not in accord with the realities of organization structure. All our accounts of problems between Vice President Martin and management in the division involved clashes with the superintendents. The general superintendent reported that he sometimes dropped in on meetings between the vice president and superintendents, and other management people, but he appeared to view his role as that of an observer who threw in an occasional light comment designed to relieve tension. On the side of the union, Martin was responsible for affairs throughout the division. His position did not correspond with that of the superintendents. Rather, he was on the level of the general superintendent himself, and yet the two men rarely sat down to a serious discussion.

The same situation was observed at a still higher level. Except for the negotiating meetings immediately preceding the strike, for a period of many months the works manager had had only one contact with the union local president. That contact occurred at the time when a division-wide wildcat strike on the vat lines was coming dangerously close to the three-hour period at the end of which power on the lines would have been shut off and the lines would have gone down for a number of weeks. At that point the works manager warned the union president of the drastic consequences of continuation of the walkout and urged him to get the men back to work. This single contact, without discussion, hardly forms the basis for resolving industrial relations problems. The significance of the organization of interaction between union and management at various levels will be discussed in later chapters.

2.   The rise and fall of the grinders[4]

At the time of the organization of the union in 1941, the grinding department of 35 men in a work force of 1,200 provided the local union president and three members of the executive board. The grinders as a whole participated much more actively in union affairs than did members of the average department. Seven years later, the department provided no local union officers and few men who participated at all in union affairs. Whereas in the early period the men had been solidly united, now the department was divided against itself.

How do we explain these changes? Let us begin by placing the work group in its technological and physical and economic and social environments, and then let us look into the social system itself. The picture to be presented first represents the period around the time of union organization in 1941.

The environment

The technology of centerless grinding provided a number of individual machines through which steel rods were run in a finishing process. The rods came into the department from an extrusion-type process that left a scaly, rough coating. The grinding finished them to a fine, mirror-like surface. In addition, errors in size that had developed at earlier stages in

---

[4] This case is based upon the article by Leonard Sayles, "A Case Study of Union Participation and Technological Change," *Human Organization*, Vol. XI, no. 1 (Spring, 1952).

the process could be corrected through skillful grinding, thus saving waste materials and manpower.

The machines operated at automatically controlled speeds, but the men were required to set the machines up for each run and to adjust size tolerances to 1/100th of an inch and less. While the machine was operating, the worker generally had nothing to do except stand by, observe the process, and be ready to intervene if anything went wrong. When the machines were operating properly—which was most of the time—workers could leave their machines and move around the department for minutes at a time without any adverse effects upon operations.

Physically the workers were in an advantageous position. Their work space was light, clean, and airy. It was also located in the center of the plant, which put the grinders in a key position in the communications network. The work itself was light and the men did not get very dirty or tired on this job.

Since at this location all of the company's production of an important type of rod went through the grinding process, this department in 1941 had a strategic economic position. The workers' relations to the economic environment were reflected in their wages. They reported receiving the highest pay of any group in the category of finishing operations. All of the men held the same job classification; they all received the same pay, except for the several "long grinders." There was just one machine that was larger and longer than the others, and men assigned to this machine received five cents an hour more than their fellows on the standard machines.

The grinders also received incentive pay. While management established the speed at which the machines operated, running the machines more continuously made the premium pay possible.

The economic importance of the job to management and its other characteristics combined to give the grinders a high status in the plant community. There were men involved in the production of steel who had higher classifications and received more pay, but in most cases their jobs were hot and heavy. These conditions gave the grinders some claim to social superiority.

As befits the favorable evaluation of their jobs, most of the grinders were long-service employees. Some of the newer men worked on a smaller second shift.

The social system: 1941

In this initial period, the sentiments of the men were reported to be quite similar on most important points. They took pride in their jobs and in their high status in the plant. They held strong feelings of friendship within the group. They were suspicious of management.

The technology and physical layout allowed for great freedom to interact on the job, and reports indicate that the men took full advantage of this freedom. The foreman was not seen on the floor very much. For the most part, these men just ran their own jobs. Most of the men lived in the same neighborhood. The men and their wives often got together for social activities, and family picnics were a common occurrence.

While the activities on the job called for setting up and tending the machines and reporting the production, it was possible for men whose machines were stationed near one another to share each other's work. In fact, when Joe Borse, who was to be first president of the union local, was out in other departments organizing for the union during working hours, other men "covered" the job for him. As already noted, the job activities, interactions, and sentiments growing up on the job led to the organization of social activities outside of working hours.

The union enters

Why and how the workers in this plant were able to organize the union is not pertinent to our case. It is important to note how unionization affected leadership within the department.

At the time of unionization, there was no dominant leader in the department. The top-seniority men held high prestige in the department, but with the exception of Straub and Salora, who were moderately active, the old-timers remained aloof from the conflict.

The leader of the organization drive, Joe Borse, had little seniority in the department. The two other grinders who were most active and influential in the organization drive were men of only moderate seniority: Korcz, who became an executive board member, and Silton, who became grievance man for several departments in the plant. Note that the union president and executive board members were elected from the plantwide constituency, as was the grievance man, although his jurisdiction was limited to several departments besides his own. Thus these three men had achieved leadership not only within their own department, but also in the total plant community.

The fruits of organization

Beyond the gains won by the workers as a whole through unionization, the grinders were able to take important steps to improve their own position in the early years of World War II.

As Sayles describes it:

With the outbreak of World War II, the demand for the company's product jumped sharply. The company, however, anxious to continue training replacements for this vital operation, refused to institute an overtime day, although this had become the policy in many other parts of the plant. The union supported a brief 24-hour strike that secured the coveted sixth day of work and the concomitant overtime payments. The company also demanded increased production but was unable to secure approval from the War Labor Board for an improved incentive plan. Adept bargaining by the union president achieved the results in practice if not in theory. The men were permitted to speed up their machines. At that time there was no change in the formula under which their earnings were computed, and this provided an automatic wage increase.

During the war, employment in the machine polishing department reached an all-time peak of 100, and there was increased confidence in the future. In the words of one of the men: "We felt we had the world by the tail. We were sure a cocky bunch then."

Later, as defense orders fell off, management undertook to change the incentive formula to take into account the increased machine speeds that had been authorized. This meant a substantial cut in earnings for the grinders. Led by Joe Borse, the men carried through a three-month-long slowdown which finally led management to re-establish the old incentive rate. In fact, the men did not just regain ground that they had lost. In the process of negotiation, the union was able to obtain from management a copy of the company's incentive formula, which had previously been confidential. With this knowledge, the men were able to increase their earnings without increasing production. They were paid for time spent on maintenance as well as on the piece rate for finished grinding. By writing on their time cards more maintenance time than was actually required, they achieved an actual pay increase.

Technological, physical, and personnel changes

Joe Borse became an international representative for the union in 1946. When he had been local union president, he had had union responsibilities for all of the company's operations at this location, but he had remained close to the grinders. As international representative, he could no longer work with them so closely. He was out of town a good deal of the time, and a new local president from other department was elected in his place.

Shortly thereafter, the department was hit by a combination of physical and technological changes. The old department was moved into a new plant a quarter of a mile away. If anything, the new surroundings were more physically desirable than the old, but the move disrupted the relations the grinders had had with men in other departments. No longer was their department the social crossroads of the plant.

As the men moved into the new plant, they were shocked to find that their process had been drastically devalued by technological changes in preceding processes. In the new plant, management had installed greatly improved extrusion machines to produce a finished surface that required no further grinding. Many special orders still required the grinding operation, so all but a few of the oldest grinding machines were installed in the new location. As the department was bypassed on much of the production of the plant, the work available to the grinders was sharply reduced. With fewer polishing machines available to the men, some who had worked on the day shift for years had to drop back to the second shift.

According to the contract and past practice, the men with the least seniority were to drop back, but this affected men with as much as 15 years of seniority, who had considered themselves fixtures on the day shift. This situation gave rise to seniority disputes that set the most influential men in the department against each other.

The most important case involved a written grievance signed by Korcz and Silton, who had played leading roles in organizing the union. They argued that because they operated the long grinders and had been receiving five cents an hour more than the men on the standard size machine, they were entitled to remain on the day shift and have men of somewhat greater departmental seniority drop to the night shift. The contract provided that in case of a curtailment of the work available, men of higher seniority bumped men of lower seniority down into a lower classification, or less desirable shift. It was specifically stated that at such a time of curtailment men were not allowed to bump up. Korcz and Silton were claiming in their grievance that the long grinder position represented a promotional step above the standard grinder, and therefore, they could not be bumped. The older seniority men naturally claimed that the job was in the same classification, no matter which machine was worked on, and that the long grinding job had never been considered a promotional step.

Management remained neutral in this case, allowing the men to fight it out among themselves. Straub, one of the top seniority men in the department, had just been elected steward, and he interpreted the grievance in favor of the high-seniority men. Although no longer holding official union jobs, Korcz and Silton appealed the case from the department to the local grievance committee, to the district director, and even to the international president—but without success. The fact that the two men fought the case so hard and for so long contributed to the unsettled conditions of the department and to the suspicions which the men felt toward one another.

The second case involved the claim of a worker named Hoffman (then on the second shift) that another worker, listed as having more seniority, had achieved such seniority through a clerical error. Again management remained neutral and allowed the union to handle the case. After an investigation of the records, which yielded conflicting evidence, the union officials decided that the existing records had to be accepted as they were.

While Korcz, Silton, and Hoffman all lost their grievances, the cases left a heritage of bitterness that had important repercussions in later years.

In the years 1947–48, a decline in the volume of military orders, together with the new extrusion process, so reduced work for the grinders that all but the most senior men had to drop into the labor pool on a part or full time basis. Although the reduction of the total *number* of grinding jobs was not great, the work became irregular for most of the men. This lowered further the desirability of working in the grinding department, and men now began to transfer out into other departments. This also heightened conflict within the group, for some second shift men claimed that the first shift men were putting pressure on management to see to it that whenever work was short, the first-shift people got to work full time and the second-shift men bore the brunt of the shortage.

A cut in prices

In the midst of internal bickerings, the department faced its most serious crisis—management again attempted to change the grinders' lucrative incentive formula. One day the superintendent appeared and without prior notice, tore down the old standard sheets (upon which incentive earnings were based) and posted new and more stringent ones. The threat of a 30 percent cut in earnings for everyone held some promise of reuniting the group that had been badly shaken by seniority disagreements. The succeeding events are described by one of the night shift men:

The same day we get together with the union president. Everyone gathers around and he tells us it's up to us and the union will back us. Whatever we do the company can't fire us. The day shift decides to hold a meeting that night. We men on the night shift knocked off to go to the meeting. Everyone was there. It was made pretty clear then that we were going to maintain our old speed. We weren't going to tell anybody but if management said anything to anybody, we were all going to walk off the job next day. We weren't going to take any threats.

Well, the next morning coming to work, three of the older men who ride to work on the bus together, three big shots, who always decide things, got together and decided that no, that wasn't the thing to do. They were going to go along with the new speed the company posted. The word soon got around and that was the end of our plan.

This resulted in general confusion in the department; with Borse no longer union president and other officers who once represented the grinders now inactive, the men lacked strong leadership. Bill Silton, who had been one of the department's ablest grievance men, recalled an exchange he had with one of the "older men":

I was telling the men right then and there that the thing to do if we wanted to protect our incentive plan was to walk off the job. But then Salora turned to me and said, "Why are you telling us what to do. You haven't anything to lose. How do we know if these jobs will be waiting for us when we come back, that somebody else won't take them?" I tried to argue with him. I told him no good union man would take our jobs. We have a good union and they'll be behind us. But Salora and Dules and the others, they didn't care. They figured, five or six of them, they'd always be working anyhow. They didn't care what happened to the incentive plan or the rest of the men; so they didn't do anything about it and that was the end of our incentive plan, right there.

Of course the day shift men had another interpretation of the same events:

Sure, these younger guys wanted to strike. They were in favor of it right off the bat. But they had nothing to lose. Most of them by this time were in the labor pool doing unskilled work for low wages. We had a lot to lose. We figured we weren't going to strike. I'm sure it wouldn't have done any good anyhow.

The majority of the men apparently were not satisfied that the union leaders could really back them up once they started something.

The rest of us weren't clear either what we were risking, whether the company could get rid of us, so we followed the older ones instead of doing what we had originally planned.

Fears were also expressed that management might move the grinding operation out of the community to some other plant.

While in 1945 they had shown their unified determination to resist any changes by a prolonged slowdown, in 1948 the men merely went through the motions of filing a grievance. This soon became a dead issue, although the company promised a better plan "some time in the future." The men did little to pressure the union into action on their case.

Management's new offer

By the spring of 1951, the volume of orders involving grinding had again picked up, and management was concerned with increasing production in the department. This led the company to offer—for a trial period —a new and potentially rewarding incentive formula. The men on the first and second shifts decided informally that they would give only a moderate increase in production during this trial period so as not to give the company any excuse for another tightening of the rate. This time it was the men on the second shift who broke away from the informal agreement and joined the "youngsters" on the third shift in breaking all previous production records. Even management was surprised by the extent of the increase. It appeared likely that the new incentive formula would be drastically cut because of the lack of solidarity of the men.

On two critical occasions then, when standing firmly together might have seemed to be of advantage to all members of the department, that solidarity broke down in the face of distrust among the men.

State of the social system

Let us now compare the state of the social system as we found it at the end of the case, with the picture presented at the beginning. We can summarize marked changes in sentiments, activities, and interactions.

So far as we can determine, worker sentiments toward management remained much the same throughout this case: distrust in the beginning and distrust at the end. This suggests, incidentally, that it is a gross oversimplification to assume any close relationship between worker sentiment toward management and aggressive or cooperative behavior in relation to management. Whether or not the workers act out their sentiments depends upon the other forces we have been examining.

Sentiments internal to the work group had drastically changed from harmonious to hostile. Along with this went a sharp decline in the confidence of group members in their ability to accomplish anything collectively. They also perceived themselves to have lost status and potentialities for the support of other groups in the rest of the plant. The grinders assumed that they could no longer get the support which had led all the workers in the plant to walk out with them to win them the sixth day of work.

We do not have the systematic data to show whether indeed workers in other departments had changed their sentiments toward the grinders, but scattered comments picked up by Sayles suggest that their perception of the situation was accurate. For example, one man said: "We're damn fools to have struck the plant so they could get a sixth day of work. What did we get out of it?" Whether or not the grinders interpreted community evaluations correctly, the important thing is that they acted in terms of their impressions of these evaluations.

There was little change in the strict sphere of job activities—though fewer men were on the first shift to perform these activities. The marked change came in out-of-plant activities, since the men no longer got together.

In interactions, the men no longer went out of their shift or departmental sphere to participate actively in the union. Their interactions with men in other departments had markedly declined. Having most of the men together for a departmental meeting became a rare event indeed, and broad social gatherings simply did not happen any more.

The changes in sentiments, interactions, and activities are reflected in the following comments. The first one comes from a man from the first shift:

In the old days, we were always having picnics and beer parties. One of the men had a cottage and we'd be down there having a wonderful time. But I don't know what's happened the past few years; no one seems to have any close friends in the department any more. We've all got interests outside, friends outside the plant; we just keep pretty busy without seeing the men we work with. The minute we leave the shop doors we sort of scatter in every direction.

The second is from a man from the second shift:

How could you have parties with those guys? Before it used to be 18 to 20 of us who were all working on Western Avenue together, and maybe we invited some fellows we worked with too. But now there's too much prejudice. Do you think we would go and have a party with that first shift? What do they care for us? What do we care for them?

Analysis

How did these changes come about?

Changes in the technological, physical, and economic environment of the group had the effect of transforming a once homogeneous group into one which was heterogeneous in important respects. Before the changes, the men thought of themselves as all doing pretty much the same job and getting the same pay. The fact that the long grinders received five cents an hour more and handled heavier jobs was not thought to be a significant difference by the men. Most men preferred the standard grinding machines, but a few men preferred to work on the long machines. There had been no competition for these assignments.

The group was not homogeneous as to shifts worked, but the smaller second shift at the outset was made up of younger men with less seniority, who apparently accepted the preferred position of the first shift men without any question. It was only when long service men of established social position in the plant and department were to be bumped back to the second shift that the equilibrium of the group was seriously disturbed.

Following Leonard Sayles' analysis, I am suggesting that if a group is homogeneous, it is likely to stick together in its relations with management; if it heterogeneous, solidarity becomes more difficult to achieve. However, the case suggests that the degree of homogeneity cannot be assessed on an absolute basis. There are differences that matter and differences that do not matter. The differences that matter are those on which men in authority may make decisions that alter the relations of individuals to the environment. In the early period of our case, the difference between the long polishers and those on the standard machines simply did not matter. When Korcz and Silton made an issue of this difference as they struggled to hold their positions on the first shift, it began to matter very much indeed.

It is also important to note the positions of Korcz and Silton in the social structure of the department. We should not regard grievance handling as an impersonal, judicial process. It is always important to note which individuals are involved in a particular grievance and what positions they hold in status and in jobs in a department. Korcz and Silton had been leaders not only in the department but on a plantwide basis. Their long and bitter fight to hold their first shift position lost them that leadership position not only in the department, but in the plant also. One man commented on Korcz, "He's lost every friend he had."

The downfall of Korcz and Silton threw the departmental leadership solidly into the hands of Straub, the steward, and others of the top seniority group.

The change in the department's relation to the economic and technological environment also affects the ability of the men to stick together on any given issue. Workers are not merely pawns who respond in a passive manner to management's manipulation of the environment. Workers also manipulate the economic and technological environment in an effort to induce changes in managerial behavior. The outcome of this mutual manipulation process depends not only upon cohesion within the work group. It also depends upon the leverage the group can exert upon its environment.

In the heyday of the grinders, they occupied a strategic position in regard to the technological and economic environment. A large part of the production of the plant had to go through their department. They could be confident that as long as they themselves stuck together, management would have to come to terms with them. This did not mean that management would have to give them everything they desired. It did mean that they had the strength to be sure that some important concessions would be made.

Changes in the technological and economic environment destroyed the strategic position of the grinders. One large part of the production that they had formerly processed now was produced in finished form without their operations. Their importance to the company was drastically reduced. No longer would a departmental strike or slowdown seriously cripple the company. If the workers threatened aggressive action, management could talk of transferring the grinding operations to another plant. Such a threat would not have been believed before the change in the economic and technological environment occurred, making the threat seem like a real possibility—particularly to the longest seniority men who had the greatest stake in continuance of the department.

We should note finally the relationship between the status of the group in the plant community and the importance of the operations it performed. When the grinding operations were essential, the grinders enjoyed high status and could rally support from other groups for their own interests. As the importance of grinding operations dropped drastically, there appeared to be a corresponding drop in the status of the group in the plant and a diminishing prospect of rallying support of other workers. The research of Leonard Sayles and George Strauss suggests that we can expect to find this relationship between status and influence, and the importance of the job performed, in local unions generally.[5]

3. The Benton blowing room

For our third case, we return to the Benton blowing room, which we explored in Chapter 10 in telling the story of Gaffer Jack Carter. This department was marked by a high level of heterogeneity, which would lead us to predict a low level of cohesion. In general, this expectation proved correct, yet we must also account for certain instances of effective collective action.

Jobs in the blowing room ranged from completely unskilled up to highly skilled craftsmanship, and there was a corresponding spread in pay. Since each work team, or shop, contained a full range of these skills, the men had little opportunity to form groups on the basis of common jobs and common pay levels.

The 40-odd men on each of the two shifts of the blowing room could be divided roughly into two factions: the old-timers and the young men. The old-timers were the men in their fifties and early sixties who had come up slowly through the ranks in the period when the old Swedes were still in control. The young men ranged from mid-forties down to early twenties. Even the gaffers among them were only in their late thirties or early forties. They had made nearly all of their progress in the period since the retirement or death of the old Swedes.

The importance of age grading in the traditional blowing room is indicated by the title of the top man. "Gaffer" is an old English term for grandfather.

The young gaffers were looked upon with contempt by the old-timers. They were not thought to be real glassworkers. They were not maintaining the real quality standards of Benton (though management seemed quite satisfied with their performance in this respect). Furthermore, they were not all-around glassworkers; they could not do skillfully all of the operations on the shop.

When the young men had difficulties with a new and more complicated piece, the old-timers watched from a distance with ill-concealed satisfaction. They did not volunteer helpful advice. When their advice was requested, they found themselves to be "too busy" to go to the other man's shop to discuss his problem and to observe his work. At other times, they responded to requests for advice with suggestions that they knew would lead the young men into further technical difficulties. At the time of our study, we learned about this advice-giving through interviews, but

---

[5] Leonard R. Sayles and George Strauss, *The Local Union*, rev. ed. (New York: Harcourt, Brace & World, 1967).

the situation was already a matter of the past. Young men no longer asked the old-timers for the secrets that would advance their progress.

The young men reacted by taking a negative view of the personalities and skills of many of the old-timers. There were at least three old-timers whose skills were universally respected, but there were a number of others whom the younger men considered to be bungling workers in spite of their long years of experience.

The separation of the men into two factions could be observed both on and off the job. For a time, we made observations of who was seen with whom during the lunch period or just before or after the working day. To a very high degree, the old men tended to cluster together, and so did the young men. The work allowed many of the men some free time between their job operations, so there was opportunity for social contact on the job. Most of these contacts were channeled within a single age group.

A lack of cohesion was shown in the failure to arrive at any department-wide production norms. This was particularly evident when a given design was shifted from a shop of old-timers to one of younger gaffers. This happened on several occasions when work was shifted from Al Campisi's shop to that of Jack Carter. Since management, like the workers, rated Campisi most skilled of all the old-time gaffers, he was assigned nearly all of the exhibition pieces, and also many of the more complicated regular designs, as they were introduced into the line in the spring and fall. To take on these new pieces, Campisi had to be relieved of some of his old items. These were passed along to the gaffers who were coming up, such as Jack Carter.

In the eyes of the old-timers, Jack Carter should not have been able to make these newly assigned pieces at all. If he did, after an appropriate period of failure and struggle, his production should level off below that regularly attained by Campisi. Under no circumstances should he make more than Campisi had made.

Jack Carter did not share these views of either his abilities or his social obligations. He took pride in raising the quality and quantity of his production rapidly. He sometimes did run into technical difficulties that threatened to take him out of the status competition, and one of these incidents has been discussed. However, in general, Carter was able to raise his production to that attained by Campisi in an outrageously short time. In fact, in some cases he even went beyond Campisi's records. Not much beyond, but just enough to show that he and his men could do it.

This was the source of considerable annoyance to Campisi and his friends. The old gaffer had been the chief protégé of Johnny Jensen, the last of the great Swedish gaffers. Jensen was remarkable not only for the great skill with which he worked the glass, but also for being an exceptionally fast worker. Campisi was thought to have acquired most of the skill of Jensen, but he was not nearly so fast as the old Swede. Therefore, he could be overtaken in competition on some pieces, even as he moved on to new items of production.

While at the time of our study most of the men were well satisfied with their jobs, there were a number of them who had complaints about various matters, and particularly about their failure to receive merit increases in pay as soon as they were eligible for such consideration.

In most cases, such men kept their complaints to themselves or just shared them with a friend or two. There was the general feeling that a man would not get any backing from his fellows on any problems he might take up.

If there was to be any concerted action among the men, we might have expected it to be directed against Jim Dayton, assistant production manager and immediate superior of the foremen. He was regarded by the men as the real boss of the blowing room. A young man of industrial engineering training, he was frustrated by the apparently easygoing pace of life in the blowing room and sought ways to establish greater control over this area. In the fall and winter 1952–53, Dayton made three moves that stirred up antagonism in the blowing room.

The first move, without any prior discussion, was a memorandum addressed to the blowing room foremen, with carbon copies to the plant guards, which was placed upon the bulletin board for all workers to read. The notice read as follows:

Within recent weeks there has been an increase in the number of finished and unfinished pieces missing. To help eliminate this deplorable condition, we must prohibit all unauthorized persons from entering the finishing area. In the future, if there are pieces of ware which in the foreman's judgment should be shown to blowing room personnel, those pieces of ware should be taken by the foreman to the person, or that person should be escorted by the foreman into the finishing area.

This notice was offensive to everyone in the blowing room, and particularly to the gaffers. While up to this point there had been no restriction on movement into the finishing area, it had been the gaffers particularly who had availed themselves of this freedom. A gaffer might wander in now and then to see how the pieces his shop made looked as they were inspected and put through the finishing process. The gaffers claimed that it was a considerable aid to their work to be able to see the pieces at these later stages. They felt that it was demeaning to have to call upon their foreman to accompany them for this purpose. The gaffers were no more pleased at the idea of having the foreman bring the pieces to them. Such actions seemed to advertise to the whole blowing room that the gaffer had been making mistakes.

On the day the memorandum was posted, one of the men added to it a penciled comment stating that the assistant production manager should go back to the Army, where such notices were more appropriate. However, while the notice provided the research interviewers with many heated anti-Dayton comments from the men, no concerted action was forthcoming. The new rule remained in effect, and the agitation simply died down.

In late January, Dayton took two further actions of general significance. One night he searched the lockers of the blowing room men for cups and saucers from the company cafeteria and for pieces of Benton ware. As Dayton told us later,

Boy, there was a lot of excitement. That is, the people who had glass in their lockers made a lot of fuss. The people who didn't have glass found in their lockers, I guess they didn't care much one way or another. It's a funny thing. The one who made most of the fuss had most of the glass in his locker, and he was the one who had the most expensive stuff. The only really expensive stuff we found was in his locker.

The next night Dayton had the outside door of the blowing room bolted shut, so that the men entering or leaving the blowing room had to use the door at the far end of the finishing area, 100 feet or more distant. This action was taken on orders of higher authority, following the vice president's chance observation of a tourist stepping through the door into the blowing room to get a closer look at the process. But as far as the men were concerned, Dayton deserved all the blame for the idea.

The men were strongly resentful, both over the locker search and the door welding. There was a feeling that the lockers were the men's private property and that management had no right to enter them; that in the event of a search, management should have had a representative of the men present. Regarding the value of the ware found in the lockers, there were conflicting points of view. Dayton called some of it "semi-finished —in the process of being finished." The men in whose lockers such glass had been found argued that it was only ware that had been discarded in inspection. Such disagreements arose because of the nature of the inspection process. At that point, some pieces were immediately discarded but others were set aside as doubtful, and the final determination was made only at the end of the day.

The men regarded the door welding as unwarranted interference with their freedom of movement and further evidence that Dayton regarded them all as potential thieves.

What was done by the men about the locker search and the door welding? As far as we could tell, the men took no action at all on their own initiative. Within a week, men in the blowing room were saying that as far as they could tell, all of the excitement had died down and nothing was going to happen.

A few days later, management did call a meeting of gaffers (at the suggestion of the researchers) to discuss some of the changes then in prospect. At this time some of the gaffers did vent their feelings regarding the two incidents. At this meeting, the production manager announced that management had decided to open the door once again. He defended the locker search. (However, within management, it was agreed that if any searches were to be made in the future, a management man would be accompanied by a union representative on this mission. This decision was not known to the men.)

Why was the door opened? Apparently because one of the safety inspectors from the main office considered this locked exit a hazard in case of fire.

While the general picture was that of a divided department with little power for concerted action, there were indeed two occasions on which all of the men stood solidly together. The first arose before our research began and at the time the men moved into the new plant, with its gallery for visitors to watch the work process. Since Sunday was the best day for visitors, management scheduled Sunday as a regular working day and made Monday the day off for the men. For equally obvious reasons, the men did not care to work on Sunday. The representatives of the men and union officers met with management to argue the case. The result was a compromise which gave the men most of what they wanted. Instead of operating a full schedule on Sunday with five shops each on two shifts, management scheduled only one shift to coincide with visiting hours and settled for just two shops on that shift. This meant that instead of working every Sunday, each worker was off four Sundays out of five.

If we can judge from interviews with workers and management people, the workers stood solidly united on this issue. If management had insisted upon its original work schedule, it seems likely that the men would simply have refused to work on Sunday.

The second incident involved working on election day in 1952. It was management's interpretation that the morning shift would have ample time to vote after quitting time, and the afternoon shift, before coming in to work; therefore, there was no need to give the men two hours off with pay. A notice to this effect was posted on the bulletin board. It seemed to contain some loophole for claims for time off in the case of men who might have difficulty in getting to the polls. The notice was posted late on the day before election day, and was worded in an exceedingly ambiguous fashion.

Just to test out what the notice meant, Jack Carter put in a written request for time off. When he came in to work on election day, Carter was informed by his foreman that his request was not to be granted. By this time, it was already evident that the two hours' pay had become a popular issue in the blowing room, and Carter decided to see it through. He demanded to have the union president brought in. At first the president interpreted the notice on the situation in the same way as had management, but finally Carter insisted that there must be a law to cover this situation. The union president telephoned the vice president for industrial relations in the main office, and he in turn consulted the company attorney. Sure enough, the attorney found that there was indeed such a law, and that the men were entitled to take two hours off. The decision came through after election day, but the result was that all the men in the blowing room—and in the other plants, too—received two hours' extra pay.

While Carter was highly unpopular with some of the old-timers in the blowing room, on this particular issue they were all behind him.

That united front broke down just a year later, again on election day. Curiously enough, management did not reach a decision on how election day should be handled until the last minute, when it was decided that the 6 A.M. to 2 P.M. shift should get off at noon and the 2 to 10 P.M. shift should come in at 4 o'clock. In order to keep some activity going between noon and 4 o'clock for possible visitors, the foreman got two of the morning shift shops to work a regular schedule—with two hours of additional straight-time pay plus two hours more of overtime pay.

When Jack Carter came in at 4 o'clock on the afternoon shift and found that another shop had been working straight through, he kidded the men, calling them "scabs." Just how seriously this was intended we do not know, but the old-time gaffer to whom it was addressed was bitterly resentful and the other men of his age group sided with him. On this issue, Carter did not even have the full support of the younger men. The other gaffer involved was one of the younger men and other young men had received overtime pay on the shops in question.

Analysis

How can we explain the cohesion observed on some issues and the lack of integration in others? For this purpose, we should look at both the position of the men and the nature of the issues, presented in terms of heterogeneity or homogeneity.

We were observing a highly heterogeneous department both in skills and age. Skills ranged from unskilled up to a level of a master craftsman. The department was further divided markedly into age groupings. This meant that a benefit the individual sought, such as a merit increase or additional overtime work, was mainly of concern to himself alone, or at most, to his shop. In a few cases, a man's gaffer might speak up for him on the merit increase question, but he received no general support.

Given the heterogeneity of the department, even some issues that appeared to have a departmentwide impact actually affected some individuals much more strongly than others. The notice barring men from the finishing area primarily affected the gaffers. They were the ones who were accustomed to entering that area. A servitor might very occasionally have gone in, but the lower ranking men hardly ever entered the area.

The locker search also had an uneven impact. No one in the blowing room defended Dayton's action, but those who were most bitter about it were indeed the ones in whose lockers some glass had been found—even though no disciplinary action was taken against them. The ones who had not been caught with the glass could view the event with much less concern. In fact, since the man whose locker contained the most glass was one of the high-prestige old-timers, some of the younger men even got a bit of satisfaction through seeing him embarrassed. In any event, there was no concerted move against management. The only actions that arose were of an individual nature, with some men threatening to buy their own private locks.

While the door welding case was resented by everyone, the door was used primarily by men working close to it. In good weather, they could step outside when there was a delay between operations. (The main door had to be used anyway at the beginning and end of the shift, since the time clock was located there.)

The issues of Sunday work and election day pay were quite different. No one wanted to work on Sunday, and everyone welcomed an additional two hours' pay. On the second election day issue, however, the impact on the men was no longer homogeneous, and group cohesion broke down. While all of the men benefited at least to the extent of two hours off with pay, some were thought to have benefited more than others through their overtime work, and this issue split the department.

Summary and conclusions

In the first case, we compared two divisions which differed markedly in the degrees of cohesion and militancy manifested. In the second case, we followed a series of changes in which a high-cohesion, highly militant department became a low-cohesion unit so divided against itself as to be unable to exercise concerted pressure on the management. In the third case, we described a department generally low in cohesion but which on certain occasions "stuck together." Let us briefly re-examine the cases to specify certain common factors related to unit cohesion and militancy.

The homogeneity-heterogeneity dimension relates to the possibilities of developing joint payoff transactions among the workers. In the chemical division, the high degree of heterogeneity meant that almost any change introduced in favor of one worker or small group of workers was likely to have no effect or a negative effect upon other workers within the division. In such a situation, it is exceedingly difficult to mobilize a union for concerted action in pursuit of a common payoff. In the highly homogeneous situation prevailing in smelting, almost any change proposed by management would have had roughly the same effects, positive or negative, upon most of the workers. Under these conditions, joint payoff possibilities were much more likely to be perceived and acted upon by the workers.

We have also noted that smelting provided conditions much more favorable than the chemical division for the mobilization of worker interactions and activities.

That the militancy displayed by smelting union leaders is not to be explained simply in personality terms is indicated by the case of the caustic plant, which was a small subunit of the smelting division. In heterogeneity of jobs and in job-based limitations on concerted interactions and activities, the caustic plant resembled the chemical division much more closely than the rest of smelting. Likewise in cohesion and militancy, the caustic plant was much closer to the chemical division than to the rest of smelting.

The case of the grinders indicates that even within the same general technological environment there can be substantial changes in cohesion and militancy over time. We also note that what is the same and what is different in the work environment is not obvious by casual inspection. The cases suggest that *the differences that count are those differences on which management makes decisions regarding rewards or penalties to individuals or groups.* In the high-cohesion period, the difference between the long grinders and the regular grinders was not considered of any importance. When it came to a management decision as to whether the men on the long grinders held a superior position and therefore could not be bumped by higher seniority regular grinders, then the difference became highly salient.

The grinders' case also illustrates the importance of *centrality* of the unit in the production process. As long as all production of the plant had to go through this department, the grinders occupied a highly strategic position. When management worked out changes that required only a fraction of the total output to go through the department, the grinders had lost much of their bargaining leverage. The change can be restated in terms of negative exchange transactions. In the early period, the grinders could penalize or threaten to penalize management with some confidence that management would not be able to retaliate with equally heavy blows. When the grinders lost their central position in the production process, many of the men recognized a marked shift in the negative exchange possibilities: The men could bring less damage upon management, and management could penalize the men with great severity. The risks involved in this changed situation were responded to differently according to the *investments* the workers had in their jobs. The low-seniority men, having less to lose, were inclined to be more militant. The high-seniority men were inclined to play safe to protect their jobs even when this meant accepting reduced earnings.

The Benton case focuses our attention upon the importance of particular *issues* as factors in promoting or inhibiting worker collective action. Where conditions are highly heterogeneous, most issues will have differential impacts upon the workers, and this reduces the probability of collective responses. However, even in highly heterogeneous departments there may occasionally arise issues which have a similar impact upon all the workers—in this case, Sunday work schedules and election day pay. The occurrence of such issues raises the probability of collective responses on the part of workers.

Specialists in collective bargaining devote much of their efforts to the classification and analysis of issues. We are not here concerned with the usual subject matter classifications: wages, incentive rates, working conditions, discipline, safety, and so on. We ask quite a different question: Is the issue likely to have a *differential* or a *uniform* impact upon members of the work unit? The answer to that question enables us to improve our estimate of the probabilities of a collective response to that particular issue.

References

Sayles, Leonard. *Behavior of Industrial Work Groups.* New York: John Wiley & Sons, 1958. The pioneering work relating cohesion and militancy to technology, work flow, and the nature of jobs.

Sayles, Leonard. "A Case Study of Union Participation and Technological Change," *Human Organization*, Vol. XI, no. 1 (spring, 1952). A full account of the Grinders' case in this chapter.

Seashore, Stanley. *Group Cohesiveness in the Industrial Work Group.* Ann Arbor: Institute for Social Research, 1954. The best survey study so far done on work group cohesiveness.

Discussion questions

1. You have the assignment of planning the physical layout and formal organization structure of a factory. Three products are to be produced; let us call them A, B, and C. Each of these products requires some of the same operations on milling machines, drill presses, and punch presses. Basically, you consider two alternative forms of organization: *product* or *functional.*

If you choose the *product* form, this means that the factory will be divided largely among three units. The department producing A will have its own milling machines, drill presses, and punch presses, plus an assembly line to put the product together, and auxiliary services. The departments producing products B and C will be similarly organized.

If you choose the functional form, this means that you will set up one department for all milling machines, one for all drill presses, and one for all punch presses. You will then have separate assembly departments for A, B, and C.

What are the implications of your decision (*product* versus *functional*) for the cohesion and militancy of work units?

What are the implications of your decision also for:

a) The shape of the formal organization structure?

b) The knowledge and skills required of departmental supervisors?

c) Job satisfaction of workers?

d) Possible lines of promotion for workers?

(Note: This chapter is about cohesion and militancy. However, any important change affecting cohesion and militancy would also have effects upon other aspects of organizational behavior, as suggested in points *a*, *b*, *c*, and *d* above. To put your knowledge of organizational behavior to work, you need to think in terms of the interrelations of effects of a single major decision.)

2. Draw up a list of the factors affecting work-unit cohesion and militancy. Select a work organization with which you have had personal experience. Examine it in terms of the factors in your list. In terms of these factors, what level of cohesion and militancy should we expect to find in this work unit? What level of cohesion and militancy did you observe in this work unit? (Illustrate your conclusion with examples of events reflecting this assumed level of cohesion and militancy.) Does the observed level fit the level we would expect in terms of the factors in your list? If not, how do you explain this lack of fit?

3. Carry out the same assignment as in Question 2 on the basis of interviewing a person who has had experience in some work organization.

22. Patterns in union-management relations

CAN WE DISCERN any patterns which prevail from group to group in examining union-management relations? That is, do we see any similarities among cases where harmonious relations are reported on both sides? Do we see any similarities in cases where conflicts are reported on both sides?

Our efforts in the past to find these patterns have been obscured by a tendency to concentrate attention exclusively on sentiments. It is observed that in apparently harmonious situations union and management leaders express faith in each other, whereas in apparently conflict-laden situations, they cast bitter aspersions on the point of view, trustworthiness, and motivation of members of the other party. It is noted that in conflict situations people have little confidence in being able to settle their problems without coercion, whereas in harmonious situations they are inclined to feel that all problems can be worked out without resort to strikes.

We cannot proceed very far along this line of thinking before recognizing that we are dealing in tautologies. We define a harmonious relationship in terms of the sentiments the parties feel toward each other, and then we try to explain the harmony of the relationship by reference to these same sentiments. Obviously, this is a futile pastime.

In seeking patterns, I suggest that we continue to look at the sentiments, but seek to determine what interactions, activities, and transactions are associated with these sentiments.

The scheme to be presented grew out of study of a very small number of cases, so that it must be regarded as highly tentative. On the other hand, since the first statement of this scheme appeared in 1949, I have had occasion to apply it to an increasing number of cases and have found it a distinct help in analyzing the behavior observed.[1] Furthermore, I have encountered no case which violates the scheme—where, for example, a

---

[1] The structural analysis presented in this chapter is based primarily upon my article, "Patterns of Interaction in Union-Management Relations," *Human Organization*, Vol. 8, no. 4 (Fall, 1949), pp. 13–19. The transactional analysis was fitted in in 1968 for this book.

pattern of harmonious sentiments is associated with the interaction and activity pattern characteristic of conflict situations. I therefore suggest with some confidence that this way of looking at things can be helpful to any student or practitioner in the field of union-management relations.

Before getting down to cases, certain limitations should be pointed out. The scheme is based upon a study of relations involving industrial unions. Its possibilities of application to craft union situations are not known. Furthermore, the scheme purports to explain behavior at the level of the industrial plant and the local union. It includes the behavior of the union's international representative and of representatives of main office management who enter into activities at the local plant level. It does not deal with the total range of union-management relations from the local plant up to the top management of the corporation and of the international union. On the other hand, even where contracts are negotiated on a companywide or industrywide basis—which is becoming an increasingly common practice—there are still many cases in which local union officers and plant management officials have a good deal of autonomy in working out their relations with each other within broad limits set by the contract, company policy, and union policy. The scheme should apply to such local plant situations.

While the scheme does not purport to explain what happens when the United Steel Workers Union negotiates with the steel industry, for example, it may perhaps cast some light—at least by contrast—upon this area of relations.

A scheme for analysis

This scheme is sketched in the diagrams on page 518. The arrows in the diagrams refer not to the simple frequencies of interaction but to the frequencies of origination of activity (or action) between points of the organization structures.

The diagrams are very much oversimplified. They describe only four levels of organization, leaving out staff organizations in order to concentrate upon the relations between the line organization of management and the union—except for one diagram in which it has been necessary to include staff. In studying any particular case it will, of course, be necessary for the researcher to draw his diagrams in terms of the actual number of levels of organization and to tie in staff with line.

These diagrams are not intended to cover all possibilities of union-management relationships, even within the limitations already stated. They represent merely an outline of a few of the common types to be observed. If the scheme proves to be of value, other researchers may introduce other observed patterns.

The analysis begins with the period before the union enters the plant, Diagram A, concentrating here as in the other diagrams upon the fre-

quency of origination of activity. In a nonunion plant there are many
varieties of patterns, but emphasis here is placed on one very common
type. Origination of action proceeds with a very high frequency down
the line from top management to the worker, with very little action being
originated up the line. As noted in the key, the thickness of the arrows
indicates a rough estimate of the relative frequency of origination.

In the A situation, management has a predominance of power in the
offering of rewards and the exacting of penalties. We find positive
exchange transactions linking members of management with individual
workers. We also find negative exchange transactions: a manager penalizes a worker and the worker tries to "get even" insofar as he dares. Both
these transactional types tend to be unbalanced. The manager has more
resources to reward the worker than the worker has to offer in return,
which yields worker sentiments of personal obligations toward management. In negative exchange, the worker cannot retaliate directly for fear
of losing his job. He may combine with others in holding back production or in otherwise hurting management, and this in itself may lead to the
kind of group formation that stimulates unionization.

Diagram B, representing the situation when the union enters, shows
what a drastic change is introduced into the social system of management
when this occurs. New and unfamiliar people enter the picture to originate action for management at various levels. Furthermore, one of the
chief effects of the union organization is to place limitations upon the
frequency with which the foremen can originate action for the workers.
The foreman thus finds himself in a position whose difficulty will be
elaborated upon later.

In the B situation, at first we may see an increase in negative exchange
transactions as workers now dare to come out into the open to penalize
management. Here we approach a more balanced negative exchange
relationship, since workers collectively can damage management much
more severely than they can individually. We also see the generation of
competitive or win-lose transactions at foreman, middle management, and
top management levels. The union representative comes in to get something from management. If he gets it, he has won and management has
lost. If he does not get it, management has won and he has lost. At this
stage we observe few trading transactions and no joint payoff transactions.

Such a drastic shift in the pattern of initiation of activities as represented by the change from A to B presents a difficult adjustment problem,
especially to top management. Accustomed to unilateral control, top
management must now respond to the initiations of a new set of people.
Efforts to cope with this shift will be described in terms of two common
patterns.

Diagram C depicts management's "soft policy." By following this
policy, management men adhere to the theory that they can win peace

and a harmonious adjustment with the union through satisfying the demands of the union leadership as often as possible. They look fondly toward the day when their generosity will be rewarded—the day the union leaders will cease pushing their demands.

In situation C, top management finds itself engaged in a series of competitive transactions with the union leaders. What the union wins, management loses.

We should also note the effects of this transactional strategy upon the relations between union leaders and the rank and file. As the union leaders gain rewards from management, they can pass these down the line, building up positive exchange transactions with the rank and file and thus strengthening their control over the rank and file. This continuing flow of rewards from management through union leaders to rank and file maintains an unbalanced positive exchange relationship between union leaders and workers. The workers can only square accounts by being especially responsive to the directives of their leaders.

To stop taking advantage of management's "soft policy" would mean for the union leaders:

1. Stopping use of transactions that yield continuing rewards.
2. Sharply reducing the frequency of their initiations of activities to management.
3. Drastically curtailing the flow of rewards from management that enables them to maintain an unbalanced positive exchange relationship with the workers.

Union leaders are not likely to be persuaded to change a strategy that yields continuing rewards in favor of one which would undermine their positions.

As long as management continues to give in, trouble may be avoided, but such behavior on management's part is not unlimited. For example, we may take the case of the Blank Manufacturing Company which operated a chemical plant employing about 350 workers. The president of the company had given in to the union leaders so often and so readily that wages in his plant had become the highest in the industry, approximately 25 percent above the level of his competitors. The men also had the finest working conditions in the industry. At the same time, however, costs were high and productivity within the plant compared unfavorably with competitive plants. Consequently, the Blank Company was losing money. The president reluctantly decided that the time had come to say no to union demands. Since he did not feel able to take this step himself, he hired an industrial relations man to act for him. The first time the new executive put his foot down, the union went out on strike. The strike was unauthorized, in violation of the contract, and the international officers of the union exercised all their influence to persuade the men to return to

A Scheme for Analysis

Thickness of arrows represents relative frequencies of origination of action

TM Top Management

MM Middle Management

F Foremen

W Workers

S Union Stewards

MU Middle Union

TU Top Union

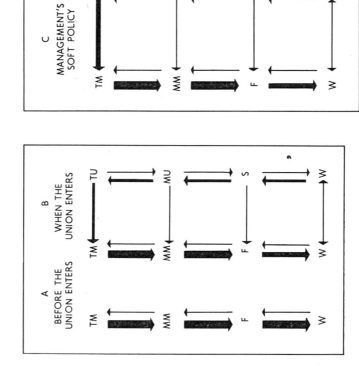

work, but the control of the local leadership over the rank and file was so tight that the strike continued with solid ranks for many weeks.

At the end of the fifth week, the international officers ruled the strike a clear violation of contract, and wrote to all employees telling them that unless they returned to work within 10 days, they would lose their jobs. Even under this pressure, only 10 percent of the 350 workers returned to the plant. The international union then began to recruit new workers to break the strike, and three months later the plant was back in operation— but with a highly inexperienced and unskilled working force. Throughout this entire period, only 10 percent of the original work force showed a willingness to break away from its local union leadership, thus illustrating the strength of that leadership, built up over years of gaining concessions from management.

This strike was, of course, disastrous for the local union leaders and for the nine-tenths of the workers who lost their jobs in the plant. It was also a terrible financial blow to the company. Furthermore, it indicated to management that its policy with the union for so many years had been basically misconceived.

If a soft policy is impracticable, let us observe the results of a "tough policy." In Diagram D, we see such a situation. To maintain union-management relations, the management must respond to origination of action from the union at certain times. But each time the union demands some action, it seems to the management people that they are giving away some of their powers and prerogatives. Therefore, it becomes highly important in management thinking to draw the line between those powers and prerogatives that can be safely yielded or shared with the union and those that must remain sacred to management. The tough policy management then seeks to draw this line in order to protect its prerogatives and takes a strong defensive position behind it, defending its privileges in an elaborate, legalistic manner. As a result, there is much pressure up the union structure toward management, the union leaders feeling compelled to originate action upon management, but with only limited success because of the narrowly defined areas in which management is willing to give ground. In a situation of this kind we find that management generally takes firm steps on questions of discipline. Within the union this approach may generate much antagonism toward management, but if the punishments are followed through fairly consistently, there are not likely to be many undisciplined outbreaks. Wildcat strikes may be more a product of confusion and inconsistency than of a tough management. However, the management that pursues a tough policy builds up strong hostilities toward itself within the union, and those strikes that are authorized may be long and bitter. In such situations it may be found that the workers are not particularly interested in stepping up productivity for management, the latter achieving production through technology and the various controls it exercises over the job.

In situation D, as in situation C, we see a high frequency of competitive transactions—but with this important difference: Outcomes are much more uncertain as management often imposes losses on the union leaders. Negative exchange transactions are also frequent as management retaliates in response to union pressures.

Many management people have surveyed the results of both a soft policy and a tough policy and recognize the drawbacks in each approach. In making their decision to be neither tough nor soft, they resolve to be "firm but fair." For the analysis of behavior, this policy has one basic difficulty: it is meaningless. One may announce that one is being firm, but to others one's attitude may appear stubborn and unyielding. One may believe one is being fair, but the reaction of others may be that they are being badly cheated. The terms "firm" and "fair" are so vague and are subject to so many different interpretations that no particular pattern of interaction and activities is defined. They are simply a set of symbols which may be described as a management ideal.

Union-management reciprocity

There is, nevertheless, an alternative to the tough and soft policies. This can be seen from examining the diagrams. As we compare C and D, we note one striking similarity: Management rarely originates action directly for the union. Management has only one channel through which to originate action: through its own structure. Whether they are acting tough or soft, the managerial people in these situations feel themselves in a defensive position, and regard any move on the part of the union as an attempt to take away ground from management. For them it is a highly unrewarding position and does not augur well for harmonious relations with the union. A way out of this problem is shown in the diagram called "Union-Management Reciprocity."

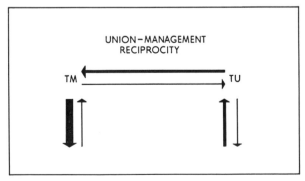

Note: TM Top Management TU Top Union
Thickness of arrows represents relative frequencies
of organization of action.

While most of the observations in this article are rather tentative and based upon a small number of cases, one generalization can be made with considerable confidence: Wherever union and management in industry get along well together and express favorable sentiments toward each other, we find management originating action directly for the union to some degree, as well as originating down its own management structure. What arises may be termed a *reciprocity in the origination of action,* and when this develops we also find what is generally described as a sharing of responsibilities between union and management.

Tough managements constantly talk about union irresponsibility and demand that the union leaders become more responsible. But what do they mean by responsibility? We find that according to their conception, management has the responsibility of organizing production, effecting technological changes, setting up the marketing and advertising facilities, and so on, through a wide range of vital and interesting activities. On the other hand, the union leaders are responsible for preventing their members from going on strikes or participating in slowdowns, and for encouraging them to follow the plant rules in general. The union leaders are supposed to make their position felt only in the grievance procedure. Their responsibilities, therefore, are entirely of a negative character. That is, the union leaders, in exercising their "responsibilities," have a punishing effect upon the members. This is hardly the foundation upon which to build a harmonious union-management relationship. If the leaders are to hold their positions, they cannot follow through on this negative conception of responsibility desired by management.

A sharing of responsibilities does not necessarily mean that the management must have the full concurrence of the union before acting upon every problem. There are varieties of adjustments in this area, but in the major problems affecting the union, no new action is taken by management without a thorough discussion with the key union people.

In transactional terms, union-management reciprocity means the frequent occurrence between union and management leaders of positive exchange, trading, and joint payoff transactions.

With the development of reciprocity between union and management at the top levels, we find the people concerned expressing favorable sentiments toward each other and speaking with some pride about the way they get along together. However, the fact that an adjustment has been reached at top levels does not necessarily mean that relations will flow harmoniously at the lower levels. Since the social systems are made up of interdependent parts, changes in one part will affect other parts; however, a change that leads to more harmonious relations at one point will not in itself necessarily have the same impact at other points. Further compensatory changes at many points in each of the systems are then essential.

Problems at lower levels

To illustrate this observation, let us look at the situation in Diagram E, "Foremen Under Pressure." Here we see that it is possible to work out a harmonious relationship at top levels in such a manner that the foremen feel themselves under increasing pressure from above as well as from the union. For a complete understanding of this situation, we should consider the pressure of staff organizations, for in recent years the foreman's freedom of action has been seriously curtailed by the development of staff activities in engineering departments, in industrial relations staffs, and so on. The foreman's situation today often means that while the union is originating action for him, the very presence of the union limits his freedom to originate action for his subordinates. Moreover, the presence of the union may also lead to increasing pressures on the foreman from the top down. We often find top management regarding the foreman as something of a scapegoat. As union-management frictions chiefly crop up at this point, some top management people regard the whole problem as one of foreman training; therefore, they seek to devise more elaborate methods of telling the foreman what to do. With all these pressures converging upon him, the foreman finds himself limited in his opportunities to compensate for them. Consequently it is not unusual to find him complaining that he has become a bumping post between labor and management, and expressing in many ways the feeling that he is what we have described as "the Man in the Middle."[2]

When we find the foreman thus caught in the middle, we see him visualizing his relationships with workers predominantly in two types of transactions: competitive and negative exchange. To keep the peace, he gives in to the steward. He would like to "get even" (resort to negative exchanges) with the steward and the workers, but he learns that if he goes far in this direction, the union will get management to punish him. In this situation, he is likely to react to his problems in a confused and inconsistent fashion.

In the mid-1940's some foremen were finding a way out of this bind through joining their own unions, such as The Foreman's Association of America, which enabled them to initiate action up the line on management as far as the highest levels, if necessary. For reasons beyond the scope of this book, unions for foremen have long since faded from the scene.

Can foremen reestablish their equilibrium within the management system? Diagram F shows the possibilities of adjustment in three directions. Foremen may be encouraged to increase the frequency with which they originate action upon their superiors. The origination of action from

[2] William F. Whyte and Burleigh B. Gardner, *The Man in the Middle: Position and Problems of the Foreman,* special issue of *Applied Anthropology,* Vol. 4 (Spring, 1945). Also available as No. 91 in the Bobbs-Merrill Reprint Series in the Social Sciences.

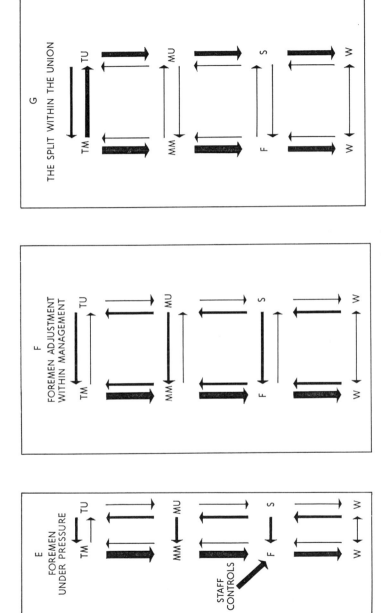

Thickness of arrows represents relative frequencies of origination of action.
TM Top Management   MM Middle Management   F Foremen   W Workers   S Union Stewards   MU Middle Union
TU Top Union

superiors to foremen may be decreased. The foreman may be encouraged to originate action for the union steward. To put this statement of possibilities into subjective language, high levels of management should encourage foremen to make their needs felt, and should allow them more freedom to organize and operate their departments. The foremen should also consult with union stewards before taking action on disciplinary and other problems involving the union within their departments. In general, we find that where a situation giving scope to these adjustments prevails, the foremen have high morale and express favorable sentiments toward both management and the union.

Cooperation between top union and top management presents hazards for union organization also, as shown by the situation in Diagram G. In this diagram we find management originating action for top union with a relatively high frequency and top union originating action down the line inside the union with similar frequency. Here, also, originations of action up the union line and from top union to top management have been relatively curtailed. This situation has certain definite characteristics in terms of symbols and sentiments. We find that after a certain number of encounters, both top union and top management people establish personal ties and a feeling of mutual trust. Union leaders become aware of an interest in management's problems, such as costs and productivity, and realize that the management people are not the ogres they expected to find. There is awakened in the union leaders a sympathetic attitude toward management's point of view. Furthermore, they begin to use the same symbols used by management to describe union-management problems. As these symbols fail to win a response from the rank and file, the union leaders come to feel that the workers don't understand sufficiently what is going on and need to have "the true picture" described to them. We sometimes hear top union leaders speak in the same disparaging terms management people use regarding the intelligence and understanding of the rank and file. The management man who hears such talk should not regard it as a healthy sign, but rather as a danger signal pointing to a possible future split within the union. In several cases a situation of this kind led to a rank and file uprising during which the top union officers were voted out of office; in other cases we found top union leaders making commitments for the rank and file which they were then unable to carry out.

In transactional terms, top management and top union have established a mutually satisfying set of positive exchanges and trading and joint payoff relationships. But the payoffs are shared primarily among the two sets of people at the top of the two organizations. This leads to an estrangement of the workers from the union leaders.

The union-management men who see this danger approaching may find a possible solution by referring back to Diagram F, in which relatively high frequency of origination of action prevails within the union from the bottom up. Origination within the union in these two directions (up and down) are closely related. When top union and top management get together to increase the frequency with which top union originates down the line of its structure, they should not ignore the necessity to increase activity up the line of the union. If this is not done, the equilibrium of the system will be destroyed.

The scheme as a guide to data

This scheme not only suggests how to organize the data; it also tells us exactly what data we need to explain conditions we discover.

For example, a study by Orvis Collins of union-management relations in the Tennessee Valley Authority showed that relations between foremen and stewards were remarkably good, both sides speaking favorably of those they dealt with in the opposite structure. According to this framework of analysis, we would then expect to find the foremen originating action for the stewards on matters of discipline and in other areas, in addition to their normal activity of responding to the stewards. When we conducted interviews on the topic, that was precisely what we found. On the other hand, although Collins found that overall union-management relations in TVA were remarkably harmonious, he did find some minor tension between members of middle management and the union. Indeed in TVA the middle management people alone seemed to feel themselves in a defensive position, fearing that the union was depriving them of some power. The union men spoke highly of most members of management, but were critical of many middle management people. According to our conceptual scheme, we should expect to find that members of middle management did not originate for the union to any appreciable extent, while their opposite numbers in the union originated action for them with a relatively high frequency. When we interviewed to test this hypothesis, we found it amply substantiated by the data. Applying the scheme in this manner points out tension areas and gives some explanation of how these tensions are related to the social system, as well as indicating possible changes that would relieve the tensions.

This case suggests one of the values of a conceptual scheme. It indicates the types of data that should be gathered and how they should be put together. It leads us to believe that when we find a certain pattern of sentiments between two points in an organizational system, we should then expect to find a certain pattern of interactions and activities, and it is there that we can direct our attention.

Summary and conclusions

We have presented a structural analysis of union-management relations at the plant level. For this purpose, we have been looking particularly at the *directions* and *frequencies* of *initiations of actions or activities* and at the distribution of types of *transactions*. We have pointed to the following types of relationships:

a) Management's unilateral control, before the union enters.
b) Initial period of establishing the union.
c) Management's soft policy.
d) Management's tough policy.
e) Foremen under pressure.
f) Foremen adjustment within management.
g) The split within the union.

While there is a natural time sequence from (*a*) to (*b*) and from (*e*) to (*f*), the other patterns do not follow in any necessary time sequence. Management is free to meet unionization with either a soft policy (*c*) or a tough policy (*d*). Whichever policy management applies, the foremen are likely to find themselves under pressure (*e*) as they get blamed from both sides for problems really beyond their powers to solve. If these pressures on the foremen are to be relieved, higher management decreases its downward initiatives and encourages upward initiation from the foremen, while the foremen begin to take the initiative in dealing with the union, developing positive exchange and trading transactions with the steward.

Both (*f*) and (*g*) represent what we call reciprocity in union-management relations: Positive values are flowing in both directions. They differ primarily on the union side. In F we have positive values flowing down from top union leaders and across from various levels of management, and (compared to *g*) we have relatively high levels of initiative going up the union structure and across to management at low and intermediate levels. The split within the union does not have to occur, but it will unless top union officers and members of management respond to initiatives from bottom and intermediate levels of the union in ways that lower officers and workers find rewarding.

Finally, we have suggested an approach to the diagnosis of the current state of union-management relations in the plant as a whole and the difficulties that may be observed at any point in the two structures. If the student can gather from workers, union officers, and management people the data that permit him to draw a rough diagram such as those used in this chapter, and if he can also make a rough assessment of the distribution of transactions at the various points within and between the two structures, then he can make his own diagnosis. This should lead him to the key problems of each case. It should also provide certain leads toward the solution of those problems. However, changes in the day-to-day pattern of union-management relationships are often generated particularly in the process of collective bargaining. It is to an analysis of that process that we turn in the following chapter.

References

Gouldner, Alvin. *Wildcat Strike*. Yellow Springs, Ohio: Antioch University Press, 1954. A case study of a wildcat strike in a gypsum plant and mine.

Whyte, William F. *Pattern for Industrial Peace*. New York: McGraw-Hill Book Co., 1951. A study of a change from extreme conflict to unusually cooperative relations in a steel container plant.

Discussion questions

1. An industrial relations man makes the following statement:

"Basically, it comes down to a question of attitudes. To have good relations between union and management, you must have mutual trust. Where there has been conflict, that can come about only through changing attitudes on both sides."

Do you agree or disagree with that statement?

2. Select a published case study of a union-management relationship. Try to apply to it the framework of the present chapter. Note particularly where the author does not provide you with data that the framework requires; how do you explain such gaps? Compare your analysis of the case, using the present framework, with the analysis given by the author of the case. What similarities and differences do you find?

3. If you have had any experience in a union-management relationship, seek to apply the present framework to that experience. Does that exercise enable you to understand that experience better? If so, how? If not, why not?

4. Interview someone who has experience in a union-management relationship as a manager, union officer, or worker. Ask him to assess the quality of that relationship. Then get him to give you as much information as is within the scope of his knowledge and experience to enable you to diagram the case along the lines developed in this chapter. Can you fit the informant's sentiments regarding the quality of the relationship with the data he gives you for your structural diagram?

23. The collective bargaining process

ONCE THERE WAS a president of a small unorganized company who believed firmly in labor unions. He was, therefore, gratified when his employees notified him that they were joining a union and wished to bargain collectively with him. The negotiating committee submitted its demands in advance, and the president studied them carefully. As he compared those demands with contracts in other companies in his industry, he could find nothing that seemed unreasonable. The employees were simply asking for conditions that would put them in line with those existing in plants which had been organized for several years. So when the negotiating committee came in to bargain, he simply told them that he was prepared to accept their terms in full and sign a contract at once. Such a magnanimous attitude, he thought, would establish a firm basis for harmonious relations.

In legal and economic terms the union had won without effort the gains that had been achieved with great difficulty by other organizations. You would think, therefore, that the union people would have been very happy. This was not so. The employer's troubles began as soon as he had signed the contract. Productivity fell off, there were wildcat strikes in one department after another, and it was many months before relations settled down into the harmonious pattern that the employer's friendly attitude should have made possible.

What happened in this case? The union organization arose out of a variety of worker dissatisfactions, and the members of the negotiating committee found themselves in the unaccustomed but pleasingly prominent position of representing their fellows in the fight to eliminate these dissatisfactions. They took their mission very seriously, and prepared their arguments with care. The negotiators went into the conference with the employer under a full head of emotional steam. Then in the meeting with management there was simply nothing for them to do, and they went out of the conference with their emotions still awaiting expression. The whole thing simply had not been done right. They reasoned that since the president had given in so easily, they had been at fault in not demanding more of him. Things which he could give away so readily must not be worth having. The same sentiments developed among the rank and file members.

The manufacturer made one fundamental and very costly mistake in this case. He looked at bargaining simply in legal and economic terms. He did not recognize that it is also a social process—a round of ceremonial activities.

He failed to recognize that bargaining involves dealing with emotions as well as with logic and economics. It is said by some authorities that emotions must be kept out of the collective bargaining process. This is nonsense. The emotions felt by people must find some expression. They simply cannot be ignored. If the emotions that are built up around the collective bargaining process are not expressed in that process, they will break out, as they did in this case, in other highly damaging ways.

This is an examination of the nature of the collective bargaining process. Bargaining involves technical questions of law and economics, but it also involves the emotions of workers, management people, and union officers, and the sentiments through which they give expression to those emotions.

To understand the process we must consider two important aspects: the network of human relations and the expression of the sentiments. For our purposes, this network of relations involves particularly those who sit around the bargaining table, but we must also consider the relations of union leaders with their members and of management negotiators with top management people who may not be directly involved in negotiations, but are often important in establishing limits and policies. All of these sets of relations I will be able to consider here, with one exception. My data come in large measure from collaboration with Sidney Garfield, late president of the International Chemical Worker's Union.[1] Accordingly, I cannot claim any knowledge regarding relations between management negotiators and top management in the bargaining process.

So as to face the maximum difficulty with our analysis, let us assume that a union and a management are entering upon negotiations in a period that has been marked by hostile sentiments and an exchange of negatively valued activities—such as slowdowns and work stoppages on the union's part. In such a situation, the actual negotiations often serve to intensify hostilities, yet occasionally we see parties utilizing the negotiations to effect a transition toward more harmonious relations. How is this done?

In this chapter, we shall attempt first to answer that question through citing examples from cases. We shall then seek to link the points emerging from the case analysis with a more general theoretical framework pro-

[1] This chapter is based primarily on Garfield and Whyte, "The Collective Bargaining Process" (in four parts), *Human Organization*, Vol. IX, no. 2–Vol. X, no. 1 (1950–51).

vided by Richard Walton and Robert McKersie.[2] Finally, I shall seek to show the relationship between the Walton-McKersie framework and the transactional approach of this book.

Symbolic equivalence of status

If the union leaders are to reach an adjustment with management, they must carry on negotiations on a plane of symbolic status equality. In the community outside of the plant, this equality of status does not exist. The management people even at the plant level are likely to be at least upper-middle class, with perhaps some holding upper-class positions. If the international representative for the union is accepted in upper-middle class circles in his home community, he would be the only one of the negotiating team on his side so placed. Others would presumably be classified as lower-middle and upper-lower.

When there are such disparities in social status between the parties, it is quite natural for the management people to express themselves in ways that symbolize their social superiority. If this is done, however, the union people will react most vigorously against it.

The following case shows the disastrous consequences that can follow from behavior symbolizing the status superiority of management.

The members of the local negotiating committee were preparing the case they were to present in bargaining with the X plant of the ABC Company. The annual contract still had six months to run, but there was a clause allowing for discussion of wages at the half-year point. The contract provided that if no agreement was reached during such interim bargaining, the existing contract would continue to the end of the year. Therefore, management did not have to act at this time. It was up to the negotiating committee to persuade management that changes were necessary.

The negotiators took their duties very seriously. They prepared figures on the rising cost of living and marshalled all of the other common arguments in favor of a wage increase. They reviewed the plant's production picture so that they could show that the union had been playing an active role in the success of the company. They planned carefully among themselves and with the international representative as to who was to make which arguments.

They went in and argued for a wage increase all afternoon long. Finally the representative of top management stepped in and cut off the discussion with these words:

Well, you fellows have done a lot of talking, and I must say I haven't found your arguments very convincing. Still, I think you're a good bunch of fellows, and I tell you what I'll do. I'll give you 10 cents.

───────────
[2] Richard Walton and Robert McKersie, *A Behavioral Theory of Labor Negotiations* (New York: McGraw-Hill Book Co., 1965).

The union negotiators were temporarily stunned, but the international representative recovered more quickly than the others. He said that 10 cents was a very good settlement, in line with the best that were then being made around the country. He felt his organization should be happy to have achieved such a settlement. And then, having spread this dash of perfume, he quickly had the meeting adjourned.

Later, at the general membership meeting, the local union president gave this account of the negotiations:

Well, we talked and we talked and we talked. And in the wind-up, Mr. Jones says he don't think so much of our arguments, but we're a good bunch of fellows so he'll give us 10 cents. . . . Oh, hell. . . .

The membership voted to accept the offer because there was nothing else they could do. The contract had six months to run. But next time it was not to be so easy.

When the contract ran out and the parties were again negotiating, management proposed a five cent general increase—making a total of 15 cents for the year. The local union negotiators reported the offer to the membership meeting, where it was unanimously rejected. Anti-management feeling ran high at this time, and the members voted unanimously to strike unless the company came through with a better offer.

It was at this point that the international representative was again called in. He found the parties apparently hopelessly deadlocked. The management men were determined not to go above five cents. They were convinced that a total of 15 cents for the year was on the generous side compared to what other companies were doing.

The international representative felt that a strike at this time might well be disastrous to the union. The company was in the process of reorganizing its staff and production lines and had no pressing backlog of orders. It would have been easy to shut that plant down and shift its orders to other plants for a considerable period, with little hardship to the company.

Furthermore, the international representative was convinced that a large majority of the workers did not really want to strike. The problem seemed to be that morale within the union had gone to pieces to such an extent that the members were not turning out in large numbers to their meetings even in a crisis. Only 65 of 300 had come out for the strike vote. Attendance may not be high for every meeting, but a crisis meeting in a local of this size should be expected to bring out more than half of the members.

The local union officers wanted to avoid a strike they could not win, but they saw no way out of the impasse. Further discussions with the company brought nothing beyond the five cent offer. The state mediation service was then called in, but the mediator was able to make no progress. Finally, as a last resort, the international representative proposed that the mediator conduct another vote on the company's offer at the gates of the plant, to make sure every worker had a chance to vote on the issue. The vote was two to one in favor of accepting the five cent wage offer.

In that way, the strike was averted. But what of the underlying problems?

Let us ask why this highly favorable economic settlement led to such severe problems within the union. The case provides another example of the application of the old maxim: "It ain't what you do but the way you do it."

It is not often that a worker in the shop has a chance to sit down across the table with local management, or even with a representative of top management in a large corporation. That unusual experience makes a deep impression. The local officers had prepared themselves for it long and conscientiously. They felt, at last, that they were to sit down with management people, who would accept them as equals. But did they?

A relationship of even temporary equality requires expressions and indications of respect on both sides. It requires that concessions be *won*, not *given away*. You don't make gifts to equals except when they are in the position of making gifts in return. When the top management man said, "I'll give you ten cents," and took pains to show the men that they had done nothing to win this offer, he was in effect telling the local officers that they were beneath management—that they did not amount to much.

When the local president passed management's statement on to the membership, he was in effect letting them know management's opinion of the union. And he was telling them that their own leadership was unable to get anything except what management deigned to give. A more crushing blow to the morale of the union leadership could hardly be imagined. The leaders could have regained their standing with the people only through fighting to get more than management was going to give. With the contract still in force, they were blocked from this course of action.

When the end of the year came around and management offered five cents, the management representatives thought they were conceding a 15 cent increase for the year. From the union standpoint, the picture looked far different. The 10 cents at midyear had been given away, so that didn't count. It was only the five cents that was won by the union. And a five cent increase would not stand comparison with what other unions were doing. The union had to get more.

The maneuver of the international representative averted a disastrous strike, but it did not solve the underlying problems. It left the militant group completely frustrated, without any way of taking action, and it left the rest of the membership as apathetic as ever. In such a situation, we would not have to be crystal ball gazers in order to predict continuing unrest within the union and further friction between union and management.

The moral of the story might be put to management in these words: Don't give anything away! That does not mean that management made a mistake in offering 10 cents. The mistake was in the way the offer was made. Instead of presenting a gift, management could have allowed itself to be persuaded that the union was entitled to 10 cents.

Attacking the man who isn't there

In a society like ours, which puts an emphasis upon the values of frank expression, there is nothing quite like the satisfactions we get when we are able to express our hostile feelings directly at the target of our hostility. The difficulty of this approach is, of course, that a direct attack of A upon B nearly always serves to stimulate B to counterattack. Thus, even as A gets some satisfaction from his own expression, he receives new insults which fan the flames of resentment and demand further expression. And so it goes with B also.

Our studies suggest that on occasion, A can receive nearly the same measure of satisfaction—without the hazards—if he carries out an oblique attack: an attack upon the man who isn't there. I sometimes think that this man who isn't there plays one of the major roles in collective bargaining. Consider these several cases.

When International Representative Shaw was called in to conduct negotiations for the local union with the Ajax Chemical Company, he was told by his committee that conditions in the plant were in an uproar. Management negotiators claimed that the plant had been losing money. They had decided that the outdated technology and job methods were responsible for the backward condition of the plant and had called in an engineering firm to study the situation and to make improvements. The engineers moved in, and at a cost of approximately $30,000, carried out sweeping changes.

However, neither management nor the engineers made any effort to inform the union or the workers of what was to happen, and it soon became apparent that the foremen also knew nothing about the situation. When workers approached their foremen for explanations, they came away more confused then ever. The plant was so shaken up that nobody knew where he stood, and in their anxiety the workers expressed strong hostility to management.

In view of the financial condition of the plant, it seemed unlikely that the union would attain substantial economic gains in its bargaining with management. In fact, Shaw was told later by management that an increase of absolutely no more than three cents an hour had been predetermined.

Shaw decided that he would not attack on the economic front. At the meeting, after some preliminary fencing, he plunged directly into a long discussion of the engineering program. He spoke about the way the program had been introduced, and outlined the general effects that should be anticipated from a program of this nature. Then he continued by discussing in detail the problems that were cropping up in department after department. He even suggested that the foremen were as confused as the workers about the program.

So closely did Shaw's discussion hit home that it seemed to management that he must be possessed of remarkable insight. Actually, the facts he had were elementary to a man with experience in this field. He had seen enough of engineering and methods changes, introduced without proper preparation, to know eactly what was to be expected, and the reports of his local committee filled in all the necessary details.

Even after he saw that he had management on the defensive, Shaw continued to talk. Feeling it essential to avoid argument, he continued uninterruptedly for almost an hour and a half. He built up his case, stating that management had spent $30,000 only to find itself in a worse position than before the program had started.

As he talked, Shaw took careful note of the expressions of the men across the table. He saw that one of the vice presidents had become exceedingly red in the face and seemed about to explode, and surmised that this was the man who had taken the initiative in calling in the engineering firm. But he made no personal charges against this vice president either then or later.

Having put full pressure on this issue, Shaw eased up with a joking remark to the effect that his lecture should have been worth a 17-cent an hour wage increase to the company. If the company offered them anything less than that, he said, the union would consider they were still owed the difference. This eased the tension somewhat.

Then Shaw said with emphasis: "You know who's to blame for what happened here? I don't blame you members of management at all. It's that engineering firm. I have seen cases like this before. It's the responsibility of the engineers. They just bungled the job." Immediately after that, he called a recess for lunch.

As soon as the meeting adjourned, the embarrassed and furious vice-president rushed to his office and put in a long distance call to the engineering firm. He gave them hell—unloading on them some of the pressure Shaw had placed on management.

The recess lasted for two hours, allowing plenty of time for Shaw's words to sink in and for management to reconsider its position.

When the meeting reconvened, it soon became apparent that management was making every effort to adjust the differences. One management man suggested bringing in the foremen to discuss the engineering and methods changes thoroughly. Shaw agreed that this would be an excellent idea. Another member of management asked whether it would not be a good idea to have joint meetings with the foremen and union officials. Shaw said that would be even better. Then, as they went on into the economic issues, management carried through in a very conciliatory manner, making an offer of an eight cent increase and two paid holidays, in addition to the six the union had already won. On the same day, many other substantial concessions were made, resulting in an agreement between management and the negotiating committee of the union.

Shaw and his committee were delighted with the contract, which was considerably better than the union had expected from the negotiations. The eight cent an hour increase met the general pattern in that area, and at that particular time, in that industry. No one else in the area had eight paid holidays and there were other features of the contract that were equally attractive.

The same approach can be utilized by management people. In studying the remarkable change in union-management relations at Inland Steel Container Company's Chicago plant (in *Pattern for Industrial Peace*[3]), I noted that early in the negotiations the management people expressed their concern on several occasions regarding slowdowns and work stoppages and other evidences of what management considered irresponsible actions. Each time, the management people were careful to state that they were not accusing any member of the union negotiating committee of being involved in these demonstrations. As a matter of fact, some of the local union negotiators had indeed been ringleaders in some of these activities. Furthermore, without being able to prove it, the management people were convinced that this sometimes had been the case. But what good could have come from direct accusations? If the union leaders had been so attacked, they would have felt impelled to defend themselves through attacking the management actions which they felt had made necessary this type of resistance.

By focusing attention on the man who wasn't there—on some unnamed and irresponsible union member—the management people could give full expression to their sentiments regarding the seriousness of the problem. Not being directly under attack, the union leaders could listen respectfully.

When they had their opportunity to reply, the union leaders fastened upon the same symbolic scapegoat. Complaining about some conditions their members faced, the negotiators placed the blame for these conditions upon the foremen. Here again, in most of the problems raised, union negotiators considered that higher management people were really more to blame than the foremen. Nevertheless, they too refrained from pinning the blame directly on the other side of the table.

At first glance, it may seem that this is an evasion of the real problems. We realize this is not the case when we distinguish between what people

---

[3] William F. Whyte, *Pattern for Industrial Peace* (New York: Harper and Bros., 1951).

are thinking and what they are saying. When the management people heard the foremen attacked, they fully recognized that the problems being discussed were at least as much their own responsibility as that of the foremen. Furthermore, they realized that the union negotiators felt this way, too—but were good enough not to say it.

By the same token, when management people attacked the irresponsibility of some unnamed workers, the union leaders fully recognized their own personal involvement in these problems. They knew, moreover, that the management people knew—but were good enough not to say it.

By means of such oblique attacks, the parties sometimes are able to grapple constructively with problems that could not be handled by a frontal attack.

Encouraging full expression

When a man states a point of view on which you disagree, there are two contrasting ways of meeting the situation. You can immediately bring in counterarguments to show him that he is wrong. Or you can express interest (not approval) in his point of view and ask him to tell you more about it. Why does he feel the way he does? What is behind his thinking?

These two moves lead in opposite directions. The first move leads to increasingly sharp disagreements, marked by brief and rapid interchanges, interruptions, and rising emotional tension.

The second move leads to relaxed tension and makes agreement possible. The man does not feel under pressure to get out his statement in a hurry and prepare for counterattack. He is able to talk to the subject and around it, in an informal, exploratory manner. Both parties are then better able to size up possibilities of getting together.

This is illustrated by the opening of the discussion on the most difficult issue in the Inland Steel Container Company case. For five meetings the parties avoided the issue, but now they met it head on, with Attorney Kaufman and General Factories Manager Novy speaking for management, and Shafer speaking for the union:

KAUFMAN: All right. "The arbitration provisions of Section 2 shall not apply to the determination of wages, wage rates, or job classifications."

Now, that is one that I believe we are going to have to insist on. I don't know how familiar you are with the history of our problems in this plant, and I can imagine, without knowing, what the union has said about it. If the union wants to explain why it wants that change, maybe we had better hear from them first on it. I want to tell you at the outset that that has been in there several years, I think, and we think that that provision is what has enabled us to beat several programs—when I say programs I am not mentioning a program that Lucius or Don or Ernie or anybody else are involved in—several concerted efforts which were pretty clearly slowdowns.

Is that a fair statement of our position, Bob?

Novy: That is putting it very mildly.

Kaufman: I am a mild fellow.

Shafer: I am interested in Mr. Novy's statement. You say, "That is putting it very mildly." [4]

Instead of counterattacking immediately, Shafer encouraged the management people to state their position fully and freely. Only when they had done so did Lucius Love speak for the union, and then management gave him a full and respectful hearing.

It took five more meetings to reach agreement on this issue (and on others too), but this manner of opening the discussion enabled the parties to explore their problems in an atmosphere of relaxed tensions that did not seem possible before Shafer encouraged management people to express themselves freely.

Building a pattern of agreement

Where there are a number of issues to be negotiated between the parties, a few will be of major significance to both parties, and the rest will be of minor significance. If the parties discuss issues according to the sequence of the number of clauses in the contract, then it will be a matter of chance whether the minor or major issues are tackled first.

Even following this sequence of numbered clauses, I found in the Inland Steel Container Company case the possibilities of readjusting the sequence according to the weight of the issues. Without any conscious planning or agreement as to procedure, the parties in effect agreed that they would discuss the numerous minor points first. When they did come to a major issue, each party stated its own position briefly, which showed them that they were far apart. Then someone proposed that they move on to the next issue and leave this one until later.

In these negotiations, the question of whether the union should have a right to call for arbitration of grievances regarding a new or changed piece rate was the most important and explosive issue of all. After being passed over quickly in one of the early meetings, this issue did not come up for really intensive discussion until the sixth meeting, out of a total of 11 that made up the whole process. By the time this most explosive issue did come up for discussion, the emotional atmosphere in the bargaining had already undergone a substantial change. In the process of compromising on minor points, the parties were able to test each other out and establish the beginnings of an effective working relationship. This was particularly important in these meetings, for the key man, International Representative Lawrence G. (Jake) Shafer, had met the management people for the first time in the opening negotiation meeting in the 1947

[4] *Ibid.*, pp. 87–88.

contract talks. Before it could be determined whether an agreement was possible, he had to size up the men across the table from him, and they had to have an opportunity to size him up.

Safety valves

It is all very well to resolve that negotiation shall be conducted without emotional explosions, but what do you do when tempers rise—as they are bound to do when men disagree on issues important to them? At such points, the search for safety valves becomes important.

Jake Shafer found one in his interest in hunting and fishing. In the early stages of bargaining at Inland Steel Container Company, when the parties were still tense and wary of each other, Shafer interrupted the discussion with a casual comment that he had stopped on his way to the plant to pick up some pictures he had taken on a recent hunting and fishing trip. Would the men around the table like to see the photographs? The management men reported later that at first they had been mystified by this maneuver. Nevertheless, they agreed to inspect the pictures, and there followed an interlude of attention to hunting and fishing. When negotiations resumed, the tension seemed to be greatly relieved.

No standard set of safety valves can be offered. They must be developed to fit the particular situation. The skillful negotiator will recognize danger signals and be ready with some tension-easing diversion before men reach the point of making statements whose damage cannot be readily repaired.

Symbolism of common interests

In a conflict situation, the union and management negotiators are inclined to look at the men across the table as completely different types of individuals. Mutual trust cannot arise quickly; yet if the parties are exposed to symbols indicating certain personal points they have in common, they may be able to talk with each other more effectively than would otherwise be possible.

Since the parties appear to be in conflict on major issues, it is highly unlikely that these issues will provide potentially integrating symbols at the outset. Instead, the integrating symbols may be quite unconnected with the conflict situation, and, perhaps for this very reason, provide a bridge toward understanding.

The hunting and fishing diversion of Jake Shafer did more than provide a cooling-off period. Robert Novy, general factories manager, commented later:

It's been my experience that whenever you run into a real sportsman, you'll find that he is a pretty regular fellow. He's a man you can deal with straight from the shoulder. That's one of the things that sold me on Shafer.[5]

---

[5] *Ibid.*, p. 184.

In Chapter 19 (Enter The Union), we viewed symbolism of common interests as important elements in establishing the bargaining relationship in the first place. Herbert Buchsbaum was influenced toward union recognition by Garfield's protection of the strikebreaker's car, symbolizing a common belief in the sanctity of private property. He was also influenced by the report of a trusted friend that Union General Manager Laderman could be counted on for "keeping his word," that he "disliked fights" and "liked opera," and finally, "was a real human being." All of these symbols helped the company president to perceive the union leaders as persons much like himself and with whom he therefore might reasonably expect to get along well. The same principles of symbolism are involved in negotiating an agreement as in establishing union recognition.

Making the institutional framework clear

Effective bargaining requires a flexibility of approach. The party that begins with a "final offer" or unalterable set of demands is simply inviting a strike, or else a humiliating surrender. The parties naturally begin with certain definite objectives and with plans as to how far they can go in meeting the demands of the other party. They size up what points can safely be yielded in return for concessions from the other party.

The first steps in bargaining involve an exploratory process on both sides. In the preliminary fencing, the bargainers size up the people across the table and try to sense the relative importance of each issue to the other party.

For effective negotiations, it is important for both parties to understand the limitations within which the other party must act. If this is not done, the union may push to the point of a strike an issue on which management cannot possibly yield, or management may precipitate a strike on an issue that the union negotiators cannot afford to yield.

Strikes are sometimes necessary and unavoidable, but there are strikes that arise simply because one party has pushed beyond the retreating point on a certain issue, through a failure to understand the crucial nature of the issue to the other party. If a strike is necessary, both sides should approach it with their eyes open. It is an evidence of bad leadership for one party to find itself trapped into a strike by having taken too early, too strong a stand on an issue that could not be won across the bargaining table. In such a case, the party must suffer a strike or else "lose face" on this issue.

Losing or saving face is not a peculiar oriental type of behavior, as it is sometimes supposed to be. It is of vital importance in bargaining and may strongly influence the emotions of individuals and the morale of their organizations. In fact, there may well be times when it is more important to the future solidarity of the organization to go through a strike than to lose face. But people cannot lose face unless they have put their face in the balance first—unless they have taken a strong, dogmatic stand. It is therefore a job of the negotiator to approach these points of possible impasse with the utmost care, to explore the situtaion thoroughly before taking any irrevocable stand, and to be ready with face-saving phraseology if the other party gets backed into a corner.

This exploration of the limits within which a bargain can be reached involves more than an estimate of the relative importance of the issues to each party. It involves an understanding of the reasons behind this importance. Such understanding cannot be conveyed simply through an argument concerning the issues themselves. The parties need to gain an understanding of the institutional framework within which the men across the table, think, feel, and act.

For example, International Representative Sutton found himself dealing with a peculiarly adamant plant manager. Sutton and his committee took pains to put forth the union's case for each demand in reasoned, unemotional language, but it was clear that they were making no progress. The plant manager's replies suggested that he considered these arguments simply an attractive cloak for personal ambitions.

Sutton then tried another tack. He placed the demands within the institutional framework of the union. He began talking about "the policy of our organization" and "the decisions of our executive board." He used words that had a familiar and pleasant ring to the executive. He suggested, by implication, that there were many similarities between the two organizations represented in that room.

At last the manager began to warm up, and it became possible for the parties to work out a contract that was a realistic adjustment of the problems of both organizations. The approach here was twofold. Sutton avoided red-flag words and used those that would not only sound familiar, but safe and respectable, to the executive. And then he used these words to place himself in the institutional structure of the union so as to make clear the limitations within which he acted. Management can apply the same principles in presenting its case to the union.

The role of the international representative

As we consider relations within the union, let us look first at the international representative, who often is the key man in bargaining at the local plant level.

In many conflict situations, there is so much personal animosity between the local union leaders and the management people that, left alone, they would not be able to reach an agreement. If the international representative has not been involved in their previous struggles, he is in a strong strategic position in such a situation. While he does not qualify as a neutral, he is often able to view the local issues with a greater degree of objectivity than is possible for those on either side who are more intimately involved.

That does not mean, however, that the international representative can move right in and "call them the way he sees them." He represents the union and depends upon the committee and the rank and file for support. They don't expect him to act as an umpire; they want him to help win their objectives from management. Therefore, he cannot begin making adjustments to management's point of view until he has shown some ability to win concessions from management. He must establish himself with his own organization first. But, if management understands this problem, management can help him to take that step.

The case of International Representative Jones and Local XYZ will illustrate this point. Jones' union had just taken over a particular plant from another union. The convinced adherents of the ousted union presented a difficult problem to the new organization.

Previously, relations between union and management had been terribly strained. In the preceding four years, the workers had been out on strike for a total of 52 weeks. Management had been fighting the union tooth and nail, and had followed a practice of stalling at all times.

When the new union took over, Jones met with the management people in a room where the tabulation was being made of the representation election. He let the local people pay attention to the tabulation, and he himself concentrated his attention upon Carter, the district superintendent who represented top management. Jones tried to be affable and kid the management man in order to establish some sort of casual relationship. Finally, he was able to persuade Carter to meet him at breakfast the following morning. After a little preliminary small talk, Jones said that he wanted to smooth out relations between the company and the new union, but he could do it only if he could show his people that he was able to get action from management. He suggested that management agree to a meeting with the union negotiating committee the following day; then a week later, meet with the union again to submit management's answer to the union's demands; and the following week, set aside two days in which to negotiate the contract. Jones added that the company was under no legal obligation to meet with the union at this time because it would take 10 days or two weeks for the certification to come through from Washington; but he wanted to have something to take back to the people to show that the company was willing to take the first step. He also felt that keeping to a close time schedule was important in view of the dragged-out nature of previous negotiations.

Carter said he'd think it over, and commented, "You talk just like a businessman." Later in the day, Carter called Jones and said that he had secured top management's agreement to go ahead with the time schedule Jones had outlined. That night Jones was able to go before a meeting and surprise the members with the statement that the company had agreed to a negotiation meeting the following day—when they were not even required to do so by law. He also laid out the schedule of meetings that were to follow. In view of past history, this impressed everyone, and kept to a minimum criticism leveled by people who had been closely associated with the previous union. When union and management were able to carry through this schedule and reach an agreement after two days of negotiating, that agreement was accepted by the membership with considerable enthusiasm, and thus the first steps were taken toward establishing a harmonious relationship. In this case the international representative could not have made any moves toward cooperation if management had not agreed to make certain concessions that strengthened his hand with the membership.

In the Inland Steel Container Company case, Jake Shafer held a strong hand with the local union from the very beginning of negotiations, even though he entered shortly before the first meeting with management as a complete stranger to the local people. Here it appears that the situation played into his hands. The local union negotiators were bitterly hostile to management and convinced that no worthwhile agreement was possible. At the same time, the membership had gone through a 199-day strike the previous year, and the plant had been shut down for about 55 days in a complicated labor dispute the year before that. Clearly, a strike was to be avoided if at all possible. Jake Shafer, as a new man, could set out to explore the possibilities. The local union people in this situation could afford to sit back and let Shafer make his try for an agreement. When negotiations broke down, the local leaders could resume control. As negotiations progressed, however, the local union officers began to see evidences of real progress even long before a final settlement was reached, and this added steadily to their confidence in Shafer.

Getting the contract accepted

In our form of collective bargaining, it is not enough for the negotiators themselves to reach agreement. The agreement must then be ratified by the membership, and sometimes an apparently good settlement is voted down. Upon what does acceptance or rejection of the settlement depend? Let us consider the following four questions:

1. How good is the contract, in terms of member expectations?
2. What has been the pre-existing pattern of human relations in the local union?
3. What has been the customary sequence of activities in the past in working out a contract?
4. To what extent are the achievements of the contract dramatized to the members?

The following case shows the influence of the first two factors together.

The plant in this case was located in a semi-rural area of declining industries. It manufactured charcoal and wood alcohol, both of which were in declining demand. The union's research department showed that the industry was sick and that management could not stand any wage increase at that time. In fact, in that particular area, no contract had carried a wage increase and there had been two negotiated wage cuts. The plant under review was part of a corporation that could close this unit with little disturbance to the total operation. The union, therefore, was in an exceedingly weak bargaining position.

Nevertheless, the local union negotiating committee was pushing vigorously for a 15 cent increase. After four fruitless meetings with management, the international representative was called in.

Now the workers not only did not want a strike, they did not expect an increase. In a small town, there are inevitably enough informal contacts between workers and foremen, or friends or relatives of workers with friends or relatives of foremen, for the workers' feelings to be public knowledge. In this case, the workers were saying to each other: "We'll be lucky if we get the same damn contract again." And management knew it.

Why then the aggressive demand for a 15 cent increase? First, because of the bitter resentment of the workers toward management. The local people felt that management had resisted the union at every opportunity and in every possible way. They were constantly on guard against management, and had fought out a strike only two years previously. And second, because two factions were fighting for control of the local union. Although they were not divided on any ideological lines, the two contending leaders disagreed on all sorts of issues within the plant. They could agree on only one thing; the boss was their chief enemy and must be fought aggressively.

The union leaders in power felt compelled to make strong demands. Anything less, they felt, would be interpreted as weakness and would result in political suicide. They probably were afraid that management would demand a wage decrease, and their demand for a 15 cent raise was only a tactic to head off such a move on management's part. But management did not propose a decrease. And as the local officers argued for the 15 cents, they found themselves so committed to this figure that they were powerless to back down. The opposition leaders were forced to agree that 15 cents was a very strong union demand, so while the argument continued the local officers had no opposition. But they knew that if they agreed not to take an increase, the opposition would immediately jump into action and gain adherents for the local union election to be held only six weeks hence.

When the local negotiating committee and management finally reached an impasse, the international representative came in for three meetings. Each time he argued the union's case vigorously—with no real hope of success.

Finally, in his third meeting, the international representative called a recess and announced to his committee:

Look, I'm tired. I don't think we can get any further. The company refuses
to budge. I think you ought to go back and recommend a strike to the people.
Let's break off negotiations, call a special meeting, and call for a strike. I will
clear it with the international union. You already have strike sanction. I say
it's okay—go ahead, call the strike!

The committee members argued back:

No, no, let's not break off negotiations. . . . Let's keep it going. We don't
want to take a strike vote. . . . Let's keep talking.

The international representative stood pat:

Look, you're wasting my time, you're wasting your time, you're wasting
the conciliator's time. You just can't get anywhere. You know it and I know
it.

The local people still wanted to keep the negotiations going and kept
arguing until the international representative came forward with a new
proposal:

I would suggest that we go back in and negotiate now and say that we will
accept the same contract, but with a 30-day wage opener. And I'm willing to
go to the membership and sell that.

The local officers accepted this proposal immediately. The right to
reopen wage negotiations at any time, on 30 days' notice, could hardly
mean anything concrete, since the economic picture for the plant was not
likely to change much within the year. But the proposal did have face-
saving value. Furthermore, the international representative's offer to take
responsibility for the settlement seemed to take the local officers out of
the line of fire.

When the international representative went before the membership
meeting, he was faced with a dual task. He wanted to sell the contract,
and he also wanted to protect the position of the local officers. This he did
by making a strong attack upon the membership—for letting the negotiating committee down.

He began by complimenting the local committee members for the
efficiency with which they had handled the negotiations. They had really
done their part, he said. But the rank and file members had forgotten that
they, too, played an important role in negotiations, although they did not
sit around the bargaining table. In his words:

Every single person in this hall and every single person within management knew, number one, that you weren't going to strike, that you didn't
want to strike, and number two, that you felt you would be lucky to get the
same contract. Whenever you talked about the negotiations, inside the plant
or outside, you blabbed, every one of you. You said, "We'll be lucky if we
get the same damn contract." Top management knew it. You gave guns to
your committee, and then you forgot to give them the ammunition.

You were fighting a losing battle from the beginning, but you do have a 30-day wage opener. I don't know if it's going to do you any good, but if conditions change, and you fellows really mean business, then you have a chance to redeem yourselves. You can't blame anybody but yourselves for what has happened.

Besides, you have to be conscious of certain things. First, you have a sick industry. You know as well as I that nobody in this area has gotten a raise—and as a matter of fact, two outfits got a cut of 15 percent. You know it and management knows it. And one more thing, throughout the country, our union has been getting increases in only 40 percent of our contracts. We just haven't been getting many increases this year. So I wouldn't feel too bad about the fact that you didn't get an increase.

The membership voted unanimously—but with no enthusiasm—to accept the contract.

When the elections were held, all the incumbent officers were voted out, and the opposition group took over. We have no evidence as to what happened, but we assume that the opposition faction campaigned on the issue that the officers in power had been too easy on management and that the new group would be more aggressive and more effective in its demands. That conclusion is supported by subsequent events. Immediately the new officers took over, they invoked the 30-day notice for reopening wage negotiations. (I have no information on this second effort.)

In this case the difficulties in worker-management relations were compounded by the declining economic picture. Since relations between workers and management had been fraught with conflict, there was a good deal of emotional support for a tough policy toward management. If he had been dealing with a prosperous plant, the international representative could have sought to negotiate enough out of management so that the settlement would not only be accepted by workers but so that the incumbent union leadership could support it without fear of losing control. The unfortunate economic situation provided no rewards that the local leaders could bring back to the membership.

The international representative also had to deal with the conflict between worker expectations and their sentiments toward management. The 15-cent-an-hour demand grew out of their hostile sentiments toward management. At the same time, as Shaw pointed out to them, they really had no expectation at all of getting anything like 15 cents. By bringing dramatically before them the conflict between their sentiments towards management and their expectations, with a face-saving clause thrown in, Shaw was able to meet the immediate crisis and get a contract settlement. While meeting their expectations, the settlement did not express worker sentiments toward management, and therefore it could be used against the incumbent leadership as a means of voting the old crowd out.

We must not assume from this story that the union leaders can strengthen their bargaining position simply by telling the members to talk militantly. An occasional individual may be able to put up a bold front and convincingly portray an impression of confidence he does not feel, but this is not possible for a large body of workers. If the members as a whole do not feel this confidence, sooner or later the impression is going to get out to management.

This does not mean that if the negotiators begin by asking for 50 cents an hour and the members generally believe that nothing better than 15 cents will be possible, that the opening demand serves no function. It is well recognized in those bargaining situations that the union opens with larger demands than it really expects to settle for and that management opens with smaller offers—if any—than it expects to have to grant. If the members really believe that in terms of what workers elsewhere are gaining and in terms of the profitability of the plant, they have about fifteen cents coming to them, it would be hard indeed for management to get them to settle for much less. On the other hand, if their expectations give them no hope for an increase, then it won't make much difference whether the negotiating committee is talking about 15 cents or 50 cents.

The solidarity and militancy of the union is not demonstrated in conversation alone. It may also be shown in certain activity changes.

Perhaps in certain departments there has been a great deal of overtime work and it has been the accepted practice for the foreman simply to ask certain workers to stay beyond the regular time to finish up important jobs. He may suddenly find that this is no longer possible. If a strike is in the offing, the workers may willingly forfeit their time-and-a-half over-time pay on the grounds that they do not want to help management get ahead with its production schedule. This type of pressure sometimes may result in an actual slowdown in the plant, but more often it means that workers are being extremely careful not to do any more than usual. The effects of increased tension may also be visible in the grievance process, where stewards and other union officials may push grievances much more energetically than they have in the past, showing that they are militantly behind their leadership.

It is important to demonstrate this unity in order to strengthen the position of the union negotiators and to give the rank and file a sense of participation. But it is not always necessary for such a demonstration to restrict and hamper management. Sometimes the demonstration can be accomplished with as much if not greater effect in terms of a constructive contribution to the efficiency of the enterprise. For example, we observed one case where a marked transition toward cooperation was effected through negotiations carried on over a period of four months. Among other things, management was concerned with a serious problem of absenteeism. Following discussions of this problem, the union leadership went before a membership meeting and put a strong case to the members.

They were told that they were hurting themselves and the position of their union through their absenteeism record. It was suggested that if the record could be improved, it would be a demonstration of the effectiveness of the union leadership and would enable the leadership to win greater gains from management. The record of later negotiation sessions reveals that management gave credit to the union leadership for a substantial improvement in the absenteeism record. This seems to have been an important factor in giving management confidence in the union leadership, and stimulating a willingness to make concessions in return for the improvements that it suddenly discovered the union leadership could bring about.

The power of the union to carry out such activities will, of course, be affected by the particular environmental situation in which it finds itself. This is particularly true for the organization of activities that will be negatively valued by management. For example, if the plant is operating well below capacity and a number of workers have already been laid off, there will be no overtime for workers to refuse to do. Slowdowns will also tend to be difficult to organize, for workers will feel that management might shut down a given operation altogether. The same anxieties tend to hold workers back against the more militant expression of grievances.

Let us now illustrate the importance of the third and fourth questions raised above. If, in the past, workers have voted down one or two proposed contracts and have then found management coming forward with a better offer, they naturally find it hard to believe that the contract offered the first time is the best they can do. At least they will not accept the first contract offer unless it is put to them in the form of a dramatic presentation.

We see both of these points in the further adventures of International Representative Shaw, who thought he had arrived at a good settlement in the situation involving the engineering changes. A few days later he received a telegram from his negotiating committee urgently demanding that he come back to help them. The membership meeting had voted not to accept the contract.

Upon his return, Shaw found the union negotiators and management quite depressed. The union negotiators still felt that the contract offer was an excellent one, but they had not sold it. The members were still so hostile toward management that they could see nothing good in the contract.

In a joint meeting, Shaw told the union negotiators and the company executives that he still felt the contract offer was a fair one. However, he would have to insist that the company make a new offer, an offer to be made in a way that would not hurt the company financially. He suggested a cost-of-living adjustment, and told the company to pick out the points of the cost-of-living index beyond which the cost of living would have to rise in order for the adjustment to go into effect. He suggested that they should not choose a ridiculously high figure, but one on which they could count on not having to pay anything. Since the cost of living at that time appeared to have leveled off, this seemed to offer no practical difficulties.

The management people objected, saying that this would lead the workers to expect gains that would never materialize. Shaw replied that this was not the case; he would tell the membership that they were not getting anything, but he did need an excuse to go back to them. Management accepted this deal, picked an index point ten points above the one prevailing at that time, and wrote this into the contract. Armed with the amended contract, Shaw then faced the general membership meeting.

Prior to the meeting, the atmosphere had been full of tension and the local negotiating committee members were only too eager to turn the complete responsibility over to Shaw. Shaw stood up to address the members and began by saying, "I don't know whether I should say I'm glad or sorry to be here. I understand you've come here tonight to take the hide off me." This brought a laugh from the crowd, and Shaw felt the tension ease somewhat. Then he said he had had a new offer from the company, but he added that the union wouldn't really get anything concrete out of it. Before he laid the offer on the table, however, he wanted the members to understand what had taken place at the initial negotiations.

Shaw began by describing the lecture he had given the management people on the engineering and methods changes. Not only did he repeat what he had said to management, but he stated which management people had been present, describing how they had looked and how they had reacted. He was particularly careful to describe the vice president who had become so upset. As he told his story, he found the crowd coming with him. They tittered and laughed at certain spots, and he could hear them saying, "That's telling them," or "That's what I tried to tell them, but they wouldn't listen!" and similar remarks that indicated that he was really expressing what they felt.

At the end of this discussion, Shaw announced that he was not there to try to persuade the members to accept the contract. It was up to them to make their decision, but they should consider the alternative. Were they ready for a strike? He emphasized that few strikes recently had been successful, and suggested that if they were going to strike they had better be prepared for it to be long and costly. He then sat down, leaving the decision up to the members.

Two or three of the old-time workers spoke up, saying that they had been through a strike and knew what it meant. They thought the members should take the matter very seriously and not jump into it without a great deal of thought. When the vote was finally taken, it was 175 to 5 in favor of accepting the contract, which was essentially the same as the one they had turned down earlier.

The action of the membership in voting down the original contract suggests that Shaw and his committee overlooked an important part of the bargaining process.

Compared to the achievements of other locals, this was a good contract. The union's skill in bargaining had won a wage increase of five cents an hour more than management had expected to concede—and in a situation where management could not easily make financial concessions.

But a contract with economic concessions was not enough. The engineering program had completely destroyed the equilibrium of the union-management social system. Until that problem was solved, the members would remain in a state of anxiety and tension.

Furthermore, in past dealings, the union had adopted the procedure of voting down the first two management offers and accepting the third. The management people were aware of this pattern, but in their desire to make amends for the engineering disturbances, they overlooked this point and offered every possible concession in the first round.

If it had been handled effectively, perhaps the members could have been won over in one meeting. But in presenting the contract to the members, the local officers did little more than lay it on the table and outline its good points.

The local officers who had participated in the bargaining were satisfied that the problems were worked out. But the rank and file had not experienced the bargaining first hand and they were still experiencing the serious disturbances caused by the engineering program.

Shaw's major contribution was to allow the members to share vicariously the experiences of the local officers and himself. Their cheers and laughter and shouts of "That's telling them!" and their almost unanimous vote prove that he brought this experience home to them quite vividly.

We do not mean to suggest that the union's acceptance of the agreement solved the problems growing out of the engineering program. A disturbance of that nature must be treated with patience and skill over a period of time. But at least Shaw was able to establish an emotional basis between management and union, upon which the necessary adjustments could be built. As they left the meeting, the workers were ready to believe that improvements were in prospect.

All too often, the chairman of the union negotiating committee does little beyond placing the new contract on the table and inviting the members to inspect its favorable points. He may say: "We had a tough fight with management to get this for you," but he seldom gives the members a sufficiently vivid picture of what went on around the bargaining table for them to feel as he does about it. He merely concentrates on the technical details of the contract and then asks the members to trust him and his committee because of their past service to the union. It is as if the members were presented with a box score of a baseball game, without being given an account of the plays that went to make up the score.

Launching the agreement

Let us assume now that the members are ready and willing to sign the contract. How should the actual signing be carried out? It can simply be a routine matter, or it can be made into an impressive ceremony. Where relations have been reasonably stable and harmonious, there will be no need for such a ceremony. But in the signing of a first contract, or when the parties have reached an agreement that they hope will effect a transition from conflict to cooperation, the situation is quite different. Throughout the world, ceremonies are used to accompany transitions in people's relations.

Benjamin M. Selekman has reported on a very interesting use of ceremony in a case involving the Commonwealth Edison Company of Chicago and the International Brotherhood of Electrical Workers.[6] The union had finally succeeded in organizing the company and was ready to sign the first contract with management. While management officials were not pleased with this development, they were determined to meet it realistically. They wished to establish a basis for cooperative relations with the union and hoped to avoid the period of confusion and friction that generally accompanies the initial recognition of a union. The international representative suggested that this might be accomplished if management would agree to a joint ceremony at the signing of the contract.

The ceremony was held in the union hall, before a large audience of members. On the stage were top union and management officials who addressed the members, telling them what their sentiments were toward each other and how they hoped their relations would develop. The members were tremendously impressed to hear the president of the company give his endorsement to the new relationship right in their union hall. This carried a conviction that would never have come from a printed statement or even from an address limited to top officials. For the members, this scene dramatized the ushering-in of a new era in union-management relations and destroyed the very common suspicion that management did not really believe in the contract and would try to bypass it wherever possible.

Once the contract has been signed, it must be put into effect by both parties. Here, again, is an opportunity for action on a group basis. If the parties wait to interpret the contract only as specific cases arise, people will not understand the changes that have taken place.

The annual round of collective bargaining presents the most favorable opportunity for effecting changes in union-management relations. The entire process builds up so that people are led to expect changes and to be ready to adjust to them. The changes, therefore, must be put into effect as

---

[6] Benjamin M. Selekman, *Labor Relations and Human Relations* (New York: McGraw-Hill Book Co., 1947).

an integral part of the process. The contract must not be allowed to drift —it must be launched.

Selekman refers to the "technical launching" and the "emotional launching." The contract is a technical document that must be studied and discussed by those who will administer it, from top management down to foreman, from top union official down to steward. Such technical knowledge is essential—but it is not enough. A contract is also a statement of the pattern of human relations that the parties wish to develop—a purpose for which the written word is particularly inadequate. One can have two situations in which the contracts are identical, and yet there are vast differences in the way the parties get along together.

Since, beyond the formalities, the contract says so little about the relations that are to be developed, it is important for the people who will be responsible for shaping these relations to get together and discuss their plans for the future.

It is now common practice for top management to hold meetings and to explain and interpret the new contract to its foremen and superintendents. Similarly, high union officials discuss these matters with their stewards.

Such meetings are essential, but in some cases they do not go far enough. We have seen cases where these separate meetings failed to clear up misunderstandings on technical points, particularly on "the spirit of the contract." These misunderstandings were cleared up most effectively through joint foreman-steward meetings.

Regardless of what the discussion leader says, a separate meeting gives the impression that there is a separate union or management position regarding the contract. On the other hand, the joint meeting dramatizes for all involved that the parties are mutually concerned with building up the relationship between them.

The problem of manipulation

In this discussion, I have emphasized the ceremonial nature of the collective bargaining process. I have suggested that certain aspects of the process need to be acted out dramatically, if the process is to work through to a successful conclusion.

Many people will find this point of view hard to accept. They will consider it insincere and involving the manipulation of men. They may also regard these statements as very dangerous advice, perhaps assuming that if the leaders of management and unions just develop enough manipulative skill, they can get the workers to accept anything that the leaders desire.

Nothing could be farther from the truth. Contracts are not negotiated in a vacuum. Workers as well as union and management leaders know what kinds of contracts are being negotiated in related industries as they set out to negotiate their own contracts. They know a good deal about the financial situation of the company. They are also aware of certain problems involving friction within the plant—whether the problems revolve around incentive rates, job evaluation, or promotional ladders. The situation is rarely so structured that the contract that will result is completely predetermined. On the other hand, the situation is always structured to a considerable extent so that agreement must be reached within certain limits. Skill in handling the collective bargaining process—on both sides—can often make the difference between reaching an agreement within these limits and failure to reach agreement, with resulting losses to both sides.

Nor am I saying, as is sometimes assumed, that good human relations in collective bargaining simply means arranging somehow to have the parties like and trust each other. The problem goes much deeper than the sentiments of Mr. A for Mr. B. Consider this case in which a high degree of trust had already been established.

The president of the company was embarrassed. He pointed out to the union negotiators that their harmonious relations were well known throughout the industry; that the union had always been able to trust him in the past. Now he asked that they trust him once more by not asking for a wage increase at that time, but instead, reopening discussion in 90 days. He stated that by then, he hoped the company would be able to offer the increase it was unable to give at present; he offered no further explanation.

The union negotiators were sympathetic but unmoved. They agreed that their relations had always been satisfactory and that they had been able to trust the president. The chief negotiator even went so far as to say he trusted the president now—without question. But, he added, the union negotiators had had several years of personal experience with the president and their trust had been built up thereby. On the other hand, the hundreds of workers in the plant, having had no such direct experience, did not have the same personal trust in management. So it was not conceivable that the union negotiators could simply ask the membership to take the president on faith. There had to be some explanation that they could pass on to the members.

The president's feelings were hurt by this apparent lack of faith, but he went on to tell the story that he had been embarrassed to reveal. The company's financial problems were not due entirely to the general business situation. Management had made serious mistakes in its buying policy and in the general operation of some departments. The president felt that steps were being taken to repair the damage and that he could reasonably expect the company to be in a more favorable position within three months. But at the moment, management was in a very difficult position.

The union negotiators accepted this explanation. In fact, only a few of the details were news to them, since the "grapevine" in the plants had reported some of management's blunders. So while it embarrassed the president to make such admissions, his story served to bring out into the open officially, what was common knowledge to the union leaders and to many employees. In such a situation, the president could not have asked the union to go along on faith. However, when he revealed the full story —including a convincing account of steps being taken to meet the crisis —he placed himself and the management in a much better position in relation to the union. He also gave the union negotiators a story they could carry back to the members. Instead of having to apologize for failing to get an increase and asking that the members trust a man whom they knew only as a remote symbol, the negotiators were able to make a strong and reasoned case for the 90-day extension. On the strength of this case, backed by the years of harmonious relations with management, the union members voted overwhelmingly for the extension. The story has a happy ending, for three months later, the parties were able to negotiate an increase that fitted in very well with current trends in the industry.

The principle involved in this case can be stated in this way: the sentiments people have towards a company, a union, an individual, or a group, are strongly colored by the personal relations they experience. The union negotiators had had frequent interaction with the president, mostly of a mutually satisfying nature. They therefore had a high personal regard for him and would have been inclined to accept his word without question. But they were intelligent enough to recognize that the members did not enjoy similar interactions with the president and could not be expected to have the same sentiments toward him. To ask them to take him on faith would have placed a dangerous strain on leader-follower relations within the union. In that event, there certainly would have been protests that the leaders were selling out to management.

Successful negotiation is not just a matter of winning the personal regard of men across the table. The negotiator can make trouble for himself through his very successes, and the man who is won over often finds himself in a most difficult personal situation.

When the union leader decides that the top executive is, after all, honest and well-meaning in his dealings with the union, his problems may very well be started instead of ending. Will the top executive have the intelligence and perseverance to carry agreed-upon solutions right through his organization? Is the management organization functioning in such a way as to make it possible for a top policy decision to be carried out effectively down to the plant level? These questions indicate the folly of accepting the top executive simply on a personality basis.

The workers in the plant don't know the big boss. Their daily contacts with management are with foremen, superintendents, personnel men, time study men, engineers, and so on. If relations at that personal contact level continue to be unsatisfactory to the workers, the personal respect of top union for top management cannot be turned to the advantage of either party.

Industrial relations problems are too complicated to be solved simply by "good men" who approach them with "good will." The union man who allows himself to be won over on this basis alone is asking for trouble for himself and his union. Unless the negotiator can foresee changes in the whole union-management system of human relations as a result of the new relationship between himself and the management negotiator, he must proceed with the utmost caution and not allow himself to be sidetracked by attractive personalities.

In short, no relationship can be treated realistically in isolation. The union negotiator must see his relations with management from the perspective of his relations with other union officers and members. The management man must be sure that by winning over a union representative, he does not isolate that man from the rank and file, thus rendering him useless to both union and management. Management must think not only of its relationship with the men across the table, but of protecting and improving the positions of those men with the rank and file.

Conclusion

Collective bargaining presents an emotional as well as an intellectual problem. We assume that the skillful bargainer needs to have thorough knowledge of the past application of given contract clauses in his own situation, coupled with knowledge of trends in other bargaining situations that may affect the contract he is seeking to obtain. These aspects we have taken for granted. Our focus has been upon the emotional aspects of the problem.

Here we have given attention to the meaning of verbal symbols, concentrating particularly upon the status parity problem. We have argued that in many cases the refusal of management, consciously or unconsciously, to accept union negotiators on an equal footing has made agreement impossible. We have examined the symbols that tend to equalize relations along with those which tend to subordinate the other party.

We have also suggested that the course of bargaining must be seen in the perspective of the past pattern of activities and interactions, and the current network of interpersonal relations. When in the past the parties have reached an agreement only after two or three management offers have been turned down by the membership, it will be very difficult to gain acceptance for the first management offer, no matter how good it is. This does not mean that the past pattern must be continued forever. It does mean that the parties should recognize when they are making a major departure from past practice and should do something to dramatize the value of their new approach.

Concerning the network of interpersonal relations, we need to recognize that it is not only the parties around the table who have to get together, but the union negotiators and the rank and file as well, for it is the rank and file who will have to vote upon the settlement. We have shown cases in which failure to recognize problems in this area has led to rejection of a good management offer, and we have shown some ways in which the members may be influenced to accept an offer that the negotiators feel is a good one.

Finally, while we have given particular attention to the human relations aspects of bargaining, we must be careful not to overemphasize this side of the picture as against economic conditions and forces. The current economic situation of the firm involved in contract negotiations, together with the pattern of settlements being reached in the same industry during that time, will tend to establish certain limits on the behavior of both parties. However, we must not assume that the parties will always act in terms of the long-run economic health of the firm.

There are times when the parties fail to reach an agreement that would be economically advantageous to both sides. There are also times when the parties reach an agreement that has unfortunate economic consequences.

We therefore cannot assume that the economic forces will just automatically work themselves out. It is the task of the negotiator to exercise such human relations skills as will bring about a contract that is economically sound. At the same time, we need to recognize that the use of such skills will not guarantee an economically sound settlement. Men may be led to disaster with great skill. We are simply saying that skills in human relations need to go together with skills in economic analysis in order to arrive at solutions that may be accepted in the long run by both parties.

Let us move on from these conclusions from the cases in order to reach some more general theoretical formulations. Here the Walton-McKersie[7] approach seems especially powerful.

The authors properly criticize some students of organizational behavior (including myself) for concentrating upon cooperative relations, to the exclusion of union-management conflict. While it might be argued that the analysis of cooperation will readily point to conclusions about conflict, any satisfactory general formulation will deal with both cooperation and conflict within the same general framework. That is what Walton and McKersie undertake to do.

They establish two ideal types of bargaining relationships: distributive and integrative. The distributive type involves a focusing upon what one party will take away from the other. The integrative type involves focusing discussion upon what the parties can do for each other, so that each party benefits. Negative inter-party sentiments are associated with the distributive type, whereas positive inter-party sentiments are associated with the integrative type. The authors call "attitudinal structuring" those interventions in bargaining by one participant or another that tend to

---

[7] Walton and McKersie, *op. cit.*

move the opposite party toward more favorable sentiments (or attitudes) concerning the speaker's party. We could just as well call "attitudinal structuring" the interventions that move the opposing party in the opposite direction, except that generally interventions that generate more positive inter-party sentiments are more or less consciously introduced by the speaker. Provocation of negative sentiments is usually inadvertent, triggered by the emotions of the speaker, and not planned.

In our terms, distributive bargaining involves the parties in competitive, negative exchange, and conflict transactions, whereas integrative bargaining turns them toward joint payoff, positive exchange, and trading transactions.

Bargaining involves a more complex set of transactions than any situation we have examined up to this point. Why should this be the case? In earlier chapters we have been concerned with describing specific events and noting how they were perceived by the parties concerned. In bargaining, most of the events occur during discussions between union and management negotiators. The activities consist largely of talk about what has happened in the past and what is likely to happen in the future. Furthermore, the events that occur around the table must be interpreted in terms of the relations of the bargainers with their constituents.

To some extent the pluses and minuses are produced directly for the people in the room—see, for example, the discussion of establishing a pattern of agreement. In most cases, the participants in the discussion must visualize the production of pluses or minuses among people outside of the room at some future time.

Bargainers are engaged in the manipulation of symbols. They use verbal symbols to express their own sentiments and to seek to change the sentiments of the other party. They also use symbols to represent past and future states of interactions, activities, and transactions.

It is sometimes said that the bargainer should not express the antagonistic sentiments he may feel. But sentiments cannot simply be repressed. The problem is to express sentiments, but not in ways that will provoke a vicious cycle of hostilities.

Sentiments are affected not only by the content of what is said. They are also affected by the pattern of interactions and activities of the bargaining meeting. Short, choppy interchanges, with frequent interruptions are not only indicative of hostile intergroup sentiments, they also reinforce such negative sentiments. A pattern of longer statements, alternating with fewer interruptions, is both indicative of more positive sentiments and tending to reinforce such sentiments.

References

Douglas, Ann. *Industrial Peacemaking*. New York: Columbia University Press, 1962. A study of the process of mediation of union-management conflicts, based upon observed and tape-recorded mediation sessions and interviews with the participants.

Walton, Richard, and McKersie, Robert. *A Behavioral Theory of Labor Negotiations.* New York: McGraw-Hill Book Co., 1963. Presents case material in a systematic framework for the study of bargaining.

Discussion questions

1. A company spokesman makes the following statement:

"We do not believe in haggling with union leaders. We don't think it is honest to start out by telling them that we can afford to give them little or nothing and then finally settle on something that maybe we figured on giving them all along.

"We prepare for negotiations very carefully. We survey our employees to determine what they are interested in. We analyze our own financial capabilities and prospects and what our competitors are doing.

"Then, when we go into the first bargaining session, we make our best offer right at the start. We explain it fully and give the union leaders the facts and figures the offer is based on. We also send out information on our offer to all the employees, to be sure they have the true picture.

"Now, if the union leaders can prove to us that we have not given sufficient consideration to some important element affecting our offer, we are willing to re-assess our position. If they can demonstrate that the facts call for a change in our offer, we will make that change. Otherwise, we will stick to our original offer. As I said, we do not believe in haggling."

a) Consider the consequences of this policy for union-management relations. What effects would you expect the policy to have upon the role of union leaders?

b) What conditions outside of the direct interpersonal relations between management and union negotiators are likely to increase or decrease the chances for success of this policy, from management's standpoint?

Part VIII

INTRODUCING CHANGE

THE STUDENT of organization needs to understand both statics and dynamics. For some purposes it is advantageous to begin analysis upon the organization "at rest." We know that changes are taking place, but we need to get a grip on stabilities—on persisting patterns—before we can move on to the more complex problem of the study of change. We should now be ready to make that next move.

In fact, we have already taken change into account for it is difficult to present *what is* without also considering *how it got to be that way*. In Part IV all three of our case studies have examined individuals and work groups over the course of a series of changes. In Part V on "Vertical Relations," we have examined how the role of the first-line supervisor has changed over a period of many years (Chapter 12), and in Chapter 14 we have shown how a combination of changes within a period of several months transformed a successful supervisor into a failure.

In Part VII on "Union-Management Relations," we have been still more concerned with change. We have examined how the union enters and how the union-management relationship tends to evolve. We have also stressed how the collective bargaining process may generate change.

We should now be ready to focus directly upon the problem of introduction of change. Change comes in a variety of forms, and we shall investigate some of this variety.

Chapter 24 considers several cases of technological, process, and product changes and seeks to present a framework for the analysis of such changes. Chapter 25 considers the problems that accompany "Changing Organizational Size, Composition, and Character."

The modern corporation does not face change simply in response to the initiatives of individual internal change agents, nor in response to external pressures. Management sets up organizational units that are specifically designed to invent, develop, and introduce changes that will have major effects upon the organization. In research and development (Chapters 26 and 27), we are dealing with the institutionalization of the process of introducing major changes. Research and development involves groupings of men devoting full time to this process. It also involves a division of labor and the linking of working groups along work flows, beginning with research and ending where research and development links up with the production organization.

In research and development, we are dealing with the introduction of changes that flow predominantly along a lateral dimension—though vertical interactions of course accompany each step of this flow. Major changes are also introduced vertically, from the top down. A change in plant managers is likely to have broad and deep effects upon the social system. In "Managerial Succession" (Chapter 28), we examine three cases of this nature and seek to draw some general conclusions.

Executives are often advised to improve the performance of their organizations through delegating authority and responsibility. Delegation is one of those good things that no one will speak against, and yet the adviser rarely makes clear what the word should mean in behavioral terms. It is such behavioral specification that we undertake in Chapter 29, on "The Meaning of Delegation."

While some changes take place accidentally, as far as organizational members are concerned, in modern industry the introduction of important changes tends to be preceded and accompanied by group discussions and individual actions that we call "The Decision-Making Process." In Chapter 30 we attempt to assess some of the forces that shape this process and influence the quality of decisions emerging from it.

24. On introducing change

It is customary to begin a discussion of the introduction of technological change with a short essay on something called "resistance to change." The underlying assumption is that human beings are naturally conservative and tend to resist change. The task of management then becomes one of "overcoming resistance to change." The further assumption behind this specification of tasks is that, whatever the change, resistance to it can be overcome by skillful structuring of social processes.

I shall take issue with such assumptions. I feel it is misleading to assume any universal human tendency to resist change. We find that many cases, so explained, turn out upon closer examination to be based upon other concrete phenomena that can be observed. The assumption of a universal human tendency is in itself not susceptible to testing.

While I would not minimize the importance of the manner in which a given change is introduced, I suggest that the *process of introducing change* has been given such emphasis as to give readers the impression that the nature of the change being introduced is of no importance.

In this chapter, I shall examine a series of changes in technology, or in manufacturing process with particular reference to the changes in interactions and activities that were produced by the technological or manufacturing process changes. In other words, my assumption is that the disturbances so often classified under "resistance to change" are directly traceable to the changes in interactions and activities produced by the technological innovation or by the accompanying change in the structure of rewards.

Changing work team composition

Let us begin with a classic case, that of the introduction of the mechanized "long-wall" work team organization in the British mining industry.[1] The change under examination was introduced into the British mines with the hope of reviving a sick industry that was suffering from

[1] Eric Trist, *Organizational Choice* (London: Tavistock Publications, 1963).

561

low productivity and high costs. To the disappointment of its sponsors, the new system failed to yield the productivity increases predicted, and the change was met by worker resistance in the form of increased absenteeism and more frequent grievances. Before the change was introduced, the "short-wall" method prevailed. This form of organization was given its title because work was organized in terms of small groups of men working along a short space of the wall of the mine. Technology at the time was largely of the "pick and shovel" variety. While there was a division of labor within the work team, the men worked close together and there was considerable rotation of jobs so that each man could feel that he had mastered all aspects of mining. Finally, each small work team was paid a group piece rate, which helped to build up a feeling of unity. The men were sharing in joint payoff transactions. Also, since each small group accomplished a self-contained unit of work, the group itself required and received little supervision from management.

The introduction of the long-wall technology involved a drastic change in the organization of work teams. Short-wall teams consisted of from two to eight self-selected men, who interacted frequently with each other. The long-wall method called for groups of 40 to 50 men, spread out over 200 yards. The great differences in work group size and spatial positions also naturally meant a drastic change in informal group organization. Furthermore, the new method involved greatly increased specialization. Now each miner had along side him a number of others doing the identical task. While the pay was still based on the total output of the work unit, the unit was now so large that the individual miner could not visualize how his own work was contributing to the result and had no assurance that unsatisfactory earnings were not due to slack work on the part of others whose performance he could not observe and with whom he had no close relations.

The shift in specialization and in the size of work units now involved management much more heavily in the coordination of activities than had been the case before, and management became the focus of many worker complaints.

The research men recommended a reorganization which came to be known as the "composite" form of organization. Modern technology was maintained, but the production units were again reduced into the size of small work groups of men who could again work side by side and build up the solidarity that had been characteristic before. On this basis, productivity increased, absenteeism went down, and there were general indications of improved job satisfaction.

Introducing a new product

In telling the story of Joe Sloan (Chapter 11) we noted the disturbances accompanying the tri-isobutylene run. Let us review them here from the standpoint of problems of introducing new products in a process industry.

Workers in the Hi-Test plant were accustomed to a pattern of activities that they carried out with very infrequent initiatives from the foreman. They were accustomed to more frequent interactions with Dan Benton, staff engineer, but his usual pattern involved him working with one of the men on an experimental basis, with a good deal of discussion between the worker and the engineer about what should be done. The workers had favorable sentiments toward both Foreman Tom Lloyd and Engineer Dan Benton. Under ordinary circumstances, Benton was careful to avoid giving orders to any of the men directly, and if he had something he wanted the fractionator operator to do, he always checked first with the number one man, the poly operator.

When Foreman Lloyd was ordered to begin the tri-isobutylene run immediately, he did not feel he could dare leave the job to the operators. He called in Engineer Dan Benton and put him in charge of all of the activities connected with the run. The foreman himself hovered over the plant in an unaccustomed fashion, interacting with the workers much more frequently than before, as he took samples and tested them to check on progress.

When Lloyd could not be present, he brought in Catalyst Operator Thompson to do the distillations for him. Thompson came from a lower status plant, over which the poly operators had once had supervisory responsibilities, and Thompson, as a vociferous advocate of the company union, was particularly unpopular in the Hi-Test plant. Now he found himself in the position of checking on the work of the poly operators and others and informing them as to where they were falling short.

Engineer Benton was in the plant almost all the time for a period of two and one-half days, taking active charge of all operations. When he retired from the scene, completely exhausted, Foreman Lloyd took over and introduced further modifications of the regular routine. He responded to an initiative from the fractionator operator (number three man) and decided to give Kendall full powers to handle his fractionating column as he desired, without any control from the poly operator. When eight hours of Kendall's approach did not bring out the product but seemed to be making progress, Lloyd held Kendall over and kept him in charge of the fractionating column, instructing Poly Operator Walling how to proceed. At the end of Walling's tour, he in turn was held over to take charge on the following shift.

The product that top management had expected to get produced within 24 or 48 hours at the most had actually required approximately 80 hours, and the experience left many people upset. Up to this point, Foreman Lloyd's reputation with higher management had been growing, but now he found himself blamed for poor performance on this vital run. Engineer Benton had put out superhuman efforts and had failed to produce results. The workers were annoyed and critical of higher management. Let us quote again the way one of them sized it up:

> It wasn't until they left it to the operator that they got the thing lined out. Sure, it would have gone much faster if they had made it that way in the first place. The operator knows these columns better than the technical man.

Was the problem due to resistance to change? Certainly the operators were not resisting the introduction of a new product. In fact, some of them commented that it was good to have new things to make so as to break the monotony. What they *did* find unsettling was the disruption of the established pattern of interactions and activities. In order to achieve quick results in an emergency, Tom Lloyd abandoned the pattern of interaction and activities that had been producing results at other times. The short-cut proved to be the long way around. It led not only to poor technical performance but also to the production of more negative sentiments within the social system.

Making the Amicon tube

In this case, we follow the introduction of a new product over a much longer period of time. First steps on the "Amicon Tube"[2] were taken in August, 1948, and it was not until January, 1950, that the product was coming off the line in a manner satisfactory to management. While we have no way of estimating what the right amount of time from conception to production should have been, all concerned were in agreement that the innovation had taken far too long.

Was this a case of resistance to technological change? On the contrary, what we see in the case are disruptions of patterns of interactions and activities. Let us review these disruptions.

1. *Reversal of the development flow of work.* The usual flow of work in the development of a new product in this plant began with the development engineers working out the general plans and testing the equipment and methods necessary to make the product. When the design proposed by the development engineers had been approved by higher management, it was turned over to the industrial engineers. It was their responsibility to work out the production methods in detail and to establish the incentive rates for the various work operations. In this they worked closely with production supervisors and with production workers.

In this case, the Amicon tube was the inspiration of Fred Fisher, an industrial engineer. In recognition of the initiative and imagination of Fisher, higher management freed him from other responsibilities and allowed him and an assistant, George Gantos, to set up a small laboratory

---

[2] Paul Lawrence and Harriet Ronken, *Administering Changes* (Boston: Harvard Graduate School of Business Administration, 1952).

unit, working with two production workers, Claire and Alice, to solve the technical problems of production. The development engineers were completely left out of the initial planning. When the development engineers did come onto the scene and became involved in testing specimens of the tube produced by Fisher and his coworkers, they found most of the units defective. Fred Fisher argued that the testing methods used by the development engineers were not appropriate to the task and that therefore they were producing inappropriate findings. Here we have an illustration of the way disturbances in human relations can produce conflicting interpretations of even such apparently objective matters as test measurements.

2. *Disruption of the work group.* During the weeks that Fred, George, Claire, and Alice worked together, they naturally built up a high rate of interaction with each other. Fred Fisher minimized status differences, often expressing appreciation for the good work done by the girls and listening seriously to any suggestions or criticisms they had. Claire and Alice took great pride in their important responsibilities in developing the new product.

Before Fred Fisher felt that the technical problems of the Amicon tube were solved, higher management decided that the operation should be turned over to production, and Claire and Alice were placed under the supervision of foreman Lou Corriveau.

3. *Disruption of the foreman's pattern of interactions and activities.* Since the foreman would hardly have a full time job supervising a unit composed initially of only two workers, Corriveau was retained in his position as a supervisor of a neighboring department. This meant that he had to divide his time between his regular department, where he felt at ease with his subordinates, and the new department, entirely populated by two girls who felt a strong loyalty to Fred Fisher and who knew much more about what they were doing than did their foreman.

The foreman naturally felt at a disadvantage in relation to Claire and Alice. When they had trouble with their work, they were inclined to appeal to Fred Fisher, which added to the anxieties of the foreman. So that he could catch up with the knowledge that the girls had, Lou Corriveau began spending time after work making Amicon tubes himself. The foreman complained to higher management that Fred Fisher was interfering with his department, and higher management ordering Fisher to keep out.

As the new department slowly expanded beyond the two original members, and as interactions between Claire and Fred Fisher were cut off, Claire became increasingly dissatisfied. She put in a claim for higher pay in recognition of her special value to the company, but this initiative was turned down. After a period of absences through illness, Claire left the company.

4. *Pressures from the top.* Top management expressed a great deal of

concern about the Amicon tube project and instituted a series of weekly meetings of the "Amicon tube management team." This team was remarkable both for size and composition. It spanned ranks from plant manager down to foreman and spread across the various organizational units, including production, production control, industrial engineering, development engineering, purchasing, accounting, and personnel. In the first meeting observed by the researchers, there were 16 people present and all or nearly all of the others were of substantially higher status in the company than either Fred Fisher or Lou Corriveau. Most of the talking was done by high-ranking management officials. Lou Corriveau and Fred Fisher spoke only in response to occasional questions directed at them. The effect of the large group that spread over such a wide range of status differences was to establish an inverse correlation between the frequency of speaking and the knowledge of the problems being discussed. Those closest to the problems contributed the fewest remarks. The situation was also structured so that both the foreman and the industrial engineer felt under fire from higher management for not having been successful with the project.

Higher management put on pressure in another important way also, establishing production schedules far beyond the ability of the department to produce. Consider the discrepancies between scheduled and actual production in the following two columns:

Month	Tubes Scheduled	Tubes Actually Produced
February..............	——	198
March................	7,500	800
April.................	20,000*	2,500
May..................	——†	5,000
June.................	100,000	3,000

* Later reduced to 7,000
† Not reported.

We have here an interesting example of a phenomenon that anthropologists have examined in primitive society: the use of magic to alleviate anxieties. As time passed without showing the anticipated advances in production, the higher plant management people grew increasingly anxious. Perhaps it gave them some release of anxiety to take a decisive management step and settle upon a respectable production figure for the following month's schedule. But this of course had the effect of accentuating the anxiety of people at lower levels, who constantly found themselves in a failure situation. While the magic interpretation is admittedly speculative, we can hardly explain the differences between production scheduled and production achieved in terms of any rational management approach. We note that the scheduled amounts ran from approximately 10 times to over 30 times the actual amounts produced. When there are such enormous differences between plans and actuality, it can hardly be claimed that the plans are being used for any rational purpose.

5. *Going back to the beginning.* When production for June dropped from 5,000 to 3,000 instead of soaring toward the 100,000 scheduled, the discrepancy was finally so large as to force management to take a different approach. At this point the tube was taken out of production and turned over to the development engineers. The "Amicon tube management team" was also disbanded, and the development engineers worked directly with foreman Lou Corriveau.

Automation and the new IRR

In *Toward the Automated Factory*, Charles Walker[3] presents a detailed examination of the introduction of drastic technological changes. This is the case of the introduction of the first continuous seamless tube mill in the United States in the Lorain, Ohio, plant of the United States Steel Corporation. This change had important effects upon the nature of jobs and job classifications, and upon the relations among the men. In a broad sense, certain of these effects could be foreseen, and those we will note here. We will later describe effects that were not anticipated.

In contrast with the old steel tube mill, with 25 men on a shift, the new mill was to produce four times as much with far fewer men. The original crew complement was 11 men, and this was later reduced to nine.

This reduction in the size of crew meant that the nine men were scattered over a large area of physical space. In the older mills, men worked together in groups of two to 10, forming a number of small work teams whose members could and did interact readily with each other. Members of the work crew in the new plant were so isolated physically that they had no opportunity to interact with one another during the time the mill was in operation, except through a public address system.

The new mill brought important changes in the physical and mental composition of the jobs. Except for one work station, manual labor was all but eliminated—and so was the manual skill of manipulating steel billets and tubing. A different kind of skill was being substituted, but until there was experience with the new plant, it was difficult to evaluate the skill required.

Changes in the jobs also involved changes in job classifications. The job classification system then in effect in the plant gave points to manual skill and to the heat and hazard of working conditions—all of these being considered greater in the old mill. For example, in the old mill, there had been a team of nine to 11 men for the operation of billet heating. The

---

[3] Charles Walker, *Toward the Automated Factory* (New Haven: Yale University Press, 1957).

heater had job class 18, and his eight to 10 helpers held classifications at job class 8. Only two men were required for this operation in the new mill; a furnace inlet man (class 4) and a furnace discharger (class 10).

On the average, men in the new mill were to receive less hourly pay than in their previous jobs. If the mill were placed on incentive, they might earn as much as they had before, or possibly more. Management expected to provide an incentive, but this could not be done until the mill had been in operation for some time.

In this case there was indeed a struggle between the union and management, but we cannot understand what was going on if we see it simply in global terms as worker resistance to technological change. The workers were indeed concerned about the reduction from 25 to 11 men on a crew, and when management later reduced the complement down to 9, they held back on production until management made certain adjustments to take care of the two men who had most recently been displaced.

The men did indeed show some initial anxieties about being able to handle the new jobs, but they soon got used to these changes and began telling the researchers that they preferred the new jobs to the old.

Disagreement was focused particularly on the question of the investment-rewards relationship (IRR). Since management was getting so much more production with fewer men on the job, the workers could not accept the idea that those remaining in the plant on the new teams should receive less money than they had had before. Management had indeed promised greater earnings through the establishment of incentive rates. The workers wanted those rates to be installed as soon as possible so that they would not lose money while waiting. The time study men wanted the plant to run for an extended period of time so as to get a realistic picture of what "normal production" should be. In pressuring management to establish the new piece rates sooner, workers engaged in a concentrated slowdown. This made it still more difficult for management to establish realistic rates.

A struggle was indeed going on, but the struggle was not over the issue of acceptance or rejection of the new technology. The issue was over the distribution of rewards within a technological frame that the workers had accepted.

Summary and conclusions

Let us now review the nature of changes introduced in these four cases.

The mining case involved a drastic change in the composition of work groups and in the relation of work groups to the system of economic rewards. It also involved a shift from a situation in which small work groups organized their own activities with little interaction with management to one in which larger aggregates of men had to be organized and directed by management.

The tri-isobutylene run involved not a technological change but a change in product. There was no resistance from the men directed at the product change. In fact, previous research indicated that the men found product changes adding interest to their work. The evidences of dissatisfaction and inefficiency appeared to be related to disruptions of customary interaction-activity patterns in the following relationships: foreman-workers, engineer-workers, within work group, and between work group and catalyst plant operator.

In the Amicon tube case, we have a number of abrupt and drastic changes in the interactions and activities of organizational members, with higher management being completely unaware of the implications of these changes. Higher management failed to make any adaptation for the unusual position of initiative occupied by Fred Fisher at the beginning of the project and for the disruption of the engineering work flow that this involved. Management took no account of the drastic interpersonal changes involved for Clair and Alice and for the foreman. The focus was always strictly on technical problems. Finally, management compounded the problems by increasing downward pressures upon the foreman and the engineers.

In the tube mill, whereas the men indeed had some worries about the first sharp reduction of the work force, neither they nor their union leaders made any active opposition to this change. After they had operated for many months with crews of 11, thus building interactions, activities, and sentiments around this work group, they did indeed fight against the lopping off of two of their own men. They held firm in opposition until management had guaranteed to do something to take care of the two men.

A change may be accepted at the work level as legitimate in principle, yet there may still be vigorous disagreements regarding the distribution of rewards and penalties that flow from the change. In other words, workers may agree that management has a right to make the change and yet argue against some of the consequences of the change. This is what happened in the tube mill. Workers protested about the composition of the work group and about the level of economic rewards they were to receive.

In each of these cases, we have developed our explanation without any reference to any presumed tendency of human beings to resist change. Technological or product changes necessarily involved changes in interactions and activities. They are also very likely to involve changes in the distribution of rewards and penalties, economic and otherwise.

To a considerable extent, the student of organizational behavior should be able to anticipate the social consequences of the introduction of change. He should ask himself these questions:

1. How will this change affect interactions and activities?
2. How will this change affect the distribution of rewards and penalties?
3. Given the answers to questions 1 and 2, what changes in sentiments can be predicted?
4. Given the answer to question 3, what, if any, protest activities can be expected?

We need to put these questions in a broader context. As Gerald Gordon has pointed out,[4] the more highly interdependent the parts of the social system, the more difficult it will be to introduce change into one part, since that change necessarily affects other parts. To this we add the corollary statement: If change is introduced into one part of a social system, the more highly interdependent the parts of the system, the more widespread will be the effects of the change throughout the system. Thus, the more highly interdependent the parts of the system, the more widely does the student of organization need to cast his net in seeking to predict the consequences of the introduction of the change.

References

Lawrence, Paul and Ronken, Harriet. *Administering Changes*. Boston: Harvard Graduate School of Business Administration, 1952. A detailed and well documented account of the Amicon Tube Case.

Trist, Eric. *Organizational Choice*. London: Tavistock Publications, 1963. A case study of the introduction of changes in the British mining industry, presented in the framework of Trist's conception of the socio-technical system.

Walker, Charles R. *Toward the Automatic Factory*. New Haven, Conn.: Yale University Press, 1957. A detailed and well documented account of the Tube Mill Case, based on interviews, observations, and survey data.

Discussion questions

1. Put yourself in the place of the plant manager at a time when industrial engineer Fred Fischer approaches you with the idea for the development of the Amicon tube. You are convinced that such a tube would have attractive commercial possibilities. What actions should you and your associates in management take in order to realize these possibilities yet avoid or minimize the negative aspects noted in the project as it was actually carried out?

2. Select for analysis a case of the introduction of change. You can use a published case (excluding those discussed in this chapter), a case from your own experience, or a case drawn from interviewing another person. For your analysis, give special attention to questions such as those raised in the next to last paragraph of this chapter.

---

[4] Personal communication.

25. Changing organizational size, composition, and character

CHANGE enters the work place not only through technology. In this chapter, we shall consider the changes that accompany increases in organizational size, shifts in the social composition of the work force, and the introduction of new symbols for the meaning of the organization.

1. By *size*, we mean here the number of individuals employed in the unit under study. Changes in complexity and structure of the organization naturally accompany changes in size. It is these relations that we shall explore in our first two cases.
2. By *composition*, we mean the social characteristics of members of the work force or of the organizational subunit under discussion. Here we shall be giving particular attention to the problem of integrating Afro-Americans into a work unit or set of jobs where they have not been before.
3. By *character*, we refer to the symbols that communicate to the members and outsiders the nature of the organization. Several cases will enable us to state some general conclusions regarding the impact of symbols in organizational change.

1. Size and structure: a restaurant case

To examine the relationship between size and structure—and the problems in human relations that develop with increasing size—let us consider the story of Tom Jones, restaurant man, who starts at the bottom and reaches the top.[1] He is a fictitious character, but the human problems he faces are representative of those that go with organizational growth everywhere.

The success story can be told in five stages. Jones begins with a small restaurant where he dispenses short orders over the counter (Stage 1). He

---

[1] From W. F. Whyte, *Human Relations in the Restaurant Industry* (New York: McGraw-Hill Book Co., 1948), pp. 21–9.

has two employees working for him, but there is no division of labor, and all three work together as cooks, countermen, and dishwashers.

The business expands, and Jones finds it necessary to move to larger quarters and hire new employees. Here we see the beginning of the division of labor (Stage 2). He now has a staff of cooks, dishwashers, and waitresses to serve the customers over the counter or in their booths. But the staff is still small, and there is only one supervisor, Jones himself. He keeps track of everything and frequently pitches in to work when he is needed at one of the stations.

In these early stages, the restaurant is characterized by the informality of its human relations. Jones is close to all his employees. They are few enough for him to know them well, and the fact that they work together so closely forms a good basis for friendship.

There are few formal controls in evidence. The workers know what the boss expects of them, and they know what to expect of the boss. The organization rolls along in a comfortable, informal manner.

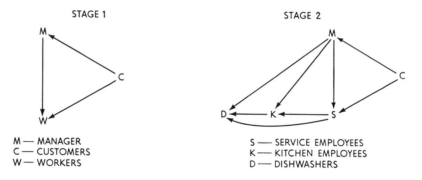

STAGE 1

STAGE 2

M — MANAGER
C — CUSTOMERS
W — WORKERS

S — SERVICE EMPLOYEES
K — KITCHEN EMPLOYEES
D — DISHWASHERS

There is just one problem in Stage 2 that Jones did not have to face in Stage 1. Now, if the organization is to function smoothly, the work of waitresses, cooks, and dishwashers must be coordinated. Sometimes Jones observes that there is friction among these various workers, but he is nearly always on the spot when trouble arises so that he can step in to smooth things over. The problem, therefore, is relatively simple at this point.

The first two stages are also characterized by the close relationship between Jones and his regular customers. He finds that his restaurant has become something of a social center in his neighborhood, and he has become an important local figure. The regular customers are his friends. They come in to eat, but they also come in to talk with him. In the regular course of business activity, he hears of the successes and failures, of the family and business affairs of the local people. When they are in trouble, they tell him, and if he can help them, he does.

Tom Jones serves good food and has his own style of menus and

service. This helps to account for his success, and yet, if you cross-exam-
ine his regular customers, they will admit that some of his competitors do
just as good a food job. They go to the Jones restaurant because they
enjoy the familiar, friendly atmosphere of the place and because they are
personally loyal to the owner-manager.

Now the business continues to expand, and Jones again takes over
larger quarters. No longer is he able to supervise all the work. He hires a
service supervisor, a food-production supervisor, and places one of his
employees in charge of the dishroom as a working supervision. He also
employs a checker to total checks for his waitresses and to see that the
food is served in correct portions and style (Stage 3).

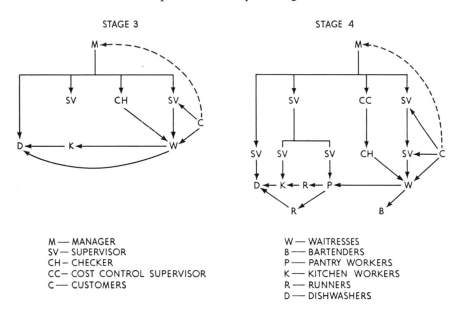

STAGE 3   STAGE 4

M — MANAGER   W — WAITRESSES
SV — SUPERVISOR   B — BARTENDERS
CH — CHECKER   P — PANTRY WORKERS
CC — COST CONTROL SUPERVISOR   K — KITCHEN WORKERS
C — CUSTOMERS   R — RUNNERS
                                    D — DISHWASHERS

In time, he finds that he can take care of a larger number of customers
if he takes one more step in the division of labor. Up to now, the cooks
have been serving the food to the waitresses. When these functions are
divided, both cooking and serving can proceed more efficiently. Therefore, he sets up a service pantry apart from the kitchen. The cooks can
now concentrate on cooking, the runners carry food from kitchen to
pantry and orders from pantry to kitchen, and the pantry girls serve the
waitresses over the counter. This adds one more group of workers to be
supervised, and to cope with the larger scale of the operation, he adds
another level of supervision, so that there are two supervisors between
him and the workers (Stage 4).

Stages 3 and 4 introduce some very significant changes in the position
and activity of Tom Jones. He is no longer able to keep up such close

relations with his customers. There are too many of them, and they come and go too fast. To be sure, he knows a large number by name, but the relationship is much more formal: "Good evening, Mr. Smith." "How are you, Mr. Jones?"

He comes to realize that he can no longer count on personal relations with customers to build up his business. He cannot sell the good will of the restaurant directly. He must sell it through his supervisors and workers. They represent him to the customers, and he must teach them to maintain the distinctive atmosphere and style which the customers find attractive. With the personal touch of the owner carrying less direct weight, he must give special attention to improving standards of food and service, so that customers who have never seen him will eat in his restaurant because "it's the best place in town."

This expansion also gives rise to new problems in the relationship between the manager and his subordinates. As the number of employees grows, Jones finds that he no longer has time to get to know them well. With those who were with him in the early days, he manages to maintain a cordial personal relationship even though he has much less time for them than before. But those more recently hired are little more than names and faces to him.

He has the uncomfortable feeling that he no longer knows his organization as he once did. He overhears one of the newer employees saying, "There's a clique of old-timers in here. You can't get a fair break unless you belong to the old gang. The boss plays favorites."

This worries Jones. He has always prided himself upon his relationship with his employees, and he is determined to solve this problem. But he does not have time to get to know the new people as he did the old. And the loyalty of the older employees has been responsible for a large measure of his success. That must be worth something. He does not feel that it is right to break off relations with the old-timers just to meet the charge of favoritism. So what can he do?

He also faces new problems. One day Frank, an employee of some years' service, comes in to complain that Miss Markley, his supervisor, has discriminated against him. He had been expecting a promotion to a higher paying job, but the supervisor told him that his work was not up to standard and that he could expect nothing better than his present job. Frank appeals to the boss to overrule Miss Markley.

Jones thinks it over. He has always had the impression that Frank was doing a good job, but Miss Markley is in a better position to know the facts of the case. Still, he does not feel that she has always used good judgment in handling workers in the past, so it is quite possible that she has been unjust to Frank. Perhaps he should tell Frank that he will take care of the case for him, but that would undermine the authority of his supervisor. So perhaps he must simply tell Frank to accept Miss Markley's decision as final. But then Frank will probably quit. That in itself may not be so serious, but as workers fail to get a hearing from Jones, they will stop coming to him with their problems and he will be completely cut off from them.

If that happens, the morale of the workers will be left entirely to his supervisors. Perhaps that is inevitable in the long run, for as the organization continues to grow and executive responsibilities pile up, there simply is not enough time left in the day to keep in direct touch with the employees.

While this is a natural result of growth, it raises new problems for the owner-manager. He wonders how he can select supervisors who are capable of doing a good personnel job. He knows how to evaluate their knowledge of food production or service, but skill in human relations seems so much more difficult to measure. He interviews the applicants for supervisory positions, and he sizes them up on the basis of his own experience. He feels that his judgment is above average, and yet he sometimes doubts his whole procedure. Perhaps he is just choosing people who make a good impression on him, thus assuming that the workers will react in the same way. Yet he knows very well that there are supervisors who manage to make a good impression on management, but are highly unpopular with the workers. The ideal supervisor is able to adjust well to subordinates and superiors alike—but how is he to be located?

Of course, people are not born with supervisory skill, nor can they be expected to have it when they take on their first supervisory job. Such skill grows with experience and training. Perhaps the deficiencies of Jones' selection procedure would not be so serious if he could provide new supervisors with the sort of experience and training that would make the most of their talents in handling people. That, he realizes, is a major problem.

When Jones was beginning, he could state his personnel problem in very simple form: How can I get the cooperation of the workers? As the organization grew, he found he had to leave that problem more and more in the hands of his supervisors. His problem was: How can I get the cooperation of my supervisors? At first he did not recognize this as a problem. He assumed that anyone who was a part of management would naturally give his best to the organization. In the course of time, he learned that this was not so. Not that supervisors willfully refused to do their best. Under certain circumstances, they were simply unable to perform at full capacity. Through observing his supervisors, he found that their efficiency was much higher when they were happy and well-adjusted in their jobs than when they were facing nervous tensions. That was enlightening, but it solved no problems. Instead, it posed a new one: How can I make supervisors happy and well-adjusted in their jobs?

As the restaurant organization expanded, Jones discovered that it also moved toward standardization. When he himself worked behind the counter, he did not need to worry about elaborate financial controls. He knew his workers and he trusted them. He knew, from day-to-day experience, just about how much business he was doing, so that if the cash register was ever short, he could check up on it right away.

With a large organization, such informal controls necessarily break down. Jones had to build up a system of cost control, and the old employees had to learn new ways.

In the kitchen, there was a larger problem. Jones made his name through maintaining a certain standard of food and service. In his single restaurant, the quality of the food depended upon the chef. If the old chef went out and a new chef came in, the character of the food changed. One man seemed too slender a thread from which to hang the future of his restaurant.

With Stage 5 in development, the chain restaurant, this problem became more acute.

From the customers' standpoint, there is little justification for a chain except in the advantage it gives them in knowing what type of food and service to expect, no matter which unit they patronize. This cannot be done without standardization, and that means standard recipes as well as standard service procedures.

Jones approached the problem of standardized recipes tentatively at first. He told the chef of his first large restaurant that he had a secure job with the organization for as long as he was able to work, but in case he were lost through illness or other causes, it would be a great loss to the restaurant to have his secrets leave with him. Would he be willing to write down some of the chief recipes upon which the restaurant depended?

The chef did not respond very well to this request. He said he was very busy and besides, he just did these things by heart and would not know how to put them down on paper. Jones was sure that the chef could furnish the information if he really tried. The owner-manager became aware of another factor in the situation.

Operating without written recipes, the chef was king of the kitchen. The manager might find fault with some of the dishes, but not knowing how they were made, he could only bring the matter to the chef's attention and hope for the best. If recipes were furnished, the manager could then supervise the chef much more closely. He could check to see that the recipes were being followed. He could bring in new recipes and revise old ones.

Furthermore, this standardization would tend to take the skill out of the job and much of the prestige with it. It had taken the chef years to learn his craft, and now, in a restaurant down the street, cooks were being trained through standard recipes in a matter of weeks. And women were taking over those jobs, too. It all went against the grain, and the chef did not want to be a party to it. So he balked. And Jones wondered whether it would be possible to change the chef's attitude or whether a kitchen with standardized recipes required a fresh start, with inexperienced workers and a college-educated food-production manager to train them.

That was a major problem and there were others like it. Increasing size required standardization of procedure, and that involved important changes in work routines and human relations. Unless these changes were made skillfully, the morale of the organization would deteriorate. Within limits, standardization was clearly necessary for business reasons, and so he faced another problem: How can I gain the benefits of standardization without losing employee morale and cooperation?

We are not here concerned with possible ways of dealing with the human problems that Tom Jones faced. My purpose at this point is simply to show how increasing size leads to changes in organization structure, and how size and structure together affect the social system of activities, interactions, and sentiments.

2. The evolution of the Electrical Equipment Company

The Electrical Equipment Company case[2] presents problems in growth, structural change, and confusion as to the character of the organization. The company had approximately 500 employees at the time of the Arensberg-McGregor study in 1939. The authors report that growth in number of employees since the founding in 1932 had been slow, but they examined major changes in organization structure that were due in part to this growth.

Located in Cambridge, Massachusetts, the company was a forerunner of the tremendous growth of high technology and science firms that developed around Boston and near Harvard and M.I.T. in the 1950's and 1960's. It was founded by engineers, and the owners and founders visualized the firm as a way of grouping together fellow engineers who could thus accomplish together what was beyond their reach individually. The philosophy of management emphasized informality of relationships and de-emphasized the exercise of authority. It was often said that "the competent man needs no supervision."

By 1939, it had become apparent to top management that the firm was not functioning quite as had been originally planned, and management invited the behavioral scientists in to assess the situation. Arensberg and McGregor concentrated on the design engineers, who seemed to have special problems and to be a special focus of management concern.

There were conflicting opinions within management as to the pattern of authority that was supposed to prevail. The authors described the problem in this way:[3]

---

[2] Conrad M. Arensberg and Douglas McGregor, "Determination of Morale in an Industrial Company," *Applied Anthropology*, Vol. 1, no. 2 (1942), pp. 12–34. See also G. C. Homans' chapter on the case in *The Human Group* (New York: Harcourt Brace, 1950), pp. 369–414.

[3] *Ibid.*, p. 16.

The question was whether the directors intended the company to run along democratic lines or along autocratic ones. There were several points of view expressed. There were those who believed that it was a genuine desire of management that the company be democratically operated, with the employees—and particularly the stockholder-employees—determining policies, and the directors acting merely to carry out the wishes of the majority.

Within the group who held this opinion were two subgroups: Those who thought the directors were effectively carrying out this philosophy, and those who thought that, in spite of their genuine desire to carry it out, autocratic methods prevailed in practice.

There were those who believed that the directors wished to create the impression that the company was run in a democratic fashion, but had no intention of relinquishing autocratic control. The people who expressed this opinion frequently commented that it was not particularly important to them whether the company was autocratically or democratically run, but that they wished there might be a frank and open avowal of one or the other philosophy of management.

Finally, there were those who believed that the directors had no intention of democratic operation of the company and no intention of creating the impression that it was so operated. This group was small, and mostly limited to the directors themselves and to some of their immediate subordinates.

The design engineers suffered particularly from confusion as to the nature of supervision. The authors present this interpretation of the problem, paraphrasing a number of comments made to them:[4]

"The competent man needs no supervision." It was the belief of a number of people that this phrase was expressive of an ideal, but that either it was not carried out in practice or there were no competent men in the organization. There are several aspects of this problem. The first concerns the extent to which individuals are able to carry out their ideas without intereference. People discussing this problem talked somewhat in the following fashion: "Although it may be true that the competent man needs no supervision, it is obvious that no individual is completely competent in everything. It follows that that idea applied to that area where the individual is demonstrably competent. But, in practice, he is not given freedom to make decisions even within that area. There is little consistency with respect to the way his decisions are treated. A relatively major decision may be carried out without interference, and a minor one overruled. A decision with respect to the design of an instrument may pass today without notice, but a decision of a very similar sort tomorrow may be violently criticized. One will be told in private to carry out a given course of action and that course of action will be criticized or even vetoed in public."

How did these confusions and inconsistencies arise? Let us examine the position of the design engineers at the outset and then note the changes that were introduced.

In the early period, the design engineers had a high degree of control

---

[4] *Ibid.,* p. 15.

over their own activities and easy access to the president of the company. The authors described the early pattern in this way:[5]

They were thus at the time able to sign travel vouchers, make changes on designs through direct orders to bench workers, suggest plans for development, and otherwise act as coordinates in authority with other staff officers. Sales were not "functionalized" at first; the engineers were their own contact men. In a phrase, the company looked more like a group of professional associates than an industrial company. Much of the common folklore of the 1939 formal organization dated from this stage.

Arensberg and McGregor showed step by step how the position of the design engineer was changed from 1932 to 1939. We need not go into this detail here. We shall simply sum up the major changes that took place.

A separate sales force was established, and the design engineers were cut off from their customers. As the number of customers increased, a separate accounting and cost control department was established. The design engineers had their budgets more closely scrutinized than before, and they were no longer able to sign their own travel vouchers. The design engineers were also cut off from "direct contact of authoritative kind with the shop."

The design engineers also found themselves farther removed from the top of the organization. A series of changes was introduced that finally crystallized in the establishment of a design committee, which the authors point out might more properly have been called a coordinating committee, since design was only one aspect that was considered by the committee. The chairman of this strategic committee had come up out of the sales department, and the design engineers had only one member on the committee.

By 1939, the design engineers had lost their position close to the top and were now on the same level as accounting, sales, production, or other departments. But while the structure had clearly changed, the old personal contacts had not been entirely eliminated. Design engineers felt that they still could go see the president and on occasion did so. They reported that he listened to them sympathetically, but they complained that he did nothing about the problems that they brought to his attention.

What had happened in this case? We have seen a process of growth accompanied by a shift from informal and flexible interpersonal relations to a more highly formalized and controlled system. As some writers would put it, the organization had become bureaucratized. In this process, the design engineers had lost status and had lost substantially in their powers of initiating activities for others, while the initiations from others to them substantially increased.

What could be done about the problems of the design engineers? Arensberg and McGregor noted that the major changes that had taken

---

[5] *Ibid.,* p. 28.

place were irreversible. As the organization grew, the coordination of its interrelated functions became increasingly important. It would no longer have been practical to allow the design engineers the freedom they had enjoyed in the beginning.

The consultants did recommend that organizational symbolism be brought into line with the realities of everyday interactions and activities. They pointed out that the symbolism of individual freedom and absence of authority that had been reasonably compatible with the company in its first months of operation was now markedly at variance with real life. When men still heard the phrase, "The competent man needs no supervision" and heard others speak of the company as if it were still a group of colleagues seeking to operate in terms of a democratically produced consensus, they noted that such symbolism was markedly at variance with what they were experiencing and observing. This naturally led the people concerned to think of their superiors and rivals as hypocrites. Arensberg and McGregor suggested resolving the conflict by changing the symbolism—in other words, by getting higher management to discuss with subordinates the way the company was being run in verbal symbols that would more closely approximate reality.

While top management reported that it acted on these recommendations and was satisfied with the outcome, we have no research report of the changes involved in this symbolic realignment. The underlying principle involved is nevertheless worthy of emphasis. Symbols must be seen in relation to the everyday experience and observation of organizational participants. If the verbal symbols are markedly at variance with experience and observation, this condition tends to promote confusion and interpersonal conflict.

The authors are not saying that a realignment of symbolism would make the engineers happy in this case. They are saying that individuals will be more satisfied with their lot when they have a cognitive map of the organization that corresponds to reality than they will be if the cognitive map transmitted to them is more favorable than the situation they are experiencing.

3. Changing ethnic composition

A company or plant tends to be identified in the minds of its employees with the "kinds" of people who work there. The introduction of any new kind of people is therefore perceived by many organizational members as involving change in the character in the organization. These changes in character are often perceived in terms of shifts in ethnic composition of the work force and in allocation of jobs.

Earlier we have examined cases of this nature: of the subordination of Italian-American and others to Irish-Americans in the shop, with special reference to access to supervisory positions; of the monopoly control earlier exercised by the old time Swedish-American craftsmen in the Benton blowing room, and their resistance to the introduction and upgrading of representatives of other ethnic groups.

Does the introduction and upgrading of Afro-Americans present just another case in interethnic relations? Or do we face a distinctively different situation here?

There are indeed important similarities, some of which we will explore, but there are also important differences in degree and kind.

No other ethnic group began its experience in the United States in slavery. Afro-Americans are the only ethnic group which has suffered from legally sanctioned discrimination—economic, political, and social. They thus have found themselves heavily disadvantaged in education and employment opportunities. This has meant that a far greater proportion of Afro-Americans has occupied lower class positions, compared to whites. This, in turn, reinforces the tendency of whites to look upon all Afro-Americans in terms of the picture whites have of lower class behavior. While legally sanctioned discrimination has been eliminated to a large extent, the effects of past discrimination are still with us.

Ethnic groups that have entered American urban and industrial life from Europe have come in at the bottom but have spread through the several social classes in the course of two or three generations. To some extent this has come about through collective action exercised in the political field, but to a considerable extent it has come about through individual mobility. In the early period following the Supreme Court's school desegregation decision of 1954, many supporters of the civil rights movement were assuming that, once legal barriers were removed, enough Afro-Americans would move up through the social and economic structure so as to relieve the tensions of race relations. While the rate of individual mobility has probably increased, at this writing it has become evident that the individual route is not massive enough to relieve the pressures and tensions. Afro-Americans are increasingly looking for collective solutions —actions based upon their own collective strength. We will return to some of the collective aspects of the problem toward the end of this chapter.

The symbolism of race relations in industry

Everett C. Hughes points to a common tendency of white managers in race relations:[6]

This frame of mind is revealed in the inclination of many managements to see a racial issue in any difficulty in which Negroes are involved. This tendency is of course given strength by a like tendency of employees, both Negro and white. In a typical case of this kind the management frantically

[6] Everett C. Hughes, "Race Relations in Industry," "When Races Meet," in W. F. Whyte (ed.), *Industry and Society* (New York: McGraw-Hill Book Co., 1946).

called the representative of an agency that tries to settle such matters to say they were having race trouble and would have to establish separate locker rooms. The investigator found that the plant had grown tremendously during the war, without any increase in locker-room facilities. For two years employees had been complaining of crowding in the locker room and of having to share their lockers with workers on other shifts. When Negroes were hired, the matter came to a head; the white employees demanded separate locker rooms. This case was settled by immediately building new but not segregated locker rooms well placed about the plant. The racial way of thinking in this case gave a ready definition for a chronic problem.

White workers are inclined to interpret the introduction of a new kind of people into their department in terms of the way it reflects upon them. Hughes puts the case in this way:[7]

If we look at the structure of the thinking of workers about Negro fellow workers, we will find in it not merely the conventional American attitude toward Negroes, but also the general inclination of workers to view with disapproval, born of anxiety, the hiring of new kinds of workers for their particular jobs. Their anxiety relates not only to security but to status and prestige as well. Jobs and departments in an industry are rated by everyone concerned. We expect that. Less attention has been given to the fact that the kinds of people hired for a given job determine to some extent the job's prestige. Thus, if women are hired for a job that only men have done, the men may take the hiring of women, not as proof that women are rising in status, but as proof that the job's status is threatened. We have heard of one industry in which Italians, who had been limited to poorer jobs, were annoyed when Negroes were hired to work alongside them; not because they disliked Negroes particularly, but on the ground that—since they knew what people thought of Negroes—the hiring of them was additional evidence that management had a low opinion of the Italians.

We must recognize the important symbols which Afro-Americans recognize themselves. There were rapid changes in this sort of symbolism in the 1960's. Whites have long recognized that Afro-Americans strongly object to being referred to as "niggers," but now many are surprised to find that some Afro-Americans object to being called "Negroes." What is going on here? Militants explain that "Negro" was the name attached to them by whites; they feel that the right to determine a name for their own segment of society is a necessary part of their liberation. Militants are saying that they want to be called "blacks"—even though many of them are nearer to white than black in color. They find acceptable the term Afro-American. Since this term is just as accurate as Italian-American, Polish-American, Irish-American, and so on, it is this term which we are using in the present book, even though it will seem unfamiliar and strange to many readers.

The situation is complicated because there is no uniformity among

---

[7] *Ibid.*, p. 120–21.

Afro-Americans on this symbolic question. It is the militants who are rejecting the word "Negro," whereas many who have found their place in middle-class society take it for granted that they will be referred to as "Negroes," and might resent being called "blacks." Lower class Negroes, who have not joined in any militant movement, similarly will not react against the designation of "Negroes." It should be noted that the quotations from Hughes were printed in 1946, when it had not occurred to anyone of either race that there was anything offensive about the word "Negro."

Militants are concerned not only with the use of the word "black," but with establishing new meanings to be attached to that word. It has long been recognized by students of Afro-Americans in U.S. society that the predominant values in our society tend to be visualized in "white" terms so that the Afro-American child in the past has tended to fall into the habit of thinking that "white" is good and "black" is evil, that "white" is high and "black" is low, and so on. To reverse this pattern of thinking, some Afro-Americans hold special classes where they drill children into saying "I am black and black is beautiful," in order to instill pride in color and cultural heritage.

Strategies of change

How are Afro-Americans to be introduced into the workplace and to be provided opportunities for upward movement? Here we need to consider both the symbolism of status and the informal structure of work groups.

The Italian-American case previously described illustrates the status symbolism point: if Afro-Americans are introduced only at the lower levels, those already holding jobs at those levels will consider the introduction of the new group as further evidence of the low regard in which management holds the existing work force.

As Hughes reports:[8]

One company prides itself on having placed its first Negroes in the employment office for all to see, thus forestalling the criticism that the front-office staff was willing to give the shop hands Negro fellow workers but wouldn't have any themselves.

The influence of formal group structure is indicated in another illustration, also drawn from Hughes:[9]

In a certain plant, Negroes were first hired in a department that, though dirty and smelly and without prestige, has a very stable working force. The men in it, mostly elderly Poles, work in groups of three that produce as units and are so paid as to make teamwork the key to a good income. It was

---

[8] *Ibid.*, p. 112.
[9] *Ibid.*, pp. 113–14.

thought that these men would not have much prejudice and that the isolation of the department would allow the hiring of Negroes without much comment. Of several Negro men hired, none stayed more than a few days. The management was disturbed, for it thought that the Negroes were confirming the common opinion that they are unreliable. Interviews with these Negro men brought out a consistent and simple story. The workers in the department had practiced every obvious and subtle art to let the newcomers know that they were not wanted and would never learn (i.e., be taught) the work. Upon hearing all this an aged member of the management, now retired, snorted that no one had ever succeeded in 40 years in putting into that department any new man not chosen by the men already there. In this rather extreme case appear two factors: (1) the attitude of the men to the Negro newcomers, and (2) what we may call the molecular structure of their organization. We may leave the first with the remark that all the evidence in the case indicates that these men had no great prejudice toward Negroes as such, but that they had an ingrained suspicion of newcomers. On the second point, it is clear that formal admission to this shop meant nothing without informal admission to one of the work teams.

This case suggests the strategy of making the first moves into departments that do not have such tightly knit informal group structures.

It is often said, "You can't change attitudes by law. Education is what is needed." Since education takes a long time, such a statement provides a rationale for doing nothing in the present or near future. That statement needs to be examined in the light of the theoretical framework of this book.

The statement implies that attitudes or sentiments can be changed through an educational process which presumably points out to the students the fallacies inherent in assumptions about superior and inferior races and such matters. So far, there is very little research evidence to support this view and voluminous evidence to indicate that the provision of information has little measurable effect upon sentiments. On the other hand, we have been seeking to demonstrate throughout this book that changing the interactions, activities, and transactions in which people are participating is bound to change their sentiments.

The skillful administrator in this field is therefore not the one who waits until whites are "ready" to have Afro-Americans introduced or upgraded into superior positions. He thinks rather about strategies for bringing about the change and then for helping the potential resisters to adjust to the change.

We need to put the problem into an action framework. What will happen if Afro-Americans are introduced into a given department? Let us assume that a given white worker holds strong racial prejudices. While this is a fact of some importance, the fact alone does not enable us to predict what the worker will do. We need to know whether he is an informal group leader or a follower. If he is a follower and the informal leader and other group members are in favor of the change, or at least willing to go along with it, we can predict that the worker in question will make no disturbance, even though he may be privately resentful.

If the worker in question is an informal group leader and wishes to protest, we still have little evidence justifying a prediction. We need to get answers to three further questions that the group leader is presumably asking himself: How will management react to the protests of the informal leader and his work group? How will union leaders react? Will government officials intervene?

If the informal group leader predicts that with a little pressure from himself and his group management will back down, that the union leaders will at least covertly support him, and that no government officials will intervene, then we can predict with a high degree of probability that the leader will mobilize his group and apply the pressure. If he predicts that in the face of a protest by his group management will stand firm and be ready to impose penalties, that the union leaders will firmly support the introduction of the new group and refuse to process grievances for workers who are disciplined for resistance, and that government officials will intervene to support the change if called on, then we can predict, with a very high probability of success, that the leader and his group members will go no farther than complaining among themselves. If two or only one of these powers can be counted on to support the change, then the probable reactions of the formal leader and his work group fall somewhere between these two extremes.

Note that we are not suggesting making predictions on the basis of the sentiments of the leader and his group members. We are assuming negative sentiments towards Afro-Americans and yet pointing out that the sentiments alone give us very little of predictive value. We have to put the problem in a transactional framework. Here the leader can get a plus or a minus from his own work group, from management, from union leaders, and from government officials. If none of the three powers outside of the group is prepared firmly to support the change, then the informal leader is facing what we might call a four-plus situation for his protest. By opposing the new group openly, the leader gets credit from his own work group for doing the manly and courageous thing to protect the rights of the group. He also gets a plus from the recognition that he gets from the other three powers who support his initiative or at least do not fight against it. If the outside powers are sufficiently firm in opposition to his protest so that the leader and his work group get severely penalized, then the leader has suffered a minus from all quarters. He may even be blamed by fellow workers for getting them into this negative situation.

The effective administrator in this sort of case therefore will not concentrate his attention upon the sentiments of the members of the work force. As he prepares to make his moves, he will seek to determine first that management will stand firmly behind these moves, that the union leaders are prepared to support the change, and that government officials can be brought in in support, if necessary. Such an action strategy has far greater promise for success and in much shorter time than any program based upon education directed at the changing of sentiments.

Do the personalities or character of the first Afro-Americans to be introduced make a difference in the success of the effort? Some change agents have sought to make their first moves by utilizing what we might call a "star strategy." This is best illustrated in the case of breaking the color barrier in major league baseball. By the time that Branch Rickey was ready to bring up the first Afro-American to his Brooklyn Dodgers, he already had under contract several Afro-Americans who appeared to have exceptional talent for playing baseball. Of these, Rickey selected as his first case, Jackie Robinson, who was overqualified in every relevant respect. He was not only an exceptional athlete. He was also a college graduate, and thus had much more education than the average professional baseball player. With the case of Jackie Robinson before him, the prejudiced ball player would naturally find it difficult to claim that Negroes were inferior in intelligence, lacking the courage to perform under pressure, and voice other stereotyped beliefs.

While the "star strategy" has clearly paid off in a number of other situations beyond baseball, it offers no promise for a general solution to the problems. There simply are not enough available Afro-American stars —or stars in any ethnic group—to open all the doors that need to be opened for the group in question. Concerned management and union leaders now well recognize this situation and are attempting to grapple with a much more difficult problem of bringing into productive employment vast numbers of individuals who, in large measure because of lack of opportunities in the past, are severely underqualified for the jobs in question. If management simply continued to hire on the basis of demonstrated qualifications, these people would continue to be "hard core unemployed." It is only as management makes allowances for educational and general cultural deficiencies arising out of past discrimination and develops special programs to raise the qualifications of disadvantaged individuals, that private industry can begin to make important contributions in this field. We assume that much if not most of the responsibility for such programs and policies must be borne by government, but here we are going beyond the scope of this book. In any case, the efforts to bring severely disadvantaged groups into productive employment are so new at this writing that we must wait for further experience before there will be research findings worth reporting.

4. Changing organizational character

The perceived status of an organization is one aspect of what we mean by character, but we also need to consider character in more inclusive terms. How do members conceptualize the organization? What does it mean to them?

We have portrayed the union organization drive as a struggle over the conception that workers and management people have of their organizations. We have referred to a vertical orientation as one in which the worker sees himself holding a position toward the bottom of an *integrated* hierarchy. Horizontal orientation refers to a worker conception of horizontal and separate segments. The farewell party (Chapter 19) was a symbolic representation of the vertical model, for it brought people of widely differing statuses together, acting as if these differences either did not exist or were unimportant.

Can symbols be used in taking over an organization or in bringing about a drastic change in the character of that organization?

One answer to these questions was provided by Pope Gregory VII as long ago as the year 601. At this time the Church had been attempting to convert the heathen Britons, and two of the missionaries, finding that they were making little progress, wrote to Rome for advice. The Pope responded with these words:[10]

We must refrain from destroying the temples of the idols. It is necessary only to destroy the idols, and to sprinkle holy water in these same temples, to build ourselves altars and place holy relics therein. If the construction of these temples is solid, good, and useful, they will pass from the cult of demons to the service of the true God; because it will come to pass that the nation, seeing the continued existence of its old places of devotion, will be disposed, by a sort of habit, to go there to adore the true God.

It is said that the men of this nation are accustomed to sacrificing oxen. It is necessary that this custom be converted into a Christian rite. On the day of the dedication of the temples thus changed into churches, and similarly for the festivals of the saints, whose relics will be placed there, you should allow them, as in the past, to build structures of foilage around these same churches. They shall bring to the churches their animals, and kill them, no longer as offerings to the devil, but for Christian banquets in name and honor of God, to whom, after satiating themselves, they will give thanks. Only thus, by preserving for men some of the worldly joys, will you lead them more easily to relish the joys of the spirit.

This case suggests that skillful administrators have always recognized the significance of symbols in organizational behavior—though few have ever spoken of them so explicitly as did Gregory the Great. It is our task in this book to make the symbols explicit, to deal with them systematically, and to relate them effectively to interactions, activities, and sentiments. If we are successful in this, the knowledge can be used both by students of organization and by men of action.

Gregory the Great was presenting to his hard-pressed missionary priests these important truths of organizational behavior. The interactions,

---

[10] My translation from Giuseppe Pitré, *Feste Patronali in Sicilia*.

activities, and sentiments of men are organized around certain key symbols which give meaning to their organizational life. If you want to incorporate these men into your organization, do *not* attack the symbols around which their behavior has been organized. Nothing is so certain to alienate men as attacking their cherished symbols. Therefore, you should accept insofar as possible the symbols these men currently cherish and begin the task of modifying the meanings attached to these symbols as you yourselves enter into the activities and interactions of these men. As you acquire leadership roles in these activities and interactions, you will be able gradually to reshape the symbols. It is in this way that you will be able to transform pagans into Christians.

5. Symbols and the introduction of change

In this and earlier chapters, we have pointed out symbols of importance to the cases under discussion. In this section, we will bring symbols into the foreground for a more extended analysis. We shall refer to some of these symbols already noted, present others, and organize the lot into categories that may help us to understand their meaning. (Note that we have just dealt with the symbols of organizational character.)

Symbols of personal identification

Symbols can operate on sentiments of personal identification, orienting the individual in a hostile or friendly direction in relation to another individual or organization. In the Buchsbaum unionization case (Chapter 19), we have noted how Garfield's intervention to protect the car from being overturned and the company president's friend assuring him that Laderman was a trustworthy individual who liked opera helped to break down Buchsbaum's conception of union leaders as different types of human beings who were necessarily hostile to himself.

Symbols of status

Years ago only sociologists and anthropologists talked and wrote about status. Now the term has come into every day conversation outside of the behavioral sciences, and specialists in advertising consciously seek to manipulate status symbols in order to sell their products. Status symbols are indeed important and powerful tools to facilitate the introduction of change, but they cannot be used effectively unless their user recognizes their limitations as well as their potentialities.

Status symbols refer to the prestige position of individuals in their social world. When the person encounters symbols referring to himself that tend to place him in line with his own conception of his status, the symbols stir no affect, and the individual may not even be aware of the symbols involved. When the symbols used tend to place the person above the status he claims for himself, he pays attention, and he is pleased—unless the discrepancy is so great as to make him suspect that he is being made a fool. When the symbols used tend to place the person below his own status evaluation of himself, he is likely to react with strong negative sentiments toward the user of those symbols and what he represents.

The watchman statement (Chapters 11 and 19) symbolized for the Hi-Test workers a status so far below that which they accorded themselves as to provoke a widespread and intense negative reaction against management. Since this negative discrepancy symbolization provoked hostile sentiments, we might consider it as falling under "personal identification." However, the negative sentiments are a product of a status-depressing use of symbols.

Status symbols provide one key to the explanation of some cases of resistance to change. Workers (and executives, also) note that the proposed change will eliminate certain symbols and replace them with others which have lower status values. Such changes naturally evoke negative sentiments and anxieties.

Can symbols be used to elevate the status of jobs? The following three cases illustrate some of the possibilities and limitations.

A restaurant owner was having trouble with high turnover and inefficiency on his dishwasher jobs. He recognized three interrelated status problems: (1) the title of the position suggested a very lowly valued position, (2) the wages he paid were at the bottom of his scale and around the bottom paid for unskilled labor in his area, and (3) the work of handling dirty dishes was universally looked down upon. To meet these problems, the owner took three interrelated actions: (1) he changed the job title to "dish machine operator," (2) he gave the position a substantial increase in hourly pay, and (3) he installed a large and complex dishwashing machine for the dish machine operators to operate. The owner reported that after these actions the dishwashing department no longer presented special problems of turnover, absenteeism, and low efficiency.

Another owner of a large restaurant thought he was applying exactly the same strategy, but to his surprise it did not seem to work. He already had modern dish machines. He called in the men of that department to tell them that their job classification had been changed from "dishwasher" to "dish machine operator" and that furthermore they were getting a substantial pay increase. For the first few days, he reported that the men seemed pleased, and the owner thought he was beginning to see the improvements in morale and efficiency that he had counted on, but the improvement was short-lived. The men were soon performing in the old and unsatisfactory pattern. Puzzled, the owner called one of the men aside and asked what he and his fellows were unhappy about. Taking his pay envelope out of his pocket, the worker showed it to the owner. On the envelope were typed these words: "Juan Romero, dishwasher." The owner had informed the payroll clerk about the pay increase for these men, but he had neglected to inform him of the change in title!

Consider the following case reported by Dale Carnegie:[11]

> This mechanic's job was to keep scores of typewriters and other hard-driven machines functioning smoothly night and day. He was always complaining that the hours were too long, that there was too much work, that he needed an assistant.
>
> J. A. Want (the boss) didn't give him an assistant, didn't give him shorter hours or less work, and yet he made the mechanic happy. How? This mechanic was given a private office. His name appeared on the door, and with it his title—"Manager of the Service Department."

As far as Dale Carnegie was concerned, this was the end of the story, but I can let my readers in on certain developments that took place later. A day or two after the events described, the mechanic was approached by a fellow worker, and the following conversation ensued:

> "Congratulations, Joe, I see you are a department manager now. How many people in your department?"
>
> "Well, there is just me. Nobody else."
>
> "You mean you are a manager, but you got nobody to manage?"
>
> "Yeah, I guess the boss just gave me the title."
>
> "At least you must have got a good raise out of it?"
>
> "Well, not exactly. The boss didn't say anything about more money."

After Joe had been subjected to variations of this conversation with several of the workers and had overheard conversations about him in which the word "sucker" kept recurring, he approached J. A. Want again. This time he reported that he felt more overworked than ever and needed *two* assistants. He wanted more money also. As he put it, "I figure that a manager should be worth a lot more to you than just a plain mechanic."

I should add that my sequel is imaginary, but can anyone really believe in the happy ending of this story provided by Dale Carnegie? The point is that symbols are not arbitrary. They bear some relation to the organizational world around them. The symbol of the title of manager implies supervisory activity, some people to supervise, and a job that should pay more money than one without such a high-sounding title. The possibilities of substituting status symbols for money are actually quite limited, and the man who tries to make such substitution is likely to find that he gets into more trouble than the effort is worth.

The status symbols discussed so far have been those referring directly to the prestige positions of individuals. There are also status symbols that refer to the prestige of an organization. To some extent the individual and

---

[11] Dale Carnegie, *How to Win Friends and Influence People* (New York: Pocket Books, Inc., 1942). I found this on p. 241 of Copy 2,365,447 of "The most popular work of non-fiction of our time."

organizational symbols fit together, for, as we have seen, the introduction of people of low status into the organization may be interpreted by members as reflecting adversely upon the status of their organization.

But it is not only people that symbolize the status of an organization. The physical arrangements of the workplace, the cleanness or dirtiness of the plant, and the quality of the materials worked on, among other things, may serve to place the organization in social space. A change in such an organizational status symbol will then have important repercussions among some of the members.

The point is illustrated in the following case, which involved a clash between Mr. Jefferson, the new manager of Everbest Restaurant, and the assistant manager, Miss Lucas, who had been with the organization for many years. Everbest was an old established organization well known for its high-quality foods. But it had been losing money, and Jefferson was sent in "with a free hand" to change things. He described in this way some of his difficulties with Miss Lucas:

I'll tell you, I had a hard time with her. When I came in, Everbest had been losing ground in competition, and I had a free hand to make changes. Well, I went ahead and changed things right off the bat. That was my mistake. I tried to do it all myself, too. One thing I went to work on was the menu. I went ahead and simplified the menu, and then I changed the price structure. That caused a lot of disturbance.

I'll tell you though what upset her most. At the time I came in, Everbest had served nothing but U.S. prime beef. Any beef on our menu was always U.S. prime. Of course, we want to serve good meat, but I didn't think we had to serve that particular grade every time, so I changed it.

Well, at the same time I changed the chocolate sauce. I'm telling you, we were serving a brand of chocolate sauce that they would have been ashamed to serve in a cheap restaurant. It was terrible. I went ahead and put in a much better grade of chocolate sauce.

You see, I wasn't running down the quality. But when I changed that U.S. prime beef, Lucas got terribly upset. You'd have thought the world was coming to an end. That was a terrible thing to do. She didn't think that Everbest could survive without serving U.S. prime beef.[12]

Even without consulting Miss Lucas, we can readily see that the manager and assistant manager viewed the problem from quite different angles. To Jefferson, this was simply a practical problem: What quality of foods should be bought and what prices should be charged in order to enable the restaurant to cope with competition most successfully? Taking this approach, he could not see that it was necessary to serve U.S. prime beef all the time. He felt that the type of meat purchased should be determined in line with the overall business requirements of the organization. The same reasoning called for an improvement in the quality of the chocolate sauce. So, according to Jefferson, he made changes resulting in

---

[12] Whyte, *op. cit.*, p. 336.

a slight lowering of standards in one item and a considerable improvement in another.

What Jefferson overlooked was that to Miss Lucas this was not primarily a practical problem. Without realizing it, he was attacking a symbol that represented Everbest restaurant to Miss Lucas and gave meaning to her connection with it. That restaurant had stood for U.S. prime beef for years, and U.S. prime beef had come to stand for the Everbest restaurant in the thoughts and feelings of Miss Lucas. She had come to take pride in being associated with a restaurant that served nothing but the very best. And when she thought of the very best, she didn't think of chocolate sauce. She thought of a few items that she considered especially important. These were the symbols of the restaurant. Her reactions to Jefferson showed that U.S. prime beef had become for her one of the chief Everbest symbols.

Our study of status in the kitchen showed that the highest status jobs were associated with the preparation and cooking of meat. It does not take a special study to show that, in this country, beef has the highest status of all meats. If beef has such symbolic significance, then the quality of beef served becomes a vital concern, and U.S. prime beef can readily become one of the symbols by which the members identify their organization.

Summary and conclusions

In this chapter, we have examined some of the concomitants of changes in size and perceived composition or character of organizations.

Organizational growth (in terms of the number of members) necessarily involves changes in formal organization structure and in the patterns of interaction and activities of members as well as in the types of transactions available to them.

Harassed by a union organization drive in one set of plants of his company that now numbered 25,000 employees, the president called a meeting of local management people to assure them that "this is still the same company it was when I signed all the paychecks myself." From a legal point of view, the president's statement was correct. From a behavioral science point of view, he was talking nonsense.

To act effectively in a growing organization or to make scientific sense of it, administrator and student both need to be able to adjust the set of symbols through which they visualize the organization so as to maintain linkages between cognitive maps and current realities. In a changing situation, he who acts today in terms of yesterday's symbolic model is bound to get into trouble.

Members and outsiders as well tend to visualize an organization in terms of the kinds of people who compose it or who hold certain special positions within it. In many U.S. plants, the "kinds" of people considered appropriate tend to be defined in ethnic terms. To this extent, Afro-Americans are experiencing some of the same problems experienced earlier by other ethnic groups then new to industry. However, we have noted that the history of Afro-Americans and the systematic legal discriminations to which they have been subjected in the past have imposed unparalleled obstacles in the way of their advance toward equality of status with other groups.

Examining ways in which Afro-Americans can be introduced into an organization and promoted up through the ranks or placed in superior positions, we have examined the symbolism of interethnic relations, as perceived by both parties. The resistance of one ethnic group to the introduction of Afro-Americans may be due in part to the interpretation that this action lowers the status of the work unit into which the new group is being introduced. Management can undermine this interpretation by taking care to introduce Afro-Americans first into higher status positions.

In introducing Afro-Americans, management needs to consider what Hughes calls the nuclear structure of the work group. Tightly knit units are likely to put up strong resistance. If more loosely knit units are available, the tightly knit unit should not be tackled first.

While some companies have had success with the "star strategy" of introducing overqualified Afro-Americans first, this approach offers no promise of bringing about a general solution to the problems. Recognizing this, some companies are now beginning to reach out to bring in people who are severely underqualified by reason of low education, lack of skills, poor work habits, and other deficiencies traceable to a history of racial discrimination.

Changes in the size, composition, or character of an organization are always accompanied by changes in the symbols through which people visualize the organization and by which organizational leaders seek to motivate their followers. We have presented examples to show how symbols both stand for and influence the perceptions of friendship or hostility, high or low status, and the character of the organization itself.

These symbols can be powerful tools to initiate or to block change, but to be effective, symbols must "ring true." Whether they "ring true" or not depends upon the context within which they are utilized. It is not possible to solve problems simply through changing an isolated symbol. In other words, there is no magic in symbols.

References

While there is voluminous literature on the problems of Afro-Americans and on race relations generally, very little research has been focussed upon the fitting of Afro-Americans into industry. Those interested in race relations in our society may consult:

Myrdal, Gunnar. *An American Dilemma*. New York: Harper and Brothers, 1944. The classic formulation of the problem.

Davis, Alison, Gardner, Burleigh B. and Mary R. *Deep South*. Chicago: University of Chicago Press, 1941. A study of caste and class in a southern industrial city in the 1930's.

Cayton, Horace, and Drake, St. Clair. *Black Metropolis*. A study of Afro-Americans in Chicago.

Williams, Robin M. *Strangers Next Door*. Englewood Cliffs, N.J.: Prentice-Hall, 1964. An analysis of the various studies making up the Cornell intergroup relations research program in the 1940's and 1950's.

Discussion questions

1. Some claim that resorting to the use of symbols in introducing change involves "manipulation" of people and is therefore unethical. What assumptions underlie that charge? Do you agree or disagree with the statement?

2. Pick an organization known to you through experience. What are the key symbols that characterize the organization to you and other members? Are there symbols that tend to place people in different status positions in the organization? How do you know that the symbols you cite have the meaning you give them? How do you know they are important?

3. Interview someone who has been in an organization which has changed in size, composition, or character during his membership. Get him to describe these changes. Can you relate your picture of the changing organization to the particular symbols that stand for the organization in the symbolic model of your informant? In other words, to what extent can you interpret the symbols he uses to infer the nature of the changes that probably took place?

26. The industrial research laboratory

In studying the introduction of change in industry, we are likely to visualize an innovator trying to influence individuals and groups in the organization to change their behavior. While individual roles are important, we must recognize that modern industry in the United States has institutionalized a process of introducing change. It is a common experience these days to hear a company executive report that more than half of the volume of sales of his company is in products that the company did not make 10 years earlier. Such far-reaching changes do not come about in response simply to the technical ingenuity and social skills of individual change agents. Managements have set up organization structures and organized social processes in order to create new ideas, to develop and test them, and finally to put them into operation. It is these organization structures and social processes that we will be examining in the present chapter.

Research departments were late in arrival on the American industrial scene. General Electric established the first industrial research department and Corning Glass Works followed within the first decade of the 20th century. These early industrial research departments were very much the creation of individual change agents, Charles Steinmetz in General Electric, Eugene Sullivan in Corning Glass Works. In face of the skepticism of "practical" glassmakers, Dr. Sullivan was hired to create a new type of glass for railroad signal lights. At the time, railroads had been plagued by an economic and safety problem: the glass then used in the signals had a tendency to crack when subjected to wide extremes of heat and cold, and no one in the production shops had been able to make a glass that would survive under these conditions for long.

After some months of chemical experimentation, Sullivan created a glass which would meet the most exacting requirements for performance on the railroad. In so doing, he also opened the way to development of pyrex glassware for home use. A dramatic solution such as that of the railroad signal light problem convinces the skeptics of the value of an industrial research department. At this point, the battle for recognition

595

has been won, but down through the years management continues to wrestle with the problem of developing organization structures and social processes that will be optimal for creating valuable new ideas and translating them into practice. These days management people do not need to learn through experience in their own company that research can be valuable. This is taken for granted, but the problem of the organization of research and development remains problematical.

In the early years of industrial research, research departments began as small appendages to production organizations. In the years since World War II, we have seen a number of spectacular examples of companies which were born in research laboratories, set up by scientists and development engineers, with the production end of the business being subordinate at least at the outset to research and development. Even when these new companies develop large production organizations, we suspect that their origin in research and development tends to differentiate them in organization structure and social processes from companies where research has had to be fitted into a large and well-established production organization. As yet, we are unable to test this notion, for there have been no systematic comparative studies of companies having these two types of organizational history.

Grafting on the research function

In this chapter we will concentrate on what has been learned regarding those companies which have grafted research departments on well-established production organizations. Various studies indicate that the history of this grafting on process points to some of the essential human problems of such companies. Managements have tended to apply organization theory arising out of study and experience in military, production, or sales organizations to research and development departments. It is now well recognized by management people as well as by students of organization that the organization structures and leadership styles that work well in production or sales organizations do not work well in research organizations. Such a realization generally leads to a series of compromises rather than to an effort to build a completely new framework of organization and processes that is designed to meet the task requirements of research and development.

In considering how the traditional approach to organization breaks down when we deal with research and development, let us consider first the role and problems of the research scientist in industry. At a later point, we shall consider the engineer, for recent research suggests that while these two categories of people have some things in common, they also have differences that distinguish them so sharply that it is misleading to lump them together.

Various studies have shown an underlying conflict of interest between company goals and the goals of scientists. The traditional manager would like to have his scientists be creative—but in solving just those problems that would lead to commercial advantage. He wants to keep their ideas secret so as to maintain the proprietary advantage of the company. He would like the scientists to be just as devoted to the interests of the company as are the foremen and other management people in the production organization.

The scientist is inclined to resent efforts of management people to determine the problems he shall select to study or the ways he shall go about studying them. This is not simply a function of the scientist's personality—that he tends to resist authority. It also comes about because he has recognized in his scientific training that success in science is determined in a very large measure by the choice of the problem one selects to study and by the approach one takes in studying that problem. There are some problems that appear ready to be solved, given the state of knowledge, the equipment and resources available, and the talents of scientists prepared to work on them. There are other problems which appear not to be ready for solution, either because the background knowledge available has not yet suggested a promising approach to experimentation, or because the equipment and resources are not available to the scientists concerned, or because the scientist does not have the talent for this type of problem. The scientist is also very much interested in publication of his research findings, for such communication is essential to building his reputation among fellow scientists. He wants to be free to attend scientific meetings and maintain and develop his association with fellow scientists in the universities and in other companies.

The conflict of interests has been phrased in terms of conflicting reference group identifications: cosmopolitans versus locals.[1] How does the scientist define success for himself? For any normal human being, his own opinion of how well he is doing is strongly influenced by the evaluations of other individuals. One way of determining a man's reference group is to identify those individuals whose good opinion of himself he most highly values. In these terms, the local is a man who defines success for himself very largely in terms of his contribution to the organization in which he works and in terms of the favorable evaluation that organizational superiors have of him. The scientist who is oriented in a cosmopolitan direction thinks of success in terms of recognition by the scientific community in his own specialty. A few members of this community will be inside the company, but all others will be outsiders.

We should recognize that the terms, cosmopolitan and local, are ideal types. There will be few individuals who perfectly fit either type. The local finds it hard to disregard altogether the opinion of his scientific

---

[1] Barney G. Glaser, "The Local-Cosmopolitan Scientists," *American Journal of Sociology,* Vol. LXIX, no. 3 (Nov., 1963), pp. 249-59.

colleagues outside of the company. The cosmopolitan would like to feel that he is making some contribution to the company at least in the long run and that he is getting recognition for this within the company. If he did not feel this way at all, he would hardly go to work in the company in the first place. Even as we grant that scientists in real life are distributed across a continuum from local to cosmopolitan, we find enough scientists far enough toward the cosmopolitan end of the continuum to make for a potentially serious conflict between scientific interests and management interests.

Scientist or administrator?

Another potential source of conflict is found in the structure and process of supervision. How is the scientist in the research laboratory to be rewarded for his success? Pay increases and promotions are the traditional rewards that management has to offer. Few scientists are so unworldly as to be indifferent to an increase in salary, but the offer of a promotion poses for them a real dilemma. The scientist's conception of a scientist is a man who works at the bench and in the scientific laboratory. As the scientist moves up in management, he is getting away from the practice of science. He may feel that in accepting a promotion he is selling out his dearly held scientific values. On the other hand, if he turns down a promotion, he will find himself being supervised by other men who are no better scientists than he and whom he may consider to be inferior to himself as scientists.

We should not assume that this conflict of values is inevitable in every scientist. Research suggests that when young scientists take on their first employment in industry, most of them cherish the hope of making some substantial contribution to the advance of science. As the scientist gains experience in the organization, he finds himself surrounded by other scientists as well trained as he, and he is likely to find the intellectual competition severe. At this point, some scientists appear to make a realistic evaluation of themselves in relation to their peers. The scientist finds that there are one or more others in the laboratory who seem to be more brilliant than he. If he has some talents and interests in administration, the scientist may decide that it is not worthwhile to try to struggle to keep in the competition as a scientist, but instead to take the management route. For such individuals, the management ladder provides a resolution of conflict rather than intensification of it.

The distribution of knowledge between superior and subordinate in the research laboratory is likely to create awkward situations. Even when the two men are of roughly equal scientific competence, it is usually the case that the scientist knows more about the problem he is investigating than does his superior—if only because he has immersed himself in that problem. This situation tends to make the scientist resistant to direction from his superior. As the superior himself is aware of the discrepancy in knowledge, the situation creates anxieties in him, and he has doubts upon his ability to supervise someone more knowledgable than he.

Management policies

There are several ways of meeting these organizational dilemmas. We have noted three common compromises:

1. *Publications and meeting attendance.* As a concession to the scientist's desire for recognition from his colleagues, the company provides travel and expense money so that he can at least attend the annual meeting of his professional society. The scientist is permitted to publish papers in professional journals. In some cases, he may even be encouraged to publish, although the most to be expected from most managements is a benevolent neutrality in this connection. Furthermore, even when management has the policy of permitting or encouraging publication, the scientist has to secure company clearance before he publishes. For this reason, even when the scientist is permitted to publish, he may be required to wait a period of some months to assure his company a head start in the exploitation of his idea. In most cases, in the university he has to secure no one's permission in order to publish.

2. *The dual ladder of promotion.* Administrators have come to recognize that many scientists can make their best contribution to the company through remaining at the work bench, carrying out their research. If such a man is promoted into management, the company may lose a good scientist and gain a poor administrator. Management must therefore establish a dual ladder or, as it is sometimes called, "parallel paths to progress," so that the man who is a superior performer as a scientist and does not want to move into administration may be rewarded by pay increases and by titles which reflect increasing status in the company. On paper this seems like a neat solution to the problem, but practice so far indicates that, at best, it is only a partial solution.

In some companies, we find one or a very few scientists whose research resulted in spectacular commercial successes for the company. These men may be individuals who launched the research department or who started a new branch of research. When the work of such a man has paid off handsomely for the company, and yet he does not relish administrative duties, we may find him in a laboratory of his own design, with full freedom to do work of his own choosing, and serving as a highly respected scientific consultant to top management.

Administrators may refer to this man as an indication that the company will reward scientists who do not want to take the administrative ladder. The symbolism of the scientific pioneer is likely to be interpreted rather differently by the scientists in the company research laboratories. They see a great gulf between themselves and this super star in terms of pay, status, and freedom to do their own work. They claim that the intermediate steps on the ladder between themselves and the star are not visible, and so they argue that their path is not really parallel to the administrative path.

Why don't these intermediate steps on the scientific ladder more often get filled in? Here we deal with an important aspect of administrative structure and practice. Administrators are accustomed to think of organization in terms of a table of organization filled with boxes for positions and lines connecting position to position in a vertical hierarchy. When a man holding a supervisory position is promoted, transferred, retired, fired, or buried, this creates a vacancy, and the logic of the chart demands that a blank box be filled in with a new name as soon as can be arranged. If no fully qualified candidate for the position is available, the position must be filled, so management assumes that the new man will grow into his new responsibility. The scientific side provides no such ready-made boxes. Scientists claim that their superiors do not advance them on the scientific ladder, while expecting them to grow into the larger responsibilities. They rather demand that the scientists prove outstanding capacity before they are recognized.

This situation does not seem to be due to conscious discrimination on the part of administrative decision makers. They are accustomed to dealing with the set of administrative boxes that must be filled. While they generally accept the principle that a scientist should be able to advance along the scientific path, they see no ready-made position boxes there, and they are troubled as to how they can judge superior performance that is not related to administrative responsibilities.

Who chooses the problem?

Who is to choose the problem to be worked on: the scientist or his superior? Marcson[2] quotes this statement by a supervisor of scientists:

In the case of some individuals, I would not dare to shift them or to direct them or even to supervise them. They are people who are very good. They know what they are doing. They know how to do it. They can be and are left completely on their own.

What to do with a great majority of scientists who are not exceptional performers? Marcson reports two common approaches.[3] The first we might term selling the problem to the subordinate. Thus speaks a supervisor:

We try to communicate to the individual that he is working on what he is interested in. This is the job of the research supervisor.

---

[2] Simon Marcson, *The Scientist in Industry* (New York: Harper & Bros., 1960) p. 114.

[3] *Ibid.*

The other approach Marcson calls "hedging." The supervisor wants the scientist to work on problem A. If the supervisor insists that the scientist spend all his time on problem A, he knows that the scientist will feel exceedingly resentful. He will be harder to work with in the future —if indeed he remains long with the organization. On the other hand, if the supervisor lets the scientist spend all his time on problem B, the supervisor would have doubts that he was performing his supervisory role properly, and, in addition, he might find himself under pressure from higher management people who also thought problem A was more advantageous to the company.

The supervisor gets out of his dilemma by hedging. He asks the scientist to go to work on problem A, but permits him to devote 10 percent of his time to work on problem B. This strategy provides some resolution of an interpersonal conflict. The scientist cannot so readily accuse his superior of thwarting him. Besides, if the scientist's work on problem B later turned up some very promising leads, the supervisor can claim some credit for sponsoring problem B and can later allow the scientist to devote increasing amounts of time to it.

While the three compromises tend to reduce the level of interpersonal conflict, we may question whether they make any positive contribution to the creativity of the scientist. We need to distinguish between methods of protecting the supervisor's position and means of stimulating scientific creativity.

With the exceptional performer, the supervisor just abdicates from his role as supervisor.

Selling the problem to the subordinate can also be regarded as a means of reducing interpersonal tensions without coming to grips with the creativity problem. Supervisors know that scientists do not like to be told what to do. Instead of telling the scientist, "You will now work on problem A," the supervisor prefers to use a manipulative approach. He tells the scientist something like this:

> I have run across some very interesting material on problem A. I have an idea that you can make a really important contribution on this problem. Why don't you take this material along with you? Look it over and think about it. When you're ready, let me know if you would like to work on it.

This approach is known in management as "making the worker feel he is participating." The scientist is then supposed to make his own independent decision that he wants to do what management wants him to do.

This approach probably fools few scientists into thinking that they are really making their own decisions. Even the greenest scientist will recognize that he is expected to find problem A most interesting and decide to work on problem A. He knows that if he reports back to his superior that he does not care to work on problem A, this will create a most awkward situation for himself and his supervisor. On the other hand, he is likely to agree to go along with the charade because his supervisor is going through the motions of respecting his scientific integrity and independence. Nevertheless, this approach seems more likely to increase the scientist's dependence upon his superior than increase his creativity.

Hedging should also be looked upon as a human relations gimmick—a way of smoothing interpersonal relations without resolving the underlying problem. While the scientist is free to spend 10 percent of his time on a project of his own choice, there is a serious question as to whether this concession of the superior is more symbolic than real. A study by Gordon[4] indicates that on those projects judged most creative by a panel of experts in the field of research in question, the investigator spent 50 percent or more of his time on the given project. This research conclusion is supported by the testimony of scientists themselves. They say that they cannot readily shift from one problem to another. When you are really involved in a problem, you devote not only your direct working time to it. You find yourself reflecting on the problem at times away from the job, and sometimes the best insights come outside of the job situation itself—but only in relation to problems on which the investigator has been deeply immersed while on the job. The creative mind cannot be switched from one problem to another without a loss of momentum. By the time that the scientist has his ideas reorganized and is ready to make progress on his own problem, the four hours a week he may devote to it will have largely gone by, and he must wait another week to crank himself up and start again on that problem. In most cases, therefore, the decision of a supervisor to allow a scientist to spend 10 percent of his time on a project of his own choice is a way of letting that project die on the vine without the supervisor taking the blame for killing it.

Differences between lab and shop

This analysis suggests that tinkering with an administrative strategy that has grown up out of production and military organizations will not lead us to good solutions of the problems of administration of research laboratories. If we are to work out a new approach, it is well to begin by recognizing explicitly some of the major differences between a production organization and a research laboratory.

1. *Production of objects or of ideas?* The scientific laboratory does not produce physical objects. Its basic product is ideas. Only as these ideas pass through stages of development, pilot operation, and production, do they become transformed into physical objects. It seems reasonable to suppose that the management of ideas would call for a different administrative strategy than that which can be used for the management of physical production.

---

[4] Gerald Gordon, "A Paradox of Research Administration," *Proceedings of the 20th National Conference on the Administration of Research*. Also in Reprint Series (No. 224), New York State School of Industrial and Labor Relations.

2. *Locus of knowledge.* In a production organization, it has been traditional to assume that knowledge of production problems and processes increases for several levels as we go up from workers into middle management. It is further assumed that higher management people, while lacking detailed knowledge of production problems and processes, can interpret the various types of reports they receive so as to understand what is going on in production. While this traditional approach tends to ignore the detailed experiential knowledge workers have and management people lack, and is also inclined to overlook the serious problems of communication that arise between organizational levels, nevertheless, the assumptions of management are sufficiently close to reality so as to make for a viable system of production.

The situation is completely different in the research laboratory. There both theoretical and detailed operating knowledge are heavily concentrated at the level of the scientist at the work bench. The higher up we go from the work bench, the less well equipped people tend to be to understand and evaluate the work of the scientist.

3. *Distribution of education.* In the production organization, there tends to be a high degree of correlation between average level of formal education and position in the organizational hierarchy, at least when we consider the range of positions from worker up to plant manager. Even as workers complain that their more highly educated superiors are not really as smart as they think they are and lack the worker's understanding of his job situation, they recognize the high prestige value of education in our society. As status levels correspond roughly to educational differences, there is likely to be a greater tendency to accept the legitimacy of the leadership exercised by higher status people.

In the scientific research laboratory, the situation is reversed. All of the men holding professional positions as scientists will have at least college degrees and many of them will have master's degrees and doctorates. Comparing bottom with higher levels in the research laboratory, we are likely to find that the scientists at the bench are at least equal to their organization superiors in years of formal education and in advanced degrees, and they may be somewhat above them in these respects. As we compare the scientist at the bench and the research laboratory with higher management outside of the laboratory, we will generally find the scientist superior both in years of formal education and in the percentage holding advanced degrees. Organizational superiors therefore cannot find support in their educational superiority for their positions in administration.

4. *Degree of predictability of outcomes.* In production, outcomes in terms of physical products are highly predictable. While we often hear a manager complaining that his expectations as to the quantity or quality of the product have not been met, we find in practice that these deviations from expectations in performance tend to fall in a fairly narrow range. To be sure, when a product is first going into production, the plant manager

may budget 10,000 units for the first month and find that unanticipated difficulties have held production down to 5,000. As experience is gained on the new product, we can generally expect that the discrepancy between projected performance and actual performance will be steadily narrowed. Some months later, if we find the manager worried about this discrepancy, we may find that whereas he budgeted for 20,000 units, 19,000 were produced.

When predictability is at this high level, it becomes possible to work out detailed specifications as to who should do what, where, when, and with whom. Whether it is practical for management to aim at a maximum of specification or programming of activity is another question. Our point here is simply that the level of predictability in the activity is sufficiently high so that detailed specification of procedures is possible.

The scientific laboratory is characterized by its extremely low level of predictability of outcomes. A scientist may be able to predict with a reasonable degree of accuracy how long it will take him to perform experiment A. He cannot predict with a high degree of confidence that experiment A will be successful. All he can say is that experiment A seems the most promising approach to the solution of his problem that he has yet devised. If experiment A does indeed turn out as he hoped, he is then in a position to make a reasonably accurate prediction of how long it will take him to test the next step in his plan. On the other hand, if experiment A proves unsuccessful, he may have to try experiments B, C, D, E, and so on, until he arrives at an experiment that works. Under these circumstances, even an estimate of the time to be taken for completion of the first successful experiment in the program can be little more than guesswork.

We have illustrated the uncertainties in terms of time. They can equally well be expressed in other terms. Let us say that the scientist is considering experiments A and B. He thinks experiment A is somewhat more likely than B to yield the desired outcome, but experiment A also requires much more elaborate and expensive equipment and a larger complement of personnel. Should he decide to save time and money by trying experiment B first? In that case, if experiment B fails, he will have lost time and money that might have been put into getting experiment A underway.

Unpredictability of outcomes faces the supervisor with problems quite different from those encountered in production. How do you supervise a man when he is not at all sure what he should do and you are even less sure?

5. *Reference groups.* This is the problem already discussed regarding company versus professional identification—locals versus cosmopolitans. While the commitment of no employees to the organization should be taken for granted, management can assume, in general, that employees above the white-collar level will want to identify with the organization.

There may be problems regarding commitment to parts of the organization at the expense of other parts: salesmen being committed to the sales department and antagonistic to production, production men committed to the production department and antagonistic to sales, and so on. However, these are commitments that are all inside the total organization. The scientist faces a real problem of dual loyalties. If he is asked or ordered to do things that do not fit the role of scientist, as it is conceived by himself and his professional colleagues outside of the company, he experiences a conflict within himself that will at least lead to friction between himself and his organizational superiors and may even lead to him leaving the company.

6. *Replaceability of personnel.* In production, the men at the work bench are for the most part unskilled or semiskilled workers. If labor turnover at this level is high, management is forced to recognize a serious problem. If one or a few workers quit from time to time, they can easily be replaced without serious cost to the organization.

This is not the case with research scientists. In an economy, which is increasingly based upon technical and scientific advance, the demand for scientists in industry tends to outrun the supply. Many companies are constantly in the position of having unfilled positions for scientists, and the recruiting of scientists is becoming a year round activity to which companies make large commitments of money and the time of their own staff people.

Years ago, there was such a gap between university salaries and those paid by industry for professional people that management was able to offer the professor or potential professor substantial financial inducements. In the last 20 years, with the population explosion in higher education, the demand for professors in universities has tended to make university salaries competitive to those in industry.

One effect of this change is shown in the narrowing differential in industry between the starting salaries offered for scientists and those given to scientists with some years of experience in the organization. In order to remain competitive with other companies and with universities, many companies have raised their starting salaries much more than they have the salaries for more experienced people. This enables the company to continue to recruit scientists with attractive starting salaries, but it creates felt inequities between starting scientists and experienced scientists as the differential between them has been sharply reduced.

It is now not at all clear that a scientists who is finishing his university education will do better financially if he takes an industrial research position in preference to a university position. In most companies, it is assumed that he gives full time to the company and that therefore his salary represents his total earnings. Most universities have a policy that a professor may devote approximately one day a week to outside activities, for which he may receive compensation. As he begins to establish his reputation, the professor may be offered honoraria for giving lectures away from his home campus. He may also work as a consultant to industry, getting several hundred dollars a day and expenses. The professor may also write books—and that on time devoted to his regular university duties. While a scholarly book will yield him little, a textbook for an introductory course can yield large sums of money. If the book catches on and is adopted by a number of colleges and universities, by revising the text every few years to put out new editions, he can keep that gold mine producing indefinitely. Furthermore, as the college population continues to increase, the textbook market becomes ever more lucrative.

It is not our purpose to determine whether the average physicist or chemist stands to make more money in the university or in industry. We are simply noting that the financial advantage of an industrial career is no longer so clear-cut as it was once assumed to be.

In today's market situation, the individual scientist has considerable bargaining power in dealing with company management. If he has been able to maintain contacts with his university colleagues and has made a respectable record in scientific publications, the scientist in industry may readily move into a university position. To be sure, there will be wide individual differences in bargaining power. The company scientist who has been with the firm for a number of years, who has not maintained close academic ties, and who has not made much of a publication record, is in a very poor position for seeking university employment. On the other hand, the creativity of the research laboratory might suffer much less from the loss of this man than it would from the loss of one who had maintained the university connections and publication record that would give him much more freedom to leave.

The situation of dual loyalties, combined with a highly competitive market for scientists, undermines the control that company administrators can exercise over scientists.

The supervisor as lab group representative

In thinking of the role of the supervisor, we are likely to concentrate on his relations with subordinates, giving little attention to his interactions and activities with superiors and with those on his same level. Richard Ritti suggests that we should think of the supervisor as the representative before management of his laboratory group. He writes: [5]

From my experience, I would guess that the supervisor or manager in a research laboratory spends as much time representing his group to others in the organization as he does in dealing with his own group. That is, lobbying for funds, manpower or a desirable research mission is a crucial part of the research management process. This takes place at various levels of research

---

[5] Personal letter, April 12, 1967.

management. Research proposals collected from one's own scientists must be sold up through the organization. Successful selling of these projects is probably the most important factor that I can identify in maintaining high morale among researchers.

This represents another contrast between the laboratory and the production supervisors. While the production supervisor is expected to speak up for his men, this speaking up is likely to occur primarily in *response* to changes initiated from above. He has little to say—and expects to have little to say—regarding what products are to be made in his department. These basic decisions are handed down to him from above. Since laboratory work cannot be programmed from higher levels, the lab supervisor or manager has the opportunity to try to get from higher management the kind of assignments that he and his men want to work on. Perhaps *obligation* would be a better word than *opportunity* because the scientists urge their supervisor to "sell" their favorite projects up the line, and they are disappointed in him when he is unsuccessful in this effort. His skill in handling interpersonal relations with his subordinates will not win the supervisor their respect if he is unsuccessful in his efforts to get them projects that offer them interesting and potentially rewarding projects.

A new strategy for supervisor-subordinate relations

Common administrative strategies in the factory have been based upon the exercise of control. If a manager in a scientific laboratory is not to exercise control, what then does he do? It is not enough for the manager to know that the factory strategy will not work. Unless he has a new and different strategy worked out for himself, he will be anxious and uneasy, and he will find himself in conflict with his subordinates.

Research suggests six supervisory functions that contribute to the productivity and creativity of a scientific group. The first two can be simply stated; the others will require more elaboration.

1. *Facilitation.* The supervisor can see to it that the scientist has access to the goods and services and information that he needs in order to do his job well.

2. *Recognition.* The supervisor can help the scientist get recognition for his work by taking an interest in his progress and seeing to it that influential people in the company hear about the scientist's achievements. He can also strive to gain for the scientist the tangible rewards of increased salary and titles that would reflect increased status, even when the scientist chooses to remain at his bench.

3. *Interpretation.* Many good scientists are poor communicators. They may be able to explain their work to fellow scientists, but they have difficulties in making effective and understandable presentations to laymen. If higher management, beyond the laboratory, were to judge scientific talent in terms of the presentations they received from individual

scientists, they would tend to favor the mediocre-scientist-good-communicator over the good-scientist-poor-communicator. Of course, there are men who are both good scientists and good communicators, and these man have less need of the interpretive help of another person. For scientists who lack these communication skills, the supervisor can play highly important functions. He can himself interpret to management people the meaning and importance of the scientist's work. Through questioning the scientist, suggesting points that need further explanation, and showing how the basic idea can be presented without being overburdened with technical detail, the supervisor can help the scientist to talk and write more effectively about his work. In fact, we suspect that such discussions between supervisor and scientist can be helpful even to the good communicator. The scientist who becomes immersed in his own work inevitably tends to neglect points he takes for granted yet which must be expressed if his exposition is to be understandable and convincing to others. The supervisor, having more detachment from the project, can more readily spot these missing elements.

4. *Composition of work teams.* Probably most projects in industrial scientific laboratories involve two or more individuals working together. The performance of the group will depend in large measure upon the way in which the members work together. If the supervisor has responsibility for the composition of work teams, his skill in matching people will be an important influence on the performance of the teams.

Matched in terms of what? We can think of three criteria: specialties, "personality" and cognitive style.

a) If the problem requires knowledge and skills from chemistry and physics, then it is obvious that the team should include at least one physicist and one chemist. For some problems the optimum specialty mix will not be so obvious, but on the whole, this criterion will be most apparent to the supervisor and most readily applied by him.

b) We put "personality" in quotes to indicate that we are not thinking of a fit among individuals that is determined by psychological testing. Everyone recognizes that some individuals "get along well" together and others do not, but some people are much more skillful than others in judging which individuals will form effective teams.

While extreme interpersonal conflict is clearly to be avoided, it does not necessarily follow that the other end of the continuum, complete harmony, is optimum for team performance. It is comfortable for individuals to feel that they have "much in common," but there is some evidence to suggest that too smooth a relationship may result in suppressing differences of opinion that might lead to more creative solutions.[6]

c) We all recognize, at least implicitly, differences in "cognitive

---

[6] Donald A. Pelz and Frank M. Andrews, *Scientists in Organizations: Productive Climates for Research and Development* (New York: John Wiley & Sons, 1966), pp. 140–41.

style." We may even recognize that IQ scores do not tell us all there is to know about intelligence: that two individuals with similar scores may do their thinking in quite different ways. We assume that these differences in "cognitive style" have a bearing upon the performance of scientists.

This assumption leads us to no practical conclusions unless we can devise reasonably objective methods for the identification of cognitive styles. The work of Gerald Gordon[7] suggests that such identification is now possible. It will not be necessary to focus attention upon the procedures used in this identification in order to consider the implications of Gordon's categories for supervisory performance.

Gordon divided his research subjects into four analytic groups: *problem solvers*, *problem recognizers*, *integrators*, and *technicians*.

Problem solvers are those who, when they have the nature of the problem defined for them, are able to work effectively toward solving the problem. They are not nearly so effective in defining problems for themselves.

Problem recognizers are good at recognizing and defining the nature of problems. They are not nearly so effective in carrying through the detailed procedures necessary to solve the problem.

Integrators are highly skilled both at recognizing and solving problems.

Technicians are ineffective at either recognizing or solving problems. They can do an adequate job only when other people recognize problems for them and work out the problem-solving strategy that they are to follow. (We should not assume that Gordon's use of the term is equivalent to the social category of those who have the title of "technician." Probably most people with this title would fall into Gordon's category of *technicians*, but there may be some who can function as *problem solvers*, perhaps fewer who have the capacity of *problem recognizers*, and there may even be a few who, if given the opportunity, could function as *integrators*. Similarly, while most of those classified as "scientists" should fall in the first three categories, there will always be some who can function only as *technicians*.)

Efficient scientific work requires both problem recognizing and problem solving activities. Thus neither a work team made up exclusively of *problem solvers* nor one made up exclusively of *problem recognizers* can be expected to function satisfactorily. The optimum team will be one containing a mix of the two cognitive styles.

This categorization suggests what cognitive styles are required to make a good scientific supervisor. Clearly if the individual's cognitive style is that of *problem solver* or *technician*, he will have trouble providing effective leadership to a group of scientists. His difficulties will become particularly apparent when his group bogs down in argumentation over how to diagnose the essential features of the problem.

---

[7] Gordon, *op. cit.*

At least in terms of cognitive style, the *integrator* is clearly well qualified for scientific group leadership. However, there seems no inherent reason for believing that the *problem recognizer* will be less effective as a scientific supervisor than the *integrator*. In most scientific groups, it is safe to assume that *problem solvers* will be present, whereas *problem recognizers* are likely to be in much shorter supply. If the *problem recognizer*, as supervisor, can help his group to diagnose the nature of the problem, he can usually assume that group members will be able to devise appropriate problem solving procedures.

Can the scientific supervisor use this conceptual scheme to help him in the composition of efficient work teams? Probably we are far from the point where management will apply psychological tests to sort people out in cognitive styles. Nevertheless, if the supervisor keeps this framework in mind, he may be able to sort out his people in such categories on the basis of his own observations of their work. In fact, we suspect that some scientific administrators even now think in these terms, although they use other terminology.

5. Mediation and arbitration. Even if the supervisor has his work teams optimally matched, there will occasionally arise disagreements that cannot be resolved within a team. What does the supervisor do then? What has been said about the reluctance of scientists to take orders suggests that the skillful supervisor will rely more upon mediation than upon arbitration. That is, he will listen to the contending parties and try to help them work through to an agreement that is mutually acceptable. This may not be simply a matter of arriving at a compromise which leaves the contending parties equally dissatisfied. A skillful mediator can sometimes facilitate a solution that both parties will find more acceptable than the ones they were arguing for.

But let us not assume that mediation can always be successful. There will be times when it is necessary for the supervisor to arbitrate the differences—to make the decision himself. There may also occasionally be cases where, in the course of his mediation efforts, the supervisor becomes convinced that the mutually agreeable solution that may be within reach is not the best solution from a technical, scientific standpoint. Here he faces an unavoidable risk. If the supervisor follows through to the mediated solution, he contributes to the harmony of the work team—in the immediate situation. But if later some of the team members become convinced that the agreed upon decision was not scientifically productive, then recriminations may break out, and the supervisor's standing with his subordinates will suffer. If the supervisor imposes his own decision, he may stir some resentment at the time. The seriousness of these resentments depends in part upon subsequent events. If the decision made turns out to be scientifically fruitful, as the members judge results, the supervisor can expect the personal resentments to subside and his own standing with his subordinates to rise in the process. The worst outcome for the supervisor, of course, is one in which his imposed solution turns out to be fruitless. In that case, he will suffer a maximum loss in personal resentments and in his own standing with the group.

To express the supervisor's dilemma in more general terms, we may say that he plays both a *task* and a *social-emotional* leadership role. In many situations, he can play both leadership roles at the same time, and those minimum risk cases are most satisfying to most leaders at most times. There will nevertheless be some occasions when what he would like to do in his *social-emotional* role conflicts with what he thinks he ought to do in his *task* role. He then faces unavoidable risks, for neither course of action is an entirely safe one.

Does this type of situation simply represent the dilemma faced by the supervisor of any type of work? Not entirely. The factory foreman functions in a much more predictable environment. He may have more relevant experience with similar problems than his subordinates, and there is a good probability that what was done in some past situation will provide a useful precedent for reaching a technical decision. Even if he turns out to be wrong, his subordinates are not likely to question his right to make the decision—though a negative outcome will have some adverse effect upon his standing with them.

The scientific supervisor functions in a much higher risk situation. He is likely to know less about the problem in dispute than his subordinates. In research, the precedents of past solutions are more difficult to identify and less likely to serve as useful guides to decisions. Furthermore, the scientific supervisor can more clearly be proven wrong. In the factory, few decisions the foreman makes will turn out to be so obviously wrong as to be so recognized by everyone concerned. While some workers may feel that a different course of action would have yielded better results, if production continues to move in a minimally acceptable fashion, no one can really prove the foreman wrong. In the research laboratory, all concerned, including the supervisor, may eventually have to acknowledge that the supervisor's decision did not lead to a solution of the scientific problem.

This leads us to conclude that a scientific supervisor must have a greater capacity for coping with risk and uncertainty than supervisors in other types of work.

6. *Stimulation of ideas.* In the light of our discussion so far, this seems like a paradoxical recommendation. If the scientist indeed knows more about his particular problem than does his supervisor, as is generally the case, how can the supervisor contribute to the scientist's ideas?

While the scientist has the advantage of deep immersion in his problem, the supervisor may have the advantage of a broader perspective, and he has less personal investment in any particular strategy for solving the problem. The scientist may sometimes find that his deep immersion in a problem tends to lead him down a blind alley, while closing off his mind to alternative intellectual pathways. The supervisor may help the scientist to gain greater perspective on his problem and to think more flexibly about it through expressing interest in the problem, and raising questions about what new approaches might be worth considering. If the supervisor makes it clear that he is not trying to tell the scientist what to do and is only trying to help him think through the problem more effectively, the supervisor may make a real contribution to scientific creativity. The supervisor may indeed seldom suggest what turns out to be the best solution to the given scientific problem and yet, even as the scientist explains why the approach proposed by the supervisor will not work, the scientist may find in the discussion process the stimulus to work out a modification that gets him onto the right track.

A still more productive approach to the stimulation of creativity is provided by group situations. Here certain skillful scientific administrators have brought some of the culture of the university into the industrial laboratory. A good university department is alive with discussions of the work in progress. On a more or less regular basis there are colloquia in which members of the department or investigators from outside the university are invited to present reports on experiments and developments in theory. Fellow faculty members are not passive listeners at such presentations. They are often free with criticisms and suggestions, pointing out weak points in the experimental design or in the theoretical argument, suggesting modifications in procedures or next steps that should be taken. When this kind of presentation and discussion is well carried out, it can be an exciting intellectual experience both for presenter and other participants in the discussion.

The scientific discussion does not end with the close of the meeting. In a sense the group meetings simply serve to give all participants background information about the work that is going on and the challenging problems that are being faced. Participants carry on from the meeting in pairs, threesomes, and occasionally larger groups in offices, corridors, over cups of coffee, and at lunch.

It is this style of scientific and administrative leadership that seems to be rarely exercised in industry today. In fact, we find few industrial research administrators who are even aware of this possibility.

Administrators have generally learned that scientists resent being told what to do. It also seems to be a principle of conventional wisdom that ideas are created by individuals and not by groups. From these two general conclusions, some research administrators construct an image of the ideal situation from the standpoint of the scientist. That situation is one in which he is left alone to do whatever he wants to do.

One industrial research administrator in a large laboratory sought to practice this philosophy. When he found nevertheless that his scientific laboratories were not as creative as he had hoped they would be and was looking for an explanation for the disappointing performance, he was mystified to hear from a scientist, "We have communication problems." He thought to himself, "How can they have communications problems? We let them alone and they can communicate in any way that they want to."

The problem is that scientific creativity is not purely an individual phenomenon, even when a man is working alone on his particular project. There are very few scientific geniuses who are so self-sufficient that they can provide themselves all the stimulation they need and perform at optimum levels in social isolation. While we are accustomed to thinking that it is the individual and not the group that *gets* an idea, the individual is not a self-generating-and-evaluating idea machine. The quantity and quality of the ideas an individual produces will depend to a large extent upon his interactions with men working in his own or related fields. Most scientists will readily acknowledge that they themselves are more creative when they are working in a "stimulating atmosphere" than when such stimulation is lacking. The individual scientist can contribute to this stimulating atmosphere but he cannot create it himself. The scientific supervisor or administrator is in a much more strategic position to create the environment that will maximize the creativity potential in the laboratory scientist. This he can do by bringing together scientists with complementary interests and by encouraging a pattern of free discussion, information sharing, and argumentation over scientific work.

Why are the scientists themselves unlikely to create this environment without administrative leadership? Let us examine the hypothetical cases of scientists Jones and Smith. They are working in different fields whose interrelations are not obvious but which would be discovered if the two sat down to talk about their problems. Jones and Smith know each other socially and each has some respect for the intellectual ability of the other. Each one even has the notion that it would be helpful for him to be able to consult the other fellow about the problem he is working on—but still they do not get together. Why not?

There seem to be two main obstacles in the way of setting up the kind of communication that would be mutually productive. On complicated scientific problems, useful advice is not to be had simply by asking for it. Before Jones can get any valuable reactions from Smith, Jones may have to spend an hour to provide Smith with the background of the problem and a description of the various strategies he has tried on it. Only after that investment of time, will Smith be in a position to be helpful. Even then, if he responds with something off the top of his head, this may serve to meet the norms of politeness more than to contribute to scientific progress. Smith may need some time to think about the problem, and it is not always easy to think while Jones is sitting there waiting for some helpful advice. Besides, Jones recognizes that Smith has his own work to do. What right has he to take an hour of Smith's time in order to get help on his own problem?

The second obstacle is one so well explored by Peter Blau[8] in his studies of consulting relationships and relative status. If Jones goes to Smith to ask for advice, he is implying by his action that Smith occupies a superior prestige position compared to himself. He is naturally hesitant to accept this implied subordination.

On the other hand, suppose Smith, from casual remarks, picks up an idea of what Jones is working on and recognizes the point at which Jones is stuck. Smith has an idea that he thinks might get Jones unstuck. Should he approach Jones and offer him this new idea? But perhaps Jones will resent his intrusion or will think that Smith is just trying to advertise his superior competence. At the level of the individual, there are quite natural inhibitions against asking for or volunteering advice.

If the scientific administrator establishes a pattern of group meetings and promotes a free and lively exchange of ideas, then he creates the setting within which individuals can help each other and stimulate each other informally.

Now, after Jones has presented a report on his project to a meeting of scientific peers, he does not have to take the initiative in seeking out Smith and giving him a one-hour briefing on the nature of the problem. As they meet over a cup of coffee he can say, "Joe, you raised a question in our meeting the other day, and I confess at the time I didn't see the point of it, but later I got to thinking that you might be on to something that I should consider more seriously. Can you tell me more about what you have in mind?"

Or Smith can take the initiative in dropping into Jones's office to say, "You remember that point in your presentation where you came up with apparently contradictory results? I have been mulling that one over, and it suddenly occurred to me that this might be the explanation. . . ."

Such a stimulating atmosphere cannot be established by management authority. It can be created by a skillful scientific administrator—providing he recognizes that this is a possible function of an administrator. It is the most important contribution that he can make to the organization.

Parallel conclusions emerged out of the Pelz-Andrews study. They found a positive correlation between frequency of interaction with colleagues and scientific performance.[9] In the preceding paragraphs, we have sought to indicate how these interactions may be structured.

Little man versus big company

Up to this point, we have been discussing the management of scientific research in large companies. This is where the bulk of industrial research activity goes on, and yet there are those who wonder whether the lone

---

[8] Peter Blau, *The Dynamics of Bureaucracy* (Chicago: The University of Chicago Press, 1955).

[9] Pelz and Andrew, *op. cit.*, pp. 51–2.

inventor is not more likely to come up with important innovations than is the large company research laboratory. In fact, this conclusion has even been endorsed by a panel of scientific administrators from big business. They report:[10]

. . . independent inventors and small firms are responsible for an important part of our inventive progress, a larger percentage than their relatively small investment in R & D would suggest.

How can this be? While we have no data that would support a global answer to such a question, we may venture some guesses.

So far in this chapter we have made no distinction between scientific creativity and productivity—a distinction which may be crucial to the problem of this section. Productivity refers simply to the amount of work that gets done per man-hour or other standard of working time. Creativity in scientific research refers to the development of valuable *new* ideas. While it is not easy to measure scientific productivity, and creativity presents even more serious measurement problems, we are here concerned with the distinction itself rather than with the methods of measurement.

Pelz and Andrews[11] report that in industrial laboratories creativity and productivity do not necessarily go together. While every scientific administrator will pay lip service to the importance of creativity, actually in many companies conditions are such as to discourage creativity.

The layman may have a glamorous picture of all scientists, seeing each man at the very frontiers of knowledge, plunging into the unknown. Actually the bulk of scientific work involves the systematic working out of problems along previously established pathways. While the outcomes of such work are not as predictable as factory production schedules, the laboratory which channels its work along these established pathways may achieve a good productivity record.

Creativity—the truly innovative idea—involves a sharp departure from established pathways. The scientist is really striking out into the unknown, where the risks of failure are exceedingly high and the time and money required to make success possible are unpredictable. Given these hazards in the creative leap into the unknown, many company laboratories naturally incline toward the surer payoffs that come from the established pathways. In such laboratories, the truly creative individual is not likely to be highly productive. If he remains on the job at all, he is likely to be so frustrated by his inability to pursue his new ideas as not to pull his weight in "getting the job done," as defined by his company superiors.

The lone inventor may face enormous problems in getting the resources needed to back his work. If he can solve that problem, he faces no one who can tell him not to pursue his idea.

---

[10] "Is the Little Man More Inventive?" *Business Week*, March 4, 1967. I am indebted to Peter Weissenberg for drawing this article to my attention.

[11] Pelz and Andrews, *op. cit.* pp. 171–2.

Such differences may also account for the common failure of large companies to recognize the value of new ideas developed outside of their own organizations. The Polaroid Land camera and the Xerography process are among the most spectacular examples of a rather common phenomenon: the development of an idea outside the big company, the offering of that idea to the big company, the rejection of the offer, and the subsequent successful exploitation of the invention by the inventor or by a small company.

In the research and development departments of some large companies, one often encounters the initials "N.I.H."—meaning "not invented here." The initials are usually applied to inventions produced within the company, but by some rival department. The initials carry the implication, "Since it was not invented in our department, it can't be any good."

While this attitude may be denounced as narrow minded prejudice, it is actually a natural outcome of the way many company research laboratories operate. The budget of each department tends to rise or fall according to its apparent success in producing product or process ideas that promise to contribute to company profits. The scientist naturally gets identified with his own work and that of his department. It can hardly be expected that a man in this position will say that some outside individual or group has produced something of such value that the company's resources should be diverted to the exploitation of the imported idea at the expense of the work of his own department. If the higher level executives are too receptive to ideas coming from outside of their organization, they too may get into difficulties in the allocation of resources between established groups and new groups that need to be developed to exploit the imported idea.

Resources in time, money, and physical facilities are always limited. Thus the management decision to push one line of research necessarily involves sidetracking or reducing support for other lines. The potentially imported project must compete with internal projects in which company people already have made substantial investments. In this context, it is hardly surprising that proposals for the importation of projects so often fail to get what an uncommitted observer would consider a fair and objective evaluation.

Summary and conclusions

In the case of most large companies, research departments have been grafted onto long established production and sales organizations. Experience and research have demonstrated that research laboratories in organizations do not function well when managed according to models evolved for production organizations.

While some scientists readily accept the goals of the business organization as their own, many remain oriented toward general scientific goals that call for freedom in selecting problems and selection in terms of the probabilities of adding to scientific knowledge, independent of potential profitability. The contrast here is the well known one of *locals* versus *cosmopolitans*. The choice between science and administration imposes a further strain upon the scientist. If the main channel to success in an industrial research laboratory is through going into administration, this means abandonment of scientific work.

The choice of the problem to be worked on is often a key issue between scientists and their supervisors. The means often used to resolve the issue may smooth over interpersonal relations, yet reduce the independence and creativity of the scientists.

One of the principal responsibilities of the manager of a group of scientists is that of "selling" their ideas to higher management so as to get for the department interesting projects and the resources and facilities needed. In relation to his subordinates, the good supervisor sees to it not only that they get what they need in facilities and funds to do their work, but also that the individual scientists gain recognition inside the company and outside it for doing valuable work. The supervisor interprets the work of his scientists to others outside of the laboratory. He seeks to provide the kind of "mix" of abilities and personalities that will lead to effective performance. He mediates and, if necessary, arbitrates disputes among his scientists. Finally, the supervisor seeks to create a stimulating atmosphere by so structuring the interactions and activities of the scientists that useful information is readily exchanged and helpful criticisms and suggestions are offered.

We have noted that in the race for innovativeness the single inventor or small company still often beat the large organization, which appears to have overwhelming advantages in resources and trained manpower. As a partial explanation to this phenomenon, we emphasized the difference between productivity and creativity. We suggested that many large companies so operate their laboratories so as to maximize productivity and minimize creativity.

While emphasizing the differences between laboratory and shop, we should note how the laboratory situation reinforces the theoretical framework we have been presenting. We have noted research findings indicating that the improvement of scientific performance depends upon reorganization of the interactions of the scientists. In the scientific laboratory we also find another case where the nature of the task being performed by the worker tends to shape the role to be played by the supervisor.

Let us conclude with a dilemma from our transactional analysis. In terms of potential positive and negative exchanges, the individual scientist is in a far stronger position than the unskilled or semiskilled worker: he can either reward or punish management more heavily. This tends to lead management to be more receptive to his interests—for example, to provide him with opportunities to publish and to attend scientific meetings. But these activities enable the scientist to increase his perceived value among his scientific colleagues outside of the company. This puts him in the position where he can make the threat to leave the company more credible, since management knows he can get a good position elsewhere. In other words, management's policies have enabled the scientist to increase his bargaining power with management. Thus "doing the right thing by the scientists" does not produce a docile body of scientists. Management is constantly engaged in transactions to keep the scientists within the company and happy enough to do work rewarding to the company.

References

Marcson, Simon. *The Scientist in Industry.* New York: Harper & Bros., 1960. A useful series of case studies.

Pelz, Donald A., and Andrews, Frank M. *Scientists in Industry: Productive Climates for Research and Development.* New York: John Wiley & Sons, 1966. Survey research findings on a large number of scientists and engineers in research organizations.

Discussion questions

1. You are called in as a consultant to the president of a large company. He believes his own research organization is not sufficiently receptive to outside ideas. He is afraid this lack of receptivity may lead his company to overlook important commercial possibilities such as Xerography and the Polaroid Land camera. What would you recommend?

2. Find yourself a scientist who has done research both within a university and within industry. Interview him for the purpose of making an analysis of the similarities and differences in the organization and administration of scientific work and in the impact laboratory management had upon his job satisfaction, creativity, and productivity. (Of course, you will not expect to draw any firm conclusions based upon one individual. Use the exercise to put in case form some of the considerations discussed in this chapter—and also important ones we may have overlooked. If you do not locate a scientist who has worked in both worlds, interview your subject about the picture he has of the world he is not in, based upon what he has heard from friends and associates.)

27. The development process

MOVING FROM RESEARCH to development, we take a further step along the work flow from invention to marketing. In terms of the commitment of resources, we still have not moved very far from the starting point. A recent study[1] of the distribution of innovation costs allocates no more than 10 percent to research and development combined. The costs were allocated in the following way:

Distribution of Innovation Costs

Research and development............ 5 to 10%
Product engineering design.............10 to 20
Manufacturing engineering tooling......40 to 60
Manufacturing start-up................ 5 to 15
Market start-up........................10 to 25

We shall not be able to examine these later stages through research findings, yet the rough cost allocations may help to place our problems in context. Since most of the costs of innovation arise after a project leaves the development stage, management naturally seeks to focus on research and development some of the concerns of production engineering, manufacturing, and sales. People in development are placed squarely in between the concerns of what is technically and scientifically possible and what is considered practical from the standpoint of engineering, production, and marketing. How these competing concerns are brought to bear in development will strongly influence the effectiveness of the development department.

We are dealing with problems of lateral coordination. The complete work flow can be visualized as involving a series of steps beginning with basic research and proceeding through applied research, development, product engineering design and manufacturing engineering tooling, pilot operation, production, and marketing. In our subsequent discussion, we

---

[1] *Technological Innovation: Its Environment and Management*, U.S. Department of Commerce, Jan., 1967.

will not attempt to draw a sharp line between development and the various engineering groups, for the same problems of lateral coordination are involved at each step in the work flow.

Complex as it is, this picture is oversimplified in one important aspect. We should not visualize one work group at each stage relating itself to the preceding and following group. At each stage two or more units may need to bring their work together before the process can move on to the next stage. For example, the development of a new data processing machine involves work in electronics, mechanical engineering, and in programming, before the unit can be put together for a pilot operation.

One picture needs to be modified in another respect also. We should not assume that every new product or process begins in basic research and moves successively through the other stages indicated. Relatively few innovations go through all these stages. Many begin in applied research, where the investigators are simply seeking to test known scientific principles in a new problem situation. Many more innovations begin in development itself, where the engineers are building on past experience, rather than depending upon research. This may be better understood later as we examine the nature of engineering activity.

The race to develop radar

The importance of coordination and communication along a process of research and development is well illustrated by the race between Britain and Germany for the development of radar in World War II.[2]

In Britain very close contact was established at the outset between the personnel of the Telecommunications Research Establishment (TRE) and serving officers in the Royal Air Force and officials in the Air Ministry. This system was consolidated at an early stage by the so-called "Sunday Soviets" instituted by the then Superintendent of TRE. A "Sunday Soviet" was an open meeting held every Sunday in the Superintendent's room to which were invited all senior Air Ministry officials and all Air Staff Officers. The importance of the occasion as a main channel of communication was soon recognized by the Ministry and the Royal Air Force, and every Sunday brought its "galaxy of everybody from Air Marshals down." Differences in rank were obscured or ignored. A particular type of equipment or an operational problem would be selected, and the division leaders and group leaders on the TRE side would be there to discuss it. There was thus a very intimate, personal connexion between the people who had the operational knowledge and the problems to face, who saw their men getting shot down, and who themselves flew and got shot down, on the one hand, and on the other, the people who worked in TRE and who had an intimate knowledge of the scientific techniques and their scope. The result of this was that the laboratory workers got an immediate emotional as well as intellectual appre-

---

[2] Tom Burns and G. M. Stalker, *The Management of Innovation* (London: Tavistock Publications, 1961), pp. 440–42.

ciation of the pressing operational difficulties, needs, and problems which they could not have acquired by any other means. Equally important, the operational people began to acquire notions of the potentialities of the techniques which they could never have had except through meeting the people who had originated them. The rapid application of the techniques to the problems which did take place was made possible by this intimate joining of operational needs with technical possibilities in an immediate, personal, informal way.

In Germany, a great deal of radar development had taken place before the outbreak of war, and some equipment of an advanced type was in quantity production by 1939, but work on development was virtually closed down for a time because it was thought there would be no further need for it. When the Germans did start up again, they established a Plenipotentiary for High Frequency Techniques. This official established a chain of new research institutions. He also introduced a system of logging all the available laboratory effort not only in his own institutions but in all the industrial firms, universities, and technical colleges in the country. He then established contact with an official in the Air Ministry corresponding to himself. The Air Ministry official defined specifications of what the Air Force wanted, and these went to the Plenipotentiary for High Frequency Techniques. The latter would then consult his list and see which laboratories were unemployed, and then post off the specification to one of them. The laboratory would thereupon make an equipment designed without any real knowledge of the operational needs and therefore, in many cases, not meeting them adequately. But much more important than these deficiencies was the fact that most of the possibilities were not realized anyway, because the operational people could not envisage the potentialities of the techniques available, nor could the technical people appreciate the problems of the men who were flying machines.

There is no reason to believe that the Germans were technically inferior either in research or in production methods at the outset of the war, or that they were lacking in resources. The clue to the strong lead which Britain obtained and held seems to lie in the appreciation of the supreme importance of bringing technical knowledge bodily into close contact with the user's requirements.

Downstream and upstream relations

Let us examine the factors affecting communication and performance along the flow of work. To locate our directions, let us speak of downstream as movement along the line from basic research to production and upstream as a movement in the opposite direction. A conceptualization of down and up fits not only for direction of flow but also carries implications in status and influence. There is a tendency for those upstream to regard themselves and their contribution as superior to those farther downstream. At the beginning point, the people in basic (sometimes called "pure" research) tend to regard themselves as the real scientists, whereas the applied research men may be looked upon as tinkerers who do not have the ability to do important scientific work, or who are being seduced away from science by the pressures and rewards of the industrial concern.

In turn, the more applied people tend to regard their "basic" colleagues as wasters of time and money on projects of no practical importance. To what extent do these distinctions represent reality in scientific work? Chester I. Barnard[3] made this comment in criticizing a report of the National Science Foundation which used the dichotomy between basic and applied research:

> As one example, we have Karl Jansky's discovery of radio signals from outer space. Jansky, according to the report, was not engaged in basic research; he merely made a basic discovery. Here the confusion arises from labeling research according to the motives for which it is carried on; there is an element of snobbery involved which ought not to be encouraged. After all, Louis Pasteur made his great contributions to the foundations of bacteriology in trying to find solutions to the practical problems of the French silk and wine industries. The whole discussion demonstrates that the dichotomy between basic and applied research can be overemphasized.

While Barnard's view may represent a more realistic appraisal than that of the "basic" research man who looks down upon his "applied" colleague, the actual distribution of sentiments is a reality that the administrator must deal with, however distorted he may feel these evaluations to be.

As we move downstream from research to development, we move from science to engineering, and here again status differentials are commonly involved. While advanced degrees in engineering are now becoming more prevalent, most engineers have had no more than a four-year college education, whereas the professionals in basic and applied research departments have generally acquired at least a master's degree, and in some organizations nearly all of them will hold doctorates. As we move downstream within engineering from development engineers to industrial engineers, we find another traditional status differential. While most men classified as engineers in industry will have college degrees, there are noncollege men who have moved up from technician or craftsmen into a classification as engineers, and such men are likely to be found in industrial engineering more frequently than in other branches.

As we have noted earlier, the work flow tends to affect influence and status. As you move downstream, you tend to find that the alternatives for action are successively narrowed and that members of the upstream group are seeking to specify what the adjoining downstream group shall do, whereas the downstream groups tend to exercise less influence on upstream behavior.

Communication along the flow of work is affected also by differences

---

[3] Chester I. Barnard in *Scientific American*, November, 1957.

in the subcultural pattern of the various groups of professional specialists and by the spatial location of groups. When a laboratory is built onto an existing factory, these cultural differences suddenly come to the attention of people who may not previously have been aware of them. Workers and management people in the factory have become accustomed to a regular routine of work periods. These are controlled to the minute by time clocks in the factory and often even in white-collar work areas. Even when management people do not punch the time clock, they tend to follow a norm of being very punctual on the job. Within management there tend to develop standardized patterns of dress. People in manufacturing management also have their own style of looking busy at all times.

Scientists are not inclined to follow a strict time schedule. They may turn up at odd hours in the morning and sometimes work far into the night, according to the way the work is going. Some of the scientists may dress in a way that strikes manufacturing management as rather unconventional, and the scientists on the average are not likely to put as much store by frequent hair cuts and highly polished shoes as do the people at high levels of manufacturing management.

Scientists also do not look very businesslike when they work. They may be seen at times casually conversing in halls and offices. They may even be observed at times reading things beyond company memoranda— or even sitting and thinking.

Science is so important in the modern world that it is impossible these days for the manufacturing manager to dismiss scientists as unimportant, and yet many management people regard scientists with ambivalent feelings: although possibly geniuses in their own fields, out of touch with reality and completely impractical.

Some companies have found that they can avoid adverse comments on scientists by other management people and also avoid complaints against the relaxed way of living that is presumed to be typical of the scientist, by building the scientific laboratory apart from the development and manufacturing units, perhaps on the other side of the city, or in a different city altogether. This arrangement is often influenced by city zoning ordinances: laboratories can be built where factories are not permitted. While this solution tends to reduce adverse comments about scientists, the physical separation imposes further difficulties in communication along the flow of work. In effect, imposing a physical separation reduces the superficial irritations and yet makes it more difficult for management to cope with the fundamental problems of research and development.

In companies undergoing rapid scientific and technological development, problems of communication are compounded by failure of changes in power and influence to keep up with shifts in the importance of a given group to the research and development process. For example, in one company there has been a traditional separation within engineering development between people in "hard ware" versus those in "soft ware" in the development of data processing equipment. In the past, the "hard ware" people have been in the dominant position, making the more important decisions regarding the design of equipment, and establishing schedules for the completion of each stage of development. The "soft ware" people, particularly the programmers, represent a new specialty which, until recently, did not even appear in college engineering curricula. In fact, many of those who have gone into programming have not had college degrees. In earlier models, the subordination of the programmers to the "hard ware" people seemed a natural and inevitable arrangement. With each new model, the work of the programmers has become more complex and more important. It appears that in the computers of the future, programming will have assumed such importance that those in charge of the programming may ultimately take power from the chief "hard ware" people. One company has already encountered a severe crisis, as an outgrowth of these shifting levels of importance and complexity of contribution. Management found itself in the awkward position of presenting a new machine to a selected public for demonstration purposes, only to find that the machine would not do as it was told. While there is never any single simple explanation for such a problem, it appears that in this case the "hard ware" people had had the ear of top management whereas the programmers had not. The "hard ware" people had proceeded to commit the company to a basic machine design and delivery schedule that was practical for "hard ware," but allowed the programmers insufficient time to both complete and test their work.

When such a catastrophe occurs, the "hard ware" people may complain about the inefficiency of the programmers, but the programmers can then say to top management that they knew all along that the plans of the "hard ware" people were unsound yet they could not get anyone to listen to them. Out of such a crisis is likely to come a shift in power so that in future activities programming people will play a more prominent role in decision making.

How can these problems of communication and coordination be solved? Unless special provisions are made, communication and initiation of activity are likely to flow predominantly downstream. The problem this can cause may be illustrated in the case of development and production of a new model television set. If we look at just one part of this flow, it seems superficially logical that those people responsible for development of the components should determine the design of the chassis which is to be built around it. If the work were actually accomplished in this fashion, the factory would certainly run into difficult problems in production of the chassis and in assembling the components and placing them in the chassis. Furthermore, the whole unit might turn out to have an appearance that would offend potential buyers.

Clearly, the outcomes will not be satisfactory unless those at downstream points have an opportunity to exercise influence upstream. It is difficult for the downstream groups to do this when they are presented with a finished design from the preceding stage. If they find that this design involves them in difficult problems that might be avoided, naturally they try to persuade the upstream people to change the design. The upstream people are likely to resist this influence for two reasons. The attempted influence seems like a challenge to their own competence in their special field. Furthermore, it is disrupting to their own work plans if they are called upon to rework a design that they thought was completed, and thus have to set aside new projects. It is therefore clearly advantageous to have consultation and discussion up and down the line of work flow well before designs are frozen at any point.

These various lateral coordination problems are well illustrated in the following case described by George Strauss:[4]

We observed the process of designing a new-model TV set in one company. The engineering department is, of course, the one most directly concerned, and it consists of five sections. *Electrical* determines in theoretical terms how the set will be made (technically: what the over-all "system" will be). *Mechanical* tries to fit the components together; it often finds that *Electrical's* theoretical plans are impractical or even that one electrical engineer's theoretical suggestions are incompatible with those of another. *Chassis* designs the cabinet; close coordination is required if the components are to fit the cabinet. This is not as easy as it sounds, since *Electrical* and *Mechanical* are constantly designing improvements which give better reception, but which conflict with the company's over-all goal of producing an ever-thinner, lighter set.

Automation designs the machinery which makes the printed circuits and attaches the tubes to it; in contrast to *Electrical*, which wants an ever-more "sophisticated" set, *Automation* wants one that is simple enough to be reduced to printed circuitry and put together mechanically. *Industrial Engineering* determines the techniques by which the set will be manufactured (other than the operations that are 100 percent automated). Like *Automation*, it seeks to eliminate what it feels to be unnecessary frills.

Further complicating over-all coordination are the pressures brought by outside departments: *Sales* wants an attractive product that will sell easily, and *Manufacturing* wants a set that is easy to put together. And management as a whole is interested in keeping costs low, profits high.

Note that in this case no one section can make modifications without affecting all the others. A change in a cabinet, for instance, may require adjustments by every other section, yet each adjustment may in turn require further compensating adjustments elsewhere. Each section has its own vested interest. *Electrical*, with its goal of technical perfection, conflicts, for example, with *Industrial Engineering's* goal of manufacturing ease.

Since a new model must be designed each year, intergroup conflicts tend to reach a crescendo as the time for a final decision approaches. During the early part of the year there is little pressure to resolve agreements, and each

---

[4] George Strauss and Leonard Sayles, *Personnel: The Human Problems of Management* (Englewood Cliffs, N.J.: Prentice-Hall, 1960), pp. 367–68.

section is free to work on its own pet projects. As the deadline draws near, an increasing number of compromises and adjustments must be made, tempers grow raw, and human-relations problems begin to complicate the technical ones. Each engineer likes to feel that he has *completed* his end of the job and hates to reconsider his position just to please another section. No engineer likes to sacrifice his own brainchild.

Complicating all these problems are the changing status relationships between departments. When TV was new, the major problem was to design a workable set, and *Electrical* was the highest-status section. Today the emphasis is on sales appeal and manufacturing ease. *Electrical* still thinks its function is the most important one, but management seems to favor other sections when it makes critical decisions and hands out promotions.

Coordination through liaison positions

Burns and Stalker describe in this way how one English firm responded to the problems of coordination and communication along the flow of work:[5]

In one concern, the number of specialists acting as connecting links had grown rather formidably. The liaison structure began with sales engineers from product divisions resident in development sections. The model shops had been placed under the administrative control of production, the growing need for precision mechanical work in them being met by the introduction of methods engineers (from production).

After development had produced a satisfactory prototype, a job passed to the stage of production drawings. At this point again, production was involved, this time operationally, through more methods engineers resident in the drawing office, who 'supplied' production engineering technique to the designers and draughtsmen who produced drawings to the instructions of the development engineers. A fourth element which acted on the drawing office was the Standardization Group, which endeavoured to limit variations in the specification of components and the design of parts. This group was also 'resident' in the Drawing Office. The draughtsmen's job, therefore, was to see that drawings were produced by the date required by the product division, in accordance with the design group's specification, within the limits set by the standardization group, and in conformity with the ideas of the methods engineers. Quite apart from the organizational complexity which this involved, by detaching so many constituent functions from the draughtsman's task, his sense of involvement and his interest in his job was weakened, and his responsibility for seeing that drawings and schedules really did provide all the information they should, and were up to specification, might be surrendered to the supernumerary controllers who surround him. He became reduced, in fact, to what the managing director said he was: 'Just a chap with a pencil.'

Fragmentation of the process of designing and preparing for production continued in the next stage. Drawings, each signed by a D.O. methods

---
[5] Burns and Stalker, *op. cit.*, pp. 169–71.

engineer, passed next into production engineering (planning), and production prototypes were then made in the pre-production shops. At this point discrepancies often appeared between the performance of equipment manufactured to drawings and laboratory prototypes, discrepancies which could arise merely from the cumulative electrical distortion of parts and components which are individually within specification, or from misreading of design requirements at any of the preceding stages, or because of necessary adjustments made by engineers or model shop craftsmen to formal specifications and designs which are not entered on drawings. The traffic generated by these contingencies was again carried by methods engineers located in pre-production, who acted as intermediaries and interpreters as well as problem-solvers. A similar organizational arrangement was being built up in the production shops proper, with project engineers 'taking care of troubles arising with test, drawing office, and development.'

Development, finally, had produced its own liaison specialist with whom to confront the liaison specialist from the works. 'If there's a design going through production for which we've been responsible, well, a project engineer represents what happens in the works as far as we're concerned. He'll come to us with a tale of woe, and gets on to one engineer in our group—the post designs engineer. He may be able to solve the thing on his own. If not, he goes to the particular engineer who was responsible for that bit of the design. The works,' he hardly needed to add, 'are a *terra incognita* to us.' The head of the concern in which this state of affairs existed introduced his outline of the organization by saying that he, like the chairman of the group of which his concern formed part, was strongly in favour of giving jobs as little specification as possible. Doubtless, when every new group was created, a perfectly sound reason had appeared to justify it, and to show why the shorter circuit would not work. While it is not possible to point to the reasons in specific instances, we are inclined to ascribe the tendency to two characteristics of managerial thinking. The first is to look for the solution of a problem, especially a problem of communication, in 'bringing somebody in' to deal with it. A new job, or possibly a whole new department, may then be created, which depends for its survival on the perpetuation of the difficulty. The second attitude probably derives from the traditions of production management, which cannot bring itself to believe that a development engineer is doing the job he is paid for unless he is at a bench doing something with his hands; a draughtsman isn't doing his job unless he is at his drawing-board, drawing, and so on. Higher management in many firms are also worried when they find people moving about the works, when individuals they want are not 'in their place.' They cannot, again, bring themselves to trust subordinates to be occupied with matters directly related to their jobs when they are not demonstrably and physically 'on the job.' Their response, therefore, when there is an admitted need for communication, is to tether functionaries to their posts and to appoint persons who will specialize in 'liaison.'

The creation of liaison positions adds additional links in the communications chain and confirms within each group its tendencies to isolationism. If other people are responsible for liaison, then the people within one work group do not need to be concerned about how their own work fits with the work of other groups. Thus, the very strategy designed to solve problems of lack of integration tends to accentuate the symptoms underlying these problems.

Coordination through authority

If problems of communication and coordination are not to be resolved through liaison functionaries, how else may they be met? The traditional response would be to refer each unresolved problem up the line of authority until the problem between two groups reached a functionary who had authority over both of them. He would then render his decision.

There are three difficulties with this solution. It takes time to refer problems up the line and get the attention of higher management officials. When two groups resolve their disputes in this way, they find themselves involved in win-lose competitive transactions. The group that wins may feel so pleased with the result and so confident in itself as to give less attention to the interests of the other group in the future. The losing group is naturally resentful, and its members tend to look for new issues that they can take up the line with a better chance of getting a favorable decision.

The farther up the line a problem is referred, especially in a rapidly changing industry, the less knowledge relevant to the problem is the executive likely to have. The arbitrator in this situation is likely to render decisions which will cause further dislocations and bring the same problem before him shortly once again, in modified form.

To the extent that an executive finds himself arbitrating the day-to-day disputes among his subordinates, the time and energy he can devote to planning for ways to improve the operations for which he is responsible become correspondingly reduced. He finds himself so harrassed with the immediate problems that he is constantly treating symptoms and never has the opportunity of dealing with the underlying problems.

If there are difficulties involved either in trying to resolve intergroup problems through appeal to hierarchical authority or through the creation of liaison positions, we may well ask: Why not settle the problems at the level where they occur? This approach has obvious advantages, and yet what can be done when we find individuals in groups whose activities need to be coordinated expressing conflicting points of view? Which individual or group is to have its way?

Case materials gathered on research and development organizations provide frequent examples of arguments between individuals and groups at different points along the flow of work. We find individuals toward the upstream end of the flow arguing that one of their group should retain control in successive stages so that the development and production people do not introduce changes that violate the scientific principles involved and thus lead to unsound products. On the other hand, we find individuals in downstream groups arguing that a member of their group should exercise some authority upstream so that upstream groups will not work out plans and specifications for the work of his downstream group that seem to members of that group impossible to carry out or involving unnecessarily complicated and costly procedures. Since strong feelings are involved and each group can make compelling arguments for its aim to extend its control over the other group, it becomes clearly impractical to resolve such intergroup disputes on the basis of formal allocations of authority.

Coordination through restructuring interactions

The resolution of this dilemma depends upon changes in prevailing patterns of interaction. To some extent the disputes are based upon the intellectual isolation that grows up when a work group concentrates its activities upon its own particular task and has little interaction with members of groups at other points in the work flow. This intellectual isolation can be reduced through interactional changes. When an upstream group has completed its work on a particular project, one of its members may be assigned to follow the project downstream for one or more stages, spending part or all of his time on such downstream points. He would not be given authority to tell downstream groups the way their tasks should really be done. He would be available for consultation and to provide further interpretations of the rationale behind certain decisions taken by his own work group. He might also work on special technical problems that arise out of the coordination of the work of two or more groups. He should not be expected to be able himself to resolve all disputes that might arise between his group and downstream groups to which he is temporarily assigned. He might well be responsible for recognizing the disputes that he himself cannot resolve and for taking initiative to bring members of the two groups together for more far-reaching discussions. While playing this role may serve to facilitate the work of downstream groups, it also provides the upstream man with a deeper understanding of downstream activities and problems, which in turn increases the value of his contribution to his upstream group when he becomes involved once again with his own group.

The same logic may be applied to the initiation of interactions upstream. A downstream man may be assigned temporarily to spend some of his time with a group one or more stages upstream, participating in the planning discussions of this group, working with them on problems for which he has some technical qualifications, and seeking to anticipate for himself and for them the problems that may arise downstream in response to each of the alternatives under discussion at the upstream point. Like his opposite number who moves downstream, the upstream mover can make a contribution in two directions. He can help the upstream group to resolve problems that otherwise might bring the project back to them after they thought that they were through with it, and he can increase his understanding of upstream activities and problems so that he provides his own group with a more effective linking activity.

Coordination through negotiation

I do not assume that all intergroup disagreements can be resolved through such interactional changes. Even when people move more flexibly up and downstream, some differences will remain. In the best of situations in complex organizations, there will continue to be disputes that must be resolved by higher level authorities, but the frequencies of these can be drastically reduced through a reorganization of interactions that tends to break down group isolation and provides for more frequent interactions along the flow of work. Most of the disagreements that do arise will not be resolved through appeals to authority but by negotiation. As Sayles has pointed out, negotiation within management is neither a new nor an unusual phenomenon. As Ritti remarks regarding one project he studied:[6]

Bargaining and exploration of alternative solutions take considerable time and energy. In this case it turns out that the entire design process took between two and three months. Just laying out the appropriate circuits to meet the initial requirements took only two days.

The difference between two days and two to three months presents us with a dramatic illustration of the importance of intergroup relations in research and development. If the group observed by Ritti had achieved a 25 percent increase in its efficiency in "laying out the appropriate circuits," its own internal task could have been completed in half a day less. A similar 25 percent improvement in the processes of communication and negotiation among the various work groups could have saved as much as 20 days of the time required for this particular group to finish its task in a form that was acceptable to other groups in the system. This case suggests that those who look to improvement in performance in research and development activities through getting each group to perform its own tasks more efficiently are working on the wrong problem.

Coordination through group discussion

We should not assume that all problems can be settled at the point where the work is actually done. For interactions and activities to flow smoothly at the work level, they need to be supported by an appropriate pattern of interaction and activities linking the various units together with

---

[6] Richard Ritti in draft of book on engineering organizations.

higher level personnel. Management meetings are an increasingly frequent phenomonon in modern industry, and yet we often hear dissatisfaction expressed by management people concerning the frequency of meetings and the time they "waste" in meetings. The man-hours spent in management meetings are a real cost to the organization, and the effectiveness of management meetings should be as much open to scrutiny as are other activities of the firm. It is not my purpose here to try to determine what people should take part in a given management meeting, how often such meetings should be called, how long they should last, nor how they should be conducted. My concern here is simply in pointing out how sometimes broader and larger meetings may serve to facilitate the solutions of problems that cannot be resolved entirely at the work level. Burns and Stalker provide us with a case of a firm which used management meetings in a way that was both flexible and effective:[7]

. . . The dimensions of the Management Committee were not permanently set. It was regarded as a cadre which was capable of expansion at need into a large meeting consisting of almost the whole personnel of the management staff and representatives of the different shops. This happened when, as we were told, 'the firm seemed to be getting into the doldrums a bit,' when overtime seemed to be called for fairly often, when production targets had not been approached closely enough, whenever, in fact, there appeared symptoms of dislocation between the programme and actual production, between earlier and later process departments, between one level and another of the personnel of the firm, and so forth. At such meetings they would usually find that after the preliminaries a good number of complaints and criticisms would start getting voiced. The first large meeting would be taken up with getting these ventilated, and by the time the second meeting occurred many of the difficulties behind the complaints would have been settled in the interval by people directly involved in them. The residue of difficulties would be discussed and possible solutions put forward. After a few meetings the volume of new problems which lent themselves to discussion by a large group of members of the firm would have dwindled, and the management committee would be shrunk to its ordinary size.

Role and functions of the engineer

Up to this point, we have been considering the engineer in the context of his relations with other specialists up and down the flow of work in research and development. Let us now focus more closely upon the role and functions of the engineer in industry.

A number of studies have shown that engineers in industry tend to have a level of job satisfaction far lower than what would be expected in terms of their salaries and status in the organization. Countless surveys have shown a correlation between the level of the work group in the

---

[7] Burns and Stalker, *op. cit.*, p. 86.

organization and the level of expressed satisfaction with the job situation. Skilled workers express more satisfaction than semiskilled, who in turn express more than unskilled. Foremen tend to express more satisfaction than their subordinates, and higher level management people tend to express more satisfaction than those at lower levels. This relationship breaks down when we turn to the engineers, whose level of satisfaction is often found only slightly above that of blue-collar workers. What is peculiar about engineers and engineering that leads to this apparently paradoxical result?

Various writers have claimed to find the answer in a role conflict experienced by engineers: A conflict between their commitment to the profession and their commitment to the company.

Ritti argues that this assumption is based upon a failure to distinguish between scientists and engineers. For scientists, this sort of role conflict is apparently frequently felt. Ritti's surveys of engineers in one large company of very advanced technology indicate that few engineers are troubled by such a conflict. Ritti asked his engineers to check 45 items in terms of degrees of importance in their satisfaction with their job and the company. The professional goal of having opportunities to "publish articles in technical journals" ranked 44th on the list of goals, with only 15 percent checking the top category of "very important." Another professionally oriented item, "established a reputation outside the company as an authority in your field," was 35th in rank, with only 29 percent checking "very important." On the other hand, "be known in the company as an expert in your specialty" ranked 19th, with 49 percent of the engineers checking "very important." The top items on the list dealt with living conditions, a friendly atmosphere in which to work, opportunity to help the company move ahead, and freedom to do one's own job the way he thought best.

The layman tends to lump scientists and engineers together, because he feels that both work in areas that are highly complex and incomprehensible to him. These findings suggest that we should take a closer look at the nature of engineering activities. As Ritti[8] points out, most engineering activities are carried out in a self-contained fashion, with little linkage to science:

Engineers are paid for their ability to achieve a practical end. They need not understand *why* something works, but what works and what does not. They are fairly well specialized in a field of endeavor, and experience gives an engineer a pretty good feel for what will work and what will not work. I would say that the bulk of engineering development is done qualitatively first —from experience—then tested to determine the precise characteristics of the result. Modifications are made if the results do not meet specifications. Engineering principles and relationships are used to inform the analysis—to suggest trial values—rather than to establish the design.

[8] Ritti, *op. cit.*

There are several good reasons for this. First, it's usually faster to do it this way. Second, because a machine, device or system must operate under real as opposed to ideal conditions, the analytical procedures that exist aren't good enough or don't apply. There are too many interactions between components of the system or too many nonideal conditions to be coped with. Analytical formulae are derived under precisely controlled conditions, but engineering is done in the real world. Engineering is an art in its own right. The fact of the matter is that the bulk of engineering has nothing to do with translating the knowledge of science into working technology. It has much more to do with upgrading technological functions in a systems sense. That is, more functions, lower cost, added throughput.

In fact, a large part of the engineering activity in the development laboratory is comprised of tasks that can be described as *formatted*. The essential nature of the formatted task is that it can be learned as a self-contained specialty, independent of background knowledge. The familiarization of relevant background knowledge may help in the early stages of *learning* the task, but be of little or no value in *performing* it. A formatted task is one which is governed largely by relatively fixed procedures, standards, rules, which are relatively free of ambiguity and contingencies. Where a contingency arises, some specialist in another body of rules can be found to handle it.

Ritti goes on to point out that much of engineering does not depend on research, not even on applied research:

This example involves a chemical engineer who was responsible for the selection and evaluation of materials. In this case he was seeking an adhesive with special optical properties. I think I assumed that he would perform this function by cooking up some gunk in his test tubes, but it turns out that he never would proceed in this way. First, he consults his charts for the optical properties of different kinds of plastic resins, and then he writes to the manufacturers of these to find out if they have anything that will fit these specifications. The manufacturers, in turn, write back and often supply the names of other users who have requested similar things. In this way he tracks down a suitable material, then proceeds to evaluate the material and document its properties. No test tubes, no gunk, no creativity required. . . . the engineer relies more on his vendor's salesmen than he does on the resident scientist.

If engineering activity is indeed quite different from scientific research and if the engineers show much less commitment to their profession than do scientists, we can assume that the dual hierarchy would have less meaning to engineers than it might to scientists. Indeed, Goldner and Ritti[9] have found that relatively few engineers desire to retain the role of specialist at the work bench. Most of them see possibilities of progress primarily in terms of moving up in management, and their satisfaction with their jobs is related strongly to the possibilities they see for this line

---

[9] Fred Goldner and Richard Ritti, "Managers and Professionals in Complex Organizations," *American Journal of Sociology* Vol. 72, no. 5 (March, 1967).

of promotion. For most engineers, promotion to a high-level title as an engineering specialist is not as desirable as promotion to a position in management at the same status level. In fact, Goldner and Ritti find that in many cases the staff engineering positions are looked upon as consolation prizes for engineers who are not considered competent to move up the management hierarchy.

The engineers are seeking not only more money and higher status; they are seeking power—particularly the power to make decisions affecting the work they shall do and the way they shall do it.

This point is illustrated as Ritti[10] explores a novel finding in a survey of engineers. Like blue-collar and white-collar workers, engineers were asked whether the amount of work they are required to do was too much, about right, or too little. Whereas the blue- or white-collar worker who checked that he had too little work to do was exceedingly rare in their studies, a substantial minority of engineers checked "I would like to do more work."

What did this finding mean? Ritti noted that the percentages of engineers checking this possibility varied markedly from one development laboratory to another within the company. For each plant, he plotted the percentage of engineers reporting, "I would like to do more work" against the percentage saying "I was *seldom* or *never* able to make the decisions I felt were necessary to assure the best technical course of action for (the company)." He found a rank order correlation of .76, which means that the more dissatisfied the men were about the possibility of making decisions important in their work situation, the more likely they were to report that they wanted to do more work. In other words, when the investigators found sentiments regarding underutilization of the skills of the engineers and of their ideas about the way work should be organized, these two phenomena appeared together.

Forms of engineering organization

Forms of organizing engineering activities are likely to give rise to feelings of lack of involvement of engineers in important company decisions. There are two common forms of organization: product or project groups, task or specialty groups. The task or specialty groups perform a set of specialized functions on any project that is being carried out by other groups, whereas the product or project groups work on a given project from its initiation until its conclusion. As Ritti notes:[11]

. . . The project organizations are much more in the main stream of the development activity than are the service or functional groups. Working on a complete project provides the opportunity to feel that your efforts are a significant part of the final product—to become "ego-involved" in the results

---

[10] Ritti, *op. cit.*   [11] Ritti, *op. cit.*

of your work. This is not so in the service groups. The work of engineers providing service does not directly become part of a product. The job seems endless. The tasks are often of relatively short duration, there is often no final end product, and it seems as though the main communications from other groups are complaints of inadequate service.

We can thus expect that members of such service or specialty groups will be less satisfied with their job situation than are those working on projects. While the project does allow for more "ego involvement," the sense of participation is likely to be highest when the project is relatively small and individuals can see their part in the total process. As Ritti comments:[12]

. . . The small project allows considerable opportunity for individual influence, the opportunity to work on a substantial piece of the project and the consequent visibility of the concrete results of your work. A large system design effort must necessarily be more fragmented and specialized.

Instability of work groups

The engineer in research and development also suffers from the instability of his work groupings. In a production organization, an individual may work with a group whose membership changes slowly over months and years, unless major technological changes are introduced. The work appears to go on forever, one day being much like the next, with minor variations. In research and development, the jobs to be done have beginnings and ends. The next project to be available when the current one is completed is unlikely to require the same number of men or the same distribution of skills and knowledge. The individual may no sooner get well adjusted to a particular group of coworkers when he is faced with the necessity of working out a new set of interpersonal relations as he becomes involved in a new project.

Insecurities are not limited to the shift involved upon completing of one project and moving to another. At times, a group of engineers will find that even though they themselves feel confident that they are making progress, higher management has decided to abandon their project, having made a judgment that its commercial possibilities are not as attractive as some alternative line of development. Engineers can thus find themselves in a failure situation not simply because they themselves have not performed as well as they had hoped, but also because of decisions quite beyond their control and on which they may have had no voice.

In many organizations, the development engineer has no fear of losing his job, yet he may feel highly insecure about what the future holds beyond the immediate project. If he gets assigned to a project that is part of an important new development in a company, his fortunes may rise

[12] Ritti, *op. cit.*

636 Organizational behavior: theory and application

even if his performance is only adequate. On the other hand, if he finds himself assigned to a project that turns out to be a dead end, he finds he has lost ground to other engineers even if his performance has been outstanding.

Engineers as internal entrepreneurs

How can the engineer cope with the insecurities of changing group membership and changing task assignments? Those who cope best with such insecurities are men who develop what we might call an entrepreneurial role within the organization. As the leader of an engineering project group looks toward the end of the project, he does not wait passively to see what management has to assign him and where management will place his current associates. If he feels that he and his fellows have developed an effective working team, he will make every effort to keep that team together in the future—perhaps to build a larger team around it. He keeps in touch with influential individuals outside of his own group, surveys the activities going on beyond his group, and seeks to arrive at an estimate of what look like profitable lines of development to be pursued. He then conspires with his work group to do a little of what is called in some organizations "bootlegging." That is, he and his teammates decide what project they would like to take on next. In order to assess the feasibility of the chosen project, they devote some fraction of their time to working on it. The "bootleg project" not only enables them to assess its possibilities much better than if they hadn't tried it. It also puts them in a much improved position so as to be able to make a forceful presentation to higher management regarding the importance of the project and the high potential for success it has if work is carried out along the lines proposed. If this strategy is successful, the work group moves, with little change in membership, from the old project to a new one. Since the new project is simply the bootleg project now officially recognized, the group begins with a head start which is likely to impress higher management with its performance. This in turn improves the chances for the entrepreneurial engineer to continue to work with the people he wants to work with and to continue to choose the projects on which he wants to work. Needless to say, as he applies this strategy successfully, he tends to move up the management hierarchy.

When we hear of bootleg projects, we are likely to think of furtive and small scale activities. This may be the case in most situations, but there have even been bootleg projects in which millions of dollars have been spent and of whose existence large numbers of people must have been aware. Such a spectacular bootlegging operation is likely to arise only when there have been basic disagreements in management circles as to which technical path to take and where a power struggle continues to be unresolved. Those who lose out on the key decision as to what technical path to follow in building a major new product may decide to back their own theories nevertheless with a bootleg project, gambling that if their strategy is successful, top management will eventually reverse the previous technical and product decision and readjust the power balance in their favor.

Obviously, it is a risky business when large sums of money and large numbers of people get involved in the bootlegging activity. When the president of one large company discovered that his firm had invested millions of dollars in one large plant to back a product development effort that he had specifically vetoed, he expressed a great sense of outrage and demoted the chief bootlegger. However, by this time the competing project that the president had approved was doing poorly, and the bootleg project was in an advanced stage of development. After reviewing development strategy with his associates, the president decided that after all the bootleggers were on the right track. He therefore reversed himself, gave his blessing to the bootleg project, and of course correspondingly elevated the chief bootleggers to higher management positions.

While there will be few cases of this large-scale nature, hiding an unapproved (or even vetoed) project under a project that has been approved is apparently a common phenomenon in research and development organizations. It is one of the major ways in which engineers seek to cope with the uncertainties inherent in their work situation.

Summary and conclusions

Development effectiveness depends in large measure upon lateral coordination. In our terms, coordination means relating the interactions and activities together of two or more units so that each one is able to move toward shared objectives, or at least so that the movement of one unit does not block the progress of other units.

Development must be seen in terms of the interdependence of parts of the social system. The problems of development cannot be solved on the basis of having each unit simply do its own job. We have illustrated this general conclusion with cases from radar to more mundane products.

In Chapter 18 dealing with "Patterns of Lateral and Diagonal Relations," we emphasized the importance of the lateral dimension of work flow relations. Here we have entered into an analysis of upstream-downstream relations in greater depth, for that is where the chief action is in development.

We have considered the advantages and limitations of five approaches to coordination in the following terms:

1. *Liaison positions.* While this approach gives explicit recognition of the lateral coordination problems by establishing functionaries to handle those problems, it relieves the project supervisors of concern with coordi-

nation and thus accentuates their tendencies to think and act solely in terms of the interests of their own units. The addition of liaison positions also adds to payroll and lengthens the lines of communication.

2. *Authority.*   We have argued that lateral coordination is not the sort of problem that can be handled on an authority basis. If the development process requires frequent authoritative interventions from higher level executives, that is a sure sign of weakness.

3. *Restructuring interactions and activities in the work flow.*   To meet the need for a smooth flow of information and consultation, we have noted the possibility of having an upstream man accompany the project for several steps downstream. Similarly, a downstream man could join the project at a point several steps upstream and accompany it down to his regular work group. However, this raises complicated questions of building new roles and new role relationships that require further study.

4. *Negotiation.*   Many intergroup differences are in fact resolved through negotiation, and this is as it should be. Still, the negotiation process has its own problems, as we have noted earlier. Besides, even with skill and good will on all sides, we must assume that there will be some disagreements that cannot be resolved on the basis of negotiation alone. But this does not mean that they must then necessarily be referred for decision to an individual superior. There remains the possibility of using the approach discussed next.

5. *Group discussion.*   We reject both extreme viewpoints: that group discussion is the answer to all ills or that group discussion is a waste of time. The skillful executive will call together a rather large meeting when a number of interrelated problems seem to be coming to a head at the same time. If the large meeting at least serves to clarify the nature of the problems, then there may be follow-up group discussions of more limited and specific problems by small groups. In other words, the executive adjusts the size, frequency, and topical content of meetings to his diagnosis of the changing nature of the organization's problems. Of course, he does not thereby escape the responsibility of making decisions, but now he acts on the basis of more adequate knowledge.

We concluded with an analysis of the role and problems of the engineer. We noted that engineers are much more likely than scientists to feel committed to the company and to see success in terms of working up the management ladder.

We found that the forms of organization of engineering work strongly influence the satisfactions engineers derive from their work. In general, those who work on projects feel they are more committed to meaningful work than those who provide services.

The engineer faces a special problem in the instability of his work groups, for engineering projects come to an end and there is frequent reshuffling of personnel. The more successful engineers build up for themselves a role of internal entrepreneurs: devising and selling new projects to keep the group together and growing, and even on occasion bootlegging a project and gambling that it will later gain recognition and support.

References

Burns, Tom, and Stalker, G. M. *The Management of Innovation.* London: Tavistock Publications, 1961. The book is important not only for its discussion of the development process but also for the light it throws on organization theory.

Discussion questions

1. As manager of development, you decide to experiment with a more flexible organization along the lines of the work flow. That is, you plan to have a representative of an upstream group accompany the project downstream and a representative of a downstream group participate in discussions upstream.

What problems would you expect that such a representative would have? Outline for him how he should play his role. How would you answer these questions he is likely to ask you:

a) In case of a conflict between my own group and the group I am working with, whose side am I on?

b) Where will my office be?

c) How is my work to be evaluated if I don't have any special part of the project to call my own?

2. You are a consultant to management regarding meetings in the R&D departments. An executive asks how he is going to know when he is having too many or too few meetings. What kind of meetings should he have and how often? How many people should be included, and how should they be selected? Help him to think the problems through by indicating the factors that need to be considered in answering such questions.

3. If you have not had such experience yourself, locate someone who has worked in a development department. Interview him about his job. Explore particularly the work flow and other lateral relations. To what extent are his problems related to these relations? (If you have had such experience yourself, examine your own problems in this framework.)

28. Managerial succession

SUBSTITUTION of personnel provides one common way of changing behavior in organizations. While a change in personnel at low levels can be expected to have little impact, a change in a key executive position may be expected to have widespread repercussions.

In the plant or local unit of the company, the manager is the key man. Whenever an old manager leaves and a new one comes in, all members of the organization recognize this as a noteworthy event. People at all levels speculate on how the new manager is going to behave and what effects he will have upon them. Comparisons with his predecessor are inevitable. This interest does not simply reflect idle curiosity, for a new manager can have profound influences upon the working experiences of all members of the organization.

The phenomenon of managerial succession has now received substantial research attention. In this chapter, we shall examine four cases in some detail and then seek to arrive at some general conclusions.

Framework for analysis

If we are to compare four cases, we must present approximately the same data for each. Since the four cases were studied by different people with different points of view, it will not be possible to meet this standard fully, but at least it will be helpful to try to follow a general framework.

Following a brief description of the plant, we will focus first upon a comparison of the old and the new manager. For each man, we will examine his activity and interaction pattern in relation with superiors, with immediate subordinates, with personnel at lower levels of the organization, and with union officers (where a union is involved). We will distinguish between pair events (the manager interacting with only one person at a given time) and set events (the manager interacting with two or more people at the same time), since we find wide differences between managers in their utilization of one or the other type of interaction.

We will examine each manager's sentiments especially in his orientation toward his subordinates. We assume that how a man regards his subordinates will be noted not only by the researcher in his study, but will also be observed by subordinates and will therefore have an effect upon their behavior.

We will be concerned with time perspective. In his dealings with subordinates, does the manager emphasize past, present, or future? Here we are not concerned so much with explicit statements the manager makes about the importance of time, for any executive likes to consider himself a man who has vision and plans for the future. We are more concerned with the way the manager's behavior affects the time orientation of his subordinates. For example, a research man once visited a steel mill at a time when a new machine was being installed. He noted that supervisors and executives of six levels of authority spent several hours in the area during the day to observe the installation process. This seemed to the research man an excessive concentration of high level manpower on the same activity. The research man found the explanation in the pattern of behavior of the works manager. When anything went wrong, he was likely to call in any of his subordinates and demand an immediate explanation. If the man being interrogated could not produce a good answer on the spot, the works manager took this as evidence that he was not "on top of his job." His subordinates adjusted to this pattern as best they could by trying to anticipate trouble that might come to the works manager's attention and preparing themselves with the data they would need when going into his office. Some of them kept elaborate "J.I.C." folders in their files—the initials standing for "just in case" the works manager called upon them. This sort of managerial behavior tended to induce a concentration of attention upon the past.

We must also examine the sanctions exercised by each manager. What rewards and what penalties does he give out? And for what kinds of behavior?

We will then seek to assess how the behavior pattern of the new manager affects the functioning of the organization. From manager A to manager B, we shall examine changes in vertical relations and changes in horizontal relations. We shall also look at changes in union-management relations (where a union is involved).

Finally, we will seek to assess the performance of the two managers. In part we can provide some reasonably well founded assessments, but we will also provide evidence as to the difficulty in drawing firm conclusions on performance in comparing managers.

1.   Chandler's Restaurant

Our first case is drawn from Chandler's Restaurant, with which we are already acquainted through the Chapter 9 discussion of the clash between the waitress, Ann Lindstrom, and her supervisor, Ellen Geiger. To sum up the background, Chandler's was a large (200 employee) and busy restaurant operating on two floors in the central shopping district of a major city.

Our case involves a change in managers from Mr. Potter to Mr. Stanton. As is too often the case, the change in personnel did not stop at this point. When Mr. Potter was manager, his immediate subordinate in the front of the house was Miss Ellis, supervisor of service. In a staff position at the same level was Miss Geiger, training supervisor.

Mrs. Schultz was assistant supervisor of service, reporting to Miss Ellis. All of the hostesses reported to Mrs. Schultz particularly, and also to Miss Ellis. Under the hostesses were the waitresses.

The organization structure is shown in the accompanying figure.

Mr. Potter left on January 1, 1944. Within an eight-month period, the change in managers had been followed by personnel changes all the way down to waitresses. The changes with which we shall particularly deal seem all closely related to the change in managers. In fact, we shall observe a change taking place at the top being followed by changes at successively lower levels.

In June, Miss Ellis, supervisor of service, and Mrs. Schultz, her assistant, quit their jobs. Mr. Stanton appointed Miss Geiger supervisor of service and abolished the training position. In July, Mrs. Loomis, one of the hostesses, left her job. Within another month, Ann Lindstrom, Rita Carey, and her sister and several other waitresses quit.

Chandler's: The Front of the House Under Manager Potter

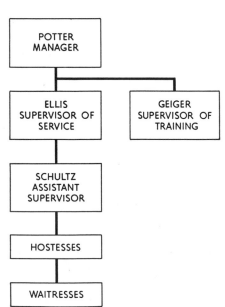

Differences between Potter and Stanton

Potter spent little time in his office. He was inclined to circulate about the restaurant, observing as he went, and also stopping to chat with people all the way down the line from his immediate subordinates to the work level.

He did not initiate changes in activities directly to people below his immediate subordinates. He described his behavior in this respect by citing an incident that arose in the restaurant to which he went upon resigning from Chandlers:

The other day I happened to be walking through the dining room when I ran into a waitress just as she was tossing off a glass of orange juice over in a corner. I couldn't help seeing it, and she knew I saw it, but I just stopped and chatted with her for a few moments on other things, and then I walked away. I looked up Miss Loring (head hostess) and mentioned the incident to her. I said if the girls were coming on the floor hungry, we ought to work that problem out, but in any case we would have to check up on picking on the food. I left the problem in her hands. That's what I do when I happen to notice something wrong. Sometimes I tell the supervisor which employee it was, but other times, I just tell what I saw without mentioning any names and let the supervisor speak to the group about it. That way I don't have to take on the job of reprimanding the workers. When I explain it, I suppose it sounds just like a way of making a good fellow out of myself to the workers, but that's the way I like to handle those situations.

Potter's practice of circulating through the restaurant led him to initiate interaction to others frequently and to respond to the initiative of others with a high frequency. It was also reported that people below his level found it possible to initiate activity changes to him. They could go to him and get him to respond to suggestions.

Potter's interactions and interpersonal activities were not limited to the pair situation. When he was concerned with a problem in the area of responsibility of two or more people, he was accustomed to calling them in to talk it over. When one individual brought in criticisms in the area of someone else's responsibility, he immediately called that person in for a three-cornered discussion.

Stanton spent most of each day in his office. He did little circulating throughout the restaurant and when he did move about, he did not stop to talk with people. Employees commented that when Stanton went by, he generally seemed preoccupied and unaware of their presence.

Stanton initiated interaction to subordinates, particularly at the lower levels, with greatly reduced frequency, compared to his predecessor. Employees reported that they hesitated to initiate interaction with him. This also led to far fewer efforts to initiate activity changes for Stanton than had been the case with Potter.

Since Stanton did not seem generally accessible to approaches from subordinates, he received his information primarily from those few who did take the initiative in interaction with him. When I asked him how he was able to know how his subordinates were functioning, he gave this response:

It's not so hard when you've had some experience. There was a manager in our Z store. He's one of the best managers in the chain. He told me once that there wasn't anything that went on in his store that he ought to know that he didn't know within 24 hours. Not that he had stool pigeons working for him either. There were just some people that really had the best interests of the store at heart. If they see some people do something that was going to hurt the store, they'd take him aside and say, "Now, look here. You ought not to do that." If that didn't work, they'd take it to the manager. I feel the same way here. There's not much that goes on in the store that concerns me that doesn't get to me in a pretty short time.

Miss Ellis seldom initiated interaction with Stanton. Miss Geiger did not hesitate to do so. The significance of this difference will be noted shortly.

Stanton also contrasted with Potter in the matter of set events or interaction in group situations. When one subordinate approached him to discuss the problem in the area of another subordinate, Stanton did not follow the practice of calling in the other person and having a three-way discussion. We shall see later the importance of this difference to Miss Ellis.

The two men contrasted markedly in their views of human nature and of particular subordinates.

Potter held a generally optimistic view of human nature: given the right conditions, people would perform well. In viewing particular subordinates, he was quite discriminating as to strengths and weaknesses and hesitated to make blanket judgments. For example, he made this comment regarding his service supervisor:

Well, I did have a problem with Miss Ellis. She was a very efficient supervisor and when I left I recommended her highly to the main office, but she had certain weaknesses. You had to watch her or she would get away with things. She would take advantage of you. I worked with her in the Y store. I knew what to expect of her and when I came out here I knew how to handle the situation.

Regarding Miss Ellis' weaknesses, he made three points: (1) She would sometimes leave the job earlier in the evening than her official quitting time, and he had to check her on this. (2) "She did a little drinking during working hours, and that was bad." (3) She was on terms of close personal friendship with some of her subordinates. They would go out together to parties after work. He felt that some of the hostesses who were not in on these activities felt that the personal associations led her to play favorites on the job. The manager felt he had to check her on this.

Such statements suggest that Potter had faith in his subordinates, and yet it was not a blind faith. The criticisms he raised regarding Miss Ellis could be considered quite serious, but yet he felt that her strengths more than balanced her weaknesses—as long as he was on the job to keep the weaknesses in check. And he regarded it as the job of the manager to minimize the weaknesses and maximize the strengths of his subordinates.

Mr. Stanton's view of his first service supervisor was quite different. Of Miss Ellis, he said:

I think she is worried about getting married. I've had some trouble with her. (He paused long, he did not look at me.) I can't say that I like her. It seems that she has been out to make things tough for me.

He then went on to describe how Miss Ellis had talked of quitting several times and always changed her mind, of how she selected the time of finally quitting for a period which would make the maximum difficulty for him (when he was off on vacation), and of how she took certain others with her. He went on:

One thing you can tell about Miss Ellis from what happened after she left was that she was just working for Miss Ellis. She was only building up loyalty to herself, not to the store. If she had been working in the best interest of Chandler's, why would those other two have quit just because she left? Just because they were all friends doesn't seem to me to be any reason for all of them leaving. Why do they all have to go just because one goes?

Regarding Miss Ellis' possible sources of dissatisfaction, he said:

I hear that she had been talking before she left, telling people that she wouldn't work from nine in the morning till nine at night for anybody. Now it's true that the work was temporarily pretty hard for a month, but I thought that was a very poor attitude to take. If it was too hard for her, why didn't she come in and talk it over and we could have worked something out?

Stanton talked a good deal about the "cliques" among the employees. Ann Lindstrom, the informal leader among the younger waitresses, seemed to him aggressive, insubordinate, and a corrupting influence among the other girls.

Stanton also saw the evil influences of cliques among several of the men employees, who quit at about the same time as Ann Lindstrom and several of the other waitresses. Regarding the downfall of Jonesy, his assistant maintenance man, he commented:

Everything was all right until Jonesy moved in with Lou and Fred. That was when the trouble started. You know, in the crowd you have just one fellow with the wrong attitude and he can change the mind of the others.

We can sum up Stanton's view by saying that he was inclined to expect the worst of subordinates. When they once got off the track of good behavior, he saw no possibility of bringing them back, and he suspected informal groupings of undermining loyalty to the organization.

Regarding time perspective, we can only note that the establishment of the training director position by Potter is evidence of future orientation, and the elimination of this position by Stanton may be interpreted as showing lesser emphasis upon the future. However, our data on this point are too fragmentary for any definite conclusions.

The two men differed markedly also in the sanctions they exercised. These sanctions were exercised primarily in the personal relationships of the two men. Subordinates from the top down to lower levels under Potter generally felt that they were working in what Douglas McGregor has called "an atmosphere of approval." The manager's behavior toward them suggested that he believed in them and expected them to do a good job. Stanton did not provide this kind of atmosphere. Subordinates came to expect that they would hear from him if he had something negative to say, but that otherwise there would be no personal contact.

Now let us examine the effects of the managers upon their subordinates. Miss Ellis said of Potter:

He was a wonderful manager. He knew everybody on the staff and you felt that you could go to him with any problem that you had. You always felt that he was behind you. He'd do whatever he could for you.

Of Stanton, Miss Ellis said:

Mr. Stanton just doesn't seem to care. He sits in his office with his own work and you don't feel that you want to go in and bother him. You think it is just up to you to handle your job in the best way you can. But I have nothing against him personally. I think that Mr. Stanton is a nice person.

A number of subordinates at lower levels gave me similar contrasting statements regarding the two managers. Since Miss Geiger declined to make any comments about either manager, we cannot present an evaluation directly. Whatever her view of Potter, we must assume that she was much more favorably inclined towards Stanton than others who did express themselves to us, for Stanton had advanced her in position, and she apparently did not feel the hesitancy about initiating interaction with Stanton that Miss Ellis spoke about.

Here we seem to be dealing with a significant personality difference between the two men. Miss Ellis' life story (not presented here) shows a continual history of strong peer group associations and loyalties, and we note in comments by both managers the strength of the ties that she maintained with her immediate working associates. The life story of Miss Geiger (See Chapter 9) reveals a person who, from her earliest years, was conditioned to responding to authority and had never had strong peer group associations or loyalties. She seemed ill at ease in informal situations. When I attended the annual picnic, I observed her most of the time either by herself or on the fringes of some group and never taking an active part in the festivities.

Concerning the differences of the impact of the two men on horizontal relations in the organization, we have no data for lower levels of the organization, but it is clear that the managerial change brought about a drastic change in the relations of Ellis, service supervisor, and Geiger, training directress. Unfortunately, I was unable to get Miss Geiger's views on this problem, but Miss Ellis spoke quite freely of the frictions between them. While these frictions existed even under Potter, they did not become a severe problem to Miss Ellis until the advent of Stanton. She described the problem in this way:

Well, frankly, she was the main reason why I left. I liked her and we were very friendly when she was my assistant. I think it was a mistake to put her in charge of training just for that one store. Here Miss Geiger had been used to being on the floor and she wanted to keep active on the floor. There were times when she would come out and tell the girls something that was just the opposite from what I had told them. That made a very awkward situation when we were contradicting each other. It was bad for both of us. One time I found her bawling out Mrs. Schultz. She was furious, and she slammed her fist right down on the table. Now, that was no business of hers at all. Mrs. Schultz was under me, not under Miss Geiger. Anything like that she should have taken up with me first. I just walked away. What else could I do? But that made a terrible impression upon the girls.

Then she used to go in to Mr. Stanton every now and then with some criticism of the way my department was being run. Of course, I was interested in improving anything that could be improved in my department, so I would have been glad to have her come to me; but it was really none of her business to take those tales to the manager. I resented that very much. It seemed a sneaking thing to do to talk behind my back.

I asked whether Miss Geiger had taken such criticisms to Mr. Potter.

No, she hardly ever did that. You see, just as soon as she went in to Mr. Potter with any criticism, he would call me in and we'd talk it over. That way, everything was open and above board. It was entirely different under Mr. Stanton. She could go in and talk to him, but I wouldn't hear about it until later.

Note that the accentuation of Miss Ellis' difficulties can be traced directly to differences in the interaction patterns of Potter and Stanton with their subordinates. Potter circulated about the restaurant so much and initiated interactions so frequently with his subordinates that it was easy and natural for them to communicate with him. If you wanted to talk to Stanton, generally you had to go to his office and wait to see him. To seek out Mr. Stanton under these circumstances was not in line with Miss Ellis' past pattern of interactions and she was unable to bring herself to do it. On the other hand, taking the initiative toward a superior authority was something that Miss Geiger had learned to do over the years and had no difficulties in carrying out.

We also see a crucial difference in the utilization of set events. Except for an occasional large and formal meeting, Stanton's interactions with subordinates were confined mainly to pair events. Thus, when Miss Geiger brought him in a criticism or suggestion regarding service activities, it never occurred to him to call on Miss Ellis and have a three-cornered discussion. The three-cornered approach practiced by Potter tended to reduce the frequency with which Miss Geiger brought him criticisms of Miss Ellis' activities, whereas the pair interaction pattern practiced by Stanton encouraged this type of channeling of communication, which Miss Ellis found so threatening.

Chapter 9 presents data on the way the change in managers and in directresses of service affected relations down the line to the level of waitress. We see that some of the key subordinates of Potter lost their sense of commitment to Chandlers' restaurant and left the organization. We have seen this followed by resignations also at the bottom level. We cannot say that this negative effect was felt strongly throughout the organization at the work level. In general, the work situation changed little for the experienced waitresses who had the preferred dining room locations and who received little supervisory attention under either regime. It was especially the newer and less experienced waitresses who responded negatively to the change.

How shall we compare these two men in performance? In the building and maintaining of commitment of key supervisors to the organization, Potter clearly had a superior record. The same might be said at the work level at least for the younger and less experienced waitresses. Here, however, we are dealing with a small number of cases on which we have personal data, and we would feel more confident if we had turnover figures for waitresses during the two time periods.

We have no data on costs, or such other customary indices of business efficiency, against which to measure our two men. Thus, while we can clearly show the impact of change on certain parts of the organization, our performance evaluation must necessarily be somewhat inconclusive. We shall return to this evaluation problem in our conclusion.

2.   The Gypsum case[1]

The Gypsum operation consisted of a mine (75 workers) and a board plant (150 workers). These were located in a small town where everybody knew everybody and the gypsum company was the major employer.

The work flow began with a mining operation and the transportation of the gypsum rock to the surface on trains. At this point, the rock was weighed and crushed into more manageable chunks. If it was for immediate use, it was pulverized and dehydrated. The powder then went into the

---

[1] This case is taken from Alvin Gouldner, *Patterns of Industrial Bureaucracy* (Glencoe, Ill.: The Free Press, 1954).

plant on a conveyor, to be made into plaster or gypsum wallboard. Wallboard production involved rolling the gypsum paste into a flat surface and putting on a paper cover. There were operations of cutting, inspecting, bundling, and loading, at the end of the line. The product was made for stock, so that there was no difficult problem of adjusting types of production to customer orders.

The predecessor, known as "old Doug" to the men, had come up from the ranks and had personal relations with all the workers. Old Doug apparently did not spend a great deal of time circulating about the plant and mine, but, whenever anything went wrong, he went straight to the assumed source of the problem and talked it out with those immediately involved. Under Old Doug there prevailed what Gouldner calls an "indulgency pattern." Relations between the manager and the workers were highly informal. Within limits, to suit their own convenience, men were allowed to punch in on the job early and go home early, when they had personal problems that made changes in working time convenient for them. They were also allowed to appropriate a certain amount of company materials for their own use.

The workers appreciated having Old Doug as a buffer between themselves and the main office. They had the impression that he took care of his men and ran the plant as he saw fit, accepting no dictation from the main office.

The picture did not look so rosy from the vantage point of the main office. Members of higher management considered the production of the mine and plant low and the costs high, but perhaps they recognized that no fundamental changes could be made while Old Doug was in charge, so they waited to move upon his retirement.

Management sought to improve efficiency by a two-pronged strategy. Major investments were made in modernizing the technology of the board plant. At the same time, management brought in a man from the outside, Peele, to introduce the new technology and to get more production from the operation.

One of Peele's first moves signalized the destruction of the indulgency pattern. He fired an employee who had followed the previously time honored custom of taking company supplies for personal use. Testifying before an arbitrator, Peele:

. . . clearly announced that these informal patterns were illicit, that he no longer would permit foremen to honor them, and that, henceforth, foremen-worker relationships were to be within the formal regulations of the company. . . . Peele made (the employee) an "example," warning other workers of what they should expect, should they continue adhering to the old informal patterns.[2]

Peele's interactions in the plant differed markedly from those of Old Doug. In the early months, he spent much of his time in various depart-

_____
[2] *Ibid.,* p. 60.

ments of the plant in an effort to get information about operations. These interactions in this period were apparently a good deal more frequent than they had been with Old Doug, and their content was also quite different. Old Doug had gone directly to employees to ask their views on a particular problem and otherwise left them alone. Peele did not ask subordinates for advice or opinion. He simply sought information. His approach to employees was regarded as formal and "all business." At the same time, Peele frequently issued orders on the spot.

Subordinates, down to the worker level, regarded Peele with hostility, and his first efforts showed no apparent improvement in efficiency. As Peele came to recognize the resistances to him, he sought to overcome them by strengthening paper controls. He made new rules and provided for reporting infractions of rules. He attempted to secure information about the organization through the requirement of daily reports.

As resistance to these changes increased and production dropped, he adopted new tactics. He made a practice of appearing unexpectedly in various corners of the plant in the hope of catching shirkers by surprise.

By this time Peele had so isolated himself from the rest of the organization that he had no confidence in anything anyone said to him. He responded to this problem by making what Gouldner calls "strategic replacements"—bringing in loyal subordinates from the outside so that he would have some allies in his efforts to push through the changes.

While Peele appeared to be a complete autocrat within the plant, subordinates noted with disapproval an extreme dependency upon the main office. Whereas Old Doug had made his own decisions on the spot, Peele frequently called the main office for advice or directions.

We can sum up the interaction-activity pattern of Peele in this way. He initiated interaction with superiors far more than Old Doug. Peele interacted in the plant with a high frequency, compared to Old Doug, and his activities could be characterized primarily as inspection. He predominantly initiated interaction throughout the organization, and he did not allow others to initiate changes in his own activities. His interactions were limited almost exclusively to pair events. He developed no regular pattern of group meetings.

Although he was carrying out a program of major technological changes, affecting everyone in the plant, Peele consulted with no one concerning the impact of these changes nor how they should be put into effect. He even provided no advance information as to what he was going to do.

The sentiments of Peele toward his subordinates are illustrated by this statement to a researcher:[3]

Some of them thought they were going to get fired. I *could* work on these guys. But others, who didn't expect to get fired, were. Each foreman is just a little bit *on edge* now. They don't know whether they are doing right.

---

[3] *Ibid.*, p. 90.

Peele clearly believed that the only way to get performance out of his subordinates was through fear. All the sanctions he applied were punitive. Gouldner does not record any instances in which Peele praised or otherwise rewarded any subordinate.

In terms of time perspective, Old Doug apparently was oriented toward the past. He had many years of experience in the plant and was inclined to apply the precedents of that experience to the solution of problems both technical and human. Peele totally rejected the past, but his own managerial approach did not go beyond the present. He acted as a man under pressure to achieve immediate solutions to immediate problems. Gouldner provides no record of efforts on the part of Peele to plan beyond the immediate introduction of the technological improvements that had been provided for him by higher management.

The succession produced a drastic change in vertical relations, with Peele exercising constant pressure downward and being unresponsive to any upward initiatives. Gouldner provides no data on changes in horizontal relationships.

The most dramatic effect of the change in managers was found in union-management relations. The notably peaceable relations that had existed under Old Doug grew increasingly tense under Peele. This trend was climaxed by a serious strike. While the strike did not take place until after Peele himself had been succeeded by Landmann, clearly Peele's managerial strategy created this labor crisis. (We might add that Landmann pursued a strategy very similar to that of Peele, in spite of abundant evidence that the Peele approach was not working out.)

What can we say of comparative performance? Was Old Doug a better manager than Peele? Clearly that question is too general. There are various ways of failing—and also various ways of succeeding as manager.

Old Doug had satisfactory relations with the men and the union—from their standpoint. Higher management was satisfied with this labor harmony but felt strongly that more efficiency was needed. Peele destroyed the human equilibrium that had existed under Old Doug—without achieving the efficient production that management expected of him. Thus Peele was finally designated as a failure by management and demoted to a lower position in the plant.

3. The automotive assembly case

At last we come to a clear-cut success story: a successor who moved in and rebuilt a sick human organization, with spectacular results in productivity and efficiency. These changes occurred in the high-pressure atmosphere of a large automotive assembly plant.[4]

Under manager Stewart, a crisis atmosphere prevailed. Stewart felt

---

[4] Robert A. Guest, *Organizational Change: The Effect of Successful Leadership* (Homewood, Ill.: Richard D. Irwin, Inc. and The Dorsey Press, 1962).

himself constantly under pressure from the home office. According to the organization theory of top management, the plant managers were to be given considerably autonomy, but as he showed consistently poor records in efficiency, labor turnover, and absenteeism, the main office people were frequently on the phone to Stewart, demanding to know what the matter was and giving him a variety of new directives.

Stewart passed these pressures right down the line. He initiated most of the interactions with subordinates and was highly critical of their performance. He tried to solve persistent problems with on-the-spot orders. Stewart's behavior discouraged the expression of criticism and advice directly to him, and he provided no regular pattern of group discussions on problems.

The successor, Cooley, had impressed higher management with his performance as production manager in another assembly plant. He was told clearly that the plant he was taking over had the worst all-around record of any assembly plant in the corporation, but he was also told that he would not be expected to show dramatic improvements at once. Top management would give him time and leave him alone.

Cooley received no specific instructions as to his own managerial strategy. Higher management let him know that they expected he would have to "get rid of some dead wood," but these decisions would be left entirely to him.

One of Cooley's first moves upon arrival at the plant was designed to allay the anxieties of subordinates. At a supervisory meeting:

He put forward what he called "a few basic goals" for the organization in terms of expected efficiency and quality. He stated candidly . . . . that Plant Y had a bad reputation. He said he had heard that many members of the group were not capable of doing their jobs . . . . (but) was "willing to prove this was not so, and until shown otherwise, I personally have full confidence in the group." He went on to say that his job was not to catch and punish people for doing a poor job, but rather to help them in any way (he) could to do a good job. Also, ... "I don't believe in firing a lot of people and using threats and fear."[5]

In this early period, Cooley refrained from making any changes. He went about familiarizing himself with plant operations and getting acquainted with the supervisors and workers. In order to open upward communication to him, he asked foremen and union officials to invite him to visit their groups. At first Cooley had to initiate most of the interaction with subordinates, but as they found him approachable and interested in them, a more balanced pattern of initiation developed.

Guest reports that subordinate response to Cooley was initially skeptical, and it required about a year for the new human equilibrium to develop. Subordinates were persuaded that Cooley meant what he said

---

[5] *Ibid.*, p. 42.

both by the manner of his personal approach and by the decisions he made. One subordinate commented that Cooley:

. . . walks around the plant and talks with the men. He just wears an old beat-up jacket and doesn't act superior.

Another added:

He comes up and says "good morning" . . . and he means it. The foremen all know he is pulling for them and has a lot of respect for foremen's judgment.[6]

Cooley's initial changes in the physical plant were improvements in working conditions: refurbishing the cafeteria, washrooms and lockers, improving parking areas and making heating and ventilating systems more effective. Changes such as these arose directly out of suggestions given him by foremen, workers, and union officers.

It is noteworthy that Cooley made his first financial investments not in technology that might lead to greater productivity, but in the physical environment of the plant, where the only immediate direct payoff would be in the increased comfort of workers and supervisors.

Many managers, upon entering a plant which had had such a bad performance record, would have taken the attitude that since the men had done poorly, they would not be rewarded in this way until they had "earned" such rewards by good performance. Cooley preferred to meet the immediate human needs he observed and hoped that this investment, which demonstrated his responsiveness to his subordinates, would in turn stimulate them toward improved performance.

Whereas the only meetings called by Stewart had been provoked by the crisis of the moment, Cooley instituted a regular pattern of weekly meetings with his top subordinates. Here he focused attention on general problems rather than on immediate situations. In planning future changes, he set up a series of *ad hoc* groups to study special problems.

These moves were designed not only to provide recommendations on particular problems but also to give men in different but interrelated functions experience in working together. In order further to improve horizontal coordination and broaden the men's experience, Cooley began to transfer men from one job to another at the same organizational level.

The sentiments of Cooley toward subordinates could be and were inferred from the new pattern of relations he developed with them. He created an atmosphere of approval by showing respect for his subordinates and for the union officers.

Whereas Stewart's time perspective had been firmly anchored in the present, Cooley clearly showed his future orientation by leaving immediate problems to the subordinates directly concerned and focusing group

---

[6] *Ibid.*, p. 60.

discussions on the changes that would need to be made in order to improve the performance of the plant.

The effects of Cooley's interaction-activity pattern are best illustrated through the comments of foremen and general foremen. One foreman reported:

When there is trouble, their (the superiors') attitude is to find out what the problem is first. They don't take it out on the men or the foremen as the scapegoat.[7]

Because supervisors had more information and increased decision-making powers, they perceived directives as nonpersonal. A foreman commented:

We still had plenty of pressure . . . (but now) there is a good reason for it, not just some boss trying to pull rank on you.[8]

A general foreman said:

But with all these little changes and big changes, we have more time to get around. And with more time, we can think a little more about planning, instead of worrying what's going to happen the next minute . . .

Also, as the men saw some of these changes being made, they began to *believe* that they were really trying to do something for them. We can talk a lot about human relations, but unless you can show something that you have done, why it is only a lot of talk.[9]

Another foreman said:

It's like a chain reaction . . . We're getting someplace. It seems like every single section foreman on the line is trying to run his section the best way he can . . . because there are fewer reasons for squawking at each other.[10]

Guest documents the growth of more favorable sentiments toward the plant manager at all levels from worker on up, and he also notes a marked improvement in relations with union leaders.

Did these changes in human relations show up in work performance? To answer this question, we need to divide it into two stages. Guest reports that for the first two years following Cooley's taking over, production efficiency showed no marked improvement. But then during the third year there was a dramatic upswing, so that at the end of three years' time Plant Y had moved from the bottom to the top rank among the company's assembly plants in various indices of performance. It is interesting to note the time lag in this case, which may well be characteristic of the introduction of human changes into a large organization. Apparently there must be considerable investment of effort and time in changing the human organization before the results begin to show up in productivity.

[7] *Ibid.*, p. 62.   [8] *Ibid.*, p. 65.   [9] *Ibid.*, p. 54.   [10] *Ibid.*, p. 55.

4.   The precision manufacturing case

The case that we are now to consider is unique in the literature on management succession, for here we have data in depth on both managers, gathered while they were in action in this particular plant. In the restaurant case, I interviewed Potter and observed him in action in the restaurant that he managed after he left Chandler's, but I did not see him in action in Chandler's. Gouldner's study provides only general retrospective data upon old Doug. Similarly, Guest provides us retrospective data on plant manager Stewart, while he concentrates upon the successor. In the precision case, we have an intensive study of one manager carried out by Chris Argyris,[11] and we have a similarly intensive study of the successor carried out by Richard Dunnington.[12] While there were some differences in the interests of the two men in the data they gathered, their studies are sufficiently comparable to permit a systematic comparison between Oldman and Newman—to give them the names used by Dunnington. (I am also indebted to Dunnington for much of the analysis of all four cases.)

The plant in question was a branch of a corporation which had its divisional headquarters some 200 miles away. This plant was of moderate size, having approximately 450 employees. It was engaged in producing precision products in large volume. The plant produced a wide variety in its product line, so that considerable flexibility and coordination was required.

Operations at the plant began with the order department, which worked out the necessary paper records for the items to be manufactured on the basis of the salesmen's field orders. These orders were then taken over by the production scheduling department, which was responsible for organizing the flow through the five departments involved in different phases of production, assembling, and shipping. Production scheduling might be regarded as the key operation, since the ability to plan the work flow of a wide variety of items through the plant made much of the difference between a profitable operation close to capacity in each department and a nonprofitable operation, with underutilization of personnel and facilities. Since precision as well as speed was required in operations, there were constant opportunities for errors which might turn a large volume of material into scrap or require expensive rework. This combination of speed, variety, precision, and interdepartmental coordination led many supervisors to believe that their plant was necessarily a high pressure operation.

Oldman had only been on the job a little more than a year before Argyris began his study, so we have some retrospective data on his

---

[11] Chris Argyris, *Executive Leadership* (New York: Harper & Bros., 1952).

[12] Richard Dunnington, unpublished draft of doctoral thesis.

predecessor, who appeared to be much like Old Doug of the gypsum plant. Like Peele in the gypsum case, Oldman moved in with a program of technological change. By the end of World War II, the plant appeared old fashioned in its production equipment and methods as well as in the easygoing style of management of Oldman's predecessor. Top management expected Oldman to accomplish major increases of efficiency and reduction in labor costs. The labor cost reductions were to be achieved only in part through improvements in technology. A main objective of Oldman and the company was to pry the local union loose from the wage pattern of the company plants in the divisional office city. Management argued that the divisional office city labor rates in general were substantially higher than those prevailing in the city where our plant was located, and therefore a lower pay scale for that local plant could be justified. Furthermore, management argued that the products produced by the local plant were in a more competitive field, with smaller profit margins, than were the products of the divisional office plants. If the local plant was to remain competitive, management must stop the practice of granting the local unions whatever rates were agreed upon in the divisional office city.

Oldman might be described as a benevolent, autocratic father. An accountant by profession, he had worked in all parts of the operation and had an intimate knowledge of technical problems. He provided very close supervision, checking into everything, frequently bypassing his immediate subordinates. On any problem that came to his attention, he did not hesitate to give an order or instruction. He was often highly critical of the performance of his subordinates, and they spoke of frequently being "needled" by Oldman.

To some extent, subordinates resented this driving and needling supervision, and yet their feelings about Oldman were by no means entirely negative. In part, they rationalized the pressures he put upon them by telling themselves that this was the nature of the business that they were in. Also, they were profoundly impressed by Oldman's knowledge of the business and felt that he was usually right in whatever he did.

Oldman cultivated his personal relations with his subordinates. He got together with them one night a week for a poker game, and he was frequently out in the plant during lunch hour, shooting craps with general foremen, foremen, and some employees. But these group activities were confined to social events. Oldman had no regular pattern of meetings with his supervisory subordinates for the discussion of problems within the plant. Whatever management meetings he called were generally in response to an immediate emergency, with a focus on what was to be done, and with Oldman dominating the discussion and dictating the solutions.

Oldman was a man of extraordinary interactional capacity. He would walk through the plant at least daily, and each walk would involve numerous personal contacts. He knew each one of the approximately 450 workers by name, and he also appeared to know a lot about each one. He would frequently stop to talk on personal as well as work matters. Workers generally felt that Oldman had a personal interest in them.

As part of his campaign to move the union toward a differential with the divisional office city, Oldman set up a series of monthly labor-management meetings with the four chief departmental union officers. Oldman also held small group meetings with all employees on an annual basis to report on the company's plans and progress and ask for suggestions aimed toward increasing efficiency. While the general foreman and foreman of the group in question would be present at such meetings, Oldman dominated the discussion.

By the time he faced his first bargaining meetings, Oldman's personal approach had enabled him to establish friendly, informal relations with the local union officers, which smoothed the way for the tough bargaining position he was bound to take. After an extended series of bargaining meetings, he was able for the first time in history to get the local plant unions to accept a settlement that was somewhat less than had been granted in the divisional office city. To do this without a strike must be considered a major achievement.

Oldman's sentiments toward his subordinates can best be judged through his often repeated statement that most people either sought openly to avoid work or just kidded themselves into thinking that they were really working.

Oldman's managerial strategy emphasized a short-time perspective: "You take care of today, and tomorrow will take care of itself." His was a crisis management, with emphasis on immediate solutions to immediate problems.

When he moved in to take Oldman's place in 1953, Newman faced an interrelated set of difficult organizational problems. The plant under Oldman had appeared to be a "one man show." General foremen and foremen seemed to be highly dependent on the boss. What would happen when the boss left?

The plant had been operating in terms of a short-run view, with no one but Oldman doing any planning and with Oldman himself being so focused on daily operations that he gave the future little attention. This had not been a problem in the early period of Oldman's regime for he had come in with major technological changes. But now more than five years had passed since these changes, and a new series of changes would have to be introduced if the plant was to remain competitive. And no one was planning these next steps.

There was a high level of friction among departments, with each department head being concerned exclusively with the performance of his own department. In training sessions that Chris Argyris, Graham Taylor, and I had during the Oldman regime, the general foremen and foremen talked freely about their practice of "throwing the dead cat into somebody else's yard," when someone tried to pin responsibility for faulty work on their particular departments. Whatever coordination that did take place was very largely dependent upon the production scheduling department and upon the personal intervention of Oldman.

Newman was also faced with the loss of key management personnel. Before he had completed five months as plant manager, the controller, the personnel manager, the manager of cost accounting, the manager of scheduling, and the manager of the order department all moved out of the plant to bigger jobs in other plants.

Newman, furthermore, was succeeding a man who was considered by top management to have been spectacularly successful in handling both production and labor relations. In fact, this perception of Oldman's success helps to explain the number of promotions of key subordinates in the first months of Newman's tenure. Since Oldman seemed to be so successful, higher management assumed that his key subordinates must be very good people too.

Finally, Newman faced unions that were ready to make an all-out effort to regain lost ground. The union leaders had never become completely reconciled to the idea that their rates should be lower than those prevailing in the division office city. Even if they did accept the idea, this differential had grown now to 40 cents, and they considered that far too big a spread.

Newman first sought to make a diagnosis of the situation he faced and of his own potentialities and limitations for dealing with this situation. We present here the diagnosis that emerged in the series of discussions with Dunnington, and it may well be that the experience of talking through his problems with the researcher helped Newman to clarify his diagnosis.

Newman began with a rather clear picture of the leadership style of Oldman and of the problems Oldman had left to him, as outlined above. He sought and to some extent succeeded in gaining an objective picture of himself in relation to this situation. The son of a minister, Newman had very firm views about morality and frankly disapproved of Oldman's participation in gambling and drinking activities. He explained:

> Since much of this stems from my own personality, you might just as well know that I tend more to the English point of view than the American. I know I tend to be reserved. I don't tend to become too familiar with people. But I'm not so sure that this is a bad thing. Frankly, I feel that in America today there may be just a little too much familiarity between levels of supervision and the employees. Probably Oldman and I are at extreme poles on this. I suppose there is a middle ground . . . but, after all, Oldman and I are not the same kind of individual. I have to operate in the way that I know best.

Newman felt ill at ease in fraternizing with workers and recognized that he could not handle the range or frequency of interactions maintained by Oldman. He felt that his only possibility of success lay in working through the managerial structure, and he believed in this approach in any case. He felt that the structure had been unduly weakened by Oldman's constant bypassing and widespread interactions outside of organizational channels.

Newman had an engineering education and came to this position after five years of experience as administrative assistant to the manager of a much larger plant. Since his former plant differed markedly both in machines and products from his present plant, he began as manager without a detailed knowledge of operations. Without such knowledge, it was impossible for him to give close supervision. He recognized therefore that he could only succeed through building up the competence and confidence of his subordinates. This approach also fitted in with his own ideas of the nature of modern management.

From the very beginning, Newman sought to put his management strategy into words in discussions with subordinates, undertaking to give them a new cognitive map within which to frame his behavior and theirs. Whenever he read an article on management that impressed him, he circulated it among his key subordinates and arranged for opportunities later to discuss the ideas contained in the article.

One of Newman's first steps was designed to increase the autonomy of his supervisors. In the past, when the plant public address system had announced that General Foreman X was wanted in the plant manager's office, that individual felt that he had to drop whatever he was doing immediately and get to the office fast. Newman told his subordinates that when he made such calls, he did not expect them to respond immediately. He recognized that the individual in question might be in the middle of something important which should not be interrupted. In that case, he simply asked that the supervisor pick up the plant phone and let the manager know when to expect him. This release of the subordinates from an immediate response was much appreciated.

As subordinates came to him for decisions on technical matters, he made it clear that he did not have the detailed knowledge necessary for rendering such decisions. The best he could do would be to help his subordinates arrive at better decisions themselves.

With rare exceptions, any management meetings called by Oldman had been impromptu affairs, and generally the men going into those meetings could only speculate as to what topics were to be covered. Newman scheduled regular weekly meetings (for an hour or less time) with his key subordinates. Furthermore, he circulated an agenda two days ahead of the meeting so the participants could think about what was going to be discussed. He also invited participants to make their own suggestions as to what they ought to be talking about.

Newman also established a pattern of monthly meetings with general foremen, foremen, and section leaders. In all of these group meetings, his own participation was far different from that of Oldman. Newman himself consumed a markedly smaller proportion of the talking time, and he encouraged others to express their opinions, even when they disagreed with him. While Oldman sometimes complained to the researchers that he was surrounded by yes men, his response to any contrary opinion was such as to discourage further dissent. Newman showed his appreciation of dissenting opinions not only by the respectful attention he gave in the meeting itself but by his follow-up behavior. Often in a subsequent meeting, he would mention an opinion expressed previously by one of the participants, saying that he had not agreed with it at the time, but that it represented a legitimate point of view that needed to be given serious thought. The fact that the manager would remember a dissenting opinion that had been expressed a week or more earlier indicated to subordinates that he took their opinions seriously enough to reflect about them between meetings.

To make sure that items brought up in these meetings were not forgotten until some decision had been reached and carried out, Newman had the controller keep a notebook to note the disposition of each agenda item. Newman reviewed this between meetings, so as not to let any unfinished business get lost. He encouraged others to keep their own notebooks so that they could relate the meetings more effectively to their day-to-day problems.

While Newman felt unable and unwilling to maintain the social pattern established by Oldman, he did recognize the necessity for some social activities outside of the plant. In the early months, he took the superintendents out for a social weekend at a lake resort. While Newman did not participate in the poker games and evening drinks at the lake, he made no effort to discourage these activities. Following a pattern set by Oldman, Newman held monthly lunches with the general foremen.

Newman made special efforts to improve interdepartmental relations. As he became aware of problems involving more than one department, he would set up small committees or task forces cross-cutting department lines and assign them to study a problem and come in with a recommended plan of action. As problems arose between departments, he did not press in to try to fix the blame. Rather, he sought to use the problem to focus on a discussion of the social processes accompanying the flow of work.

Newman's success in improving interdepartmental relations is best illustrated by his handling of the problem of the production scheduling department. Shortly after he took charge of the plant, he had a new man in this key position. In the early months of his experience with this new supervisor, he was inclined to think that the man was inadequate and would never be able to do an effective job. Then as Newman became engaged in discussions of the scheduling department problems with the department general foreman and the other general formen, he came to feel that his estimate of the man might not be correct. The superintendent of production scheduling had succeeded a man who had held this position throughout Oldman's regime and had had the reputation of being highly efficient. It was only after this man left for a higher position in another plant that Newman and others concerned began to recognize that the preceding scheduling superintendent had kept his operating techniques very largely in his own head and had not established any system that a successor could follow. The predecessor had left very little in writing behind him that could guide the new man, and the new man had not been close enough to the predecessor to absorb his ways of operating.

When Newman came to this revised diagnosis of the problem, he recognized that it was necessary for a whole new set of operating procedures to be worked out, and he decided that this should be a joint effort of the production scheduling superintendent and the general foremen in the various production and assembling departments. He asked these men to get together to criticize current practices in production scheduling and to work out a more satisfactory system.

As Newman's problem-solving approach crossed departmental lines at the level of the general foremen, a spirit of interdepartmental cooperation sprang up also at the level of foreman. The evolution of the foremen's daily planning meetings is described in this way by Dunnington:

As nearly as the story can be pieced together, during one of the scheduling department gripe sessions, the general foreman of scheduling whispered to one of his subordinates that he and the other foremen ought to sit down with the general foreman of conditioning at periodic intervals to plan a schedule of work. The subordinate followed through on this and for a while the three men met each morning. While the conditioning general foreman was on vacation, his two foremen took his place. A foreman in final assembly heard about the meeting and asked to join. He was admitted on a trial basis. This proved helpful, so the group invited the manufacturing foreman. By this time, Newman had gotten wind of the meetings and helped to bring foremen from the two remaining departments into the meetings.

A section leader who did not attend the meetings reported on the positive effects of them from his point of view:

Until a few weeks ago, I never knew which orders to fill first. I just responded to whoever put on the most pressure, and it was a constant rush to get things down the line in time . . . now that the foreman attends a daily foremen's meeting with people from scheduling, he knows in advance what is coming and can tell me.

The foremen who attended these meetings appeared to have a common reaction. The meeting gave everybody an opportunity to raise questions about the scheduling of orders and made them feel responsible for following through on decisions made at the meeting. As a result of this opportunity for interdepartmental communication and joint planning, more suggestions seemed to be offered in a helpful spirit and accepted across departmental lines at lower levels.

At the level of employees, Newman continued Oldman's practice of having annual meetings in small groups with workers throughout the plant, but he made these meetings a team operation, with other members of management playing prominent roles. He also continued the monthly meetings with representatives of the union, but here he pushed the initiative in handling these meetings down to the level of general foremen and foremen. That is, Newman himself attended, but required the general foreman and foremen to carry the major load in presenting anything management had to present and responding to questions and opinions from the union representatives.

In the first months on the job, Newman had few contacts with workers outside of these formal meetings. As he gained more confidence in his own approach, and as he became more aware that some problems felt at the worker level were not getting up through the structure to reach his attention, he increased his interactions on the plant floor. He never reached the high level of frequency characteristic of Oldman, nor did he ever feel at ease in this situation as Oldman did, but still this increasing frequency of contact apparently helped him to win worker acceptance. It also gave him opportunities to pick up feedback on the way the plant was operating, according to the workers.

Newman's emphasis on future orientation is well illustrated by his manner of organizing a study of the capital equipment needs of the plant. He felt that the plant needed "a very thorough and deep study of major capital equipment."

I assigned the most experienced man in the plant, my staff assistant, to spearhead this study and set up committees he needed so that everyone in the plant could contribute toward developing a complete picture and formulating the kind of plan we should have to line up better equipment. I felt right at that time that that was the most important thing as far as the plant was concerned. It took nearly six months to complete the study and virtually everyone in the plant was drawn into it in one way or another, including machine operators, foremen and operating personnel.

This widespread involvement of people in discussion and study across departmental lines of course also contributed to breaking down the interdepartmental barriers and improving horizontal relations.

Under Oldman, the annual budget for the plant had been worked out by the plant manager working with the plant controller. The general foremen had no part in the process at all. The manager simply announced what their departmental budgets would be for the next year. Newman changed the approach to budget making by involving the general foreman and foremen in the process of working out the budget figures for their department. With this approach, they were more inclined to accept the final budget figures as legitimate and fair. This also involved them in looking more than 12 months into the future.

Newman's problem-solving approach also led subordinates in a future direction. The difference between the two managers in this respect is discussed in the following way by two general foremen:

GENERAL FOREMAN 1: Remember how we used to really alibi. That's what you had to be, an alibi artist under Oldman. He'd ask you a question, and if you didn't have an answer, by God, that was too bad. So, you'd figure out a good alibi to satisfy him.

GENERAL FOREMAN 2: Yeah, that's right. It's pretty hard to alibi the way things are now. The way Paul brings us into the planning function there's really not much use in alibiing. I've been thinking about this, and I guess maybe Newman is not so much concerned with detail as he is with planning.

If a man feels under pressure to have alibis ready, then he is constantly concerned with justifying past behavior, and has little time or inclination to look into the future. Since Newman used the problems that arose not for the purpose of fixing blame but for analysis in order to organize the work processes more effectively in the future, it became irrelevant whether a man was a good "alibi artist" or not.

The sentiments Newman had regarding work and his subordinates have been illustrated by the various moves that he made. We might sum up his outlook by saying that he believed that the men under him were basically competent and responsible people who would do a good job if conditions were right for the job being done. It was his responsibility as manager to create these conditions.

What were the effects of the new managerial approach? We must answer that question in terms of two time periods.

For about the first eight months it was not at all clear that Newman was going to succeed. Without the strong hand of Oldman to guide them, the general foremen and foremen were all at sea. One general foreman described how the change affected him in this way:

Newman (delegates) something to you and sets a date when he wants a report on it and expects you to have it ready. That's a hell of a lot different from Oldman. I didn't pay any attention unless he said something twice. It's quite a change. *It's almost like having the props taken out from under you.* This is a different kind of pressure. You've got to be able to plan ahead. Now, I think in the long run the "consult" basis is best. But in the short run, the "tell" approach is best. You get things done immediately. But in "consult," maybe it takes a while to get it in operation, but once it is, I think things will work more smoothly. But, boy, what a change this has been!

The change in managers affected some supervisors differently from others. Those who were most inclined to independent action and who had chafed somewhat under Oldman were the first to respond to the Newman approach. Those who had been most dependent upon Oldman naturally had the most difficult time in adjusting. In fact, Newman eventually had to demote the most dependent general foreman to a foreman position.

While the subordinates were having their problems adjusting to the change in managers, all of the indices of plant performance were down from the records of the Oldman regime. Newman was also facing up to his first and most difficult round of union negotiations. Looking back on it several years later, Newman commented:

By the end of my first eight months, I came as near to having a breakdown as I think I will probably ever come. It was much too much. I have always had a pretty good constitution, but it was rough.

As Newman got through the round of labor negotiations without a strike, the pressures on him began to ease, and a new equilibrium in the human organization began to take definite form. Supervisors were showing increasing independence in handling their problems and were welcoming the enlarged responsibilities given them. There were marked improvements in horizontal relations. Perhaps the best illustration of achievement in this area is provided by a comparison of a crisis of the same type, as encountered under Oldman and under Newman. Once Oldman discovered a major error in a large and important order at a time just when he was about to leave town. He ordered the general foremen to come in on their own time and make the necessary changes so that the order could be saved. For the first scheduled meeting, most of the men called upon turned up to work but had great difficulties in arriving at any consensus as to how the job should be done. In subsequent sessions, attendance dropped off until practically no one put in an appearance. It remained for Oldman, upon his return, to mobilize the men once again and to direct the work himself.

Under Newman, one of the general foremen spotted a similar major error at a time when Newman was out of town. He immediately got in touch with the other general foremen and they themselves arranged to put in extra time. They now had no difficulty in working together, and they completed the job rapidly and efficiently—and with full attendance.

As the foremen and general foremen responded in increasingly favorable ways to Newman, they also expressed what the change in managers meant to them. To one general foreman, the change in managers made the difference between externally applied pressures and internal drive for achievement. He put it this way:

FOREMAN: I wouldn't mean to imply that there was too much pressure in the way Paul Newman works but a different kind of pressure. Actually I still feel the same way. With Jim Oldman you had direct pressure from him on anything *he wanted*. With Paul Newman, he makes you aware of *your responsibility* to get something done and it is usually in a broader area than when Jim was here. But he makes you feel that you have direct responsibilities and you feel like you are letting yourself and him down if you don't get it done. It creates an incentive within yourself rather than just obeying orders. It makes the job a great deal more interesting and I think it makes you feel part of management. Order-taking can get monotonous in the long run.

RESEARCHER: Do you feel this pressure coming from other supervisors, other parts of the organization any differently now than before?

FOREMAN: Well, I don't believe there was ever actually what you would term pressure coming from other supervisors. It would all come through Oldman because they would hightail it into his office and he would apply the pressure. Now Paul Newman is trying to set up a few blocks so that he expects the supervisors in different areas to get together and work out a solution or attempt to work out a solution. Only when they can't work it out does he want to get involved in it. It creates a great deal more give and take among the supervisors. . . .

The general foremen also internalized Newman's view of performance responsibilities as extending beyond a man's particular department. In one departmental meeting (not attended by Newman) one general foreman made this statement:

The first item on the agenda is waste. By waste, I don't mean materials waste, but time waste. It costs $75 an hour to run (the machines in the machinery department). If our work is faulty, the machines have to be readjusted. This may take from 15 minutes to an hour. Some of the equipment costs over $100 an hour to run. This is lost if the equipment has to be stopped to re-do our work. It may take a little more time in our department, but we'd rather have it cost a little more here than hold up a piece of equipment in the machinery department. It's really better for us to spend a little more time doing a good job here and perhaps not be worried quite so much about costs . . . also, we're concerned about the service angle in our business. Things are tightening up, and the demands on us are going to be greater to get the orders out on time. So we really have two problems here: one of cost, and one of service.

The general enthusiasm extended even to the old-timers. One general foreman, who was about to retire, told the researcher:

You know, it's amazing to me the broad vision that man has. For a person who's only been with the company six years, he has a real grasp of things—and, mind you, this is a complicated business. Now, I've talked to you about the other managers. . . . Oldman was a smart cookie, but this guy tops them all! Why the things he's got planned are terrific. . . . Maybe if he knew how far-reaching they were, he wouldn't slip into them. But I think this plant is really going places with this guy.

The favorable reaction to Newman even extended to union officers. One such officer made the following comment:

Newman just walked into a bad situation, that's all. If Oldman hadn't moved out when he did, this plant would have been out on strike . . . we're just afraid that Newman's too good for this plant and they'll move him out on us. If he stays around for a while, this plant is going to go places.

How can we compare these two men in performance? Both men were successful, according to the standards management generally applies. They had radically different styles, which led to different patterns of results, and required different conditions for success. Oldman ran a one-man show, and yet, while he was on the job, there could be no question about the technical efficiency and profitability of the organization. With his concentration on present problems at the expense of the future, we may wonder whether, had he remained in his position, his performance would have declined. We may also wonder whether his highly personal style of leadership would have been equally successful in a larger plant. In fact, he went on to manage a plant three times the size of this local plant, and we did hear reports that he was not as effective in the larger unit. However, we have no systematic data to back up such reports.

Newman was clearly the superior performer in developing the organization, but would he have been able to bargain successfully the wage differential that Oldman brought about? It may have required the highly personal all-pervasive influence of the manager, supplied by Oldman, to bring off this feat. This question is simply speculative, but we introduce it as a way of pointing out the complexities of trying to make such comparisons.

General conclusions

Our analysis of these four cases suggests that the quest for "the effective manager" reflects a highly oversimplified picture of the human organization. There are many criteria for effectiveness. The most immediately obvious ones are indices of organizational output: volume of production, costs, waste, and so on. We may also regard the maintenance of the human organization as providing another set of criteria. Clearly it makes a difference whether the manager's subordinates in supervision and at the work level look to him with hostility or with more favorable sentiments. Figures on absenteeism and labor turnover may also reflect this organizational maintenance function, when properly adjusted for the characteristics of the personnel in question and the conditions of the labor market. We need to consider organizational development. Does the manager's leadership style serve to develop the capacities of his subordinates, or does this style tend to stifle such development?

There are also at least three important situational factors that need to be taken into account: time, size and type of operation.

In the time dimension, for example, Oldman made an outstanding record during his seven-year tenure but there were increasing indications toward the end of his period that trouble lay ahead. Had he remained on the job another five years, we might have been forced to make quite a different evaluation of this performance.

If we had been required to evaluate Newman within the first eight months of his tenure, we could hardly have called him a success. This observation points to a general conclusion, independent of the particular case. The favorable effects of the introduction of a new style of managerial leadership cannot be expected to show up at once. Newman was well into the second year before improvements brought about by his managerial strategy began to become observable. In Cooley's case, while favorable changes in interpersonal sentiments and in interdepartmental relations could be noted well before this time, it was a full two years before the improvements began to show up in output and cost figures. This suggests that, barring a disaster that is obvious to all observers, higher management needs to give a new plant manager at least two years before expecting to be able to evaluate the results of his leadership style.

Concerning the type of operation that is managed, we have dealt here with three factories and one production and service organization. By putting these cases together in the same chapter, we have made the implicit assumption that the problems of managing these units and therefore of managerial succession have much in common. On the level of generality of our analysis, this assumption is probably correct.

Suppose Oldman had been in charge of a research and development operation approximately the same size in personnel as the plant where we observed him. Let us also assume that he had the technical knowledge of the field that would have made such an appointment seem reasonable on technical grounds. We can assume that the leadership style displayed by Oldman in the factory would not have been effective in the research and development organization. Either Oldman would have developed a radically different managerial approach or he would have failed on this job. Similar points might be made regarding the roles of the hospital superintendent, the chief of the government bureau, and no doubt other key executives of other types of organizations. It is not our purpose here to explore these differences among types of organizations. We simply raise the question to guard against the comforting but misleading assumption that there is one managerial style that will be effective in any type of organization.

Within these limitations, can we generalize about the success and failure of the managers we have had under examination? Let us begin with the cases of clear failure. Peele and Stewart had a great deal in common, and Landman, the man who succeeded Peele in the gypsum plant, appeared to resemble Peele very closely in his managerial style. In all these cases, we observed strong downward pressures and no receptivity to initiatives from below. We noted the imposition of changes without consultation or even advance information. The three men all seemed to follow the motivational theory that only fear would get subordinates to perform adequately.

Next we come to two men who cannot be readily called either successes or failures. Let us describe them as "adequate for the existing situation." Old Doug managed to rock along, maintaining good relations with worker and supervisors and getting out the production that was at least minimally adequate to management, given the then existing state of the plant technology. We may regard Stanton, like Old Doug, as deficient in the development of the organization. Stanton's relations with his supervisors and with the inexperienced employees were clearly inadequate, but he had no problem in getting along with the experienced waitresses. After he had made his own appointments for key supervisory positions, he had a management group that could work with him and vice versa. Even during the period of the chain of resignations, there was no obvious breakdown in operating efficiency.

Neither of these men was called upon to manage at a time when major changes were being introduced. Each man followed the routines he had developed from a position in either a previous restaurant or plant. If either of these two men had been called upon to take over management of an organization where major changes had to be introduced, we suspect that their performance would have been less than adequate. This of course is purely speculative, for we did not see them in such situations.

Among the successes, let us first consider Oldman, whose case may present something of a paradox, especially to the theorists of "participation management." We might first ask whether he does not in some respects resemble our failures. Like Peele, Landman, and Stewart, he exercised strong pressures downward, and he was not responsive to initiatives of his key subordinates. Like Peele, he got around the plant a great deal. Like the failures, he was also highly critical of his subordinates. But here the similarities end. While the pressures Oldman exercised on his immediate subordinates led them to respond to him as yes men, in his extensive interactions throughout the plant at lower levels, Oldman was responsive to the complaints and suggestions that were made to him. This enabled him to gain feedback from lower levels, which was impossible for our three failures. It also gave lower level people some of the feeling of involvement that was so lacking in our failure cases. Oldman did not impose changes without notice. He was always careful to inform people as to what was going to take place. While consultative relations were notably lacking in his dealings with the general foremen, some such exchange did take place in the labor-management meetings. Unlike the failures, Oldman developed warm personal relationships throughout the organization, and this social activity served to cushion the resentments that might have arisen in response to his directive leadership style. While Oldman had a low opinion of human nature in general, he was not punitive toward his subordinates—except verbally. In contrast to our failure cases, in the seven years that he managed the plant, Oldman fired only one supervisor. Nor did he exercise any pressure on subordinates to get rid of individual workers. Finally, and also in contrast to the failures, Oldman had an extraordinarily high degree of technical competence, and this in itself accounted in a significant degree for his success.

Potter resembled Oldman in having an extraordinarily large range and high frequency of interaction throughout the organization, but he differed in other respects. Potter used his frequent contacts throughout the organization as a way of observing the way the organization was functioning and as a means of establishing personal understanding. In contrast to Oldman, Potter took pains not to bypass his immediate subordinates in his interactions with workers. Potter more closely resembled Cooley in his future orientation and in his inclination to work through groups. However, on these aspects we do not have as full documentation as we do in the Cooley and Newman cases.

Cooley and Newman pursued leadership strategies that were strikingly similar. They involved their subordinates in studies of problems and in consultation on decision making. Both men gave considerable emphasis to organization building and maintenance. Both faced particular problems with a *process* orientation, attempting to discover difficulties in the process that might be remedied in the future rather than trying to pin blame on individuals or departments. This process orientation was linked naturally to future orientation, for as one shifts attention from the immediate problem to the process, one naturally thinks of what should be done in the future. Beyond this, both men took specific steps to get subordinates involved in planning activities. Finally, both men were characterized by supportive sentiments toward their subordinates, as also was Potter.

While we do not have enough data for all our cases, the transactional framework seems to throw light especially upon the comparison between Oldman and the Newman-Cooley leadership style.

Oldman established a near monopoly situation in the administration of rewards or penalties upon lower management people. This leadership style produced a continuing series of competitive transactions and negative exchanges among his chief subordinates. To win a plus or to escape a minus from the boss, each supervisor sought to place the blame for failures on some other individual or organizational unit.

Newman deliberately gave up monopoly powers over rewards and penalties. He got subordinates involved on a group basis in working out solutions to present problems and in planning for the future development of the plant. This structuring of interactions and activities produced a situation where each individual could gain rewards from the group for his contribution to the group or incur penalties for his failure to contribute. This structuring also brought about a symbolic shift: the men came to conceive of success as moving toward goals they had helped to establish instead of simply in terms of pleasing the boss and escaping his censure.

Under Newman, members of management came to feel that they were engaging in joint payoff activities. Note how this perception was dependent upon the structuring of interactions and activities. It does no good for the boss to say, "We are all part of the same team. We will rise or fall together." This symbolism will evoke no positive response unless subordinates find themselves engaging in common activities that they expect to yield joint payoffs.

On the nature of succession

We have devoted some attention to the question of what makes a good or a poor manager at the risk of losing sight of our primary goal in this chapter: the study of managerial succession. Whether we would characterize a given manager as good or bad, there are problems of change that must be faced when he is replaced. The entry of a new manager necessarily involves some readjustments throughout the organization. How should the new manager move in? Potter gave me this analysis of the succession process:[13]

There is one thing that I try to impress on my new managers. I tell them, "When you go in to take over a new place, don't make any changes in the first three months. The store can run itself for that length of time without you. Now maybe your predecessor was a poor manager and the employees didn't like him. Still, if you come in and change things around right away, they'll remember your predecessor, and they'll be thinking that his ways were the right ways."

I tell them, "Carry a notebook around with you, and when you see something that should be changed, go back into your office and make a note of it. And don't let anybody see you writing in that notebook. Don't make any changes at first, but spend those three months in letting the supervisors and employees get to know you. When they get used to you, you can begin making your changes—gradually."

As Potter was pointing out, the first job of the new manager is to fit himself into the interpersonal network of the organization. Before he can develop an effective managerial strategy himself, he needs to get some background on the managerial style of his predecessor and upon the way the organization functioned under that predecessor. Whether or not the successor proposes to follow the pattern of his predecessor, he needs to know what that pattern was. Otherwise he is introducing changes into an unknown field. We should emphasize Potter's caution about patience. The man who seeks to introduce his improvements at once is almost certain to fail.

As he gains some comprehension of the differences between his own and his predecessor's leadership style and the problems this difference will make for his subordinates, the new manager should help his subordinates to visualize a new cognitive map of the functioning of the organization.

When the experimental psychologist is working with dogs or pigeons who are not acting as he wishes, he may introduce penalties to extinguish the behavior in question. *But he cannot encourage (reinforce) the behavior he is seeking to develop until examples of such behavior spontaneously occur.* That is, if he wants to train the pigeon to peck at a certain point,

---

[13] W. F. Whyte, *Human Relations in the Restaurant Industry* (New York: McGraw-Hill Book Co., 1948), pp. 332–3.

he waits and observes the pigeon taking innumerable other actions until the pigeon "accidentally" pecks at the desired location. The experimenter then immediately releases a pellet of food (or has it automatically released upon the pecking pressure). As this sequence of activities is repeated several times, we find the pigeon "learning" that when he pecks he gets rewarded and thus going about pecking in a more and more direct fashion —as long as he is hungry.

The experimenter cannot speed up the processes by saying to the pigeon, "If you peck on the spot, you will get fed." This possibility of symbolic verbal communication is open to human beings, and the manager should use it to speed up the adjustment process.

Without this kind of cognitive symbolization, the adjustment process is unnecessarily and painfully prolonged. The subordinate finds himself getting penalized for behavior that won rewards from the former manager. This is confusing at first, but he gradually learns what it means. That is, he learns what the new manager wants him *not* to do. But negative sanctions do not produce a stable line of new behavior. Until the subordinate takes an action that is rewarded (reinforced) by the new manager, he has not begun to learn the new pattern. If the action that is to be reinforced is one he has not taken before or one that was penalized under the old manager, the subordinate naturally has great trouble getting started in the new pathway.

The new manager needs to tell his subordinates not only the results he wants achieved but also *how* he wants them to behave. Here he should not think of specific directions for each act. No manager can steer all the actions of his subordinates. He needs to put the single actions desired into a symbolic map that he seeks to communicate to his subordinates. The evidence of one case suggests that only as Dunnington helped Newman to conceptualize this symbolic map of organizational behavior, and as Newman then began explicitly presenting this map to his subordinates, did he overcome the succession crisis and begin the establishment of a new pattern that was both economically effective and satisfying to himself and his subordinates.

References

Argyris, Chris. *Executive Leadership.* New York: Harper & Bros., 1952. A case study of the plant under the leadership of the man Dunnington calls Oldman.

Gouldner, Alvin W. *Patterns of Industrial Bureaucracy.* Glencoe, Ill.: The Free Press, 1954. One of the cases discussed in this chapter, presented in full.

Guest, Robert A. *Organizational Change: The Effect of Successful Leadership.* Homewood, Ill.: Richard D. Irwin, Inc., and the Dorsey Press, 1962. One of the cases discussed in this chapter, presented in full.

Discussion questions

1. Review Chapter 9. To what extent can you draw parallels between the problems of the immediate subordinates of adapting to the change from Potter to Stanton and the problems of the waitresses of adapting to the change from Miss Ellis to Miss Geiger?

2. You are called in by your superior and told, "I want you to go in and take over as manager of Plant X. You have my full backing. You have a free hand to make any changes you decide on. Just report to me six months from now on how you have got the place straightened out." What would you say to him and why?

3. Have you ever worked on the same job when a new boss took over for your former superior? If so, describe the effect of this change upon you and upon others at your level.

4. Find someone who has worked on the same job through a change in his immediate superiors. Get him to describe and explain the effects this change had upon him and upon others doing similar work.

29. On the meaning of delegation

THE PLANT MANAGER was talking about his experiences under a previous manager:

Of course, he talked about delegation. I suppose he went home and told his wife, "We're doing things differently now in the plant. We're delegating."

One day he called me into the office and he said, "Damn it, Ed, we've gotta delegate around here. Now you take this letter from the telephone company and handle it for me. They want to put six more lines in here. Hell, we can't afford it. You tell them that."

I told him I would handle it, but I felt like asking him whether I should bring the letter back for him to sign.

Ridiculous as this case sounds, it illustrates a common problem within management. I have never met an executive who did not believe that he delegated. Most subordinates report that their bosses do not delegate to them enough. Why these opposing interpretations?

The differences arise because the term "delegation" has no commonly accepted *behavioral* definition. If the parties could get together as to the observable items of behavior referred to by "delegation," then it might be possible for them and us to know what they are talking about.

In this chapter, we shall examine a case, and then seek to arrive at some general conclusions—and our own definition of the word. This is the story of "Food World," a large and growing chain of supermarkets.[1] As the organization grew, top management came to feel farther and farther removed from the stores. Since they were unable to keep in close touch with the stores, it seemed reasonable to believe that the organization would function more effectively if more authority and responsibility could be delegated to the store level.

Before any significant degree of decentralization and delegation could take place, it was necessary to change the organization structure. Before the change, there was no single responsible head in the store. Each store

---

[1] Paul R. Lawrence, *The Changing of Organizational Behavior Patterns* (Boston: Harvard University Graduate School of Business Administration, 1958).

had a produce manager, a grocery manager, and a meat manager. At the level above them was the district manager, with his two assistants. The district manager supervised the grocery manager, while one of his assistants supervised the produce manager and the other directed the meat manager.

Under the new organization structure, the district manager had no assistants at the district level. The new position of store manager was created, and he supervised the meat manager, produce manager, and other personnel in his own store. The central office provided men with the titles of meat merchandiser and produce merchandiser, but they were thought to function in purely an advisory capacity to the appropriate departmen-

Figure 26–1.   Partial Organization Chart, 1955

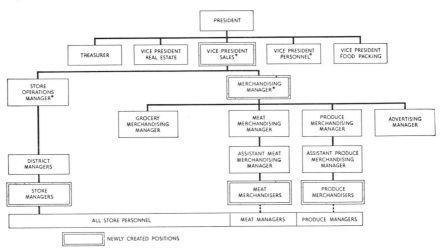

* Men with major roles in planning organization.

tal managers in the store. (See Figure 26–1.) It was emphasized in management planning that the store manager was really to be in charge of his store.

Measuring delegation

The philosophy of delegation required that district managers refrain from detailed supervision of the store managers and encourage their initiative. To what extend did it work out in that fashion? Paul Lawrence and his research associate, James V. Clark, undertook to answer that question through field observations and measurements. After some preliminary work, they concentrated upon three district managers (DM1, 2, and 3) in their relations each with three store managers. DM1 fell in with the new pattern as if it had been made for him. He avoided detailed supervision and took pride in developing the store managers. DM3 seemed still to be involved in every detail of store operation. DM2 was inconsistent, sometimes directing in detail and sometimes holding back.

The observers now sought to classify and measure the content of conversations between district managers and store managers. They divided all of the conversation into the following five topics: people, merchandise, records systems, physical plant, and small talk. The accompanying table gives their findings.

Percent Talking Time (by Topics) in DM-SM Conversations

	DM1	DM2	DM3
People......................	48	17	11
Merchandise..................	16	41	32
Records systems..............	22	25	47
Physical plant...............	7	11	10
Small talk...................	7	6	0.5

Several items catch our attention in this table. We note a sharp difference between DM3 and the two others in percentage of time devoted to small talk. Apparently DM3 was all business while he was in the store.

We also note that each DM had his own favorite topic to which he devoted almost half of the conversational time. While we have no comparable measurements for other studies, this may well be typical of managers. We may find that the manager typically devotes a disproportionate amount of time to the topic of particular interest to him, and this may not bear any relationship to the needs of the subordinate or the characteristics of the situation. We find in general that most new topics were initiated by the district manager—the percentages ranging from 77 for DM1 to 86 for DM3.

Does the choice of topic which receives most conversational attention have any effect upon the degree of delegation? I would argue that it does. In the fields of *merchandise* and *records systems*, the favorite topics of DM2 and DM3, the district manager could well assume that he knew far more than the less experienced store manager, and this assumption would probably be accepted by the store manager. We would then expect the district manager to dominate the conversation on these topics. The topic of *people* seems to be different in its effects. While the superior might dominate a conversation on the abstract nature of people, most of the talk about specific individuals would probably concern those who were working in the particular store. It would be obvious to both parties that the store manager knows more than the distrct manager about the people who work in the store. The topic of *people* therefore is likely to be conducive to the display of considerable initiative on the part of the store manager.

The researchers also sought to classify conversational units by types of utterances and measure the amounts of talking time on each type. Here the classification system divided utterances into these four categories: questions, information, opinions, and directions or suggestions. Figure 26–2 summarizes the results of this effort.

Figure 26–2.   Percentage of DM and SM Talking Time by Categories

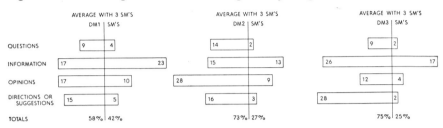

The distribution of talking time shows a significant difference between DM1 on the one hand and DM2 and DM3 on the other, with DM1 talking less than three fifths of the time and the other two talking approximately three quarters of the time. As we compare the two extremes, we see that DM3 offered three times as many opinions as his store managers, whereas DM1 offered less than twice as many; DM3 offered fourteen times as many suggestions or directions as his subordinates, whereas DM1 offered only three times as many.

The picture two years later

The researchers also made a follow-up study of the district manager–store manager relationship two years later. They assumed that some real changes that did not appear at the outset might become evident after a period of time, and this indeed proved to be the case.

Unfortunately, they could not give the follow-up data on all three district managers because in the meantime, DM1 had been promoted. This promotion, of course, was related to DM1's superior ability to fit the new management pattern.

The figures on DM2 and DM3 for the two periods show striking changes. These are summarized in Figure 26–3.

Here we find a marked reduction in the proportion of talking time on the part of the superior. We also note much more of a balance between superior and subordinate in offering opinions and suggestions or directions.

What accounts for the changes?

As Lawrence put the case, the changes are not due to any one factor, but rather to a combination of factors. With his guidance, we can enumerate a number of these factors.

Figure 26–3.   Comparison of DM-SM Talking Time by Categories in 1955 and 1957

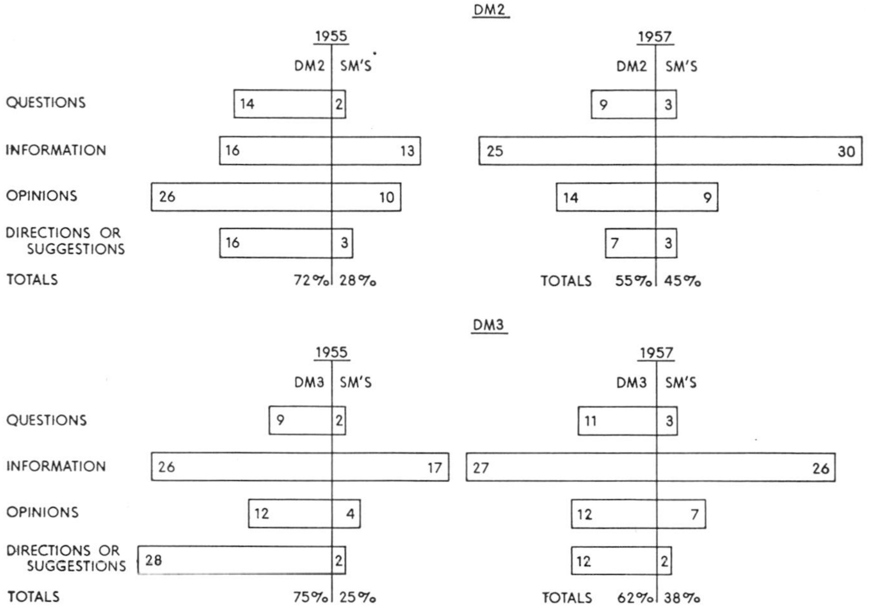

1. *Organization structure.* Without a fundamental change of organization structure, there would have been no store manager to whom authority might have been delegated. This is obvious on the face of it, and yet we are often inclined to overlook the obvious. This case suggests that we are likely to find changes in organization structure going along with a program of delegation and decentralization.

2. *Top management endorsement of the program.* No one was fired in establishing the program, but several men who had been district managers were demoted because it was thought that they could not handle the job according to the new pattern. Higher management people, both in pair situations and group discussions, made it quite clear that they were behind the program and thus strengthened the impression that district managers who were able to fit into the new pattern would be rewarded, whereas those who failed to fit into it would not. The promotion of DM1, who best fitted the pattern among the three men studied, probably made the criteria of management rewards and punishments even more clear to the men.

3. *Budgeting and employee rating procedures.* Higher management developed a new program whereby district managers were required to get from store managers estimates of their own store budgets and ratings on their employees. The district manager could dominate the process of preparing these estimates and evaluations, but the way the procedure was established made it clear that initiative was expected to flow up from the store manager.

4. *Status supports for the store manager.* The researchers report upon a meeting in which the vice-president for sales discussed with district managers current union negotiations, raising the question of whether or not management should undertake to keep store managers informed regarding the process of negotiations. Some district managers opposed this on the grounds that the store managers were too close to the employees and should not be trusted with confidential information. The sales vice president argued that if the store managers were ever going to consider themselves part of management, they must be trusted, which meant bringing them in on confidential information. He decided that this should be done. Probably there were other examples of status enhancement for the store manager, although this was the only one reported by the researchers.

5. *Top management's consultative approach.* Before the changes were announced, higher management people spent considerable time visiting in the stores and consulting with men farther down the line regarding possibilities of organizational changes. This helped to develop receptivity on the part of men below the district manager level.

The authors note that the district managers were not consulted—except for DM1, who was brought in on a confidential basis. Probably DM1 was consulted individually because his views were known to be compatible with the new approach. Nevertheless, the authors correctly point out that this involvement in consultation made it easier for him to adjust to the new system. Similarly, the exclusion of the other district managers from this consultation made the adjustment more difficult for them.

6. *Influence of superior's behavior.* The store operations manager (SOM) was the immediate superior of all the district managers. The researchers made a number of observations of him in pair situations with a district manager and also in group meetings with his district managers. They found that SOM talked only 43 percent of the time in the pair situation and only 29 percent of the time in a group situation. In superior-subordinate relations, it is common to find instances in which the superior talks 75 percent of the time or more in a pair situation and close to 50 percent in a group situation. The figures for SOM suggest that he did indeed display a pattern which threw the initiative to subordinates.

SOM exerted further influence in his annual session in which he conducted an evaluation discussion with each immediate subordinate. The authors report that in the early period he told DM3 that he was making progress but was upsetting subordinates by the way in which he criticized them. They also report that DM3 was very defensive in his reactions and would not admit this fault. The fact of defensiveness, nevertheless, does not mean that the criticism had no effect. At least DM3 became aware that he was not pleasing his superior in an important matter.

7. *Peer group influence.* In discussions with SOM, most of the district managers spoke favorably of the new system and gave an optimistic

picture of the development of the store managers. DM3 was the only one who painted a rather negative picture of the store managers. Finding himself in this minority position, he may well have wondered whether some of the fault was not on his side.

8. *Influence by subordinates.* Store managers recognized that the new program called for them to display more initiative and sense of responsibility. In general, they responded favorably when opportunities were offered along this line. On occasion, they claimed responsibilities that were not offered to them by district managers. The authors report instances where the store manager said, in effect, to his superior, "You let me handle this."

9. *The organized training program.* The company also carried through an ambitious training program for the district managers. While some of this dealt with technical matters, there was a good deal of emphasis upon the new management approach. The author describes one meeting in which DM2 described quite movingly the difficulties in adjustment he was having—and yet was apparently accepting the new approach. DM3 blurted out, "Speak for yourself." The comment suggested strong resistance. Nevertheless, at the end of this particular session, DM3 came up to the instructor and said, "Don't be discouraged about me. I've got some things to learn, and I am learning some of them."

If we examine the problems of DM3 in particular, we seem to see this type of progression. At first, he was highly confident, considering himself a first-rate district manager. The combination of factors described above undermined his confidence in his own acquired pattern of managerial behavior. The new approach structured a new way to proceed and win managerial rewards, and gradually and gropingly he was moving in this direction.

10. *Time, techniques, and personal adjustment.* When systems and procedures are new, the superior naturally feels some anxieties about the abilities of subordinates to take appropriate actions. As precedents for handling certain types of problems become established, behavior becomes more routinized. The superior is then less likely to feel that the store will go to pot if he does not exert firm control.

Conclusions

On the basis of this chapter, let us see if we can arrive at a behavioral definition of "delegation." Let me first note that I do not intend to define my term in relation to "authority" or "responsibility." Those terms themselves need definition in behavioral terms.

Delegation involves the level of the hierarchy at which a given activity may be initiated, independent of clearance from above, with respect to that activity. That is, we can say that the activity has been delegated to B when he characteristically initiates this activity with associates and subordinates without prior interaction with A, his superior. Comparing a later with an earlier period in an organization, we can say that some degree of delegation has taken place for a given activity when that activity is characteristically initiated at a lower level than it was in the earlier period.

Note that the degree of delegation, according to this definition, can only be assessed with regard to a given type of activity. In Chapter 21, "Work Unit Cohesion and Militancy," we noted concurrent efforts to raise the level of initiation for operating decisions and lower the level for industrial relations decisions.

There seem to be three main conditions favoring delegation:

1. *Changes in formal organization structure.* A reduction in the number of levels in the hierarchy tends to make it more difficult for superiors to initiate activity in all the details of operations for their subordinates and, therefore, tends to encourage subordinates to initiate at their level.

The individual can initiate activities at his level, without consulting superiors, most effectively when the activities assigned to him cover the total operations of his particular organizational unit. If he can take action in one sphere only when other individuals at his same level take related actions, then on many occasions he will need to go to his superior before taking the action in question. We have seen this in the Food World case. Before the reorganization, there were three men sharing top operating responsibilities in a given store, with each man reporting to a superior from the district office. This meant that problems of coordination among the three individuals often had to be referred to one or more levels above the store. Only when the store manager position was established, with the manager being assigned direction of all of the activities of the store, was it possible to build up the initiation of activities at the store level.

Delegation can also be fostered by specific managerial decisions that call for certain activities being initiated at lower levels.

In the Food World case, we have noted that the store managers were required to develop the store budgets and annual plans, which had previously been prepared at higher levels.

2. *Changes in face-to-face relations.* The changes in formal organization structure, noted above, actually have their effects in changes in face-to-face relations, but they only tend to channel those relations. They do not determine in detail the characteristics of face-to-face relations. Within the framework of the formal organization structure, we can see certain ways that the superior, in interaction with his subordinate, can stimulate the subordinate to initiate more activities at his own level. In other words, it is not enough to announce the policy that such-and-such a decision shall be made at such-and-such a level. The pattern of interactions within the organization will determine whether the man at that level actually initiates the activity on his own or takes it first to his superior for approval.

Based upon the Food World data, we can say that delegation is fostered when, in the relations between superior and subordinate, the superior reduces his percentage of total talking time—and particularly the proportion of opinions, directions, and suggestions that he offers—compared to those of his subordinates. Note that we are here dealing with proportions. The proposition may not require an absolute reduction of the number of opinions A expresses in conversation with B.

3. *Rewards and penalties.* Whether B will feel free to initiate activites without checking with A will depend in part upon how A responds when B actually does so. Is B rewarded or penalized for such initiative?

In many cases, when we hear superiors complain that the subordinates are not showing any initiative, we find that whatever the subordinate does, the superior tends to find something wrong with it. This type of penalizing behavior will wipe out any positive effects from verbal encouragement of initiative.

Supporting evidence

How do these general conclusions drawn from one case stand the test of other cases? Let us consider here briefly the case of General Superintendent John Dyer (presented in detail in Chapter 25 of *Men at Work*).

Dyer headed a large metals fabricating division in a large company. When he took over, the foremen and general foremen seemed to have little confidence in themselves and were not inclined to take anything other than routine actions without checking with superiors. A few months later these same men were showing a high degree of initiative in making their own decisions and proposing changes to their superiors. The influences that brought about this transformation can be described under the same three general headings we used on the Food World case.

1. *Changes in formal organization structure.* Before John Dyer took over as general superintendent, there had been a position of supervisor between the superintendents and general foremen. That position was eliminated in all divisions at about the time Dyer became general superintendent. The department superintendents were not able to supervise the general foremen as closely as had the supervisors, so that the structural change tended to increase the freedom of action of general foremen.

This structural change was accompanied by formally specified changes in the duties and responsibilities of the general foremen. For example, whereas previously requisitioning and ordering of new materials were handled by the superintendents, these powers were now delegated to the general foremen. They were authorized to sign for new materials and new employees, without securing clearance from above. They were also authorized to write and sign purchase orders for new equipment up to a limit of $1,000.

2. *Changes in face-to-face relations.* John Dyer instituted what he called a "free speech policy." He explained it in this way:

I want people to question my ideas. If I am not confident that a man will question my ideas, I am afraid to give him any idea until I have had a chance to study it out in full detail. That slows us all up. It is much better if I can feel free to pass along an idea and be confident that the man will use any part of it that seems sound to him or reject it altogether if he feels it does not make sense in his situation.

Whereas in the Food World case, changes in face-to-face relations at the level of the store were brought about within pair events linking district managers with store managers, in the Fabricating Division case, the new pattern was set in part through set events that recurred on a regular schedule. Dyer instituted a monthly meeting including himself, the superintendents, and the general foreman, and another set of monthly meetings in each department which included the superintendent, general foremen, and foremen. Pleased with his experience in the two three-level meetings, one general foremen initiated a monthly meeting with his foremen and workers, shutting down the production lines for half an hour for this purpose. After he reported on his experience with this new type of meeting in the monthly session with the general superintendent, superintendents, and other foremen, the practice rapidly spread throughout the division.

Dyer established the three-level pattern for the purpose of de-emphasizing rank in the expression of opposing points of view. He wanted it understood that each man was perfectly free to express his own opinion, even when it differed from that of his immediate superior. In fact, if he held back such an opinion, he could be criticized later for failing to contribute to the group. On the other hand, Dyer made it clear that decisions would not be made in the meetings. They would be made by those individuals formally charged with responsibility for making the decisions in question. The meetings were to contribute to decision-making effectiveness in giving each individual the benefit of the ideas and experiences of others.

Subordinates will not be impressed so much by how a superior says he will behave as by their observation of how he actually does behave in the face of a dissenting opinion. In Dyer's case, there was a close correspondence between his professed theory and his practice. One general foreman expressed the general opinion of people at his level in this way:

. . . we have these meetings very frequently and everyone is free to ask questions. We are even invited to make the questions just as embarrassing as possible. And we respond to that invitation. John invites us openly to argue with his opinions. He always says that his own idea is probably not the best and that our thoughts have great value. Besides it has often happened that he has abandoned his idea in order to take one of ours, recognizing that his own was not so practical. Now that really invites us to think and scratch our heads and rack our brains. That is why I think the discussions are so profitable.

3. *Rewards and penalties.* We have already considered this point in part in examining the behavior of the general superintendent in the meetings. It was very rewarding to the general foremen to discover that they could disagree with John Dyer and still get a respectful hearing and even, on occasion, get him to accept their ideas over his own.

The penalizing aspects of Dyer's strategy are illustrated by an encounter he had with one of his superintendents. That superintendent felt embarrassed when Dyer expressed disagreement with him in front of his subordinates or even sided with a general foreman who had disagreed with the superintendent. Wouldn't it be better, the superintendent proposed, if he and Dyer got together before the meeting so they could agree on what positions to take in the presence of the general superintendents? Dyer replied that, on the contrary, such an approach would destroy the value of the meetings. Some time later, that superintendent asked for and received a transfer out of this division. It became clear to all concerned that if you could not adjust to the "free speech policy," you would be better off elsewhere.

Does the introduction of the supporting evidence from a second case constitute "proof" of the general conclusions drawn from the Food World case? Of course not. The second case only gives us some small encouragement that we are on the right track. On the other hand, the purpose of this chapter has been much more modest that presenting "proof" of anything. We have sought to do just two things:

1. Present a behavioral definition of the delegation of authority and responsibility.
2. Present some preliminary conclusions regarding how the degree of delegation in an organization may be increased or decreased.

If the student of a new case looks for the behavioral items noted in our description of the Food World and John Dyer cases, he should be able to make some reasonably concrete statements about the degree of delegation he finds. He should also be able to indicate whether the introduction of a specified change will tend to increase or decrease the degree of delegation he has found.

References

Chapple, Eliot D., and Sayles, Leonard. *The Measure of Management*. New York: MacMillan Co., 1961. Presents an interactional approach to the study of management, readily applicable to the study of delegation.

Sayles, Leonard. *Managerial Behavior*. New York: McGraw-Hill Book Co., 1964. Examines the exercise of authority in relation to the other important aspects of managerial behavior.

Discussion questions

1. In an organization with which you have had personal experience, specify the degree of delegation of authority and responsibility prevailing in regard to a specific managerial position. Indicate the kinds of evidence you used in making your judgment.

2. Interview someone with experience in an organization regarding the degree of authority and responsibility delegated to him by his boss. First get him to make a general statement about the degree of delegation prevailing. Then get him to present to you the information on which he bases this general conclusion.

3. Interview someone with experience in an organization regarding the degree of authority and responsibility he delegates to his subordinates. First get him to make a general statement about the degree of delegation prevailing. Then get him to present you the information on which he bases this general conclusion. What problems do you have in making a realistic appraisal regarding delegation when you depend solely upon the testimony of the boss?

30. The decision-making process

THIS CHAPTER examines decision making as a *social process*. Why have a chapter on decision making in a section on the introduction of change? Are not decisions being made in various levels of the organization at all times in the ordinary course of business operations? Indeed they are, but it is useful to make a distinction between routine and change decisions. Here we will concentrate on change decisions.

Another way of expressing the same idea is to distinguish between programmed and unprogrammed decisions. Some recurring decisions are based on such familiar elements that we can describe them as programmed. By this we mean that rules can be established to specify that, when conditions X, Y, and Z are observed together, the individual should take action A. Such decisions are not only theoretically programmable. In modern industry they are increasingly being programmed in an electronic sense.

Inventory control presents a simple example of such programming possibilities. In the past, a functionary in charge of the inventory had the responsibility of making decisions as to when to reorder certain standard items. He would keep records and act on certain rule-of-thumb indicators as to the amount and timing of a given order.

Studies of past operations in inventory control can readily lead to the electronic programming of the main elements of the system. If it is determined that when the inventory stock of item X falls below 1,000 units, an order for an additional 1,000 should at once be placed, both obsevation and decision can be plugged into the system. As units of item X are removed from inventory, the appropriate information is fed into the computer. When the computer notes that the stock of item X has dropped below 1,000, the computer produces the necessary instructions for placement of the new order.

Does this mean that computers will relieve managers of most of their decision-making activities? To answer that question, we must emphasize the difference between programmable and unprogrammable decisions. The inventory control case is a simple programmable example. Decision rules could be established on the basis of voluminous past experience. In effect, those who design the program were saying: "We will make our future decisions on the basis of our analysis of past experience." The machine program is based on the sometimes questionable assumption that the future will resemble the past. On the other hand, human beings in making decisions without aid of computers tend naturally to make the same assumption and, in general terms, it is a reasonable one. If the future bore little or no resemblance to the past, then men would be unable to learn from experience and planning would be impossible. Furthermore, as conditions do change, new experience can be analyzed and a revised program developed on the basis of new decision rules.

When we talk about planned change, we are necessarily entering into an area where decisions are only partly programmable, if indeed they can be programmed at all. Men are trying to anticipate conditions that they have never yet experienced. They are trying to estimate costs, production, volume of sales, and so on for conditions sufficiently different from past experience so that a simple extrapolation from the past to the future will not provide firm guidance.

Furthermore, as we enter into these areas of uncertainties, we find different individuals and groups presenting conflicting recommendations, with each proposal backed by its own set of figures. The decision does not make itself on technical grounds, and whatever decision emerges may have important effects on the positions of the competing individuals and groups in the organization.

The traditional approach

Decision making has long been a matter of central interest to writers on management. While there are variations from one writer to another, the standard approach has evolved along the lines summarized in the following statement by Craig C. Lundberg:[1]

1. In scanning one's environment, a discrepancy between what is perceived and what one conceives to be normal or standard is perceived and a problem thereby formulated.
2. Information is acquired (implies searching the environment and/or one's memory).
3. Sometimes the problem is redefined.
4. Information that is gathered is ordered into alternative solutions.
5. A review of the applicable goals indicates the criteria to be used in evaluating the alternative solutions.

---

[1] Craig C. Lundberg, "Patterns of Organizational Decisioning: A Conceptual Scheme and Its Application in the Study of Comparative Cases in Industry" (Ph.D. thesis, New York State School of Industrial and Labor Relations, Cornell University, 1966), pp. 315–16.

6. The alternatives are evaluated in terms of the criteria and a choice is made.
7. Implementation of a solution is effected.

This approach is typically expressed in graphic form as the decision making tree. There are ultimate objectives and intermediate objectives and shorter range objectives and there are means to be used in aiming toward one set of objectives or another. The diagram is so set forth as to indicate that, as the decision maker selects a given objective, his course of action branches off from what it would be if he selected a different objective.

What is wrong with this approach? We note four important difficulties:

1. The description of activities is usually expressed in passive form, as in the summary presented above. The description does not make it clear whether the activities of an individual, group, or organization are being described. In fact, such discussions often are written as if it made no difference which unit was being described.
2. The statements are normative rather than observational. That is, they are based upon the writer's assumptions of what people *ought* to do in decision making rather than upon observations of what they actually do do.
3. These statements are phrased entirely in intellectual terms, whereas human action in the real world is a combination of intellectual and nonintellectual elements.
4. Decision making is often conceived in dramatic terms, with the act of making the decision being the climax and chief focus of attention. As we will show below, it is more useful and more realistic to view decision making as a process.

The impact of information

In the usual approach to decision making theory, information is considered as a neutral or passive element. The individual making the decision is to gather all of the relevant information—and relevance is to be determined solely on technical grounds. Cyert and March argue against this view in the following words:[2]

Individuals will treat estimates, information, and communication generally as active parts of their environment. They will tend to consider the decision for which the information is relevant, the probable outcomes of various possible biases in information, and the payoff to them of various possible decision results. They adjust the information they transmit in accordance with their perceptions of the decision situation.

[2] R. M. Cyert and J. G. March, *A Behavioral Theory of the Firm* (Englewood Cliffs, N.J.: Prentice-Hall, 1963), p. 75.

We also need to look at information in terms of the structure of the organization and the interaction among its members, for information does not float around by itself. Information is carried by particular individuals at particular points in the organization. It therefore becomes important to determine which individuals, at which organizational positions, participate in the decision-making process—and which ones are excluded. This is particularly well illustrated in the Bay of Pigs case.

The Bay of Pigs

The Bay of Pigs case is worth analysis, for what happened is well documented, and here we have no problem about evaluating the correctness of the decision—one of the stumbling blocks in research on decision making. The problem then is one of determining how such a collosal blunder could have happened.

When it was all over, President Kennedy asked himself, "How could I have been so stupid?" I suggest that this is not a fruitful question for a decision maker to ask, for it leads us to discussions of thinking ability. We are likely to come out with no more productive conclusion than that it is better to be smart than stupid.

I shall not attempt to set forth the *process* in full but only tell enough of the story to indicate the importance of a *process* approach.

One of the first questions to ask is: Who is included in the process? In other words, who is included in the process with the function of providing information? Who is included as an advice giver? As a discussion-group member? Let us follow the account of Arthur Schlesinger, Jr.,[3] on this point.

Since this was to be a secret operation, the "need to know" standard came into operation: Only those individuals who had a demonstrable need to know what was going on could be included in the planning process. Schlesinger points out that the application of this standard excluded the Cuban desk in the State Department. The Plans Division of CIA (popularly known as the "dirty tricks" division) had the main responsibility for planning and carrying out the operation, but the Intelligence Division of CIA, which had the responsibility of providing information about what was going on in Cuba, was also left out of the planning process. This meant that while CIA administrators at high levels were free to use whatever information was coming into the Intelligence Division on a routine basis, they were precluded from asking the intelligence analysts to evaluate the feasibility of the plan. As Schlesinger puts it:[4]

---

[3] Arthur Schlesinger, Jr., *A Thousand Days* (Boston: Houghton Mifflin, 1965). The Bay of Pigs discussion and other parts of this chapter have appeared in my chapter on "Building Better Organizational Models," Gerald Somers (ed.), *Essays in Industrial Relations* (Ames: Iowa State University Press, 1969).

[4] *Ibid.*, p. 248.

The "need to know" standard—i.e., that no one should be told about a project unless it becomes operationally necessary—thus had the idiotic effect of excluding much of the expertise of government at a time when every alert newspaper man knew something was afoot.

What would have happened if the Cuban desk at State and the appropriate people for Cuba in the Intelligence Division at CIA had been involved in evaluating the plans? No one can answer such an hypothetical question, but we may speculate that there was at least one point where detailed factual knowledge regarding Cuba would have proven indispensible. In one of the final planning meetings, President Kennedy asked what would happen if the rebel forces, having landed on the beaches, were unable to fight their way inland. The answer was that, in this case, the insurgent forces would make their way into the Sierra Maestra Mountains, there continuing the resistance, much as Castro had done before he came to power. As Schlesinger points out, this was a physical impossibility. Some miles of swampland separated the Bay of Pigs beaches from access to the mountains. In other words, there were only two alternative outcomes: the insurgent forces would be able to fight their way inland or they would be driven into the sea. If the imaginary third alternative had been exploded, perhaps this exposure of the wishful thinking involved in the planning operations would have led President Kennedy to re-think the whole matter.

What individuals had the legitimate right to advise the President on these issues? In what social setting was it legitimate for a given individual to exercise his advising role?

In the Bay of Pigs case, all of those who were formally called upon by the President to give him advice in White House group discussions were heads of large bureaucracies or key figures in such structures: The Secretaries of Defense and of State, the Director of the CIA, the Joint Chiefs. No one of these men was free to give his full attention to an uncommitted analysis of the proposal. Like any good organization man, each of these executives had to be concerned also with his relations with members of his own bureaucracy and with interagency relations. The plan was developed within CIA. When men in the Defense Department examined it, they had inevitably to consider past, present and future relations with CIA. If they reacted negatively to the plan, would this be accepted by other administration figures as coming out of a dispassionate intellectual analysis, or would it suggest some possible jealousies between agencies? If they supported the plan, would this have a favorable effect upon future interagency relations?

As Schlesinger himself points out, in these top level meetings there was no one called upon to speak whose only loyalty was to the President himself. The White House staff? The role that White House staff members might play on such matters had not crystallized at this time. Schlesinger attended these top-level meetings but did not speak upon his own initiative, nor did the President call upon him. Once President Kennedy asked him casually what he thought of the plan, and Schlesinger responded with a negative evaluation. The President commented that he had read a newspaper report on conditions inside Cuba that tended to support Schlesinger's argument. He suggested that Schlesinger have lunch with the newspaper man and draw him out further, without telling him that an invasion had been planned. The fact that the President would reach for such information outside of channels suggests his consciousness of the extent to which he was limited by the way the process had been structured, but unfortunately this uneasiness did not lead him to examine the decision-making process itself.

Schlesinger, on his own initiative, wrote two strong memos to the President, recommending against the invasion. He blames himself for not having spoken up in the formal, top-level meetings. I would suggest that his role at this time had not been so defined as to legitimatize such intervention. A top executive cannot expect to save himself from a blunder by counting on some subordinate having the initiative to violate the unwritten understandings of channels of communication.

Suppose the process had been so organized as to provide for an independent and critical role by men responsible only to the President? President Kennedy had an able group of personal advisors. He might have asked them to take the plans as presented to him, to examine them from stem to stern, to do their best to tear them apart. It seems likely that a process organized in this fashion would have brought in such a negative report on the project that the President might well have made a different decision.

The President did, in fact, draw this kind of conclusion from the Bay of Pigs experience. As Schlesinger points out, he later made much more use of his assistants for providing critical analyses of projects presented to him by members of his Cabinet and other administrative figures.

On the indeterminacy of facts

We are often advised to "let the facts speak for themselves." Of course, the facts do not speak for themselves, but only through the people who present them.

While making all due allowances for the distorting effects of personal biases, can we not develop scientific methods to determine the "facts" in such an unequivocal way that they permit only one interpretation? This is more difficult than we may wish to recognize even in cases where we have technical questions that we would expect to be determined by technical procedures. For example, consider the conflict in the Amicon Tube case (Chapter 24) between industrial engineer Fred Fisher and the development engineers over the testing of the items produced by the method designed by Fisher. There was no question about the fact that the items did not pass this particular test. There was, however, strong argument over whether this particular test and the conditions surrounding it were appropriate for the purposes of determining quality. Thus the parties fell to arguing over the appropriateness of the test and the accompanying procedures, even though the facts of the test results were clear-cut.

If it is difficult enough to determine the facts on events taking place in the recent past, when the decision maker enters into the realm of future possibilities, he is an area where facts are hard to come by and where those that are available may not be relevant for his purpose. When men enter into discussions of the future, they are engaged in the manipulation of expectations. This manipulability of expectations is illustrated in the following comment by a company official regarding a decision he was urging upon the company:[5]

In the final analysis, if anybody brings up an item of cost that we haven't thought of, we can balance it by making another source of savings tangible.

In a very technologically advanced company, an engineer made this comment on the role of facts in decision making:[6]

Decisions have to be made by edict very often because you can't make a good engineering judgment. Two years from now you don't know how things may have changed, so you'll never know whether you did the right or wrong thing. . . . We make a lot of assumptions that are good to about plus or minus 50 percent. You have to include all of the dimensions, all of the variables, and you have to guess three to five years early in the game. You're going to get a lot of overlap in your alternatives because of this, and you can't make a solid engineering judgment. You need an edicted answer.

The indeterminacy of the future makes it impossible to base decisions purely on factual information. Thus, when important decisions are to be made, the modern organization becomes an arena in which advocates of different alternatives struggle to make their conception of the future prevail. An engineer described the process in this way:[7]

Every engineer has to do some selling—spend a certain amount of his time this way. People are continually fighting for their beliefs, for what in their opinion is best for the company . . . we are going to have to convince people that we can do the job. . . . Some day you have to get out there and wage political warfare, and you have to battle for your convictions. If you don't—if you are not willing to battle for your beliefs—then the other guy is just going to take all the money and go home.

---

[5] Cyert and March, *op. cit.*, p. 81.

[6] R. R. Ritti and Fred H. Goldner, "Managers and Professionals in Complex Organizations," Paper delivered at 1967 meeting of American Sociological Association.

[7] R. R. Ritti, *Engineers and the Industrial Corporation*, to be published in 1970 by Columbia University Press, New York.

Structural effects

In the business or governmental organization, decisions take place within a hierarchy and can only be understood if we take the nature of this hierarchy into account. If the ability to reach a "good" decision on the part of a high-level decision maker depends upon his ability to get accurate information from low levels of the organization, then the decision-making process will clearly be influenced by the forces that influence the accuracy of this upward informational flow. Many writers have noted the filtering effects commonly observed in large organizations. Harold L. Wilensky puts it this way:[8]

. . . In reporting at every level, hierarchy is conducive to concealment and misrepresentation. Subordinates are asked to transmit information that can be used to evaluate their performance. Their motive for "making it look good," for "playing it safe," is obvious. A study of 52 middle managers (mean age 37) found a correlation of + .41 (p. .01) between upward work-life mobility and holding back "problem" information from the boss; the men on their way up were prone to restrict information about such issues as lack of authority to meet responsibilities, fights with other units, unforeseen costs, rapid changes in production, scheduling or work flow, fruitless progress reports, constant interruptions, insufficient time or budget to train subordinates, insufficient equipment or supplies, and so on.

The effects of hierarchy are not limited to the communication process up and down from level to level. Hierarchical effects are also to be observed when individuals of a number of different organizational levels are present in the same discussion meeting. This was well illustrated in the Amicon Tube case. When progress on the tube did not satisfy him, the plant manager instituted a series of large group meetings. He called in 16 people ranging in position from himself at the top down to the foreman and the industrial engineer who were immediately involved in the problem. As Ronken and Lawrence observed, there was a high correlation between the volume of an individual's participation in the discussions and his position in the hierarchy. This means that Lou Correveau, the foreman, and Fred Fisher, the industrial engineer, who knew far more about the problems than anyone else, were the least frequent participators in the discussion. In fact, it appears that they only spoke when someone called on them for information or opinion. It seems hardly coincidental that the Amicon Tube project began to progress more rapidly as soon as these large meetings were terminated and group discussions were limited to those who, in both position and immediate experience, were close to the development and operating problems.

We must also consider the effects of group commitment. When alternative courses of action are being discussed, it is not only ideas that are in

---

[8] Harold L. Wilensky, *Organizational Intelligence: Knowledge and Policy in Government and Industry* (New York: Basic Books, 1967), p. 43.

conflict. The contest is among the advocates of the ideas. The winner in such a contest gains prestige in the eyes of those around him, and the losers lose some of their "face." But the effects go far beyond the personal feeling of pride or disappointment on the part of the key participants. Which idea prevails may also determine which group of engineers and managers moves ahead in budget, status, immediate promotions, and enhanced possibilities of future promotions—and which group is sidetracked, relegated to more routine operations, or even broken up. Under these circumstances, it is hardly realistic to expect the advocates of a given course of action to present a detached and dispassionate analysis.

We must also consider the group commitment effect that arises when a number of individuals have invested a large part of their time and energy in a project over a considerable period of time. Here again, let us turn to the Bay of Pigs case. By the time that the project approached its final decision point with President Kennedy, a large number of CIA people, from Director Allen Dulles on down, had invested major parts of their time for two years in planning the invasion of Cuba and in carrying out the preliminary training and logistical activities necessary for that purpose. The Cuban exiles who made up the army that was in training in Guatemala had also made very substantial investments of their time for a long period—and on a full time basis. The proponents of the invasion plan quite reasonably noted that, if the operation were cancelled at the 11th hour, the U.S. government could not expect the members of this army to disperse and go about their business as if nothing had happened. Having made these major investments, and having been prevented from seeking the rewards of these investments, they would naturally have taken their frustrations out in troublesome criticisms of the U.S. government policies.

When the planners and organizers of the projected invasion first began making their plans, they based their hopes for a successful outcome on three assumptions:

1. If U.S. direct military involvement in the invasion was necessary for the support of the Cuban exile army, that support would be given.
2. An uprising within Cuba could be brought off in time so as to coincide with the invasion.
3. If the invaders did not succeed in fighting their way inland, they could retreat into the mountains and carry on guerrilla activity.

With the advantage of hindsight, we can say that the invasion had a reasonable chance of success only if all three of those assumptions had been correct.

In all of the discussions he held regarding the invasion, President Kennedy explicitly ruled out the first assumption: Under no conditions would U.S. military forces land in Cuba. President Kennedy apparently thought that the second assumption might be valid, but in fact the CIA operations people did not trust the Cubans in this country who were in contact with disaffected Cubans in Cuba and were, through these channels, to give the signal for the uprising. Since the Cubans in this country were not given information as to when the invasion was to take place, clearly the assumption of an internal uprising was unrealistic. The third assumption, regarding the retreat to guerrilla activities in the mountains, became an impossibility when the Bay of Pigs location was selected for the invasion.

It appears that by the time the final decision point was approaching, the key CIA people had forgotten about the assumptions on which their initial assessment of the prospects of an invasion had depended. How else can we account for their extraordinary failure to examine the geography of the landing area to determine whether in fact it would be possible for the invading troops to retreat to the mountains? Thus the assumptions which justified beginning work on the project were abandoned at that most critical point when the invasion or cancellation decision had to be made.

Did the key CIA people continue urging the invasion, disregarding the assumptions necessary for success, because they were stupid? Since the key men involved had carried out other highly complex operations with a high degree of skill, the stupidity explanation is hardly plausible. Clearly we are dealing with an emotional commitment to a project, that necessarily grew out of the investment of time and effort of many men in developing the project up to the final decision point. In fact, Allen Dulles inadvertantly revealed the emotional basis of his motivation when he spoke to the President with great eloquence, insisting that he believed in the success of the Cuban invasion even more than he had in the success of the Guatemalan operation—which had proved successful. In effect, the CIA leaders had so much invested in the project as to rule out any possibility of their making an objective assessment of the situation.

The decision maker as hero

In the popular mind, a good deal of glamour attaches to decisions and to the role of the decision maker. The popular assumption seems to be that for any decision there must be a decision maker, and that furthermore there must be a particular point in time when this hero makes his decision.

In organizational life, human actions are not nearly so neatly arranged. It is often impossible to determine in any realistic fashion who has made a given decision. It may be even impossible to determine who has the "power" to make a given decision. Let us consider a case in point.

Choosing a dean

To illustrate the essentials of a new approach to power and decision making, let us consider a concrete case: the choosing of a dean for the New York State School of Industrial and Labor Relations in Cornell

University. No one could deny that this is an important decision within a university. I have been involved in this decision on two occasions, first simply as a member of the faculty, and second, as a member of the responsible committee, and therefore I can describe what takes place from first-hand knowledge.

As I begin the story, let me ask the reader to keep two questions in mind: Who has the authority to make this decision? Or who actually does make the decision? At the conclusion of my account of the case, I shall challenge anyone to give a meaningful answer to either of those questions.

When a vacancy in this position occurs, the process goes through the following steps:

1. The president appoints a committee from the college. He tends to appoint departmental chairmen or men at approximately that level of responsibility, though this is not required by legislation.
2. The president meets with the committee. There follows a discussion of the procedure to be followed and of the qualities that would be desirable in a man holding this position. The president encourages the committee to consider outside candidates as well as insiders and not to assume that any desirable candidate may be unavailable. He asks the committee to present him with names of three or more individuals, all of whom would be acceptable to the faculty of the school. Furthermore, he asks that these names not be ranked, so that he will have an opportunity to make an independent judgment without appearing to challenge the recommendations of the committee.
3. The committee meets and discusses the procedure it will follow. The first order of business is to canvass all members of the faculty for their suggestions of candidates, and each member of the committee is assigned a list of professors to canvass.
4. After the canvassing has been completed, the committee meets to work out a "master list" of names to be considered. Committee members may add names that have not been suggested by the faculty members canvassed. The committee may also, at its peril, drop off names of men suggested. If the committee members are sure at this point that they would not, under any conditions, recommend a given individual to the president, they may deem it inadvisable to proceed further with this name. Of course, if the man to be dropped off the list has been urged by influential faculty members, this committee vetoing may subject it to serious criticism. Finally, out of this committee discussion comes a preliminary list of perhaps 10 to 12 names deemed worthy of further consideration.
5. The committee members now re-canvass their constituents, each man going back to the people he originally consulted. The procedure is to show the constituent a list of those under consideration and ask him to make a ranking of these names.
6. When the re-canvassing has been completed, the committee meets,

works out a summary of the rankings and then strives to arrive at a list of three to five names to be recommended to the president. This is not simply a mechanical matter of following the rankings provided by the faculty. The committee introduces its own judgments, but, at the very least, the rankings provide evidence of what candidates would be acceptable to the faculty and what ones would not.

7. The committee chairman presents the president with a list of three to five acceptable candidates and also furnishes biographical data on each one.

8. Over a period of several weeks, the president undertakes to have a personal conversation with each potential candidate to whom he is willing to give serious consideration. He then asks the committee to invite his first choice to the campus for a visit.

9. The candidate comes to town (with his wife) and goes through a cycle of social activities, discussions with key faculty and administration figures, and he also gives a talk on some topic of his choosing to the faculty. If these activities point toward some mutual agreement, the candidate and the president and possibly others may be involved in preliminary negotiations to establish the nature and conditions of the position.

10. The president negotiates with his nominee to secure his acceptance of the offer.

12. The president appears before a meeting of the faculty to announce his choice and make whatever remarks he wishes in favor of this recommendation. The president generally does not find it necessary or advisable to speak at length in favor of the candidate.

13. After presenting his proposal and responding to whatever questions may be directed at him, the president leaves, and the floor is open for further discussion. Since discussions and arguments over the merits of this man have been in progress in the offices and corridors for many days, the discussion on the floor of the faculty is likely to be brief or to be skipped altogether. There follows a secret ballot, in which each faculty member is asked to vote yes or no on the president's recommendation.

14. At the next meeting of the Board of Trustees, the president presents his recommendation for the deanship. By faculty legislation, he is required also to announce to the Board the result of the vote on this candidate. In other words, the majority vote against the candidate does not require the president to withdraw the candidacy, but he must announce the vote, whatever it is, to the Board of Trustees.

15. The trustees vote their approval of the candidate.

Let us now place the questions: Who has the authority? Who makes the decision?

The trustees? They only ratify the president's recommendation. Refusal to ratify the president's recommendation on a matter of this importance would be equivalent to asking for his resignation. On the other hand, the requirement that the recommendation must go before the Board is not a mere formality. The president who recommends a dean who has received an adverse vote from the faculty places himself in an awkward position before the Board of Trustees. Such a situation can be interpreted as a reflection upon the president's judgment and upon the quality of his relations with the faculty. In my 20 years at Cornell, I know of only one occasion when the president made a recommendation for a man who had received an adverse vote—and in this case it was not for a dean of a college but for a comparable position. The trustees did support the president's recommendation, but a number of faculty members had the impression that in the months and years following this trustee action, the president showed increased concern for faculty opinion.

Does the president have the power? He is limited to those in the list prepared by the committee. To be sure, he has the legal right to recommend a man who is not on that list, but unless he is able to convince the committee of the outstanding qualities of this individual, such an action would guarantee an overwhelmingly negative vote against the candidate in the faculty meeting.

On the other hand, the president plays a very important role in negotiating with the candidate. Not every professor wants to become a dean. Those who are persuadable will want to explore very carefully not only the economic conditions of employment but the organizational pattern into which they must fit. The candidate's evaluation of the president is obviously an important element in his decision to accept or reject the job offer.

The faculty committee obviously plays a key role. To some extent the members of the committee, individually and collectively, can exercise independent judgment, but it is easy to exaggerate the degrees of freedom the committee enjoys. The committee cannot put across a man unacceptable to the president. Nor can the committee afford to put on the list a man who cannot be counted upon to get at least a majority favorable vote from the faculty. Before the president begins his own discussions with potential candidates, he wants to have the assurance of the committee that those recommended to him will win such faculty support. If the man recommended by the president receives an adverse vote from the faculty, this is embarrassing to the committee as well as to the president.

Feedback or justification?

The cycle does not end with the making of a decision. We need also to consider evaluation of the effects of the decision.

Ideally, if executives are to improve their decision-making skills, they should have constant feedback on the effects of their past decisions. In

698   Organizational behavior: theory and application

most organizational situations, it is impossible to meet or even approach this ideal. There appear to be two main problems in the way of an objective feedback process on the effects of past decisions.

1. *Proof is difficult to come by.*   There may be some simple decisions whose effects will show up in a short time, but executives most of the time are concerned with reaching decisions on complex problems, where the effects will show up over a long period of time and in ambiguous forms. Few decisions will turn out to be brilliant successes or spectacular failures. (We have indeed considered the Bay of Pigs case here, but where do we find others where the failure was so complete and so universally acknowledged?)

There is also a problem in finding agreement upon some standard of measurement. Here the contrast between the Edsel and the U.S. policy in Vietnam is instructive. To be sure, Robert McNamara and his associates in the Ford Motor Company were embarrassed when the Edsel failed to achieve public acceptance, but this did not prevent them from cutting their losses by abandoning the project. In the Vietnam case, it was clear to all concerned that the policy was enormously costly in human lives, money, and the disruption of U.S. society, and it was also clear that the immediate favorable results of the policy hardly balanced the costs. Why then did the President, the Secretary of State, and the Secretary of Defense (Mr. McNamara) hold so firmly to the policy for so long a period? Supporters of the policy could argue in terms of *what might have been* and in terms of the *long run.* They could (and did) say that while the policy was indeed extremely costly, any other policy would have been more costly. Also they could (and did) argue that while favorable results were hard to discover in the short run, in the long run the policy would prove successful.

I am not claiming that such arguments are falacious. I am simply pointing out that it is impossible to disprove—or to prove—their validity. You cannot measure the impact of decisions not taken, nor can you really determine in the short run what the long-run results will be of the decisions that are made. Thus, in the Edsel case, the decision makers were applying some sort of measurable standard: When the project has lost X million dollars and is losing X dollars a month, it is time to abandon the project. No such agreed upon standard was available for judging policy in the Vietnam case.

While foreign policy is more likely to be plagued by questions of what *might have been* and by guesses about the *long run,* the same kinds of considerations can come up with many complex business decisions. Therefore, we cannot assume that simply "getting the facts" will give us the answer.

2. *The decision maker has made investments in the decision.*   People in high places know very well that their future power and influence will depend to a considerable extent upon their reputation for having made

"good" decisions. Therefore, they find it difficult to be neutral in evaluating their own past decisions. They are pleased to receive evidence of the correctness of the decision and upset to receive evidence of its incorrectness. Subordinates take cues from such reactions and respond by rushing to the boss any favorable indication and filtering out or in some way spraying perfume over unfavorable indications. The executive can thereby readily find what he is looking for.

Perhaps we can say that a successful executive is one who makes good decisions—but that is hard to prove. We can say with more confidence that a successful executive is one who makes his past decisions look good. Of course, we do not assume that a skillful executive can make any bad decision look good. There must be important limitations to such powers of executive alchemy, but without research data upon this transformation process we can only point to the importance of the phenomenon, without attempting further analysis.[9]

Implications for administrative action

Can we draw from this discussion some practical lessons for the administrator?

In much more elaborate words, he is often advised to be smart rather than stupid and to pick smart advisers rather than stupid ones. The value of such advice is questionable, for nobody is stupid on purpose, and nobody deliberately picks stupid advisers.

We move in a more practical direction if we turn our attention from the qualities of individuals and focus upon decision making as a process. If the process is well organized, then average men will produce superior decisions. If the process is poorly organized, then only geniuses can save the organization from disaster.

We cannot give the administrator any simple how-to-do-it manual, but the preceding discussion at least suggests certain questions that deserve his thoughtful attention.

Since the quality of the decision will depend in large measure upon the range and quality of information fed into the process, the administrator needs to consider what individuals and what organizational positions should be involved in the seeking and providing of information. He should recognize (as is dramatically illustrated in the Bay of Pigs case) that the inclusion or exclusion of individuals in group discussions can have crucial effects on the quality of the decision. As he observes the discussion process, the administrator needs to keep in mind that organizational structure (and membership in particular organizational units) necessarily influences the range and quality of information fed into the process, the positions taken in discussion, and later reactions to decisions.

---

[9] For the idea in this last paragraph, I am indebted to Richard Ritti.

The administrator should recognize hierarchical effects. He should expect that information reaching him through the normal hierarchical channels will be filtered and selected. If he cannot fully rely on the picture presented to him through normal channels, should he short-circuit these channels by going direct to the individuals most immediately involved in the problem situation? Or should he have a staff member responsible only to him moving about freely, outside of normal hierarchical channels, so as to get closer to the information? Either of these strategies may have disturbing effects upon those who are acting in the normal hierarchical channels, but the administrator has to weigh the importance of these effects against the possible importance of a good or poor decision on the issue in question.

The administrator should recognize the status constraints that enter into group meetings where men of widely differing statuses are present. He should not expect a low-status man to speak up on a given situation even if he is the best informed of those present. On the other hand, it is possible for the administrator to conduct group meetings in such a fashion as to minimize the status constraints and to stimulate open communication from members of low status.

The administrator needs to recognize group commitment effects. He should not consider it illegitimate for an individual to be influenced in his views by the position he holds and the group within which he works. On the contrary, he should recognize that such influences are natural and to be expected. It is up to the administrator to recognize the influence of these effects and to seek to compensate for them in his own reflection about decision making and his management of the decision-making process.

When contending parties are urging different courses of action upon him, the clash of information and opinion tends to protect the administrator in part from the biasing effects of the commitment of a particular group. To this extent, the executive should regard competition and conflict as normal and (in some situations) constructive organizational activities.

But suppose that there is no conflict among those advising the administrator? On matters of small importance, the lack of dissent can safely be taken as a signal for going ahead. The executive cannot searchingly investigate all sides of every decision situation. To a large extent, he must rely upon others to do this for him. However, whether the executive is satisfied with a consensus judgment from his chief advisers should depend upon the magnitude of the consequences for a wrong decision. The Bay of Pigs case again serves as an illustration. Among the major participants in the decision-making process, there was a consensus favoring the invasion, and yet everyone recognized that the failure of this project could have disastrous consequences. In such a situation, the executive needs to call upon others to restudy the problem, to tear apart the arguments presented in favor of the decision in question, and thus bring to him any important negative indications that may have been lost in the consensus of his chief advisers.

How does one judge advice or the adviser? We all recognize the pitfalls of being misled by feelings of liking or disliking of individuals, so we are first inclined to say that "personality" should be left out of the picture and we should give our attention to the facts. On the other hand, we have shown that the "fact" approach has its own built in difficulties. Let us consider one type of situation in which skillful executives quite wisely consider the personal element.

Perhaps it would be more accurate to say that they consider the past "track record" of the adviser. An industrial relations man in a major oil company told me the following story. At one time he had found himself temporarily in the position of superintendent of field operations in a major oil-producing area of a foreign country. He had had no formal training in engineering or geology, the specialties normally possessed by incumbents of this position. He was confronted with the necessity of making a decision on a proposal that involved a substantial investment for the company. One man was strongly advocating this course of action, whereas another man of equally high rank was arguing in opposition. Without the technical expertise to make an independent judgment, how could the superintendent come to a reasonable decision? After getting all he could out of discussions and written reports, the superintendent spent a considerable amount of time going over the past records to determine how previous proposals of the present recommender had turned out in practice. He did a similar evaluation in somewhat less detail for the chief opponent of the project. It seemed clear to him from this examination of the record that the projects advocated in the past by the present proponent had turned out to be practical and valuable. Therefore he approved the recommendation.

Of course, there are many situations in which the executive should not make the decisions himself, but the executive should be clear as to which decisions he really wants to make himself. Otherwise, he may find himself simply "going along" with recommendations of others, who then in effect are really deciding the questions.

The question of who should make the decision, in a large organization, requires a structural answer. Consider the case of Harry Truman,[10] who was determined that he in fact would decide on the critical issues that fell within his principle responsibility.

In the case of a bill that stirred debate in Congress and that seemed likely to come to the Presidential desk for signature or veto, Mr. Truman organized his White House staff into two competing groups. Those in the

---

[10] I am indebted to Philleo Nash, who was a White House advisor to President Truman, for the following account.

"pro" team were required to prepare a report presenting a systematic analysis of all the considerations that should lead the President to sign the measure, and they were also responsible for drafting a Presidential statement to be released if and when he decided to sign. The "anti" team was responsible for a report presenting all of the considerations weighing against signing the bill, and they were also required to prepare a draft of the veto message. So that his assistants would be more likely to do a strictly professional job, uninfluenced by their personal sentiments, Mr. Truman undertook to assign each man to a team that was to take a position opposite to his own personal point of view.

There were a number of occasions on which the White House assistants had no idea what the President's decision would be until the last moment, as the President sat at his desk with the bill and the two opposing team reports laid out before him. The first signal of the President's decision came when Mr. Truman reached for the veto message or for the message setting forth his reasons for signing the bill.

On important matters, Mr. Truman did not want decisions made for him. He felt it was the responsibility of the President to make these decisions. Furthermore, he wanted the situation to remain completely open until he made his decision. The way he structured the process achieved these objectives for Mr. Truman.

Summary and conclusions

The case of choosing the dean at Cornell illustrates a process in which it is impossible to determine who makes the decision. In the examples from Presidents Kennedy and Truman there is no question about who made the ultimate decision, but we must examine the process if we are to understand what happened.

Unless we understand what people are included in the process to provide information, what people give advice, what people are involved in discussions of a given decision, and the sequence of the interactions and activities leading up to the decision, our literature in the field of decision making will continue to be a mixture of fact and folklore.

This conclusion has important practical as well as theoretical implications. The administrator who wishes to improve the quality of the decisions for which he has some responsibility would be well advised not to devote himself exclusively to the improvement of his own abilities of logical reasoning, nor even to the question of getting more able advisers or information producers. He should recognize that the quality of his decisions will depend in large measure upon the way the decision-making process is organized. If he wants to improve that quality, he should first lay out for himself the sequence of interactions and activities that have led to decisions in his recent experience. He might then consider what reorganization of this process would produce better decisions.

The Truman case and the Bay of Pigs case both point in the same direction concerning the importance for the executive of having on his immediate staff, loyal to him alone, individuals who help him to evaluate the information that comes to him through the regular channels and who are themselves free to do research and re-evaluation of data furnished by others.

Textbook discussions of decision making tend to give the impression that information gathering and weighing are technical, rational processes. The executive just recognizes what information is relevant, gathers that information, and submits it to logical analysis.

Life is not that simple. Unless the executive visualizes decision making as a social process, he cannot expect to utilize the human resources of the organization (including himself) with full effectiveness.

References

Gore, William J. *Administrative Decision Making: A Heuristic Model.* New York: John Wiley & Sons, 1964. A theoretical framework for the study of decision making, together with material from a number of field studies.

Wilensky, Harold J. *Organizational Intelligence: Knowledge and Policy in Government and Industry.* New York: Basic Books, Inc., 1967. An analysis of the uses and abuses of knowledge in organizations. The book is based primarily upon cases from government, but the same principles should apply to private industry and other nongovernmental organizations.

Discussion questions

1. Select for analysis a decision made in an organization where you were a participant in the decision-making process. Describe the process through which this particular decision got made. What people were involved? Why these people and not others? What information and what interpretations of information were provided by what people? To what extent can you answer the question: who made the decision? Was it a good or a bad decision? How do you know?

2. Select an informant with organizational experience. Get him to identify a decision that he considers important and in whose making he participated. Interview him so as to answer the questions posed in Question 1.

Part IX

PROGRESS REPORT

In this concluding part, we aim to do three things:

1. Assess the current state of knowledge as derived mainly from research in the United States (Chapter 31).
2. Examine cultural differences that may shape organizational behavior in forms different from those familiar to us in the United States (Chapter 32).
3. Assess the problems and possibilities involved in applying behavioral science research findings for improved organizational functioning (Chapter 33).

In each chapter we shall be seeking to look ahead to see how our field of knowledge may develop more rapidly from a scientific standpoint and to generate findings that will be of increasing practical value.

31. What have we learned so far?

THERE ARE TWO WAYS in which to assess what we have learned so far. One approach would be to state a number of propositions that have been reasonably well supported by research evidence and present these as the product of research to date. Another approach would be to examine trends in our field and evaluate theoretical developments with the hope both of assessing present position and indicating possible future lines of development.

The first alternative presents us with one important difficulty. It is not a simple matter to state a list of propositions. This is not simply because the tested propositions in our field are few—though indeed they are fewer than we would like. It is more because a meaningful statement of a proposition requires considerable background material indicating the conditions under which the proposition can be expected to hold. While many people would like to call upon behavioral scientists for unconditional propositions—those that would hold under any conditions—this is not possible in the natural sciences, and we can hardly expect to pull it off in the behavioral sciences. Thus, any proposition we state would have to be backed up by several paragraphs of background and qualifying statements. To do the job right would require not a single chapter but several long chapters and possibly a book.

In this chapter, I shall follow the second approach. I shall seek to take a bird's eye view of the evolution of our field up to this point and then evaluate where we stand.

The process of learning what was not true

Development of our field has been more cyclical than unilinear. That is, we cannot trace a single line of upward movement, however slow and gradual that progression might be. Instead, we see cyclical movements, rapid developments in one direction being followed by a period of demolition of the main lines of preceding work, after which the field starts off in a new direction.

We see this in the development of and reactions to Taylorism and the scientific management movement. Our field of study got its start through tearing down much of the framework of the scientific management movement.

The same process can be observed in reaction to Max Weber's theoretical ideas. The first published works in our field of Alvin Gouldner and Peter Blau were both oriented toward the Weber framework, but in large measure they found themselves demonstrating what was *not* true in what Weber said. It was only later that Blau went on to build his own framework and stopped bouncing his ideas off Weber.

The human relations movement

As Taylorism had been a mechanistic model with great emphasis upon formal organization structure, those who got their start in the human relations movement in demolishing Taylor tended to go to the other extreme, ignoring technology or formal organization structure in order to concentrate strictly on interpersonal relations and what they first called "informal organization."

Those who approached the field with survey research techniques had the same sort of interpersonal focus. They concentrated particularly on studies of the man-boss relationship and supervisory leadership styles.

As exclusive focus on the man-boss relationship failed to yield the research findings sought, theorists broadened their approach and began talking about "participation management" and McGregor's theory X and theory Y.

Recent research seems to have demolished a good deal of what was standard doctrine years earlier in the human relations movement. The demolition has not been complete. Readers will have noted that we have managed in this book to salvage some useful findings regarding supervisory leadership styles and participation management. Nevertheless, we must admit that in relation to the time, effort, and talent invested in these lines of research, the yield has been pitifully small. How explain this poor rate of return?

Bringing in technology, work flow, and formal organization structure

I attribute the low yield primarily to the long neglect of technology, work flow, and formal organization structure. Having proven many years ago that formal organization structure did not determine everything, we went on to act as if it influenced nothing.

It was not that technology, work flow, and formal organization structure were entirely neglected in our case studies. Some of the men involved in this human relations movement have been exceedingly talented field workers, and they have not been ones to neglect factors whose importance is to be found in the field situation. But it is one thing to report something from the field and quite another thing to make systematic theoretical sense of what has been observed.

For example, in my own research as early as 1949 I wrote an article which examined human relations in large restaurants within a framework of technology, work flow, and formal organization structure. Furthermore, I went into detail to demonstrate how certain items of technology affected human relations on the job. For example, I showed that it made a great deal of difference in the relations between waitresses and countermen in the service pantry whether the waitresses called in their orders or whether the restaurant provided a spindle on which waitresses were supposed to place their order slips. In fact, I find some people consider my discovery of the human relations significance of the spindle as one of my most interesting contributions to the field.

I do not bring up these cases from my own earlier work in order to claim that "I knew it all the time." It is no use to know some facts and even to know that they are important facts unless you also know what to do with those facts. What to do requires placing the facts in some systematic framework. But a systematic framework requires comparative analysis of cases.

In the 1940's and 1950's, those of us who worked on case studies did indeed face up to technology, work flow, and organization structure within each case, but we sought to arrive at generalizations at the level of interpersonal relations—which was not the level where the structural elements could be placed in an appropriate theoretical context.

On the other hand, those who studied organizations through survey research techniques were accumulating a lot of comparative data across cases, but the data were again at the interpersonal level, and the researchers had no way of taking technology, work flow, and formal organization structure into account.

It was only as research people began to look at cases in terms of a comparative framework that we moved on from a demolition phase of the cycle toward a new line of construction.

In looking at his cases of local unions, Leonard Sayles noted that while he could say something in general terms about the quality of the union-management relationship at the plant level, he found a wide range of differences at the departmental and work group levels. He began to wonder why, in the same plant and over a period of years, certain work groups would be consistently cohesive and militant in pressing their demands on management, others would be apathetic and inactive, and still others would be apathetic most of the time but on occasion break out into erratic pressure movements. To answer these questions he examined such concrete items of data as the technology, the homogeneity or heterogeneity of the jobs within the work group, the range of pay differences within the group, and so on. We have built Chapter 21 on "Work Cohesion and Militancy" very largely upon Sayles' work.

Probably the major impetus for this new line of development has come out of the work of Joan Woodward with her extraordinarily ambitious and systematic examination of the relationship between technology and organization structure in a large number of industrial companies. When she was able to show that formal organization structure tended to vary in form in terms of the technology of the organization, it became evident to many people that if we were going to progress further in this field we would not only have to take technology and formal organization structure into account, but we would have to link both of them to the behavior we observe in the plant situation.

Burns and Stalker provided a further impetus in the same general direction as they focused their studies on the introduction of changes in technology and processes. They discovered that they could not make sense out of their data unless they distinguished between firms in which innovation and change was relatively rapid and continuous and those where the operation continued along the same general lines with few and slow changes. They present data to indicate that in the stable organization a structure with a high emphasis upon the vertical hierarchy may do a reasonably effective job economically, whereas this sort of structure will break down in an industry subject to rapid changes. Does this mean that these changing organizations require a participative management approach? Insofar as that means reduced emphasis upon exercise of authority from above and more consultation between levels, this appears to be correct. On the other hand, as we have pointed out earlier, the participation management school has given no attention to problems of lateral and diagonal relationships. These rapidly changing organizations can only be understood if we give as much attention to the lateral and diagonal relations as we do to the vertical ones.

The study of lateral and diagonal relations is of very recent origin. George Strauss's study of the purchasing agent is a classic case along this line. Leonard Sayles has reshaped thinking about managerial behavior by giving special prominence to these lateral and diagonal relations and emphasizing processes of negotiation rather than the traditional studies of the exercise of authority.

While it is too early to see clearly where the work of Woodward and others is leading us, we can begin to grasp the next steps that are now emerging. Here we find ourselves moving from concepts toward variables. Woodward has shown where we need to look and what kind of concepts we need to use. Others are carrying on to focus on variables such as technical diffuseness-specificity and other aspects of tasks that can be stated in variable form.

The end of human relations?

Does this mean that the study of interpersonal relations in organizations is dead? Perhaps I am simply reluctant to bury such a large part of my past, but I should at least like to try a different formulation of the situation. It is clear that we came long ago to a dead end in studies focused primarily on interpersonal relations. We may yet find important values in those studies if we can now fit them in with the newer line of theoretical development which places interpersonal relations in a context of technology, work flow, and formal organization structure. In effect, that is what this book is all about. I have tried to re-examine other studies and my own work, going back as far as 1942 to place interpersonal relations in this structural context.

Standards for assessing progress

In the 1930's at Harvard, Lawrence J. Henderson, a noted physiologist, offered a course in "Concrete Sociology." If it seems peculiar for a physiologist to be teaching sociology, I can only add that the title of the course was even more peculiar in that period. It was a time when much sociological work was global in its interests and rather far removed from any concrete data. Henderson did not seek to provide much of the data himself, but he invited men who had been involved in field studies or field experience to present their own concrete data and see what kind of analysis they could work out of it.

L. J. Henderson's specifications for the sociologist at that time appear to me equally compelling now. Judging from his own work and that of others in the natural sciences, Henderson proposed these requirements for progress in the scientific study of society:[1]

The sociologist, like the physician, should have first, intimate, habitual, intuitive familiarity with things; secondly, systematic knowledge of things; and thirdly, an effective way of thinking about things.

Let us examine our progress over the last three decades in terms of the three criteria suggested by Henderson:

1. *Intimate, habitual, intuitive familiarity with things.* Before publication of *Management and the Worker*, factories and other work organizations were simply unknown territory to all but a very few behavioral scientists. As we noted in Chapter 1, for some years after the publication of that book, discussions of factory life and problems were all written

---

[1] L. J. Henderson, "Sociology 23: Introductory Lectures" (2nd. ed., rev. 1938), mimeograph p. 18.

from within the context of the Hawthorne plant of the Western Electric Company, simply because no other work setting had ever been systematically described from a behavioral point of view.

The world of work looks far different now. Large numbers of behavioral scientists have acquired that "intimate, habitual, intuitive familiarity" with the world of work. This familiarity has developed not only within the factory and within different types of factories but also within other work organizations such as restaurants, hotels, department stores, hospitals, and government agencies.

As research has extended across this range of organizations and increased in depth in each type, new observations fit into a context that was lacking three decades ago. When I began my research in industry in 1942, I had the impression that almost anything I was finding out was completely new. No doubt I exaggerated the novelty of my experience, and in any case, there is no necessary relationship between newness and scientific importance. In fact, when a phenomenon appears to be completely new, it is rather difficult to say anything of importance about it. The interpretation of the meaning of the phenomenon depends upon the context into which we place it, and in 1942 I was equipped with very little in the way of relevant context.

In 1969, when I make an observation, or read about, or hear described some type of behavior in an organization, my reaction is usually quite different. I say to myself: "That case sounds very much like one I found in X Company," or "That case seems similar to one reported by Z." On occasion, I may think, "This new case seems similar to case Y in some respects but different in others. I wonder what can account for the differences."

These reactions are only in part consciously directed. It is not as if, upon hearing of or observing a new case, I had to ask myself: What other cases does this case resemble? What similarities and differences do I find in comparing this case with others? The new case comes to me against a background of my own experience and whatever I have been able to absorb from the reported observations of other research men. The fit (or lack of fit) between the background and the new case naturally poses the questions and sets off a train of speculative thinking.

It is a long way from speculation to scientific conclusions, yet I suspect that the man who is not entertaining any "interesting" speculations is not likely to arrive at any important scientific conclusions.

Up to this point, the process is largely intuitive, not grounded in any explicit theoretical formulations. In fact, I have found that when behavioral scientists with quite diverse theoretical frameworks get together to discuss the same case, we are generally able to agree as to what is going on and as to why particular items of behavior are taking place or why particular sentiments are being manifested. It is only as we try to arrive at more general formulations that disagreements begin to emerge.

2. *Systematic knowledge of things.* The "things" in question here are the behavior of individuals and groups in the organizational context.

Behavioral scientists have mapped the terrain far beyond the Hawthorne plant. We have explored a variety of factories, gone underground into the mines, spread out into service industries, and examined hospitals and government agencies. The student who wishes to familiarize himself with any one of the major types of organizational work settings can find in the literature a good deal of systematic description. While each new organization he studies is new to him and each assumption needs to be verified, the student at least begins with background knowledge of some of the principal features of the organization and of the human problems which characterize it. When the student goes beyond his own culture, he finds that much less is known, yet cross-cultural studies are now rapidly accumulating.

There is also a body of systematic knowledge of problem areas that cross-cut types of organizations.

Supervisory leadership is probably the most studied of such cross-cutting problems. While we have argued that the payoff in this area has been meager in relation to the man-hours of work expended, some systematic knowledge does seem to be emerging. Earlier efforts were handicapped by a failure to take into account differences in types of organizations and in types of supervisory positions and also by the bias most of us share in favor of "democratic" forms of interpersonal relations. Now, as a new emphasis upon technology and organizational structure is rapidly developing, the man-boss relationship is being fitted into a context where it becomes possible to make useful reinterpretations of what previously seemed ambiguous and inconclusive findings. A good example of this reinterpretation is Dubin's[2] conclusion that the leadership style-productivity relationship that enthusiasts for "democratic" leadership hoped to find universally may actually be observed in Woodward's category of *unit and small-batch production,* but not in other types.

We have learned a great deal about characteristic forms of worker responses to financial incentives. At the plant level, we have found certain common patterns of union-management relations.

While early research was focused primarily upon worker behavior, in recent years behavioral scientists have been concentrating particularly upon relations within management. The old view of management as a pyramid of authority relations has been abandoned in favor of a network of vertical, diagonal, and horizontal relations, with authority being only one of the elements involved.

3. *An effective way of thinking about things.* In our field I interpret a way of thinking as consisting of two elements: (*a*) a conceptual scheme

---

[2] Robert Dubin *et al., Leadership and Productivity* (San Francisco: Chandler Publishing Co., 1965). See his chapter on "Leadership and Productivity: Empirical Findings and Theoretical Considerations."

or framework and (*b*) a body of theory. A framework tells us what elements to look for and, in a preliminary way, how to fit these elements together. In my definition, theory is a body of interrelated propositions regarding the relations among the elements specified in the framework.

The word *interrelated* deserves emphasis. Theory building is *not* the simple accumulation of tested hypotheses. Theory evolves only as these isolated fragments are fitted together into a meaningful pattern.

I see the framework in structural terms, yet my view is quite different from the approach of what I and others have called the "social structuralists." As Etzioni[3] has described that approach, the focus of attention is upon problems of power and authority at a rather high level of abstraction. Those who take this approach rarely bring the problems of power and authority down to the play-by-play examination of the behavior and interrelations of workers, foremen, managers, engineers, scientists, and personnel men, and other actors on the organizational scene.

As I see it, a useful conceptual framework in our field must enable us to analyze behavior on the individual, group, and organizational level. I have sought to span these levels using basically the same set of concepts. If that approach is successful, then as we examine a single case, we can draw conclusions about the problems of particular individuals, of their work group, and of the organization within which we find them.

I feel we need a structural framework because, whatever else it is, an organization is a set of structured relations among those who make up its membership. I see structure in terms of vertical, horizontal, and diagonal relations among individuals and organizational units. In these terms, the student needs to place his problem within a structural framework, first identifying the positions of the individuals involved in the problem along the vertical, horizontal, and diagonal axes that make up the structure, and then gathering data upon the interactions and activities to be observed among these positions in the structure. Furthermore, we take the time dimension into account as we examine the state of vertical, horizontal, and diagonal relations over various points in time.

Let us illustrate by summarizing the procedure followed in analyzing the case of "The Foreman Who Failed" (Chapter 14). Here we were concerned with two points in time: 1948, when Tom Walker was considered a great success, and 1950, when he was considered a failure. For each period separately we examine Walker's interactions and activities in the following relationships: vertical down (with workers), vertical up (with his immediate superior and with those at higher levels), horizontal work flow (with other foremen in the same work flow), horizontal union-management (with union stewards), diagonal up service (with maintenance superintendent), diagonal up union-management (with union president),

---

[3] Amitai Etzioni, *Modern Organizations* (Englewood Cliffs, N.Y.: Prentice Hall, 1964).

and horizontal auditing (with inspector). The analysis then builds upon the differences we find in activities and interactions along these relationships for the two points in time.

Clearly, we are far from having a good theory in this field. I would only claim that I see more clearly than I did a few years ago the lines of development that this theory should take. For years I have been working with something which has been called "interaction theory," although some critics have claimed there is no theory in it. As Homans, Blau, and others have worked on exchange theory and on theories of psychological reinforcement, I have begun to see the convergence of certain theoretical ideas. This I have tried to state and apply with a new approach which links what I call *transactions* with *interactions, activities,* and *sentiments.*

It would be fruitless for me to try to evaluate this emerging body of theory at this time. I have tried to apply this conceptual framework throughout the book, making the applications as explicit as I can. Others will have to evaluate whether this framework represents a step ahead in the field or simply adds to the conceptual confusion.

In any case the value of a theory is not to be judged entirely in terms of its immediate usefulness. A theory or conceptual framework may be wrong in important aspects and yet contribute to the development of science insofar as it stimulates others to discover the errors and to develop formulations that will more adequately explain and predict behavior.

Summary and conclusions

This chapter has presented an assessment of progress in terms of an examination of major trends in the field.

Development in our field has been more cyclical than unilinear. The field got its start in reacting against earlier formulations of Taylor and Weber. In demonstrating what was *not* true about earlier approaches, we developed new approaches that were equally one-sided but in a different direction. Thus the human relations movement tended to interpret life in the organization as if interpersonal relations occurred in a vacuum.

Recent work of Woodward and others has indicated that future theorizing on organizational behavior should be based upon a foundation of knowledge of technology, work flow, and formal organization structure. To some extent, the rather meager findings that have come out of the interpersonal relations focus can take on new meaning as they are fitted into the context of technology, work flow, and formal organizational structure.

Following Henderson's framework, we have found increasing numbers of men in our field developing "intimate, habitual, intuitive, familiarity with things," and "systematic knowledge" of various aspects of organizational life has grown enormously in the last three decades. We have also found a convergence in certain lines of theoretical development. We cannot claim having gone beyond the very preliminary stages of theory building, and the student must judge for himself whether the theoretical framework presented here presents valuable guidance both for future theoretical development and for practical applications of research findings.

Reference

Etzioni, Amitai. *Modern Organizations.* Englewood Cliffs, N.J.: Prentice Hall, 1964. This brief book presents an evaluation of knowledge in our field from the standpoint of one of the leading social structuralists. He takes a very different point of view from mine.

Discussion questions

1. Make your assessment of those aspects of organizational behavior where you think the most and the least solid knowledge are available.

2. Select three propositions regarding organizational behavior that seem to you to be reasonably well supported by research evidence. State the *conditions* under which each one holds true. Indicate what evidence is available in support of each proposition.

32. An intercultural context for organizational research

Up to this point, our focus of attention has been upon research in the United States, where indeed more organizational behavior studies have been done than in all of the rest of the world combined. Now that the literature on organizational studies in other cultures is growing rapidly, it is important to put our U.S. research findings in an intercultural context.

We need to face these two crucial questions:

1. Can the findings of U.S. research be generalized to other cultures, or do we need to make substantial modifications to take cultural differences into account?
2. Does our conceptual framework enable us to interpret organizational behavior abroad, or do we need substantial changes in this theoretical orientation in order to make sense out of data from other cultures?

It is much easier to demonstrate the existence of important cultural differences than it is to deal with them systematically. Demonstration can be done through anecdotes: through telling stories about how a particular situation with which we are familiar in the United States is handled quite differently in some other culture. The problem of anecdotes is not only that of representativeness: How do we know that the handling of the situation described was typical of the given culture and not a deviant case? The problem also is one of systematizing comparisons, which cannot be done with scattered anecdotes. We must establish the dimensions along which we are going to compare cultures and then gather data for each culture in terms of these particular dimensions.

The selection of cases

At this early stage in comparative studies of organizations in different cultures, it would be foolish to try to cover the world broadly. Let us instead deal with a small number of cases that provide interesting enough differences to test the usefulness of our approach. At a later time, we may then venture to tackle a larger number of countries and culture areas.

I shall concentrate on three countries: the United States, Peru, and Japan. The United States provides a natural anchoring point for all comparisons not only because it is the home country of most readers of this book, but also because it is the country on which we have the most voluminous body of organizational research. Peru is a developing country, in the early stages of industrialization and is representative in many ways of the large culture area that we call Latin America. Peru is also the foreign country that I know best, on the basis of some years of research in industrial and business organizations, high schools, and rural communities.

When we compare the culture of Peru and of the United States, it will be apparent that some of the major differences fall in areas that seem to be crucial to economic development. Such an observation has naturally led many people to take the United States as the model of the successful highly developed country and to assume that the problems of developing countries like Peru are to be solved on the basis of imitation—making their own cultures like that of the United States in all those respects relevant to industrial and economic development. The Japanese case is a useful antidote to such simplistic thinking. The culture of Japan differs from that of the United States in striking ways, and yet Japan has been extraordinarily successful in industrial and economic development. Although almost completely without such critically important resources as iron ore and petroleum, Japan today is clearly one of the leading industrial nations of the world. Furthermore, consistently since the end of World War II, the rate of economic growth of Japan has surpassed that of any other country of the world. Anyone tempted to suggest that the U.S. model of industrial development is the one best way to move in this field would do well to consider the case of Japan.

Dimensions of comparison

We will examine our data in four categories:

1. Social structure.
2. Prevailing sentiments and value orientations.
3. Structuring of interpersonal relations in organizations.
4. Distribution of types of transactions.

Under social structure, we will be concerned with the distribution of status in the society, with the distribution of labor as affected by status, and with the ease or difficulty of mobility within the status system.

Under sentiments and value orientations, we will be concerned particularly with sentiments toward authority. We will be concerned with the degree of "faith in people"—the prevalence of trust or mistrust in interpersonal relations. We will be asking toward what individuals or groups the holders of certain positions feel that they have responsibilities. We will look at the preferences of people for individualistic or collective activities. We will want to know what people consider to be the primary sources of rewards and also their conceptions of who should be rewarded. We will be examining sentiments toward work, manual and other types, also. We will note the prevalence of achievement motivation and also the value placed on words versus actions, style of actions versus results. We will also look into conceptions of causation and the degrees of predictability perceived in life.

In examining the structuring of interpersonal relations in organizations, we will look at the handling of vertical relations (authority) and lateral relations (nonauthority). We will also be concerned with discovering common styles of problem solving and conflict resolution.

We shall be considering the reward structures that typically evolve in each culture. Do we find distinctively different distributions of types of transactions as we compare cultures that appear to be markedly different from each other?

When we deal with intercultural comparisons, we are necessarily involved in oversimplification. The picture we give of the culture of the country will never be fully represented in any particular organization we choose to study. Here we must necessarily be concerned with central tendencies. It we can get a firm hold on the general framework of a given culture, then we shall be able to deal meaningfully with the deviations we are bound to observe when we get down to the examination of cases.

In our examination of Peru and Japan, we will be using the United States as the anchor point for comparisons. We shall pull together some summary statements about U.S. culture following the presentation of these two foreign cases.

1. Peru

The interpretation of Peru to be presented here is based in part upon field studies of organizations and communities and in part upon the analysis of language and language usage in relation to culture. The language-culture study was carried out in collaboration with Robert R. Braun, a Peruvian citizen whose family migrated from Austria, and who became both a consultant and collaborator in my first research in the country in 1961–62. Since the language-culture question is based upon the Spanish language, which is used in many other countries besides Peru, what we say in this area can be taken to apply broadly throughout Latin America and in Spain, but we will focus our attention particularly on Peru and not try to deal with the similarities and differences among Spanish-speaking countries.

The Andes mountains that divide the country north to south, and the desert area along the coast, impose serious obstacles to Peruvian development, yet compared to Japan, Peru is well endowed with natural resources. The country is richly endowed with copper, has substantial oil resources, some coal and iron, and other resources largely absent in Japan. Nevertheless, industrialization has come late to Peru, and even in the last decade when industrial production and investment have been rising rapidly, most of this growth can be attributed to "outside influences," the nature of which we shall explore in this chapter.

High dominance, low faith in people

While the country is in the process of change, Peru has been what we might call a high-dominance society—one with a rather rigid social structure, with a high degree of prestige and power concentrated at the upper levels and strong inhibitions upon upward social mobility—although it is not difficult to find individuals who have broken through the status barriers.

Peru is characterized by a low degree of "faith in people," compared with the United States. For example, the Cornell Values Study of 2,975 students in 11 U.S. colleges showed 89 percent of the respondents picking the high faith alternative on the item, "Some people say that you can trust most people. Other people say that you can't be too careful in your relations with other people." Our survey of 1,833 high school boys in Peru[1] shows only 31 percent choosing this same alternative. While there is some age difference in the two population studies, the Peruvian high school boys can actually be considered a more elite segment of the population than U.S. college students, for a smaller percentage of the Peruvian population reaches the last year of high school, where our survey was applied, than the proportion that reaches college in the United States. The same item applied to 202 white-collar workers in a Peruvian public utility yielded a 37 percent trusting response.[2] A comparison between a U.S. Sears, Roebuck and Company store (n = 176) and a Peruvian Sears unit (n = 164) again showed the U.S. employees giving the more trusting response, 93 to 47 percent.[3]

Other items designed to measure "faith in people" yielded the same general result in the high schools, the utility, the store, and in 26 villages. Not only is this general finding rather well supported by data from a wide variety of sources, it is highly significant in the structuring of interpersonal relations in organizations.

If you do not trust people, you hesitate to delegate authority and responsibility—how do you know that subordinates will really do the job and will not undermine your position? If you do not trust people, you

---

[1] For a report on the Peruvian high school survey, see W. F. Whyte, "Culture, Industrial Relations, and Economic Development: The Case of Peru," *Industrial and Labor Relations Review*, Vol. 6, no. 4 (July, 1963). That article gives a 30 to 45 percent trusting response for 12 high schools in Lima, the elite private schools giving a more trusting response. The 31 percent figure given in this chapter is an average of responses from 29 high schools in Lima and six provincial cities.

[2] Lawrence K. Williams, William F. Whyte, and Charles S. Green, "Do Cultural Differences Affect Workers' Attitudes?" *Industrial Relations*, Vol. 5, no. 3 (May, 1966), p. 110.

[3] Research report being prepared for publication at this writing.

will find it difficult to handle negotiations and other relationships where the direct exercise of authority is not involved. How can you count on the other fellow to do as he says, if you have no control over him?

Attitudes toward authority

Peruvians appear to be somewhat ambivalent toward authority. A more ready acceptance in Peru of firm supervisory control is indicated in several items comparing 364 blue-collar workers and 202 white-collar workers in a Lima utility with matched samples of U.S. utility workers. We have summarized our findings in these words:[4]

1. For both our white-collar and blue-collar Peruvian samples, we found a small but significant positive correlation (approximately .20) between perceived closeness of supervision and general satisfaction with the supervisor. In our U.S. company, the correlations were at about the same level, but negative (white-collar, −.17; blue-collar, −.23). In other words, there was some tendency for these Peruvian workers to prefer the boss who supervised them closely, whereas the U.S. workers leaned toward the one who exercised more general supervision. Similar preferences for general supervision have been reported in many U.S. studies.

2. "How much emphasis does your supervisor put on getting out a lot of work?" Here again we found a positive correlation between production emphasis and satisfaction with supervisor, and at a substantially higher level (.39 for white-collar workers and .41 for blue-collar workers). The question was not asked of blue-collar workers in our U.S. company, but for white-collar workers we found a smaller but significant negative correlation (−.20), which again is in accord with many U.S. studies. Apparently Peruvian workers find pressure for production more acceptable than do U.S. workers.

3. "Does your supervisor let his superiors know how members of his work group feel?" Interestingly a high percentage of our Peruvians checked, "I don't know" (57 percent for white-collar and 48 percent for blue-collar workers). We have no exact comparison with the U.S. here, since the alternative of "I don't know" was not offered in our U.S. company. However, U.S. workers were free to leave the question blank, and yet very few of them did so. It is our experience that U.S. workers generally think they know the answer to this question, whereas a number of Peruvians asked us, "How should I know?"
   "He lets his superiors know how his employees feel only when he feels his superiors will agree with him." In the United States, when a worker checked this alternative, we could be almost certain that he would give a negative evaluation of his supervisor. Not so in Peru. Those checking this item were somewhat more likely than those who

[4] Whyte, *op. cit.*, pp. 107–8.

did not to give a favorable evaluation of the supervisor. On the question as a whole, in the U.S. company there was a relatively high correlation (.58) between the supervisor's letting his superior know workgroup feelings and satisfaction with the supervisor. For the Peruvian white-collar workers, there was an insignificant (.03) correlation, while for the blue-collar workers we found an almost significant negative relationship ($-.10$).

These findings suggest that Peruvian workers see the exercise of strong control over them as legitimate and even acceptable. At the same time, they have no expectation that a good supervisor will stand up for them before his superiors.

Data from other studies show a strong urge of Peruvians to escape from the control of superiors. On the Peruvian countryside, as we asked people to choose between working for themselves and working for other individuals or for a company, the choice in favor of "starting your own business" ran over 90 percent in 16 of the 26 villages surveyed and over 80 percent in 6 of the remaining 10. In no community did this choice fail to poll a majority. In a comparative survey of Sears, Roebuck and Company in Lima with a U.S. Sears store, we asked, "If you had your choice, would you prefer to own your own business or work for someone else?" In the U.S. store, the responses were nearly evenly divided, with only a slight majority (52 percent) voting for "own my own business." The Lima Sears employees voted to an extraordinarily high degree (90 percent) for "own my own business." These differences cannot be explained in terms of differing degrees of satisfaction with the company or the job in the two comparison cases. The Sears Lima employees showed themselves on balance somewhat more satisfied with the company management, with their own jobs, and with Sears as a whole than was the case in the comparable U.S. store, satisfaction being high in both cases. Furthermore, interviews with a 10 percent sample of the employees of the Sears main store in Peru showed that the employees considered themselves extraordinarily fortunate to be working for Sears rather than for other organizations in which they might have been employed.

The escape from authority interpretation is further supported by the following item, also from the Sears' study:

The ideal job is one where you are your own boss, since no one can tell you what to do. Do you:	Peru	U.S.
1. Agree	49%	8%
2. Partially agree	32	53
3. Disagree	16	39
4. N.A.	6	—

Individualism or escape from authority

The value on individualism is high. At first glance, we may feel that this is stating a similarity with the United States, but the meaning of individualism is quite different in the two cultures. In the United States, we are inclined to assume that a man will express his individualism by taking the initiative to express his opinions and introduce changes into some group or organization of which he is a member. This high initiative of individuals is not expected in a Peruvian organizational context. There, individualism is more likely to take the form of escaping from the controls of the organization.

Many observers have commented that Peruvians tend to have very limited commitments to any grouping outside of the family. The capacity to build and maintain organizations appears to be low. The APRA political party is sometimes cited as a case tending to contradict this generalization, since the party has been a powerful force in Peruvian politics from the time of its founding in the early 1920's up to the present time. However, we should note that the party is still dominated by its founder, Victor Raúl Haya de la Torre and the small circle of associates who worked with him through four decades. Only when Haya de la Torre is no longer on the scene will we have an opportunity to test the durability of the organization, as opposed to the charismatic appeal of its founder. Beyond the APRA party, Peru fits very well the general organizational pattern that is often described as "personalism"—the tendencies of organizations to form around a particular personality and to break up when the individual leaves the helm.

The Peruvian tends to look upon life as less predictable and less subject to his own control than is typical for the U.S. citizen. The Peruvian tends to see his success depending in part upon chance and in part upon personal relations he is able to establish with some superior authority. Even skill in developing relations with superior authorities does not guarantee success, for Peruvians are inclined to think that these interpersonal relationships are unstable so that the "connection" that brings success today may deliver a rebuff tomorrow.

Organizational characteristics

Let us now see how these cultural characteristics are reflected within organizations. In Peruvian companies, we find primary reliance upon the line of authority with marked status differences inhibiting upward communication. Where status differences are large within an organization, we can expect to find—other things being equal—that those in higher positions will feel a very limited sense of responsibility for the welfare of those at low levels. This is illustrated by an interview I had with a manager of a textile mill in Peru. I asked him about training programs his company might have developed for the workers. He acknowledged that the company had no such programs, and then he went right on to talk very negatively about the workers and their inability to learn. He insisted upon their *falta de cultura* (lack of cultural background). By the time of this interview, the textile industry had existed in Peru for over 100 years, and this particular company had been in business for about 70 years— seven decades of experience without any effort on the part of management to meet the presumed problem of *falta de cultura* by developing educational activities. If viewed strictly from a rational standpoint, the situation of the company was paradoxical because, on the one hand the executive talked as if he considered *falta de cultura* a serious problem, and yet he showed no inclination to do anything about it. The paradox can only be explained in terms of the low level of management's evaluation of its work force. If you believe that your workers are inferior beings who are incapable of learning, then you are being quite rational in avoiding the expense and effort of providing training programs.

Of course, this was an extreme case, as many companies are currently hard at work in developing training activities. Nevertheless, we must note that the emphasis on training of workers has come into Peruvian industry primarily through the stimulation of government agencies and through imitation of what foreign firms have been doing.

This high emphasis on authority relations is accompanied by difficulties in developing of lateral (nonauthority) relations. Within manufacturing organizations, difficulties between departments are likely to be resolved through appeal to higher level authorities rather than through direct confrontations of people involved. In sales and service organizations, it is often left to the customer to do the coordination among units of the company, rather than to have these lateral relations worked through internally. This is illustrated by a crisis we observed in a large merchandising organization charged with the task of providing 400 uniforms for a school which my children attended. Four hundred uniforms in a single order certainly constituted a very large piece of business for this firm, but it apparently did not occur to management to send a representative to the school to take the measurements of the children and later to deliver the uniforms. Instead, several hundred mothers and several hundred children had to make trips into the center of the city to place their orders and get the measurements taken.

The uniforms were not to be ready before a certain date, and to make things more exciting, the school, in announcing this date, then set up a contest, offering a prize to the class that was completely uniformed first. This assured that all of the children and the mothers would arrive at the store seeking uniforms at approximately the same time. While the uniforms consisted of a standard order, each boy getting a jacket, a pair of trousers, shirts, neckties, socks, and shoes, and the girls getting the same thing but substituting a skirt for trousers, no effort was made within the store to bring all of the items together in one package. Instead, each mother, with her impatient children in tow, had to wait in three or four lines. When she had at last reached the counter on one line, she then had to start all over again at the end of another line. Besides, few uniforms fitted perfectly, so many mothers and children had also to wait for the tailor to make new measurements and otherwise to correct errors.

In this case, nobody was lazy. Everyone was frantically busy and very excited. The pressure and tension were wonderfully impressive to behold. They were also unavoidable, given the initial structuring of the process which placed all of the coordinating interactions and activities in the hands of the customers.

One of the most distinguished foreign observers of Peru, John Rowe,[5] reports that this pattern of coordination by customers or clients dates back to the early days of the establishment of Spanish control in Peru. As soon as the governmental offices were set up, each acted completely independently of any other office, in spite of the effect each might have upon the work of the other. Thus, the Peruvian who had to deal with two or more governmental agencies on the same problem always had to wait in line upon each agency.

In problem solving and conflict resolution generally, we note a tendency to avoid individual face-to-face confrontations, and an inclination to resolve conflict problems through appealing to higher authority.

Now let us turn to our analysis of language and culture, in order to demonstrate how this type of study may cast light upon the structuring of organizational behavior.[6]

Leadership and authority

Our introduction to this study came about through an apparent mistranslation of an item in a questionnaire. The English statement was, "Some are born to lead and others to follow." The bilingual secretary had given this translation: *"Unos han nacido para mandar y otros para obedecer."*

I objected, "That means, 'Some are born to command and others to obey.'" She agreed that I was right but insisted that she was right also. In other words, "lead" or "command" can both be rendered by the verb, *"mandar,"* and likewise, "follow" and "obey" can both be rendered by *"obedecer."*

There is an important difference between the words in each pair in English: one suggests voluntarism, the other suggests coercion. It is

---

[5] Personal conversation.

[6] The discussion of language and culture is based upon W. F. Whyte and Robert R. Braun, "On Language and Culture," in H. S. Becker, B. Geer, D. Riesman, R. S. Weiss (eds.), *Institutions and the Person* (Chicago: Aldine Publishing Co., 1968).

significant that Spanish provides no neat and economical way of making this distinction.

In Spanish culture, *"mandar"* conveys the sense of sending someone somewhere to do something, while the commander stays behind. An indication of this meaning is that *"mandar"* is also used for sending physical objects: *"El manda un paquete a su esposa."* (He is sending a package to his wife.) In consequence, the counterpart of *"mandar"* is necessarily *"obedecer,"* with the original meaning being "to obey." If the commander stays behind, it is awkward to think of his people following him.

In Spanish a politician *"arrastra a la muchedumbre"* (carries away the crowds), and *"lleva a su partido a la victoria"* (takes his party to victory). *"Guíar"* (to guide) cannot be used in this sense, since it is an unheroic word that does not touch the imagination. *"Guíar"* is only used in connection with school children, blind people, tourists, and vehicles.

While origins of new words must remain speculative, we think we can trace the beginning of change to the era of *"Il Duce"* and *"Der Fuehrer"* which dramatized the need to have a way to refer to "the leader." In this period, newspapermen began to use the term, *"líder,"* which is clearly a transliteration and is pronounced approximately the same as "leader." Under the post–World War II impact of North American culture, with its emphasis upon enlightened leadership, conference leadership seminars, the exercise of managerial leadership, etc., the word *"líderazgo"* (leadership) was added. Thus the gap for voluntaristic leadership in Spanish has been partly filled in—through borrowing nouns (but not verbs) from English.

The English-speaking student of management first becomes aware of another language-culture problem when he hears references to *"el Chairman."* The dictionary translates "chairman" as *"presidente."* But *"presidente"* is, of course, also used to mean "president." In other words, Spanish provides no economical way of distinguishing between a chief executive officer and a person who, though holding a position of prestige, is responsible for the performance of the group, without being able to give orders. In the U.S. world of industry, the chairman of the board does indeed enjoy a much more powerful position in relation to his board members than does the chairman of some civic committee. However, if the chairman is indeed expected to run the show, he is generally given the title of "Chairman of the Board and Chief Executive Officer."

Let us also consider the word, *"patrón."* If we limit ourselves only to words referring to human beings, we find in the dictionary the following meanings: sponsor, protector; patron saint, patron; landlord; owner, master; boss, foreman; host, skipper (of a boat). Here we find a linking of the religious symbol (the patron saint) and authority symbols, with a single word expressing what are in English a number of quite different positions. The paternalistic attitude that characterized Latin American employers' associations in their beginnings is still reflected, for example, in the official title of the *Confederación Patronal de la Republica Mexicana*.

Let us seek to put these fragments in some sort of coherent pattern. The difficulty we have in Spanish in distinguishing between voluntaristic and coercive leadership suggests the much greater emphasis upon formal authority that we observe in Spanish and Latin-American societies. The problems we have with *"patrón"* and with *"presidente"* also reflect this preoccupation with formal authority, but there is an additional element involved. In Latin-American culture, reflecting a society that has been more rigidly stratified than ours, there tends to be less role differentiation in leadership terminology. Thus we can link together concepts so distinct (to us) as an executive officer and a discussion leader or a top management man and a low-level supervisor.

The language of conflict resolution

In industrial relations in the United States, union and management are supposed to reach agreement by "discussing" their differences and by "negotiating." In the process, they are expected to manifest sentiments of "mutual respect."

In the Peruvian context, the words in quotation marks in the above paragraph all present problems. In the first place, *"respeto"* does not convey a sense of mutuality. It is generally used to describe the feelings of a subordinate to someone of superior status.[7]

The student of Spanish must learn not to invite Latin Americans to *"discutir"* something with him. While *"discutir"* does mean "to discuss," it can also mean "to debate." The foreigner can avoid unfriendly implications if he simply invites people to "talk about" a given subject with him.

The dictionary translates "to negotiate" as *"negociar,"* but in Peru *"negociar"* conveys the implication of a stronger individual or organization taking advantage of a weaker one. Furthermore, the past participle, *"negociado,"* has the definite connotation of a shady deal, involving graft or other illicit procedures. No such meanings are implied in U.S. usage. These differences suggest that a U.S. diplomat may unwittingly project the wrong images when he proposes to *"negociar"* with Latin Americans.

It is noteworthy that Peruvian newspapers rarely use the words *"negociar"* or *"negociaciones"* to refer to collective bargaining. Instead, they refer to *"trato directo,"* literally "direct dealings" between the parties. In speech, we find the word *"directo"* emphasized, which tells us that in the past it has been customary to resolve conflicts through recourse to a third party more powerful than union or management—a point which we shall explore more fully later.

---

[7] This translation problem of *respeto* came to our attention through Wayne Holtzman, "Cross-Cultural Research on Personality Development" (No. 25 of offprint series; University of Texas Institute of Latin American Studies, 1965).

Work activities

Let us now turn to the world of work.

We first note that types of work are more sharply categorized in Spanish than in English. An "*obrero*" is a man who works with his hands. An "*empleado*" is a man who does the cleaner work with papers and with the use of his mind. The clear implication is that the "*obrero*" does not use his brains.

This linguistic distinction is paralleled in the social structure of work. The distinctions go well beyond the workplace. Peru has one social security system for *obreros*, a different one for *empleados*. The social security system for *empleados* has its hospital; the social security system for *obreros* has a different hospital.

There is only one large public hospital for tuberculosis, but this has its social structural divisions reflected in the distribution of patients among the various hospital wings. The administrator of the hospital reported that the three social classes are physically segregated: *empleados* in one area, *obreros* in another, and the bottom level of more or less indigent patients in a third. As the administrator put it, "We can have empty beds in the *empleado* wards when *obreros* are dying in the waiting line—and there is nothing we can do about it."

Nor was this stratification system imposed by the Ministry of Public Health upon a reluctant public. The administrator told us that no such social class separation had been planned when the hospital was opened, but that the administration had later yielded to pressures by patients and their families (presumably of the *empleado* group) to establish the segregated wards.

To be sure, there is some evidence that the status gap between *obreros* and *empleados* is narrowing in Peru. In recent years, labor and social security legislation has narrowed the economic gap between the two categories. Some union leaders report an increasing tendency toward forming local unions in which *obreros* and *empleados* are in the same unit.

Nevertheless, the social gulf remains large indeed. In a values survey of male high school seniors, we asked each respondent whether he would rather be an *empleado* or an *obrero*. For those who gave the expected response of "*empleado*" we asked if they would still prefer to be *empleados* if, as *obreros*, they could earn a successively larger differential, running from 50 to 300 soles more per week. There was one final category of "Under no circumstances would I prefer to be an *obrero*."

High school seniors represent something of an educational elite for Peru, since only between five to 12 percent of those who had entered school in the first grade had advanced this far. Under these circumstances, the overwhelming preference for *empleado* was to be expected. What interested us particularly was the pattern of responses we found in a large industrial arts high school in Lima. The purpose of this school was to train the boys to become skilled workers (*obreros capacitados*) in industry. (No doubt it was assumed that many of them would later rise to supervisory positions and *empleado* status, but it was also assumed that they would begin work as *obreros*.) Only 13 percent of these boys opted for *obrero* under equal pay conditions, while one third required 300-soles-a-week pay differential (then fantastically large), and another third checked that they would not prefer to be *obreros* under any circumstances.[8]

The sharpness of these distinctions clearly goes back to the conquest and beyond that to Spain. Don Quixote claimed that "the pen and the sword are the only weapons fit for a gentleman."

In English, we find it much more difficult to make the distinctions that are so neatly and sharply made in Spanish. "Employees" sounds like a more refined term than "workers," and yet either term can be used to refer to the total body of nonsupervisory personnel of an organization. Furthermore, we never hear anyone speak of "our employees and our workers," to express the *empleado-obrero* distinction.

The most common way of making the social distinction is to speak of "white-collar workers" and "blue-collar workers." There are two points to be made about this way of expressing the difference. In the first place, it is far more cumbersome than the Spanish, using six words where the Spanish can put the idea into two. In the second place, we find the contrast between the apparently superficial and the assumed intrinsic aspects of these distinctions. The American phraseology suggests a social distinction that is subject to change if people put on different clothes. The implication in Spanish is that there is a basic distinction in the quality of the human beings involved.

This is not to say that in the United States there are no social distinctions involved in categories such as "blue-collar worker" and "white-collar worker." Any textbook in industrial sociology will devote at least a few paragraphs to the status symbols surrounding the workplace. The point is that the distinction is not nearly as sharp nor as clearly defined as it is in Latin-American culture. Nor do we find attached to manual labor the stigma that is so evident in Peru. This is observed not only in the workplace; it becomes particularly evident in the things men do away from the job. A college professor in the United States who had painted his house or had worked in the garden to raise vegetables for the family table would not hesitate to acknowledge these activities. In fact, he might even boast about them to friends and acquaintances. Such behavior just could not be expected to occur in Peru. Nor do Peruvian stores feature the "do-it-yourself" kits so common in the United States. If a Peruvian had

---

[8] Whyte, *op. cit.*, pp. 586–7.

enough money to buy such a kit, he would be middle-class and would not do it himself.

On reading a Lima newspaper one day, we came across the statement that there is no exact Spanish equivalent for the German word, "*gründlichkeit*." Is there an exact English equivalent for this word? "Thoroughness" seems to fit perfectly. The word involves three ideas: (1) attention to detail, (2) high standards, (3) and the capacity for getting things done. Why no such word in Spanish? Is "thoroughness" not an important virtue in Latin culture?

When a newcomer first hears Peruvians saying that they do things "*a la criolla*," he takes this as a simple statement to the effect that they do things in the manner that is customary in Peru. Then he notices that the phrase often occurs with another idea in the same sentence. For example: "We do not do it the way it should be done; we do it *a la criolla*."

It was not always thus. Hugo Neira, writing in *Expreso*,[9] claims that at the time of the War of Independence, the phrase was used with pride to point to the evolving national culture. Neira goes on to say:

> . . . the word which inspired a part of the ideology of liberation thus was turned into something like an affront, a reproach, as the recognition that what was being done here was incomplete, hurried, useless . . .
> . . . thus *criollism* is like the confession of a collective failure. . . . perhaps the tragedy these days may be that the synonym for *criollo* is the unfinished, that which is made in haste, of low quality, in forms and styles of the inferior.

The lack of emphasis upon high standards and thoroughness points to a serious problem in Peruvian industry. Let us consider two examples.

In our studies of small business, we were much impressed by Señor Rodriguez, who had built up a carpentry shop and furniture business. His shop was still small, but it had been growing, and he prided himself on having his machines set up to work on a regular production line—"American style." He was specializing in making doors for new houses and apartment buildings. He told us that his production of doors was 200 a month and that it could easily rise to 500—were it not for one problem. Builders furnished him with measurements of the doors, but he could never count on the door frames being built to these measurements. He found the variability so great that he had to keep two men busy most of the time measuring door frames.

We asked him whether he had tried to do anything about persuading the builders to achieve some standardization. He said he had once got into a heated argument with a construction foreman. The foreman considered himself insulted and brought Señor Rodriguez into the police station, charging him with defamation of character. After this one bitter experi-

---

[9] Lima, July 4, 1964. Translation by Whyte.

ence, Señor Rodriguez had to accept approximate measures and make the best of them.[10]

In another factory, we observed a problem of temperature control. The workers, who were on piece rates, found that they could make more production if they operated with a chemical solution at higher than the specified temperature. This led to a product of inferior quality and presented management with a serious problem.

How had the workers been checking on the temperature? According to the plant manager, the custom had been simply to stick a hand in the solution and say to oneself, "This seems about right." However, let us not simply blame this lack of thoroughness on the workers. It was evident that management had done little to enforce exacting standards. In fact, the temperature gauge that had been in use was very difficult to read. We happened to be in the management offices at the time when they were purchasing a new temperature gauge which would be much easier to read, thus taking a necessary step toward the enforcement of standards.

The lack of exacting standards makes itself felt particularly in the market place. We find a widespread preference for foreign products, in attitudes which we have measured in a questionnaire. The assumption seems to be that the foreign product will generally be made to more exacting standards than the Peruvian product. The desire and ability to insist upon exacting standards seems to be one prerequisite for building up the public acceptance of Peruvian manufactured articles.

Before leaving "*a la criolla,*" we should note another common meaning. We often hear people say something like this:

Fulano is right, but he will lose out because he does not know how to handle things "*a la criolla.*"

Here the speaker is saying that Fulano is right, in the sense that he is "going by the book" or following the formal rules of the institution, but he will fail because he does not know how to make the necessary informal adjustments. In other words, doing things "*a la criolla*" should not succeed, according to the norms of scientific management, and yet it may be the only way to take advantage of the fact that the other people are not following "sound management principles" either.

Another reflection of this underlying problem is found in the words "*serio*" and "*seriedad.*" The dictionary provides no clue to the problem, for we find straightforward translations as "serious" and "seriousness." The student may be puzzled when he hears that so-and-so is "*un hombre serio.*" A serious man? The phrase tells nothing about a man's sense of humor or the expression on his face. What is being said is that the man is not fooling around, he is working in concentrated fashion at whatever he is engaged in.

---

[10] The foreman's reaction also illustrates the points discussed later in the section, "Words: Instrumental or Expressive?"

We recently asked a Peruvian friend why he preferred one internal Peruvian airline to the other. He replied, *"Más seriedad."* More seriousness? That hardly makes sense in English. What he was saying was that the airline of his preference tended to its business more effectively.[11]

Can we express these concepts economically in English? The word "businesslike" seems close to this meaning of *"serio,"* but its use tends to be limited to commercial and industrial and bureaucratic activities. Furthermore, it refers to the impression that a man gives in going about his work, whereas *"serio"* tells us something important about his motivation. There is the same difficulty with the words "efficient" or "efficiency": they tell about the quality of the performer or the performance but not about the attitude of the individual toward his work.

We can say that Jones is "a serious artist" to distinguish him from Smith, who is a "Sunday painter," but if we say, "Jones is a serious man," we will only confuse our listeners. Why do we have such a problem with this idea? We suggest that the explanation involves the implicit assumptions of U.S. culture. We assume that a man is just naturally serious about his work, and a business organization is obviously serious about its activities, so why state the obvious? No such presumption is made in Peru. We often hear about people in positions both high and low in the society who are not giving very serious attention to the jobs they are supposed to be carrying out. Therefore it seems important to state not only what activity a man is carrying out but whether or not he is *"serio"* about it.

In Peru the seriousness of a man's demeanor is thought to be related to the seriousness of his purpose. There is no such presumption in the United States. In fact, we often find men talking in a light and casual manner about matters that are obviously of deep concern to them. (Perhaps this facility for mixing the light with the heavy makes it easier for North Americans to take criticism and confront critics than it is for our Latin-American colleagues.)

Peruvians are puzzled if not offended when the speaker prefaces his remarks with a joke, as is customary in the United States. To appear *"serio"* in demeanor is not necessarily accepted as the equivalent of being *"serio"* in thoughts and actions, but to speak in a light manner on a heavy topic raises questions about a man's *"seriedad."*

The words "achieve" and "achievement" have an important meaning in the culture of North America as they do no doubt also in England. The word "achievement" contains three interrelated ideas. It means (1) an outstanding result (2) through one's own efforts (3) arrived at through sustained effort over a period of time.

Each of these ideas seems essential to the meaning of the word. An achievement cannot be something trivial, unless the word is used sarcasti-

---

[11] He had something there; within a year after his statement, the airline which lacked *seriedad* had two serious crashes and was grounded by the government.

cally. It cannot be arrived at by luck or otherwise without effort, nor can it be something presented to one as a result of the efforts of other people. It cannot be something that just suddenly happens, although it may be something that happens in a short space of time if it represents the culmination of a period of effort. For example, winning the 100-yard dash in an important meet may be called an achievement, but there we imply that the result is due to a long period of training and effort.

Perhaps "*logro*" is the best Spanish translation of achievement. It can mean getting something by personal and long sustained effort. *But* it can also mean getting something by luck or "by hook or by crook."

One consultant tells us that the State Department has been using "*rendir*" and "*rendimiento*" for "achieve" and "achievement," but the most usual translations of the verb and noun are "to yield, to produce; yield, production." We suspect that here the State Department was excessively concerned with the immediate interests of getting out the production—a typical U.S. attitude in itself—and thus sacrificed some of the essential meaning of "achievement." Besides, there are other implications of the verb "*rendir*" that are still more incompatible with "achievement." "*Estar rendido*" means to be tired or worn out, which suggests in Latin culture that producing is exhausting and not exhilarating as the representative of U.S. culture is expected to consider it.

The difficulties of translation are further illustrated as we try to express the idea in Spanish. In interviewing candidates for management positions in British or North American firms, Braun was accustomed to using as one of his questions, "What do you feel has been your most outstanding achievement?" This sort of question is familiar to most English-speaking people, and they have no difficulty in understanding its meaning. Not so in Spanish. Braun found that when he tried to give this sentence a fairly literal dictionary translation, the responses he got often seemed to have little to do with the concept of "achievement." He finally arrived at the following question: "*Cual fue su actuación más saltante o importante en cuanto a calidad y esfuerzo y/o de resultados?*" This statement translates back into fairly literal English as follows: "What has been your most outstanding or important accomplishment as regards quality and effort and/or results?"[12]

Related to the notion of "achievement" is the U.S. concept of "challenge." The dictionary here gives no hint of the translation problem for it appears to offer us as a simple equivalent, "*reto*." "*Reto*" is perfectly appropriate for a challenge to combat, or to an athletic engagement. It does not express the "challenges" that the well-socialized North American

---

[12] The high school survey (*op. cit.*) suggests that within Peru there are marked social class differences, the public school boys being more achievement oriented than the elite private school boys. Since Peruvian firms are largely family owned, we can assume that most of the high management positions in such firms will be taken over by boys from these elite schools.

sees before him in his path toward "achievement." Built into U.S. culture is the notion that the overcoming of difficulties makes success sweeter. In fact, the good North American is expected to feel disappointed if he finds the path to his goal too easy.

The typical Peruvian finds this view incomprehensible. He feels that life is hard enough as it is without going out of his way to find obstacles to overcome. If you "challenge" him to reach some goal, he is likely to consider this a distinctly unfriendly act. The foreigner may try to *"esti-mular"* him, but he had better not *"retar"* the Peruvian.

The difficulties we have in getting the notions of "achievement" and "challenge" into Spanish can hardly be accidental. We are dealing here with differences in culture. The difference goes back to Spain, but its influence seems to have persisted in Peru. The emphasis has not been upon *achieving* but upon *being*, not upon the concrete results of your independent efforts, but upon the kind of person you are.

On national heroes and bullfighters

A fundamental proposition of the Peruvian value system may be expressed in these two ways: what you are is more important than what you do, and style is more important than substance.

We see this value acted out in the bullring. While bullfighting originated in Spain, it enjoys great and growing popularity in Peru. The uninitiated North American might assume that the purpose of the matador is to kill the bull. Not at all! The death of the bull is only the end point in the drama. The important thing is the style in which the drama is enacted.

We see this set of values represented in the heroes held up as models to the children of Peru. While the history of Peru since independence does provide at least two men of genuine and substantial achievement (the Presidents Ramón Castilla and Nicolas de Piérola), most of the other heroes are honored for exploits of quite a different sort of significance. Let us consider several of these.

Interestingly enough, three of the greatest Peruvian heroes, Miguel Grau, Francisco Bolognesi, and Alfonso Ugarte, all won their fame in the War of the Pacific against Chile, in which Peru suffered a catastrophic defeat. Commanding a division in a battle on the coast, Alfonso Ugarte saw that the Peruvian flag of one of his battalions was about to fall into the hands of the enemy. Spurring his horse forward, he grabbed the flag as he plunged off the cliff "preferring to bury himself with the flag in the sea rather than see it soiled by the enemy." The battle was already lost when Ugarte made his charge, and his heroic and self-sacrificing act accomplished no concrete result.

In the battle of Arica, General Francisco Bolognesi found himself surrounded by the Chilean forces with no hope of reinforcements. Calling together his staff, he said that he was resolved to fight to the death to defend the honor of his country but that those younger than he might retire with honor so as to serve their country in the future. The staff decided by acclamation to fight with him to the last. When the Chilean commander asked for the surrender of his division, Bolognesi replied with the statement that has gone down in Peruvian history: "I am resolved to fight until I have fired the last cartridge." Two days later, he was killed in action.

Admiral Miguel Grau commanded the ship, *Huascar,* against the Chileans. He set out to ravage Chilean shipping. For four months the Chileans were unable to undertake any effective operations against the Peruvian coast, due to the effectiveness of this campaign. At last, the Chilean navy set six ships the task of running down the *Huascar.* When they made contact, the end was inevitable. Outnumbered and outgunned, Grau and his men nevertheless fought to the finish, when the Admiral himself and a number of his men were killed in action.

What have these men in common? While each one may have achieved important things in his life, it is not for these that he is celebrated. In essence, each man was a failure—but a glorious failure. The concrete results of their celebrated actions had no effect upon the course of Peruvian history—but a good deal of effect upon the minds of Peruvians. For these men, it was not the *results* that counted but rather the *style* of the action. All are celebrated for the gallant style in which they accepted risks and met death.

In the field of industry, there are no heroes, as far as the schoolchildren are concerned. Why is this? The most fundamental answer is that up to the present time industry has ranked low in the scale of Peruvian cultural values. The lack of heroes cannot be explained on the basis of a lack of available candidates. Peru provides several examples of men who started from humble beginnings and achieved striking success in important industrial enterprises, but two points should be noted in this regard: (1) With hardly any exceptions, the most successful Peruvian industrial entrepreneurs have been immigrants or sons of immigrants; for men thoroughly embedded in the culture, entrepreneurship is not an attractive calling. (2) While newspapers report the strictly business news of their enterprises, neither in the press nor in popular magazines do we find human interest stories regarding the careers of Peruvian entrepreneurs.

Apparently this neglect of the entrepreneur by the media is a reflection of a lack of interest on the part of their middle- and upper-class readers. When I learned that the wife of a university professor had been in the same high school class with Peru's most spectacularly successful industrial entrepreneur, I plied her with questions designed to throw light on his early struggles and first successes. My effort was completely unproductive. The woman could only tell me that someone had once told her that the millionaire entrepreneur had been helped at the start through a relationship he established with a wealthy woman. The episode left me with two compatible interpretations: (1) the only item of information— or misinformation—given me fitted the prevailing pattern of explaining success through personal relations and had nothing to do with achievement motivation, and (2) the manner in which the woman spoke about the man she had once known rather well and still saw occasionally suggested that she found his business career a boring topic of conversation —perhaps even distasteful.

The "from rags to riches" success story, so popular in the United States, is not popular in Peru. While the self-made man himself may take pride in his rise from humble origins, his family would like to create the illusion that they have always been important people. The emphasis is upon what a man is or appears to be and not upon what he achieves.

This is not simply a value expressed for the benefit of schoolchildren. We find it in the writings of Jorge Basadre, Peru's leading historian, who recently published an impressive four-volume history of his country. Speaking of General Bolognesi and his fellow officers who fell before the Chileans at Arica, he writes:[13]

> In them, human dignity and honor rose superior to death. Before pronouncing those famous words, the silent and profound vision of the hero recognized and overcame all the infamies of the world and of the war with that strange solitude that grows out of the honor and the energy of the free man and the pure desire to do good . . .
>
> Bolognesi and his men proved that neither armies nor nations nor men should concentrate exclusively upon immediate utility or on the visible consequences of their great decisions . . . he who dies, if he dies where he should, is also victorious and performs a service . . .
>
> Bolognesi and his companions are forever accompanied by love and a spontaneous respect of the people because, in sacrificing themselves they gave to Peru something more important than a lesson in strategy: they gave her national symbols, a mysterious inspiration for the collective soul. And thus can grief be the best source of rejoicing, of renovation, of new undertakings.

Words: instrumental or expressive?

We have concentrated so far upon problems of meaning of particular words. We should also recognize that words *in general* are used in rather different ways in our comparison of cultures. Peruvians and Spanish speakers generally have much more of a feeling about the importance of their language itself and of the particular words they use than do North American English speakers.

In the United States, words are looked upon as instrumental, of value insofar as they enable one to get things done. We say, "actions speak louder than words." We celebrate the "strong, silent man" and speak

---

[13] Quoted in *Expreso*, Lima, August 11, 1962. Translated by Whyte.

approvingly of the "man of few words" as if there were some necessary connection between strength and silence. We tell people, "don't waste words," or "save your breath," suggesting that there is no point in speaking unless it advances us toward some practical objective.

Children learn to say, "Sticks and stones can break my bones, but names can never hurt me." Of course, words do hurt in the United States, but except under the most extreme provocation, it is expected that the man who is injured by the words will simply disregard the incident. This conception was well illustrated during the time when the late Senator Joseph McCarthy was charging the Eisenhower administration with harboring Communists. Many people wondered why the President did not strike back. Mr. Eisenhower put it this way to his friends: "I will not get down into the gutter with that man."

In Peru words are not considered simply instruments toward reaching practical objectives, nor can they be taken lightly on any other grounds. It is significant that the "sticks and stones" saying has no counterpart in Latin America. Words carry more weight and are fraught with more perils.

Offensive words cannot simply be ignored. A gentleman must rise to defend his honor. Although duels were outlawed in Peru many years ago, the papers still occasionally report a challenge to a duel. In case of such a challenge, both parties appoint seconds who seek to negotiate in the hope of being able to show that the incident was based on some kind of misunderstanding. In this way, most challenges are resolved without a duel, but duels sometimes do take place. Several years ago, Fernando Belaúnde Terry (later President), fought a duel with sabers against a prominent politician of an opposing party. We have the impression that the duel contributed to the favorable public image of each man. Certainly the political fortunes of both of them prospered impressively after that event.

An incident in a factory illustrates the weight of words in Peru. The factory manager said that he had for some time been wanting to get rid of a certain local union leader. How was he finally successful? He provoked an argument with the man so that the union leader lost his temper and accused the manager of a *"falta de dignidad"* (lack of honor). The manager immediately replied that the union leader, with these words, had committed what the law considers a *"falta grave"* (serious offense) and was therefore discharged.

To be sure, the case was not resolved quite this simply. The union leader brought other local union officials into the manager's office to demand his reinstatement. At this point the manager took the initiative and opened up another line of attack. He reported that, under the preceding plant manager, this particular union leader had accepted money from management to spy on union officers of different political convictions and report his observations to management. Surprised and confounded by this accusation (which happened to be true), the union leader found himself defenseless, and the case was dropped with his discharge.

Thus, it was not the word alone which led to the union leader's downfall, but it is interesting to note that the manager provoked the word to initiate the process. Furthermore, while he had introduced a new charge before the union group, he insisted that the discharge would have been sustained by the labor inspector, on the basis of an unjustifiable affront to the personal honor of a management man, even without any other evidence. He may have been mistaken. Much would have depended upon the amount of support the discharged union leader got from fellow union leaders and the rank and file. However, in the case of a well-established and powerful union in the United States (as this one was), it is difficult to imagine a management man seeking to discharge a union leader on the basis of a single phrase uttered in the middle of an argument. The North American conceptions of words and personal honor are so different as to rule out such an action.

In another Peruvian case, the North American owner of a small factory told about the problems he was having with a union officer in his plant. His troubles with the man had culminated in the following incident: Before a crowd of workers, the union leader pulled a *management* notice off of the *management* bulletin board, ripped it into pieces, threw the pieces on the floor, and stamped on them. Earlier when the owner's pregnant wife was walking through the plant, the union leader had made an indelicate joke about her to the other workers. The owner heard of this from his wife and from one of the workers.

Now, if only one or two of those workers would be willing to testify in the Ministry as to what that union man said, I would have no problem. I could fire him in a minute.

How would these two cases be regarded by a U.S. arbitrator? The *words* about the owner's wife would have been regarded as an unfortunate breach of etiquette, but having nothing to do with the collective bargaining relationship and therefore justifying no institutional sanctions. The *actions* of the union leader in publicly defying management authority would call for the imposition of heavy penalties.

This difference in the weight of words is built into the labor code of Peru, as we find in the case of severance pay for women. The legally specified indemnities (in 1962) were 15 days' pay for blue-collar workers and 30 days' pay for white-collar workers per year of service, plus accumulated vacation pay. However, independent of this, the worker stands to get 90 days' pay for a "*despedida intempestiva,*" that is, if she is terminated in an inopportune or untimely manner.

This can lead to interesting maneuvers between worker and supervisor or manager. In some cases, the worker may not be at all reluctant to leave and even have been thinking of quitting, but she would like to take the 90 days' bonus with her. The manager may be looking for an opportunity to get rid of the worker, but he does not want to pay the 90-day penalty. In this situation, the worker tries to behave in such a way as to irritate the manager but without going to the point of giving him the concrete evidence to fire her without her indemnities. The manager tries to catch her in some legally specified cause for discharge without indemnities, while he seeks to avoid the injurious words that would win her the bonus. The game may come to an abrupt end when the manager makes what he considers the innocent statement that "we don't want any bad workmanship around here." The worker considers herself fired and charges to the union and labor inspector that the boss accused her of bad workmanship. In Braun's experience in the textile industry, this maneuver was likely to win the game for her—and the 90-day bonus.

Such differences in the weight of words provide one clue as to why it has proved easier to maintain free speech in the United States and Britain than in Latin America. Those who regard words as relatively light and inconsequential should find it easier to maintain free expression than those who see words as heavy and potentially punishing.

If words are indeed such dangerous elements, how can Peruvians avoid getting into conflicts all the time? The answer seems to be that the culture favors the avoidance of direct face-to-face expressions of disagreement. North Americans have the rather naïve idea that almost any conflict can be resolved if the parties will just come together and thrash things out, face to face.

We see this belief dramatized in politics when Richard Nixon tries to shake hands with hostile Peruvian university students and discuss politics with them. We see it when Teddy Kennedy, in a whirlwind tour of the Peruvian sierra in 1962, stops his car time and again, to shake hands with an Indian and (through interpreters) ask him what he thinks of the United States, Communism and other high level topics of international relations.

Peruvians have no such idea of the value of personal confrontation. In their culture, the emphasis is on avoiding direct expressions of interpersonal conflict.

This same tendency to avoid open disagreement is found in cases when one Peruvian asks another to do something for him. It somehow does not seem quite appropriate to refuse outright. The appropriate response is one or another form of "yes"—but then often the thing does not get done.

In Peru, the word is used so seldom that we are startled when we hear somebody say no. One attuned to the culture learns not to take "yes" seriously. You cannot judge by the words alone; you must learn to listen for the melody. In other words, you look and listen for cues surrounding the word "yes" in the current situation and in the past behavior of the speaker in order to predict what he is likely to do. While a well-attuned Peruvian is far better at divining the meaning of "yes" than an outsider, even Peruvians have a good deal of trouble judging what a man will do on the basis of what he says. In part, this grows out of the cultural inhibition against saying no. If a man cannot say no, then the word "yes" loses its meaning. Under these circumstances the predictability that is so important for organizational life is difficult to achieve.

Words and planning

Differences in use of words between North Americans and Latin Americans give rise to difficulties particularly in the activity we call planning.

Consider this example that arose out of the school lunch program. The program is entirely administered by Peruvians, but U.S. advisors sought to assist in the planning. One of these advisors told the following story, which he claimed was typical of his experience in this field.

Upon arriving at a large provincial city, the advisors were told that the plan had been worked out—and even put on paper. The paper indicated that four rooms in four schools could be made available for serving the lunches and that the job of baking the rolls could be contracted out to a local bakery. Questioning by the advisors revealed that the planner had either not thought of, or was quite vague about the following points:

1. How many children were to be served (he had made a guess, but it was only a small fraction of the actual total).
2. How many children could be served in each room at any one time?
3. How many stoves (if any) were there in these rooms?
4. How many burners did each stove have and how much heat did they generate?
5. How much water was available?
6. What size pots were to be used?
7. How many rolls could the bakery bake in a day?
8. How many trays would be needed to carry the rolls?

As these questions were raised, the planner sought to give snap answers, but this only added to his difficulties. When asked whether any local bakery had the necessary baking capacity, he replied that this must be the case because there were several good bakeries in town. A brief inspection of the proposed local bakeries was enough to show that this particular solution was out of the question. When asked what size of container should be used to do the cooking, the planner, thinking that a lot of people must be served, suggested a 25-gallon pot. In other words, he suggested a size of container so large that, when filled, it would be too heavy to lift. Nor had he considered how a pot that size would fit on the stove.

It might be argued that the planner failed in this case because he did not have an expert knowledge of cooking and baking. While such knowledge is certainly useful in running such a program, the lack of it can hardly explain the planner's behavior.

With or without specialized knowledge, there were a number of steps essential to effective planning, none of which the planner had taken. You begin by asking for records indicating the total number of children to be fed. You go out to the schools to inspect the rooms that you hear are potentially available. You count the number of tables and chairs in the room or note, in terms of the size of the room and the size of tables and numbers of chairs that may be available, how much seating capacity can be provided. You look at the stoves and count the number of burners. You turn on the burners and try to get at least a rough idea of how much heat they generate—if indeed they work at all. You look over pots of different size, checking on their relation to the burner surface of the stove. You fill some of these pots with water to check upon the ease or difficulty of handling them when they are full. You go to the bakery and look at the ovens. You ask the baker how many rolls he is now baking per hour. You relate these figures to the numbers of rolls needed per day. And so on. This is the way a North American-style plan gets made—at least in its preliminary stages. Before the plan is put into effect, it may be supported by much more precise measurements than indicated in the operations noted above.

But this is not the Peruvian style of planning. Why not? In the first place, this form of handling physical objects and going out to low-prestige places is not in accord with the status of an official important enough to be charged with planning a large program. In the second place, what we call planning is entirely alien to the type of education that has prevailed in Peru.

In the traditional school, the child learned that the *word* was everything. His success or failure in school depended upon his ability to memorize what he found in the textbook and took down from the teacher's dictation. While memorization is now being officially discouraged in Peruvian education, the old teaching patterns are hard to change, and in any case, the adult planners of today have come up through an educational system that placed an extremely high value on words.

The North American conception of planning involves the step-by-step relating together of words, actions, activities and objects, through time and in space. Anyone who has grown up without this instrumental approach to words is bound to find it difficult to work out what we consider to be a plan. He is more likely to present us with a good idea, eloquently expressed.

Sentiments and transactions

To translate these findings into transactional terms, we can say that behavior in Peruvian organizations is marked by a relatively low incidence of trading and joint payoff transactions. We find a high incidence of positive exchange transactions, linking pairs of people together. In fact, this seems to be the primary transaction utilized by Peruvians in efforts to maintain or improve their position. The general aim is to establish a relationship with someone in a superior position and to do things for him in the hope that he will reciprocate. Relations among people at one's own level tend to be marked by competitive transactions and by negative exchange transactions. The prevailing outlook can be described in terms of George Foster's essay on "Peasant Society and the Image of the Limited Good."[14] While he wrote this now much-cited article in order to explain life in peasant communities, Peruvians themselves have commented that it fits well for many sectors of Peruvian society. The rationale of "The Image of the Limited Good" is that the things of value in the world are always in limited supply. Therefore, if someone else in your community or organization gains some benefit, he must have done so at your expense, and similarly, if you gain some benefit, he is going to think that you have done it at his expense.

2.   Japan

This discussion of management in Japan draws particularly upon a recent study by M. Y. Yoshino,[15] who, in addition to reading extensively in original Japanese sources, carried out interviews in Japanese with many executives and businessmen. On the union side, we are particularly dependent upon a comprehensive study carried out by Alice Cook.[16]

Historical roots of industrialization

We will begin on Japan by tracing some of the historical roots of Japan's present value system and of her industrialization.

Japan's industrialization began in the late 1860's. We are inclined to think of the impetus coming simply from the arrival of foreign naval vessels in Japan and the "opening up" of Japan to Western society. This does indeed seem to have been a triggering event, but we find that the Japanese-style feudal system was breaking up at the time the outsiders arrived. The Samurai elite, which had dominated the country under the Emperor and the royalty, were beginning to lose ground to a rising class of merchants.

While it was once believed that members of the Samurai class had been

---

[14] George Foster, "Peasant Society and the Image of the Limited Good," *American Anthropologist*, Vol. 67, pp. 293–315.

[15] M. Y. Yoshino, *Japan's Managerial System: Tradition and Innovation* (Cambridge: M.I.T. Press, 1968).

[16] Alice Cook, *Japanese Trade Unionism* (Ithaca, New York: Cornell University Press. 1966).

entirely responsible for industrialization, having simply changed their roles from warriors and political leaders to industrialists, Yoshino cites a recent study of 189 prominent entrepreneurs of the early Meiji era. The figures show that 23 percent of these men came from the Samurai class whereas the remaining 77 percent were drawn from the commoners, with those who had fathers who were merchants in the towns making up 50 percent of the total. The sons of Samurai were much more strongly represented in a comparable study of political leaders (79 percent) and of intellectual leaders (67 percent).

There are two ways of looking at these figures. They certainly show that the new industrial entrepreneurs were drawn from a wide range of social origins and the sons of Samurai were not nearly so strongly represented in industrial entrepreneurship as they were in politics and intellectual pursuits. On the other hand, while the Samurai in this period made up 6 percent of the population, the 23 percent of entrepreneurs coming from this class shows that the Samurai were markedly overrepresented in terms of their share of the population.

For our purposes, the important point to make is that the new vocation of industrial entrepreneurship was *not* rejected by the then ruling elite. In fact, it seems to have been seized upon as a means of providing sons of Sumurai with the economic resources to maintain their social position.

Certain intellectual leaders not only accepted the new set of activities but went on to develop an ideology emphasizing the respectability and social values of business enterprise. The leader of this movement was Yukichi Fukuzawa, the great educator of the Meiji period. Born into a low-ranking Sumurai family, he had extensive opportunities to travel abroad in his youth. Upon returning to Japan, he interpreted what he had found in the Western world that should be of value to Japan's development. Yoshino[17] describes Fukuzawa's book, *An Exhortation to Learning* as:

. . . an attack on Japan's traditional views on learning. Fukuzawa emphasized pragmatism in learning and taught that learning had to be liberated from a highly theoretical orientation and applied to daily life, particularly in the field of business.

This book had the extraordinary sale of 3.4 million copies in the five-year period between 1872 and 1876. Since Japan's population at this time was approximately 35 million, this indicates a ratio of one copy for every two to three families.

Fukuzawa emphasized the respectability accorded to business in the West, and to raise the level of performance and also the social standing of business leaders in Japan, he founded Japan's first modern institution of higher learning, Keio University. The school was specifically designed to train potential business leaders.

---

[17] Yoshino, *op. cit.*, pp. 60–61.

In the value accorded to business in Japan in this developing period, we see a sharp difference between Japan and Peru and a strong similarity between Japan and the United States. In Peruvian culture, industrial entrepreneurship has a much lower value than in either Japan or the United States, and the notion that it is respectable for universities to offer work in business administration has only been gaining ground in Peru in the last two decades.

Education and achievement orientation

The high achievement orientation noted in the early period of industrial development has remained characteristic of Japanese business leaders. The Japanese school system appears to be even more achievement-oriented than our own. U.S. observers in Japan have noted that the work load of Japanese schoolchildren is substantially greater than is the case in our own school systems. In fact, the load is so heavy that Japanese students, between schoolwork and homework, have very little time for any recreational activities.

Since a much smaller proportion of high school graduates goes on to the universities, and since college education tends even more to fix a man's status in life than in the United States, we might think of the Japanese high school as being highly competitive. However, it is important to note that the Japanese student is not in direct competition with fellow students for the favor of his teachers. His academic fate is determined by his standing in an *impersonal* national examination. We can therefore say that the Japanese high school puts heavy emphasis upon achievement motivation, but is not designed to produce this motivation through the stimulation of interpersonal competition.

By the time the individual moves into industry, his general position in the organization has already been determined. Managers enter upon graduation from the university, and workers enter after finishing their schooling at a lower level.

The firm as a family

While it does take individual performance and an impersonal examination to assure inclusion in the university elite and in management, once the university graduate has become a member of the organization, he finds himself in a highly collectivistic culture. It is as if the organization were built on the model of the extended family. The roots for this symbolization of the organization go back to the feudal period and the organization of "commercial houses" at that time. Yoshino describes in this way the typical commercial organization of this period:[18]

---

[18] Yoshino, *op. cit.*, p. 67.

Employment in the commercial house was clearly divided into two basic categories. In the first category were the apprentices, who were for the most part drawn from related or friendly families; they were considered members of the house and were given the status and privileges of kin, retaining this relationship for life. The second category consisted of servants who, unlike apprentices, were not considered members of the house; usually they were not allowed most of the privileges associated with house membership.

The emphasis in apprenticeship, in commercial houses, was on learning through practical experience. Apprentices were highly differentiated in status according to length of service; they made very slow progress up the clearly defined hierarchical ladder. After many years of faithful service to a house, they were given an opportunity to set up their own business as a branch of the main enterprise, with the main house supplying, in most cases, much of the needed capital and business connections. The branch house was allowed to operate under the name of the main house. In fact, the offshoot was a branch of the main establishment in every respect, regardless of the fact that in the great majority of cases, no blood relationship existed between the head of the main house and that of a newly created branch. At least for the first several generations, a close business and ceremonial relationship was maintained between the main enterprise and its branch houses. As a result, the simulated kinship tie established when an apprentice was first taken into the business lasted well beyond his lifetime, involving his descendants.

The most striking characteristic of the Japanese system of personnel administration, from our standpoint, is the lifetime employment commitment. Yoshino describes it in this way:[19]

1. All managerial employees are recruited directly from universities. Only at the time of college graduation can one choose his lifelong career without undue disadvantage. At the time of entry into the firm, both the firm and the employee make a permanent and irrevocable commitment to one another. Permanent employees can be dismissed only under very dire circumstances, such as a serious moral offense. Neither incompetence nor the changing need of the corporation constitutes a justifiable ground for the dismissal of an employee. It is not a contractual relationship in which each party agrees to an employer-employee relationship, bearing certain conditions and terms, which can be terminated at the option of the parties involved. The Japanese employment relationship is an unconditional one, requiring *total* commitment on the part of the employer and employee.

2. Under the permanent employment system, managerial personnel are recruited not to fill specific positions, but to become members of the organization who will be given a wide variety of assignments in the course of their working careers. All prospective managerial personnel enter the corporation as management trainees, presumably aspiring for top management positions. As a result, occupational specialty is much less of a concern to Japanese management personnel than to their counterparts in the United States. One's security and identity depend largely on permanent membership in the firm, rather than on occupational specialty. Under this system, criteria for recruit-

¹⁹ Yoshino, *op. cit.*, pp. 229–30.

ment and selection must be, of necessity, quite general and are largely based on one's personal qualifications, such as intellectual capacity, congenial personality, emotional stability, and family background. Specialized professional competence and training are relatively unimportant. This is particularly true among nontechnical management personnel. . . .

3. Retirement comes at a relatively early age, and for those under the directorship level, retirement is most strictly enforced. Under the permanent employment system, early retirement is thought necessary to insure the infusion of fresh talents to managerial ranks and to provide opportunities for younger employees.

The lifetime commitment is also offered to workers—with the reservations to be noted below. When a worker becomes a member of the body of regular employees of the firm, he cannot be discharged except for a grave moral offense. The employee's rate of pay is determined less by his performance than by his family responsibilities and length of service.

The salarly structure in large Japanese corporations traditionally has been quite complex. Typically, in addition to the base salary, there are several types of allowances, including allowances for housing, transportation, cost of living, and so on. Like the base salary, these allowances are not related to one's productivity or performance; they have been designed primarily to meet certain needs of the employee and his family. The compensation system of Japanese corporations also provides for extensive fringe benefits for employees and their families, including housing, medical care, company stores, recreational facilities, educational programs, and company-sponsored savings programs at an interest rate substantially higher than the commercial rate. These fringe benefits constitute a very important element in the overall system of compensation.[20]

Within management, one enters with his own graduating class from the university and moves up slowly and very predictably along with this group. Promotions are governed largely by seniority. If the individual proves unequal to his responsibilities, he continues to move up but is given positions which, while of appropriate status for his seniority, keep him out of involvement with the most important activities of management.

Collective responsibility

People who have grown up in a culture where it is felt that promotion to higher management levels should come only to those fully competent to discharge the individual responsibilities of that position will find it difficult to understand how the Japanese system can function when the less competent move up as rapidly as—or nearly as rapidly as—the more competent. Part of the answer to this question is found in the Japanese system of collective responsibility. The Japanese organization is not

---

[20] Yoshino, *op. cit.*, p. 238.

nearly so dependent upon the performance of a key individual as our U.S. organizations.

Yoshino describes the fit between the value system and the organizational structure in these terms:[21]

One of the distinct features of the Japanese corporate organization is that it is structured in collective organizational units rather than in terms of individual positions. This is very evident in the organization chart, in which the corporate organization is depicted in terms of divisions, departments, and sections, rather than individual positions; only one or two of the highest top management positions—usually those of the chairman of the board and the president—are identified. These two positions are explicitly recognized because of the importance that the Japanese have traditionally attached to the formal leadership position of the collectivity. It must be noted that even though these two positions are indicated on the chart, they are not identified by the names of the incumbents, as is frequently done in the organization chart of an American firm. Beyond the one or two top-most positions, however, none of the other top management positions is shown on the chart individually—they are merely indicated collectively as the board of directors or as the executive committee. As a result, from the organization chart alone, there is no way of telling how many top management positions exist in a firm. Likewise, reporting relationships between various levels are indicated not in terms of individual positions, but in terms of collective units. Similarly, the organizational manual, which is now commonly found in almost all large Japanese corporations, describes assignments and responsibilities in terms of a division, a department, or a section, rather than as individual positions.

Although this may appear somewhat strange to American students of management, both the organization chart and the organizational manual of Japanese corporations accurately reflect management's view of the organizational structure. Because of a high degree of collectivity orientation, the Japanese management does, in fact, view a corporate organization in terms of hierarchically related collective units, rather than individual positions. To the Japanese, a task is performed by a group, not by individuals, and responsibilities are consequently shared by the entire group. True, each group has a formal leader with appropriate status and title, but the task is assigned not to him but to the group of which he happens to be the head. It is the group's performance that matters, rather than that of the individual or the formal leader. The basic unit in the organization is a collectivity, not an individual. Herein lies one of the fundamental differences between American and Japanese management.

A closely related feature of the collectivity orientation is that the responsibilities of each organizational unit are defined only in very general terms. Detailed job descriptions, as typically specified in large American corporations, do not exist in Japanese firms. For example, the functions of the export department in one firm are described in its manual as follows: "The Export Department shall take charge of exportation and the necessary investigations

---

[21] Yoshino, *op. cit.*, pp. 202–5.

and negotiations (connected with it)." Descriptions found in other companies studied are equally brief and general. Even in those rare cases in which a job description of an individual position is found, it is stated only in very broad terms. For example, the description of the position of section chief is stated by one firm as: "A chief shall be assigned to a section [note that even here, the emphasis is on a section, a collectivity]. The chief of the section takes charge of and is responsible for its administration to his immediate superior."

This characteristic also stems from the traditional Japanese view that a task is to be performed through *cooperative* efforts among individual members of an organization. Thus, Japanese managers are much less concerned about who performs a task and where the responsibility lies than about how individuals within the organization work together harmoniously toward the accomplishment of the goals of the collectivity. . . .

Another distinct feature commonly observed in the organizational structure of large Japanese corporations is the strong emphasis on hierarchy. The relative status of each organizational unit is distinctly defined in relation to others, and much emphasis is placed on the *vertical* relationship between units; little concern is shown for the horizontal relationship between functionally related units.

The relationship patterns discussed above are very apparent in the organizational structure of large Japanese corporations, where the formal status of every member, in relation to other members in the hierarchy, is defined in the most meticulous and particularistic manner.

The two major determinants of relative hierarchical status have been the level of education and seniority. Each member has his place in the organization, and he must behave in a manner congruous with his status. One finds, therefore, a very interesting situation in a typical Japanese corporate organization, where the relative status of each individual is rigidly defined and observed, *but where his function and responsibilities are not.* This peculiar emphasis on hierarchy is quite consistent with traditional Japanese cultural values, with their emphasis on hierarchical status. . . .

The description so far applies generally to the larger and better established Japanese firms. While these firms do make enormous commitments to the long-run welfare of their employees, managerial and white-collar and blue-collar, there are also institutionalized ways of limiting the impact of this commitment. Much of the growth of the individual firm in Japan has been built on subcontracting. When expansion is needed, executives may often determine that it is advantageous to meet the need through expanding subcontracting rather than through internal growth. The firm is thus not responsible for the employees of the subcontractor. The firm also grows through the establishment of affiliates or subsidiaries.

In Japan there is a large difference in wage levels and fringe benefits between the large and small firms. The subcontracting firm will usually be much smaller than the purchasing firm and will thus have greater flexibility in its labor costs.

Yoshino[22] points out that neither by law nor by custom are subsidiaries required to follow the same policies as the parent company. Like the small subcontracting firms, the subsidiaries tend to pay much lower wages and offer smaller fringe benefits than do the parent companies. Yoshino comments:[23]

Thus, the subsidiaries are often asked to carry burdens to "improve" the performance of the parent company. . . .

The corporation could "transfer" some of their less-competent employees to subsidiaries in their mid-career, which in effect relieves them of their obligations to find management positions commensurate with age within the parent organization.

The mandatory retirement age of 55 provides another important element of flexibility. The incompetent executive will simply retire at 55, whereas the able individual will generally be invited to take on a position of high responsibility in a subsidiary or with a subcontractor, thus enabling the parent firm to continue to benefit, directly or indirectly, from his services.

Companies also maintain some flexibility in their labor force obligations through limiting the lifetime commitment to those classified as "permanent" employees. The individual does not become accepted into this category until he has worked continuously for the parent company for a specified period of time. Yoshino comments:[24]

One year appears to be the accepted cut off point. In the past, it has been a common practice to lay off temporary workers periodically to make sure that they remain temporary.

Ideally, under the Japanese system, all higher positions are filled by movement up through the ranks. There are strong sentiments against "pirating" executives from other companies—though there is evidence that this practice is beginning to grow. How then can a firm fill the ranks of management when it is undergoing a very rapid growth? There is no ban on recruiting men out of government, and apparently this is a common source of meeting the needs for rapid expansion. However, Yoshino notes that men who have come in in this way are not likely to feel that they are really part of the in-group for a very long time.

This system of lifetime employment, clothed in the symbolism of the house and the family, has sometimes been interpreted as a direct outgrowth of the Japanese value system. Others have argued that in fact the lifetime commitment is of relatively recent origin and arose to a large

---

[22] Personal correspondence.

[23] Yoshino, *op. cit.*

[24] Yoshino, *op. cit.*

extent in response to severe labor shortages and consequent needs to build and hold onto a stable labor force. While economic factors undoubtedly did play an important role, we should note that the system that has developed is highly compatible with the Japanese value system. Furthermore, we do not have to prove that an institution had purely social origins in order to demonstrate the social effects it has upon its members.

Decision making

Decision making in the Japanese organization is based upon the *ringi* system. Yoshino describes it this way:[25]

In a large Japanese corporation. . . . lower echelon management personnel are confronted with a host of decisions in the conduct of day-to-day business. Since their authority and responsibilities are ill-defined and they receive no policy guidelines from their superiors, they must refer all but a few routine decisions to top management. In doing so, however, the lower echelon managerial personnel must follow a certain procedure. He must draft a document known as a *ringisho*. In this document, he must describe the matter to be decided and his recommendation as to what ought to be done. Here we should note that the *ringisho* is not a mere inquiry as to what decision is to be made; neither does it suggest alternatives to be considered. The *ringisho* is presented in such a way as to seek top management's approval on a specific recommendation of a subordinate.

When the formal *ringisho* is ready, it must be circulated among various sections and departments that will be affected by the decision, or whose cooperation will be necessary in its implementation. As each manager evaluates it, he indicates his approval (if he concurs) by affixing his seal. By complex and circuitous paths, the *ringisho* slowly works its way up to top management, eventually reaching the president. When the president approves the *ringisho* by affixing his seal, the decision is finalized. The *ringi* document is then returned to the original drafter for its implementation. . . .

The basic philosophy of the *ringi* system draws heavily on the process of decision making commonly employed in the traditional family system. Just as the family provided the basic structural framework for all kinds of secondary organizations, the underlying concept of decision making in the family served as the model for decision making in other types of organizations as well.

Some critics of Japanese management have recently been finding fault with the *ringi* system. They argue that it takes a long time for the document to go through all the necessary steps and that the process operates in such a way that it is very difficult for a high executive to refuse to affix his seal. By the time the document reaches him with all the other appropriate seals on it, he feels he can hardly withhold his approval. Yoshino points out that certain modifications have been introduced to

---

[25] Yoshino, *op. cit.*, p. 255.

meet these criticisms. In some cases, to speed up the flow, management has reduced the number of individuals who must examine the proposal. It is sometimes now possible to submit a *ringi* proposal directly to top management, skipping various levels, in case of an emergency. In some firms, *ringi* proposals are taken up in executive committee meetings rather than having each member of the committee act on it individually. Thus the members can bring some collective judgment to bear. However, as Yoshino notes, no Japanese is proposing the abandonment of the *ringi* system. The Japanese are just trying to make it work better. It remains in the center of the decision-making process. Even budget making is carried out through the *ringi* procedure.

In its structural aspects, the Japanese model differs markedly from both the U.S. and Peruvian models. At first glance, the Japanese model seems to be constructed primarily along the vertical dimension, but further examination indicates that this is far from the autocratic authority model we find in some cultures. It is the group and not the individual that relates to this vertical dimension. While levels of position are graded in terms of status, and the Japanese profess to have high respect for authority, we have observed that their system provides for a great deal of upward initiation of activities through the *ringi* system. So widely and frequently used is this method of problem solving that some high-level executives are beginning to complain that they do not really have control over the organization.

The *ringi* system also provides a clue to the Japanese approach to lateral relations. When a proposal for action has effects upon more than one organizational unit, that proposal must have the signatures of heads of the organizational units affected before it goes up the line for action.

In problem solving, the Japanese tend to avoid the direct public confrontations of individuals with different points of view that are characteristic of U.S. culture, but yet they do not tend to follow the Peruvian pattern. Whereas in Peru issues between individuals and organizational units tend to be evaded or passed on for arbitration to higher levels, in Japan the aim is to resolve the issues and reach consensus through discussion within the group of those affected. Since most, if not all, of those at the same organizational level have come in at the same time with the same university graduating class and moved up together, the individuals know each other very well, and they also know that they are going to have to continue to work together as a group, so that victory or defeat for one man or organizational unit is not an acceptable outcome.

In all management activities, individualism is minimized, and successes and failures are thought of in group terms. Individuals are rewarded primarily in terms of their group membership. That is, the individual is rewarded from day to day as he meets the expectations of his fellows, and he incurs their displeasure if he fails to meet those expectations. In the longer run, the individual manager is promoted along with his group, which is another factor which tends to keep him thinking about the group as a source of rewards.

Survey evidence

Some of these cultural interpretations have been confirmed in surveys by Arthur M. Whitehill, Jr., "of 2,000 production workers, equally divided between Japan and the United States, and employed by four roughly comparable firms in each of the two countries."[26]

The Japanese worker tends much more than his U.S. counterpart to link his personal and family life with that of the firm, as the following item indicates:

When a worker wishes to marry, I think his (her) supervisor should:	U.S.	Japan
1. Help select a possible mate and serve as go-between...	2%	6%
2. Offer personal advice to the worker if requested...	29	70
3. Merely present a small gift from the company.......	9	19
4. Not be involved in such a personal matter.........	60	5

The Japanese worker tends also to identify himself much more strongly with *his* company, as illustrated by the following item:

I think of my company as:	U.S.	Japan
1. The central concern in my life and of greater importance than my personal life.................	1%	9%
2. A part of my life at least equal in importance to my personal life.............................	23	57
3. A place for me to work with management, during work hours, to accomplish mutual goals..	54	26
4. Strictly a place to work and entirely separate from my personal life...........................	23	6

The Japanese worker has a greater tendency to accept the status distinctions within the company as valid models for behavior outside the plant, as illustrated by the following item:

[26] Arthur M. Whitehill, Jr., "Cultural Values and Employee Attitudes: United States and Japan," in M. S. Wadia (ed.), *Management and the Behavioral Sciences* (Boston: Allyn and Bacon, 1968). This originally appeared in *Journal of Applied Psychology*, February, 1964. See the full report of Whitehill's important work in *The Other Worker* (Honolulu: East-West Press, 1968).

If my immediate supervisor enters a crowded bus on which I am riding I should:	U.S.	Japan
1. Always offer him my seat since he is my superior.. 2%		10%
2. Offer him my seat unless I am not feeling well... 2		44
3. Remain seated and offer to hold any packages he may have....................................33		41
4. Remain seated since a fair rule is "first come, first served."..................................63		5

If Japanese workers are not individually rewarded for hard work, why should they work so hard? The following item confirms our interpretation that *social expectations* weigh far more heavily in Japan than in the U.S.:

I believe workers are willing to work hard on their jobs because:	U.S.	Japan
1. They want to live up to the expectations of their family, friends, and society....................10%		41%
2. They feel it is their responsibility to the company and to coworkers to do whatever work is assigned to them..............................61		37
3. The harder they work, the more likely they are to be promoted over others to positions of greater responsibility........................... 9		11
4. The harder they work, the more money they expect to earn.................................20		11

Unions and union-management relations

The attachment of workers to the firm leads to patterns of union organization and union-management relations that are quite different from those observed either in the U.S. or Peru. While recognizing some exceptions to this generalization, Alice Cook presents the following statement:[27]

"Enterprise unionism" is the common description of Japanese trade union structure. Briefly it means that unions . . . . are organized into autonomous units by companies or enterprises rather than in plant or craft locals. Most union functions, but particularly the economic ones of bargaining, striking, and grievance-handling, are performed in the enterprise union. It is financially self-supporting, elects its own officers, is the membership unit and keeps all membership records, determines the range of union activities, and

---

[27] Cook, *op. cit.*, p. 28.

sets up functional departments, which its officers head, for servicing its members.

Since the enterprise is the fundamental organizational unit, white- and blue-collar workers belong to the same union. In line with traditional Japanese respect for status, union officers are nearly always white-collar workers. Since membership includes only permanent employees and since the white-collar workers tend to move up into supervision (and out of the bargaining unit) with increasing seniority, we find (1) that union leaders, just as much as the rank and file, identify their interests with the enterprise, and (2) the union leaders are generally much younger than the higher management people with whom they deal. These conditions tend to confirm the dependent position of the union within the enterprise.

In the Japanese union membership meeting, issues are not brought to a vote, as in the U.S. and Peru. The Japanese pattern calls for making decisions by consensus. While the leaders have the responsibility of determining when and where consensus is reached, they are expected to give every member an opportunity to make his views known. A group of Japanese union experts explain the process in this way:[28]

Japanese custom goes back to the village where everybody participates in decision making and in family conferences. The individual assumes that if he is a part of an organization he has a right to have his say in it, and expects to be consulted. Failure on the part of the organization's leaders to report to him, to "consult" him is the equivalent of leaving him out of the group society. Often merely hearing the report or seeing the document satisfies the need to be "consulted." This consultation does not imply necessarily—as it probably would in the West—that it is a consultation of equals; on the contrary, it is characteristically a consultation of persons in a superordinate-subordinate relationship. So far as union participation is concerned, however, it is an essential part of the process of consensus.

While some U.S. consultants sought to introduce grievance procedures into the union-management relationship and did in fact get such clauses into many contracts, what actually happens is far different from the U.S. pattern:

. . . Japanese mores do not readily condone a single individual's raising personal grievances, nor does the system of lifetime employment conduce to such a system. A worker who is going to remain for life in a given enterprise avoids as long as possible coming to any open disagreement either with his peers or his superiors. Hence individual grievances initiated by the worker himself are almost unknown. Instead, the union officer, aware of discomfiture in the workshop, will seek an opportunity in which he can present a general grievance rather than a specific, personal one, and will put it on the collective bargaining agenda for direct consideration between the top labor and management representatives in their negotiating sessions. Since the individual

---

[28] Cook, *op. cit.*, pp. 31–2.

grievance is almost unknown, the group or department grievance becomes the norm. Many such grievances can be handled in advance of conflict through informal communication between union and plant officials when either suspects that a circumstance has arisen that may produce disputes.[29]

Joint consultation is a prominent feature of union-management relations in Japan, a recent study[30] estimating that 37 percent of all unions participate formally in some scheme of joint consultation with management. Often there is no sharp line drawn between consultation and collective bargaining. The parties begin discussing their problems informally and, as they are unable to resolve particular issues, find themselves engaged in collective bargaining.

When the parties are unable to resolve a serious dispute, a strike may result, but the form of the strike is different from what we observe in the U.S. or Peru. Cook comments:[31]

The strike is a tactic of harassment and of publicity; it is not meant to interfere seriously with production.

She quotes one union leader as explaining:[32]

It is not our intention to hurt the enterprise, but rather to call the attention of the public to our grievances.

The prevailing pattern then is for strikes to consist of brief scheduled work stoppages and public demonstrations. The material damage to the employer is small, but the attendant publicity suggests to many people that the employer has not been a good father to all of his family, which is expected to move the employer to more serious consideration of union demands.

This description should not give the impression that labor-management conflict is absent in Japan. We do indeed get reports of clashes between labor and management, but when these occur on a large scale, they are fought out in the political arena involving political parties. When issues of class versus class arise in Japan, they must be transferred out of the familistic enterprise and into the public arena.

Sentiments and transactions

While the individual within management or in the work force cannot improve his position by out-working others, his experiences in family and school have led him to accept high work standards, thoroughness in everything he does, and a pragmatic approach to the solution of problems. Therefore, although he does not push himself ahead of others in order to

---

[29] Cook, *op. cit.*, p. 49.

[30] Cook, *op. cit.*, p. 47 (citing study of Japan Productivity Center).

[31] Cook, *op. cit.*, p. 51.

[32] Cook, *op. cit.*, p. 8.

succeed in management, he has to meet high expectations in others regarding his own performance.

Life in the Japanese organization is highly predictable. If the individual lives up to the expectations of his group, he can count on being rewarded. In this regard, we can say that Japan is a good deal more predictable than the United States, while the United States in turn is a good deal more predictable in organizational life than Peru.

While we have no survey data to measure "faith in people," all accounts would lead us to expect that if such items were applied in Japan the responses would be highly on the trusting side.

In transactions, life in the Japanese firm is organized in terms of joint payoffs. The individual is rewarded as his group is rewarded. Competitive transactions are notable for their absence.

3.   The United States

The United States has always been in the background of our statements regarding Peru or Japan, but let us briefly consider those aspects of U.S. culture most relevant to our discussion.

One student of the subject has given this picture of the role of business in the United States:[33]

Business has been the national work of the United States just as baseball is its national sport; and the top of American society is occupied largely by businessmen. Historically, this status is unusual, perhaps unique, for elsewhere businessmen have been despised, or, if condoned, relegated to an inferior level of the social order. In Europe, they suffered consecutively from the disapproval of medieval theologians, 18th-century aristocrats, and modern socialists. In America, they have sometimes been censured by the few, but those episodes of criticism have ended by renewed approval of the many. . . .

Businessmen were already established in their high status when the United States emerged as a nation in 1789. Even as early as that, the United States could have been described as a nation of businessmen ruled by businessmen. That description would have violated certain of the more acceptable images of American life, but it would have fitted the larger facts.

The author overstates his case by using the word "unique," for Japan, especially in recent years, seems to be offering the same social prestige to businessmen. However, the general line of the argument is worth emphasis: A situation we tend to take for granted is quite rarely found in other countries. Certainly it is not found in Peru or indeed anywhere in Latin America.

Our culture also places a high value upon work, much higher than what we find in Peru, perhaps not as high as observed in Japan.

The U.S. and Japan find themselves nearly at opposite poles on the

---

[33] William Letwin, "The Past and Future of the American Businessman," *Daedalus* (Winter, 1969), pp. 1–2.

individualism-collectivism dimension. While in Peru the emphasis on individualism tends to lead to withdrawal from organizational relations and control, in the United States people tend to see individualism as coupled with initiative and responsibility. It is perfectly all right to work within an organization, but the individual himself should show initiative in working out his own destiny, and he should accept the responsibilities that go with the position.

U.S. culture fosters direct confrontation of opposing points of view in discussion and arguments. In the organization, if Jones disagrees with Smith, it is thought to be the manly thing to do for Jones to inform Smith of this disagreement and for the two of them to thrash the issue out face to face. This is not to say that all such agreements are in fact thrashed out directly. The point is that U.S. culture places a high positive value on the direct working out on these interpersonal disagreements, and in fact these confrontations appear to occur far more frequently in U.S. organizations than they do in the organizations of either Peru or Japan. This confrontation approach appears to be particularly marked in handling of lateral relations, where formal authority does not come into play. It is characteristic of U.S. culture that these nonauthority relations are more flexibly handled than tends to be the case in high-dominance cultures such as Peru. We have noted that the Japanese have quite a different approach to the handling of lateral relationships.

U.S. culture places substantially less emphasis upon status distinctions than is the case either in Peru or Japan. We feel that, since all men are created equal, if the subordinate disagrees with his boss, he should tell the boss about it, and the boss should be responsive to these criticisms and suggestions. While subordinates often fail to raise these criticisms and superiors often fail to be responsive to those that are raised, we do find much more upward initiative in U.S. organizations than is found in Peru and indeed in most other countries of the world. However, Japan shows a substantial channeling of upward initiative, but avoiding the direct confrontations favored by U.S. culture by using the *ringi* system.

Superiors are expected to assume more responsibility for the welfare and progress of their subordinates than is the case in Peru, but Japan exceeds the U.S. in this regard.

We see a substantial strain of competition in U.S. management, which is completely absent in Japan. Compared to Peru, the impact of this competition is moderated, because North Americans are inclined to feel that they are living in a world of expanding rewards so that all concerned can benefit from competition. To the Peruvian, life looks much more like a zero sum game: what I win, you lose and vice versa.

Organizational life in the U.S. is much less predictable than in Japan but much more predictable than in Peru. Furthermore, there is a stronger belief in the United States than in Peru that one's personal effort affects the results achieved.

On the pitfalls of oversimplification

Any statement regarding a national culture is bound to be an oversimplification. We cannot consider the range of differences within a culture. Also, we cannot consider the changes that are necessarily in progress in all cultures. To give the basic description and give the variations and the changes at the same time would involve us in writing a lengthy book about each of the cultures.

Nevertheless, let us consider some of the implications of these necessary oversimplifications. Peru appears to be changing in the direction of less hierarchical dominance and more emphasis in working out problems outside of the authority relationship. Some modifications are apparently coming into the Japanese system. Nearly all of those in management stay with the same company until retirement, but instances of "pirating" from other firms appear to be increasing. While Japanese organizational life is highly collective, there appear to be some trends in the direction of individualism.

While U.S. culture in the past has been characterized by a very high degree of "faith in people," this may well be changing as our country seems to be experiencing increasing difficulties in solving basic problems of intergroup relations. While we have described the U.S. as having a culture which places a high emphasis upon achievement motivation, we often hear it said that young people today are not nearly as much interested in achievement as their fathers and grandfathers were. Whether this is true for achievement motivation in general, or whether it is true simply for achievement in material terms, we do not yet know. There are also indications that business is losing its pre-eminent position in our national scale of values. At this writing, college recruiters for management trainees are reporting increasing difficulties in attracting adequate numbers of able young men. Whether these phenomena are evidences of a major shift in American values or simply a cyclical fluctuation, it is still too early to tell. To hedge on this question, let us say that in this chapter we have been considering certain aspects of the culture of the United States as manifested in the 1950's.

Conclusions and implications

In this chapter, we have sought to compare three nations along the same dimensions: social structure, prevailing sentiments and value orientations; structuring of interpersonal relations in organizations; and distribution of types of transactions. I shall make no attempt to summarize the wide variety of materials discussed here. The significance of such materials may better be assessed as we seek to draw some of the implications for policies of economic development and promotion of industrialization.

Contrasting Japan with the United States, we have demonstrated that there is no single correct model for successful industrialization and economic growth. Does this perhaps mean that in this field "anything goes"? While the student is likely to be impressed particularly by the differences between the U.S. and Japan, we have also noted two important similarities: in both nations we find a high achievement orientation and high prestige accorded to business and industrial executives. (Note that these two phenomena do not necessarily occur together. A society may have a high achievement orientation yet accord low prestige to businessmen. In that case, individual achievements will be channeled predominantly into other fields of activity.)

In Peru, we have found relatively low values both for the prestige of business occupations and for achievement orientation. We have argued that in the traditional Peruvian culture *being* is more important than *achieving* and the *style* of action is more important than the *results* achieved.

The U.S.–Japan contrast serves to challenge some of our most cherished notions about the importance of individualism in economic progress. The Japanese child grows up and goes through school in a situation that is highly achievement oriented, but he is competing only against an impersonal standard such as the university entrance examinations. When he becomes a member of the organization, he fits into a tightly knit collective. We ask ourselves: How can the individual be motivated if he is not individually rewarded? The point is that the individual is rewarded in Japan, as in any culture, but in Japan the primary rewards to the individual come through his collectivity.

The Japanese case also suggests that we look for some of the *disfunctional* effects of competition. In any discussion of management development in the U.S., we are likely to hear company executives bring up problems with individuals who manage to make their units look good in the short run so that they get promoted and then leave their successors in a very disadvantageous position. The problem of the individual who gets himself ahead in a way that indirectly damages the organization is a common theme in U.S. management discussions. This kind of problem could not occur in the Japanese organization.

We must also recognize some of the advantages that come with a high degree of predictability and understanding. If you know what is going to happen, there is less time wasted in trying to figure it out and make adjustments for uncertainties.

In seeking to understand the difference between the Japanese and the U.S. pattern of problem solving, where authority is *not* involved, we should note that the need for confrontation of differences of opinions and interests depends upon the inclination of the parties to take the other man's point of view and interests into account. If we have a culture in which it is assumed that each manager looks after the interests of his own department, then the adjustment of interests among departments can only be achieved through confrontation and working through on a face-to-face basis or by referring the issues up the line to a common organizational superior. U.S. culture favors the direct confrontation approach, whereas the resort to arbitration is favored in the Peruvian culture.

If we assume that each man develops within management so that he comes to consider managers of organizational units other than his own as part of his own group, then each individual is naturally sensitive to the differences in interests and points of view of other people on the same level as he. In that case, we do not need to assume that issues must be confronted in order for them to be resolved. The culture inclines each individual to be highly sensitive to the interests and ideas of other individuals and to consider it a failure on his part not to be so attuned. In this kind of setting, differences can be resolved without either the kind of dramatic confrontations that are common in U.S. organizations or the common resort to arbitration by superiors that we find in Peru.

To what extent does cultural analysis enable us to understand major trends in national economic and industrial growth? Let us imagine ourselves some 50 to 75 years ago trying to predict the future growth of Peru and Japan on the bases of two bodies of knowledge: the type of cultural data presented here and a comprehensive inventory of the natural resources available within the country. The resources approach would have led us to expect a bleak and desperate future for Japan; the cultural approach would have pointed us along the road Japan has actually taken. The resource approach would have led us to expect rapid and substantial industrial growth for Peru. The cultural analysis would have led us to expect either an absence of such growth *or* a growth rate largely dependent upon importation of capital and of people of different cultural orientations.

Let us specify this cultural interpretation in more detail for Peru. Knowledge of Peruvian culture could have provided the basis for a prediction that very few Peruvians who were well integrated into their own culture would take to entrepreneurial careers. Adding our observation about low faith in people to the variables of achievement orientation and prestige of business careers, we could have expected that few Peruvians with money would invest in enterprises they did not directly control. Since controlling an enterprise generally involves devoting some time and personal interest to it, Peruvians with money would be more likely either to send their money abroad or to put it into real estate. This means that the industrial development of Peru (now proceeding at a fairly rapid pace) would be produced by foreign firms, supplemented by immigrants and the sons of immigrants.

This cultural analysis of economic development should also lead to recognition of a major political problem. Whenever the economy of a nation is dominated by foreign interests, we can expect political leaders to raise an outcry against "economic colonialism." As this appeal fits in with growing nationalistic sentiments of the populace, we can expect increasingly tense relations between Peru and the country which is the major source of her industrial investment (the United States).

These conclusions for Peru appear to be generalizable to other Latin American countries. In fact, industrial development throughout Latin America seems to have depended predominantly upon foreign firms, immigrants, and the sons of immigrants.

These observations lead us to a general conclusion regarding the so-called profit motive. Theorists of private enterprise have assumed that, wherever opportunities to make profits exist, individuals will move into those fields to build up enterprises to exploit those opportunities. We now see that the existence of opportunities to make profits is a *necessary but not a sufficient condition* for the stimulation of entrepreneurial activities. If the culture favors entrepreneurship, then the existence of opportunities will call forth entrepreneurial responses. If the culture downgrades entrepreneurship, then the opportunities will be grasped by outsiders or by those not completely adapted to the national culture.

How can a nation meet this problem of foreign economic domination and scarcity of national entrepreneurial activity? Changes in values and abilities necessary for entrepreneurial success can be brought about through education, but how this might be done is beyond the scope of this book. In any case, education is a slow process. We cannot expect political leaders who are interested both in industrialization and national economic independence to rely upon educational changes that can show their effects only a generation later and, in any case, can have little effect upon the existing foreign enterprises. We can expect such political leaders to act both through taking over foreign firms and through setting up state enterprises. They will do this not so much because of an ideological commitment that socialism is better than capitalism but because, given their goals of industrialization under the control of their own countrymen, they will find this course of action the only way to get the job done.

We may also suggest certain implications for management development programs and for organization theory. This chapter might be interpreted as suggesting that organization structure is relatively unimportant and that the really important elements are found in the value system of the culture. That has not been my intention. I would argue that, whatever their nature, the existing structures tend to channel behavior, to form and change attitudes, and even to modify the underlying values of the organizational participants. What this chapter does mean is that there is no *one best way* to set up and operate an organization. We have seen such drastically different models as the U.S. and Japanese both yielding high performance. Models of organization structure and plans for management policies and programs need therefore to be interpreted against the background of the culture within which the organizations are developing. As long as management development programs around the world are based, explicitly or implicitly, on U.S. models (as is now generally the case), we can expect low yields from these programs, in relation to the money and manpower invested.

This is not an argument for leaving the culture alone. Industrialization will unavoidably introduce cultural changes, and sometimes political leaders themselves undertake to push through plans of cultural change. This is an argument for understanding what it is you might be changing as you set up a new industrial enterprise, for examining the fit between the existing culture and your model for the enterprise, and for thinking in terms of changing the model as well as in terms of changing the culture.

Let us conclude with answers to the two questions posed at the beginning of this chapter.

We have found that we can *not* simply generalize findings within U.S. culture (for example, on individualism and on general versus close supervision) to other cultures. On the other hand, our conceptual framework has provided us with at least some of the tools necessary to examine organizational behavior in different cultures.

This excursion into intercultural comparisons may also have served to indicate the way in which research findings on the individual and group level can be examined in order to draw conclusions regarding organizational problems, national cultures, economic development and industrialization, and international relations.

References

For further background on the culture of Latin America, see:

Heath, Dwight, and Adams, Richard (eds.). *Contemporary Cultures and Societies of Latin America*. New York: Random House, 1965.

For readings concerning organizational behavior in Japan, see:

Abegglen, James. *The Japanese Factory*. Cambridge, Mass.: M.I.T. Press, 1958. Also Yoshino, M. Y. *The Managerial System in Japan: Tradition and Innovation*. Cambridge: M.I.T. Press, 1968. Regarding union-management relations in Japan, see particularly Cook, Alice. *Japanese Trade Unionism*. Ithaca, New York: Cornell University Press, 1966. Also Levine, Sol. *Industrial Relations in Postwar Japan*. Urbana: University of Illinois Press, 1958.

For a study of Japanese workers in comparison with U.S. workers, see:

Whitehill, Arthur M., Jr., and Takezawa, Shin-ichi. *The Other Worker*. Honolulu: East-West Center Press, 1968.

For organizational studies in other cultures, see particularly:

Crozier, Michel. *The Bureaucratic Phenomenon*. Chicago: University of Chicago Press, 1964. Deals with plants and offices in France. Also Kolaja,

Jiri. *The Polish Factory*. Lexington: University of Kentucky Press, 1960. Especially useful in examining the dilemmas of worker-management relations in a socialist economy.

Discussion questions

1. This chapter has dealt with only a few of the aspects of organizational behavior in the U.S. that have been discussed in the present book. For Japan or Peru select a problem in organizational behavior *not* discussed in this particular chapter. On the basis of your background knowledge of the culture, what would you expect to find if you undertook a study of this particular problem in the country of your choice. Why?

2. Select a U.S. book or article dealing with management methods or management development programs. State the underlying assumptions regarding motivation and behavior that the author makes (implicitly or explicitly) in stating what he thinks ought to be done. To what extent should these assumptions be valid for human beings anywhere? To what extent do these assumptions hold good only for the United States—if indeed they hold good anywhere? What do the answers to these questions tell you about the possible exportability of the ideas and techniques presented by the author?

3. How does Crozier (see references) use his interpretation of French culture and society to explain the rigidities he finds to be characteristic in French organizations?

4. What does Kolaja's study (see references) suggest regarding the relations among (*a*) the ideology of government and party in a socialist state, (*b*) problems arising from differences of interests between workers and managers, and (*c*) structures and techniques utilized in attempting to resolve those problems?

33. On the application of behavioral science research in organizations

WHILE WE CAN ACCEPT the customary admission that the behavioral sciences are in a relatively primitive state, compared to the natural sciences, we have argued in this book that nevertheless some solid research findings have been produced. However modest our scientific achievements, we must further acknowledge that only a small fraction of what is currently known from behavioral science research is put into practice in the administration of organizations. In this final chapter, we shall focus upon the gap between knowledge and application, seeking to discover the factors underlying it and concluding with some preliminary suggestions for reducing the gap.

We will not be concerned with the uses of behavioral science knowledge in industry generally, but rather with concrete efforts to develop new knowledge and bring it to bear. Thus, we recognize that in recent years there has been a transformation of the curriculum in business schools so that behavioral science knowledge, methods and theories are increasingly taught to potential business leaders. We can thus assume that the behavioral sciences are having some general influence upon business administration, but this is far from what we find with research in chemistry, physics, and engineering, where the findings generated within the organization are put into practice in the organization. The research-to-action record in the behavioral sciences is much less impressive.

We shall review certain of these efforts to indicate what has been done and what might be done. Our aim here will not be to prove that research has yielded valuable results, but rather to give a picture of some of the ways in which behavioral scientists have sought to bring their research techniques and findings to bear in their organizations.

Intervention strategies

Behaviorial scientists interested in application have pursued a number of different strategies. We will review some of these strategies in order to illustrate some of the possibilities. We will not aim to select the "one best method," for we must assume that what is the best strategy will depend upon the situation in which it is to be used, the training and capacities of the research and action personnel, and the objectives of the research people and change agents.

A British psychiatrist, Elliott Jaques, has been a pioneer in this field. His book, *The Changing Culture of a Factory*,[1] describes the process of data gathering, diagnosis, and intervention. The techniques Jaques used and the ground rules he established for his work grew directly out of his psychiatric experience. Jaques worked particularly upon the discussion processes within management, and between management and union, in Glacier Metals, Ltd. He sat in as an observer on many of the meetings. His interventions were limited to efforts to clarify for the participants the nature of the social process in which they were engaging. For this purpose, he limited himself to comments upon aspects of the discussion that had been experienced by those to whom he addressed his remarks. That is, he refrained from gathering confidential information from individuals or groups and limited himself to matters that were "public," at least among those with whom he was talking. While Jaques has later stated that he does not feel it necessary now to limit himself in this way and feels it appropriate for the change agent to deal with confidential materials under certain conditions, nevertheless, his accounts suggest that even within the self-imposed restrictions he was able to help union and management personnel to develop the kind of discussion that enabled them to work through to better solutions of technical and human relations problems.

While Jaques provides no measurements of the effects of changes introduced through his research-action approach, he does provide systematic descriptions of the intervention process and of how behavior changed in the course of his activities. Furthermore, the record shows that Jaques has been extraordinarily successful in his ability to maintain a mutually satisfactory relationship with the organization, for he has been carrying on research of various sorts with Glacier Metals for approximately 20 years. His research activities have covered an extraordinary range, from the beginning that we have described to his more recent efforts, in *Measurement of Responsibility*,[2] to develop a scientific approach to job evaluation.

A major line of action-research has developed through group dynamics, with its emphasis upon group discussion methods as a means to the improvement of communication among organizational members. There is no question about the wide degree of acceptance won within management

---

[1] Elliott Jaques, *The Changing Culture of a Factory* (London: Tavistock Publications; New York: Dryden Press, 1951).

[2] Elliott Jaques, *Measurement of Responsibility* (London: Tavistock Publications; Cambridge, Mass.: Harvard University Press, 1956).

by proponents of one or another style of sensitivity training. So far it must be said that the acceptance of this approach to organizational change has outrun research evidence of its effectiveness, yet certain valuable research contributions have emerged. The work of Chris Argyris, one of the leaders in this field, has been reviewed in Chapter 17.

Rensis Likert has been a pioneer and a continuing leader in efforts to apply survey research methods to organizational problems. The Institute for Social Research, of which he is director, has carried on a long-term research-action relationship with the Detroit Edison Company. Under the direction of Floyd Mann for the University of Michigan, the investigators have involved members of management in all stages of the research process. A management advisory committee has worked with the research men to define the problems to be studied and to work out the best approach to these studies. While these studies have involved a good deal of preliminary exploration with different methods, the heart of the operation has always been the application of a questionnaire survey.

The first step in the feedback of research findings in the organization has involved a presentation of preliminary results to the research advisory committee. From this point, the management committee members have worked out with the research men a pattern of feedback within each department studied. Within a given department, the feedback sessions are organized, step by step, from the top down to the first-line supervisors. In each session, a member of management in the department presents the findings and leads the discussion. A member of the research team sits in on these discussions as a "resource person." He is called upon particularly to say whether a given interpretation of the research findings can be supported by the data.

It is now well recognized that a written report, by itself, no matter how well written or how persuasive its data and interpretations, rarely is utilized by the organization in which the study was done. Mann and his associates on the Detroit Edison studies have produced various written and published reports, but the feedback process they organized seems to have been much more important in involving management members in the research and in getting them to utilize the research findings. This process has also been an important factor in maintaining the university-company relationship over a number of years.

Along with the late Douglas McGregor, Likert has been one of the chief advocates of "participation management." Probably the most impressive case study representing this approach that has appeared at this writing is *Management by Participation*,[3] the principal collaborators in the project and in the writing being Alfred J. Marrow, Chairman of the Board of Harwood Manufacturing Company, and David G. Bowers and

---

[3] Alfred J. Marrow, David G. Bowers, and Stanley Seashore, *Management by Participation* (New York: Harper & Row, 1967).

Stanley E. Seashore, of the Survey Research Center of the University of Michigan. Marrow himself represents a unique combination of business executive and behavioral scientist. He received his Ph.D. in psychology and worked closely with Kurt Lewin on the first efforts to bring group dynamics research into the industrial plant. The classic Coch-French-Harwood experiment has been reported upon in Chapter 2. The change program Harwood carried out in Weldon, its new subsidiary, has been briefly described in Chapter 13.

This was a change process impressive in its magnitude and also in the results achieved. In two years' time, Weldon went from a minus 15 percent return on capital invested to plus 17 percent. Operator turnover rates dropped from 10 percent a month to 4 percent, and absences for production employees dropped from 6 percent daily to 3 percent. Figures on production and efficiency and operator earnings showed similar gains. The researchers noted favorable changes in the attitudes of Weldon management personnel toward the plant and company. Measures of employee attitudes, motivations, and satisfactions generally showed changes in favorable directions, but these were much smaller than had been anticipated, in view of the magnitude of the other changes.

While this is an impressive and well documented case in which human relations research and training programs apparently contributed to dramatic improvements in the economic performance of the plant, the very magnitude and variety of interventions involved at Weldon makes it extremely difficult to relate the research to the results achieved. Let us return to this problem after considering a final case.

My own most far reaching effort to relate research to action in an organization took place in 1945 and 1946 in what we are calling The Tremont Hotel.[4] Our aim here was to build into an organization a new role for the interpretation and application of organizational behavior research. We found ourselves establishing this role for the personnel man of the hotel, Meredith Wiley, who had worked on our research program at the University of Chicago and went to the Hotel Tremont to take over an established position and develop new functions within it. Edith Lentz, who had worked with me in the restaurant industry study, carried on research in the hotel under my general direction. While the project was paid for by the hotel, Miss Lentz' salary came from the University of Chicago, and she had no responsibilities to the hotel management.

We operated at several levels at the same time. The research began at the level of worker, supervisor, and department head. Miss Lentz spent her time observing and interviewing first in the coffee shop, then in the housekeeping department, later in the front office, and then with the checkers and cashiers. Her research reports went to Wiley and to me.

---

[4] William F. Whyte and Edith Lentz Hamilton, *Action Research for Management* (Homewood, Ill.: Richard D. Irwin, Inc. and The Dorsey Press, 1965).

The three of us met together to discuss the research findings and to help Wiley to plan how to utilize them. He then consulted with supervisors and department heads, providing some feedback on the research, and encouraging them to establish regular discussion meeting with their subordinates so that the problems that were brought to our attention could be dealt with directly by the supervisors and managers.

It was my responsibility, primarily, to deal with Mr. Smith, the top active executive of the hotel, with whom we arranged the project. I sought to interpret to him how the project was going and to relieve his impatience when he did not see immediate results. I also utilized several meetings of the department heads with Mr. Smith and with his resident manager, Mr. Kraus, to interpret organizational behavior research findings, first outside of the organization, and later within it, in an effort to promote a new pattern of management which we were seeking to stimulate in the hotel. As time went on, and as Wiley achieved increasing recognition from supervisors and department managers for the assistance he provided them, he was able increasingly to handle relations with the two top men, Smith and Kraus, without outside intervention from the university.

The project may be considered successful from several points of view. A new role for the personnel man was established. While it took a university-company collaboration to begin this process, Wiley remained in the position, carrying out much the same consultative activities with members of management (but unsupported by current research findings) for two years after the research contract with the university terminated. In fact, Wiley was able to survive and serve in a situation in which Smith first fired Resident Manager Kraus, and later Kraus returned to take over Smith's position when Smith lost out in a struggle with his previously silent partner for control of the hotel.

There was a general recognition of relaxed tensions throughout the hotel, but we have no measures of such data. At the time we began our research project in mid-1945, employee turnover was running over 20 percent a month. By the winter of 1947–48, it had dropped to below 4 percent. However, some caution must be used in interpreting those figures. In the first place, although we had the impression that other hotels in the city had not experienced comparable gains, no other hotel at the time was keeping systematic turnover figures, so that we could not say with any confidence how much of the gain at the Tremont should be credited to our program and how much to a change in conditions in the city. Furthermore, the turnover rate remained approximately at its high level throughout the 12 months of our research project and only began dropping—and rapidly—six months after the termination of the project —though still while Wiley was carrying on his part of the program. Can we take credit for a delayed effect here? This issue deserves further attention later.

Our principal failure was in our relations with Mr. Smith. While Wiley and I apparently enjoyed his confidence, he was never able to understand what we were doing in any systematic way. Furthermore, we were not able to make any far-reaching changes in his own leadership style, which had been and continued to be a source of some disturbance in the hotel.

Lessons learned

Whatever their limitations, all the projects described here can be considered successes. But if we go on to ask whether such cases "prove" the practical value of organizational behavior research, we face a question which has no simple answer. In scientific terms, the most convincing proof of success is provided by the experiment. The situation existing before the experimental situation is systematically described and measured. A simple and measurable stimulus is applied in a precisely controlled fashion within a single brief time period. The resulting situation is then systematically described and measured. The whole process may be accompanied by before-and-after measures of a control group to which the experimental stimulus is not applied, so as to check the possibility of changes taking place in the experimental situation through extraneous factors.

We now know that these standards have rarely if ever even been approached in interventions in organizations. This has not been due to lack of ability or lack of scientific commitment on the part of investigators. It seems to be in the very nature of organizational behavior that it does not lend itself to this kind of neat research design.

Two projects will illustrate the extraordinary difficulties of determining causation for induced changes in complex organizations. For our first case, we go back to the beginning: the relay assembly test room of the Hawthorne plant of Western Electric Company. The experiment was carried out according to the finest traditions of science, but the investigators ultimately discovered that the changes in behavior and productivity that arose were traceable less to the experimental stimuli of rest pauses, refreshments, and so on, than to the changes in interpersonal relations among workers singled out for special attention in the test room and to the changes in worker-supervisor relations. This experience suggests that it is well-nigh impossible to achieve the degree of control common in physics and chemistry which enables the investigator to state with assurance that the changes observed are due to the experimental stimuli and not to other unplanned factors.

The Weldon Company case[5] gives us another view of the complexities involved in interventions in industry. The new top management and those

---

[5] Marrow, Bowers, and Seashore, *op. cit.*

involved in the design of research aimed to assess what a participative management approach could do in improving the Weldon Company as a social and economic unit. At the same time, they recognized that they were dealing not with a single problem, but with a complex set of interrelated problems requiring a variety of interventions. They moved in with the assistance of consulting engineers, human relations trainers and management consultants, as well as research personnel. What changes were introduced? The authors give a chronological record. For our purposes, it will be sufficient to reproduce the descriptive titles of each intervention:[6]

1. Conversion to unit system of production with improved production planning.
2. Attitude surveys among production employees (applied in 1962, 1963, and 1964).
3. Enlargement of Weldon's permanent professional staff by addition of a personnel director and a second engineer.
4. Reorganization of the shipping room (layout changes to facilitate workflow).
5. Introduction of incentive pay for cutting and shipping.
6. In-unit training programs for operators.
7. Earnings development counseling with individual operators (consulting engineers observing operator work methods and helping operators to improve methods and production speeds).
8. Screening tests in employment.
9. Tightening of termination policy for chronic absentees.
10. Tightening of termination policy for persistently low-performing operators.
11. Vestibule training program (for new operators, with occasional retraining for experienced operators).
12. Training of managers and supervisors in interpersonal relations (sensitivity training laboratories involving all members of plant management and supervision).
13. Blanket 15 percent adjustment in rates for operators in one production unit.
14. Increase in miminum guaranteed wage by federal legislation.
15. Group problem-solving program with operators (discussion program with supervisors, their assistants and operators).
16. Union recognition and bargaining (the union coming in without opposition from management).

In addition to these changes summarized at one point by the authors, we should note that there was a substantial increase in the number of supervisors for production workers, with the aim of developing more effective supervision. In the merchandizing division in New York City,

---

[6] Marrow, Bowers and Seashore, *op. cit.*, pp. 159–61.

five of the six executives present at the time of the merger left the company in the course of the change program.

The authors comment:[7]

The changes were not introduced in any neatly experimental way designed to allow separate evaluation of each element. On the contrary, the theory guiding the program holds that the elements are all mutually interdependent and, in principle, not separable. . . .

Our purpose here is not to criticize the research design in the Weldon case but rather to use it to illustrate the difficulties of "proving" the effectiveness of any particular intervention in a complex human organization. We agree with the investigators at Weldon that an organization is made up of mutually dependent parts. Therefore, there will be few opportunities for showing a dramatic impact through an intervention in one small part of a large, complex organization, and ruling out the possibility of unplanned changes affecting the results. Applications of behavioral science knowledge and research findings must therefore involve a variety of interventions at various points in an organization, and carried out often through an extended period of time.

We face also the problem of the time lag between interventions and certain types of results. As the authors in the Weldon case state:[8]

From these results and observations, we suggest that basic gains in the "output" of an organization with respect to satisfactions, motivations, and positive feelings, often may be harder to achieve than gains in cost performance and work output. Such gains may well take place over a long span of time; employees may reserve judgment about the personal meaning of the policy and work system changes until the passage of time has allowed proof of their validity and proof of the stability of the new conditions of life.

In the Weldon case, operator turnover rates dropped sharply within two years of the inauguration of the program. The same can be said of the Tremont Hotel case, but we noted there that the reduction in turnover did not begin to show itself until some months after the research project had come to a conclusion. If indeed the drop in labor turnover could be attributed to our action research program, there was a time lag of many months before results could be shown. The longer the lag between interventions and measurable results, the greater the possibility that the results are influenced by other factors which were not planned as a part of the intervention program. The change agent is thus likely to get credit (or blame) for results of factors operating in the situation before his intervention, while a lag between intervention and measurable results means that it is often difficult to credit (or blame) the outcomes observed to the changes introduced.

---

[7] Marrow, Bowers and Seashore, *op. cit.*, p. 182.
[8] Marrow, Bowers and Seashore, *op. cit.*, p. 201.

There have also been serious problems in specifying the nature of interventions in organizations and how those interventions which are thought to arise out of the application of behavioral sciences relate to other changes. In the Weldon case, while there were definitely interventions growing out of behavioral science research and training activities, these were mingled with other changes which can only be described as "good management." In Chapter 13 we have noted the tendency of some enthusiasts to call anything except the arbitrary use of authority "participation management." If we cannot clearly specify the nature of the changes we are seeking to introduce, then we can hardly expect either to measure the impact of these changes or to relate them to behavioral science research findings.

On the establishment of organizational research inside organizations

It is not enough to demonstrate that there is some practical value in behavioral science research in organizations. In other fields of science, research has become a well established function within the organization itself. The record shows no such acceptance and consolidation of behavioral science research in industrial organizations.

When I began my own research in industry in 1942, I imagined that the day was not far off when every forward-looking management would have its own research department working on the problems of its human organization. Just a few years later, I thrilled to the words of a man who was then thought to be a leading spokesman of modern management thinking. In describing the principal functions that every personnel department should contain, he said that it was very important to have a research unit. But then he went on to say what he meant:

If your company is to keep up with the leaders in the personnel field, you should have within the personnel department several people who make it their responsibility to keep informed about what other companies are doing.

This follow-the-leader mentality has been very prevalent in American industry. If General Motors has put a new personnel technique into practice, as we all know, General Motors is a very large and a highly successful company run by very able people, and so it follows that this new technique must have some magical values that can be applied in other companies.

Fortunately, that has not been the whole story. There are a number of companies whose managements have made serious efforts to develop behavioral science research within their organizations, but their experience suggests that the problem of developing such research and maintaining the program in industry is still unresolved. Let us review some of the cases for clues as to the difficulties that have been encountered.

Case A: Western Electric Company

We will mention only one company by name, the Western Electric Company, since there we can base our interpretations upon the printed record. In a very real sense, our field was born within the Western Electric Company, and the research done there in the late 1920's and early 1930's still merits the respect that it won many years ago.

Into the 1950's, writers on management were writing about the Western Electric research program as if it were still in existence, whereas in fact there was practically no research in organizational behavior carried on within the company after the early 1930's. How did such a spectacular beginning lead to such a disappointing fadeout?

It is my thesis that the very success of the first research at Hawthorne led to the end of the program. Two of the pioneers in this program, William J. Dickson and Fritz J. Roethlisberger described the situation in this way:[9]

In late 1935, the management at Hawthorne posed the following question to those who had been involved in the Hawthorne studies: "In the light of these research experiences, are there any changes or additions which should be made to the company's personnel program to make it more effective?"

On the face of it, this seems like the answer to the research man's prayer. Here management was recognizing the importance of research that had been done and was asking for suggestions as to how the research findings might be applied. Furthermore, the request did not take the research team by surprise, as members of the group had already spent many hours in discussing the action implications of their research. They had a ready response: the personnel counseling program.

While the proposal involved many aspects that could only be worked out through experience, the research men were able even then to lay out the main outline of the counseling program, which we have discussed in Chapter 17. The management decision makers responded with full support for the counseling program, and so the research men had achieved their organizational innovation.

The successful application proved the downfall of organizational behavior research at the Western Electric Company. The time, effort, and creative energies of those who had been involved in research were now shifted toward the developing of the counseling program. This was an organizational innovation of large magnitude that could not simply be plugged into the organization and then be forgotten about. The program required the establishment and maintenance of a new role, that of the

[9] *Counseling in an Organization* (Boston, Mass.: Harvard Graduate School of Business Administration, 1966), p. 36.

personnel counselor. It meant establishing a personnel counseling organization and handling its many and perplexing relations with the line organization and with various staff activities.

Since the counseling program was expensive and made no readily measurable contribution to the company, those responsible for it naturally found much of their time and thoughts involved in interpreting and defending counseling to critics, friendly and otherwise, inside and outside of the company.

Those who planned the counseling program did not intend that it should become a substitute for research. In fact, it was assumed at the beginning that the data coming in to counselors in their interviews would somehow be utilized for research, though there never seems to have been a very clear idea as to how this would be done. The counseling organization did in fact submit periodic reports to management on the state of morale of the organization, as reflected in the complaints of employees, and sometimes also on special topics such as worker reactions to technological change. Such reports, insofar as they were considered at all by management, were looked upon simply as an information service. Furthermore, none of them went beyond the confines of the company, and this was not due primarily to any restrictive policy on the part of management. Whereas the findings of *Management and the Worker* were of extraordinarily great interest to behavioral scientists and imaginative management people outside of the Western Electric Company, the counseling program was producing in-house service materials.

At last, after 20 years, the counseling program died. Whatever contribution it made in its time to the operation of the Western Electric Company, it produced no research and, we would argue, the program made it impossible for the company at Hawthorne to carry on further research.

How could it happen that the very men who opened the door to an important new field of research led themselves into the trap that closed the door against research in the organization where they had begun their work? Let us postpone the answer to this question until we have considered other cases.

Case B: from research program to operating program

Company B was relatively early after Western Electric in getting into organizational behavior research. In the 1940's, the company had a small group of able, imaginative, and enthusiastic men in the personnel department, dedicated to the idea that research in organizational behavior had important values to offer the company and believing that it was up to them to lead the way in the realization of these values. The research team set about the task of developing methods for the assessment of the human functioning of the various parts of the company organization. The period of development of the organizational assessment instrument and of the methods for its interpretation and utilization was one of intellectual ferment and creativity within the personnel department.

But then came the time when the instrument had passed beyond the developmental stage and was ready to be utilized as a regular part of the management program of periodic assessment of various aspects of the business. The research men who had developed the instrument now became involved in applying it and interpreting it to other management people and in training others to apply it and interpret it. Here again the research men had achieved success with their management. Their instrument and their methods had become incorporated into established management programs.

While this was going on, what was happening in research in this company? The answer can be given in one word: nothing. The men who had been involved in development of the assessment methods were now too busy applying them and interpreting them, so that they had no time for the opening of new research pathways. Company executives outside of the personnel department were quite satisfied with the assessment instrument and saw no need for moving into less familiar fields.

Case C: who is carrying the ball?

Organizational behavior research arose in Company C in an atmosphere of rivalry between two leading figures in the personnel department—let us call them Jones and Smith. It was recognized within the department that when the vice president for personnel retired, the new vice president would be either Jones or Smith. Jones developed a very penetrating interest in, and enthusiasm for, organizational behavior research. He built up a small research unit and devoted most of his time and creative energies to the development of these new activities, giving relatively little attention to other personnel functions for which he was formally responsible. Jones became recognized inside the company, and outside as well, as a leading spokesman for the new ideas of management that were growing out of the research findings.

Smith followed a completely different strategy. He stuck strictly to the "bread and butter" established programs of personnel administration, seeing to it that all branches of management had the highest quality of personnel services that his unit could provide.

When the vice president retired, Smith was promoted into this position. Jones left the company. Those who had worked on the research program under Jones either left also or else moved over into more traditional types of personnel activity. That was the end of the research program at Company C. We might add that some years later, Smith, long since firmly established in his vice presidency, was giving indications that he would be receptive to support for some new research activities. So perhaps the cycle is beginning again, but years were lost in competitive struggle.

Case D: the expendable program

Some years ago, Company D had a very enterprising and imaginative director of personnel research and training. He served under a vice president who was exceedingly influential in top management and who supported him solidly. Carter, as we shall call him, developed innovative programs both in research and training. He developed a combination of internal and external programs, building up a small internal research and training staff which engaged in collaborative activities with leaders in organizational training and research from the universities.

Then the supportive vice president was moved up to a position which, while higher in prestige and general influence, removed him from involvement in the research and training activities. The appointment of a new vice president coincided with a sharp decline in the market for the company's products. The new vice president thought it was his duty to show his concern for the serious (though temporary) economic problems of the company by drastically reducing the budget of his own department. Carter suddenly found his research and training staff reduced to one half-time secretary. Displaying extraordinary perserverance in the face of adversity, Carter managed to hang on and retain his interest in the activities he was no longer able to promote. In time he again found opportunity to rebuild—though on a small scale—some of the activities that had been eliminated. But, by now, the earlier purge in his department was well known in the company and outside, and he found it hard to get good people to come in and work for him.

Case E: basic is best

Observing the instabilities of organizational behavior research programs in other companies, the personnel executive in Company E decided upon a different approach. His was a large company, well known for its generous support of basic as well as applied research in the natural sciences. The executive decided that behavioral science research people needed to be sheltered from the immediate demands to make their findings useful until they had had time to build up a fund of basic knowledge. Therefore, he established a basic research laboratory for the behavioral sciences and went out, with attractive salaries and promises of financial support and freedom for research, to hire some of the best behavioral scientists he could find anywhere.

The executive recognized that in the long run the existence of the basic research laboratory would have to be justified in terms of the practical applications developing out of the research program. Judging from successes achieved in translating research findings of the natural sciences into practical application, he had faith that this long run would not be too far off in the behavioral sciences.

What the executive offered seemed at first glance like the dream of the research man. More salary than the universities could offer him; practically unlimited research funds for his projects without having to go through the painful and often frustrating process of applying to fund-granting agencies; and finally, complete freedom to work on the problems that interested him. On this basis, the company was able to hire several first-rate behavioral scientists.

The results? Disappointing to all concerned. The company followed through on its promises of attractive salaries and generous research support, and company officials scrupulously refrained from trying to influence what the research men would study. The behavioral scientists thus enjoyed the freedom that some of them had been dreaming about, but they also found themselves isolated. They were isolated from the sometimes frustrating, but also sometimes stimulating, contacts with fellow professors and students that they had become accustomed to in the academic community. While they were free to establish any relationships with company management people that seemed appropriate to their research mission, they had no recognized place in the company system. They came to feel that they did not belong anywhere—not in the university world which they had left, and not in the company system which provided their pay and facilities, expected much from them, but required nothing of them. Before long they began leaving the company for the universities.

Then there was a change in top management in the personnel department, with its accompanying re-evaluation of the work that had been done. Had basic research led anywhere? No? And so it was cut out, and those concerned with research in the company began casting about for a new approach.

Case F: from small beginnings

The behavioral science research program in Company F began in a small way with the appointment of behavioral scientists to do research in several of its major plants. The research men were loosely attached to the personnel department. As a man we will call Jessup moved from the plant location into the central personnel office, he found himself devoting much of his time to the role of interpreter—interpreting research findings to management people, interpreting management's concern with human problems to research men in such ways that they could define researchable problems. Jessup also found new opportunities for studies that were of sufficient interest to plant management to win financial support at the plant level. Jessup and his associates involved management people in the planning of research and in feedback discussions.

Over the course of a number of years, the program slowly expanded, meanwhile producing respectable research findings that began attracting interest in university circles. Within the company, the research team had had some small successes and also some disappointments. Jessup found on occasion that when he reported findings that he thought would be of great practical interest to management, reception was not nearly as warm as he had expected. But then a breakthrough came. Top management was becoming much more cost-conscious and pushing cost reduction programs down to the plant level. The research team carried out a survey in Plant X. Figures showed that substantial cost reduction had been achieved in Plant X, but the survey responses also showed a substantial lowering of employee satisfaction scores—with the company, with the job, and with a number of aspects associated with the work situation. The cost reduction program had been carried out in Plant X through a traditional industrial engineering approach. The figures suggested that the gains made in money costs had to some extent been achieved at the expense of good will to the company and to the supervisors. Then the research team had the opportunity to do a similar study in Plant Y, which had achieved equally impressive results in cost reduction through applying quite a different management approach with group discussions and involvement of people at various levels in the organization in working out changes. The survey showed that there had been no loss in employee satisfaction with the job or with the company in Plant Y.

The research team put together a report comparing the results in Plant X and Plant Y and making certain interpretations about management strategy in introducing changes. The report attracted more attention than earlier reports of the research team—and not all of it favorable, for the report offended some of the traditionalists in industrial engineering, and it also fitted into the pattern of interplant rivalries and competition.

But then the report reached the president's desk, and he responded with enthusiasm. He had taken great pride in the high morale and dedication to the company of the work force, but he had come to be increasingly concerned with rising costs. Would Company F have to sacrifice its good relations with its employees in order to make the economic gains essential to maintaining its competitive position? The research report suggested that it was not necessary to buy cost reduction at the expense of good employee relations. Apparently, if you applied the lessons of behavioral science research, you could have your cake and eat it, too. The President thereupon expressed strong support for further development of research along these lines.

Several years later top management became alarmed over a rash of resignations of very highly regarded engineers and scientists. The president called in Jessup and arranged to devote a week of top-management discussion time to behavioral research findings that might bear on this problem.

The week led to an interesting social invention: the setting up of management study teams with a behavioral scientist attached to each team as a "resource person." Jessup and his colleagues participated in the training of the research teams with sessions on interviewing methods, interpretation of previous research findings, and organization theory.

Each team made its study in an organizational unit to which none of the team members belonged. The work was exceedingly intensive. Team members spent all day interviewing local management people individually and in groups, and talked far into the night about what they were finding out. At the conclusion of the study, the team members spent some days together listening to tapes of interviews, going over records, and preparing their report. At a later time, the several teams met for a period to compare notes and to determine to what extent the problems each team had encountered were specific to a given location or general to the company.

The behavioral science "resource people" were active participants in the whole process, but they did *not* direct the studies. They did some of the interviewing and joined in the evening discussions of problems and plans for next steps. They also contributed points from related research carried out earlier and suggested interpretations based upon theory. They found that the perceived value of their contributions did not depend upon having authority to impose their views. If the research man had something interesting and useful to say, he was listened to and encouraged to contribute more. If he was not able to make a useful contribution, requiring people to listen to him would hardly have been helpful.

At this writing, it is too early to report on management changes that may have come about through the research team approach. At the same time, it is worth noting two payoffs that seem already apparent:

1. *Training effects.* Comments of the management participants in the study teams suggest that this was an extraordinarily valuable advanced management training program. Some of the men commented that they had learned more about management and organizational behavior through this experience than through all of their previous participation in formal educational programs. They also reported that the studies gave them ideas that they were going to try out when they returned to their own regular jobs.

2. *Strengthening researcher-manager relationships.* The concentration of interactions within the study teams over a period of time naturally led to friendships not only among managers but also between managers and research men. Furthermore, the managers testified that the experience gave them a better understanding of behavioral science research, whereas the behavioral scientists said that they gained a better understanding of management and managers.

So far this sounds like a success story, and indeed Company F seems to me to have the soundest program I have yet encountered, but this does not mean that behavioral science research in Company F has become as fully established as research in engineering and physics. Behavioral scientists are still engaged in finding their place in the organization even as the general level of acceptance increases. Some of the most active participants in the research program in the past have since left the company for university research and teaching positions, but the company continues to attract able young behavorial scientists. The future is uncertain, yet the trend seems upward.

Lessons from the cases

What lessons can we draw from these cases? At this point it may be helpful to consider our cases against the context of the development in industry of research programs in physics, chemistry, engineering and so on. I do not mean to suggest that behavioral science research must follow the same pathways, but to some extent the establishment of a new field of research activities in a company faces problems similar to those that were met and solved in earlier periods in other fields, and thus the analogies may provide us some guidance.

Should we begin, like Company E, with basic research? This seems to me flying in the face of all previous experience in other fields of research in industry. While the establishment of industrial research in other companies may not have had such dramatic turning points as in the case of Dr. Sullivan and the pyrex glass (see Chapter 26), I assume that the general process has been the same. As useful results have been produced, programs have expanded, and the research men have had increasing freedom to pursue the ideas they consider important. How could we ever imagine that behavioral science research would reverse this process, establishing a beachhead in industry with basic research, and in some far future getting to practical application?

For understanding what happened in Western Electric and in Company B, we should look upon research and development in the behavioral sciences, as in the natural sciences, as a process which must be organized and maintained. In Western Electric, the research men sought to move from research to an operating program in one jump. In the process, they lost the research program and succeeded in establishing only an operating program which eventually died also.

When management asks for the action implications of a research project, the temptation to produce recommendations is almost irresistible. But this request can lead us into a trap even now and—in hindsight—it is painfully clear that it was a trap in 1935. As we look back upon the Western Electric research program, as impressed as we should be by the magnitude of the accomplishments, we should nevertheless recognize that the first Western Electric researches were primarily a ground-clearing operation. They demonstrated that certain established organization theories were false or inadequate, and they demonstrated that certain established ways of running an organization necessarily gave rise to results contrary to management's objectives. However, the pioneering researches did not provide a new theory of management nor did they provide ways of solving the problems the researchers had discovered. Looking back now with the wisdom of hindsight, we can say that the reply to management should have been along these lines:

Our research program has not reached the stage from which action implications can legitimately be drawn. The important next step is to continue the basic research we have been doing and also focus on certain applied problems. As we reach findings on applied projects, then we should be in a position to propose action programs.

In Company B, there was indeed a progression from basic research to applied research and development as the organization assessment instrument was developed and put into practice. But the research men who began on the basic research phase had simply moved over into applied research, and then into establishing an operational program. When the program was established, there was no research still going on in Company B.

These cases point up the importance of the establishment of distinctive developmental roles and research application roles in organizational behavior research. Some research men are so versatile that they can play each role from basic research to the establishment of an operating program reasonably effectively—but they cannot perform all these roles at once. This does not mean that a man must always be required to perform the same role. It may be stimulating to individuals and helpful to the organization to have its research people getting experience in various types of research and in the establishment of action programs, and it may be stimulating to management officials to take part in some aspects of research programs. The point is that research and development, if it is to be fruitful, must be organized as a continuous process, so that one activity is not abandoned in order to get the next stage of the process going. If the research man on Project A moves with the project as it evolves into applied research, development, and finally into operations, his place in earlier stages must be taken by others.

Cases C and D illustrate some of the interpersonal rivalries and instabilities of personnel that have plagued organizational behavior research programs. Such problems can be serious, but I cannot believe that they are insurmountable obstacles. If we examined the history of industrial research programs in chemistry and physics, I am sure we would find similar problems of interpersonal rivalries and instabilities of personnel. I suspect we would find the main difference in the fact that these programs have produced such impressive results that no modern company can afford to let organizational problems destroy a research program. These days a manager can hardly afford to look upon research in the natural sciences as an expendable item which can be sharply curtailed when the company runs into financial difficulties. In fact, he may feel that this is the very time to give increasing emphasis to research and development so that the company can eventually produce new products that will improve its economic position.

While organizational behavior research will always be handicapped, in competition with chemistry and physics, in not being able to show such "concrete" results, we can assume that the problems of personnel instabilities and rivalries will be overcome, or at least reduced in seriousness, when organizational behavior research programs reach the point of providing useful knowledge to management.

Problems of recruiting and maintaining research talent

The problems here are the same as those encountered in attracting chemists and physicists into industry except that the roles of research chemists and research physicists are now well established, whereas the organizational behavior research role remains unclear and unstable. The past instability has naturally had a discouraging effect upon bright young people who might be attracted to research in industry. The problems of recruitment today are compounded by two prevailing sentiments in the social sciences. There is a widespread feeling, particularly marked in sociology, that the only research worthy of the name is "pure" or basic research, while applied research is hardly worthy of consideration. While it can easily be demonstrated that important additions to basic knowledge have been gained through studying applied problems, the prejudice nevertheless remains a significant force. There is also an antibusiness bias which is now marked in the colleges of the country. Until the last decade or so, most men going to college took it for granted that they would go into business careers upon graduation and saw no need to apologize for such an ambition. In recent years, company recruiters have had increasing difficulties in attracting able undergraduates, competing against graduate schools and against such apparently more glamorous service opportunities as the Peace Corps, the Vista Program and so on. The prospects of attracting able young men and women into organizational behavior research in industry therefore do not look good, at least in the short run. However, let us see what could be done if these research activities were more effectively organized.

Prospects for organizational behavior research in industry

What changes would it take in order to establish organizational behavior research more firmly in business and governmental organizations?

In the first place, I would argue for giving attention to the development of a social process. It is a serious mistake to assume that research will become established in an organization as soon as certain research findings can be proven useful. We have reviewed cases where this has happened and yet where the research program has been lost. If we give less attention to "proof" of success, and more attention to developing the process necessary to sustain the research program, we will have more chance of success.

Our review also suggests giving much greater attention to developmental roles. In the past, the research man has had to try to be jack-of-all-trades, moving from basic research all the way through into program establishment, and we have seen the self-defeating character of this approach. What kinds of people should be involved in applied research and in the establishment of programs based upon research findings? If management personnel without special research training were to have opportunities to work in these roles in collaboration with behavioral scientists, I suspect this would have three very constructive results. The management people involved in research and the utilization of research findings would help the research people to remain in touch with the realities of organizational life. The management men would find the experience exceedingly valuable training for future effectiveness in administration. Finally, the interpenetration of research and management people in these programs would build a steadily growing understanding of and receptivity for research within management. The experience of Company F already attests to some of these values.

Where in the organization of a large company should organizational behavior research be located? Usually we find it located in the personnel department, and to most people this seems like the natural place. However, as we have seen, personnel departments tend to become very largely involved in procedures and practices and to have little touch with some of the major problem areas of organizational behavior research—such as the impact of technology or the organization structure upon the behavior. Would location in the personnel department therefore tend to limit the growth and effectiveness of this research finding?

Suppose organizational behavior research were placed in the same department as research in physics, chemistry, engineering, and so on? On the assumption that all these fields of research have something in common, this would seem like a logical decision, and it indeed might provide the organizational behavior unit support and protection it badly needs—providing the head of the research department is sympathetic to this new line of work. On the other hand, the organizational behavior research unit would have to develop its relations primarily outside of the research department—with the personnel department, with operating management, with staff organizations, and so on. Organizational behavior research needs support from the top of an organization, but it cannot just operate at this level. In fact, most of the data may be gathered from observations, interviews, and surveys of low-prestige people. The research men and research administrators therefore must master the difficult problem of relating effectively to a large range of status positions.

It is impossible at this point to make any flat statement about where organizational research belongs. The best we can do is lay out some of the problems and possibilities and suggest that, in any case, the solution of one company may well be different from that of another.

Should an organization have its own behavioral research unit or should it contract the work out? The outsider, whether professor or consultant, has the great advantage that he is not limited by a position in the hierarchy. Within the same hour, he may be talking to a worker on the production line and the president of the company, and no one will necessarily think this strange. The inside research man, however important his findings, is likely to be so far below the key executives in the structure that he cannot communicate with them without encountering all sorts of organizational difficulties.

On the other hand, if the research people are all outsiders, their work is likely to suffer from other deficiencies. It is difficult for them to develop the intuitive familiarity with the company situation that is possessed by people working inside it. Also, they are not likely to provide the continuity of activity which is necessary for developing a real impact upon the organization.

Facing the difficulties of his fixed and modest position in the company structure, the inside man is often unable to exploit the superior familiarity he has with the company situation. In fact, without outside stimuli, he may even come to take so for granted the life he sees around him as to fail to raise the important scientific questions.

These criticisms suggest that the ideal arrangement would be a combination of inside-outside perspective. The company would maintain a small research staff of its own, but contract out certain research projects. Such an arrangement could also involve utilizing the outside research men as consultants to the company researchers and as interpreters of the company research program to higher management. Such a dual arrangement seems to me to offer the greatest prospect of success.

References

Argyris, Chris. *Interpersonal Competence and Organizational Effectiveness.* Homewood, Ill.: Richard D. Irwin, Inc. and The Dorsey Press, 1962. A full account of a major action-research project carried out by Argyris.

Jaques, Elliott. *The Changing Culture of a Factory.* London: Tavistock Publications; New York: Dryden Press, 1951. The author's account of his pioneering action-research program in Glacier Metals, Ltd.

Mann, Floyd, and Likert, Rensis. "The Need for Research on the Communication of Research Results," in Adams, Richard N., and Preiss, Jack J.

(eds.). *Human Organization Research*. Homewood, Ill.: The Dorsey Press, 1960. Pages 57–66 describe the feedback of research results as carried out by the Survey Research Center.

Marrow, Alfred J.; Bowers, David G.; and Seashore, Stanley. *Management by Participation*. New York: Harper & Row, 1967. An account of the reorganization of the management of a subsidiary, accompanied by research and training programs.

Sofer, Cyril. *The Organization from Within*. Chicago: Quadrangle Books, Inc., 1962. An account of how the author carried out a researcher-consultant role in several organizational projects.

Whyte, William F., and Hamilton, Edith Lentz. *Action Research for Management*. Homewood, Ill.: Richard D. Irwin, Inc. and The Dorsey Press, 1965. An account of a project involving development of a new role for a personnel manager in a hotel, and the utilization of research findings by him. See especially Chapter 14, "On the Theory and Practice of Action-Research," which interprets the other studies listed here as references (except Marrow *et al.*) as well as the hotel study.

Discussion questions

1. Should an organizational research program be located in (*a*) the personnel department, (*b*) the research and development department, or (*c*) some other unit (specify)? What considerations lead you to your conclusion?

2. Consider the problem of establishing a continuing action-research program within an organization in terms of the following framework:

Select a research project from one of the cases cited in the references for this chapter or from another source. Examine the case in terms of the following questions:

a) How were the various research and action roles defined by the chief participants? Why did the director of the project pick these role definitions and not others?

b) What problems did the chief participants in the action-research effort have in (*a*) gaining rapport, (*b*) gathering the data, and (*c*) feeding back the data to organization members.

c) To what extent were the strategies pursued by the action-research people conducive to maintaining a continuing program within the organization?

d) What general lessons do you draw from this case regarding the problems of developing and maintaining a research program in an organization?

Indexes

Index of cases

Note: Unless otherwise indicated, the reference is to a summary of the case. Only those cases discussed in some detail are indexed here. For other references, see the Index of Subjects.

Amicon Tube (Ronken and Lawrence), 564–67
Decision making, 690–92
Automatic Tube Mill (Walker), 567–69
Banana Time (Roy), 184–91
Benton Blowing Room (Whyte)
Jack Carter, gaffer, 252–76
Seniority and Jack Carter, 471
Work group cohesion, 504–10
Blank Oil Company (Whyte)
Vertical versus horizontal integration, 110–14
Joe Sloan case, 277–98
Unionization drive, 419–50
Favoritism by foreman and seniority, 469–70
Tri-iso-butylene run (introducing change), 563–64
Farewell party, 587
Symbols (watchman), 589
Boys' Groups (Sherif)
Sociometric structures, 174–76
Intergroup relations, 205–8
Buchsbaum (Gardner, Whiteford, and Whyte)
Summary, 450–56
Dual loyalties, 473
Symbols of identification, 588
Chandler's Restaurant (Whyte)
Pressures on waitresses, 102–7
Ann Lindstrom versus Ellen Geiger, 232–50
Esso Experiment (Blake), 209–13
Ethnicity and Group Pressures (Collins), 198–201

Food World (Lawrence), 673–83
Foreman Who Failed (Whyte)
Tom Walker case, 331–45
Furniture Experiment (Rosen), 37–40
Grinders (Sayles)
Intergroup relations, 219–22
Cohesion, 494–504
Milo (Dalton)
Maintenance case, 359–63
General conclusions, 564–67
Motivation, Productivity, and Satisfaction (Zaleznik et al.)
Bases of social groupings, 191–98
Nortons Corner Gang (Whyte), 179–84
Overseas Corporation (Whyte)
Standardization program, 351–55
Area coordination system, 355–59
General conclusions, 364–67
Smelting versus Chemical Division (Whyte), 481–94
Steel Containers (Sayles)
Incentive rate and intergroup problem, 222–24
Truax (Dean)
Frank Vitucci, Abe Carter, and their union, 458–66
Western Electric (Roethlisberger, Dickson)
History, 7–9
Illumination experiment, 30–31
Relay Assembly Test Room, 31–33
Personnel counseling, 385–89, 397

789

Index of subjects

A

Absenteeism, 48, 562
Achievement, needs for, 135
Action-research program, 327
Action symbols, 143
Activities
  aspects of, 117–22
  attitude formation, 121–22
  barrel department supervisor, 334–35, 338–40
  challenge, 120
  changes in patterns of, 561–70
  defined, 114
  degrees of complexity, 117–18
  evaluation of, 129–30, 143–44
  failure, 120–21
  feelings about, 128, 143; see also Sentiments
  initiation of foremen and subordinates, 315–16
  interaction in relation to, 114–15
  leaders and followers, 115–16
  leadership and status, 116–17
  oil company worker, 291–95
  performance, 121–22
  repetitive, 119–20
  sentiment formation, 121–22
  social arrangements of work, 118√
  success, 120–21
  traction, degrees of, 118–20
  transactions in relation to, 167–68, 170
  wholeness of, 120
  work and nonwork distinguished, 118
Activity, 96
Adams, Stuart N., 196 n
Advisory relationships, 408–9, 410–11
  development of, 409
Afro-Americans
  integration of, 571
  introduction into industry, 581–86
  reactions of, 582–83
  upgrading of, 581
Age symbol, 142
Aggressiveness, 96
Ajax Chemical Company, 533
Amicon tube, introduction of, 564–67, 569, 692
Andrews, Frank M., 608 n, 614–15
Area coordination system maintenance organization, 355–59

Arensberg, Conrad M., 9, 11, 22, 91, 379 n, 577, 579
Argyris, Chris, 14, 45, 368, 391, 655, 657, 766
Aristotle, 3
Armed forces steel container assembling and welding for, 222–24
Aspiration, level of; see Level of aspiration
Assembly line operations; see Continuous process operations
Attitude formation, 121–22
Attitudes; see Sentiments
Auditing
  budget, in relation to, 407
  defined, 406
Authority coordination and communication through, 628–29, 638
Automation
  investment-rewards relationship, effect on, 568
  studies in field of, 16
Automotive assembly line; see Continuous process operations
Autonomous group study, 178–84, 202
Autonomous groups, 116

B

Bakke, E. Wight, 9
Balanced relationships, 149–50
Baldamus, W., 118
Bales, R. Freed, 92, 177
"Banana time," 184–91, 202
"Barber college" crisis, 191, 202
Bargaining, 149, 158–59, 169; see also Collective bargaining
Bargaining unit in oil company, 425
Barnard, Chester I., 622
Barrel department, 331–45
Basadre, Jorge, 736
Batch production, 57, 62–64, 733; see also Mass production
Bavelas, Alex, 34
Bay of Pigs case, 688–90, 693–94, 703
Behavioral sciences; see Organizational behavior
Bell, Daniel, 18
Bell, Gerald D., 67–68, 81
Belonging needs, 135–36
Bendix, Reinhard, 12, 18 n

Bennis, Warren, 14
Bisson, André, 481 n
Blake, Robert, 14, 209 n, 210–11
Blau, Peter, 12, 19, 45, 73 n, 149–50, 409, 614, 708
Blue-collar workers, 634
  in Japan, 742 ff
  in Peru, 721 ff
Blumer, Herbert, 18 n
Bootleg projects, 636–37, 639
Borgatta, E. F., 177 n
Bowers, David, 325, 326 n, 766, 769 n, 770 n, 771 n
Boys camp experiment, see Intergroup relations
Braun, Robert R., 719, 725 n
Breer, Paul, 121
Brown, George C., 9
Buck, Vernon E., 119
Budget
  auditing in relation to, 406–7
  defined, 368
  impact on people of, 371–74
  importance of, 369
  negative effects of, 375–76
  problems with, 371–72
  process by which made, 374–75
  significance of, 368
  specialist in, 377
  views of, 369–70
Bulldogs versus Red Devils experiment, 205–9
Bureaucracy
  features characteristic of, 6
  Weber's study of, 6–7
Bureaucratic career, 6
Burns, Tom, 620 n, 626, 631 n, 710
Burtt, Harold E., 389
Burtt, R. D., 319 n
Buy-sell relationships, 151–52
  nature of, 403–4

C

Canada, French, local union study in, 481–84
Card-ranking method of study, glass industry, 262–64
Carey, Alex, 32 n
Carnegie, Dale, 590
Cartwright, Dorwin, 13, 33 n
Cassel, Frank, 72
Caustic plant, work unit cohesion and militancy, 484–85
Centralization of maintenance organization, 350–51
Ceremonial ways of handling social transitions, 306–7
Challenge, 120
Change, technological; see Technological change

Change agents, 595
Change
  in personnel atmosphere, foreman's and steward's versions of, 341–43
  in social system of grinding department, 495–96, 501–2
Chapple, Eliot D., 11, 22, 44, 91, 93–98, 123, 125
Chapple, Martha F., 95 n
Character of organization, 571
Charts; see Diagrams
Chemical versus smelting division, work unit cohesion and militancy, study of, 481–84, 510–11
Chicago Inland Steel Container Company, 468
"Chicken-egg" problem of supervisory leadership and productivity, 37–40
Christensen, C. R., 132 n, 191 n
Chronograph interview, 93–98
Chronograph studies, 122–23
CIO organization drive at oil company, 419–20; see also Union
Clicking machine workers study, 184–91
Coch, Lester, 33, 327 n
Cognitive dissonance, principle of, 131
Cohesion
  group memberships, 203
  intergroup relations, 219, 227
  militancy and; see Work unit cohesion and militancy
  norms of behavior in relation to, 479
  productivity in relation to, 479
  work group, 325–26
  work unit, 479–513
Coleman, James S., 12
Collective bargaining
  attitudinal structuring, 555–56
  ceremonial launching of agreement for, 550–51
  common interests, 538–39
  contract for
    acceptance of, 542–49
    launching of, 550–51
  distributive relationships, 555–56
  effects of, 528
  elements involved in, 529
  encouraging full expression, 536–37
  harmonious relations sought through, 529
  institutional framework made clear, 539–40
  integrative relationships, 555–56
  international representative's role, 540–42
  manipulation of men, problem of, 551–54, 556
  negotiation process, 530–50
  oblique attack upon nonexistent man, 533–36

Collective bargaining—*Cont.*
  pattern of agreement, 537–38
  ratification of agreement for, 542–49
  safety valves in, 538
  symbolic equivalence of status, 530–33
  symbolic scapegoat, 533–36
  symbolism of common interests, 538–39
Collectivism, 121–22
College-trained foremen, 308–11
Collins, Orvis, 11, 198–99, 214–15, 525
Committee on Human Relations in Industry, 9
Commonwealth Edison Company of Chicago, 550
Communication
  authority, 628–29, 638
  factors affecting, 621–26
  group discussion, 630–31, 638
  in Japan, 742 ff
  liaison positions, 626–28, 637–38
  negotiation, 630, 638
  oil company channels, early days of, 420–22
  openness between superiors and subordinates, 315–16
  in Peru, 719 ff
Communication programming, 79
Company union
  negotiating for, 441–43
  oil company, 422–23
Comparative studies
  of organizational behavior
    Japan, 742–56
    Peru, 719–42
    questionnaire survey approach, 48
    United States, 756–62
  in research, 25–28
Compensation system; *see* Rewards
Competitive transactions, 149, 154–56, 168–69
Complexity of job, 67–68
Composite form of organization, 562
Composition of work force, 571
Conflicts of interests
  scientist versus company, 596–98
  management policies toward, 599–600
Consideration in supervisory behavior, 319–20
Construction organization; *see* Maintenance organization
Continuous process operations, 16, 58
  barrel department of steel fabricating plant, 331–45
  differences in supervisory jobs, 321
  interaction between supervisor and men, 60
  interactional requirements, 99
  managerial succession, 651–54
  personnel requirements, 70
  work flow in, 58–59

Continuous seamless tube mill, introduction of, 567–68, 569
Cook, Alice, 742, 753, 754 n, 755
Cooperation, supervisor's role in building, 331–32
Coordination, 69
  through authority, 628–29, 638
  factors affecting, 621–26
  in glass industry tasks, 256–58
  through group discussion, 630–31, 638
  through liaison positions, 626–28
  through negotiation, 630, 638
  through restructuring interactions, 629–30, 638
Copley, F. B., 3 n
Cornell University, 694–97, 702
"Cornerville," study of, 178–84
Corning Glass Works, 595
Cost control; *see* Budget
Costs of innovation, 619
Craft coordination in maintenance organization, 356–58
Craftsmen; *see also* Glass industry
  maintenance organizations, 351
Creativity defined, 615; *see also* Research department
Crying behavior of waitresses in restaurants, 102–7
Cuba; *see* Bay of Pigs Case
Culture; *see* Japan; Peru; *and* United States
Customers
  relation with, in restaurant, 101–7 ✓
  restaurant, standardization of, 576
Cyert, R. M., 687, 691 n

D

Dalton, Melville, 11, 41–43, 45, 359–64, 466 n, 468
Data processing machines, 47–48
Davis, Allison, 9
Davis, Sheldon A., 392 n
Dean, Lois, 49–50, 458, 473
Dean of school, choosing of, 694–97, 702
Decentralization
  of labor relations, 492–94
  of maintenance organization, 349–50, 351
Decision-making process, 685–703
  Bay of Pigs case, 688–90, 693–94, 703
  dean of school, choosing of, 694–97, 702
  facts, indeterminacy of, 690–91
  feedback or justification, 697–99
  glamor attached to, 694
  hierarchical effects, 692–94
  implications for administrative action, 699–702
  information, impact of, 687–88
  "participation management" in, 326–27

Decision-making process—*Cont.*
  programmed versus unprogrammed,
    685–86
  structural effects, 692–94
  traditional approach to, 686–87
Decision-making theorists, 14–15
Definitions
  activities, 114
  auditing, 406
  budget, 368
  cohesion, 203
  creativity, 615
  delegation, 679–80
  formal organization structure, 61, 71
  interaction, 91
  level of aspiration, 129, 143
  productivity, 615
  self-evaluation, 129, 143
  status, 129, 143
  symbols, 141
  technology, 56
  transactions, 148
  work flow, 56
Delegation, 328
  budgeting procedures, 677
  changes in patterns, 676–79
  conditions favoring, 680–81
  definition of, 679–80
  employee rating procedures, 677
  face-to-face relations, changes in, 680–
    82
  grocery chain of supermarkets, 673–84
  influence by subordinates, 679
  influence of superior's behavior, 678
  meaning of, 673–84
  measuring of, 674–76
  metals fabricating division, 681–83
  organization structure, 677
    changes in, 680–81
  organized training program, 679
  rewards and penalties, 681, 683
  status supports for store manager, 678
  top management's consultative
    approach, 678
  top management's endorsement of pro-
    gram, 677
Democratic group discussions, 34
Department store, interaction differences
  in, 98–99
Departmental groups, 191–98, 202–3
  grinding department study, 219–22
  intergroup relations study, 219–22
  steel container assembling and welding,
    222–24
Dependence, needs for, 135–36
Design engineers, changes in position of,
  578–80
Detroit Edison Company, 766
  human relations training study, 389–90

Development process, 619–39
  authority, 628–29, 638
  bootleg projects, 636–37, 639
  communication, problems of, 621–26
  coordination, problems of, 621–26
  costs of innovation, 619
  downstream-upstream relations, 621–26
  effectiveness of, 637
  engineer, role and functions of, 631–34
  engineering organization, forms of,
    634–35
  engineering and scientific activities dis-
    tinguished, 632–33
  engineers as internal entrepreneurs,
    636–37, 638
  group discussion, 630–31, 638
  instability of work groups, 635–36
  liaison positions, 626–28, 637–38
  negotiation, 630, 638
  radar, 620–21
  restructuring interactions, 629–30, 638
  television set, 624–26
Deviant groups, 193–94, 197
Diagonal relations, 348 ff
  patterns of, 399–415
Diagrams
  decision making in participation man-
    agement, 328
  departmental group layout, 192
  job satisfaction approaches, 139
  managerial succession in restaurant,
    642
  organization structure of grocery su-
    permarket, 674
  restaurant size and structure, changes
    in, 572–73
  sociometric, 174–75
  talking time of district and store man-
    agers in supermarket, 675–77
  transactions, types, forms, and values
    of, 149
  union-management reciprocity, 521
  union-management relations
    foremen adjustment within manage-
      ment, 524
    foremen under pressure, 524
    scheme for analysis of, 517, 519
    split within union, 524
Dickson, William J., 8, 30, 31 n, 32, 45,
  94, 135–36, 138, 144, 386, 389, 773
Dissatisfaction, 136–40
Dominance, 96
Dominance-submission patterns, 116
Douglas, Ann, 45
Downstream-upstream relations, work
  flow, 400, 621–26
Dual-factor theory of job satisfaction
  and motivation, 134, 136–40
Dubin, Robert, 319–21, 329, 713
Dulles, Allen, 693–94

Duncan, Otis Dudley, 73 n
Dunnington, Richard, 655, 658, 661
Dutton, J. M., 400
Dynamic tendencies, 159–60

E

Early experience
  gaffer in glass industry, 271–74
  interactions affected by, 110–14
  man who walked off job, 281–85
  restaurant personnel, 231–51
Economic man concept, limitations of, 8
Eells, Kenneth, 130 n
Effective manager, quest for, 666; see also
  Managerial succession
Eisenhower, Dwight D., 737
Electrical Equipment Company case,
  577–80
Electronic computers, 47–48
Employee relations; see Personnel de-
  partment
Engineering, impact of; see Technologi-
  cal change
Engineering activities and scientific ac-
  tivities distinguished, 632–33
Engineering organization, forms of, 634–
  35
Engineers
  bootleg projects, 636–37, 639
  instability of work groups of, 635–36
  internal entrepreneurs, role of, 636–37,
    638
  role and functions of, 631–34
England, George W., 473
Environment; see Work environment
Ethnic composition, changing of, 581–86
Ethnic differences, 142 43
Ethnicity
  group membership determined by,
    195–98, 203
  group pressures and, 198–201, 203
Etzioni, Amitai, 18 n, 714
Evaluation; see Job evaluation
Event-process analysts, 11–12
Experimental studies in research, 28–41

F

Factory, work flow in, 400
Facts, indeterminacy of, 690–91
Failure, 120–21
Fair treatment, needs for, 135–36
Feedback
  necessary in decision-making process,
    697–99
  of research findings, 766
Feelings; see Sentiments
Festinger, Leon, 131 n, 453 n
Field experimenter, 29–30
Field work department system, 360–63
Financial rewards; see Rewards

First-line supervisory position; see Fore-
  men; Supervisors
Fisher, Lloyd H., 18 n
Fitch, H. G., 400
Fleischman, Edwin A., 319 n, 389
Flexibility; see Management flexibility
Follett, Mary Parker, 61
Followers, 115–16
Ford Motor Company, 698
Foreign policy, 698–99
Foremen; see also Supervisors
  change in role of, 464
  changing nature of positions of, 304–5
  college-trained, 308–11
  communication, interaction, and the
    initiation of activities, 315–16
  disruption of pattern of, 565
  effective versus ineffective, 321–22
  elaborate program for selection and
    training of, 307
  glass industry, 260–62, 303
  interaction of, 107–8, 304
  moving up from worker to, 305–8
  nonvertical relations, 333
  in oil company, 303–4
  pattern of failure, 337–41
  pattern of success, 333–37
  positive exchange transactions with
    workers, 314–15
  production, 320–21
  rotation of, 21
  status symbols, 311–14
  switching of, 38–39
  technology and work flow, 59–61,
    332–33
  "the" foreman, existence of, 303–5
  training program results, 390
  vertical relations, 333
Foremen-worker relations, changes effected by union activity, 447–48
Form, William H., 73 n
Formal organization structure
  defined, 61, 71
  impact of technology on, 61–64
  influence of personnel men in, 382
  informal versus, 70–72
  interpersonal relations and, 708–10
Foster, George, 742 n
Friendship needs, 135–36
French, John R. P., Jr., 13–14, 33, 327 n
French Canada, local union study in, 481–
  84
Fringe benefits, 74
  union pressure for, 381
Fukuzawa, Yukichi, 743
Functional foremanship, 4–5

G

Gaffer in glass industry
  case study of, 252–76

Gambling activities, 423
Gardner, Burleigh B., 8–9, 11, 450 n, 522 n
Garfield, Sidney, 529
Gasoline plant; see Oil company
General Electric Company, 595
Gerth, H. H., 6 n
"Gigo approach," 48
Glacier Metals, Ltd., 765
Glaser, Barney G., 597 n
Glass blowing; see Glass industry
Glass industry, 252–76, 471, 504–10
Goals
    conflicts in, 596–97
    setting of, 323–24
Goldner, Fred, 633–34, 691 n
Gordon, Gerald, 602 n, 609
Gouldner, Alvin, 12, 149, 446, 648 n, 651, 655, 708
Government agency, unbalanced exchange in, 150–51
Green, Charles S., 720 n
Gregory VII, Pope, 587
Grievances
    handling of, 464–65
    meaning of, 466–68
Grinding department, 219–22, 494–504, 511
Group behavior; see Groups; Intergroup Relations
Group discussion, coordination through, 630–31, 638
Group dynamicists, 13–14
Group leader, gaffer in glass industry, 252–76
Groups
    autonomous, 178–84, 202
    "banana time," 184–91, 202
    "barber college" crisis, 191, 202
    breaks, patterns of, 187
    choice patterns of members, 174–75
    cohesion in, 203
    core members of, 173
    determination of membership of, 173–204, 201–2
    deviant, 193–94, 197
    ethnicity and, 198–201, 203
    ethnicity as determinant of, 195–98, 203
    fringes of, 173
    industrial organization, 184–91, 202
    intergroup relations; see Intergroup relations
    nonwork activities versus limited work activities, 192–93
    norms in, 197, 203
    observational approach to determine membership, 201
    one department, many groups, 191–98, 202–3
    peripheral members of, 173

Groups—Cont.
    popularity and influence relationship, 177
    popularity and leadership distinguished, 176–77, 202
    rank in, relationships with, 182–84
    regular, 193–95, 197
    social-emotional leader, 177–78
    sociometric determination of members of, 173–78, 201–2
    status congruence, 195–96, 203
    status in, 196, 203
    subgroups, 180
    task leader, 177–78
    work, 184–91, 202
Guest, Robert H., 16 n, 45–46, 107 n, 120, 321 n, 651 n, 652, 654–55
Gypsum case, 648–51

H

Haberstroh, C. J., 6 n, 400 n
Hamilton, Edith Lentz, 391 n, 767
Hard criterion variables, 48
Hare, Paul, 177 n
Harris, Edwin F., 319 n, 389
Harvard Business School, 7, 15
Harvey, Edward, 65–66, 79, 81
Harwood Manufacturing Company study, 10, 33–35
    participation management, 326–27
Havighurst, Robert C., 9
Hawthorne works, studies at, 8, 11, 30–33
    personnel counseling program, 385–89
Hedging, 601–2
Henderson, Lawrence J., 711, 715
Herzberg, Frederick, 134–41, 145, 147
Hesitancy, 96
Historical background of book, 3–24
Hi-Test Aviation Gasoline Plant, 110–14, 277–98, 419–50, 469–70, 563–64, 587, 589
Holtzman, Wayne, 727 n
Homans, George C., 9 n, 11, 12, 18 n, 132, 149, 162, 191 n, 225–26
Homogeneity versus heterogeneity, smelting versus chemical division, 482, 510
Horizontal interactions, 108–14
Hoslett, Schuyler Dean, 368 n
Hotel study, 767–69
House, Robert J., 136 n, 138 n
Hughes, Charles C., 128 n
Hughes, Everett C., 9, 11, 22, 581, 583
Hughes, Jane M., 128 n
Human relations; see Interpersonal relations
Human relations consultant
    obstacles against utilization of, 394–96
    personnel man as, 393–96

Human relations movement, 708
Human relations training, 389–90

I

Illumination experiments, 30–31
Incentive systems; *see also* Rewards
  change in formula, 499–500
  effectiveness of, 78
  rate setting for, 77–78
Independence, needs for, 135–36
Indeterminacy of facts, 690–91
Individualism, 121–22
Individuals' behavior; *see* Activities; Interactions; Sentiments; Transactions
Indoctrination, 324
Industrial conflict, frequency of, 25–26
Industrial organizations, military organizations studies, application of, 9
Industrial relations, training in field of, 381–82
Industrial relations department, union contribution to management organization, 379
Industrial research laboratory; *see* Research department
Influence, popularity in relation to, 177
Informal organization versus formal, 70–72
Information, impact of, 687–88
Inhibitedness, 96
Initiation
  activities
    foremen and subordinates, 315–16
    rare, pattern of, 365
  flow into maintenance, 404
  service relationships, 405
  structure, 319
Initiative, 96
Inland Steel Container Company, 535–38, 542
Innovation; *see* Development process; Research department
Institute for Social Research at Michigan University, 10, 766
Instructions, giving of, 323
Insurance company study, 35–37
Interaction chronograph, 93–98, 122–23
Interaction theory, 16
Interactions
  activities related to, 114–15
  barrel department supervisor, 333–34, 337–38
  changes in patterns of, 561–70
  chronograph measurement of, 93–98, 122–23
  continuous process operations, 99
  defined, 91
  department store, differences in, 98–99
  earlier experiences, effect of, 110–14

Interactions—*Cont.*
  foremen and subordinates, 107–8, 315–16
  group relations; *see* Intergroup relations
  horizontal, 108–14
  initiative in, 92
  leadership, 92
  macro-interaction, 122
  micro-interaction, 93–98, 122
  oil company, 100, 291–95
  opportunities for, smelting versus chemical division, 483
  pair event, 91
  patterns of, 97, 98
  personality and organization, 98–107
  restaurants, 100–107
  restructuring of, coordination through, 629–30, 638
  set event, 91
  situational, 92
  social implications, 125–26
  supervisor-worker; *see* Supervisor-worker interaction
  transactions in relation to, 167–68, 170
  vertical, 108–14
Intercultural context for organizational research, 717–63
Interdependent activities, technological versus human control of, 69
Intergroup relations, 205–27
  boys' camp experiment, 205–9, 224–25
  cohesion, 219, 227
  conflict, 209, 210, 219–22, 225–26
  disagreements, resolution of; *see* Coordination; Cooperation
  Esso Standard Oil Company experiments, 209–13, 224–25
  grinding department study, 219–22
  industrial management people, experiment with, 209–13, 224–25
  joint payoff, 222, 224
  maintenance organizations, 349–67
  negative exchange, 217, 225–26
  nonconformity, 218–19
  norms regulating member behavior in, 218, 226–27
  piece-rate incentive systems, 214–18, 219–20, 226
  steel container assembling and welding department, 222–24
  12-year old boys, experiment with, 205–9, 224–25
  two-transaction strategy, 222
  work group versus management, 213–19, 226
International Brotherhood of Electrical Workers, 550
International Chemical Workers Union, 529

International Harvester Company, human relations training program, 389
International Typographical Union, 12
Interpersonal relations
changes effected by union activity, 447–50
end of study of, 711
formal organization structure and, 708–10
shift from informal to formal, 579
technology and, 708–10
work flow and, 708–10
Interrelatedness, 88
Interview-observational methods of research, 41–47
limitations of, 45–47
possibilities of, 44–45
Inventory control, 351–54, 407, 685
Investment-reward relationship (IRR), 132–33, 144
automated factory, effect of, 568, 569

J

Japan, organizational comparison with United States, 742–56
Jaques, Elliott, 15, 19, 67, 77, 765
Jasinski, Frank J., 99–100, 125
Jewelry manufacturer, unionization of, 450–54
Job description, 76–77
Job evaluation, 76–77
time orientation, 132, 144
Job placement, 72–74
Job satisfactions, 191
improvements in, 562
motivation and, 134, 136–40
variables in, 139
Job security, smelting versus chemical division, 483–84
Job skills, training in, 389
Johnson, Robert, 43
Joint payoff, 149, 153–54, 168, 222, 224, 510
Justice, needs for, 135–36

K

Kahl, Joseph, 130 n
Kahn, Robert L., 319
Kamarovsky, Mirra, 18 n
Kennedy, John F., 688, 690, 693
Kennedy, Edward M. (Teddy), 739
Kerr, Clark, 18 n, 25–26
Kerr, Willard A., 473

L

Labor-Management Center at Yale University, 9
Laboratory, research; see Research department

Laboratory experimenter, 28–29
Lateral coordination, 619–20; see also Coordination
Lateral relationships, 348 ff.
advisory; see Advisory relationships
auditing; see Auditing
buy-sell; see Buy-sell relationships
nature of, 414–15
patterns of, 399–415
scheduling; see Service activities, scheduling of
service; see Service activities, scheduling of
stabilization; see Stabilization relationships
standard setting; see Standard setting
work flow; see Work flow
Lawrence, Paul, 564 n, 673 n, 674, 676, 692
Leadership, 92, 115–16
glass industry
gaffer in, 252–76
quantitative measures, 264–66
popularity distinguished from, 176–77, 202
status and, 116–17
union organizers, 458
Leavitt, Harold J., 323 n
Leighton, Alexander, 128 n
Lenski, Gerhardt, 196 n
Letwin, William, 756 n
Level of aspiration defined, 129, 143
Lewin, Kurt, 10, 13, 33, 767
Liaison positions, communication and coordination through, 626–28, 637–38
Likert, Rensis, 10, 13, 766
Lipset, S. M., 12
Listening ability, 96
Locke, Edwin A., 121
Long-wall technology, British mining industry, 561–62, 568
Loyalties
research department versus production organization, 606
in union-management relations, 472–75
Lundberg, Craig C., 686

M

Macro-interaction, 122
Maier, Norman A., 14, 389 n
Maintenance organization
area coordination system, 355–59
centralization, 350–51
craft coordination, 356–58
craftsmen in, 351
decentralization, 349–50, 351
effectiveness of, 349
field work department system, 360–63
manufacturing plant, relations in, 359–63

Maintenance organization—*Cont.*
  obsolescence, 351
  scheduling of activities, 406
  standardization program, 351–55
  status, 364
  work load changes, 349
Man
  relations of to job, group, and organization, 277–99
  walking off job, 277–99
Man-boss relationship; *see also* Foremen; Supervisors; Supervision
  glass industry, 258–62
  studies contributing to, 10, 13
Management
  changes in, 424
  glass industry, 252–76
  intergroup relations
    Esso Standard Oil Company experiments, 209–13, 224–25
    work group versus, 213–19, 225–26
  personnel counseling service to, 388
  shakeup in oil company, 424–25
Management flexibility, 96
  smelting versus chemical division, 483
Management organization before unions, 380–81
Managerial succession, 640–72
  automotive assembly case, 651–54
  framework for analysis of phenomenon of, 640–41
  Gypsum case, 648–51
  precision manufacturing case, 655–66
  restaurant case, 641–48
Manipulation of men, 551–54, 556
Mann, Floyd, 766
Manufacturing organizations, 57–58
Manufacturing plant, maintenance organization relations, 359–64
March, James G., 14, 687, 691 n
Marcson, Simon, 600–601
Marrow, Alfred J., 326 n, 327, 766–67, 769 n, 770 n, 771 n
Maslow, A. H., 134–35, 137, 140–41, 144–45
Mass production, 58, 63–64; *see also* Batch production
Mausner, B., 136 n
Mauss, Marcel, 149–50
Mayo, Elton, 7–8, 22, 32
McCarthy, Joseph, 737
McFarland, Dalton E., 380, 382
McGregor, Douglas, 9, 13, 577, 579, 766
McKersie, Robert, 530, 555
McNamara, Robert, 698
Measurability, 88
Meeker, Marcia, 130 n
Membership rewards, 74–75
Merit increases, 75
  determination of eligibility, 259

Metcalf, H., 61 n
Michels, Robert, 12
Micro-interactions, 93–98, 122
Midvale Steel Company, 3
Militancy of workers; *see* Work unit cohesion and militancy
Military organizations, application of studies of, 9
Miller, Frank B., 92 n, 257, 265, 368 n
Mills, C. Wright, 6 n, 18 n
Mills, Theodore M., 92 n
Mining industry in Britain, long-wall technology, introduction of, 561–62, 568
Mobility in restaurants, opportunities in, 231–33
Mobility systems, 72–74
Modifiability, 88–89
Moment, David, 15
Monopoly, 152–53
Morale; *see* Sentiments
Morse, Nancy, 35
Motion study, 78, 83
Motivation and job satisfaction, 134, 136–40

N

Nash, Philleo, 701 n
National Science Foundation, 622
National Training Laboratories, 14, 177, 213
Natural conditions, experiment in, 39
Nature of the job
  complexity for supervisor and for subordinate, 67–68
  work flow and, 58–61
Needs, structure of, 134–36
Negative exchange, 149, 156–57, 169, 217, 225–26
  intergroup relations, 217
Negative thinkers, 474
Negotiation, coordination through, 630, 638
Negroes; *see* Afro-Americans
Neira, Hugo, 730
New management approach, work unit cohesion and militancy, 487–88
New product, introduction of, 562–64, 569
  Amicon tube, 564–67, 569
New York State School of Industrial and Labor Relations, 694–97, 702
Night watchmen in university, personality studies of, 99
Nixon, Richard M., 739
Nonconformity, 218–19
Normative system, construction of, 5
Norms
  cohesion in relation to, 479
  concept of, 130

Norms—*Cont.*
  group membership, 197, 203
  intergroup relations, 218, 226–27
Nosow, S., 73 n
"Not invented here," 616

O

Objectifiability, 88
Obsolescence, 351
Office organizations, 57
Ohio State Leadership Studies, 10
Oil company, 110–14, 209–13, 277–98, 419–50, 469–70, 563–64, 587, 589
Open conflict, 149, 157–58, 169
Operating organization, relations between maintenance and operations, 359–63
Optimum span of control, 5
Oral communication, 91; *see also* Interactions
Orders, giving of, 323
Organizational behavior
  application of research in organizations, 764–85
  comparative studies of
    Japan, 742–56
    Peru, 719–42
    United States, 756–62
  cyclical movements in progress of, 707
  dichotomy in field of, 71
  effective way of thinking about things, 713–15
  elements of setting of, 55–86
  extrinsic satisfactions; *see* Transactions
  familiarity with things, 711–12
  framework of, 87–89
  framework for study of, 714
  future of field of, 20–22
  historical background, 3–24
  interrelatedness, 88
  intrinsic satisfactions; *see* Activities; Interactions
  measurability, 88
  modifiability, 88–89
  objectifiability, 88
  origins of field of study, 3–24
  parsimony, 87–88
  personality and, 98–107
  present-day views and theories, 17–20
  programming of, 322–25
  research methods, 25–54
  structuring of the work environment, 55–86
  systematic knowledge of things, 713
  theoretical approach to, 714
Organizational character, changing of, 586–88
Organizational programming, areas of, 66
Organizational research, intercultural context for, 717–63
Organizational size, 571–94

Organizational structure, 571–94
Organizational surveyors, 13
"Out of line" conditions, 407
Output programming, 79
Overeagerness, 96

P

Pair event, 91
Paranoid tendencies, 99
Parsimony, 87–88
Participant observer; *see* Interview-observational methods of research
Participation management, 16, 33–35, 325–27
  conceptual clarification, 327–28
  decision making in, 327–28
Patterns in union-management relations, 514–27
Pavlov, Ivan, 148
"Pecking orders," 115–16
Pelz, Donald A., 608 n, 614–15
People, impact of budget-making process on, 371–74
Performance, urges for, 413–14
Performance rewards, 75
Personal identification, 130, 144
  symbols of, 588
Personal worth; *see* Self-evaluation
Personality
  organization and, 98–107
  traits, 96
Personnel changes in grinding department, 497–99, 502–4
Personnel counseling, 385–89
  frustration of counselors, 388–89
  program of Western Electric Company research in relation to, 387
  supervision in relation to, 388
Personnel department
  authority of, 383–84
  employee relations, responsibility for, 383
  evolution of, 379–82
  extended, 382
  functions of, 383–85
  human relations consultant, 393–96
  influence in design of formal organization, 382
  integrated, 382
  organization of, 382–83
  professionalization of, 381
  split function organization, 382
  stabilization position of, 407
  staff coordinated, 382
  training of members of, 389–93
  veto power, 384
Personnel man; *see* Personnel department
Peru, organizational comparison with United States, 719–42
Peruvian utility questionnaire, 50

Picard, Laurent, 481 n
Piece-rate incentive systems, 75
  intergroup relations studied, 214–18,
    219–20, 226
Plastics manufacturer, unionization of,
    450–54
Polaroid Land camera, 616
Ponder, Quentin, 321
Popularity
  influence in relation to, 177
  leadership distinguished from, 176–77,
    202
Positional rewards, 75
Positive exchange, 149–50, 168, 181
  status and, 314–15
Positive thinkers, 474
Post-war adjustments, work unit cohesion
  and militancy, 485–87
Power, struggle for, 413–14
Power relations, 163–65, 169
Precision manufacturing case, managerial
  succession in, 655–66
Predictability, 78–79
Process
  man and, 277–99
  technology and, 280–81
Product groups, 634–35
Production control, importance of, 369
Production control departments; see
  Maintenance organization
Production department
  scheduling of activities, 406
  work flow, 400–401
Production organization research depart-
  ment distinguished; see Research de-
  partment
Productivity, 48
  cohesion in relation to, 479
  defined, 615
  evaluation of quality of work, 259–60
  increase in, 562
Programming
  defined, 79
  organizational behavior, 322–25
  types of, 79
Project groups, 634–35
Promotions of worker to foreman, 305–8
Psychiatric analysts, 15
Psychological man concept, limitations
  of, 9
Psychotherapy, application of, 15
Purcell, Father T. V., 473, 475 n
Purchasing agent, view of job of, 412–13
Pyrex glassware, development of, 595

Q

Quantitative observational studies; see
  Interview-observational methods
  of research

Questionnaire survey method of research,
  possibilities and limitations of, 47–52
Quickness, 96

R

Race relations in industry, symbolism of,
    581–83
Radar, race to develop, 620–21
Railroad signal light, 595
Ranking, 130–31, 144
Reference group, 134
Regular groups, 193–95, 197
Reimer, Everett, 35
Reinforcement theory, 148
Relay assembly test room experiments,
    31–32
Repair problems; see Maintenance organ-
  ization
Repetitive production activities, 119–20,
    184–91, 202
Repp, Judith A., 95 n
Research
  application in organizations, 764–85
  broad comparative studies, 25–28
  case studies, 772–80
    lessons learned from, 780–82
  establishment inside organizations, 772–
    80
    lessons learned from, 780–82
  experimental studies, 28–41
  feedback of findings, 766
  industrial application of, 764–85
  intercultural context for, 717–63
  intervention strategies, 764–69
    lessons learned from, 769–72
  interview-observational methods, 41–47
  lessons learned from, 769–72
  maintaining personnel in, 782
  personnel counseling in relation to, 387
  prospects in industry, 782–84
  questionnaire survey, 47–52
  recruiting problems, 782
  Western Electric Company case, 773–
    74
Research Center for Group Dynamics,
    10, 13
Research department
  access to goods, services, and informa-
    tion, 607
  arbitration, 610–11
  attendance at professional meetings of
    scientists, 599
  categories of workers in, 609–10
  communication skills, 607–8
  conflicts of interest in, 596–99
    management policies toward, 599–600
  creativity in, 614–16
  degree of predictability of outcomes,
    603–4

Research department—*Cont.*
  differences between laboratory and
    production organization, 602–6
  distribution of education, 603
  dual ladder of promotion, 599–600
  grafting onto well-established produc-
    tion organization, 596–98
  growth of, 595
  hedging in choosing problem, 601–2
  integrators, 609–10
  introduction of, 595
  locus of knowledge, 603
  loyalties, 606
  mediation, 610–11
  "not invented here," 616
  post–World War II developments, 596
  problem recognizers, 609–10
  problem solvers, 609–10
  production of objects or ideas, 602
  publications of scientists' papers, 599
  reference groups, 604–5
  replaceability of personnel, 605–6
  size of company, effect of, 614–16
  stimulation of ideas, 611–14
  supervisor as laboratory group repre-
    sentative, 606–7
  supervisor-subordinate relations in,
    strategy for, 607–14
  supervisory functions contributing to
    productivity in and creativity of,
    607–14
  technicians, 609
  who chooses problems for work on,
    600–602
  work team composition, 608–10
Restaurants
  backgrounds of two levels of person-
    nel, 231–51
  chain, growth of, 576
  crying and noncrying waitresses, 102–7
  differences in supervisory jobs, 321
  difficult problems of coordination,
    104–5
  expansion in size and structure of, 571–
    77
  high pressure of operation of, 102–7
  high turnovers, 101–2
  interactions in, 60–61, 100–107
  kitchen, status symbols in, 143, 592
  managerial succession in, 641–48
  mobility opportunities, 231–33
  organizational study of, 231–51
  personnel changes, 237, 249
  "refined" atmosphere in, 231–33
  size and structure of, 571–77
  status, 231–33, 589–92
  technology of, 57
  transactional experience of two levels
    of personnel, 231–51
  work flow in, 58

Rewards; *see also* Incentive systems
  investment relationship with, 132–33,
    144
  types of, 74–76
Richardson, F. L. W., Jr., 11, 109
Rite of passage, 306–7
Ritti, Richard, 630, 632–35, 691 n, 699 n
Robert's Rules of Order, 465
Roethlisberger, Fritz J., 8, 30, 31 n, 32,
    45, 94, 132 n, 135–36, 138, 144, 191 n,
    386, 389, 773
Rogers, Carl, 94, 385
Rohrer, John H., 175 n, 205
Role programming, 79
Ronken, Harriet, 564 n, 692
Roseborough, Mary, 92 n
Rosen, Ned, 21, 37–40
Rotation of factory foremen, 21
Routine jobs, 191
Rowe, John, 725
Roy, Donald, 11, 41–43, 45, 119, 184–91,
    215, 468
Rubenstein, A. H., 6 n, 400 n
Rules
  establishment of, 323
  in union-management relations, 468–72

S

Safety needs, 135
Sales department, work flow, 400–401
Satisfaction, 134, 136–40; *see also* Job
  satisfactions
Sayles, Leonard, 27–28, 45, 219, 322, 399,
    403, 405–7, 411, 413–14, 457, 479–80,
    494 n, 496, 502–3, 504 n, 630, 709–10
Schlesinger, Arthur, Jr., 688 n, 689–90
Schwartzbaum, Allan M., 107
Scientific activities and engineering ac-
  tivities distinguished, 632–33
Scientific management, 708
  basis of, 17
  Taylor's ideas of, 4–5
Scientific thinking, progress of, 79–82
Scientists; *see also* Research department
  attendance at professional meetings, 599
  conflict of interests with company,
    596–98
  impracticality of, 623
  promotional ladder for, 599–600
  publication of papers of, 599
Sears, Roebuck and Company experi-
  ment, 61–62
Seashore, Stanley, 325, 326 n, 479–80, 767,
    769 n, 770 n, 771 n
Selekman, Benjamin M., 550–51
Self-evaluation defined, 129, 143
Selznik, Philip, 12
Seniority, 142
  in glass industry, 254
  in oil company, 426

Seniority—*Cont.*
union-management relations involving, 471
Sensitivity training, 327, 390, 393
Sentiments, 121–22
barrel department supervisor, 335–36, 340–41
categories of, 128–29, 143
dual-factor theory of job satisfaction and motivation, 134, 136–40
elements of, 128, 143
framework of time, 131–32, 144
intergroup relations, 225
investment-reward relationship, 132–33, 144
nature of, 128–31, 143–44
needs, structure of, 134–36
oil company worker, 291–95
patterns of, 131, 144
social relativity, 133–34, 144
structural effects, importance of, 140–41
time orientation, 131–32, 144
transactions in relation to, 167–68, 170
Service activities, scheduling of, 405–6
Service organizations, 57
work flow in, 58
Service relationships, 404–5
initiation of activities and interactions in, 405
Set events, 91, 163
Sex symbol, 142
Shartle, Caroll, 10
Shawcross Corporation, Benton Blowing Room of; *see* Glass industry
Shepard, Herbert, 14, 390
Sherif, C. W., 205 n
Sherif, Muzafer, 175 n, 176, 205–7, 224
Short-wall technology, 562
Siegel, Abraham, 25–26
Simon, Herbert A., 14
Situational interactions, 92
Size of organization, 571
Skinner, B. F., 148
Snow, C. F., 30
Snyderman, B., 136 n
Social-anthropological approach, 11–12
Social-emotional leader, 177–78
Social process, decision making as, 685–703
Social relativity, 133–34, 144
Social science origins, United States, 6
Social status and leadership, 116–17
Social structuralists, 12–13
Social transitions, rites and ceremonies to handle, 306–7
Society for Applied Anthropology, 11–12
Sociology, requirements for progress in study of, 711–15

Sociometry, group membership determination, 173–78, 201–2
Sofer, Cyril, 15
Specialty groups, 634–35
Stabilization relationships, 407–8
Stagner, Ross, 473 n
Stalker, G. M., 620 n, 626, 631 n, 710
Standard operating procedures, establishment of, 323
Standard setting, 406–7
Standardization committee, 408
Standardization program in maintenance organization, 351–55
Status
changing relations of, 411–13
collective bargaining, 530–33
defined, 129, 143
differences in, 142–43
groups, 196, 203
leadership and, 116–17
maintenance organization, 364
positive exchange transactions and, 314–15
in restaurants, 231–33
symbols of, 311–14, 588–92
Status congruence, 195–96, 203
Stealing of gasoline, 423
Steel fabricating plant barrel department, supervision in, 331–45
Steel mill grinding department study, 219–22
Steinmetz, Charles, 595
Stodtbeck, Fred L., 92 n
Stouffer, Samuel A., 9 n
Strauss, George, 45, 49, 322–23, 327, 328, 411, 412 n, 413, 457 n, 503, 504 n, 625, 710
Strike prone industries, 26
Structuralist approaches, 12–13, 15–16
Structuring of work environment; *see* Work environment
Subjective aspects of human relations, 128–46
Success, 120–21
Sullivan, Eugene, 595
Supermarket chain, meaning of delegation in, 673–84
Supervision
barrel department, 331–45
changes in, 429–31
confusion and inconsistencies in pattern of, 577–80
consideration in, 319–20
delegation, 328
dichotomy in, 318–19
differences in jobs, 320–21
dimensions of, 319
"general" versus "close," 321–22
initiation structure, 319
laxity of, effects of, 423–25

Supervision—*Cont.*
oil company, problems in early days of, 420–22
participation management; *see* Participation management
personnel counseling in relation to, 388
scientist in position of, conflict of interest of, 598–99
Supervisor-worker interaction
continuous process operations, 60
restaurant industry, 60–61
Supervisors; *see also* Foremen
activities, 334–35, 338–40
complexity of job for, 67–68
cooperation built by, 331–32
craft, 356–58
employee centered, 318
expansion of organization size and structure, effect of, 574–75
interactions, 333–34, 337–38
production centered, 318
research department, strategy in, 607–14
research laboratory, 606–7
restaurant personnel relationships, 231–51
sentiments, 335–36, 340–41
social system, 331–45
success to failure, 331–32
supportive behavior, 325–26
symbols, 335–36, 341
training programs, 389–90
transactions, 336–37
Supervisory behavior; *see* Supervision
Supportive behavior, 325–26
Survey Research Center, 326
human relations training study, 389–90
Survey researchers, 13
Swedish glassmaking, 253–54
Swift local of union; *see* United Packinghouse Workers of America
Symbols
barrel department supervisor, 335–36, 341
budget as, 368
changes in, 580
cost, importance of, 365
definition, 141
interpersonal relations changes effected by union activity, 448
management sentiments toward unions, changing of, 450–54
personal identification, 588
race relations in industry, 581–83
significance of, 587–88
status, 311–14, 588–92; *see also* Status
technology and work process and, 295–99
types of, 140–43

T

Tannenbaum, Robert, 14
Task groups, 634–35
Task leader, 177–78
Task performance, 121–22
Tasks; *see* Activities
Tavistock Institute of Human Relations, 15
Taylor, Frederick Winslow, 3–5, 708, 715
Taylor, Graham, 657
Taylorism, 3–5, 708
Team composition in the glass industry, 254–55
Team leadership in the glass industry, 266–71
Technological change
abandonment of, 567
automation, 567–68, 569
continuous seamless tube mill, introduction of, 567–68, 569
disruption of foreman's pattern of interaction and activities, 565
disruption of work group, 565
in grinding department, 497–99, 502–4
introduction of, 561–70
mining industry, 561–62, 568
new product, 562–64, 569
Amicon tube, 564–67, 569
pressures from the top, 565–67
resistance to, 561
reversal of development flow of work, 564–65
work team composition, 561–62, 568
Technological structuralists, 15–16
Technology
defined, 56
impact on formal organization structure, 61–64
interpersonal relations and, 708–10
personnel requirements of, 70
process and, 280–81
types of, 57–58
work flow and, 56–58, 324–25, 332–33
Television set, development of new model of, 624–26
Temperament traits, 96–97
Tennessee Valley Authority, union-management relations, 470–71, 525
Thefts, 423
Theodore, Eustace, 121, 122 n, 158 n
Theory
background of book, 3–24
framework of organizational behavior, 87–89
Therapy, personnel counseling as, 388
Time orientation, 131–32, 144
Time-span of responsibility, 67, 77
Time study, 78
Tool kit case, 353–54

Totalitarian exchange, 158 n
Traction, 118–20
Trading, 149, 151–52, 168, 403–4
Training programs, 389–93
Transactional values, determination of, 16–63, 169
Transactions, 147–70
  bargaining, 149, 158–59, 169
  barrel department supervisor, 336–37
  competitive, 149, 154–56, 168–69
  defined, 148
  determination of values of, 160–63, 169
  dynamic tendencies, 159–60
  foreman's deficit in, 343–44
  identification of types of, 165–66
  joint payoff, 149, 153–54, 168, 222, 224
  level of analysis of, 166–67, 169–70
  measuring values of, 165–66
  negative exchange, 149, 156–57, 169
  open conflict, 149, 157–58, 169
  positive exchange, 149–50, 168, 181
  power relations, 163–65, 169
  relationship to interaction, activities, and sentiments, 167–68, 170
  table of types of, 149
  trading, 149, 151–52, 168
  two-transaction strategy, 222
  values, determination of, 160–63, 169
Tremont Hotel, 767, 771
Trice, Harrison, 99, 307
Trist, Eric, 561 n
Trow, Martin, 12
Truman, Harry, 701–2, 703
TRW Systems training program, 392–93
Turner, Arthur N., 16 n, 46, 107 n, 321 n
Turnover, 48
  restaurant personnel, 101–2
Two-transaction strategy, 222

U

Unbalanced relationships, 156–57
Union
  bargaining unit, 425
  bureaucratic leader, 458
  centralization of control, 464–65
    extent of, 465–66
  changes in interpersonal relations, 447–50
  charismatic leader, 458
    downfall of, 458–63
  collective bargaining process; see Collective bargaining
  company; see Company union
  contribution to management organization, 379
  divided loyalty, 472–75
  dual loyalty, 472–75
  effects of, 381
  foremen-worker relations, changes in, 447–48

Union—Cont.
  glass industry, entrance into, 254
  grievances, handling of, 464–65
  grievances, meaning of, 466–68
  horizontal integration, 445
  industrial relations department of, 379
  interest in, 431
  international representative's role, 540–42
  long-run changes, 445–47
  loyalty to, 472–75
  management organization before, 380–81
  management sentiments toward, symbolism for changing of, 450–54
  meeting procedure, 465
  organization drive, 286–87, 419–20, 431–34, 587
    aim of, 457
    grinding department, 496–97
    jewelry and plastics manufacturer, 450–54
    local management's counteroffensive, 434–39
    management's last efforts, 443–44
    oil company, 419–20, 431–34
    party for leaving employees, 439–41
  representation election in oil company, 110–14
  significant symbols of change effected by union activity, 448
  steward, decline of, 463–65
  symbolism of management regarding, 450–54
  worker-management off-the-job relations, changes in, 448–50
Union-management relations, 418 ff
  collective bargaining process; see Collective bargaining
  conflict precipitated in, 488–92
  decentralization in, 492–94
  developments in, 475
    results of, 476
  evolution of, 457–78
  experiences affecting, 553
  firm but fair policy of management, 520
  foremen adjustment within management, 522–24
  foremen under pressure, 522, 524
  militancy of workers, 27, 479–513
  patterns in, 514–27
  problems at lower levels, 522–25
    diagrams, 524
  reciprocity, 520–21
    diagram, 521
  rules in, evolution of, 468–72
  scheme for analysis, 515–20
    diagram, 518
    guide to data, 525

Union-management relations—*Cont.*
  seniority as issue of, 471
  sharing of responsibilities, 520–21
  "soft policy" of management, 517
  split within union, 523–25
  structural analysis at plant level, 514–27
  tough policy of management, 520
  types of, 526
  work group cohesion, 27
  work unit cohesion and militancy, 479–513
Unit production, 66
United Packinghouse Workers of America, 473–75
United States
  organizational comparison with Japan and Peru, 756–62
  social science origins of, 7
United States Employment Service, 72
United Steel Workers Union, 515
Unity of command, violation of concept of, 5
Urwick, L., 61 n

V

Values, transactional, 160–63, 169
Variables, dependent and independent, 66
Vertical interactions, 108–14
Vertical relations; *see* Foremen; Supervision; Supervisors
Visibility of results, 68–69
Vroom, Victor, 138

W

Wadia, M. S., 752 n
Wage inequity issue, smelting versus chemical division, 484
Waitresses; *see also* Restaurants
  crying behavior, 102–7
  interactional requirements, 100–107
  restaurant personnel relationships, 231–51
Walker, Charles R., 15–16, 45–46, 107 n, 120, 321, 567
Walton, R. E., 400–402
Walton, Richard, 530, 555
Warner, W. Lloyd, 9, 11, 22, 130 n
Weber, Max, 6–7, 12, 17, 458, 708, 715
Weldon Company case, 767, 769–72
White-collar workers, 634
  in Japan, 742 ff
  in Peru, 721 ff
Whiteford, Andrew H., 450 n
Whitehead, T. N., 32 n
Whitehill, Arthur M., Jr., 752
Whitsett, D. A., 136 n
Wholeness of tasks, 120
Whyte, William F., 50 n, 52 n, 102 n, 104 n, 137, 143 n, 154 n, 179 n, 206 n, 214 n, 232 n, 263 n, 277 n, 391 n,

Whyte—*Cont.*
  450 n, 468 n, 470 n, 522 n, 529 n, 571 n, 591 n, 720 n, 721 n, 725 n, 729 n, 767 n
Wigdor, L. A., 136 n, 138 n
Wildcat strikes, 519, 528
Wilensky, Harold L., 692
Williams, Lawrence K., 50 n, 720 n
Winslow, E. K., 136 n
Woodward, Joan, 16, 26–27, 57, 62–66, 80–81, 320, 329, 710, 713, 715
Work activity, programming of, 323–25
Work environment
  compensation system, 74–76
  complexity of job for supervisor and for subordinate, 67–68
  elements of, 55–86
  formal versus informal organization, 70–72
  grinding department, 494–95, 511
  impact of technology on formal organization structure, 61–64
  implications of, 82–85
  interdependence and coordination, 69
  job description and evaluation, 76–77
  job placement, 72–74
  mobility systems, 72–74
  personnel requirements of the technology, 70
  physical changes in, 497–99, 502–4
  predictability, 78–79
  programming, 78–79
  rate setting for incentive systems, 77–78
  rewards system, 74–76
  scientific thinking, progress of, 79–82
  specific determinants of, 65–70
  structuring of, 55–86
  technological versus human control of interdependent activities, 69
  technology and work flow, 56–58
  visibility of results, 68–69
  work flow and the nature of the job, 58–61
Work flow
  changing of, 411–13
  defined, 56
  downstream-upstream dimension, 400, 621–26
  first-line supervisors, 59–61
  glass industry problems, 254–58
  interpersonal relations and, 708–10
  nature of the job and, 58–61
  problems of, 399–402
  reversal of, 564–65
  Taylor's approach, 4–5
  technology and, 56–58, 324–25, 332–33
Work group
  breaks, patterns of, 187
  chatter themes, 189
  cohesion of, 325–26
  disruption of, 565

Work group—*Cont.*
  glass industry, 252–76
  instability of, 635–36
  management versus, intergroup rela-
    tions of, 213–19, 226
  restaurant personnel relationships, 231–
    51
  study of a, 184–91, 202
  "times," frame of, 187–88
Work team composition, 571
  change in, 561–62, 568
  research department, 608–10
Work unit cohesion and militancy, 479–
  513
  caustic plant, 484–85
  centrality of the unit, 511
  conflict in worker-management and
    union-management relations, 488–
    92
  glass industry, 504–10, 511–12
  grinding department, 494–504, 511
  levels of militancy, 481
  new management approach, 487–88
  post-war adjustments, 485–87
  smelting versus chemical division, 481–
    84, 510 11
  union-management relations, 27, 479–
    513

Worker
  moving up to foreman, 305–8
  personal and organizational history of,
    in oil company, 281–85
  positive exchange transactions with
    foremen, 314–15
  rapid rise of, 291–92
  reactions to blocked progress, 292–93
Worker-management off-the-job relations changes effected by union activity, 448–50
Worker-management relations, conflict
  precipitated in, 488–92
Working conditions
  glass industry, 262
  smelting versus chemical division, 482
Worthy, James C., 61–62

X

Xerography processes, 616

Y

Yoshino, M. Y., 742–51

Z

Zaleznik, Abraham, 15, 132 n, 191 n
Zander, Alvin, 14, 33 n

*This book has been set in 10 point and 9 point
Janson leaded 2 points. Part numbers are 18
point News Gothic; part titles are 11 point
News Gothic. Chapter numbers and titles are
18 point News Gothic. The size of the type
page is 27 by 46½ picas.*